Leading
Constitutional
Decisions ====

Leading
Constitutional
Decisions ⎯⎯⎯⎯⎯⎯⎯

13th edition

ROBERT E. CUSHMAN

in collaboration with

ROBERT F. CUSHMAN

New York

APPLETON-CENTURY-CROFTS

Division of Meredith Publishing Company

Preface
to the 12th edition ═══════

No one can understand fully and clearly how our American national government works, or how it came to be the kind of government it is, unless he is familiar with the way in which the Supreme Court of the United States does its work, and with some of its decisions which are milestones in the growth of our American constitutional system. This collection of cases is intended primarily to serve the needs of students of American government and American history.

The Supreme Court does not work in a vacuum. Its decisions upon important constitutional questions can be fully understood only when viewed against the background of history, politics, and economics out of which they grew. The brief introductory notes attempt to reconstruct this background, to suggest the significance of the cases in our constitutional development, and, to a limited extent, to indicate the relation of the decisions printed to other, and perhaps equally important, ones which could not be included.

The first edition of this book was published thirty-eight years ago. At that time, with President Coolidge in the White House and Chief Justice Taft presiding over the Supreme Court, the American people faced the future with a sense of well-being and security. Since that time many of the old normalities have gone into the discard. A long and ruinous depression spawned the far-reaching social program of the New Deal, part of which is now largely forgotten, but much of which remains embedded in the pattern of our modern life. Then came a global war which drained our resources of men and money and demanded the exercise of drastic emergency powers by Congress and the President. Now we are deeply involved in a cold war with world Communism which strains our economy and creates new problems of national security. A nation which, in retrospect, seemed provincial and self-contained in 1925, faces in 1963 world dangers and world responsibilities, along with acute and complex domestic problems.

The impact of all this upon the growth of our constitutional law has been profound. For one thing, the Supreme Court of 1925 no longer exists. No man who sat on it is still alive. Twenty-one associate justices and four new chief justices have taken office during this period. These are the men who, in reality, make our constitutional law; and the changes which have come about in that law reflect in some measure the Court's new personnel, but reflect much more the revolutionary changes which have gone on in the life of the nation. Many problems which the ever changing Court has faced have been novel and difficult. In dealing with them it has applied old principles of constitutional law to new situations; it has announced new principles in areas not before explored; and it has discarded some old principles now felt to be unsound. In the years before 1925 the Court had reversed eleven of its earlier decisions; since then it has reversed more than twice that number.

This book would not serve its purpose if it did not retain a core of landmark cases, Marbury v. Madison, McCulloch v. Maryland, and the like, which not only embody some of the fundamental principles of our constitutional law, but also display the judicial craftsmanship of some of our greatest justices. This edition retains twenty cases which were included in the first printing in 1925. However, not all of the Supreme Court's decisions on constitutional questions are of equal, or equally lasting, importance. Some deal with problems, once of intense public interest, but now so well settled as to be almost forgotten; some have been qualified, clarified, or otherwise changed in more recent cases. For this reason, the opinions in ten cases which were printed in the last edition of this book have been omitted, although each is summarized in the notes to the cases retained. Many of the notes have been drastically rewritten, for this is the most thoroughgoing revision the book has ever had.

In this twelfth edition four new cases are printed and an old one (Luther v. Borden) is restored. In Cooper v. Aaron (the Little Rock case), the Court sternly rejected the doctrine of state "interposition" in defiance of federal law as that law is expounded by the Supreme Court. In Mapp v. Ohio, reversing an earlier ruling, the Court held that a state may not use in its own courts evidence secured by what would be an unreasonable search and seizure under the Fourth Amendment. Engel v. Vitale held that the reciting of the "Regents' Prayer" in a public school amounted to an establishment of religion, and thus violated the First and Fourteenth Amendments. The storm of protest against the decision has led committees in Congress to dis-

cuss a constitutional amendment to reverse it. Finally, in Baker v.
Carr, perhaps as important and far-reaching a decision as the Court
has ever rendered, the apportionment of state legislatures was
brought under judicial scrutiny in order to correct gross inequalities.
As a result, at the present time more than half the states have done,
or are in the process of doing, something about the inequitable apportionments of their legislatures.

Some sixty new cases are discussed either in the new notes or in
the opinions of the Court. The present edition includes or comments
on cases decided through the fall of 1962.

Arlington, Va.   Robert E. Cushman
November, 1962

Preface
to the 13th edition

The cases added to this thirteenth edition were selected to give some insight into the nature of the constitutional revolution which the present Court—probably the most "activist" in the nation's history—is staging under the chief justiceship of Earl Warren, and which has made the Court a center of public controversy for over a decade. The cases chosen let the student see for himself how such changes take place, how extensive they really are, by what logic they are justified, and what philosophy of government lies at their base. They center around three major areas of change, all marking advances in individual rights.

The first area of change (presaged by Mapp v. Ohio) has been in state criminal procedure, brought about largely by extending to the states through due process most of the provisions of the Bill of Rights. Gideon v. Wainwright, a widely publicized case upholding the right to counsel in a state trial, carefully explains and justifies this new approach. In Escobedo v. Illinois the Court held void the confession of a suspect who was questioned by the police without being allowed to see his lawyer. The decision raised a storm of protest from police and prosecutors, who rely heavily on such questioning to get convictions. Is a confession void if the suspect was not told he could keep silent? If he was not told he could see a lawyer? The Court is struggling with these problems now. In Murphy v. Waterfront Commission of New York the Court did away with one of two anomolies (the double jeopardy problem still remains) stemming from the divided sovereignty of our federal system, holding that testimony gotten from a person under a grant of immunity by one government could not be used by the other government. In a provocative dissent, Justice Harlan challenges the Court to show *which* constitutional provision would be violated by such use. Griswold v. Connecticut marks the birth of a new constitutional right —the right to marital privacy.

The second major area of change is the Court's insistence on human equality in the machinery of representative government—the "one man, one vote" rule of legislative apportionment. Following its promise in Baker v. Carr, the Court in Reynolds v. Sims began the long struggle to abolish unequal representation in state legislative bodies. To date, about three-fourths of the states have reapportioned their legislatures in accordance with the Court's standards, and efforts to reverse the Sims ruling by constitutional amendment have been defeated in Congress.

The third area is a new phase of the race equality revolution touched off by the Court in the School Segregation Cases—the support of congressional efforts to help. The Civil Rights Act of 1964 was upheld in Heart of Atlanta Motel v. United States and Katzenbach v. McClung, though it is an interesting commentary on our unique constitutional system that laws against race segregation have to rest on the power to regulate interstate commerce. In South Carolina v. Katzenbach the Court upheld the Voting Rights Act of 1965, which sought to brush away state obstructionist tactics and actually register Negroes to vote.

Some eighty-five new cases are listed in the Table of Cases, and cases either printed or commented upon include those decided through March of 1966.

Huntington Station, N.Y.   Robert F. Cushman
June, 1966

Contents

Table of Cases

Large and small capitals (with boldface page numbers) indicate the cases reprinted in this volume; italics indicate cases commented on in the editor's notes; ordinary type indicates cases quoted or discussed in the opinions.

Leading
Constitutional
Decisions

1

Amendments to
the Constitution

COLEMAN v. MILLER
307 U.S. 433; 83 L. Ed. 1385; 59 Sup. Ct. 972. 1939.

At an early date an important procedural point with regard to constitutional amendments was settled. In Hollingsworth v. Virginia, 3 Dallas 378 (1798), the Eleventh Amendment was challenged on the ground that Congress had not sent it to the President for his approval or veto before submitting it to the states for ratification. The Supreme Court said: "The negative of the President applies only to the ordinary cases of legislation. He has nothing to do with the proposition, or adoption, of amendments to the Constitution." The Court held that the amendment had been constitutionally adopted. More than a century later, those who opposed the Eighteenth and Nineteenth Amendments tried to convince the Supreme Court that the two amendments were invalid, first because they dealt with matters about which amendments to the federal Constitution could not constitutionally be made, and second, because they had not been ratified by correct procedures. The Supreme Court decided on the first point that there are no implied restrictions upon what may be put into constitutional amendments. In National Prohibition Cases, 253 U. S. 350 (1920), the Court, without writing an opinion, stated: "The prohibition of the manufacture, sale, transportation, importation, and exportation of intoxicating liquors for beverage purposes, as embodied in the 18th Amendment, is within the power to amend reserved by Article V of the Constitution." A similar result was reached in Leser v. Garnett, 258 U. S. 130 (1922). It was here urged that the Nineteenth Amendment (Woman Suffrage) was void because of its subject matter since "so great an addition to the electorate, if made without the state's consent, destroys its autonomy as a political body." The Court rejected the argument and pointed out that the Nineteenth Amendment is similar in form to the Fifteenth, which had been recognized as valid for fifty years.

In Dillon v. Gloss, 256 U. S. 368 (1921), the Court said that it could be fairly inferred from the amending clause of the Constitution (Article V) "that the ratification must be within some reasonable time after the proposal," and held that the Eighteenth Amendment was not unconstitutionally adopted because of the fact that Congress in submitting it to the states stipulated that it should be inoperative unless ratified within seven years. Congress could validly place a reasonable limit on the period of ratification and seven years is a reasonable limit.

In United States v. Sprague, 282 U. S. 716 (1931), it was argued that the Eighteenth Amendment was void because it was ratified by state legislatures rather than by state ratifying conventions. While amendments proposing minor or procedural constitutional changes may properly be ratified by state legislatures, it was urged that the framers of the Constitution intended that amendments conferring on the United States new direct powers over individuals, as in the Eighteenth Amendment, should be ratified in conventions. Further, the Tenth Amendment, which reserves to the states the powers not delegated to the United States, requires that amendments which reduce the states' reserved power can validly be ratified only by the people's especially chosen representatives in state ratifying conventions. The Supreme Court rejected the entire argument. When Article V states that a proposed amendment becomes part of the Constitution when ratified by the legislatures of three-fourths of the States or by conventions in three-fourths thereof, as the one or the other mode may be proposed by the Congress, it means exactly what it says. Congress has an absolutely free choice between the two methods. The Tenth Amendment in no way limits Article V. It was pointed out that all amendments thus far adopted (to 1931) were ratified by state legislatures, and several made changes quite as fundamental as did the Eighteenth Amendment.

Hawke v. Smith, 253 U. S. 221 (1920), held that the action of a state legislature in ratifying a federal amendment cannot validly be subjected subsequently to a popular referendum through which the voters of the state might set it aside. The Ohio constitution provided for just this, and when in January, 1919, the Ohio legislature ratified the Eighteenth Amendment the machinery was set in motion to have the ratification submitted to such a referendum vote. Hawke, a citizen of Ohio, brought action to enjoin Smith, the secretary of state of Ohio, from spending the state's money for such an election, which he claimed was invalid under the federal Constitution. The case was of widespread importance since more than twenty state constitutions provided for the referendum upon legislative acts, and in several the issue had arisen whether such a referendum could set aside a ratification by the state legislature of a federal amendment. In holding the Ohio referendum void the Court said that when Article V speaks of ratification by "legislatures" it means the "representative body which made the laws of the people" with which the founding fathers were familiar. It does not mean a direct vote by the people. Had the framers wished to have federal amendments ratified by direct popular vote they would have said so. It was argued that ratification of a federal amendment was a legislative act and that the state could validly make the referendum part of its legislative machinery. The Court declared that ratification is not a legislative act. It is a specific duty imposed on state legislatures by the language of Article V, and no state may change the methods therein set out by which that duty is to be performed. There is no constitutional objection to a prior advisory referendum on a federal amendment, since it would have no legal effect. Some states provide for this.

The cases just discussed left unanswered several important questions about the federal amending process. First, can a state which has ratified an amendment later withdraw that ratification? New Jersey, Ohio, and Oregon sought to withdraw their ratifications of the Fourteenth Amendment in 1868. The Secretary of State, acting on instructions from Congress embodied in a concurrent resolution, counted the ratifications as binding and proclaimed the amendment in force. New York tried to withdraw her ratification of the Fifteenth Amendment, and Tennessee sought to withdraw ratification of the Nineteenth Amendment. The Secretary of State counted both ratifications. The Supreme Court, however, never passed on the constitutional issue involved. Second, can a state whose legislature has formally rejected a federal amendment later ratify it? Third, do proposed federal amendments die of old age, as it were, by remaining before the states unratified for too long a time? The last two questions were the major issues in the present case.

Mr. Chief Justice Hughes delivered the opinion of the Court, saying in part:

In June, 1924, the Congress proposed an amendment to the Constitution, known as the Child Labor Amendment. In January, 1925, the legislature of Kansas adopted a resolution rejecting the proposed amendment and a certified copy of the resolution was sent to the Secretary of State of the United States. In January, 1937, a resolution . . . was introduced in the senate of Kansas ratifying the proposed amendment. There were forty senators. When the resolution came up for consideration, twenty senators voted in favor of its adoption and twenty voted against it. The lieutenant governor, the presiding officer of the senate, then cast his vote in favor of the resolution. The resolution was later adopted by the house of representatives on the vote of a majority of its members.

This original proceeding in mandamus was then brought in the supreme court of Kansas by twenty-one members of the senate, including the twenty senators who had voted against the resolution, and three members of the house of representatives, to compel the secretary of the senate to erase an endorsement on the resolution to the effect that it had been adopted by the senate and to endorse thereon the words "was not passed," and to restrain the officers of the senate and house of representatives from signing the resolution and the secretary of state of Kansas from authenticating it and delivering it to the governor. The petition challenged the right of the lieutenant governor to cast the deciding vote in the senate. The petition also set forth the prior rejection of the proposed amendment and alleged that in the period from June, 1924, to March, 1927, the amendment had been rejected by both houses of the legislatures of twenty-six states, and had been ratified in only five states, and that by reason of that rejection and the failure of ratification within a reasonable time the proposed amendment had lost its vitality. . . .

[The Court first considered whether the petitioners had sufficient standing in the way of direct interest to invoke the jurisdiction of the Court, and held they had. Secondly, by a vote of four to four, it affirmed, without considering the merits, the decision of the state supreme court that the lieutenant governor had authority to break a tie in the state senate.]

Third.—The effect of the previous rejection of the amendment and of the lapse of time since its submission.

1. The state court adopted the view expressed by text-writers that a state legislature which has rejected an amendment proposed by the Congress may later ratify. The argument in support of that view is that Article V says nothing of rejection but speaks only of ratification and provides that a proposed amendment shall be valid as part of the Constitution when ratified by three-fourths of the states; that the

power to ratify is thus conferred upon the state by the Constitution and, as a ratifying power, persists despite a previous rejection. The opposing view proceeds on an assumption that if ratification by "conventions" were prescribed by the Congress, a convention could not reject and, having adjourned sine die, be reassembled and ratify. It is also premised, in accordance with views expressed by text-writers, that ratification if once given cannot afterwards be rescinded and the amendment rejected, and it is urged that the same effect in the exhaustion of the state's power to act should be ascribed to rejection; that a state can act "but once, either by convention or through its legislature."

Historic instances are cited. In [December 18] 1865, the Thirteenth Amendment was rejected by the legislature of New Jersey which subsequently ratified it, but the question did not become important as ratification by the requisite number of states had already been proclaimed. The question did arise in connection with the adoption of the Fourteenth Amendment. The legislatures of Georgia, North Carolina and South Carolina had rejected the amendment in November and December, 1866. New governments were erected in those states (and in others) under the direction of Congress. The new legislatures ratified the amendment, that of North Carolina on July 4, 1868, that of South Carolina on July 9, 1868, and that of Georgia on July 21, 1868. Ohio and New Jersey first ratified and then passed resolutions withdrawing their consent. As there were then thirty-seven states, twenty-eight were needed to constitute the requisite three-fourths. On July 9, 1868, the Congress adopted a resolution requesting the Secretary of State to communicate "a list of the states of the Union whose legislatures have ratified the fourteenth article of amendment," and in Secretary Seward's report attention was called to the action of Ohio and New Jersey. On July 20 Secretary Seward issued a proclamation reciting the ratification by twenty-eight states, including North Carolina, South Carolina, Ohio and New Jersey, and stating that it appeared that Ohio and New Jersey had since passed resolutions withdrawing their consent and that "it is deemed a matter of doubt and uncertainty whether such resolutions are not irregular, invalid and therefore ineffectual." The Secretary certified that if the ratifying resolutions of Ohio and New Jersey were still in full force and effect, notwithstanding the attempted withdrawal, the amendment had become a part of the Constitution. On the following day the Congress adopted a concurrent resolution which, reciting that three-fourths of the states having ratified (the list including North Carolina, South Carolina, Ohio and New Jersey), declared the Fourteenth Amendment to be a part of the Constitution and that it should be duly promulgated as such by the Secretary of State. Accordingly, Secretary Seward, on July 28, issued his proclamation embracing the states mentioned in the congressional resolution and adding Georgia.

Thus the political departments of the government dealt with the effect both of previous rejection and of attempted withdrawal and determined that both were ineffectual in the presence of an actual ratification. . . . This decision by the political departments of the government as to the validity of the adoption of the Fourteenth Amendment has been accepted.

We think that in accordance with this historic precedent the question of the efficacy of ratifications by state legislatures, in the light of previous rejection or attempted withdrawal, should be regarded as a political question pertaining to the political departments, with the ultimate authority in the Congress in the exercise of its control over the promulgation of the adoption of the amendment. . . .

2. The more serious question is whether the proposal by the Congress of the amendment had lost its vitality through lapse of time and hence it could not be ratified by the Kansas legislature in 1937. The argument of petitioners stresses the fact that nearly thirteen years elapsed between the proposal in 1924 and the ratification in question. It is said that when the amendment was proposed there was a definitely adverse popular sentiment and that at the end of 1925 there had been rejection by both houses of the legislatures of sixteen states and ratification by only four states, and that it was not until about 1933 that an aggressive campaign was started in favor of the amendment. In reply, it is urged that Congress did not fix a limit of time for ratification and that an unreasonably long time had not elapsed since the submission; that the conditions which gave rise to the amendment had not been eliminated; that the prevalence of child labor, the diversity of state laws and the disparity in their administration, with the resulting competitive inequalities, continued to exist. Reference is also made to the fact that a number of the states have treated the amendment as still pending and that in the proceedings of the national government there have been indications of the same view. It is said that there were fourteen ratifications in 1933, four in 1935, one in 1936, and three in 1937.

We have held that the Congress in proposing an amendment may fix a reasonable time for ratification. Dillon v. Gloss, 256 U. S. 368. There we sustained the action of the Congress in providing in the proposed Eighteenth Amendment that it should be inoperative unless ratified within seven years. No limitation of time for ratification is provided in the instant case either in the proposed amendment or in the resolution of submission. But petitioners contend that, in the absence of a limitation by the Congress, the Court can and should decide what is a reasonable period within which ratification may be had. We are unable to agree with that contention.

It is true that in Dillon v. Gloss the Court said that nothing was found in Article V which suggested that an amendment once proposed was to be open to ratification for all time, or that ratification in some states might be separated from that in others by many years and yet be effective; that there was a strong suggestion to the contrary in that proposal and ratification were but succeeding steps in a single endeavor; that as amendments were deemed to be prompted by necessity, they should be considered and disposed of presently; and that there is a fair implication that ratification must be sufficiently contemporaneous in the required number of states to reflect the will of the people in all sections at relatively the same period; and hence that ratification must be within some reasonable time after the proposal. These considerations were cogent reasons for the decision in Dillon v. Gloss, that the Congress had the power to fix a reasonable time for ratification. But it does not follow that, whenever Congress has not exercised that power, the Court should take upon itself the responsibility of deciding what constitutes a reasonable time and determine accordingly the validity of ratifications. That question was not involved in Dillon v. Gloss and, in accordance with familiar principle, what was there said must be read in the light of the point decided.

Where are to be found the criteria for such a judicial determination? None are to be found in Constitution or statute. In their endeavor to answer this question petitioners' counsel have suggested that at least two years should be allowed; that six years would not seem to be unreasonably long; that seven years had been used by the Congress as a reasonable period; that one year, six months and thirteen days was the average time used in passing upon amendments which have been ratified since the first ten amendments; that three years, six months and twenty-five days has been the longest time used in ratifying. To this list of variables, counsel add that "the nature and extent of publicity and the activity of the public and of the legislatures of the several states in relation to any particular proposal should be taken into consideration." That statement is pertinent, but there are additional matters to be examined and weighed. When a proposed amendment springs from a conception of economic needs, it would be necessary, in determining whether a reasonable time had elapsed since its submission, to consider the economic conditions prevailing in the country, whether these had so far changed since the submission as to make the proposal no longer responsive to the conception which inspired it or whether conditions were such as to intensify the feeling of need and the appropriateness of the proposed remedial action. In short, the question of a reasonable time in many cases would involve, as in this case it does involve, an appraisal of a great variety of relevant conditions, political, social and economic, which can hardly be said to be within the appropriate range of evidence receivable in a court of justice and as to which it would be an extravagant extension of judicial authority to assert judicial notice as the basis of deciding a controversy with respect to the validity of an amendment actually ratified. On the other hand, these conditions are appropriate for the consideration of the political departments of the government. The questions they involve are essentially political and not justiciable. They can be decided by the Congress with the full knowledge and appreciation ascribed to the national legislature of the political, social and economic conditions which have prevailed during the period since the submission of the amendment.

Our decision that the Congress has the power under Article V to fix a reasonable limit of time for ratification in proposing an amendment proceeds upon the assumption that the question, what is a reasonable time, lies within the congressional province. If it be deemed that such a question is an open one when the limit has not been fixed in advance, we think that it should also be regarded as an open one for the consideration of the Congress when, in the presence of certified ratifications by three-fourths of the states, the time arrives for the promulgation of the adoption of the amendment. The decision by the Congress, in its control of the action of the Secretary of State, of the question whether the amendment had been adopted within a reasonable time would not be subject to review by the courts. . . .

For the reasons we have stated . . . we think that the Congress in controlling the promulgation of the adoption of a constitutional amendment has the final determination of the question whether by lapse of time its proposal of the amendment had lost its vitality prior to the required ratifications. The state officials should not be restrained from certifying to the Secretary of State the adoption by the legislature of Kansas of the resolution of ratification. . . .

A concurring opinion by Mr. Justice Black, joined by Justices Roberts, Frankfurter, and Douglas, urged that the Court should have disapproved Dillon v. Gloss in so far as it decided judicially that seven years is a reasonable time limit for Congress to place upon ratification of an amendment. That question, too, is political. "The process [of amendment] is 'political' in its entirety, from submission until an amendment becomes part of the Constitution, and is not subject to judicial guidance, control or interference at any point."

Justices Butler and McReynolds dissented.

2

Principles of
the Federal System—
National Supremacy, etc.

McCULLOCH v. MARYLAND
4 Wheaton (U. S.) 316; 4 L. Ed. 579. 1819.

When Congress in 1791 chartered the First Bank of the United States, it was only after a most full and bitter argument as to whether it had the power to do so. Hamilton, who had proposed the creation of the bank, had written an elaborate opinion defending it as an exercise of a power reasonably implied from those expressly delegated to Congress. Jefferson and his friends had stoutly maintained that congressional powers must be strictly construed and that the granting of the charter was an act of unwarrantable usurpation. Nevertheless the charter of the first bank was never attacked in the courts as being unconstitutional, and the institution continued to exist until its charter expired in 1811. The financial conditions ensuing after the War of 1812 made the re-establishment of the bank desirable, and the Second Bank of the United States was accordingly chartered in 1816. Almost immediately it incurred the bitter odium of large sections of the country, especially of the west and south. The bank was largely under the control of the Federalists, who were accused of using it as a political machine and of wielding its great influence for political purposes; its stock was largely held by British capitalists and other foreign investors; and it was accused of being responsible for a period of financial depression which brought ruin to thousands. It is true that the bank had begun operations under corrupt and inefficient management and had encouraged a high degree of inflation of credits. This had resulted in heavy losses to investors; in the state of Maryland the Baltimore branch collapsed with a loss to Maryland investors alone of a sum variously estimated from $1,700,000 to $3,000,000. Wiser counsels prevailed shortly, however, and the bank faced about and embarked upon a financial course as conservative as it had hitherto been headlong. It refused to accept the bank notes of the imprudent state banks and insisted upon the liquidation of its credits. One after another these over-inflated state banks failed, and hundreds of reckless speculators were ruined. Money was almost unobtainable. While most of this financial disaster was the inevitable result of the orgies of inflation and speculation in which the frontier communities in particular had been indulging, the Bank of the United States was popularly regarded as the cause of disaster, as the ruthless "money trust" which was ruining the prosperity of the country. A popular demand for legislative control of the bank was set up, and eight states passed either laws or constitutional amendments restricting the activities of the bank or imposing heavy burdens upon it. The law involved in this case, passed by the legislature of Maryland, which was particularly hostile to the bank because of its earlier debacle, is typical of this legislative onslaught.

The Maryland statute forbade all banks not chartered by the state itself to issue bank notes save upon special stamped paper obtainable upon the payment of a very heavy tax. This requirement could be commuted by the payment of an annual tax to the state of $15,000. A penalty of $500 forfeiture was inflicted for each offense, an amount which in the case of the now large and prosperous Baltimore branch of the Bank of the United States would have come possibly to millions of dollars. McCulloch, the cashier of the branch in Baltimore, issued notes without complying with the state law and this action was brought on behalf of the state of Maryland to recover the penalties.

The case was argued for nine days before the Supreme Court by the greatest lawyers of the day; William Pinkney, Daniel Webster, and William Wirt defended the bank, while Luther Martin, Joseph Hopkinson, and Walter Jones represented the state of Maryland. The opinion of Marshall in the case is commonly regarded as his greatest state paper.

The announcement of the decision was the signal for a veritable storm of abuse directed against the Supreme Court. Judge Roane, of the Virginia court of appeals, published a series of newspaper attacks upon the decision so bitter that Marshall was led to write a reply in his defense. The Virginia legislature passed a resolution urging that the Supreme Court be shorn of its power to pass upon cases to which states were parties. Ohio, which had previously passed a law taxing each branch of the Bank of the United States within its limits $50,000 a year, defied the Supreme Court and proceeded to collect the tax in spite of its decision, a position from which it was later obliged to withdraw; Osborn v. The Bank of the United States, 9 Wheaton 738 (1824). The attack upon the Court in this case was directed in large part against the failure of that tribunal to invalidate an act of Congress (incorporating the bank) and not against the exercise of the judicial veto. The decision was peculiarly odious to the strict constructionists because it not only sustained the doctrine of the implied powers of Congress but also recognized the binding effect of an implied limitation upon the states preventing them from interfering with the functioning of federal agencies.

The doctrine of implied powers in Congress is not new in this case. Not only had it been ably expounded by Hamilton as above mentioned, but in the case of United States v. Fisher, 2 Cranch 358 (1805), which had been decided fourteen years before, Marshall himself had given expression to the doctrine; but as that case did not relate to any such important political issue as did the bank case, the decision at that time had evoked no comment.

Mr. Chief Justice Marshall delivered the opinion of the Court, saying in part:

In the case now to be determined, the defendant, a sovereign state, denies the obligation of a law enacted by the legislature of the Union, and the plaintiff, on his part, contests the validity of an act which has been passed by the legislature of that state. The Constitution of our country, in its most interesting and vital parts, is to be considered; the conflicting powers of the government of the Union and of its members, as marked in that Constitution, are to be discussed; and an opinion given, which may essentially influence the great operations of the government. No tribunal can approach such a question without a deep sense of its importance, and of the awful responsibility involved in its decision. But it must be decided peacefully, or remain a source of hostile legislation, perhaps of hostility of a still more serious nature; and if it is to be so decided, by this tribunal alone can the decision be made. On the Supreme Court of the United States has the Constitution of our country devolved this important duty.

The first question made in the cause is, has Congress power to incorporate a bank? . . .

In discussing this question, the counsel for the State of Maryland have deemed it of some importance, in the construction of the Constitution, to consider that instrument not as emanating from the people, but as the act of sovereign and independent states. The powers of the general government, it has been said, are delegated by the states, who alone are truly sovereign; and must be exercised in subordination to the states, who alone possess supreme dominion.

It would be difficult to sustain this proposition. The convention which framed the Constitution was, indeed, elected by the state legislatures. But the instrument, when it came from their hands, was a mere proposal, without obligation, or pretensions to it. It was reported to the then existing Congress of the United States, with a request that it might "be submitted to a convention of delegates, chosen in each state, by the people thereof, under the recommendation of its legislature, for their assent and ratification." This mode of proceeding was adopted; and by the convention, by Congress, and by the state legislatures, the instrument was submitted to the people. They acted upon it, in the only manner in which they can act safely, effectively, and wisely, on such a subject, by assembling in convention. It is true, they assembled in their several states; and where else should they have assembled? No political dreamer was ever wild enough to think of breaking down the lines which separate the states, and of compounding the American people into one common mass. Of consequence, when they act, they act in their states. But the measures they adopt do not, on that account, cease to be the measures of the people themselves, or become the measures of the state governments.

From these conventions the Constitution derives its whole authority. The government proceeds directly from the people; is "ordained and established" in the name of the people; and is declared to be ordained, "in order to form a more perfect union, establish justice, insure domestic tranquility, and secure the blessings of liberty to themselves and to their posterity." The assent of the states, in their sovereign capacity, is implied in calling a convention, and thus submitting that instrument to the people. But the people were at perfect liberty to accept or reject it; and their act was final. It required not the affirmance, and could not be negatived, by the state governments. The Constitution, when thus adopted, was of complete obligation, and bound the state sovereignties.

It has been said, that the people had already surrendered all their powers to the state sovereignties, and had nothing more to give.

But, surely, the question whether they may resume and modify the powers granted to government, does not remain to be settled in this country. Much more might the legitimacy of the general government be doubted, had it been created by the states. The powers delegated to the state sovereignties were to be exercised by themselves, not by a distinct and independent sovereignty, created by themselves. To the formation of a league, such as was the Confederation, the state sovereignties were certainly competent. But when, "in order to form a more perfect union," it was deemed necessary to change this alliance into an effective government, possessing great and sovereign powers, and acting directly on the people, the necessity of referring it to the people, and of deriving its powers directly from them, was felt and acknowledged by all.

The government of the Union, then (whatever may be the influence of this fact on the case), is emphatically and truly a government of the people. In form and in substance it emanates from them, its powers are granted by them, and are to be exercised directly on them, and for their benefit.

This government is acknowledged by all to be one of enumerated powers. The principle, that it can exercise only the powers granted to it, would seem too apparent to have required to be enforced by all those arguments which its enlightened friends, while it was depending before the people, found it necessary to urge. That principle is now universally admitted. But the question respecting the extent of the powers actually granted, is perpetually arising, and will probably continue to arise, as long as our system shall exist.

In discussing these questions, the conflicting powers of the general and state governments must be brought into view, and the supremacy of their respective laws, when they are in opposition, must be settled.

If any one proposition could command the universal assent of mankind, we might expect that it would be this: that the government of the Union, though limited in its powers, is supreme within its sphere of action. This would seem to result necessarily from its nature. It is the government of all; its powers are delegated by all; it represents all, and acts for all. Though any one state may be willing to control its operations, no state is willing to allow others to control them. The nation, on those subjects on which it can act, must necessarily bind its component parts. But this question is not left to mere reason: the people have, in express terms, decided it, by saying, "this Constitution, and the laws of the United States, which shall be made in pursuance thereof," "shall be the supreme law of the land," and by requiring that the members of the state legislatures, and the officers of the executive and judicial departments of the states, shall take the oath of fidelity to it.

The government of the United States, then, though limited in its powers, is supreme; and its laws, when made in pursuance of the Constitution, form the supreme law of the land, "anything in the constitution or laws of any state, to the contrary notwithstanding."

Among the enumerated powers, we do not find that of establishing a bank or creating a corporation. But there is no phrase in the instrument, which, like the Articles of Confederation, excludes incidental or implied powers; and which requires that everything granted shall be expressly and minutely described. Even the Tenth Amendment, which was framed for the purpose of quieting the excessive jealousies which had been excited, omits the word "expressly," and declares only that the powers "not delegated to the United States, nor prohibited to the States, are reserved to the States or to the people"; thus leaving the question, whether the particular power which may become the subject of contest, has been delegated to the one government, or prohibited to the other, to depend on a fair construction of the whole instrument. The men who drew and adopted this amendment, had experienced the embarrassments resulting from the insertion of this word in the Articles of Confederation, and probably omitted it to avoid those embarrassments. A constitution, to contain an accurate detail of all the subdivisions of which its great powers will admit, and of all the means by which they may be carried into execution, would partake of the prolixity of a legal code, and could scarcely be embraced by the human mind. It would probably never be understood by the public. Its nature, therefore, requires, that only its great outlines should be marked, its important objects designated, and the minor ingredients which compose those objects be deduced from the nature of the objects themselves. That this idea was entertained by the framers of the American Constitution, is not only to be inferred from the nature of the instrument, but from the language. Why else were some of the limitations, found in the ninth section of the first article, introduced? It is also, in some degree, warranted by their having omitted to use any restrictive term which might prevent its receiving a fair and just interpretation. In considering this question, then, we must never forget, that it is a constitution we are expounding.

Although, among the enumerated powers of government, we do not find the word "bank," or "incorporation," we find the great powers to lay and collect taxes; to borrow money; to regulate commerce; to declare and conduct war; and to raise and support armies and navies. The sword and the purse, all the external relations, and no inconsiderable portion of the industry of the nation, are intrusted to its government. It can never be pretended that these vast powers draw after them others of inferior importance, merely because they are inferior. Such an idea can never be advanced. But it may, with great reason, be contended, that a government, intrusted with such ample powers, on the due execution of which the happiness and prosperity of the nation so vitally depends, must also be intrusted with ample means for their execution. The power being given, it is the interest of the nation to facilitate its execution. It can never be their interest, and cannot be presumed to have been their intention, to clog and embarrass its execution by withholding the most appropriate means. Throughout this vast republic, from the St. Croix to the Gulf of Mexico, from the Atlantic to the Pacific, revenue is to be collected and expended, armies are to be marched and supported. The exigencies of the nation may require that the treasure raised in the north should be transported to the south, that raised in the east conveyed to the west, or that this order should be reversed. Is that construction of the Constitution to be preferred which would render these operations difficult, hazardous, and expensive? Can we adopt that construction (unless the words imperiously require it) which would impute to the framers of that instrument, when granting these powers for the public good, the intention of impeding their exercise by withholding a choice of means? If, indeed, such be the mandate of the Constitution, we have only to obey; but that instrument does not profess to enumerate the means by which the powers it confers may be executed; nor does it prohibit the creation of a corporation, if the existence of such a being be essential to the beneficial exercise of those powers. It is, then, the subject of fair inquiry, how far such means may be employed.

It is not denied, that the powers given to the government imply the ordinary means of execution. That, for example, of raising revenue, and applying it to national purposes, is admitted to imply the power of conveying money from place to place, as the exigencies of the nation may require, and of employing the usual means of conveyance. But it is denied that the government has its choice of means; or, that it may employ the most convenient means, if, to employ them, it be necessary to erect a corporation.

. . . The power of creating a corporation, though appertaining to sovereignty, is not, like the power of making war, or levying taxes, or of regulating commerce, a great substantive and independent power, which cannot be implied as incidental to other powers, or used as a means of executing them. It is never the end for which other powers are exercised, but a means by which other objects are accomplished. No contributions are made to charity for the sake of an incorporation, but a corporation is created to administer the charity; no seminary of learning is instituted in order to be incorporated, but the corporate character is conferred to subserve the purposes of education. No city was ever built with the sole object of being incorporated, but is incorporated as affording the best means of being well governed. The power of creating a corporation is never used for its own sake, but for the purpose of effecting something else. No sufficient reason is, therefore, perceived, why it may not pass as incidental to those powers which are expressly given, if it be a direct mode of executing them.

But the Constitution of the United States has not left the right of Congress to employ the necessary means, for the execution of the powers conferred on the government, to general reasoning. To its enumeration of powers is added that of making "all laws which shall be necessary and proper, for carrying into execution the foregoing powers, and all other powers vested by this constitution, in the government of the United States, or in any department thereof."

The counsel for the state of Maryland have urged various arguments, to prove that this clause, though in terms a grant of power, is not so in effect; but is really restrictive of the general right, which might otherwise be implied, of selecting means for executing the enumerated powers.

In support of this proposition, they have found it necessary to contend, that this clause was inserted for the purpose of conferring on Congress the power of making laws. That, without it, doubts might be entertained, whether Congress could exercise its powers in the form of legislation.

But could this be the object for which it was inserted? . . . That a legislature, endowed with legislative powers, can legislate, is a proposition too self-evident to have been questioned.

But the argument on which most reliance is placed, is drawn from the peculiar language of this clause. Congress is not empowered by it to make all laws, which may have relation to the powers conferred on the government, but such only as may be "necessary and proper" for carrying them into execution. The word "necessary" is considered as controlling the whole sentence, and as limiting the right to pass laws for the execution of the granted powers, to such as are indispensable, and without which the power would be nugatory. That it excludes the choice of means, and leaves to Congress, in each case, that only which is most direct and simple.

Is it true, that this is the sense in which the word "necessary" is always used? Does it always import an absolute physical necessity, so strong, that one thing, to which another may be termed necessary, cannot exist without that other? We think it does not. If reference be had to its use, in the common affairs of the world, or in approved authors, we find that it frequently imports no more than that one thing is convenient, or useful, or essential to another. To employ the means necessary to an end, is generally understood as employing any means calculated to produce the end, and not as being confined to those single means, without which the end would be entirely unattainable. Such is the character of human language, that no word conveys to the mind, in all situations, one single definite idea; and nothing is more common than to use words in a figurative sense. Almost all compositions contain words, which, taken in their rigorous sense, would convey a meaning different from that which is obviously intended. It is essential to just construction, that many words which import something excessive, should be understood in a more mitigated sense—in that sense which common usage justifies. The word "necessary" is of this description. It has not a fixed character peculiar to itself. It admits of all degrees of comparison; and is often connected with others words, which increase or diminish the impression the mind receives of the urgency it imports. A thing may be necessary, very necessary, absolutely or indispensably necessary. To no mind would the same idea be conveyed, by these several phrases. . . . This word, then, like others, is used in various senses; and, in its construction, the subject, the context, the intention of the person using them, are all to be taken into view.

Let this be done in the case under consideration. The subject is the execution of those great powers on which the welfare of a nation essentially depends. It must have been the intention of those who gave these powers, to insure, as far as human prudence could insure, their beneficial execution. This could not be done by confiding the choice of means to such narrow limits as not to leave it in the power of Congress to adopt any which might be appropriate, and which were conducive to the end. This provision is made in a constitution intended to endure for ages to come, and, consequently, to be adapted to the various crises of human affairs. To have prescribed the means by which government should, in all future time, execute its powers, would have been to change, entirely, the character of the instrument, and give it the properties of a legal code. It would have been an unwise attempt to provide, by immutable rules, for exigencies which, if foreseen at all, must have been seen dimly, and which can be best provided for as they occur. To have declared that the best means shall not be used, but those alone without which the power given would be nugatory, would have been to deprive the legislature of the capacity to avail itself of experience, to exercise its reason, and to accommodate its legislation to circumstances. . . .

But the argument which most conclusively demonstrates the error of the construction contended for by the counsel for the state of Maryland, is founded on the intention of the convention, as manifested in the whole clause. To waste time and argument in proving that, without it, Congress might carry its powers into execution, would be not much less idle than to hold a lighted taper to the sun. As little can it be required to prove, that in the absence of this clause, Congress would have some choice of means. That it might employ those which, in its judgment, would most advantageously effect the object to be accomplished. That any means adapted to the end, any means which tended directly to the execution of the constitutional powers of the government, were in themselves constitutional. This clause, as construed by the state of Maryland, would abridge and almost annihilate this useful and necessary right of the legislature to select its means. That this could not be intended, is, we should think, had it not been already controverted, too apparent for controversy. We think so for the following reasons:

1. The clause is placed among the powers of Congress, not among the limitations on those powers.

2. Its terms purport to enlarge, not to diminish the powers vested in the government. It purports to be an additional power, not a restriction on those already granted. No reason has been or can be assigned, for thus concealing an intention to narrow the discretion of the national legislature, under words which purport to enlarge it. The

framers of the Constitution wished its adoption, and well knew that it would be endangered by its strength, not by its weakness. Had they been capable of using language which would convey to the eye one idea, and, after deep reflection, impress on the mind another, they would rather have disguised the grant of power, than its limitation. If, then, their intention had been, by this clause, to restrain the free use of means which might otherwise have been implied, that intention would have been inserted in another place, and would have been expressed in terms resembling these: "In carrying into execution the foregoing powers, and all others," etc., "no laws shall be passed but such as are necessary and proper." Had the intention been to make this clause restrictive, it would unquestionably have been so in form as well as in effect.

The result of the most careful and attentive consideration bestowed upon this clause is, that if it does not enlarge, it cannot be construed to restrain the powers of Congress, or to impair the right of the legislature to exercise its best judgment in the selection of measures to carry into execution the constitutional powers of the government. If no other motive for its insertion can be suggested, a sufficient one is found in the desire to remove all doubts respecting the right to legislate on that vast mass of incidental powers which must be involved in the Constitution, if that instrument be not a splendid bauble.

We admit, as all must admit, that the powers of the government are limited, and that its limits are not to be transcended. But we think the sound construction of the Constitution must allow to the national legislature that discretion, with respect to the means by which the powers it confers are to be carried into execution, which will enable that body to perform the high duties assigned to it, in the manner most beneficial to the people. Let the end be legitimate, let it be within the scope of the Constitution, and all means which are appropriate, which are plainly adapted to that end, which are not prohibited, but consist with the letter and spirit of the Constitution, are constitutional. . . .

If a corporation may be employed indiscriminately with other means to carry into execution the powers of the government, no particular reason can be assigned for excluding the use of a bank, if required for its fiscal operations. To use one, must be within the discretion of Congress, if it be an appropriate mode of executing the powers of government. That it is a convenient, a useful, and essential instrument in the prosecution of its fiscal operations, is not now a subject of controversy. All those who have been concerned in the administration of our finances, have concurred in representing its importance and necessity; and so strongly have they been felt, that statesmen of the first class, whose previous opinions against it had been confirmed by every circumstance which can fix the human judgment, have yielded those opinions to the exigencies of the nation. . . .

After the most deliberate consideration, it is the unanimous and decided opinion of this Court, that the act to incorporate the Bank of the United States is a law made in pursuance of the Constitution, and is a part of the supreme law of the land. . . .

It being the opinion of the Court that the act incorporating the bank is constitutional; and that the power of establishing a branch in the state of Maryland might be properly exercised by the bank itself, we proceed to inquire:

2. Whether the state of Maryland may, without violating the Constitution, tax that branch?

That the power of taxation is one of vital importance; that it is retained by the states; that it is not abridged by the grant of a similar power to the government of the Union; that it is to be concurrently exercised by the two governments: are truths which have never been denied. But, such is the paramount character of the Constitution, that its capacity to withdraw any subject from the action of even this power, is admitted. The states are expressly forbidden to lay any duties on imports or exports, except what may be absolutely necessary for executing their inspection laws. If the obligation of this prohibition must be conceded—if it may restrain a state from the exercise of its taxing power on imports and exports, the same paramount character would seem to restrain, as it certainly may restrain, a state from such other exercise of this power, as is in its nature incompatible with, and repugnant to, the constitutional laws of the Union. A law, absolutely repugnant to another, as entirely repeals that other as if express terms of repeal were used.

On this ground the counsel for the bank place its claim to be exempted from the power of a state to tax its operations. There is no express provision for the case, but the claim has been sustained on a principle which so entirely pervades the Constitution, is so intermixed with the materials which compose it, so interwoven with its web, so blended with its texture, as to be incapable of being separated from it, without rending it into shreds.

This great principle is, that the Constitution and the laws made in pursuance thereof are supreme; that they control the constitution and laws of the respective states, and cannot be controlled by them. From this, which may be almost termed an axiom, other propositions are deduced as corollaries, on the truth or error of which, and on their application to this case, the cause has been supposed to depend. These are, 1. That a power to create implies a power to preserve. 2. That a power to destroy, if wielded by a different hand, is hostile to, and incompatible with, these powers to create and preserve. 3. That where this repugnancy exists, that authority which is supreme must control, not yield to that over which it is supreme. . . .

The power of Congress to create, and of course to continue, the bank, was the subject of the preceding part of this opinion; and is no longer to be considered as questionable.

That the power of taxing it by the states may be exercised so as to destroy it, is too obvious to be denied. But taxation is said to be an absolute power, which acknowledges no other limits than those expressly prescribed in the Constitution, and like sovereign power of every other description, is trusted to the discretion of those who use it. . . .

The argument on the part of the state of Maryland, is, not that the states may directly resist a law of Congress, but that they may exercise their acknowledged powers upon it, and that the Constitution leaves them this right in the confidence that they will not abuse it. . . .

That the power to tax involves the power to destroy; that the power to destroy may defeat and render useless the power to create; that there is a plain repugnance, in conferring on one government a power to control the constitutional measures of another, which other, with respect to those very measures, is declared to be supreme over that which exerts the control, are propositions not to be denied. But all inconsistencies are to be reconciled by the magic of the word CONFIDENCE. Taxation, it is said, does not necessarily and unavoidably destroy. To carry it to the excess of destruction would be an abuse, to presume which, would banish that confidence which is essential to all government.

But is this a case of confidence? Would the people of any one state trust those of another with a power to control the most insignificant operations of their state government? We know they would not. Why, then, should we suppose that the people of any one state should be willing to trust those of another with a power to control the operations of a government to which they have confided their most important and most valuable interests? In the legislature of the Union alone, are all represented. The legislature of the Union alone, therefore, can be trusted by the people with the power of controlling measures which concern all, in the confidence that it will not be abused. This, then, is not a case of confidence, and we must consider it as it really is.

If we apply the principle for which the state of Maryland contends, to the Constitution generally, we shall find it capable of changing totally the character of that instrument. We shall find it capable of arresting all the measures of the government, and of prostrating it at the foot of the states. The American people have declared their Constitution, and the laws made in pursuance thereof, to be supreme; but this principle would transfer the supremacy, in fact, to the state.

If the states may tax one instrument, employed by the government in the execution of its powers, they may tax any and every other instrument. They may tax the mail; they may tax the mint; they may tax patent rights; they may tax the papers of the custom-house; they may tax judicial process; they may tax all the means employed by the government, to an excess which would defeat all the ends of government. This was not intended by the American people. They did not design to make their government dependent on the states. . . .

It has also been insisted, that, as the power of taxation in the general and state governments is acknowledged to be concurrent, every argument which would sustain the right of the general government to tax banks chartered by the states, will equally sustain the right of the states to tax banks chartered by the general government.

But the two cases are not on the same reason. The people of all the states have created the general government, and have conferred upon it the general power of taxation. The people of all the states, and the states themselves, are represented in Congress, and, by their representatives, exercise this power. When they tax the chartered institutions of the states, they tax their constituents; and these taxes must be uniform. But when a state taxes the operations of the government of the United States, it acts upon institutions created, not by their own constituents, but by people over whom they claim no control. It acts upon the measures of a government created by others as well as themselves, for the benefit of others in common with themselves. The difference is that which always exists, and always must exist, between the action of the whole on a part, and the action of a part on the whole—between the laws of a government declared to be supreme, and those of a government which, when in opposition to those laws, is not supreme.

But if the full application of this argument could be admitted, it might bring into question the right of Congress to tax the state banks, and could not prove the right of the states to tax the Bank of the United States.

The Court has bestowed on this subject its most deliberate consideration. The result is a conviction that the states have no power, by taxation or otherwise, to retard, impede, burden, or in any manner control, the operations of the constitutional laws enacted by Congress to carry into execution the powers vested in the general government. This is, we think, the unavoidable consequence of that supremacy which the Constitution has declared.

We are unanimously of opinion, that the law passed by the legislature of Maryland, imposing a tax on the Bank of the United States, is unconstitutional and void.

This opinion does not deprive the states of any resources which they originally possessed. It does not extend to a tax paid by the real property of the bank, in common with the other real property within the state, nor to a tax imposed on the interest which the citizens of Maryland may hold in this institution, in common with other property of the same description throughout the state. But this is a tax on the operations of the bank, and is, consequently, a tax on the operation of an instrument employed by the government of the Union to carry its powers into execution. Such a tax must be unconstitutional. . . .

COOPER v. AARON
358 U. S. 1; 3 L. Ed. 2d 5; 78 Sup. Ct. 1401. 1958.

While in McCulloch v. Maryland the general rule was established that the states may not interfere with or burden the agencies and instrumentalities of the federal government, the question remained as to what, in a concrete case, constitutes interference or burden. In Johnson v. Maryland, 254 U. S. 51 (1920), the Supreme Court held invalid Maryland's enforcement against a mail truck driver of a requirement that he obtain a state driving license by taking an examination and paying a fee of $3. This was direct interference with the federal postal system. The case did not squarely settle the question whether the mail truck driver could be punished by the local authorities for violating local traffic regulations. The Court's opinion, however, clearly suggests that the federal employee can be compelled to obey such local police regulations as do not interfere with the federal service. In an old case in the United States circuit court in 1817, United States v. Hart, 1 Peters (C.C.) 390, a constable in Philadelphia was held not guilty of a breach of the federal statute forbidding obstruction of the mails when he acted to prevent reckless driving: he stopped a stage "going very rapidly through Market Street, some of the witnesses supposed it to be at a rate of eight or nine miles an hour."

One type of federal-state conflict takes form in what is called the "supersession" of state law by federal law. In 1939, Pennsylvania passed a drastic act requiring the registration of all aliens in the state. In 1940, Congress passed a milder Alien Registration Act. In Hines v. Davidowitz, 312 U. S. 52 (1941), the Court held that the federal statute supplanted the state statute. It said: "the regulation of aliens is so intimately blended and intertwined with responsibilities of the national government that where it acts, and the state also acts on the same subject, the act of Congress . . . is supreme; and the law of the state . . . must yield to it." In Pennsylvania v. Nelson, 350 U. S. 497 (1956), the Court held that the Smith Act (Alien Registration Act of 1940) superseded a Pennsylvania statute under which Nelson, a Communist party leader, had been convicted. The statute punished sedition against either the United States or the state, or both. The conviction was set aside. Sedition laws in some forty states would be similarly affected, although Congress could by law restore to the states the right to legislate in this field. Authors of the Smith Act loudly denied any congressional intention to prevent state sedition laws, and a bill has been pending in Congress for some time, but not yet passed, providing that federal statutes shall not be deemed to supersede state laws unless Congress indicates in the language of such statutes its intention to do this.

In Testa v. Katt, 330 U. S. 386 (1947), the Supreme Court held that Congress could validly require the state courts to enforce the criminal sections of the Federal Emergency Price Control Act. The Court invoked the "supremacy clause" of the Constitution (Art. VI, sec. 2) to override the protest of Rhode Island that it could not be compelled to enforce the criminal laws of another government. In 1912 the Court had announced a similar, though less drastic, doctrine in holding that state courts could be required by Congress to take civil damage cases arising under the Federal Employers' Liability Act. See Second Employers' Liability Cases, 223 U. S. 1.

In most cases in which states have been held to have trespassed upon federal authority, such action has been inadvertent rather than intentional, often in areas where the lines of power have not yet been clearly drawn. The School Segregation Cases (Brown v. Board of Education of Topeka, p. 249), however, together with subsequent efforts to enforce desegregation, aroused some southern states and communities to open defiance of federal authority. The ugly conflict which emerged in Little Rock, Arkansas, and the Court's handling of it are set out in Cooper v. Aaron, below. In United States v. Louisiana, 364 U. S. 500 (1960), the Court upheld a federal district court injunction against the enforcement of various Louisiana acts designed to defeat school integration. In doing so, the Court held invalid the Louisiana "interposition" statutes which asserted that the Supreme Court's decision in the School Segregation Cases was a usurpation of state power, and which sought to "interpose" state sovereignty. The Court quoted with approval the district court's comment: "The conclusion is clear that interposition is not a constitutional doctrine. If taken seriously, it is an illegal defiance of constitutional authority."

Opinion of the Court by Mr. Chief Justice Warren, Mr. Justice Black, Mr. Justice Frankfurter, Mr. Justice Douglas, Mr. Justice Burton, Mr. Justice Clark, Mr. Justice Harlan, Mr. Justice Brennan, and Mr. Justice Whittaker. The opinion said in part:

As this case reaches us it raises questions of the highest importance to the maintenance of our federal system of government. It necessarily involves a claim by the Governor and Legislature of a State that there is no duty on state officials to obey federal court orders resting on this Court's considered interpretation of the United States Constitution. Specifically it involves actions by the Governor and Legislature of Arkansas upon the premise that they are not bound by our holding in Brown v. Board of Education, 347 U. S. 483. That holding was that the Fourteenth Amendment forbids States to use their governmental powers to bar children on racial grounds from attending schools where there is state participation through any arrangement, management, funds or property. We are urged to uphold a suspension of the Little Rock School Board's plan to do away with segregated public schools in Little Rock until state laws and efforts to upset and nullify our holding in Brown v. Board of Education have been further challenged and tested in the courts. We reject these contentions.

The case was argued before us on September 11, 1958. On the following day we unanimously affirmed the judgment of the Court of Appeals for the Eighth Circuit, which had reversed a judgment of the District Court for the Eastern District of Arkansas. The District Court had granted the application of the petitioners, the Little Rock School Board and School Superintendent, to suspend for two and one-half years the operation of the School Board's court-approved desegregation program. In order that the School Board might know, without doubt, its duty in this regard before the opening of school, which had been set for the following Monday, September 15, 1958, we immediately issued the judgment, reserving the expression of our supporting views to a later date. This opinion of all of the members of the Court embodies those views.

The following are the facts and circumstances so far as necessary to show how the legal questions are presented.

On May 17, 1954, this Court decided that enforced racial segregation in the public schools of a State is a denial of the equal protection of the laws enjoined by the Fourteenth Amendment. Brown v. Board of Education, supra. . . .

On May 20, 1954, three days after the first Brown opinion, the Little Rock District School Board adopted, and on May 23, 1954, made public, a statement of policy entitled "Supreme Court Decision —Segregation in Public Schools." In this statement the Board recognized that "It is our responsibility to comply with Federal Constitutional Requirements and we intend to do so when the Supreme Court of the United States outlines the method to be followed."

Thereafter the Board undertook studies of the administrative problems confronting the transition to a desegregated public school system at Little Rock. It instructed the Superintendent of Schools to prepare a plan for desegregation, and approved such a plan on May 24, 1955, seven days before the second Brown opinion. The plan provided for desegregation at the senior high school level (grades 10 through 12) as the first stage. Desegregation at the junior high and elementary levels was to follow. It was contemplated that desegregation at the high school level would commence in the fall of 1957, and the expectation was that complete desegregation of the school system would be accomplished by 1963. . . .

While the School Board was thus going forward with its preparation for desegregating the Little Rock school system, other state authorities, in contrast, were actively pursuing a program designed to perpetuate in Arkansas the system of racial segregation which this Court had held violated the Fourteenth Amendment. First came, in November 1956, an amendment to the State Constitution flatly commanding the Arkansas General Assembly to oppose "in every Constitutional manner the Un-Constitutional desegregation decisions of May 17, 1954 and May 31, 1955 of the United States Supreme Court," Ark.Const. Amend. 44, and, through the initiative, a pupil assignment law, Ark.Stats. §§ 80–1519 to 80–1524. Pursuant to the constitutional command, a law relieving school children from compulsory attendance at racially mixed schools, Ark.Stats. § 80–1525, and a law establishing a State Sovereignty Commission, Ark.Stats. §§ 6–801 to 6–824, were enacted by the General Assembly in February 1957.

The School Board and the Superintendent of Schools nevertheless continued with preparations to carry out the first stage of the desegregation program. Nine Negro children were scheduled for admission in September 1957 to Central High School, which has more than two thousand students. Various administrative measures, designed to assure the smooth transition of this first stage of desegregation, were undertaken.

On September 2, 1957, the day before these Negro students were to enter Central High, the school authorities were met with drastic opposing action on the part of the Governor of Arkansas who dispatched units of the Arkansas National Guard to the Central High School grounds, and placed the school "off limits" to colored students. As found by the District Court in subsequent proceedings, the Governor's action had not been requested by the school authorities, and was entirely unheralded. . . .

The Board's petition for postponement in this proceeding states: "The effect of that action [of the Governor] was to harden the core of opposition to the Plan and cause many persons who theretofore had reluctantly accepted the Plan to believe that there was some power in the State of Arkansas which, when exerted, could nullify the Federal law and permit disobedience of the decree of this [District] Court, and from that date hostility to the Plan was increased and criticism of the officials of the [School] District has become more bitter and unrestrained." The Governor's action caused the School Board to request the Negro students on September 2 not to attend the high school "until the legal dilemma was solved." The next day, September 3, 1957, the Board petitioned the District Court for instructions, and the court, after a hearing, found that the Board's request of the Negro students to stay away from the high school had been made because of the stationing of the military guards by the state authorities. The court determined that this was not a reason for departing from the approved plan, and ordered the School Board and Superintendent to proceed with it.

On the morning of the next day, September 4, 1957, the Negro children attempted to enter the high school but, as the District Court later found, units of the Arkansas National Guard "acting pursuant to the Governor's order, stood shoulder to shoulder at the school grounds and thereby forcibly prevented the 9 Negro students . . . from entering," as they continued to do every school day during the following three weeks.

That same day, September 4, 1957, the United States Attorney for the Eastern District of Arkansas was requested by the District Court to begin an immediate investigation in order to fix responsibility for the interference with the orderly implementation of the District Court's direction to carry out the desegregation program. Three days later, September 7, the District Court denied a petition of the School Board and the Superintendent of Schools for an order temporarily suspending continuance of the program.

Upon completion of the United States Attorney's investigation, he and the Attorney General of the United States, at the District Court's request, entered the proceedings and filed a petition on behalf of the United States, as *amicus curiae,* to enjoin the Governor of Arkansas and officers of the Arkansas National Guard from further attempts to prevent obedience to the court's order. After hearings on the petition, the District Court found that the School Board's plan had been obstructed by the Governor through the use of National Guard troops, and granted a preliminary injunction on September 20, 1957, enjoining the Governor and the officers of the Guard from preventing the attendance of Negro children at Central High School, and from otherwise obstructing or interfering with the orders of the court in connection with the plan. The National Guard was then withdrawn from the school.

The next school day was Monday, September 23, 1957. The Negro children entered the high school that morning under the protection of the Little Rock Police Department and members of the Arkansas State Police. But the officers caused the children to be removed from the school during the morning because they had difficulty controlling a large and demonstrating crowd which had gathered at the high school. On September 25, however, the President of the United States dispatched federal troops to Central High School and admission of the Negro students to the school was thereby effected. Regular army troops continued at the high school until November 27, 1957. They were then replaced by federalized National Guardsmen who remained throughout the balance of the school year. Eight of the Negro students remained in attendance at the school throughout the school year.

We come now to the aspect of the proceedings presently before us. On February 20, 1958, the School Board and the Superintendent of Schools filed a petition in the District Court seeking a postponement of their program for desegregation. Their position in essence was that because of extreme public hostility, which they stated had been engendered largely by the official attitudes and actions of the Governor and the Legislature, the maintenance of a sound educational program at Central High School, with the Negro students in attendance would be impossible. The Board therefore proposed that the Negro students already admitted to the school be withdrawn and sent to segregated schools, and that all further steps to carry out the Board's desegregation program be postponed for a period later suggested by the Board to be two and one-half years.

After a hearing the District Court granted the relief requested by the Board. Among other things the court found that the past year at Central High School had been attended by conditions of "chaos, bedlam and turmoil." . . . [The Court described in some detail the unhappy incidents and concluded that the situation was "intolerable."]

The District Court's judgment was dated June 20, 1958. The Negro respondents appealed to the Court of Appeals for the Eighth Circuit and also sought there a stay of the District Court's judgment. . . . The Court of Appeals did not act on the petition for a stay but on August 18, 1958, after convening in special session on August 4 and hearing the appeal, reversed the District Court. On August 21, 1958, the Court of Appeals stayed its mandate to permit the School Board to petition this Court for certiorari. . . . Recognizing the vital importance of a decision of the issues in time to permit arrangements to be made for the 1958–1959 school year, we convened in Special Term on August 28, 1958, and heard oral argument on the respondent's motions, and also argument of the Solicitor General who, by invitation, appeared for the United States as *amicus curiae,* and asserted that the Court of Appeals' judgment was clearly correct on the merits, and urged that we vacate its stay forthwith. . . . On September 12, 1958, as already mentioned we unanimously affirmed the judgment of the Court of Appeals in the *per curiam* opinion set forth in the margin at the outset of this opinion. [Not printed here.]

In affirming the judgment of the Court of Appeals which reversed the District Court we have accepted without reservation the position of the School Board, the Superintendent of Schools, and their counsel that they displayed entire good faith in the conduct of these proceedings and in dealing with the unfortunate and distressing sequence of events which has been outlined. We likewise have accepted the findings of the District Court as to the conditions at Central High School during the 1957–1958 school year, and also the findings that the educational progress of all the students, white and colored, of that school has suffered and will continue to suffer if the conditions which prevailed last year are permitted to continue.

The significance of these findings, however, is to be considered in light of the fact, indisputably revealed by the record before us, that the conditions they depict are directly traceable to the actions of legislators and executive officials of the State of Arkansas, taken in their official capacities, which reflect their own determination to resist this Court's decision in the Brown case and which have brought about violent resistance to that decision in Arkansas. In its petition for certiorari filed in this Court, the School Board itself describes the situation in this language: "The legislative, executive, and judicial departments of the state government opposed the desegregation of Little Rock schools by enacting laws, calling out troops, making statements vilifying federal law and federal courts, and failing to utilize state law enforcement agencies and judicial processes to maintain public peace." . . .

The constitutional rights of respondents are not to be sacrificed or yielded to the violence and disorder which have followed upon the actions of the Governor and Legislature. . . . Thus law and order are not here to be preserved by depriving the Negro children of their constitutional rights. The record before us clearly establishes that the growth of the Board's difficulties to a magnitude beyond its unaided power to control is the product of state action. Those difficulties, as counsel for the Board forthrightly conceded on the oral argument in this Court, can also be brought under control by state action.

The controlling legal principles are plain. The command of the Fourteenth Amendment is that no "State" shall deny to any person within its jurisdiction the equal protection of the laws. . . . Thus the prohibitions of the Fourteenth Amendment extend to all action of the State denying equal protection of the laws; whatever the agency of the State taking the action. In short, the constitutional rights of children not to be discriminated against in school admission on grounds of race or color declared by this Court in the Brown case can neither be nullified openly and directly by state legislators or state executive or judicial officers, nor nullified indirectly by them through evasive schemes for segregation whether attempted "ingeniously or ingenuously."

What has been said, in the light of the facts developed, is enough to dispose of the case. However, we should answer the premise of the actions of the Governor and Legislature that they are not bound by our holding in the Brown case. It is necessary only to recall some basic constitutional propositions which are settled doctrine.

Article VI of the Constitution makes the Constitution the "supreme Law of the Land." In 1803, Chief Justice Marshall, speaking for a unanimous Court, referring to the Constitution as "the fundamental and paramount law of the nation," declared in the notable case of Marbury v. Madison, 1 Cranch 137, that "It is emphatically the province and duty of the judicial department to say what the law is." This decision declared the basic principle that the federal judiciary is supreme in the exposition of the law of the Constitution, and that principle has ever since been respected by this Court and the Country as a permanent and indispensable feature of our constitutional system. It follows that the interpretation of the Fourteenth Amendment enunciated by this Court in the Brown case is the supreme law of the land, and Art. VI of the Constitution makes it of binding effect on the States "any Thing in the Constitution or Laws of any State to the Contrary notwithstanding." Every state legislator and executive and judicial officer is solemnly committed by oath taken pursuant to Art. VI, ¶3 "to support this Constitution." Chief Justice Taney, speaking for a unanimous Court in 1859, said that this requirement reflected the framers' "anxiety to preserve it [the Constitution] in full force, in all its powers, and to guard against resistance to or evasion of its authority, on the part of a State. . . ." Ableman v. Booth, 21 How. 506.

No state legislator or executive or judicial officer can war against the Constitution without violating his undertaking to support it. Chief Justice Marshall spoke for a unanimous Court in saying that: "If the legislatures of the several states may, at will, annul the judgments of the courts of the United States, and destroy the rights acquired under those judgments, the constitution itself becomes a solemn mockery. . . ." United States v. Peters, 5 Cranch 115. A Governor who asserts a power to nullify a federal court order is similarly restrained. If he had such power, said Chief Justice Hughes, in 1932, also for a unanimous Court, "it is manifest that the fiat of a state Governor, and not the Constitution of the United States, would be the supreme law of the land; that the restrictions of the Federal Constitution upon the exercise of state power would be but impotent phrases. . . ." Sterling v. Constantin, 287 U. S. 378.

It is, of course, quite true that the responsibility for public education is primarily the concern of the States, but it is equally true that such responsibilities, like all other state activity, must be exercised consistently with federal constitutional requirements as they apply to state action. The Constitution created a government dedicated to equal justice under law. The Fourteenth Amendment embodied and emphasized that ideal. State support of segregated schools through any arrangement, management, funds, or property cannot be squared with the Amendment's command that no State shall deny to any person within its jurisdiction the equal protection of the laws. The right of a student not to be segregated on racial grounds in schools so maintained is indeed so fundamental and pervasive that it is embraced in the concept of due process of law. Bolling v. Sharpe, 347 U. S. 497. The basic decision in Brown was unanimously reached by this Court only after the case had been briefed and twice argued and the issues had been given the most serious consideration. Since the first Brown opinion three new Justices have come to the Court. They are at one with the Justices still on the Court who participated in that basic decision as to its correctness, and that decision is now unanimously reaffirmed. The principles announced in that decision and the obedience of the States to them, according to the command of the Constitution, are indispensable for the protection of the freedoms guaranteed by our fundamental charter for all of us. Our constitutional ideal of equal justice under law is thus made a living truth.

IN RE NEAGLE
135 U. S. 1; 34 L. Ed. 55; 10 Sup. Ct. 658. 1890.

State interference with federal activities or agents may arise not only in the exercise of the state's power of taxation or police regulation, but also in the normal administration of justice in the state courts. In Tarble's Case, 13 Wallace 397 (1872), a state judge sought by issuance of a writ of habeas corpus to release from military service in the United States Army an enlisted boy alleged to be under military age. The Supreme Court of the United States emphatically denied the right of the state court to interfere thus with the administration of federal military affairs, or decide questions of federal military law.

To prevent United States officers acting under federal revenue laws from being held accountable to state authorities, Congress at an early date provided by statute that in case any civil or criminal action be brought against a revenue officer in the state courts such a case could be removed into a federal court for trial. In Tennessee v. Davis, 100 U. S. 257 (1880), a federal revenue officer was indicted for murder in a state court for having killed a man, in self-defense as he claimed, in the discharge of his duty. The Supreme Court sustained the validity of the act and allowed the case to be removed for trial to the federal district court.

In the Neagle case, which arose out of a very extraordinary set of circumstances, the doctrine of federal supremacy was pushed even further. Mr. Justice Field, of the United States Supreme Court, under the judicial system then prevailing held circuit court on the Pacific coast. In a case tried in San Francisco he had ruled against a client represented by a lawyer named Terry, who had earlier been chief justice of the supreme court of California, and Terry had made an assault on the federal marshal in the courtroom. For this he was imprisoned for six months for contempt of court and upon his release made open threats against Justice Field's life. The matter was laid before the Attorney General, and Neagle, a United States deputy marshal, was detailed to travel with Justice Field and protect him from violence. Terry, following up his threat, tried to make a murderous attack upon the justice in a railroad restaurant where the justice had stopped while traveling on circuit duty, and was about to draw his revolver when Neagle shot and killed him. Neagle was promptly arrested by the local authorities and held for murder. He was released upon a writ of habeas corpus by the federal circuit court on the ground that he was held in custody for "an act done in pursuance of a law of the United States," within the meaning of the federal statute providing for the issuance of the writ in such cases.

The most significant feature of the case is that the "law of the United States" in pursuance of which Neagle acted was not an act of Congress, but merely an executive order issued by authority of the President. In sustaining Neagle's release the Court holds that the President in the exercise of the duty imposed upon him to see that the laws are faithfully executed may without special statutory authority appoint an officer to protect the life of a federal judge.

Mr. Justice Miller delivered the opinion of the Court, saying in part:

. . . Without a more minute discussion of this testimony, it produces upon us the conviction of a settled purpose on the part of Terry and his wife, amounting to a conspiracy, to murder Justice Field. And we are quite sure that if Neagle had been merely a brother or a friend of Judge Field, traveling with him, and aware of all the previous relations of Terry to the judge,—as he was,—of his bitter animosity, his declared purpose to have revenge even to the point of killing him, he would have been justified in what he did in defense of Mr. Justice Field's life, and possibly of his own.

But such a justification would be a proper subject for consideration on a trial of the case for murder in the courts of the state of California, and there exists no authority in the courts of the United States to discharge the prisoner while held in custody by the state authorities for this offense, unless there be found in aid of the defense of the prisoner some element of power and authority asserted under the government of the Untied States.

This element is said to be found in the facts that Mr. Justice Field, when attacked, was in the immediate discharge of his duty as judge of the circuit courts of the United States within California; that the assault upon him grew out of the animosity of Terry and wife, arising out of the previous discharge of his duty as circuit justice in the case for which they were committed for contempt of court; and that the deputy marshal of the United States, who killed Terry in defense of Field's life, was charged with a duty under the law of the United States to protect Field from the violence which Terry was inflicting, and which was intended to lead to Field's death.

To the inquiry whether this proposition is sustained by law and the facts which we have recited, we now address ourselves. . . .

We have no doubt that Mr. Justice Field when attacked by Terry was engaged in the discharge of his duties as circuit justice of the ninth circuit, and was entitled to all the protection under those circumstances which the law could give him.

It is urged, however, that there exists no statute authorizing any such protection as that which Neagle was instructed to give Judge Field in the present case, and indeed no protection whatever against a vindictive or malicious assault growing out of the faithful discharge of his official duties; and that the language of section 753 of the Revised Statutes, that the party seeking the benefit of the writ of habeas corpus must in this connection show that he is "in custody for an act done or omitted in pursuance of a law of the United States," makes it necessary that upon this occasion it should be shown that the act for which Neagle is imprisoned was done by virtue of an act of Congress. It is not supposed that any special act of Congress exists which authorizes the marshals or deputy marshals of the United States in express terms to accompany the judges of the Supreme Court through their circuits, and act as a bodyguard to them, to defend them against malicious assaults against their persons. But we are of opinion that this view of the statute is an unwarranted restriction of the meaning of a law designed to extend in a liberal manner the benefit of the writ of habeas corpus to persons imprisoned for the performance of their duty. And we are satisfied that if it was the duty of Neagle, under the circumstances, a duty which could only arise under the laws of the United States, to defend Mr. Justice Field from a murderous attack upon him, he brings himself within the meaning of the section we have recited. This view of the subject is confirmed by the alternative provision, that he must be in custody "for an act done or omitted in pursuance of a law of the United States or of an order, process, or decree of a court or judge thereof, or is in custody in violation of the Constitution or of a law or treaty of the United States."

In the view we take of the Constitution of the United States, any obligation fairly and properly inferable from that instrument, or any duty of the marshal to be derived from the general scope of his duties under the laws of the United States, is "a law" within the meaning of this phrase. It would be a great reproach to the system of government of the United States, declared to be within its sphere sovereign and supreme, if there is to be found within the domain of its powers no means of protecting the judges, in the conscientious and faithful discharge of their duties, from the malice and hatred of those upon whom their judgments may operate unfavorably. . . .

Where, then, are we to look for the protection which we have shown Judge Field was entitled to when engaged in the discharge of his official duties? Not to the courts of the United States; because, as has been more than once said in this Court, in the division of the powers of government between the three great departments, executive, legislative and judicial, the judicial is the weakest for the purposes of self-protection and for the enforcement of the powers which it exercises. The ministerial officers through whom its command must be executed are marshals of the United States, and belong emphatically to the executive department of the government. They are appointed by the President, with the advice and consent of the Senate. They are removable from office at his pleasure. They are subjected by act of Congress to the supervision and control of the Department of Justice, in the hands of one of the cabinet officers of the President, and their compensation is provided by acts of Congress. The same may be said of the district attorneys of the United States, who prosecute and defend the claims of the government in the courts.

The legislative branch of the government can only protect the judicial officers by the enactment of laws for that purpose, and the argument we are now combating assumes that no such law has been passed by Congress.

If we turn to the executive department of the government, we find a very different condition of affairs. The Constitution, section 3, Article II, declares that the President "shall take care that the laws be faithfully executed," and he is provided with the means of fulfilling this obligation by his authority to commission all the officers of the United States, and, by and with the advice and consent of the Senate, to appoint the most important of them and to fill vacancies. He is declared to be commander-in-chief of the army and navy of the United States. The duties which are thus imposed upon him he is further enabled to perform by the recognition in the Constitution, and the creation by acts of Congress, of executive departments, which have varied in number from four or five to seven or eight, the heads of which are familiarly called cabinet ministers. These aid him in the performance of the great duties of his office, and represent him in a thousand acts to which it can hardly be supposed his personal attention is called, and thus he is enabled to fulfill the duty of his great department, expressed in the phrase that "he shall take care that the laws be faithfully executed."

Is this duty limited to the enforcement of acts of Congress or of treaties of the United States according to their express terms, or does it include the rights, duties and obligations growing out of the Constitution itself, our international relations, and all the protection implied by the nature of the government under the Constitution? . . .

We cannot doubt the power of the President to take measures for the protection of a judge of one of the courts of the United States, who, while in the discharge of the duties of his office, is threatened with a personal attack which may probably result in his death, and we think it clear that where this protection is to be afforded through the civil power, the Department of Justice is the proper one to set in motion the necessary means of protection. The correspondence already recited in this opinion between the marshal of the northern district of California, and the Attorney General, and the district attorney of the United States for that district, although prescribing no very specific mode of affording this protection by the Attorney General, is sufficient, we think, to warrant the marshal in taking the steps which he did take, in making the provision which he did make, for the protection and defense of Mr. Justice Field.

But there is positive law investing the marshals and their deputies with powers which not only justify what Marshal Neagle did in this matter, but which imposed it upon him as a duty. In chapter fourteen of the Revised Statutes of the United States, which is devoted to the appointment and duties of the district attorneys, marshals, and clerks of the courts of the United States, section 788 declares:

"The marshals and their deputies shall have, in each state, the same powers, in executing the laws of the United States, as the sheriffs and their deputies in such state may have, by law, in executing the laws thereof."

If, therefore, a sheriff of the state of California was authorized to do in regard to the laws of California what Neagle did, that is, if he was authorized to keep the peace, to protect a judge from assault and murder, then Neagle was authorized to do the same thing in reference to the laws of the United States. . . .

That there is a peace of the United States; that a man assaulting a judge of the United States while in the discharge of his duties violates that peace; that in such case the marshal of the United States stands in the same relation to the peace of the United States which the sheriff of the county does to the peace of the state of California; are questions too clear to need argument to prove them. That it would be the duty of a sheriff, if one had been present at this assault by Terry upon Judge Field, to prevent this breach of the peace, to prevent this assault, to prevent the murder which was contemplated by it, cannot be doubted. And if, in performing this duty, it became necessary for the protection of Judge Field, or of himself, to kill Terry, in a case where, like this, it was evidently a question of the choice of who should be killed, the assailant and violator of the law and disturber of the peace, or the unoffending man who was in his power, there can be no question of the authority of the sheriff to have killed Terry. So the marshal of the United States, charged with the duty of protecting and guarding the judge of the United States court against this special assault upon his person and his life, being present at the critical moment, when prompt action was necessary, found it to be his duty, a duty which he had no liberty to refuse to perform, to take the steps which resulted in Terry's death. This duty was imposed on him by the section of the Revised Statutes which we have recited, in connection with the powers conferred by the state of California upon its peace officers, which become, by this statute, in proper cases, transferred as duties to the marshals of the United States. . . .

The result at which we have arrived upon this examination is, that in the protection of the person and the life of Mr. Justice Field while in the discharge of his official duties, Neagle was authorized to resist the attack of Terry upon him; that Neagle was correct in the belief that without prompt action on his part the assault of Terry upon the judge would have ended in the death of the latter; that such being his well-founded belief, he was justified in taking the life of Terry, as the only means of preventing the death of the man who was intended to be his victim; that in taking the life of Terry, under the circumstances, he was acting under the authority of the law of the United States, and was justified in so doing; and that he is not liable to answer in the courts of California on account of his part in that transaction.

We therefore affirm the judgment of the circuit court authorizing his discharge from the custody of the sheriff of San Joaquin County.

Mr. Justice Lamar delivered a dissenting opinion in which Mr. Chief Justice Fuller concurred.

COYLE v. SMITH

221 U. S. 559; 55 L. Ed. 853; 31 Sup. Ct. 688. 1911.

The power which Congress possesses to admit new states into the Union is a purely discretionary power. No territory has any right to claim statehood, but must wait until it seems wise to Congress to confer that status. It is not surprising, therefore, that it should be assumed that Congress in the exercise of an unquestioned power to grant or withhold such a privilege might make the enjoyment of the right contingent upon the meeting of such conditions by the incoming state as might seem to the congressional mind desirable. This seems to have been the theory upon which Congress proceeded with reference to the admission of states, and as early as 1802 we find Ohio compelled, as the price of admission into the Union, to enter into an agreement, irrevocable without the consent of Congress, not to tax for a period of five years lands within the state which were sold by the United States government. The imposing of conditions of various kinds upon the incoming states became a settled policy of Congress, and the stipulations agreed to covered a considerable range of topics. They related to the disposition of public lands, many of them being much more detailed than the Ohio provision; to the use of navigable waters; to the protection of the rights of citizens of the United States; to slavery; to civil and religious liberty; to the right to vote. When Utah came into the Union in 1894 it was obliged to make an irrevocable agreement that there should be perfect religious toleration maintained in the state, that the public schools should be kept free from sectarian control, and that polygamous marriages should be forever prohibited. In 1910 Arizona was authorized by a congressional enabling act to draw up a state constitution preparatory to entering the Union. The constitution framed contained provisions for the popular recall of judges. While Congress somewhat reluctantly passed a resolution admitting Arizona into the Union, President Taft, being bitterly opposed to the recall of judges, vetoed the resolution. A new resolution was then passed providing that Arizona be admitted on condition that the objectionable provision be stricken out of the constitution. This was done and Arizona became a member of the Union. The state thereupon promptly restored the recall of judges by amending the new state constitution, and has retained it ever since.

But if Congress can thus impose conditions upon the new states as they assume statehood, the question arises: Are the states equal? Do we actually have states in the Union which do not have the power enjoyed by other states; as, for instance, to decide how judges shall be removed from office, or what shall constitute a lawful marriage? It is a rather curious fact in view of the length of time during which this policy has been followed by Congress that the question of the binding nature of these restrictions should have been fully dealt with by the Supreme Court for the first time in 1911 in the case of Coyle v. Smith. This case grew out of a restriction imposed by Congress upon Oklahoma in the enabling act passed in 1906 which provided that the new state should locate its capital at Guthrie and that it should irrevocably agree not to move it from that place before the year 1913 nor to appropriate any unnecessary money for public buildings. This agreement was ratified by the voters of the state at the time that the new constitution was adopted; and, thus bound, Oklahoma entered the Union. In 1910 a bill initiated by the people was approved by the voters of Oklahoma providing that the state capital should forthwith be moved to Oklahoma City and appropriating $600,000 for public buildings. This was, of course, in plain violation of the "irrevocable" agreement which the state had made and a proceeding was instituted to test the validity of the law. In sustaining the right of the state to move its capital at its discretion regardless of its agreement, the Supreme Court enunciated the important doctrine of the political equality of the states.

A distinction, however, should be noted between those conditions imposed upon incoming states which relate to political or governmental authority and which would therefore place the state upon an unequal footing in the Union, and those conditions in the nature of business agreements or contracts which relate to property. In Stearns v. Minnesota, 179 U. S. 223 (1900), it was held that an agreement in the enabling act of Minnesota whereby the state received from the United States valuable public lands in return for which it agreed not to tax the land still owned in the state by the federal government and not to tax the property of non-residents at a higher rate than that of residents, could be enforced against a subsequent effort of the state to violate it, since it did not involve any question of equality of status. In Ervien v. United States, 251 U. S. 41 (1919), the Court upheld the validity of an injunction issued against the expenditure by the state of New Mexico of money drawn from the sale of public lands granted by Congress to the state upon its admission into the Union, when such expenditure was for a purpose (the advertising of the resources of the state) other than that specified in the enabling act. This did not involve the political equality of the state and was held to constitute a breach of trust.

It may be said that the vital question whether one of the states of the Union may constitutionally secede was effectively and permanently answered upon the battlefields of the Civil War. Four years after the war had ended, however, the Supreme Court found itself under the necessity of deciding, in the case of Texas v. White, 7 Wallace 700 (1869), whether the southern states had at any time during the period of attempted secession been actually out of the Union. Was secession, in point of law, constitutionally possible? The facts in this case were as follows:

In 1850 the United States gave the state of Texas $10,000,000 in 5% bonds in settlement of certain boundary claims. Half of these were held in Washington; half were delivered to the state, and made payable to the state or bearer and redeemable after December 31, 1864. A Texas law was passed providing that the bonds should not be available in the hands of any holder until after their endorsement by the governor. Texas joined the Confederacy and during the war used some of the bonds, which were not endorsed, for the purchase of military supplies. After the war Texas sued in the Supreme Court to get the bonds back and to enjoin White and others from presenting the bonds for payment. The Court could take jurisdiction only if Texas was a "state" within the meaning of Article III. Texas was still unrepresented in Congress and White claimed that by secession she had ceased to be a state and could not sue.

The Court held that secession was constitutionally impossible and that Texas had never ceased to be a state in the Union. Chief Justice Chase said that the Articles of Confederation created what was solemnly declared to be a "perpetual Union"; that the Constitution was ordained "to form a more perfect Union"; and he concluded that: "The Constitution, in all of its provisions, looks to an indestructible union, composed of indestructible states." The fact that Texas, by her own efforts at secession, had temporarily given up the rights and privileges of membership in the Union did not alter the fact that she could not sever the constitutional ties which bound her to that Union. The Court accordingly took jurisdiction in the case and decided that Texas was entitled to recover the bonds.

The doctrine of the equality of states was invoked in two different ways in the legal battle over the claims of California, Texas, and Louisiana to valuable offshore oil deposits. California stated that the original states all had title to the offshore lands (an assertion which the Supreme Court rejected) and therefore by operation of the equality rule California had similar title to submerged oil deposits. See United States v. California, 332 U. S. 19 (1947). On the other hand Texas, which was an independent republic when admitted to the Union, undoubtedly did have title to her offshore lands. In United States v. Texas, 339 U. S. 707 (1950), the Court held that under the equality doctrine Texas upon becoming a state automatically forfeited any special rights previously enjoyed.

In the Submerged Lands Act of 1953, Congress gave these tidelands back to the states, but the Court in construing the statute held that while it gave Texas and Florida rights over submerged lands three marine leagues from the coast, the rights of Louisiana, Mississippi, and Alabama extend only three geographic miles. This resulted not from any inequality among the states, but from different congressional policies in force at the time these states entered the Union. See United States v. Louisiana etc., 364 U. S. 502 (1960).

Mr. Justice Lurton delivered the opinion of the Court, saying in part:

. . . The only question for review by us is whether the provision of the enabling act was a valid limitation upon the power of the state after its admission, which overrides any subsequent state legislation repugnant thereto.

The power to locate its own seat of government, and to determine when and how it shall be changed from one place to another, and to appropriate its own public funds for that purpose, are essentially and peculiarly state powers. That one of the original thirteen states could now be shorn of such powers by an act of Congress would not be for a moment entertained. The question, then, comes to this: Can a state be placed upon a plane of inequality with its sister states in the Union if the Congress chooses to impose conditions which so operate, at the time of its admission? The argument is, that while Congress may not deprive a state of any power which it *possesses*, it may, as a condition to the admission of a new state, constitutionally restrict its authority, to the extent, at least, of suspending its powers for a definite time in respect to the location of its seat of government. This contention is predicated upon the constitutional power of admitting new states to this Union, and the constitutional duty of guaranteeing to "every state in this Union a republican form of government." The position of counsel for the appellants is substantially this: That the power of Congress to admit new states, and to determine whether or not its fundamental law is republican in form, are political powers, and as such, uncontrollable by the courts. That Congress may in the exercise of such power impose terms and conditions upon the admission of the proposed new state, which, if accepted, will be obligatory, although they operate to deprive the state of powers which it would otherwise possess, and, therefore, not admitted upon "an equal footing with the original states."

The power of Congress in respect to the admission of new states is found in the third section of the fourth article of the Constitution. That provision is that, "new States may be admitted by the Congress into this Union." The only expressed restriction upon this power is that no new state shall be formed within the jurisdiction of any other state, nor by the junction of two or more states, or parts of states, without the consent of such states, as well as of the Congress.

But what is this power? It is not to admit political organizations which are less or greater, or different in dignity or power, from those political entities which constitute the Union. It is, as strongly put by counsel, a "power to admit states."

The definition of "a state" is found in the powers possessed by the original states which adopted the Constitution, a definition emphasized by the terms employed in all subsequent acts of Congress admitting new states into the Union. The first two states admitted into the Union were the states of Vermont and Kentucky, one as of March 4, 1791, and the other as of June 1, 1792. No terms or conditions were exacted from either. Each act declares that the state is admitted "as a new and *entire member* of the United States of America." . . . Emphatic and significant as is the phrase admitted as "an entire member," even stronger was the declaration upon the admission in 1796 of Tennessee as the third new state, it being declared to be "one of the United States of America," "on an equal footing with the original states in all respects whatsoever," phraseology which has ever since been substantially followed in admission acts, concluding with the Oklahoma act, which declares that Oklahoma shall be admitted "on an equal footing with the original states."

The power is to admit "new states into *this* Union."

"This Union" was and is a union of states, equal in power, dignity, and authority, each competent to exert that residuum of sovereignty not delegated to the United States by the Constitution itself. To maintain otherwise would be to say that the Union, through the power of Congress to admit new states, might come to be a union of states unequal in power, as including states whose powers were restricted only by the Constitution, with others whose powers had been further restricted by an act of Congress accepted as a condition of admission. Thus it would result, first, that the powers of Congress would not be defined by the Constitution alone, but in respect to new states, enlarged or restricted by the conditions imposed upon new states by its own legislation admitting them into the Union; and, second, that such new states might not exercise all of the powers which had not been delegated by the Constitution, but only such as had not been further bargained away as conditions of admission.

The argument that Congress derives from the duty of "guaranteeing to each State in this Union a republican form of government," power to impose restrictions upon a new state which deprive it of equality with other members of the Union, has no merit. It may imply the duty of such new state to provide itself with such state government, and impose upon Congress the duty of seeing that such form is not changed to one anti-republican, . . . but it obviously does not confer power to admit a new state which shall be any less a state than those which compose the Union.

We come now to the question as to whether there is anything in the decisions of this Court which sanctions the claim that Congress may, by the imposition of conditions in an enabling act, deprive a new state of any of those attributes essential to its equality in dignity and power with other states. In considering the decisions of this Court bearing upon the question, we must distinguish, first, between provisions which are fulfilled by the admission of the state; second, between compacts or affirmative legislation intended to operate *in futuro,* which are within the scope of the conceded powers of Congress over the subject; and third, compacts or affirmative legislation which operates to restrict the powers of such new states in respect of matters which would otherwise be exclusively within the sphere of state power.

As to requirements in such enabling acts as relate only to the contents of the constitution for the proposed new state, little need[s] to be said. The constitutional provision concerning the admission of new states is not a mandate, but a power to be exercised with discretion. From this alone it would follow that Congress may require, under penalty of denying admission, that the organic laws of a new state at the time of admission shall be such as to meet its approval. A constitution thus supervised by Congress would, after all, be a constitution of a state, and as such subject to alteration and amendment by the state after admission. Its force would be that of a state constitution, and not that of an act of Congress. . . .

So far as this Court has found occasion to advert to the effect of enabling acts as affirmative legislation affecting the power of new states after admission, there is to be found no sanction for the contention that any state may be deprived of any of the power constitutionally possessed by other states, as states, by reason of the terms in which the acts admitting them to the Union have been framed. . . . [Here follows discussion of a case involving the construction of the act under which Alabama was admitted to the Union.]

The plain deduction from this case is that when a new state is admitted into the Union, it is so admitted with all of the powers of sovereignty and jurisdiction which pertain to the original states, and that such powers may not be constitutionally diminished, impaired, or shorn away by any conditions, compacts, or stipulations embraced in the act under which the new state came into the Union, which would not be valid and effectual if the subject of congressional legislation after admission. . . .

It may well happen that Congress should embrace in an enactment introducing a new state into the Union legislation intended as a regulation of commerce among the states, or with Indian tribes situated within the limits of such new state, or regulations touching the sole care and disposition of the public lands or reservations therein, which might be upheld as legislation within the sphere of the plain power of Congress. But in every such case legislation would derive its force not from any agreement or compact with the proposed new state, nor by reason of its acceptance of such enactment as a term of admission, but solely because the power of Congress extended to the subject, and therefore would not operate to restrict the state's legislative power in respect of any matter which was not plainly within the regulating power of Congress. . . .

No such question is presented here. The legislation in the Oklahoma enabling act relating to the location of the capital of the state, if construed as forbidding a removal by the state after its admission as a state, is referable to no power granted to Congress over the subject, and if it is to be upheld at all, it must be implied from the power to admit new states. If power to impose such a restriction upon the general and undelegated power of a state be conceded as implied from the power to admit a new state, where is the line to be drawn against restrictions imposed upon new states?

. . . If anything was needed to complete the argument against the assertion that Oklahoma has not been admitted to the Union upon an equality of power, dignity, and sovereignty with Massachusetts or Virginia, it is afforded by the express provision of the act of admission, by which it is declared that when the people of the proposed new state have complied with the terms of the act, that it shall be the duty of the President to issue his proclamation, and that "thereupon the proposed state of Oklahoma shall be deemed admitted by Congress into the Union under and by virtue of this act, *on an equal footing with the original states.*" The proclamation has been issued and the Senators and Representatives from the state admitted to their seats in the Congress.

Has Oklahoma been admitted upon an equal footing with the original states? If she has, she, by virtue of her jurisdictional sovereignty as such a state, may determine for her own people the proper location of the local seat of government. She is not equal in power to them if she cannot. . . .

To this we may add that the constitutional equality of the states is essential to the harmonious operation of the scheme upon which the Republic was organized. When that equality disappears we may remain a free people, but the Union will not be the Union of the Constitution.

Judgment affirmed.

Mr. Justice McKenna and Mr. Justice Holmes dissent.

3

Federal Citizenship
and the Bill of Rights

UNITED STATES v. WONG KIM ARK
169 U. S. 649; 42 L. Ed. 890; 18 Sup. Ct. 456. 1898.

The Constitution of the United States from the first recognized citizenship of the United States but did not define it. It was generally assumed, however, that the English rule prevailed, which recognized as citizens those born within the allegiance of the country and subject to its protection. This rule, commonly called "jus soli," was in contrast to the rule prevailing on the European continent, which followed the doctrine of "jus sanguinis," or the determination of citizenship by the nationality of the parents. However, in 1790 Congress enacted a law giving American citizenship to those born to American parents outside the country.

In 1857 the Supreme Court had established an important exception to the rule that birth in the country conferred citizenship, by holding in the famous Dred Scott Case, 19 Howard 393, that a native-born Negro is not an American cititzen. The Fourteenth Amendment "recalled" the Dred Scott decision on this point and definitely defined United States citizenship in terms of birth in the country and subjection to its jurisdiction, thus enacting the English or "jus soli" doctrine into the Constitution. The exact purport of the phrase "subject to its jurisdiction" was for some time the subject of dispute and uncertainty. In the Slaughterhouse Cases (p. 52) the Court had gone out of its way to express the opinion that a child born in the United States to parents who were subjects of a foreign state is not born subject to the jurisdiction of the United States and would not, therefore, acquire citizenship by birth.

This view, however, was rejected by the Court in the case of United States v. Wong Kim Ark. Wong Kim Ark had been born in San Francisco in 1873 of Chinese parents who were subjects of the emperor of China but were permanently domiciled in the United States. He went to China in 1894 and upon his return to this country in 1895 the collector of the customs refused him admission to the country on the ground that he was a Chinese laborer, not a citizen, and not within any of the privileged classes named in the Chinese Exclusion Acts then in force. He sued out a writ of habeas corpus, claiming American citizenship on the ground of birth.

After Pearl Harbor the "Sons of the Golden West" in California brought a court action seeking the reconsideration and reversal of the Wong Kim Ark case in an effort to prevent Japanese children born in this country from acquiring American citizenship. The lower federal courts stood by the Wong Kim Ark doctrine and the Supreme Court, without writing an opinion, declined to review the case. See Regan v. King, 319 U. S. 753 (1943). Under recent statutes "Chinese persons and persons of Chinese descent, and persons of races indigenous to India," may now be naturalized.

An important case relating to the acquisition of United States citizenship is that of Perkins v. Elg, 307 U. S. 325 (1939). Miss Elg was born in the United States of Swedish parents in 1907. Her father had been naturalized in this country in 1906. In 1911 her mother took her to Sweden where she remained until 1929. Her father returned to Sweden in 1922, remained there, and voluntarily returned to his allegiance to Sweden. In 1929 Miss Elg, being then twenty-one years of age, obtained an American passport, returned to the United States, and continued to reside here. Action was taken to deport her as an alien illegally in the country. The Supreme Court upheld her claim to citizenship. She became a citizen of the United States by being born in New York. She might, it is true, have chosen Swedish citizenship on coming of age, since her parents had meanwhile returned to Swedish citizenship. But her relinquishment of her right to enjoy the status of American citizenship upon coming of age must be her own voluntary act. That right is not destroyed by a change in the citizenship status of her parents while she is still a minor.

A person may lose his American citizenship in various ways. He may give it up voluntarily, as did Mr. Elg in the case just cited. By act of Congress a naturalized citizen may forfeit his citizenship if he secured it by fraud. Thus Frank Costello was "denaturalized" because at the time he filed formal application for citizenship he concealed the fact that bootlegging was his occupation, and swore that he was in "real estate." See Costello v. United States, 365 U. S. 265 (1961). In the case of native-born citizens, deprivation of citizenship may raise constitutional questions. Thus in Perez v. Brownell, 356 U. S. 44 (1958), the Court, voting five to four, held that Congress (Nationality Act of 1940) could validly deprive a person of citizenship for voting in a foreign election, on the ground that this was a reasonable exercise of the power of Congress over foreign affairs. In Trop v. Dulles, 356 U. S. 86 (1958) and Kennedy v. Mendoza-Martinez, 372 U. S. 144 (1963), however, the Court, again voting five to four, struck down the statutes prescribing loss of citizenship for deserting the armed forces in time of war and leaving the country in time of war to avoid the draft. Four justices in the first case held this punishment was cruel and unusual, while five in the second case held it denied procedural due process.

Mr. Justice Gray delivered the opinion of the Court, saying in part:

. . . The question presented by the record is whether a child born in the United States, of parents of Chinese descent, who at the time of his birth are subjects of the emperor of China, but have a permanent domicile and residence in the United States, and are there carrying on business, and are not employed in any diplomatic or official capacity under the emperor of China, becomes at the time of his birth a citizen of the United States, by virtue of the first clause of the Fourteenth Amendment of the Constitution: "All persons born or naturalized in the United States, and subject to the jurisdiction thereof, are citizens of the United States and of the State wherein they reside."

In construing any act of legislation, whether a statute enacted by the legislature, or a constitution established by the people as the supreme law of the land, regard is to be had, not only to all parts of the act itself, and of any former act of the same lawmaking power, of which the act in question is an amendment, but also to the condition and to the history of the law as previously existing, and in the light of which the new act must be read and interpreted.

The Constitution of the United States, as originally adopted, uses the words "citizen of the United States" and "natural-born citizen of the United States." By the original Constitution, every Representative in Congress is required to have been "seven years a citizen of the United States," and every Senator to have been "nine years a citizen of the United States"; and "no person except a natural-born citizen, or a citizen of the United States at the time of the adoption of this Constitution, shall be eligible to the office of President." The Fourteenth article of Amendment, besides declaring that "all persons born or naturalized in the United States, and subject to the jurisdiction thereof, are citizens of the United States and of the State wherein they reside," also declares that "no State shall make or enforce any law which shall abridge the privileges or immunities of citizens of the United States; nor shall any State deprive any person of life, liberty, or property, without due process of law; nor deny to any person within its jurisdiction the equal protection of the laws." And the Fifteenth article of Amendment declares that "the right of citizens of the United States to vote shall not be denied or abridged by the United States, or by any State, on account of race, color, or previous condition of servitude."

The Constitution nowhere defines the meaning of these words, either by way of inclusion or of exclusion, except in so far as this is done by the affirmative declaration that "all persons born or naturalized in the United States, and subject to the jurisdiction thereof, are citizens of the United States." In this, as in other respects, it must be interpreted in the light of the common law, the principles and history of which were familiarly known to the framers of the Constitution. . . .

The fundamental principle of the common law with regard to English nationality was birth within the allegiance—also called "ligealty," "obedience," "faith," or "power"—of the king. The principle embraced all persons born within the king's allegiance, and subject to his protection. Such allegiance and protection were mutual,—as expressed in the maxim, "Protectio trahit subjectionem, et subjectio protectionem,"—and were not restricted to natural-born subjects and naturalized subjects, or to those who had taken an oath of allegiance; but were predicable of aliens in amity, so long as they were within the kingdom. Children, born in England, of such aliens, were therefore natural-born subjects. But the children, born within the realm, of foreign ambassadors, or the children of alien enemies, born during and within their hostile occupation of part of the king's dominions, were not natural-born subjects, because not born within the allegiance, the obedience, or the power, or, as would be said at this day, within the jurisdiction, of the king. . . .

It thus clearly appears that by the law of England for the last three centuries, beginning before the settlement of this country, and continuing to the present day, aliens, while residing in the dominions possessed by the crown of England, were within the allegiance, the obedience, the faith or loyalty, the protection, the power, and the jurisdiction of the English sovereign; and therefore every child born in England of alien parents was a natural-born subject, unless the child of an ambassador or other diplomatic agent of a foreign state, or of an alien enemy in hostile occupation of the place where the child was born.

The same rule was in force in all the English colonies upon this continent down to the time of the Declaration of Independence, and in the United States afterwards, and continued to prevail under the Constitution as originally established. . . .

The first section of the Fourteenth Amendment of the Constitution begins with the words, "All persons born or naturalized in the United States, and subject to the jurisdiction thereof, are citizens of the United States and of the State wherein they reside." As appears upon the face of the amendment, as well as from the history of the times, this was not intended to impose any new restrictions upon citizenship, or to prevent any persons from becoming citizens by the fact of birth within the United States, who would thereby have become citizens according to the law existing before its adoption. It is declaratory in form, and enabling and extending in effect. Its main purpose doubtless was, as has been often recognized by this Court, to establish the citizenship of free negroes, which had been denied in the opinion delivered by Chief Justice Taney in Dred Scott v. Sandford, 19 Howard 393 (1857), and to put it beyond doubt that all blacks, as well as whites, born or naturalized within the jurisdiction of the United States, are citizens of the United States. . . . But the opening words, "All persons born," are general, not to say universal, restricted only by place and jurisdiction, and not by color or race. . . .

The real object of the Fourteenth Amendment of the Constitution, in qualifying the words "all persons born in the United States" by the addition "and subject to the jurisdiction thereof," would appear to have been to exclude, by the fewest and fittest words (besides children of members of the Indian tribes, standing in a peculiar relation to the national government, unknown to the common law), the two classes of cases,—children born of alien enemies in hostile occupation, and children of diplomatic representatives of a foreign state,— both of which, as has already been shown, by the law of England and by our own law, from the time of the first settlement of the English colonies in America, had been recognized exceptions to the fundamental rule of citizenship by birth within the country. . . .

The foregoing considerations and authorities irresistibly lead us to these conclusions: The Fourteenth Amendment affirms the ancient and fundamental rule of citizenship by birth within the territory, in the allegiance and under the protection of the country, including all children here born of resident aliens, with the exceptions or qualifications (as old as the rule itself) of children of foreign sovereigns or their ministers, or born on foreign public ships, or of enemies within and during a hostile occupation of part of our territory, and with the single additional exception of children of members of the Indian tribes owing direct allegiance to their several tribes. The amendment, in clear words and in manifest intent, includes the children born within the territory of the United States of all other persons, of whatever race or color, domiciled within the United States. Every citizen or subject of another country, while domiciled here, is within the allegiance and the protection, and consequently subject to the jurisdiction, of the United States. . . .

It is true that Chinese persons born in China cannot be naturalized, like other aliens, by proceedings under the naturalization laws. But this is for want of any statute or treaty authorizing or permitting such naturalization, as will appear by tracing the history of the statutes, treaties, and decisions upon that subject, always bearing in mind that statutes enacted by Congress, as well as treaties made by the President and Senate, must yield to the paramount and supreme law of the Constitution. . . .

Mr. Chief Justice Fuller, with whom concurred Mr. Justice Harlan, rendered a dissenting opinion.

THE SLAUGHTERHOUSE CASES
16 Wallace 36; 21 L. Ed. 394. 1873.

At the close of the Civil War it seemed clear that without the intervention of the federal government the southern states would by legislative restrictions strip the newly freed Negro of most of the ordinary rights and immunities of free citizens. To meet this situation the Fourteenth Amendment was proposed by Congress to place the civil rights of the Negro upon a firm basis; secondarily, it aimed to coerce the southern states into allowing the Negro to vote by the threat of reduced representation in Congress. By the first section of the amendment United States citizenship was defined in terms which included the Negro, and the states were forbidden to make laws abridging the privileges and immunities of that citizenship or denying due process of law or the equal protection of the laws. Congress was empowered to enforce these prohibitions by legislation.

It has been claimed that as a matter of historical fact the framers of the amendment meant by "privileges or immunities of citizens of the United States" the whole body of ordinary civil rights and especially those enumerated in the Bill of Rights of the federal Constitution. They intended to place in the hands of Congress the broadest possible power to prevent the impairment of these rights, and they thought they had done so. Instead of looking to the state legislature for legislative protection of his civil liberty, the citizen, especially the freedman, would henceforth look to Congress or to the federal courts. Recent historical research casts doubt upon the correctness of this view, but the matter is still disputed.

The Slaughterhouse Cases, the first cases involving the interpretation of the Fourteenth Amendment, had nothing whatever to do with the rights of freedmen. The case arose on the following facts: The reconstruction or "carpet-bag" government in Louisiana, unquestionably under corrupt influence, had granted a monopoly of the slaughterhouse business to a single concern in New Orleans, thus preventing over one thousand other persons and firms from continuing in that business.

The validity of the law was attacked under the Thirteenth and Fourteenth Amendments. The Court, however, quickly limited the field of controversy by holding that the Thirteenth Amendment forbade chattel slavery only, and not the monopolistic oppression of butchers.

The importance of the case can hardly be overestimated. By distinguishing between state citizenship and national citizenship, and by emphasizing that the rights and privileges of federal citizenship do not include the protection of ordinary civil rights such as freedom of speech and press, religion, the right of assembly, etc., but only the privileges which one enjoyed by virtue of his federal citizenship, the Court averted, for a time, the revolution in our constitutional system said to have been intended by the framers of the amendment, and reserved to the states the control of civil rights generally. In a later case, Maxwell v. Dow, 176 U. S. 581 (1900), the Court specifically ruled that the privileges and immunities of citizens of the United States do not include the rights contained in the first eight amendments to the federal Constitution.

Had the Slaughterhouse Cases been decided twenty-five years later, the Louisiana statute would in all probability have been invalidated as a deprivation of liberty and property without due process of law and a denial of the equal protection of the laws. But the majority of the Court disposed rather summarily of these clauses by holding in substance that the due process of law clause was not a limitation on the state's police power, and that the equal protection of the laws clause, equally inapplicable, would probably never be invoked except for the protection of the Negro. It is important to bear in mind that Mr. Justice Miller's comments about the due process and equal protection clauses no longer state the law. The Court has long since given those clauses the broadest possible applicability. There have, in fact, been more cases interpreting the Fourteenth Amendment than on any other phase of constitutional law.

It looked for a time (1935–1940) as though the Court might also broaden the scope and applicability of the privileges and immunities clause of the Fourteenth Amendment. In Colgate v. Harvey, 296 U. S. 404 (1935), the Court held void a provision of a Vermont income tax law which taxed income from money loaned outside the state at a higher rate than that loaned inside the state. Besides denying the equal protection of the laws, this act was held to abridge the privileges and immunities of citizens of the United States. The right to carry on business freely across state lines was declared to be a privilege or immunity of federal citizenship, a doctrine sharply differing from the rule of the Slaughterhouse Cases. In 1939, in Hague v. C.I.O., 307 U. S. 496, involving the validity under the Fourteenth Amendment of various repressions of free speech, assembly, etc., in Jersey City, two justices of the Supreme Court from the majority held that the right of citizens to assemble and discuss their rights under the National Labor Relations Act was a privilege or immunity of citizens of the United States within the meaning of the Fourteenth Amendment. There was also speculation as to whether protection against unreasonable searches and seizures was also a privilege and immunity of federal citizenship, but no decision was made on that point. There was sharp dissent in both cases against this tendency to enlarge the scope of the privileges and immunities clause, and in Madden v. Kentucky, 309 U. S. 83 (1940), in a case similar to Colgate v. Harvey, the Court specifically overruled that case and returned to the time-worn narrow construction of the privileges and immunities clause embodied in the Slaughterhouse Cases.

Mr. Justice Miller delivered the opinion of the Court, saying in part:

. . . The plaintiffs in error accepting this issue, allege that the statute is a violation of the Constitution of the United States in these several particulars:

That it creates an involuntary servitude forbidden by the Thirteenth article of Amendment;

That it abridges the privileges and immunities of citizens of the United States;

That it denies to the plaintiffs the equal protection of the laws; and,

That it deprives them of their property without due process of law;

contrary to the provisions of the first section of the Fourteenth article of Amendment.

This Court is thus called upon for the first time to give construction to these articles. . . .

Twelve articles of amendment were added to the federal Constitution soon after the original organization of the government under it in 1789. Of these all but the last were adopted so soon afterwards as to justify the statement that they were practically contemporaneous with the adoption of the original; and the Twelfth, adopted in eighteen hundred and three, was so nearly so as to have become, like all the others, historical and of another age. But within the last eight years three other articles of amendment of vast importance have been added by the voice of the people to that now venerable instrument.

The most cursory glance at these articles discloses a unity of purpose, when taken in connection with the history of the times, which cannot fail to have an important bearing on any question of doubt concerning their true meaning. . . . Fortunately that history is fresh within the memory of us all, and its leading features, as they bear upon the matter before us, free from doubt. . . . [Here follows a brief comment upon the Thirteenth Amendment.]

The first section of the Fourteenth article, to which our attention is more specially invited, opens with a definition of citizenship—not only citizenship of the United States, but citizenship of the states. No such definition was previously found in the Constitution, nor had any attempt been made to define it by act of Congress. It had been the occasion of much discussion in the courts, by the executive departments, and in the public journals. It had been said by eminent judges that no man was a citizen of the United States except as he was a citizen of one of the states composing the Union. Those, therefore, who had been born and resided always in the District of Columbia or in the territories, though within the United States, were not citizens. Whether this proposition was sound or not had never been judicially decided. But it had been held by this Court, in the celebrated Dred Scott case, only a few years before the outbreak of the Civil War, that a man of African descent, whether a slave or not, was not and could not be a citizen of a state or of the United States. This decision, while it met the condemnation of some of the ablest statesmen and constitutional lawyers of the country, had never been overruled; and if it was to be accepted as a constitutional limitation of the right of citizenship, then all the negro race who had recently been made freemen, were still, not only not citizens, but were incapable of becoming so by anything short of an amendment to the Constitution.

To remove this difficulty primarily, and to establish a clear and comprehensive definition of citizenship which should declare what should constitute citizenship of the United States, and also citizenship of a state, the first clause of the first section was framed.

"All persons born or naturalized in the United States, and subject to the jurisdiction thereof, are citizens of the United States and of the state wherein they reside."

The first observation we have to make on this clause is, that it puts at rest both the questions which we stated to have been the subject of differences of opinion. It declares that persons may be citizens of the United States without regard to their citizenship of a particular state, and it overturns the Dred Scott decision by making all persons born within the United States and subject to its jurisdiction citizens of the United States. That its main purpose was to establish the citizenship of the negro can admit of no doubt. The phrase "subject to its jurisdiction" was intended to exclude from its operation children of ministers, consuls, and citizens or subjects of foreign states born within the United States.

The next observation is more important in view of the arguments of counsel in the present case. It is, that the distinction between citizenship of the United States and citizenship of a state is clearly recognized and established. Not only may a man be a citizen of the United States without being a citizen of a state, but an important element is necessary to convert the former into the latter. He must reside within the state to make him a citizen of it, but it is only necessary that he should be born or naturalized in the United States to be a citizen of the Union.

It is quite clear, then, that there is a citizenship of the United States, and a citizenship of a state, which are distinct from each other, and which depend upon different characteristics or circumstances in the individual.

We think this distinction and its explicit recognition in this amendment of great weight in this argument, because the next paragraph of this same section, which is the one mainly relied on by the plaintiffs in error, speaks only of privileges and immunities of citizens of the United States, and does not speak of those of citizens of the several states. The argument, however, in favor of the plaintiffs rests wholly on the assumption that the citizenship is the same, and the privileges and immunities guaranteed by the clause are the same.

The language is, "No State shall make or enforce any law which shall abridge the privileges or immunities of citizens of the United States." It is a little remarkable, if this clause was intended as a protection to the citizen of a state against the legislative power of his own state, that the word citizen of the state should be left out when it is so carefully used, and used in contradistinction to citizens of the United States, in the very sentence which precedes it. It is too clear for argument that the change in phraseology was adopted understandingly and with a purpose.

Of the privileges and immunities of the citizen of the United States, and of the privileges and immunities of the citizen of the state, and what they respectively are, we will presently consider; but we wish to state here that it is only the former which are placed by this clause under the protection of the federal Constitution, and that the latter, whatever they may be, are not intended to have any additional protection by this paragraph of the amendment.

If, then, there is a difference between the privileges and immunities belonging to a citizen of the United States as such, and those belonging to the citizen of the state as such, the latter must rest for their security and protection where they have heretofore rested; for they are not embraced by this paragraph of the amendment.

The first occurrence of the words "privileges and immunities" in our constitutional history, is to be found in the fourth of the articles of the old Confederation.

It declares "that the better to secure and perpetuate mutual friendship and intercourse among the people of the different States in this Union, the free inhabitants of each of these States, paupers, vagabonds, and fugitives from justice excepted, shall be entitled to all the privileges and immunities of free citizens in the several States; and the people of each State shall have free ingress and regress to and from any other State, and shall enjoy therein all the privileges of trade and commerce, subject to the same duties, impositions, and restrictions as the inhabitants thereof respectively."

In the Constitution of the United States, which superseded the Articles of Confederation, the corresponding provision is found in section two of the fourth article, in the following words: "The citizens of each State shall be entitled to all the privileges and immunities of citizens of the several States."

There can be but little question that the purpose of both these provisions is the same, and that the privileges and immunities intended are the same in each. In the article of the Confederation we have some of these specifically mentioned, and enough perhaps to give some general idea of the class of civil rights meant by the phrase. . . .

The constitutional provision there alluded to did not create those rights, which it called privileges and immunities of citizens of the states. It threw around them in that clause no security for the citizen of the state in which they were claimed or exercised. Nor did it profess to control the power of the state governments over the rights of its own citizens.

Its sole purpose was to declare to the several states, that whatever those rights, as you grant or establish them to your own citizens, or as you limit or qualify, or impose restrictions on their exercise, the same, neither more nor less, shall be the measure of the rights of citizens of other states within your jurisdiction.

It would be the vainest show of learning to attempt to prove by citations of authority, that up to the adoption of the recent amendments, no claim or pretense was set up that those rights depended on the federal government for their existence or protection, beyond the very few express limitations which the federal Constitution imposed upon the states—such, for instance, as the prohibition against ex post facto laws, bills of attainder, and laws impairing the obligation of contracts. But with the exception of these and a few other restrictions, the entire domain of the privileges and immunities of citizens of the states, as above defined, lay within the constitutional and legislative power of the states, and without that of the federal government. Was it the purpose of the Fourteenth Amendment, by the simple declaration that no state should make or enforce any law which shall abridge the privileges and immunities of citizens of the United States, to transfer the security and protection of all the civil rights which we have mentioned, from the states to the federal government? And where it is declared that Congress shall have the power to enforce that article, was it intended to bring within the power of Congress the entire domain of civil rights heretofore belonging exclusively to the states?

All this and more must follow, if the proposition of the plaintiffs in error be sound. For not only are these rights subject to the control of Congress whenever in its discretion any of them are supposed to be abridged by state legislation, but that body may also pass laws in advance, limiting and restricting the exercise of legislative power by the states, in their most ordinary and usual functions, as in its judgment it may think proper on all such subjects. And still further, such a construction followed by the reversal of the judgments of the supreme court of Louisiana in these cases, would constitute this Court a perpetual censor upon all legislation of the states, on the civil rights of their own citizens, with authority to nullify such as it did not approve as consistent with those rights, as they existed at the time of the adoption of this amendment. The argument, we admit, is not always the most conclusive which is drawn from the consequences urged against the adoption of a particular construction of an instrument. But when, as in the case before us, these consequences are so serious, so far-reaching and pervading, so great a departure from the structure and spirit of our institutions; when the effect is to fetter and degrade the state governments by subjecting them to the control of Congress, in the exercise of powers heretofore universally conceded to them of the most ordinary and fundamental character; when in fact it radically changes the whole theory of the relations of the state and federal governments to each other and of both these governments to the people; the argument has a force that is irresistible, in the absence of language which expresses such a purpose too clearly to admit of doubt.

We are convinced that no such results were intended by the Congress which proposed these amendments, nor by the legislatures of the states which ratified them.

Having shown that the privileges and immunities relied on in the argument are those which belong to citizens of the states as such, and that they are left to the state governments for security and protection, and not by this article placed under the special care of the federal government, we may hold ourselves excused from defining the privileges and immunities of citizens of the United States which no state can abridge, until some case involving those privileges may make it necessary to do so.

But lest it should be said that no such privileges and immunities are to be found if those we have been considering are excluded, we venture to suggest some which owe their existence to the federal government, its national character, its Constitution, or its laws.

One of these is well described in the case of Crandall v. Nevada, 6 Wallace 35 (1868). It is said to be the right of the citizen of this great country, protected by implied guarantees of its Constitution, "to come to the seat of government to assert any claim he may have upon that government, to transact any business he may have with it, to seek its protection, to share its offices, to engage in administering its functions. He has the right of free access to its seaports, through which all operations of foreign commerce are conducted, to the sub-treasuries, land offices, and courts of justices in the several states." . . .

Another privilege of a citizen of the United States is to demand the care and protection of the federal government over his life, liberty, and property when on the high seas or within the jurisdiction of a foreign government. Of this there can be no doubt, nor that the right depends upon his character as a citizen of the United States. The right to peaceably assemble and petition for redress of grievances, the privilege of the writ of habeas corpus, are rights of the citizen guaranteed by the federal Constitution. The right to use the navigable waters of the United States, however they may penetrate the territory of the several states, all rights secured to our citizens by treaties with foreign nations, are dependent upon citizenship of the United States, and not citizenship of a state. One of these privileges is conferred by the very article under consideration. It is that a citizen of the United States can, of his own volition, become a citizen of any state of the Union by a bona fide residence therein, with the same rights as other citizens of that state. To these may be added the rights secured by the Thirteenth and Fifteenth articles of Amendment, and by the other clause of the Fourteenth, next to be considered.

But it is useless to pursue this branch of the inquiry, since we are of opinion that the rights claimed by these plaintiffs in error, if they have any existence, are not privileges and immunities of citizens of the United States within the meaning of the clause of the Fourteenth Amendment under consideration.

"All persons born or naturalized in the United States, and subject to the jurisdiction thereof, are citizens of the United States and of the State wherein they reside. No State shall make or enforce any law which shall abridge the privileges or immunities of citizens of the United States; nor shall any State deprive any person of life, liberty, or property without due process of law, nor deny to any person within its jurisdiction the equal protection of its laws."

The argument has not been much pressed in these cases that the defendant's charter deprives the plaintiffs of their property without due process of law, or that it denies to them the equal protection of the law. The first of these paragraphs has been in the Constitution since the adoption of the Fifth Amendment, as a restraint upon the federal power. It is also to be found in some form of expression in the constitutions of nearly all the states, as a restraint upon the power of the states. This law, then, has practically been the same as it now is during the existence of the government, except so far as the present amendment may place the restraining power over the states in this matter in the hands of the federal government.

We are not without judicial interpretation, therefore, both state and national, of the meaning of this clause. And it is sufficient to say that under no construction of that provision that we have ever seen, or any that we deem admissible, can the restraint imposed by the state of Louisiana upon the exercise of their trade by the butchers of New Orleans be held to be a deprivation of property within the meaning of that provision.

"Nor shall any State deny to any person within its jurisdiction the equal protection of the laws."

In the light of the history of these amendments, and the pervading purpose of them, which we have already discussed, it is not difficult to give a meaning to this clause. The existence of laws in the states where the newly emancipated negroes resided, which discriminated with gross injustice and hardship against them as a class, was the evil to be remedied by this clause, and by it such laws are forbidden.

If, however, the states did not conform their laws to its requirements, then by the fifth section of the article of amendment Congress was authorized to enforce it by suitable legislation. We doubt very much whether any action of a state not directed by way of discrimination against the negroes as a class, or on account of their race, will ever be held to come within the purview of this provision. It is so clearly a provision for that race and that emergency, that a strong case would be necessary for its application to any other. But as it is a state that is to be dealt with, and not alone the validity of its laws, we may safely leave that matter until Congress shall have exercised its power, or some case of state oppression, by denial of equal justice in its courts, shall have claimed a decision at our hands. We find no such case in the one before us, and do not deem it necessary to go over the argument again, as it may have relation to this particular clause of the amendment. . . .

The judgments of the supreme court of Louisiana in these cases are affirmed.

Mr. Justice Field, with whom concurred Mr. Chief Justice Chase, Mr. Justice Swayne, and Mr. Justice Bradley, rendered a dissenting opinion as did the two latter justices also.

UNITED STATES v. CLASSIC
313 U. S. 299; 85 L. Ed. 1368; 61 Sup. Ct. 1031. 1941.

It has long been established that there is no necessary connection between citizenship and suffrage. While it is usual to require that voters shall be citizens, more than twenty states at some time have allowed aliens to vote before their naturalization was complete; and on the other hand the right to vote has been withheld from substantial classes of citizens, as for instance, minors, women (before the adoption of woman suffrage), and those who have no permanent residence in any state. The determination of the actual qualifications for suffrage is left by the United States Constitution to the various states. When the federal Constitution was framed, any attempt to establish uniformity among the widely varying state qualifications for suffrage would have been difficult if not impossible, and would have been so resented by the various states as to imperil the ratification of the Constitution. Consequently it was provided that the congressional suffrage should be given to those qualified under state law to vote for members of the most numerous branch of the state legislature, while the method of choosing presidential electors was left to the discretion of the state legislatures. It should be noted that the Fifteenth and Nineteenth Amendments do not guarantee any one the right to vote in a positive way; they merely stipulate that persons shall not be denied the right to vote because of race, or color, or sex.

In Minor v. Happersett, 21 Wallace 162 (1875), the Supreme Court held that the right to vote was not one of the privileges and immunities of citizens of the United States which the states were forbidden by the recently adopted Fourteenth Amendment to abridge. That amendment did not deprive the states of their right to establish qualifications for the suffrage, nor did it operate to enfranchise any classes of citizens who had previously been denied the right to vote. On the other hand, the case of Ex parte Yarbrough, 110 U. S. 651 (1884), established the doctrine that there is a certain sense in which the right to vote for federal officers may be regarded as a right of United States citizenship which will be accorded federal protection.

Yarbrough and others were members of the Ku Klux Klan which existed in the south after the Civil War. They were prosecuted in a federal district court in Georgia for the crime of conspiring together to intimidate a Negro named Berry Saunders in the exercise of his right to vote for a member of Congress. It was shown that the conspirators used physical violence and that they went in disguise upon the public highways. They were convicted and sentenced to prison. The federal crime they committed was defined by a section of the Enforcement Act of 1870 (later invoked in the Classic case) which forbade under heavy penalties two or more persons to "conspire to injure, oppress, threaten, or intimidate any citizen in the free exercise or enjoyment of any right or privilege secured to him by the Constitution or laws of the United States . . ." or to "go in disguise on the highway, or on the premises of another, with intent to prevent or hinder [such citizen in] his free exercise or enjoyment" of any such right; or to "conspire to prevent by force, intimidation, or threat, any citizen who is lawfully entitled to vote" from voting for presidential electors or members of Congress. Yarbrough contended that Congress had no delegated authority thus to protect the right to vote in federal elections. The Supreme Court, in a powerful opinion by Mr. Justice Miller, sustained Yarbrough's conviction and held the federal statute valid. It made clear that the right to vote for representatives in Congress is a right which one gets from the federal Constitution, even though the precise measure of this right is fixed by the suffrage qualifications of the several states. In other words, the right to vote for congressmen is a privilege of United States citizenship, provided one has the qualifications which the state requires of those who vote for the more numerous branch of the state legislature. Congress has full authority under the doctrine of implied powers to protect this privilege of federal citizenship against individual or state aggression.

While the states fix the qualifications for voting for federal officers, Congress is not without power to control by law the conduct of federal elections. Article I, section 4 of the Constitution provides that: "The times, places and manner of holding elections for Senators and Representatives, shall be prescribed in each State by the legislature thereof; but the Congress may at any time by law make or alter such regulations, except as to the places of choosing Senators." Congress has found it more satisfactory to use the election laws and election machinery of the states for the choice of Senators and Representatives than to replace these by its own separate laws and machinery. In 1871 Congress made it a federal crime for any officer of an election at which members of Congress were voted for, to violate any duty imposed upon him in regard to such election by any *state* or *federal law*. In Ex parte Siebold, 100 U. S. 371 (1880), the Court upheld the conviction in a federal court under this law of Siebold and others who, being state election officers, stuffed the ballot box at a congressional election in Maryland in violation of a Maryland statute. Congress could validly adopt in this manner the election laws of the states, and could add its own penalties to the violation of these laws. Such co-operative action by state and nation is constitutional. In Burroughs v. United States, 290 U. S. 534 (1934), the Court held valid a federal statute of 1925 which requires the public disclosure of presidential campaign contributions, the names of contributors, and other details. The Court said: "To say that Congress is without power to pass appropriate legislation to safeguard such an election from the improper use of money to influence the result is to deny to the nation in a vital particular the power of self-preservation."

In Newberry v. United States, 256 U. S. 232 (1921), the question arose whether the power of Congress to make regulations affecting congressional elections extends to the *primary elections* in which congressmen are nominated, or only to the *elections* in which they are finally chosen. A federal corrupt practices act of 1910 limited by criminal penalties the sums which might be spent in congressional election campaigns. In 1918, Senator Newberry from Michigan spent a great deal more than the statutory amount in winning from Henry Ford the Republican nomination for the Senate, and he was convicted of violating the federal statute. The Supreme Court in a five-to-four decision (explained in the opinion in the Classic case given below) set the conviction aside. Only eight justices, however, passed on the constitutional question whether Congress could regulate congressional primaries, and they divided four to four. In spite of this the Newberry case was popularly regarded as holding congressional primary elections immune from any federal control, although this supposed result was bitterly criticized.

In 1939, Attorney General Murphy created the Civil Liberties Unit (soon called the Civil Rights Section) in the Criminal Division of the Department of Justice, and ordered it to "direct, supervise and conduct prosecutions of violations of the provisions of the Constitution or Acts of Congress guaranteeing civil rights to individuals." As part of a varied and aggressive program for the protection of civil liberties, the Unit won a signal victory in its successful prosecution of the case of United States v. Classic. Classic, a crooked New Orleans politician, guilty of the crudest kind of election frauds, must have felt that the arm of the law was indeed long to bring about his conviction in a federal court for having violated two sections of the old Enforcement Act of 1870 which forbade obstruction or interference with the rights guaranteed to citizens by the Constitution or statutes of the United States. The result was possible only because the Court was willing to ignore the supposed ruling of the Newberry case and to hold that the right of the citizen to vote in a congressional primary election, and to have his ballot honestly counted, is a right which Congress has validly protected in its laws relating generally to congressional elections. In short, a primary election is an election within the meaning of the Constitution and statutes. The three justices who dissented in this case did so not because they doubted the constitutional power of Congress to regulate congressional primaries, but because they did not agree that Congress, in a statute passed seventy years ago, had exercised this power.

In Screws v. United States, 325 U. S. 91 (1945), the Civil Rights Section invoked the provisions of the Enforcement Act of 1870 for a very different purpose. Screws was sheriff in a county in Georgia. Aided by a deputy and a policeman he arrested Hall, a Negro, late one night for the alleged theft of a tire. There was evidence that Screws had a grudge against Hall and had threatened to "get" him. The three officers handcuffed Hall, brought him to the courthouse, and there proceeded to beat him to death. The state authorities failed to prosecute Screws and he was thereupon indicted and convicted under the section of the federal statute which provides: "Whoever, under color of any law, statute, ordinance, regulation, or custom, willfully subjects, or causes to be subjected, any inhabitant of any State, Territory, or District to the deprivation of any rights, privileges, or immunities secured or protected by the Constitution and laws of the United States . . . shall be fined not more than $1000, or imprisoned not more than one year, or both." The indictment of Screws rested on the theory that the three officers had deprived Hall, under color of the law of Georgia, of rights guaranteed to him by the Fourteenth Amendment: namely, "the right not to be deprived of life without due process of law; the right to be tried upon the charge on which he was arrested, by due process of law and if found guilty to be punished in accordance with the laws of Georgia." The results reached by the Supreme Court in this case were rather confusing. Six justices agreed that the federal statute could validly be applied to the kind of conduct of which Screws was guilty. Five justices, however, ruled that Screws was entitled to a new trial because the trial court had not properly charged the jury that Screws' violation of the statute must be shown to have been "willful." At the new trial Screws was acquitted. The case does, however, extend the authority of the federal government to punish state officers for violations of civil liberty which lie within the range of federal protection.

The foregoing cases leave unanswered certain widely discussed questions. May Congress make lynching a federal crime? Has it any power to insure the conviction in a state court of the murderer of a civil rights worker or to bring to justice members of an all-white jury that acquits such a murderer despite overwhelming evidence of his guilt? These questions are more difficult than the man in the street is likely to realize.

The steadily growing movement to eliminate racial discrimination has made the effective protection of civil rights a major problem. The modest Civil Rights Section which had existed in the Department of Justice since 1939 was made into a Civil Rights Division in 1957 under the direction of an Assistant Attorney General. With the passage of the Civil Rights Act of 1964 and the Voting Rights Act of 1965, Congress has undertaken a vastly broadened exercise of its powers in this field. The validity of these two statutes is discussed below; see p. 524 and p. 551.

Mr. Justice Stone delivered the opinion of the Court, saying in part:

Two counts of an indictment found in a federal district court charged that appellees [Classic and others], Commissioners of Elections, conducting a primary election under Louisiana law, to nominate a candidate of the Democratic party for representative in Congress, willfully altered and falsely counted and certified the ballots of voters cast in the primary election. The questions for decision are whether the right of qualified voters to vote in the Louisiana primary and to have their ballots counted is a right "secured by the Constitution" within the meaning of § § 19 and 20 of the Criminal Code, and whether the acts of appellees charged in the indictment violate those sections. . . .

Section 19 of the Criminal Code condemns as a criminal offense any conspiracy to injure a citizen in the exercise "of any right or privilege secured to him by the Constitution or laws of the United States." Section 20 makes it a penal offense for anyone who, "acting under color of any law" "willfully subjects, or causes to be subjected, any inhabitant of any State . . . to the deprivation of any rights, privileges and immunities secured and protected by the Constitution and laws of the United States." The government argues that the right of a qualified voter in a Louisiana congressional primary election to have his vote counted as cast is a right secured by Article I, sections 2 and 4 of the Constitution, and that a conspiracy to deprive the citizen of that right is a violation of § 19, and also that the willful action of appellees as state officials, in falsely counting the ballots at the primary election and in falsely certifying the count, deprived qualified voters of that right and of the equal protection of the laws guaranteed by the Fourteenth Amendment, all in violation of § 20 of the Criminal Code.

Article I, section 2 of the Constitution, commands that "The House of Representatives shall be composed of Members chosen every second Year by the People of the several States, and the Electors in each State shall have the Qualifications requisite for Electors of the most numerous Branch of the State Legislature." By section 4 of the same article "The Times, Places and Manner of holding Elections for Senators and Representatives, shall be prescribed in each State by the Legislature thereof; but the Congress may at any time by Law make or alter such Regulations, except as to the Places of chusing Senators." Such right as is secured by the Constitution to qualified voters to choose members of the House of Representatives is thus to be exercised in conformity to the requirements of state law subject to the restrictions prescribed by section 2 and to the authority conferred on Congress by section 4, to regulate the times, places and manner of holding elections for representatives.

We look then to the statutes of Louisiana here involved to ascertain the nature of the right which under the constitutional mandate they define and confer on the voter and the effect upon its exercise of the acts with which appellees are charged, all with the view of determining, first, whether the right or privilege is one secured by the Constitution of the United States, second, whether the effect under the state statute of appellees' alleged acts is such that they operate to injure or oppress citizens in the exercise of that right within the meaning of § 19 and to deprive inhabitants of the state of that right within the meaning of § 20, and finally, whether § § 19 and 20 respectively are in other respects applicable to the alleged acts of appellees.

Pursuant to the authority given by section 2 of Article I of the Constitution, and subject to the legislative power of Congress under section 4 of Article I, and other pertinent provisions of the Constitution, the states are given, and in fact exercise a wide discretion in the formulation of a system for the choice by the people of representatives in Congress. In common with many other states Louisiana has exercised that discretion by setting up machinery for the effective choice of party candidates for representative in Congress by primary elections and by its laws it eliminates or seriously restricts the candidacy at the general election of all those who are defeated at the primary. All political parties, which are defined as those that have cast at least 5 per cent of the total vote at specified preceding elections, are required to nominate their candidates for representative by direct primary elections. Louisiana Act No. 46, Regular Session, 1940, § § 1 and 3. . . .

The right to vote for a representative in Congress at the general election is, as a matter of law, thus restricted to the successful party candidate at the primary, to those not candidates at the primary who file nomination papers, and those whose names may be lawfully written into the ballot by the electors. Even if, as appellees argue, contrary to the decision in Serpas v. Trebucq, voters may lawfully write into their ballots, cast at the general election, the name of a candidate rejected at the primary and have their ballots counted, the practical operation of the primary law in otherwise excluding from the ballot on the general election the names of candidates rejected at the primary is such as to impose serious restrictions upon the choice of candidates by the voters save by voting at the primary election. In fact, as alleged in the indictment, the practical operation of the primary in Louisiana, is and has been since the primary election was established in 1900 to secure the election of the Democratic primary nominee for the Second Congressional District of Louisiana.

Interference with the right to vote in the congressional primary in the Second Congressional District for the choice of Democratic candidate for Congress is thus as a matter of law and in fact an interference with the effective choice of the voters at the only stage of the election procedure when their choice is of significance, since it is at the only stage when such interference could have any practical effect on the ultimate result, the choice of the Congressman to represent the district. The primary in Louisiana is an integral part of the procedure for the popular choice of Congressman. The right of qualified voters to vote at the congressional primary in Louisiana and to have their ballots counted is thus the right to participate in that choice.

We come then to the question whether that right is one secured by the Constitution. Section 2 of Article I commands that Congressmen shall be chosen by the people of the several states by electors, the qualifications of which it prescribes. The right of the people to choose, whatever its appropriate constitutional limitations, where in other respects it is defined, and the mode of its exercise is prescribed by state action in conformity to the Constitution, is a right established and guaranteed by the Constitution and hence is one secured by it to those citizens and inhabitants of the state entitled to exercise the right. Ex parte Yarbrough, 110 U. S. 651. While, in a loose sense, the right to vote for representatives in Congress is sometimes spoken of as a right derived from the states, see Minor v. Happersett, 21 Wallace (U. S.) 162, this statement is true only in the sense that the states are authorized by the Constitution, to legislate on the subject as provided by section 2 of Article I, to the extent that Congress has not restricted state action by the exercise of its powers to regulate elections under section 4 and its more general power under Article I, section 8, clause 18 of the Constitution "to make all laws which shall be necessary and proper for carrying into execution the foregoing powers." See Ex parte Siebold, 100 U. S. 371.

Obviously included within the right to choose, secured by the Constitution, is the right of qualified voters within a state to cast their ballots and have them counted at congressional elections. This Court has consistently held that this is a right secured by the Constitution. And since the constitutional command is without restriction or limitation, the right, unlike those guaranteed by the Fourteenth and Fifteenth Amendments, is secured against the action of individuals as well as of states. Ex parte Yarbrough, 110 U. S. 651.

But we are now concerned with the question whether the right to choose at a primary election, a candidate for election as representative, is embraced in the right to choose representatives secured by Article I, section 2. We may assume that the framers of the Constitution in adopting that section, did not have specifically in mind the selection and elimination of candidates for Congress by the direct primary any more than they contemplated the application of the commerce clause to interstate telephone, telegraph and wireless communication which are concededly within it. But in determining whether a provision of the Constitution applies to a new subject matter, it is of little significance that it is one with which the framers were not familiar. For in setting up an enduring framework of government they undertook to carry out for the indefinite future and in all the vicissitudes of the changing affairs of men, those fundamental purposes which the instrument itself discloses. Hence we read its words, not as we read legislative codes which are subject to continuous revision with the changing course of events, but as the revelation of the great purposes which were intended to be achieved by the Constitution as a continuing instrument of government. If we remember that "it is a Constitution we are expounding," we cannot rightly prefer, of the possible meanings of its words, that which will defeat rather than effectuate the constitutional purpose.

That the free choice by the people of representatives in Congress, subject only to the restrictions to be found in sections 2 and 4 of Article I and elsewhere in the Constitution, was one of the great purposes of our constitutional scheme of government cannot be doubted. We cannot regard it as any the less the constitutional purpose or its words as any the less guaranteeing the integrity of that choice when a state, exercising its privilege in the absence of congressional action, changes the mode of choice from a single step, a general election, to two, of which the first is the choice at a primary of those candidates from whom, as a second step, the representative in Congress is to be chosen at the election.

Nor can we say that that choice which the Constitution protects is restricted to the second step because section 4 of Article I, as a means of securing a free choice of representatives by the people, has authorized Congress to regulate the manner of elections, without making any mention of primary elections. For we think that the authority of Congress, given by section 4, includes the authority to regulate primary elections when, as in this case, they are a step in the exercise by the people of their choice of representatives in Congress. . . . In Newberry v. United States, 256 U. S. 232, four Justices of this Court were of opinion that the term "elections" in section 4 of Article I did not embrace a primary election since that procedure was unknown to the framers. A fifth Justice who with them pronounced the judgment of the Court, was of opinion that a primary, held under a law enacted before the adoption of the Seventeenth Amendment, for the nomination of candidates for Senator, was not an election within the meaning of section 4 of Article I of the Constitution, presumably because the choice of the primary imposed no legal restrictions on the election of Senators by the state legislatures to which their election had been committed by Article I, section 3. The remaining four Justices were of the opinion that a primary election for the choice of candidates for Senator or Representative were elections subject to regulation by Congress within the meaning of section 4 of Article I. The question then has not been prejudged by any decision of this Court.

To decide it we turn to the words of the Constitution read in their historical setting as revealing the purpose of its framers, and in search for admissible meanings of its words which, in the circumstances of their application, will effectuate those purposes. As we have said, a dominant purpose of section 2, so far as the selection of representatives in Congress is concerned, was to secure to the people the right to choose representatives by the designated electors, that is to say, by some form of election. Cf. the Seventeenth Amendment as to popular "election" of Senators. From time immemorial an election to public office has been in point of substance no more and no less than the expression by qualified electors of their choice of candidates.

Long before the adoption of the Constitution the form and mode of that expression had changed from time to time. There is no historical warrant for supposing that the framers were under the illusion that the method of effecting the choice of the electors would never change or that if it did, the change was for that reason to be permitted to defeat the right of the people to choose representatives for Congress which the Constitution had guaranteed. The right to participate in the choice of representatives for Congress includes, as we have said, the right to cast a ballot and to have it counted at the general election whether for the successful candidate or not. Where the state law has made the primary an integral part of the procedure of choice, or where in fact the primary effectively controls the choice, the right of the elector to have his ballot counted at the primary, is likewise included in the right protected by Article I, section 2. And this right of participation is protected just as is the right to vote at the election, where the primary is by law made an integral part of the election machinery, whether the voter exercises his right in a party primary which invariably, sometimes or never determines the ultimate choice of the representative. Here, even apart from the circumstance that the Louisiana primary is made by law an integral part of the procedure of choice, the right to choose a representative is in fact controlled by the primary because, as is alleged in the indictment, the choice of candidates at the Democratic primary determines the choice of the elected representative. Moreover, we cannot close our eyes to the fact already mentioned that the practical influence of the choice of candidates at the primary may be so great as to affect profoundly the choice at the general election even though there is no effective legal prohibition upon the rejection at the election of the choice made at the primary and may thus operate to deprive the voter of his constitutional right of choice. This was noted and extensively commented upon by the concurring Justices in Newberry v. United States.

Unless the constitutional protection of the integrity of "elections" extends to primary elections, Congress is left powerless to effect the constitutional purpose, and the popular choice of representatives is stripped of its constitutional protection save only as Congress, by taking over the control of state elections, may exclude from them the influence of the state primaries. Such an expedient would end that state autonomy with respect to elections which the Constitution contemplated that Congress should be free to leave undisturbed, subject only to such minimum regulation as it should find necessary to insure the freedom and integrity of the choice. Words, especially those of a constitution, are not to be read with such stultifying narrowness. The words of sections 2 and 4 of Article I, read in the sense which is plainly permissible and in the light of the constitutional purpose, require us to hold that a primary election which involves a necessary step in the choice of candidates for election as representatives in Congress, and which in the circumstances of this case controls that choice, is an election within the meaning of the constitutional provision and is subject to congressional regulation as to the manner of holding it.

Not only does section 4 of Article I authorize Congress to regulate the manner of holding elections, but by Article I, section 8, clause 18, Congress is given authority "to make all laws which shall be necessary and proper for carrying into execution the foregoing powers, and all other powers vested by this Constitution in the Government of the United States, or in any department or officer thereof." This provision leaves to the Congress the choice of means by which its constitutional powers are to be carried into execution. "Let the end be legitimate; let it be within the scope of the Constitution, and all means which are appropriate which are plainly adapted to that end which are not prohibited but consist with the letter and spirit of the Constitution, are constitutional." McCulloch v. Maryland, 4 Wheaton (U.S.) 316. That principle has been consistently adhered to and liberally applied, and extends to the congressional power by appropriate legislation to safeguard the right of choice by the people of representatives in Congress secured by section 2 of Article I.

There remains the question whether § § 19 and 20 are an exercise of the congressional authority applicable to the acts with which appellees are charged in the indictment. Section 19 makes it a crime to conspire to "injure" or "oppress" any citizen "in the free exercise of any right or privilege secured to him by the Constitution." In Ex parte Yarbrough, 110 U.S. 651, it was held that the right to vote in a congressional election is a right secured by the Constitution, and that a conspiracy to prevent the citizen from voting or to prevent the official count of his ballot when cast, is a conspiracy to injure and oppress the citizen in the free exercise of a right secured by the Constitution within the meaning of § 19. In reaching this conclusion the Court found no uncertainty or ambiguity in the statutory language, obviously devised to protect the citizen "in the free exercise or enjoyment of any right or privilege secured to him by the Constitution," and concerned itself with the question whether the right to participate in choosing a representative is so secured. Such is our function here. Conspiracy to prevent the official count of a citizen's ballot, held in United States v. Mosley to be a violation of § 19 in the case of a congressional election, is equally a conspiracy to injure and oppress the citizen when the ballots are cast in a primary election prerequisite to the choice of party candidates for a congressional election. In both cases the right infringed is one secured by the Constitution. The injury suffered by the citizen in the exercise of the right is an injury which the statute describes and to which it applies in the one case as in the other.

The suggestion that § 19, concededly applicable to conspiracies to deprive electors of their votes at congressional elections, is not sufficiently specific to be deemed applicable to primary elections, will hardly bear examination. Section 19 speaks neither of elections nor of primaries. In unambiguous language it protects "any right or privilege secured by the Constitution," a phrase which as we have seen extends to the right of the voter to have his vote counted in both the general election and in the primary election, where the latter is a part of the election machinery, as well as to numerous other constitutional rights which are wholly unrelated to the choice of a representative in Congress.

In the face of the broad language of the statute, we are pointed to no principle of statutory construction and to no significant legislative history which could be thought to sanction our saying that the statute applies any the less to primaries than to elections, where in one as in the other it is the same constitutional right which is infringed . . . Differences of opinion have arisen as to the effect of the primary in particular cases on the choice of representatives. But we are troubled by no such doubt here. Hence, the right to participate through the primary in the choice of representatives in Congress—a right clearly secured by the Constitution—is within the words and purpose of § 19 in the same manner and to the same extent as the right to vote at the general election. It is no extension of the criminal statute . . . to find a violation of it in a new method of interference with the right which its words protect. For it is the constitutional right, regardless of the method of interference, which is the subject of the statute and which in precise terms it protects from injury and oppression. . . .

If a right secured by the Constitution may be infringed by the corrupt failure to include the vote at a primary in the official count, it is not significant that the primary, like the voting machine, was unknown when § 19 was adopted. Abuse of either may infringe the right and therefore violate § 19 . . .

The right of the voters at the primary to have their votes counted is, as we have stated, a right or privilege secured by the Constitution, and to this § 20 also gives protection. The alleged acts of appellees were committed in the course of their performance of duties under the Louisiana statute requiring them to count the ballots, to record the result of the count, and to certify the result of the election. Misuse of power, possessed by virtue of state law and made possible only because the wrongdoer is clothed with the authority of state law, is action taken "under color of" state law. Here the acts of appellees infringed the constitutional right and deprived the voters of the benefit of it within the meaning of § 20 . . .

The Chief Justice took no part in the consideration or decision of this case. Justices Douglas, Black, and Murphy dissented.

BARRON v. BALTIMORE
7 Peters 243; 8 L. Ed. 672. 1833.

One of the bitter criticisms urged against our federal Constitution as it came from the hands of the Convention was that it contained no bill of rights. It was feared that without specific guarantees the civil rights and liberties of the people and the states would be at the mercy of the proposed national government. Ratification was secured, but with a tacit understanding that a bill of rights should promptly be added which should restrict the national government in behalf of individual liberty. That the early statesmen thought of a federal bill of rights only in terms of restrictions on national power is emphasized by Hamilton's ingenious argument in The Federalist (No. 84) that since the proposed central government was one which possessed only the powers delegated to it, it would be not only unnecessary but unwise to prohibit it from doing things which were clearly outside the scope of its delegated authority.

When the First Congress convened, the House of Representatives proposed seventeen amendments in the nature of a bill of rights. One of these, the fourteenth, provided that "no state should infringe the right of trial by jury in criminal cases, nor the rights of conscience, nor the freedom of speech or of the press." This amendment, which was the only one restricting the powers of the states, was rejected by the Senate. The substance of the others was consolidated into twelve amendments, ten of which were finally ratified by the states.

The First Amendment indicates by its own language that it is directed only against the federal government, for it begins, "Congress shall make no law . . ." The other amendments are couched in terms of general prohibition; and in spite of the perfectly clear historical evidence as to the intention of those who framed them, it came to be argued that these guarantees of civil liberty ought to be construed as restrictions upon state and federal governments alike. Whether this view is correct is the issue involved in Barron v. Baltimore, the last constitutional decision in which Chief Justice Marshall participated.

The city of Baltimore in the paving of its streets had diverted from their natural course certain streams, with the result that they made deposits of sand and gravel near Barron's wharf and thereby rendered the water shallow and prevented the approach of vessels. The wharf, which had previously enjoyed the deepest water in the harbor, was rendered practically useless. A verdict of $4500 for Barron had been reversed by the state court of appeals and a writ of error was taken to the Supreme Court of the United States. It was alleged by Barron that this action upon the part of the city constituted a violation of that clause of the Fifth Amendment which forbids taking private property for public use without just compensation. He insisted that this amendment, being a guarantee in behalf of individual liberty, ought to be construed to restrain the states as well as the national government.

At the present time he quite obviously would have sought his redress under the Fourteenth Amendment. While the Bill of Rights does not restrict state power, the Fourteenth Amendment does. Beginning in 1925 the Supreme Court has held that some of the basic rights protected against federal invasion by the Bill of Rights comprise part of the "liberty" which the Fourteenth Amendment forbids the states to abridge without due process of law. This process, known as "incorporation" or "absorption," is discussed on pages 151, 156, and 478. These decisions do not reverse the law of Barron v. Baltimore; they do, however, reverse much of its practical effect.

In delivering the opinion of the Court, Mr. Chief Justice Marshall said:

The judgment brought up by this writ of error having been rendered by the court of a state, this tribunal can exercise no jurisdiction over it, unless it be shown to come within the provisions of the twenty-fifth section of the Judicial Act.

The plaintiff in error contends that it comes within that clause in the Fifth Amendment to the Constitution, which inhibits the taking of private property for public use, without just compensation. He insists that this amendment, being in favor of the liberty of the citizen, ought to be so construed as to restrain the legislative power of a state, as well as that of the United States. If this proposition be untrue, the Court can take no jurisdiction of the cause.

The question thus presented is, we think, of great importance, but not of much difficulty.

The Constitution was ordained and established by the people of the United States for themselves, for their own government, and not for the government of the individual states. Each state established a constitution for itself, and, in that constitution, provided such limitations and restrictions on the powers of its particular government as its judgment dictated. The people of the United States framed such a government for the United States as they supposed best adapted to their situation, and best calculated to promote their interests. The powers they conferred on this government were to be exercised by itself; and the limitations on power, if expressed in general terms, are naturally, and, we think, necessarily applicable to the government created by the instrument. They are limitations of power granted in the instrument itself; not of distinct governments, framed by different persons and for different purposes.

If these propositions be correct, the Fifth Amendment must be understood as restraining the power of the general government, not as applicable to the states. In their several constitutions they have imposed such restrictions on their respective governments as their own wisdom suggested; such as they deemed most proper for themselves. It is a subject on which they judge exclusively, and with which others interfere no farther than they are supposed to have a common interest.

The counsel for the plaintiff in error insists that the Constitution was intended to secure the people of the several states against the undue exercise of power by their respective state governments; as well as against that which might be attempted by their general government. In support of this argument he relies on the inhibitions contained in the tenth section of the first article.

We think that section affords a strong if not a conclusive argument in support of the opinion already indicated by the Court.

The preceding section contains restrictions which are obviously intended for the exclusive purpose of restraining the exercise of power by the departments of the general government. Some of them use language applicable only to Congress; others are expressed in general terms. The third clause, for example, declares that "no bill of attainder or ex post facto law shall be passed." No language can be more general; yet the demonstration is complete that it applies solely to the government of the United States. In addition to the general arguments furnished by the instrument itself, some of which have been already suggested, the succeeding section, the avowed purpose of which is to restrain state legislation, contains in terms the very prohibition. It declares that "no State shall pass any bill of attainer or ex post facto law." This provision, then, of the ninth section, however comprehensive its language, contains no restriction on state legislation.

The ninth section having enumerated, in the nature of a bill of rights, the limitations intended to be imposed on the powers of the general government, the tenth proceeds to enumerate those which were to operate on the state legislatures. These restrictions are brought together in the same section, and are by express words applied to the states. "No State shall enter into any treaty," etc. Perceiving that in a constitution framed by the people of the United States for the government of all, no limitation of the action of government on the people would apply to the state government, unless expressed in terms; the restrictions contained in the tenth section are in direct words so applied to the states.

It is worthy of remark, too, that these inhibitions generally restrain state legislation on subjects intrusted to the general government, or in which the people of all the states feel an interest.

A state is forbidden to enter into any treaty, alliance, or confederation. If these compacts are with foreign nations, they interfere with the treaty-making power, which is conferred entirely on the general government; if with each other, for political purposes, they can scarcely fail to interfere with the general purpose and intent of the Constitution. To grant letters of marque and reprisal, would lead directly to war; the power of declaring which is expressly given to Congress. To coin money is also the exercise of a power conferred on Congress. It would be tedious to recapitulate the several limitations on the powers of the states which are contained in this section. They will be found, generally, to restrain state legislation on subjects intrusted to the government of the Union, in which the citizens of all the states are interested. In these alone were the whole people concerned. The question of their application to states is not left to construction. It is averred in positive words.

If the original Constitution, in the ninth and tenth sections of the first article, draws this plain and marked line of discrimination between the limitations it imposes on the powers of the general government, and on those of the states; if in every inhibition intended to act on state power, words are employed which directly express that intent; some strong reason must be assigned for departing from this safe and judicious course in framing the amendments, before that departure can be assumed.

We search in vain for that reason.

Had the people of the several states, or any of them, required changes in their constitutions; had they required additional safeguards to liberty from the apprehended encroachments of their particular governments; the remedy was in their own hands, and would have been applied by themselves. A convention would have been assembled by the discontented state, and the required improvements would have have been made by itself. The unwieldy and cumbrous machinery of procuring a recommendation from two-thirds of Congress, and the assent of three-fourths of their sister states, could never have occured to any human being as a mode of doing that which might be effected by the state itself. Had the framers of these amendments intended them to be limitations on the powers of the state governments, they would have imitated the framers of the original Constitution, and have expressed that intention. Had Congress engaged in the extraordinary occupation of improving the constitutions of the several states by affording the people additional protection from the exercise of power by their own governments in matters which concerned themselves alone, they would have declared this purpose in plain and intelligible language.

But it is universally understood, it is a part of the history of the day, that the great revolution which established the Constitution of the United States was not effected without immense opposition. Serious fears were extensively entertained that those powers which the patriot statesmen, who then watched over the interests of our country, deemed essential to union, and to the attainment of those invaluable objects for which union was sought, might be exercised in a manner dangerous to liberty. In almost every convention by which the Constitution was adopted, amendments to guard against the abuse of power were recommended. These amendments demanded security against the apprehended encroachments of the general government, not against those of the local governments.

In compliance with a sentiment thus generally expressed, to quiet fears thus extensively entertained, amendments were proposed by the required majority in Congress, and adopted by the states. These amendments contain no expression indicating an intention to apply them to the state governments. This Court cannot so apply them.

We are of opinion that the provision in the Fifth Amendment to the Constitution, declaring that private property shall not be taken for public use without just compensation, is intended solely as a limitation on the exercise of power by the government of the United States, and is not applicable to the legislation of the states. We are therefore of opinion, that there is no repugnancy between the several acts of the general assembly of Maryland, given in evidence by the defendants at the trial of this cause, in the court of that state, and the Constitution of the United States. This Court, therefore, has no jurisdiction of the cause; and it is dismissed.

EX PARTE MILLIGAN
4 Wallace 2; 18 L. Ed. 281. 1866.

It is one of the evils of war that there seems frequently to be a certain incompatibility between the demands of military necessity and a punctilious regard for the civil rights of the individual. Certainly in war emergencies the citizen finds his liberty curtailed and his rights abridged in ways which in times of peace would seem intolerable. There is plenty of evidence that President Lincoln, largely supported by public opinion, definitely proceeded during the Civil War upon the theory that questions of constitutional power were to be dealt with in the light of the great objective of preserving the Union. No President has ever invaded private constitutional rights more flagrantly, or from worthier motives than he. This may be illustrated by the famous case of Ex parte Merryman, Fed. Case No. 9487 (1861). Merryman was a southern agitator residing in Maryland who persisted during the early days of the war in conduct and utterances which in the judgment of the military authorities hindered the success of the northern cause. He was thereupon arrested and locked up in the military prison at Fort McHenry. Merryman promptly petitioned Chief Justice Taney for a writ of habeas corpus. Taney issued the writ, directed to the general in command of the fort. The general did not honor the writ, replying that he was authorized by the President to suspend the writ of habeas corpus, but would seek further instructions; and he declined to obey the writ further. Taney thereupon issued a writ of contempt against the general and sent the United States marshal to serve it. The marshal reported that he had not been allowed to enter the outer gate of the fort, although he had sent in his card, and that he had not been able to serve the writ. Taney, while protesting that the marshal had a perfect right to summon a *posse comitatus* and storm the fort, excused him from that duty, and contented himself with writing a full account of the entire case which he addressed to President Lincoln and which concluded with the observation that it now remained for the President, acting in fulfillment of his solemn oath of office, to enforce the laws, execute the judgment of the court, and release the prisoner. Lincoln made no answer whatever to this document, but Merryman was later released from military confinement and turned over to the civil authorities.

No case of this kind came to the Supreme Court while the war was in progress, although in 1864 an attempt was made to bring before that tribunal on a writ of habeas corpus the validity of the arrest of the notorious agitator, Vallandigham. The Court held that it was without jurisdiction and dismissed the case. It is interesting to speculate what the results might have been had the Supreme Court locked horns with the President in such a case; if, for example, the Milligan case had come up for decision during the early part of the war instead of in 1866.

The facts in the Milligan case were as follows: Milligan, a civilian, was arrested by order of General Hovey, who commanded the military district of Indiana; was tried in October, 1864, by a military commission which had been established under presidential authority; was found guilty of initiating insurrection and of various other treasonable and disloyal practices; and was sentenced to be hanged on May 19, 1865. This sentence was approved by President Johnson. On May 10, 1865, Milligan sued out a writ of habeas corpus to the United States circuit court in Indiana, alleging the unconstitutional character of the proceedings under which he had been convicted and claiming the right of trial by jury as guaranteed by the Constitution. Thus for the first time the Supreme Court faced the question of the right of the President to suspend the writ of habeas corpus and to substitute trial by military authority for trial in the ordinary civil courts in districts outside the actual field of military operations.

The Supreme Court itself found difficulty in agreeing upon the important questions presented. They all held that a military commission set up by the President under such circumstances and without special authority from Congress was unlawful and without any power whatsoever. Five of the judges took the view that neither Congress nor the President had the power to set up military tribunals except in the actual theatre of war where the civil courts were no longer functioning. Four judges, while denying such power to the President, held that it could be exercised by Congress. The Court decided, however, that Milligan had been unlawfully convicted and he was released.

The subsequent story of the case is not without interest. Milligan's sentence had been commuted to life imprisonment by the President in June, 1865, and he had been imprisoned by General Hovey in the Ohio penitentiary until his final release on April 10, 1866, as a result of the decision of the Supreme Court. On March 13, 1868, he brought an action of damages against General Hovey for unlawful imprisonment. The case was tried in the federal circuit court and the jury rendered a verdict for Milligan, but awarded only nominal damages inasmuch as the two-year statute of limitations allowed him to recover damages only for his imprisonment between March 13 when he brought the action, and April 10 when he was released.

The fact that the decision in the Milligan case set up a powerful judicial protection against military and executive invasion of individual constitutional rights was not sufficient to distract contemporary attention from the vital political consequences of the rule regarding congressional power which was laid down. Congress was in the midst of the important work of reconstruction. The radical leaders of the Republican party were committed to a policy of reconstruction which should keep the southern states under the control of federal military forces until conditions seemed to warrant the adoption of a less drastic policy. But the doctrine of the Milligan case, by condemning military government in peaceful sections where the civil courts were open, was obviously incompatible with any such form of military reconstruction. It looked as though the Court was trying to prevent the carrying out of the congressional policy, and the decision was received with an outburst of anger by the congressional leaders. There was some talk of impeaching the judges; Congress went forward with its plans for military government in the south in contemptuous disregard for the decision, and utterances from prominent men were not lacking to the effect that the Court would come off loser in any combat over the validity of the reconstruction plan adopted. It is an interesting fact that the constitutionality of these reconstruction acts was never passed upon by the Supreme Court. See the case of Mississippi v. Johnson (p. 298), and particularly the case of Ex parte McCardle, 7 Wallace 506 (1869), in which a case involving this vital question was literally snatched from the Court, after it had been argued, by a special statute taking away the Court's jurisdiction. It seems probable that the Court would have held the military reconstruction program invalid, however; for, acting upon the decision in the Milligan case, the judges in the southern circuits declined to hold court in those states which were being governed by military authority. The refusal of Mr. Chief Justice Chase on this ground to hold court in Virginia prevented the trial of Jefferson Davis for treason and particularly infuriated the congressional leaders.

Mr. Justice Davis delivered the opinion of the Court, saying in part:

. . . The controlling question in the case is this: Upon the facts stated in Milligan's petition, and the exhibits filed, had the military commission mentioned in it jurisdiction, legally, to try and sentence him? Milligan, not a resident of one of the rebellious states, or a prisoner of war, but a citizen of Indiana for twenty years past, and never in the military or naval service, is, while at his home, arrested by the military power of the United States, imprisoned, and, on certain criminal charges preferred against him, tried, convicted, and sentenced to be hanged by a military commission, organized under the direction of the military commander of the military district of Indiana. Had this tribunal the legal power and authority to try and punish this man? . . .

. . . The Constitution of the United States is a law for rulers and people, equally in war and in peace, and covers with the shield of its protection all classes of men, at all times, and under all circumstances. No doctrine involving more pernicious consequences was ever invented by the wit of man than that any of its provisions can be suspended during any of the great exigencies of government. Such a doctrine leads directly to anarchy or despotism, but the theory of necessity on which it is based is false; for the government, within the Constitution, has all the powers granted to it which are necessary to preserve its existence; as has been happily proved by the result of the great effort to throw off its just authority.

Have any of the rights guaranteed by the Constitution been violated in the case of Milligan? and if so, what are they?

Every trial involves the exercise of judicial power; and from what source did the military commission that tried him derive their authority? Certainly no part of the judicial power of the country was conferred on them; because the Constitution expressly vests it "in one Supreme Court and such inferior courts as the Congress may from time to time ordain and establish," and it is not pretended that the commission was a court ordained and established by Congress. They cannot justify on the mandate of the President, because he is controlled by law, and has his appropriate sphere of duty, which is to execute, not to make, the laws; and there is "no unwritten criminal code to which resort can be had as a source of jurisdiction."

But it is said that the jurisdiction is complete under the "laws and usages of war."

It can serve no useful purpose to inquire what those laws and usages are, whence they originated, where found, and on whom they operate; they can never be applied to citizens in states which have upheld the authority of the government, and where the courts are open and their process unobstructed. This Court has judicial knowledge that in Indiana the federal authority was always unopposed, and its courts always open to hear criminal accusations and redress grievances; and no usage of war could sanction a military trial there for any offense whatever of a citizen in civil life, in nowise connected with the military service. Congress could grant no such power; and to the honor of our national legislature be it said, it has never been provoked by the state of the country even to attempt its exercise. One of the plainest constitutional provisions was, therefore, infringed when Milligan was tried by a court not ordained and established by Congress, and not composed of judges appointed during good behavior. Why was he not delivered to the circuit court of Indiana to be proceeded against according to law? . . . If it was dangerous, in the distracted condition of affairs, to leave Milligan unrestrained of his liberty, because he "conspired against the government, afforded aid and comfort to rebels, and incited the people to insurrection," the law said, arrest him, confine him closely, render him powerless to do further mischief; and then present his case to the grand jury of the district, with proofs of his guilt, and, if indicted, try him according to the course of the common law. If this had been done, the Constitution would have been vindicated, the law of 1863 enforced, and the securities for personal liberty preserved and defended.

Another guarantee of freedom was broken when Milligan was denied a trial by jury. . . . The Sixth Amendment affirms that "in all criminal prosecutions the accused shall enjoy the right to a speedy and public trial by an impartial jury,"—language broad enough to embrace all persons and cases; but the Fifth, recognizing the necessity of an indictment, or presentment, before any one can be held to answer for high crimes, "except cases arising in the land or naval forces, or in the militia, when in actual service, in time of war or public danger"; and the framers of the Constitution, doubtless, meant to limit the right of trial by jury, in the Sixth Amendment, to those persons who were subject to indictment or presentment in the Fifth.

The discipline necessary to the efficiency of the army and navy required other and swifter modes of trial than are furnished by the common law courts; and, in pursuance of the power conferred by the Constitution, Congress has declared the kinds of trial, and the manner in which they shall be conducted, for offenses committed while the party is in the military or naval service. Every one connected with these branches of the public service is amenable to the jurisdiction which Congress has created for their government, and, while thus serving, surrenders his right to be tried by the civil courts. All other persons, citizens of states where the courts are open, if charged with crime, are guaranteed the inestimable privilege of trial by jury. . . .

It is claimed that martial law covers with its broad mantle the proceedings of this military commission. The proposition is this: that in a time of war the commander of an armed force (if, in his opinion, the exigencies of the country demand it, and of which he is to judge) has the power, within the lines of his military district, to suspend all civil rights and their remedies, and subject citizens as well as soldiers to the rule of his will; and in the exercise of his lawful authority cannot be restrained, except by his superior officer or the President of the United States.

If this position is sound to the extent claimed, then when war exists, foreign or domestic, and the country is subdivided into military departments for mere convenience, the commander of one of them can, if he chooses, within his limits, on the plea of necessity, with the approval of the Executive, substitute military force for, and to the exclusion of, the laws, and punish all persons, as he thinks right and proper, without fixed or certain rules.

The statement of this proposition shows its importance; for, if true, republican government is a failure, and there is an end of liberty regulated by law. Martial law, established on such a basis, destroys every guarantee of the Constitution, and effectually renders the "military independent of, and superior to, the civil power,"—the attempt to do which by the king of Great Britain was deemed by our fathers such an offense, that they assigned it to the world as one of the causes which impelled them to declare their independence. Civil liberty and this kind of martial law cannot endure together; the antagonism is irreconcilable; and, in the conflict, one or the other must perish. . . .

It will be borne in mind that this is not a question of the power to proclaim martial law, when war exists in a community and the courts and civil authorities are overthrown. Nor is it a question what rule a military commander, at the head of his army, can impose on states in rebellion to cripple their resources and quell the insurrection. The jurisdiction claimed is much more extensive. The necessities of the service, during the late rebellion, required that the loyal states should be placed within the limits of certain military districts and commanders appointed in them; and, it is urged, that this, in a military sense, constituted them the theatre of military operations; and, as in this case, Indiana had been and was again threatened with invasion by the enemy, the occasion was furnished to establish martial law. The conclusion does not follow from the premises. If armies were collected in Indiana, they were to be employed in another locality, where the laws were obstructed and the national authority disputed. On her soil there was no hostile foot; if once invaded, that invasion was at an end, and with it all pretext for martial law. Martial law cannot arise from a threatened invasion. The necessity must be actual and present; the invasion real, such as effectually closes the courts and deposes the civil administration.

It is difficult to see how the safety of the country required martial law in Indiana. If any of her citizens were plotting treason, the power of arrest could secure them, until the government was prepared for their trial, when the courts were open and ready to try them. It was as easy to protect witnesses before a civil as a military tribunal; and as there could be no wish to convict, except on sufficient legal evidence, surely an ordained and established court was better able to judge of this than a military tribunal composed of gentlemen not trained to the profession of the law.

It follows, from what has been said on this subject, that there are occasions when martial rule can be properly applied. If, in foreign invasion or civil war, the courts are actually closed, and it is impossible to administer criminal justice according to law, then, on the theatre of active military operations, where war really prevails, there is a necessity to furnish a substitute for the civil authority, thus overthrown, to preserve the safety of the army and society; and as no power is left but the military, it is allowed to govern by martial rule until the laws can have their free course. As necessity creates the rule, so it limits its duration; for, if this government is continued after the courts are reinstated, it is a gross usurpation of power. Martial rule can never exist where the courts are open, and in the proper and unobstructed exercise of their jurisdiction. It is also confined to the locality of actual war. Because, during the late rebellion it could have been enforced in Virginia, where the national authority was overturned and the courts driven out, it does not follow that it should obtain in Indiana, where that authority was never disputed, and justice was always administered. And so in the case of a foreign invasion, martial rule may become a necessity in one state, when, in another, it would be "mere lawless violence.". . .

The two remaining questions in this case must be answered in the affirmative. The suspension of the privilege of the writ of habeas corpus does not suspend the writ itself. The writ issues as a matter of course; and on the return made to it the court decides whether the party applying is denied the right of proceeding any further with it.

If the military trial of Milligan was contrary to law, then he was entitled, on the facts stated in his petition, to be discharged from custody by the terms of the act of Congress of March 3, 1863. . . .

But it is insisted that Milligan was a prisoner of war, and, therefore, excluded from the privileges of the statute. It is not easy to see how he can be treated as a prisoner of war, when he lived in Indiana for the past twenty years, was arrested there, and had not been, during the late troubles, a resident of any of the states in rebellion. If in Indiana he conspired with bad men to assist the enemy, he is punishable for it in the courts of Indiana; but, when tried for the offense, he cannot plead the rights of war; for he was not engaged in legal acts of hostility against the government, and only such persons, when captured, are prisoners of war. If he cannot enjoy the immunities attaching to the character of a prisoner of war, how can he be subject to their pains and penalties? . . .

Mr. Chief Justice Chase, for himself and Mr. Justice Wayne, Mr. Justice Swayne, and Mr. Justice Miller, delivered an opinion in which he differed from the Court in several important points, but concurred in the judgment in the case.

DUNCAN v. KAHANAMOKU
327 U. S. 304; 90 L. Ed. 688; 66 Sup. Ct. 606. 1946.

World War I was fought in Europe, and brought no serious menace to our domestic national security and produced no significant clashes between military and civil authority. With World War II, however, the story was very different. This was in every sense a "total" war; its successful outcome was by no means assured and danger of external attack and internal treachery was at times very real. Military leaders faced unprecedented situations and met them by resort to unprecedented extensions of military authority. Some of the problems thus created came to the Supreme Court, and in deciding them the Court threw new light upon the extent of military authority and its relation to civil authority.

The spectacular case of the Nazi saboteurs, Ex parte Quirin, 317 U. S. 1 (1942), appeared at first to reopen the major issue settled by the Milligan case. In June, 1942, eight saboteurs landed in this country from a German submarine. They brought with them explosives, incendiaries, fuses, detonators, timing devices, and acids. They had about $175,000 in American money for expenses and bribes, and they carried elaborate lists of American factories, railroad centers, bridges, power plants, and other key war facilities. They were all born in Germany, had previously lived in this country, and had, upon returning to Germany, been trained in a special school for saboteurs. One had been naturalized in the United States but had forfeited his American citizenship by induction into the Germany Army in 1941. Another claimed American citizenship on the basis of the naturalization of his parents when he was five years old, and he denied that he had forfeited his American citizenship. In its opinion, the Court held that citizenship was irrelevant because a citizen may be tried by a military commission if he violates the law of war.

About ten days after they had been landed they were arrested by the F.B.I. Thereupon President Roosevelt issued two proclamations. The first denied to enemies who enter this country to commit sabotage or other hostile acts the right of access to the civil courts, and directed that they be tried by military tribunals in accordance with the law of war. The second created a Military Commission of eight army officers to try the saboteurs, ordered the Attorney General and the Judge Advocate General to prosecute them, and designated two army officers to act as defense counsel. Four charges were filed against the saboteurs, all stating offenses under the law of war. At the outset of the trial defense counsel attacked the constitutionality of the President's Proclamation and the jurisdiction of the Military Commission, but the trial proceeded. Late in July the country was startled by the announcement that the Supreme Court (then in summer recess) would reconvene in two days to permit the filing of petitions for writs of habeas corpus on behalf of the prisoners. After proceedings that lasted two days, the Court denied the petitions and adjourned. The trial continued and the saboteurs were convicted. Six were executed and two imprisoned. In October the Court handed down its opinion in the case. It held that the President had the authority to establish the Military Commission by virtue of statutes passed by Congress, and that the offenses charged were offenses against the law of war. It held that the grand jury indictment and the jury trial provisions of the Fifth and Sixth Amendments are not applicable to trials before military tribunals for crimes against the law of war. The Court then commented upon the Milligan case; it pointed out that Milligan was a citizen and resident of Indiana, had never lived in a rebellious state, was not an enemy belligerent, and was therefore not subject to the law of war. The Court said: "We construe the Court's statement as to the applicability of the law of war to Milligan's case as having particular reference to the facts before it." The most important point about the case is that the Supreme Court did examine into the right of the military authorities to try the saboteurs. It upheld the military tribunal, but not until it satisfied itself that the tribunal had jurisdiction and was proceeding according to law.

In December, 1945, the Court scrutinized the authority of an American military commission in the Philippines to try Japanese General Yamashita for offenses against the law of war comprising his failure to restrain his troops from committing atrocities against Americans and Filipinos. See In re Yamashita, 327 U. S. 1 (1946). Again the Court recognized the right to challenge the military proceedings by a petition for a writ of habeas corpus. It held that the military commission had been properly set up in accordance with federal statutes which provided for trial, by such commissions, of enemy combatants charged with violating the law of war. It found the authority of the military is not ended by the cessation of hostilities but only by the formal establishment of peace by the political departments of the government through proclamation or treaty. It held, further, that the offenses charged against General Yamashita constituted violations of the law of war. It declared that the procedure and rules of evidence employed by the military commission are not subject to judicial scrutiny but are reviewable only by higher military authorities. This meant that the use by the prosecution against General Yamashita of depositions (written testimony) and hearsay evidence (neither of which could validly be introduced in a trial in a civil court) did not violate the due process clause of the Fifth Amendment. A military commission does not have to observe the American concept of due process of law in trying an enemy combatant. The ruling on this last point elicited vigorous dissents by Justices Murphy and Rutledge.

In the Quirin and Yamashita cases military authority was directed against enemy combatants charged with offenses against the law of war. Much more disturbing was the complete subjection to military authority of American citizens of Japanese origin living on the west coast. In February, 1942, the President issued an executive order which authorized the creation of military areas from which any or all persons might be excluded and with respect to which the right of persons to enter, remain in, or leave should be subject to such regulations as the military authorities might prescribe. Later Congress by statute imposed penalties for the wilful violation of military regulations set up in these areas. On March 2, the entire west coast to a depth of about forty miles was set up as Military Area No. 1. The commanding general thereupon proclaimed a curfew regulation in this area which should apply to all aliens, and to all persons of Japanese ancestry, but not to other residents. Later he ordered the compulsory evacuation from this area of all persons of Japanese ancestry. Of this Japanese population, numbering some 112,000, about 70,000 were American citizens by reason of their birth in this country. See United States v. Wong Kim Ark (p. 47). By the middle of the summer most of these Japanese people had been removed from their homes and locked up in "War Relocation Centers," the American equivalent of concentration camps. The constitutional right of the government to override in this drastic manner the customary civil liberties of these American citizens, none of whom was specifically charged with disloyalty, was vigorously attacked. In Hirabayashi v. United States, 320 U. S. 81 (1943), the Court held valid the discriminatory curfew regulation as a temporary emergency war measure. It admitted that discriminations based on race "are by their very nature odious to a free people," and are usually unconstitutional; but that in view of the geographical facts bearing upon the military security of the west coast, and the fact that Japan was our enemy in that theatre of the war, it was not unreasonable to deal separately and differently with a group of citizens having unique and potentially dangerous associations with Japan. "In time of war residents having ethnic affiliations with an invading enemy may be a greater source of danger than those of a different ancestry."

The more important question of the constitutionality of the military evacuation of Japanese-American citizens from military areas on the west coast was decided in Korematsu v. United States, 323 U. S. 214 (1944). The Court by a majority of six to three held the military action valid. This was on the ground of the acute danger to the national security arising from the "presence of an unascertained number of disloyal members of the group, most of whom we have no doubt were loyal to this country," and the impossibility (in the judgment of the military authorities) of "an immediate segregation of the disloyal from the loyal." The Court denied that the evacuation of the Japanese-American citizens was grounded on race prejudice, and stated that the action was solely the result of the decision by the Army that this was a security measure of vital necessity. "The military authorities considered that the need for action was great, and time was short. We cannot—by availing ourselves of the calm perspective of hindsight—now say that at that time these actions were unjustified." Three justices dissented vigorously. Mr. Justice Murphy attacked the soundness of the military finding that the mass evacuation of all persons of Japanese origin was necessary. He pointed out that the evacuation was not ordered until four months after Pearl Harbor, and was not completed for eleven months. It would, he urged, have been entirely possible to conduct individual loyalty hearings with the purpose of interning only those persons shown to be dangerous to the public security.

While the Court held valid the discriminatory mass evacuation of all persons of Japanese descent, it also held in Ex parte Endo, 323 U. S. 283 (1944), that an American citizen of Japanese ancestry whose loyalty to this country has been established could not constitutionally be held in a War Relocation Center, but must be unconditionally released. The government had allowed persons to leave the Relocation Centers under conditions and restrictions which aimed to guarantee that there should not be "a dangerously disorderly migration of unwanted people to unprepared communities." Permission to leave was granted only if the applicant had the assurance of a job and a place to live, and wanted to go to a place "approved" by the War Relocation Authority. The Court held that the sole purpose of the evacuation and detention program was to protect the war effort against sabotage and espionage. "A person who is concededly loyal presents no problem of espionage or sabotage . . . He who is loyal is by definition not a spy or a saboteur." It therefore follows that the authority to detain a citizen of Japanese ancestry ends when his loyalty is established. To hold otherwise would be to justify his detention not on grounds of military necessity but purely on grounds of race. By the time the Endo case reached the Supreme Court the War Relocation Centers were being broken up, and the military areas on the west coast and elsewhere had been disestablished.

Apart from the Army's own posts and reservations, the only area to be placed under complete military control during World War II was the Territory of Hawaii. Of the 460,000 people in the islands some 124,000 were Japanese, and of these nearly 90,000 were American citizens. The attack on Pearl Harbor naturally led the military authorities to regard Hawaii as peculiarly vulnerable, and on the day after the attack the Army established martial law and took over legislative, executive, and judicial functions. The administration of criminal justice by the civil courts was completely blacked out. Courtrooms and offices were taken over by the Army; grand jury proceedings, trial by jury, the subpœnaing of witnesses, and the issuance of writs of habeas corpus were all forbidden, and criminal cases of every description were handled by summary military procedure. This continued until March, 1943, when a partial restoration of authority to the civil officers was ordered, mainly with respect to civil matters. Most classes of civilian crimes were still tried by the Army. Martial law was finally abolished in the islands by Presidential Proclamation in October, 1944.

To responsible military leaders this drastic subordination of civilian affairs to army control undoubtedly seemed imperative, but to the civil officers of the territory it seemed a wanton and unnecessary denial of constitutionally protected civil liberties. It was urged that any active danger of the invasion of the islands was ended by the Battle of Midway in June, 1942. It was also pointed out that there were no known acts of sabotage, espionage, or other disloyal conduct by any of the Japanese in Hawaii either on or after the day of the Pearl Harbor attack. The civil courts of the territory were ready at all times to perform their normal functions had they been allowed to do so, and experienced federal judges testified that there was no good reason why any of the civilian criminal cases handled by army courts could not just as well have been handled by the courts of the territory. The bitter resentment engendered by this military suppression of civil government finally came to a climax in a dramatic struggle between Federal District Judge Delbert E. Metzger and Lieutenant General Robert C. Richardson, Commanding General of the Central Pacific Area over the detention of two prisoners, Duncan and White.

Judge Metzger issued a writ of habeas corpus in the case of two civilian American citizens who had been interned by summary military action. General Richardson replied with an order forbidding any judge in the territory to issue a writ of habeas corpus. The judge countered by fining General Richardson $5000 for contempt of court. To break this deadlock an emissary was sent from the Department of Justice in Washington, and a compromise was reached by which the President remitted the fine imposed on General Richardson and the general withdrew his order against Judge Metzger. It was agreed that writs of habeas corpus might be issued, but that prisoners would not be released unless higher courts on appeal so ordered. This agreement made it possible for the civil courts to take jurisdiction in the later cases of Duncan and White. Their case was finally dealt with by the Supreme Court in the opinion printed below.

The cases so far have dealt with military authority in time of war. Serious problems have arisen, however, with respect to the power of American military forces stationed abroad in time of peace. In United States ex rel. Toth v. Quarles, 350 U. S. II (1955), the Court held void a section of the Uniform Code of Military Justice (1950) which authorized a person discharged from the armed forces to be tried later by court-martial for crimes committed while still in service. Toth, after serving in Korea in the Air Force, was honorably discharged. He returned to his home in Pittsburgh, and five months later was arrested by military authorities on charges of murder and conspiring to commit murder while still an airman in Korea. He was taken to Korea for court-martial. The Court held that to court-martial Toth would invalidly deny him his right to trial by jury, to which as a civilian he was now entitled; and since there was no civilian federal court in Korea in which he could be tried, he was set free.

Under the Status of Forces Agreements concluded, after the war, with the NATO countries and Japan, the United States has jurisdiction to try criminal cases involving military personnel by its own courts-martial provided the host country waives its own jurisdiction—as it almost invariably does. Difficult problems arose, however, when crimes were committed by civilian dependents of soldiers, or by civilians employed by the armed forces. In Kinsella v. Kreuger, 351 U. S. 470 (1956), and Reid v. Covert, 351 U. S. 487 (1956), the Court, by a bare majority, first held that two wives accused of murdering their soldier husbands on a foreign military base could validly be tried by court-martial; but after a rehearing at the next term of court it reversed these decisions and the women were set free. See Reid v. Covert, consolidated with Kinsella v. Kreuger, 354 U. S. 1 (1957). The Court applied the same rule in Kinsella v. United States ex rel. Singleton, 361 U. S. 234 (1960), in the case of a soldier's wife accused of a non-capital offense; and in McElroy v. United States ex rel. Guagliards, 361 U. S. 281 (1960), in the case of a civilian employee accused of a non-capital offense.

To the criticism that in these cases persons accused of serious crimes escaped trial, the Court replied that Congress has power to establish civilian courts in which the constitutional rights of such persons, including jury trial, will be guaranteed.

Mr. Justice Black delivered the opinion of the Court, saying in part:

The petitioners in these cases were sentenced to prison by military tribunals in Hawaii. Both are civilians. The question before us is whether the military tribunals had power to do this. The United States District Court for Hawaii in habeas corpus proceedings held that the military tribunals had no such power and ordered that they be set free. The Circuit Court of Appeals reversed, and ordered that the petitioners be returned to prison. Both cases thus involve the rights of individuals charged with crime and not connected with the armed forces to have their guilt or innocence determined in courts of law which provide established procedural safeguards, rather than by military tribunals which fail to afford many of these safeguards. Since these judicial safeguards are prized privileges of our system of government we granted certiorari.

The following events led to the military tribunals' exercise of jurisdiction over the petitioners. On December 7, 1941, immediately following the surprise air attack by the Japanese on Pearl Harbor, the Governor of Hawaii by proclamation undertook to suspend the privilege of the writ of habeas corpus and to place the Territory under "martial law." Section 67 of the Hawaiian Organic Act, 31 Stat. 141, authorizes the Territorial Governor to take this action "in case of rebellion or invasion, or imminent danger thereof, when the public safety requires it." His action was to remain in effect only "until communication can be had with the President and his decision thereon made known." The President approved the Governor's action on December 9. The Governor's proclamation also authorized and requested the Commanding General, "during . . . the emergency and until danger of invasion is removed, to exercise all the powers normally exercised" by the Governor and by "the judicial officers and employees of the Territory."

Pursuant to this authorization the commanding general immediately proclaimed himself Military Governor and undertook the defense of the Territory and the maintenance of order. On December 8, both civil and criminal courts were forbidden to summon jurors and witnesses and to try cases. The commanding general established military tribunals to take the place of the courts. These were to try civilians charged with violating the laws of the United States and of the Territory, and rules, regulations, orders or policies of the Military Government. Rules of evidence and procedure of courts of law were not to control the military trials. In imposing penalties the military tribunals were to be "guided by, but not limited to the penalties authorized by the court martial manual, the laws of the United States, the Territory of Hawaii, the District of Columbia, and the customs of war in like cases." The rule announced was simply that punishment was "to be commensurate with the offense committed" and that the death penalty might be imposed "in appropriate cases." Thus the military authorities took over the government of Hawaii. They could and did, by simply promulgating orders, govern the day to day activities of civilians who lived, worked, or were merely passing through there. The military tribunals interpreted the very orders promulgated by the military authorities and proceeded to punish violators. The sentences imposed were not subject to direct appellate court review, since it had long been established that military tribunals are not part of our judicial system. Ex parte Vallandigham, 1 Wallace 243. The military undoubtedly assumed that its rule was not subject to any judicial control whatever, for by orders issued on August 25, 1943, it prohibited even accepting of a petition for writ of habeas corpus by a judge or judicial employee or the filing of such a petition by a prisoner or his attorney. Military tribunals could punish violators of these orders by fine, imprisonment or death.

White was a stockbroker in Honolulu. Neither he nor his business was connected with the armed forces. On August 20, 1942, more than eight months after the Pearl Harbor attack, the military police arrested him. The charge against him was embezzling stock belonging to another civilian. . . . Though by the time of White's arrest the courts were permitted "as agents of the Military Governor" to dispose of some non-jury civil cases, they were still forbidden to summon jurors and to exercise criminal jurisdiction. On August 22, White was brought before a military tribunal designated as a "Provost Court." The "Court" orally informed him of the charge. He objected to the tribunal's jurisdiction but the objection was overruled. He demanded to be tried by a jury. This request was denied. His attorney asked for additional time to prepare the case. This was refused. On August 25 he was tried and convicted. The tribunal sentenced him to five years imprisonment. Later the sentence was reduced to four years.

Duncan was a civilian shipfitter employed in the Navy Yard at Honolulu. On February 24, 1944, more than two years and two months after the Pearl Harbor attack, he engaged in a brawl with two armed Marine sentries at the yard. He was arrested by the military authorities. By the time of his arrest the military had to some extent eased the stringency of military rule. Schools, bars and motion picture theatres had been reopened. Courts had been authorized to "exercise their normal functions." They were once more summoning jurors and witnesses and conducting criminal trials. There were important exceptions, however. One of these was that only military tribunals were to try "Criminal Prosecutions for violations of military orders." As the record shows, these military orders still covered a wide range of day to day civilian conduct. Duncan was charged with violating one of these orders . . . which prohibited assault on military or naval personnel with intent to resist or hinder them in the discharge of their duty. He was, therefore, tried by a military tribunal rather than the Territorial Court, although the general laws of Hawaii made assault a crime. A conviction followed and Duncan was sentenced to six months imprisonment.

Both White and Duncan challenged the power of the military tribunals to try them by petitions for writs of habeas corpus filed in the District Court for Hawaii on March 14 and April 14, 1944, respectively. Their petitions urged both statutory and Constitutional grounds. The court issued orders to show cause. Returns to these orders contended that Hawaii had become part of an active theatre of war constantly threatened by invasion from without; that the writ of habeas corpus had therefore properly been suspended and martial law had validly been established in accordance with the provisions of the Organic Act; that consequently the District Court did not have jurisdiction to issue the writ; and that the trials of petitioners by military tribunals pursuant to orders by the Military Governor issued because of military necessity were valid. . . . The District Court, after separate trials found in each case, among other things, that the courts had always been able to function but for the military orders closing them, and that consequently there was no military necessity for the trial of petitioners by military tribunals rather than regular courts. It accordingly held the trials void and ordered the release of the petitioners.

The Circuit Court of Appeals, assuming without deciding that the District Court had jurisdiction to entertain the petitions, held the military trials valid and reversed the ruling of the District Court. It held that the military orders providing for military trials were fully authorized by § 67 of the Organic Act and the Governor's actions taken under it. . . .

. . . The petitioners contend that "martial law" as provided for by § 67 did not authorize the military to try and punish civilians such as petitioners and urge further that if such authority should be inferred from the Organic Act, it would be unconstitutional. We need decide the Constitutional question only if we agree with the government that Congress did authorize what was done here.

Did the Organic Act during the period of martial law give the armed forces power to supplant all civilian laws and to substitute military for judicial trials under the conditions that existed in Hawaii at the time these petitioners were tried? The relevant conditions, for our purposes, were the same when both petitioners were tried. The answer to the question depends on a correct interpretation of the Act. But we need not construe the Act, in so far as the power of the military might be used to meet other and different conditions and situations. The boundaries of the situation with reference to which we do interpret the scope of the Act can be more sharply defined by stating at this point some different conditions which either would or might conceivably have affected to a greater or lesser extent the scope of the authorized military power. We note first that at the time the alleged offenses were committed the dangers apprehended by the military were not sufficiently imminent to cause them to require civilians to evacute the area or even to evacuate any of the buildings necessary to carry on the business of the courts. In fact, the buildings had long been open and actually in use for certain kinds of trials. Our question does not involve the well-established power of the military to exercise jurisdiction over members of the armed forces, those directly connected with such forces, or enemy belligerents, prisoners of war, or others charged with violating the laws of war. We are not concerned with the recognized power of the military to try civilians in tribunals established as a part of a temporary military government over occupied enemy territory or territory regained from an enemy where civilian government cannot and does not function. For Hawaii since annexation has been held by and loyal to the United States. Nor need we here consider the power of the military simply to arrest and detain civilians interfering with a necessary military function at a time of turbulence and danger from insurrection or war. And finally, there was no specialized effort of the military, here, to enforce orders which related only to military functions, such as, for illustration, curfew rules or blackouts. For these petitioners were tried before tribunals set up under a military program which took over all government and superseded all civil laws and courts. If the Organic Act, properly interpreted, did not give the armed forces this awesome power, both petitioners are entitled to their freedom.

In interpreting the Act we must first look to its language. Section 67 makes it plain that Congress did intend the Governor of Hawaii, with the approval of the President, to invoke military aid under certain circumstances. But Congress did not specifically state to what extent the army could be used or what power it could exercise. . . . The language of § 67 thus fails to define adequately the scope of the power given to the military and to show whether the Organic Act provides that course of law be supplanted by military tribunals.

Since the Act's language does not provide a satisfactory answer, we look to the legislative history for possible further aid in interpreting the term "martial law" as used in the statute. . . . [Here follows a review of this legislative history.]

Since both the language of the Organic Act and its legislative history fail to indicate that the scope of "martial law" in Hawaii includes the supplanting of courts by military tribunals, we must look to other sources in order to interpret that term. We think the answer may be found in the birth, development and growth of our governmental institutions up to the time Congress passed the Organic Act. Have the principles and practices developed during the birth and growth of our political institutions been such as to persuade us that Congress intended that loyal civilians in loyal territory should have their daily conduct governed by military orders substituted for criminal laws, and that such civilians should be tried and punished by military tribunals? Let us examine what those principles and practices have been, with respect to the position of civilian government and the courts and compare that with the standing of military tribunals throughout our history.

People of many ages and countries have feared and unflinchingly opposed the kind of subordination of executive, legislative and judicial authorities to complete military rule which according to the government Congress has authorized here. In this country that fear has become part of our cultural and political institutions. The story of that development is well known and we see no need to retell it all. . . . [Here follows an historical summary showing that in England and the United States military power has not been allowed to supplant civilian criminal justice.]

Courts and their procedural safeguards are indispensable to our system of government. They were set up by our founders to protect the liberties they valued. Our system of government clearly is the antithesis of total military rule and the founders of this country are not likely to have contemplated complete military dominance within the limits of a Territory made part of this country and not recently taken from an enemy. They were opposed to governments that placed in the hands of one man the power to make, interpret and enforce the laws. Their philosophy has been the people's throughout our history. For that reason we have maintained legislatures chosen by citizens or their representatives and courts and juries to try those who violate legislative enactments. We have always been especially concerned about the potential evils of summary criminal trials and have guarded against them by provisions embodied in the Constitution itself. See Ex parte Milligan, 4 Wallace (U. S.) 2. Legislatures and courts are not merely cherished American institutions; they are indispensable to our government.

Military tribunals have no such standing. For as this Court has said before: ". . . the military should always be kept in subjection to the laws of the country to which it belongs, and that he is no friend to the Republic who advocates the contrary. The established principle of every free people is, that the law shall alone govern; and to it the military must always yield." Dow v. Johnson, 100 U. S. 158. Congress prior to the time of the enactment of the Organic Act had only once authorized the supplanting of the courts by military tribunals. Legislation to that effect was enacted immediately after the South's unsuccessful attempt to secede from the Union. In so far as that legislation applied to the Southern States after the war was at an end it was challenged by a series of Presidential vetoes as vigorous as any in the country's history. And in order to prevent this Court from passing on the constitutionality of this legislation Congress found it necessary to curtail our appellate jurisdiction. Indeed, prior to the Organic Act, the only time this Court had ever discussed the supplanting of courts by military tribunals in a situation other than that involving the establishment of a military government over recently occupied enemy territory, it had emphatically declared that "civil liberty and this kind of martial law cannot endure together; the antagonism is irreconcilable; and, in the conflict, one or the other must perish." Ex parte Milligan, 4 Wallace (U. S.) 2.

We believe that when Congress passed the Hawaiian Organic Act and authorized the establishment of "martial law" it had in mind and did not wish to exceed the boundaries between military and civilian power, in which our people have always believed, which responsible military and executive officers had heeded, and which had become part of our political philosophy and institutions prior to the time Congress passed the Organic Act. The phrase "martial law" as employed in that Act, therefore, while intended to authorize the military to act vigorously for the maintenance of an orderly civil government and for the defense of the island against actual or threatened rebellion or invasion, was not intended to authorize the supplanting of courts by military tribunals. Yet the government seeks to justify the punishment of both White and Duncan on the ground of such supposed Congressional authorization. We hold that both petitioners are now entitled to be released from custody.

Reversed.

Mr. Justice Murphy, concurring, said in part:

The Court's opinion, in which I join, makes clear that the military trials in these cases were unjustified by the martial law provisions of the Hawaiian Organic Act. Equally obvious, as I see it, is the fact that these trials were forbidden by the Bill of Rights of the Constitution of the United States, which applies in both spirit and letter to Hawaii. Indeed, the unconstitutionality of the usurpation of civil power by the military is so great in this instance as to warrant this Court's complete and outright repudiation of the action.

From time immemorial despots have used real or imagined threats to the public welfare as an excuse for needlessly abrogating human rights. That excuse is no less unworthy of our traditions when used in this day of atomic warfare or at a future time when some other type of warfare may be devised. The right to jury trial and the other constitutional rights of an accused individual are too fundamental to be sacrificed merely through a reasonable fear of military assault. There must be some overpowering factor that makes a recognition of those rights incompatible with the public safety before we should consent to their temporary suspension. If those rights may safely be respected in the face of a threatened invasion no valid reason exists for disregarding them. In other words, the civil courts must be utterly incapable of trying criminals or of dispensing justice in their usual manner before the Bill of Rights may be temporarily suspended. . . .

Chief Justice Stone also concurred. Justices Burton and Frankfurter dissented. Mr. Justice Jackson did not sit in this case.

UNITED STATES v. LANZA
260 U. S. 377; 67 L. Ed. 314; 43 Sup. Ct. 141. 1922.

It is one of the universal maxims of the common law that no man should be brought into jeopardy of his life more than once for the same offense. Protection against double jeopardy is guaranteed by the Fifth Amendment against invasion by the federal government, while a similar clause is found in the bills of rights of most of the state constitutions. A person is held to be in jeopardy when his trial has progressed to the point where he actually confronts the jury. If convicted, he may waive his immunity from double jeopardy by an appeal to a higher court which may allow him a new trial; but if acquitted, further proceedings against him by the prosecuting authorities are barred, the federal government not even being allowed to appeal the case on the ground of error of law. See United States v. Sanges, 144 U. S. 310 (1892).

One of the obvious results of living under our federal form of government is that every person is subject to the criminal jurisdiction of two separate governments, the state and the national. It is entirely possible, therefore, for a single act to constitute an offense against the statutes of the United States and at the same time to be punishable under state law. This is true in the case of counterfeiting the national currency, corrupt practices in the conduct of congressional elections, assaults against federal officers, the larceny of goods moving in interstate commerce, violations of the former Prohibition Amendment, etc. In these cases it has long been held that a person may be tried and punished by both governments without violating the protection against double jeopardy. That guarantee is violated only by a second trial for the same offense against the same sovereignty, not by a trial for the same act when it constitutes a separate and distinct crime against another sovereign. This doctrine had of course considerable practical effect in connection with the enforcement of the Prohibition Amendment, under which concurrent jurisdiction rested in the state and national governments.

The rule in the Lanza case, though sharply criticized, still stands. Abbate v. United States, 359 U. S. 187 (1959), held that a man convicted of a crime in Illinois could later be tried for the same act (the blowing up of telephone communications) under a federal statute. Lanza was specifically reaffirmed, but by a six-to-three decision. On the same day the Court, divided five to four, held that one acquitted in a federal court of robbing a federally insured bank could later be tried and convicted in an Illinois court for the same robbery. See Bartkus v. Illinois, 359 U. S. 121 (1959).

While the government may not try a man twice for the same crime, a man who is convicted may seek and be given a second trial in hope of an acquittal. In Green v. United States, 355 U. S. 184 (1957), Green was tried in a District of Columbia court on charges on which he could have been convicted of arson, second degree murder, and first degree murder. A jury found him guilty of arson and second degree murder. He asked for and was granted a new trial, in which he was convicted of first degree murder. In a five-to-four decision the Supreme Court, changing a long-standing rule, held that the second conviction violated the double jeopardy clause. It stated that the jury in the first trial had in essence found him not guilty of first degree murder, and he could not, therefore, in a second trial be found guilty of first degree murder.

Congress has inserted provisions in some criminal statutes to prevent federal prosecution after a state prosecution for the same conduct. An example is the law against the burglary of a vehicle carrying interstate or foreign shipments.

In Petite v. United States, 361 U. S. 529 (1960), Petite, a lawyer in deportation proceedings against the same man held in both Philadelphia and Baltimore, induced his client to swear falsely that he had been born in the United States. For this suborning of perjury he was convicted and punished in the federal district court in Pennsylvania, and later in the federal district court in Maryland. When the case came to the Supreme Court the Solicitor General moved that the second judgment be vacated and the indictment dismissed. He admitted that the double jeopardy clause had not been violated, but stated that "the initiation of the second prosecution in this case was contrary to sound policy and that for that reason, and in the interests of justice, the indictment should be dismissed." The Supreme Court granted the motion.

In 1959, in a memorandum sent to all United States attorneys, the Attorney General, commenting on the injustices sometimes arising from the Supreme Court's rule in Lanza, Abbate, and Bartkus, ordered that "no federal case should be tried when there has already been a state prosecution for substantially the same act or acts without the United States Attorney first submitting a recommendation to the appropriate Assistant Attorney General in the Department." Before approval, such recommendation must be presented to the Attorney General himself.

This new policy in dealing with double jeopardy cases is not, of course, binding on the courts, nor on any succeeding Attorney General.

In the present case Lanza had been convicted by the state courts of Washington for manufacturing, transporting, and possessing intoxicating liquor in violation of the state law and was sentenced to fine. He was immediately thereafter indicted and brought to trial in the United States district court under the Volstead Act for manufacturing, transporting, and possessing the same liquor. He claimed that the second prosecution placed him in jeopardy twice for the same offense in violation of the Fifth Amendment inasmuch as both the state statute and the Volstead Act derived their force from the same authority, the Eighteenth Amendment. This contention was rejected, and the conviction in the district court was sustained.

Mr. Chief Justice Taft delivered the opinion of the Court, saying in part:

. . . The Eighteenth Amendment is as follows:

"Section 1. After one year from the ratification of this article the manufacture, sale, or transportation of intoxicating liquors within, the importation thereof into, or the exportation thereof from the United States and all territory subject to the jurisdiction thereof for beverage purposes is hereby prohibited.

"Section 2. The Congress and the several States shall have concurrent power to enforce this article by appropriate legislation."

The defendants insist that two punishments for the same act, one under the National Prohibition Act and the other under a state law, constitute double jeopardy under the Fifth Amendment; and in support of this position it is argued that both laws derive their force from the same authority,—the second section of the amendment,—and therefore that, in principle, it is as if both punishments were in prosecutions by the United States in its courts. . . .

To regard the amendment as the source of the power of the states to adopt and enforce prohibition measures is to take a partial and erroneous view of the matter. Save for some restrictions arising out of the federal Constitution, chiefly the commerce clause, each state possessed that power in full measure prior to the amendment, and the probable purpose of declaring a concurrent power to be in the states was to negative any possible inference that, in vesting the national government with the power of country-wide prohibition, state power would be excluded. In effect the second section of the Eighteenth Amendment put an end to restrictions upon the state's power arising out of the federal Constitution, and left her free to enact prohibition laws applying to all transactions within her limits. To be sure, the first section of the amendment took from the states all power to authorize acts falling within its prohibition, but it did not cut down or displace prior state laws not inconsistent with it. Such laws derive their force, as do all new ones consistent with it, not from this amendment, but from power originally belonging to the states, preserved to them by the Tenth Amendment, and now relieved from the restriction heretofore arising out of the federal Constitution. . . .

We have here two sovereignties, deriving power from different sources, capable of dealing with the same subject-matter within the same territory. Each may, without interference by the other, enact laws to secure prohibition, with the limitation that no legislation can give validity to acts prohibited by the amendment. Each government, in determining what shall be an offense against its peace and dignity, is exercising its own sovereignty, not that of the other.

It follows that an act denounced as a crime by both national and state sovereignties is an offense against the peace and dignity of both, and may be punished by each. The Fifth Amendment, like all the other guaranties in the first eight amendments, applies only to proceedings by the federal government (Barron v. Baltimore, 7 Peters 243) and the double jeopardy therein forbidden is a second prosecution under authority of the federal government after a first trial for the same offense under the same authority. Here the same act was an offense against the state of Washington, because a violation of its law, and also an offense against the United States under the National Prohibition Act. The defendants thus committed two different offenses by the same act, and a conviction by a court of Washington of the offense against that state is not a conviction of the different offense against the United States, and so is not double jeopardy. . . .

If Congress sees fit to bar prosecution by the federal courts for any act when punishment for violation of state prohibition has been imposed, it can, of course, do so by proper legislative provision; but it has not done so. If a state were to punish the manufacture, transportation, and sale of intoxicating liquor by small or nominal fines, the race of offenders to the courts of that state to plead guilty and secure immunity from federal prosecution for such acts would not make for respect for the federal statute, or for its deterrent effect. But it is not for us to discuss the wisdom of legislation; it is enough for us to hold that, in the absence of special provision by Congress, conviction and punishment in a state court, under a state law, for making, transporting, and selling intoxicating liquors, is not a bar to a prosecution in a court of the United States, under the federal law, for the same acts. . . .

MAPP v. OHIO
367 U. S. 643; 6 L. Ed. 2d 1081; 81 Sup. Ct. 1684. 1961.

The Fourth Amendment traces its ancestry to the old common law maxim that every man's house is his castle; but it came more immediately from the bitter resentment, so eloquently voiced by James Otis in 1761, against the general warrants or "writs of assistance" under which British officers searched the houses of the colonists for smuggled goods. The amendment (1) forbids unreasonable searches and seizures and (2) describes the nature of the warrant necessary to make a search and seizure reasonable. Generally speaking, a search is unlawful without a warrant; but a search may be made without a warrant as an incident to a lawful arrest, and in Carroll v. United States, 267 U. S. 132 (1925), the Supreme Court said that an automobile (or other vehicles, or boats) can be searched without a warrant if there is probable cause to believe the law has been violated. A search warrant to be valid can issue only upon probable cause supported by oath and must particularly describe "the place to be searched, and the person or things to be seized." Such probable cause is shown, not by a mere statement that "affiants have received reliable information from a credible person," but by showing how the information was received and why the person should be believed; see Aguilar v. Texas, 378 U. S. 108 (1964). Moreover, the "things to be seized" must be described with care. Thus a warrant was held to be too general where it permitted seizing over 2,000 books and papers, including defendant's insurance policies, marriage certificate, and household bills, in the hope of finding Communist party records. See Stanford v. Texas, 380 U. S. 926 (1965).

Where a search is conducted as an incident to a lawful arrest no search warrant is needed, but such search is limited to the person of the prisoner or the place under his immediate control at the time of his arrest. In Harris v. United States, 331 U. S. 145 (1947), this was held to justify the search of the five-room apartment in which Harris was arrested, but in Preston v. United States, 376 U. S. 364 (1964), it was held not to justify the search of the car in which Preston had been arrested, after it had been towed away to a garage. "Once an accused is under arrest and in custody, then a search made at another place, without a warrant, is simply not incident to the arrest." In 1950, in United States v. Rabinowitz, 339 U. S. 56, the Court overruled a series of earlier cases which had held that a search, although incident to a lawful arrest, was void if there was time to get a warrant. The relevant test, said the Court, was the reasonableness of the search, not the practicability of getting a warrant. For such a search to be valid, of course, the arrest itself must be lawful. Arrests are normally made with an arrest warrant, but an officer can arrest without a warrant if he has probable cause to believe the person has committed a crime. Since the act of stopping an automobile constitutes "arrest," probable cause must be had *before* the car is stopped and cannot be got by searching the car. See Henry v. United States, 361 U. S. 98 (1959). Nor can fleeing from the police be construed as guilt to give probable cause to arrest without warrant; Wong Sun v. United States, 371 U. S. 471 (1963).

The security against compulsory self-incrimination in the Fifth Amendment embodies the protest of our ancestors against the brutality of the early English law which tortured a prisoner to make him confess his guilt. In modern practice it not only protects every person from being compelled to testify against himself, but it also provides, as one writer aptly puts it, that "a man's books and papers cannot be made to speak against him."

The Supreme Court has treated these two guarantees as closely related to each other. In other words, it takes the view that it subjects a man to compulsory self-incrimination to use against him evidence secured by the government by an unreasonable search and seizure. This led to the announcement in Weeks v. United States, 232 U. S. 383 (1914), of the so-called "exclusionary" rule, which barred the use against Weeks in a federal court of incriminating papers seized by federal officers without a warrant. The rule, however, was limited in its application by the fact that the Fourth Amendment protected the individual only against federal action. From this restriction grew up what came to be called the "silver platter" doctrine, which in essence held that the federal government could use in its courts evidence unlawfully seized by a private individual or a state official, as long as no federal illegality was involved. Thus in Burdeau v. McDowell, 256 U. S. 465 (1921), the Court held that evidence obtained by private theft and turned over to the federal authorities was admissible since there had been no unreasonable search by any federal officer. In Byars v. United States, 273 U. S. 28 (1927), the Court said: "We do not question the right of the federal government to avail itself of evidence improperly seized by state officers operating entirely upon their own account." It should be added that, following common law rules, about two-thirds of the states have permitted the use in their own courts of evidence secured by unreasonable searches.

In a recent case, Elkins v. United States, 364 U. S. 206 (1960), the Court, in a five-to-four decision, sharply restricted the "silver platter" doctrine. It held that evidence obtained by state officers through a search which, if conducted by federal officers, would have violated the Fourth Amendment cannot be used in a federal court. See also comment on Benanti v. United States, 355 U. S. 96 (1957), p. 114.

In the Mapp case the home of the defendant was entered forcibly, and without a warrant, by police officers who had been instructed that a "wanted" person was hiding there, and that "a large amount of policy paraphernalia" was hidden there. The ensuing search turned up a number of "lewd and lascivious books and pictures" and it was on the possession of these that the defendant was tried and convicted. In Wolf v. Colorado, 338 U. S. 25 (1949), the Supreme Court had held, six to three, that a state denies due process of law by conducting an unreasonable search and seizure, but refused to hold that a state could not use in its own courts evidence thus secured. The present case overrules that portion of the Wolf decision.

Mr. Justice Clark delivered the opinion of the Court, saying in part:

Appellant stands convicted of knowingly having had in her possession and under her control certain lewd and lascivious books, pictures, and photographs in violation of § 2905.34 of Ohio's Revised Code. . . . The Supreme Court of Ohio found that her conviction was valid though "based primarily upon the introduction in evidence of lewd and lascivious books and pictures unlawfully seized during an unlawful search of defendant's home. . . ."

On May 23, 1957, three Cleveland police officers arrived at appellant's residence in that city pursuant to information that "a person [was] hiding out in the home who was wanted for questioning in connection with a recent bombing, and that there was a large amount of policy paraphernalia being hidden in the home.". . . Upon their arrival at that house, the officers knocked on the door and demanded entrance but appellant, after telephoning her attorney, refused to admit them without a search warrant. They advised their headquarters of the situation and undertook a surveillance of the house.

The officers again sought entrance some three hours later when four or more additional officers arrived on the scene. When Miss Mapp did not come to the door immediately, at least one of the several doors to the house was forcibly opened and the policemen gained admittance. Meanwhile Miss Mapp's attorney arived, but the officers, having secured their own entry, and continuing in their defiance of the law, would permit him neither to see Miss Mapp nor to enter the house. It appears that Miss Mapp was halfway down the stairs from the upper floor to the front door when the officers, in this highhanded manner, broke into the hall. She demanded to see the search warrant. A paper, claimed to be a warrant, was held up by one of the officers. She grabbed the "warrant" and placed it in her bosom. A struggle ensued in which the officers recovered the piece of paper and as a result of which they handcuffed appellant because she had been "belligerent" in resisting their official rescue of the "warrant" from her person. Running roughshod over appellant, a policeman "grabbed" her, "twisted [her] hand," and she "yelled [and] pleaded with him" because "it was hurting." Appellant, in handcuffs, was then forcibly taken upstairs to her bedroom where the officers searched a dresser, a chest of drawers, a closet and some suitcases. They also looked into a photo album and through personal papers belonging to the appellant. The search spread to the rest of the second floor including the child's bedroom, the living room, the kitchen and a dinette. The basement of the building and a trunk found therein were also searched. The obscene materials for possession of which she was ultimately convicted were discovered in the course of that widespread search.

At the trial no search warrant was produced by the prosecution, nor was the failure to produce one explained or accounted for. At best, "There is, in the record, considerable doubt as to whether there ever was any warrant for the search of defendant's home.". . .

The State says that even if the search were made without authority, or otherwise unreasonably, it is not prevented from using the unconstitutionally seized evidence at trial, citing Wolf v. People of State of Colorado, 1949, 338 U. S. 25, in which this Court did indeed hold "that in a prosecution in a State court for a State crime the Fourteenth Amendment does not forbid the admission of evidence obtained by an unreasonable search and seizure." On this appeal . . . it is urged once again that we review that holding. . . .

Since the Fourth Amendment's right of privacy has been declared enforceable against the States through the Due Process Clause of the Fourteenth, it is enforceable against them by the same sanction of exclusion as is used against the Federal Government. Were it otherwise, then just as without the Weeks rule the assurance against unreasonable federal searches and seizures would be "a form of words," valueless and undeserving of mention in a perpetual charter of inestimable human liberties, so too, without that rule the freedom from state invasions of privacy would be so ephemeral and so neatly severed from its conceptual nexus with the freedom from all brutish means of coercing evidence as not to merit this Court's high regard as a freedom "implicit in 'the concept of ordered liberty.' " At the time that the Court held in Wolf that the Amendment was applicable to the States through the Due Process Clause, the cases of this Court, as we have seen, had steadfastly held that as to federal officers the Fourth Amendment included the exclusion of the evidence seized in violation of its provisions. Even Wolf "stoutly adhered" to that proposition. The right to privacy, when conceded operatively enforceable against the States, was not susceptible of destruction by avulsion of the sanction upon which its protection and enjoyment had always been deemed dependent under the Boyd, Weeks and Silverthorne cases. Therefore, in extending the substantive protections of due process to all constitutionally unreasonable searches—state or federal —it was logically and constitutionally necessary that the exclusion doctrine—an essential part of the right to privacy—be also insisted upon as an essential ingredient of the right newly recognized by the Wolf case. In short, the admission of the new constitutional right by Wolf could not consistently tolerate denial of its most important constitutional privilege, namely, the exclusion of the evidence which an accused had been forced to give by reason of the unlawful seizure. To hold otherwise is to grant the right but in reality to withhold its privilege and enjoyment. Only last year the Court itself recognized that the purpose of the exclusionary rule "is to deter—to compel respect for the constitutional guaranty in the only effectively available way—by removing the incentive to disregard it." Elkins v. United States, 364 U. S. at page 217. . . .

Moreover, our holding that the exclusionary rule is an essential part of both the Fourth and Fourteenth Amendments is not only the logical dictate of prior cases, but it also makes very good sense. There is no war between the Constitution and common sense. Presently, a federal prosecutor may make no use of evidence illegally seized, but a State's attorney across the street may, although he supposedly is operating under the enforceable prohibitions of the same Amendment. Thus the State, by admitting evidence unlawfully seized, serves to encourage disobedience to the Federal Constitution which it is bound to uphold. Moreover, as was said in Elkins, "[t]he very essence of a healthy federalism depends upon the avoidance of needless conflict between state and federal courts." 364 U. S. at page 221. . . . Yet the double standard recognized until today hardly put such a thesis into practice. In non-exclusionary States, federal officers, being human, were by it invited to and did, as our cases indicate, step across the street to the State's attorney with their unconstitutionally seized evidence. Prosecution on the basis of that evidence was then had in a state court in utter disregard of the enforceable Fourth Amendment. If the fruits of an unconstitutional search had been inadmissible in both state and federal courts, this inducement to evasion would have been sooner eliminated. . . .

Federal-state co-operation in the solution of crime under constitutional standards will be promoted, if only by recognition of their now mutual obligation to respect the same fundamental criteria in their approaches. "However much in a particular case insistence upon such rules may appear as a technicality that inures to the benefit of a guilty person, the history of the criminal law proves that tolerance of short-cut methods in law enforcement impairs its enduring effectiveness." Denying shortcuts to only one of two co-operating law enforcement agencies tends naturally to breed legitimate suspicion of "working arrangements" whose results are equally tainted.

There are those who say, as did Justice (then Judge) Cardozo, that under our constitutional exclusionary doctrine "[t]he criminal is to go free because the constable has blundered." People v. Defore, 242 N. Y. at page 21. In some cases this will undoubtedly be the result. But, as was said in Elkins, "there is another consideration—the imperative of judicial integrity." 364 U. S. at page 222. The criminal goes free, if he must, but it is the law that sets him free. Nothing can destroy a government more quickly than its failure to observe its own laws, or worse, its disregard of the charter of its own existence. . . .

The ignoble shortcut to conviction left open to the State tends to destroy the entire system of constitutional restraints on which the liberties of the people rest. Having once recognized that the right to privacy embodied in the Fourth Amendment is enforceable against the States, and that the right to be secure against rude invasions of privacy by state officers is, therefore, constitutional in origin, we can no longer permit that right to remain an empty promise. Because it is enforceable in the same manner and to like effect as other basic rights secured by the Due Process Clause, we can no longer permit it to be revocable at the whim of any police officer who, in the name of law enforcement itself, chooses to suspend its enjoyment. Our decision, founded on reason and truth, gives to the individual no more than that which the Constitution guarantees him, to the police officer no less than that to which honest law enforcement is entitled, and, to the courts, that judicial integrity so necessary in the true administration of justice.

The judgment of the Supreme Court of Ohio is reversed and the cause remanded for further proceedings not inconsistent with this opinion.

Reversed and remanded.

Mr. Justice Black, concurring, said in part:

. . . I am still not persuaded that the Fourth Amendment, standing alone, would be enough to bar the introduction into evidence against an accused of papers and effects seized from him in violation of its commands. For the Fourth Amendment does not itself contain any provision expressly precluding the use of such evidence, and I am extremely doubtful that such a provision could properly be inferred from nothing more than the basic command against unreasonable searches and seizures. Reflection on the problem, however, in the light of cases coming before the Court since Wolf, has led me to conclude that when the Fourth Amendment's ban against unreasonable searches and seizures is considered together with the Fifth Amendment's ban against compelled self-incrimination, a constitutional basis emerges which not only justifies but actually requires the exclusionary rule.

The close interrelationship between the Fourth and Fifth Amendments, as they apply to this problem, has long been recognized and, indeed, was expressly made the ground for this Court's holding in Boyd v. United States. There the Court fully discussed this relationship and declared itself "unable to perceive that the seizure of a man's private books and papers to be used in evidence against him is substantially different from compelling him to be a witness against himself." . . . And, although I rejected the argument at that time, its force has, for me at least, become compelling with the more thorough understanding of the problem brought on by recent cases. In the final analysis, it seems to me that the Boyd doctrine, though perhaps not required by the express language of the Constitution strictly construed, is amply justified from an historical standpoint, soundly based in reason, and entirely consistent with what I regard to be the proper approach to interpretation of our Bill of Rights. . . . [After discussing cases involving the "shock the conscience" standard, Mr. Justice Black goes on to say:]

. . . As I understand the Court's opinion in this case, we again reject the confusing "shock-the-conscience" standards of the Wolf and Rochin cases and, instead, set aside this state conviction in reliance upon the precise, intelligible and more predictable constitutional doctrine enunciated in the Boyd case. . . . The Court's opinion, in my judgment, dissipates the doubt and uncertainty in this field of constitutional law and I am persuaded, for this and other reasons stated, to depart from my prior views, to accept the Boyd doctrine as controlling in this state case and to join the Court's judgment and opinion which are in accordance with that constitutional doctrine.

Mr. Justice Douglas, concurring, said in part:

Though I have joined the opinion of the Court, I add a few words. This criminal proceeding started with a lawless search and seizure. The police entered a home forcefully, and seized documents that were later used to convict the occupant of a crime. . . .

We held in Wolf v. People of State of Colorado, 338 U.S. 25, that the Fourth Amendment was applicable to the States by reason of the Due Process Clause of the Fourteenth Amendment. But a majority held that the exclusionary rule of the Weeks case was not required of the States, that they could apply such sanctions as they chose. That position had the necessary votes to carry the day. But with all respect it was not the voice of reason or principle.

As stated in the Weeks case, if evidence seized in violation of the Fourth Amendment can be used against an accused "his right to be secure against such searches and seizures, is of no value, and . . . might as well be stricken from the Constitution." 232 U.S. at page 393.

When we allowed States to give constitutional sanction to the "shabby business" of unlawful entry into a home (to use an expression of Mr. Justice Murphy, Wolf v. People of State of Colorado, 338 U.S. at page 46), we did indeed rob the Fourth Amendment of much meaningful force. . . .

Wolf v. People of State of Colorado, supra, was decided in 1949. The immediate result was a storm of constitutional controversy which only today finds its end. I believe that this is an appropriate case in which to put an end to the asymmetry which Wolf imported into the law. . . .

Memorandum of Mr. Justice Stewart.

Agreeing fully with Part I of Mr. Justice Harlan's dissenting opinion, I express no view as to the merits of the constitutional issue which the Court today decides. I would, however, reverse the judgment in this case, because I am persuaded that the provision of § 2905.34 of the Ohio Revised Code, upon which the petitioner's conviction was based, is, in the words of Mr. Justice Harlan, not "consistent with the rights of free thought and expression assured against state action by the Fourteenth Amendment."

Mr. Justice Harlan, whom Mr. Justice Frankfurter and Mr. Justice Whittaker join, dissenting, said in part:

In overruling the Wolf case the Court, in my opinion, has forgotten the sense of judicial restraint which, with due regard for *stare decisis*, is one element that should enter into deciding whether a past decision of this Court should be overruled. Apart from that I also believe that the Wolf rule represents sounder Constitutional doctrine than the new rule which now replaces it.

From the Court's statement of the case one would gather that the central, if not controlling, issue on this appeal is whether illegally state-seized evidence is Constitutionally admissible in a state prosecution, an issue which would of course face us with the need for re-examining Wolf. However, such is not the situation. For, although that question was indeed raised here and below among appellant's subordinate points, the new and pivotal issue brought to the Court by this appeal is whether § 2905.34 of the Ohio Revised Code making criminal the *mere* knowing possession or control of obscene material, and under which appellant has been convicted, is consistent with the rights of free thought and expression assured against state action by the Fourteenth Amendment. That was the principal issue which was decided by the Ohio Supreme Court, . . . and which was briefed and argued in this Court.

In this posture of things, I think it fair to say that five members of this Court have simply "reached out" to overrule Wolf. With all respect for the views of the majority, and recognizing that *stare decisis* carries different weight in Constitutional adjudication than it does in nonconstitutional decision, I can perceive no justification for regarding this case as an appropriate occasion for re-examining Wolf. . . .

At the heart of the majority's opinion in this case is the following syllogism: (1) the rule excluding in federal criminal trials evidence which is the product of an illegal search and seizure is a "part and parcel" of the Fourth Amendment; (2) Wolf held that the "privacy" assured against federal action by the Fourth Amendment is also protected against state action by the Fourteenth Amendment; and (3) it is therefore "logically and constitutionally necessary" that the Weeks exclusionary rule should also be enforced against the States.

This reasoning ultimately rests on the unsound premise that because Wolf carried into the States, as part of "the concept of ordered liberty" embodied in the Fourteenth Amendment, the principle of "privacy" underlying the Fourth Amendment, it must follow that whatever configurations of the Fourth Amendment have been developed in the particularizing federal precedents are likewise to be deemed a part of "ordered liberty," and as such are enforceable against the States. For me, this does not follow at all.

It cannot be too much emphasized that what was recognized in Wolf was not that the Fourth Amendment *as such* is enforceable against the States as a facet of due process, a view of the Fourteenth Amendment which, as Wolf itself pointed out, has long since been discredited, but the principle of privacy "which is at the core of the Fourth Amendment." . . .

. . . Here we are reviewing not a determination that what the state police did was constitutionally permissible (since the state court quite evidently assumed that it was not), but a determination that appellant was properly found guilty of conduct which, for present purposes, it is to be assumed the State could constitutionally punish. Since there is not the slightest suggestion that Ohio's policy is "affirmatively to sanction . . . police incursion into privacy," what the Court is now doing is to impose upon the States not only federal substantive standards of "search and seizure" but also the basic federal remedy for violation of those standards. For I think it entirely clear that the Weeks exclusionary rule is but a remedy which, by penalizing past official misconduct, is aimed at deterring such conduct in the future.

I would not impose upon the States this federal exclusionary remedy. The reasons given by the majority for now suddenly turning its back on Wolf seem to me notably unconvincing. . . .

An approach which regards the issue as one of achieving procedural symmetry or of serving administrative convenience surely disfigures the boundaries of this Court's function in relation to the state and federal courts. . . . I do not believe that the Fourteenth Amendment empowers this Court to mould state remedies effectuating the right to freedom from "arbitrary intrusion by the police" to suit its own notions of how things should be done.

. . . I do not see how it can be said that a trial becomes unfair simply because a State determines that evidence may be considered by the trier of fact, regardless of how it was obtained, if it is relevant to the one issue with which the trial is concerned, the guilt or innocence of the accused. Of course, a court may use its procedures as an incidental means of pursuing other ends than the correct resolution of the controversies before it. Such indeed is the Weeks rule, but if a State does not choose to use its courts in this way, I do not believe that this Court is empowered to impose this much-debated procedure on local courts, however efficacious we may consider the Weeks rule to be as a means of securing Constitutional rights.

Finally, it is said that the overruling of Wolf is supported by the established doctrine that the admission in evidence of an involuntary confession renders a state conviction constitutionally invalid. Since such a confession may often be entirely reliable, and therefore of the greatest relevance to the issue of the trial, the argument continues, this doctrine is ample warrant in precedent that the way evidence was obtained, and not just its relevance, is constitutionally significant to the fairness of a trial. I believe this analogy is not a true one. The "coerced confession" rule is certainly not a rule that any illegally obtained statements may not be used in evidence.

. . . What is crucial is that the trial defense to which an accused is entitled should not be rendered an empty formality by reasons of statements wrung from him, for then "a prisoner . . . [has been] made the deluded instrument of his own conviction." That this is a *procedural right*, and that its violation occurs at the time his improperly obtained statement is admitted at trial, is manifest. For without this right all the careful safeguards erected around the giving of testimony, whether by an accused or any other witness, would become empty formalities in a procedure where the most compelling possible evidence of guilt, a confession, would have already been obtained at the unsupervised pleasure of the police.

This, and not the disciplining of the police, as with illegally seized evidence, is surely the true basis for excluding a statement of the accused which was unconstitutionally obtained. In sum, I think the coerced confession analogy works strongly *against* what the Court does today. . . .

OLMSTEAD v. UNITED STATES
277 U. S. 438; 72 L. Ed. 944; 48 Sup. Ct. 564. 1928.

At the time of the Olmstead decision there was no federal statute which forbade wiretapping. When Congress passed the Federal Communications Act of 1934, however, it included the now famous Section 605 which states: "no person not being authorized by the sender shall intercept any communication and divulge or publish the existence, contents, substance, . . . of such intercepted communication to any person." In Nardone v. United States, 302 U. S. 379 (1937), the Court held that this section forbade wiretapping by federal officers as well as others, and that evidence secured by federal officers by wiretapping could not be used in a federal court. In 1957 the exclusionary rule was extended still further. In Benanti v. United States, 355 U. S. 96, New York police, acting under a state warrant, tapped Benanti's telephone wires and secured evidence on which he was convicted in a federal court for possessing alcohol on which no federal taxes had been paid. The Supreme Court reversed his conviction on the ground that "evidence obtained by means forbidden by Section 605 [of the Federal Communications Act], whether by state or federal agents, is inadmissible in federal court."

The question remained whether wiretap evidence may lawfully be used in a state court, and many states allow its use. However, in Dinan v. New York, 371 U. S. 877 (1962), the Court, with one justice noting his dissent, refused without opinion to review a four-to-three decision of the New York Court of Appeals which upheld the use in a state court of evidence secured by the police through wiretapping which had been authorized by a state judge in accordance with a New York statute. The majority of the New York court had rested its decision on the distinction between evidence secured by an unreasonable search and seizure (as banned in the Mapp case), and that got by a violation of the federal wiretapping ban, which, as held in the Olmstead case below, is not an unreasonable search and seizure.

In order to violate the Fourth Amendment an electronic eavesdropping device must actually penetrate or trespass upon a person's premises. In the Olmstead case the Court ruled that ordinary wiretapping does not do this. However, in Silverman v. United States, 365 U. S. 505 (1961), the District of Columbia police obtained evidence of gambling by a "spike-mike," described as a microphone with a spike about a foot long attached to it, together with an amplifier, a power jack, and earphones. This was inserted into the heating duct of the defendant's house so that all conversation inside was made audible. This was held to be a violation of the Fourth Amendment.

The desirability of wiretapping remains highly controversial. The practice is denounced on the one hand as an indefensible invasion of privacy. It is defended, however, (if carefully restricted) by law enforcement officers, including every Attorney General of the United States for the past thirty years, as a necessary weapon against subversion and major crimes.

The facts in the present case are as follows: Olmstead was the ringleader of a gigantic conspiracy of rum-runners and bootleggers operating mainly from Seattle, involving two seagoing vessels and several coastwise craft, underground storage caches, and elaborate offices. The yearly income from the business was over two million dollars. Federal prohibition officers had the telephone wires of the conspirators tapped in the basement of the building in which Olmstead's offices were located. For about five months a stenographic record was kept of the telephone conversations of the defendants, a record filling 775 typewritten pages. There was no other evidence, but this conclusively proved the guilt of the conspirators.

Mr. Chief Justice Taft, in delivering the opinion of the Court, said in part:

The Fourth Amendment provides: "The right of the people to be secure in their persons, houses, papers, and effects, against unreasonable searches and seizures, shall not be violated, and no warrants shall issue, but upon probable cause, supported by oath or affirmation, and particularly describing the place to be searched, and the persons or things to be seized." And the Fifth: "No person . . . shall be compelled in any criminal case to be a witness against himself," . . .

. . . Weeks v. United States, 232 U. S. 383 . . . [involved] a conviction for using the mails to transmit coupons or tickets in a lottery enterprise. The defendant was arrested by a police officer without a warrant. After his arrest other police officers and the United States marshal went to his house, got the key from a neighbor, entered the defendant's room and searched it, and took possession of various papers and articles. Neither the marshal nor the police officers had a search warrant. The defendant filed a petition in court asking the return of all his property. The court ordered the return of everything not pertinent to the charge, but denied return of relevant evidence. After the jury was sworn, the defendant again made objection, and on introduction of the papers contended that the search without warrant was a violation of the Fourth and Fifth Amendments, and they were therefore inadmissible. This Court held that such taking of papers by an official of the United States, acting under color of his office, was in violation of the constitutional rights of the defendant, and upon making seasonable application he was entitled to have them restored, and that by permitting their use upon the trial, the trial court erred. . . .

In Silverthorne Lumber Co. v. United States, 251 U. S. 385, the defendants were arrested at their homes and detained in custody. While so detained, representatives of the government, without authority, went to the office of their company and seized all the books, papers and documents found there. An application for return of the things was opposed by the district attorney, who produced a subpœna for certain documents relating to the charge in the indictment then on file. The Court said:

'Thus the case is not that of knowledge acquired through the wrongful act of a stranger, but it must be assumed that the government planned, or at all events ratified, the whole performance."

And it held that the illegal character of the original seizure characterized the entire proceeding, and under the Weeks case the seized papers must be restored. . . .

There is no room in the present case for applying the Fifth Amendment unless the Fourth Amendment was first violated. There was no evidence of compulsion to induce the defendants to talk over their many telephones. They were continually and voluntarily transacting business without knowledge of the interception. Our consideration must be confined to the Fourth Amendment.

The striking outcome of the Weeks case and those which followed it was the sweeping declaration that the Fourth Amendment, although not referring to or limiting the use of evidence in court really forbade its introduction if obtained by government officers through a violation of the amendment. Theretofore many had supposed that under the ordinary common law rules, if the tendered evidence was pertinent, the method of obtaining it was unimportant. This was held by the supreme judicial court of Massachusetts, in Com. v. Dana, 2 Met. 329, 337. There it was ruled that the only remedy open to a defendant whose rights under a state constitutional equivalent of the Fourth Amendment had been invaded was by suit and judgment for damages. . . . But in the Weeks case, and those which followed, this Court decided with great emphasis, and established as the law for the federal courts, that the protection of the Fourth Amendment would be much impaired unless it was held that not only was the official violator of the rights under the amendment subject to action at the suit of the injured defendant, but also that the evidence thereby obtained could not be received.

The well-known historical purpose of the Fourth Amendment, directed against general warrants and writs of assistance, was to prevent the use of governmental force to search a man's house, his person, his papers, and his effects, and to prevent their seizure against his will. . . .

The amendment itself shows that the search is to be of material things—the person, the house, his papers or his effects. The description of the warrant necessary to make the proceeding lawful is that it must specify the place to be searched and the person or things to be seized.

It is urged that the language of Mr. Justice Field in Ex parte Jackson . . . offers an analogy to the interpretation of the Fourth Amendment in respect of wire-tapping. But the analogy fails. The Fourth Amendment may have proper application to a sealed letter in the mail because of the constitutional provision for the Postoffice Department and the relations between the government and those who pay to secure protection of their sealed letters. See Revised Statutes, sections 3978 to 3988, . . . whereby Congress monopolizes the carriage of letters and excludes from that business everyone else, and section 3929, . . . which forbids any postmaster or other person to open any letter not addressed to himself. It is plainly within the words of the amendment to say that the unlawful rifling by a government agent of a sealed letter is a search and seizure of the sender's papers or effects. The letter is a paper, an effect, and in the custody of a government that forbids carriage except under its protection.

The United States takes no such care of telegraph or telephone messages as of mailed sealed letters. The amendment does not forbid what was done here. There was no searching. There was no seizure. The evidence was secured by the use of the sense of hearing and that only. There was no entry of the houses or offices of the defendants.

By the invention of the telephone fifty years ago, and its application for the purpose of extending communications, one can talk with another at a far distant place.

The language of the amendment can not be extended and expanded to include telephone wires reaching to the whole world from the defendant's house or office. The intervening wires are not part of his house or office, any more than are the highways along which they are stretched. . . .

Congress may, of course, protect the secrecy of telephone messages by making them, when intercepted, inadmissible in evidence in federal criminal trials, by direct legislation, and thus depart from the common law of evidence. But the courts may not adopt such a policy by attributing an enlarged and unusual meaning to the Fourth Amendment. The reasonable view is that one who installs in his house a telephone instrument with connecting wires intends to project his voice to those quite outside, and that the wires beyond his house and messages while passing over them are not within the protection of the Fourth Amendment. Here those who intercepted the projected voices were not in the house of either party to the conversation.

Neither the cases we have cited nor any of the many federal decisions brought to our attention hold the Fourth Amendment to have been violated as against a defendant unless there has been an official search and seizure of his person or such a seizure of his papers or his tangible material effects or an actual physical invasion of his house "or curtilage" for the purpose of making a seizure.

We think, therefore, that the wire-tapping here disclosed did not amount to a search or seizure within the meaning of the Fourth Amendment.

. . . Some of our number . . . have concluded that there is merit in the twofold objection overruled in both courts below that evidence obtained through intercepting of telephone messages by government agents was inadmissible because the mode of obtaining it was unethical and a misdemeanor under the law of Washington. To avoid any misapprehension of our views of that objection, we shall deal with it in both of its phases. . . .

The common law rule is that the admissibility of evidence is not affected by the illegality of the means by which it was obtained. . . .

The rule is supported by many English and American cases. . . . It is recognized by this Court in Adams v. New York, 192 U. S. 585. . . . The Weeks case announced an exception to the common law rule by excluding all evidence in the procuring of which government officials took part, by methods forbidden by the Fourth and Fifth Amendments. Many state courts do not follow the Weeks case. People v. Defore, 242 N.Y. 13, 150 N.E. 585. But those who do, treat it as an exception to the general common law rule and required by constitutional limitations. . . . The common law rule must apply in the case at bar.

Nor can we, without the sanction of congressional enactment, subscribe to the suggestion that the courts have a discretion to exclude evidence, the admission of which is not unconstitutional, because unethically secured. This would be at variance with the common law doctrine generally supported by authority. There is no case that sustains, nor any recognized text book that gives color to such a view. Our general experience shows that much evidence has always been receivable although not obtained by conformity to the highest ethics. The history of criminal trials shows numerous cases of prosecutions of oathbound conspiracies for murder, robbery, and other crimes where officers of the law have disguised themselves and joined the organizations, taken the oaths and given themselves every appearance of active members engaged in the promotion of crime for the purpose

of securing evidence. Evidence secured by such means has always
been received.

A standard which would forbid the reception of evidence if obtained by other than nice ethical conduct by government officials
would make society suffer and give criminals greater immunity than
has been known heretofore. In the absence of controlling legislation
by Congress, those who realize the difficulties in bringing offenders
to justice may well deem it wise that the exclusion of evidence should
be confined to cases where rights under the Constitution would be
violated by admitting it. . . .

Mr. Justice Holmes, in dissenting, said in part:

. . . I think . . . that, apart from the Constitution, the government
ought not to use evidence obtained, and only obtainable, by a criminal
act. There is no body of precedents by which we are bound, and
which confines us to logical deduction from established rules. Therefore, we must consider the two objects of desire both of which we
cannot have and make up our minds which to choose. It is desirable
that criminals should be detected, and to that end that all available
evidence should be used. It also is desirable that the government
should not itself foster and pay for other crimes, when they are the
means by which the evidence is to be obtained. If it pays its officers
for having got evidence by crime I do not see why it may not as well
pay them for getting it in the same way, and I can attach no importance to protestations of disapproval if it knowingly accepts and
pays and announces that in future it will pay for the fruits. We have
to choose, and for my part I think it a less evil that some criminals
should escape than that the government should play an ignoble part.

For those who agree with me, no distinction can be taken between
the government as prosecutor and the government as judge. If the
existing code does not permit district attorneys to have a hand in such
dirty business, it does not permit the judge to allow such iniquities
to succeed. . . . And if all that I have said so far be accepted, it makes
no difference that in this case wire-tapping is made a crime by the
law of the state, not by the law of the United States. It is true that a
state cannot make rules of evidence for courts of the United States,
but the state has authority over the conduct in question, and I hardly
think that the United States would appear to greater advantage
when paying for an odious crime against state law than when inciting
to the disregard of its own. . . . I have said that we are free to choose

between two principles of policy. But if we are to confine ourselves to precedent and logic, the reason for excluding evidence obtained by violating the Constitution seems to me logically to lead to excluding evidence obtained by a crime of the officers of the law.

Mr. Justice Brandeis, dissenting, said in part:

. . . The government makes no attempt to defend the methods employed by its officers. Indeed, it concedes that if wire-tapping can be deemed a search and seizure within the Fourth Amendment, such wire-tapping as was practised in the case at bar was an unreasonable search and seizure, and that the evidence thus obtained was inadmissible. But it relies on the language of the amendment; and it claims that the protection given thereby cannot properly be held to include a telephone conversation. . . .

When the Fourth and Fifth Amendments were adopted, "the form that evil had therefore taken" had been necessarily simple. Force and violence were then the only means known to man by which a government could directly effect self-incrimination. It could compel the individual to testify—a compulsion effected, if need be, by torture. It could secure possession of his papers and other articles incident to his private life—a seizure effected, if need be, by breaking and entry. Protection against such invasion of "the sanctities of a man's home and the privacies of life" was provided in the Fourth and Fifth Amendments, by specific language. . . . But "time works changes, brings into existence new conditions and purposes." Subtler and more far-reaching means of invading privacy have become available to the government. Discovery and invention have made it possible for the government, by means far more effective than stretching upon the rack, to obtain disclosure in court of what is whispered in the closet.

. . . The progress of science in furnishing the government with means of espionage is not likely to stop with wire-tapping. Ways may some day be developed by which the government, without removing papers from secret drawers, can reproduce them in court, and by which it will be enabled to expose to a jury the most intimate occurrences of the home. Advances in the psychic and related sciences may bring means of exploring unexpressed beliefs, thoughts and emotions. . . . Can it be that the Constitution affords no protection against such invasions of individual security? . . .

Applying to the Fourth and Fifth Amendments the established rule of construction, the defendants' objections to the evidence obtained by a wire-tapping must, in my opinion, be sustained. It is, of course, immaterial where the physical connection with the telephone wires leading into the defendants' premises was made. And it is also immaterial that the intrusion was in aid of law enforcement. Experience should teach us to be most on our guard to protect liberty when the government's purposes are beneficent. Men born to freedom are naturally alert to repel invasion of their liberty by evil-minded rulers. The greatest dangers to liberty lurk in insidious encroachment by men of zeal, well-meaning, but without understanding.

Independently of the constitutional question, I am of opinion that the judgment should be reversed. By the laws of Washington, wire-tapping is a crime. . . . To prove its case, the government was obliged to lay bare the crimes committed by its officers on its behalf. A federal court should not permit such a prosecution to continue. . . .

Decency, security, and liberty alike demand that government officials shall be subjected to the same rules of conduct that are commands to the citizen. In a government of laws, existence of the government will be imperiled if it fails to observe the law scrupulously. Our government is the potent, the omnipresent, teacher. For good or for ill, it teaches the whole people by its example. Crime is contagious. If the government becomes a law-breaker, it breeds contempt for law; it invites every man to become a law unto himself; it invites anarchy. To declare that in the administration of the criminal law the end justifies the means—to declare that the government may commit crimes in order to secure the conviction of a private criminal —would bring terrible retribution. Against that pernicious doctrine this Court should resolutely set its face.

Mr. Justice Butler, in dessenting, said in part:

. . . The question at issue depends upon a just appreciation of the facts.

Telephones are used generally for transmission of messages concerning official, social, business and personal affairs including communications that are private and privileged—those between physician and patient, lawyer and client, parent and child, husband and wife. The contracts between telephone companies and users contemplate the private use of the facilities employed in the service. The communications belong to the parties between whom they pass. During their transmission the exclusive use of the wire belongs to the persons served by it. Wire-tapping involves interference with the wire while being used. Tapping the wires and listening in by the officers literally constituted a search for evidence. As the communications passed, they were heard and taken down. . . .

ULLMANN v. UNITED STATES
350 U. S. 422; 100 L. Ed. 511; 76 Sup. Ct. 497. 1956.

The privilege against compulsory self-incrimination grew up in England as a revolt against procedures, especially those in the ecclesiastical courts and the Court of Star Chamber, whereby persons were questioned by the judges in order to get evidence on which to accuse them and to secure confessions of guilt. Immunity from such questioning gradually became embedded in the common law, and it was this immunity that was written into the Fifth Amendment to the Constitution.

The sole purpose of this immunity is to protect a person against being compelled to give evidence which will expose him to prosecution for crime. If he is safe from prosecution as the result, for instance, of a pardon or a statute of limitations, he cannot claim the immunity. It is not intended to protect him from the embarrassment, public censure, or disgrace resulting from his testimony. Furthermore, it is a strictly personal privilege and cannot be properly claimed to avoid giving evidence against one's friends, employer, labor union, or other associates.

Can the government compel a person to give testimony which he wishes to withhold by granting him immunity from prosecution? In 1862, Congress passed a statute designed to compel testimony before Congress itself, and in 1868 it passed a similar act applicable to judicial and administrative agencies. These statutes provided that the evidence which the witnesses were compelled to give could not be used against them in any criminal proceeding. In Counselman v. Hitchcock, 142 U. S. 547 (1892), the Court held that the immunity thus granted was not an adequate substitute for the protection of the Fifth Amendment. It protected the witness only from the use against him of his own testimony; it left the government free, however, to glean from that testimony leads from which it could build up its own case against him. After this decision Congress changed the statute to provide that "no person shall be prosecuted or subjected to any penalty or forfeiture for or on account of any transaction, matter, or thing concerning which he may testify or produce evidence. . . ." The Supreme Court in Brown v. Walker, 161 U. S. 591 (1896), held that the statute gave adequate protection and did not violate the self-incrimination clause of the Fifth Amendment.

In 1954 Congress passed a new witness immunity act which enables

Congress and other governmental agencies to compel testimony from witnesses in certain national security investigations. A federal judge must sign the order to testify, and in return the witness gets the broad immunity which the Court held valid in Brown v. Walker. It was this statute which was challenged in the present case.

One troublesome problem has been the impact of the federal system on witness immunity. When a person pleads the Fifth Amendment and refuses to testify, his testimony cannot be used to incriminate him since he has given none; but when he is forced to testify under a federal immunity statute the testimony becomes available to state officers who may use it against him. Can a person refuse to testify under a federal immunity statute on the ground that the immunity given does not protect him from possible state prosecution resulting from his evidence? In United States v. Murdock, 284 U. S. 141 (1931), a person refused to give certain information regarding his federal income tax to the Bureau of Internal Revenue on the ground that it would incriminate him under state law. The Court rejected his claim and held that "investigations for federal purposes may not be prevented by matters depending upon state law. . . . The principle established is that full and complete immunity against prosecution by the government compelling the witness to answer is equivalent to the protection furnished by the rule against compulsory self-incrimination."

In 1944 another aspect of this doctrine was applied in Feldman v. United States, 322 U. S. 487. Feldman had testified under a state immunity statute concerning certain frauds under state law, and the federal government introduced his testimony against him in a federal prosecution for using the mails to defraud. The Court held that since the federal government had not compelled the testimony it was not barred from using it merely because it was extracted under a state immunity statute. "A state," it was pointed out, "cannot by operating within its constitutional powers restrict the operation of the national government within its sphere." The doctrine of the supremacy of national law means neither a state immunity statute nor the threat that a state may use evidence got under a federal immunity statute can limit the federal search for evidence. Murdock and Feldman were overruled in Murphy v. Waterfront Commission of New York, p. 501.

It is clear that Congress need not grant a witness immunity from state prosecution in order to compel his testimony, but the question arises whether it may do so if it wishes. In Adams v. Maryland, 347 U. S. 179 (1954), the Court held that Congress could, under the supremacy doctrine, forbid a state to use testimony given before a congressional committee. Adams had been summoned before the Senate Crimes Investigation (Kefauver) Committee and had bared his soul concerning his bookmaking activities. The state of Maryland, which had been unable to get other evidence against Adams, read the transcript of the committee hearings into the trial record as a confession, and he was convicted of illegal gambling by the state court. The Supreme Court reversed the conviction on the ground that the federal statute under which Adams had testified forbade the use of his testimony "in any criminal proceeding against him in any court. . . ." The phrase "in any court" includes state courts as well as federal; and forbidding use of the testimony by the state was held to be a necessary and proper way of securing it for federal purposes. The Immunity Act of 1954 uses this same language.

The opinion in the Ullmann case strongly declares that the privilege against self-incrimination is a protection for the innocent as well as the guilty. This position has not been accepted by public opinion generally, which is inclined to believe that a man does not plead self-incrimination unless he has something to cover up. As a result of this belief persons who invoke the self-incrimination privilege are subjected to a variety of reprisals, forfeitures, and disabilities. In Slochower v. Board of Education, 350 U. S. 551 (1956), a professor in Brooklyn College, a municipal institution, was dismissed under a provision of the New York City charter requiring the automatic discharge of any city employee who claimed the protection against self-incrimination under the Fifth Amendment when questioned about his offiicial conduct. Slochower pleaded self-incrimination before a Senate investigating committee when asked about Communist associations and activities. The Supreme Court held that Slochower's automatic dismissal denied him due process of law. It did not hold that pleading self-incrimination could not be a proper ground for dismissal; but it held that he was entitled to a fair hearing to determine whether in view of all the facts it was a proper ground for dismissal in his case. He must be allowed to rebut if he can the presumption of unfitness arising from his plea.

In Cohen v. Hurley, 366 U. S. 117 (1961), the Court held, five to four, that the state of New York did not deny Cohen due process of law by disbarring him for refusing to answer questions regarding his professional conduct on the basis of the self-incrimination clause of the state constitution, not the Fifth Amendment.

Mr. Justice Frankfurter delivered the opinion of the Court, saying in part:

. . . The Immunity Act, in its pertinent portions, provides:

"(c) Whenever in the judgment of a United States attorney the testimony of any witness, or the production of books, papers, or other evidence by any witness, in any case or proceeding before any grand jury or court of the United States involving any interference with or endangering of, or any plans or attempts to interfere with or endanger, the national security or defense of the United States by treason, sabotage, espionage, sedition, seditious conspiracy, . . . is necessary to the public interest, he, upon the approval of the Attorney General, shall make application to the court that the witness shall be instructed to testify or produce evidence subject to the provisions of this section, and upon order of the court such witness shall not be excused from testifying or from producing books, papers, or other evidence on the ground that the testimony or evidence required of him may tend to incriminate him or subject him to a penalty or forfeiture. But no such witness shall be prosecuted or subjected to any penalty or forfeiture for or on account of any transaction, matter, or thing concerning which he is compelled, after having claimed his privilege against self-incrimination, to testify or produce evidence, nor shall testimony so compelled be used as evidence in any criminal proceeding (except prosecution described in subsection (d) hereof) against him in any court.

"(d) No witness shall be exempt under the provision of this section from prosecution for perjury or contempt committed while giving testimony or producing evidence under compulsion as provided in this section." . . .

[The Court here gives the facts of the case: In November, 1954, the United States attorney subpoenaed Ullmann to appear and give evidence before a federal grand jury in New York City with respect to his and others' alleged Communist party membership and activities. He pleaded self-incrimination and refused to testify. The provisions of the Immunity Act were duly put in motion and he was again ordered to testify. He again refused, on the ground that the act was unconstitutional. The district court held the act valid and Ullmann was convicted of contempt. The case came to the Supreme Court on appeal.]

Four major questions are raised by this appeal: Is the immunity provided by the Act sufficiently broad to displace the protection afforded by the privilege against self-incrimination? Assuming that the statutory requirements are met, does the Act give the district judge discretion to deny an application for an order requiring a witness to answer relevant questions put by the grand jury, and if so, is the court thereby required to exercise a function that is not an exercise of "judicial Power"? Did Congress provide immunity from state prosecution for crime, and if so, is it empowered to do so? Does the Fifth Amendment prohibit compulsion of what would otherwise be self-incriminating testimony no matter what the scope of the immunity statute?

It is relevant to define explicitly the spirit in which the Fifth Amendment's privilege against self-incrimination should be approached. This command of the Fifth Amendment ("nor shall any person . . . be compelled in any criminal case to be a witness against himself . . . .") registers an important advance in the development of our liberty—"one of the great landmarks in man's struggle to make himself civilized." Time has not shown that protection from the evils against which this safeguard was directed is needless or unwarranted. This constitutional protection must not be interpreted in a hostile or niggardly spirit. Too many, even those who should be better advised, view this privilege as a shelter for wrongdoers. They too readily assume that those who invoke it are either guilty of crime or commit perjury in claiming the privilege. Such a view does scant honor to the patriots who sponsored the Bill of Rights as a condition to acceptance of the Constitution by the ratifying States. The Founders of the Nation were not naive or disregardful of the interests of justice. . . .

No doubt the constitutional privilege may, on occasion, save a guilty man from his just deserts. It was aimed at a more far-reaching evil—a recurrence of the Inquisition and the Star Chamber, even if not in their stark brutality. Prevention of the greater evil was deemed of more importance than occurrence of the lesser evil. Having had much experience with a tendency in human nature to abuse power, the Founders sought to close the doors against like future abuses by law-enforcing agencies.

As no constitutional guarantee enjoys preference so none should suffer subordination or deletion. . . . To view a particular provision of the Bill of Rights with disfavor inevitably results in a constricted application of it. This is to disrespect the Constitution.

It is in this spirit of strict not lax observance of the constitutional protection of the individual that we approach the claims made by petitioner in this case. The attack on the Immunity Act as violating the Fifth Amendment is not a new one. Sixty years ago this Court considered, in Brown v. Walker, 161 U. S. 591, the constitutionality of a similar Act, the Act of February 11, 1893, 27 Stat 443. . . . [Brown challenged the validity of the immunity statute of 1893, refused to testify, and was found guilty of contempt.]

The Court considered and rejected petitioner's arguments, holding that a statute which compelled testimony but secured the witness against a criminal prosecution which might be aided directly or indirectly by his disclosures did not violate the Fifth Amendment's privilege against self-incrimination and that the 1893 statute did provide such immunity. "While the constitutional provision in question is justly regarded as one of the most valuable prerogatives of the citizen, its object is fully accomplished by the statutory immunity, and we are, therefore, of opinion that the witness was compellable to answer . . . ."

Petitioner, however, attempts to distinguish Brown v. Walker. He argues that this case is different from Brown v. Walker because the impact of the disabilities imposed by federal and state authorities and the public in general—such as loss of job, expulsion from labor unions, state registration and investigation statutes, passport eligibility, and general public opprobrium—is so oppressive that the statute does not give him true immunity. This, he alleges, is significantly different from the impact of testifying on the auditor in Brown v. Walker, who could the next day resume his job with reputation unaffected. But, as this Court has often held, the immunity granted need only remove those sanctions which generate the fear justifying invocation of the privilege: "The interdiction of the Fifth Amendment operates only where a witness is asked to incriminate himself— in other words, to give testimony which may possibly expose him to a criminal charge. But if the criminality has already been taken away, the Amendment ceases to apply. Hale v. Henkel, 201 U. S. 43, 67. . . .

Again, the petitioner seeks to distinguish this case from Brown v. Walker by claiming that under the Immunity Act of 1954 the district judge to whom the United States Attorney must apply for an order instructing him to testify has discretion in granting the order and thus has discretion in granting the immunity which automatically follows from the order. . . .

[Ullmann alleged that since the district court exercises "discretion" in granting immunity orders the judge has been invalidly given non-judicial power in violation of the separation of powers. The Court finds the statute does not justify this interpretation and that the judge acts "within the scope of judicial power."]

Petitioner further argues that the immunity is not constitutionally sufficient so long as a witness is subject to the very real possibility of state prosecution. He urges that the statute does not, and constitutionally could not, grant such immunity. The immunity portion of the statute contains two parts. The first prohibits prosecutions and is worded virtually in the terms of the 1893 Act. The second makes explicit that the compelled testimony shall not be used against the witness in any proceeding in any court. Such a clause was construed in Adams v. Maryland, 347 U. S. 179, to apply to state courts. In Brown v. Walker, it was urged that the prohibition against prosecution did not grant protection against prosecution in the state courts. First finding that Congress could constitutionally provide such immunity, the Court then interpreted the statute [and found that it did so]. . . .

The Report of the Committee on the Judiciary of the House of Representatives supports the broad interpretation of the Act before us:

"Even though the power of Congress to prohibit a subsequent State prosecution is doubtful, such a constitutional question should not prevent the enactment of the recommended bill. The language of the amendment . . . is sufficiently broad to ban a subsequent State prosecution if it be determined that the Congress has the constitutional power to do so. In addition, the amendment recommended provides the additional protection—as set forth in the Adams case, by outlawing the subsequent use of the compelled testimony in any criminal proceeding—State or Federal.

"By the use of these two distinct concepts, the committee believes that the fullest protection that can be afforded the witness will be achieved." HR Rep No. 2606, 83d Cong, 2d Sess 7.

Petitioner questions the constitutional power of Congress to grant immunity from state prosecution. Congressional abolition of state power to punish crimes committed in violation of state law presents a more drastic exercise of congressional power than that which we considered in Adams. In that case, only the use of the compelled testimony, not prosecution itself, was prohibited. Here the State is forbidden to prosecute. But it cannot be contested that Congress has power to provide for national defense and the complementary power "To make all Laws which shall be necessary and proper for carrying into Execution the foregoing Powers, and all other Powers vested by this Constitution in the Government of the United States, or in any Department or Officer thereof." U. S. Const, Art 1, § 8, cl 18. The Immunity Act is concerned with the national security. It reflects a congressional policy to increase the possibility of more complete and open disclosure by removal of fear of state prosecution. We cannot say that Congress' paramount authority in safeguarding national security does not justify the restriction it has placed on the exercise of state power for the more effective exercise of conceded federal power. . . .

Petitioner also urges that if Brown v. Walker is found nondistinguishable and controlling, then that case should be reconsidered and overruled. He also urges upon us a "return" to a literal reading of the Fifth Amendment. Brown v. Walker was the second case to deal with an immunity statute. Four years previously, in Counselman v. Hitchcock, 142 U. S. 547, a unanimous Court had struck down the predecessor to the 1893 statute because the immunity granted was incomplete, in that it merely forbade the use of the testimony given and failed to protect a witness from future prosecution based on knowledge and sources of information obtained from the compelled testimony. It was with this background that the 1893 statute, providing complete immunity from prosecution, was passed and that Brown v. Walker was argued and decided. As in Counselman, appellant's numerous arguments were presented by James C. Carter, widely acknowledged as the leader of the American bar. The Court was closely divided in upholding the statute, and the opinions reflect the thoroughness with which the issues were considered. Since that time the Court's holding in Brown v. Walker has never been challenged; the case and the doctrine it announced have consistently and without question been treated as definitive by this Court, in opinions written, among others, by Holmes and Brandeis JJ. . . . The 1893 statute has become part of our constitutional fabric and has been included "in substantially the same terms, in virtually all the major regulatory enactments of the Federal Government." . . .

We are not dealing here with one of the vague, undefinable, admonitory provisions of the Constitution whose scope is inevitably addressed to changing circumstances. The privilege against self-incrimination is a specific provision of which it is peculiarly true that "a page of history is worth a volumn of logic." . . . For the history of the privilege establishes not only that it is not to be interpreted literally, but also that its sole concern is, as its name indicates, with the danger to a witness forced to give testimony leading to the infliction of "penalties affixed to the criminal acts." . . . Immunity displaces the danger. Once the reason for the privilege ceases, the privilege ceases. We reaffirm Brown v. Walker, and in so doing we need not repeat the answers given by that case to the other points raised by petitioner.

The judgment of the Court of Appeals is
Affirmed.

Mr. Justice Reed concurs in the opinion and judgment of the Court except as to the statement that no constitutional guarantee enjoys preference. Murdock v. Pennsylvania, 319 U. S. 105; Thomas v. Collins, 323 U. S. 516; cf. Kovacs v. Cooper, 336 U. S. 77.

Mr. Justice Douglas, with whom Mr. Justice Black concurs, dissenting, said in part:

I would reverse the judgment of conviction. I would base the reversal on Boyd v. United States, 116 U. S. 616, or, in the alternative, I would overrule the five-to-four decision of Brown v. Walker, 161 U. S. 591, and adopt the view of the minority in that case that the right of silence created by the Fifth Amendment is beyond the reach of Congress. . . .

The guarantee against self-incrimination contained in the Fifth Amendment is not only a protection against conviction and prosecution but a safeguard of conscience and human dignity and freedom of expression as well. My view is that the Framers put it beyond the power of Congress to *compel* anyone to confess his crimes. The evil to be guarded against was partly self-accusation under legal compulsion. But that was only a part of the evil. The conscience and dignity of man were also involved. So too was his right to freedom of expression guaranteed by the First Amendment. The Framers, therefore, created the federally protected right of silence and decreed that the law could not be used to pry open one's lips and make him a witness against himself.

A long history and a deep sentiment lay behind this decision. . . . [This is summarized at some length.]

The Court by forgetting that history robs the Fifth Amendment of one of the great purposes it was designed to serve. To repeat, the Fifth Amendment was written in part to prevent any Congress, any court, and any prosecutor from prying open the lips of an accused to make incriminating statements against his will. The Fifth Amendment protects the conscience and the dignity of the individual, as well as his safety and security, against the compulsion of government. . . .

It is no answer to say that a witness who exercises his Fifth Amendment right of silence and stands mute may bring himself into disrepute. If so, that is the price he pays for exercising the right of silence granted by the Fifth Amendment. The critical point is that the Constitution places the right of silence *beyond the reach of government.* The Fifth Amendment stands between the citizen and his government. When public opinion casts a person into the outer darkness, as happens today when a person is exposed as a Communist, the government brings infamy on the head of the witness when it compels disclosure. That is precisely what the Fifth Amendment prohibits. . . .

UNITED PUBLIC WORKERS OF AMERICA v. MITCHELL
330 U. S. 75; 91 L. Ed. 754; 67 Sup. Ct. 556. 1947.

When the new national government got under way in 1789, Thomas Jefferson, the Secretary of State, ran his department with the aid of four clerks, a French interpreter, and two messengers. By 1792 the federal payroll had risen to about 780. When the Federal Civil Service Act was passed in 1883 the government was employing about 130,000 persons. At the peak of the war effort in 1945 the federal civilian payroll listed 3,700,000 persons, and in 1949 this number was still over 2,000,000. The Census Bureau reported in 1961 that 9,100,000 men and women were earning their living as employees of our federal, state, and local governments. Inevitably the status and rights of so large a number of government employees have posed many problems of policy and of law.

From the beginning it was recognized that federal officers and employees, because of their relation to the government, could be placed under limitations which did not apply to other citizens. The first Congress in 1789 forbade certain officers of the Treasury to engage in trade or commerce or other business activities deemed incompatible with the impartial performance of their official duties. Rules of this kind have multiplied with the years. An act of 1867 punished by dismissal from office any officer or employee who required or requested any working man in a navy yard to give money for political purposes. In 1870 the soliciting or giving of political contributions or gifts was forbidden throughout the federal service, and in 1876 Congress provided that any federal officer or employee who requested, gave, or received from any other officer or employee any money or gifts for political purposes should be dismissed and should also be liable to criminal prosecution. The constitutionality of this statute was upheld by the Supreme Court in Ex parte Curtis, 106 U. S. 371, in 1882. These restrictions, designed to establish the "political neutrality" of federal officers and employees, were carried over in strengthened form into the Federal Civil Service Act of 1883, one section of which forbade persons in the civil service to engage in "political activity" and prohibited the levying upon them of political assessments. The enforcement of these rules was left in the hands of the Civil Service Commission.

The Hatch Act of 1939, part of which is dealt with in the opinion below, pulled together, tightened, and elaborated the restrictions upon the political activity of federal officers and employees. The issues presented to the Court were not new, but had taken on gigantic proportions. On one side were the political implications involved in giving over three million federal employees freedom to campaign actively in behalf of the administration in power, perhaps under compulsion from their superior officers. On the other hand lay the question whether the Bill of Rights does not assure these three million citizens a freedom of speech which includes the right, at least in their free time, to engage in political campaigning as other citizens do. In 1912 Congress had authorized federal employees to form unions, some of which are affiliated with national labor unions with heavy political stakes in federal elections. The Mitchell case should be read against this background.

There are other problems relating to the legal status of federal officers and employees. A civil service rule of 1884, aimed at the old "spoils system" of political appointments, forbade any inquiry into the "political or religious opinions or affiliations" of any applicant for a federal job. The Hatch Act, however, forbids the federal employment of any person who advocates the overthrow of constitutional government by force or violence, or who belongs to any organization that does; and appropriation acts from 1941 on forbid payment of any federal money for the salary of any such person.

In March, 1947, the Supreme Court refused to review the case of a federal officer dismissed on a finding by the Civil Service Commission of "reasonable doubt as to his loyalty to the Government of the United States." See Friedman v. Schwellenbach, 330 U. S. 838 (1947). A month later the President's Loyalty Order of 1947 was issued, a comprehensive program for "purging" the federal service of disloyal officers and employees. The Loyalty Order set up procedures and "tests" for determining the loyalty of federal employees. Among these tests was "sympathetic affiliation" with organizations listed by the Attorney General as "fascist, communist, or subversive," a list of nearly 300. The Security Order of 1953 substituted "security" for "loyalty" as the standard for judging a federal employee. The old loyalty tests were retained, but an employee could now be dismissed as a "security risk" (as in the case of a drug addict or heavy drinker) without branding him as disloyal. The Supreme Court has not ruled squarely on the validity of the loyalty or security orders, but there can be little doubt that they would be upheld. Certainly the government may require its employees to meet rigid standards of loyalty and fitness. While still on the Supreme Court of Massachusetts, Mr. Justice Holmes, holding valid the dismissal of a policeman for making political speeches, remarked, "The petitioner may have a constitutional right to talk politics, but he has no constitutional right to be a policeman."

The Court has, however, in a number of cases set aside the dismissal of federal employees because improper procedures had been followed or authority not granted had been exercised. Thus in Greene v. McElroy, 360 U. S. 474 (1959), the Court held void the revocation by the Department of Defense of Greene's security clearance (a revocation which cost him his job with a government contractor) in a proceeding in which he was not permitted to confront and cross-examine his accusers. But the decision rested not on constitutional grounds but on the point that neither the President nor Congress had authorized the procedure.

In Bailey v. Richardson, 341 U. S. 918 (1951), the Court divided four to four, and without writing an opinion, sustained a lower court decision that Miss Bailey had been constitutionally removed from her federal office for disloyalty on the basis of accusations made by persons whose identity was not disclosed either to Miss Bailey or to the loyalty boards which dismissed her.

May Congress itself, without using the method of impeachment, dismiss a federal officer or employee on grounds of alleged disloyalty? In 1943 Congress attached a rider to an appropriation bill stipulating that three federal officers, Messrs. Lovett, Watson, and Dodd (mentioned by name), who had been charged by the House Committee on Un-American Activities with being "subversive," should not be paid from federal funds after a stated date unless renominated by the President and reconfirmed by the Senate. The three men contested this action by remaining at their posts for a few weeks after the date set and then suing in the Court of Claims for salary earned during this period. In United States v. Lovett, 328 U. S. 303 (1946), the Supreme Court held unanimously that this congressional action was unconstitutional as a bill of attainder since it "clearly accomplishes the punishment of named individuals without a judicial trial."

Mr. Justice Reed delivered the opinion of the Court, saying in part:

The Hatch Act, enacted in 1940, declares unlawful certain specified political activities of federal employees. Section 9 forbids officers and employees in the executive branch of the federal government, with exceptions, from taking "any active part in political management or in political campaigns." Section 15 declares that the activities theretofore determined by the United States Civil Service Commission to be prohibited to employees in the classified civil service of the United States by the civil service rules shall be deemed to be prohibited to federal employees covered by the Hatch Act. These sections of the act cover all federal officers and employees whether in the classified civil service or not and a penalty of dismissal from employment is imposed for violation. There is no designation of a single governmental agency for its enforcement. . . .

The present appellants sought an injunction before a statutory three judge district court of the District of Columbia against appellees, members of the United States Civil Service Commission to prohibit them from enforcing against petitioners the provisions of the second sentence of § 9(a) of the Hatch Act for the reason that the sentence is repugnant to the Constitution of the United States. A declaratory judgment of the unconstitutionality of the sentence was also sought. The sentence referred to reads, "No officer or employee in the executive branch of the federal government . . . shall take any active part in political management or in political campaigns." . . .

None of the appellants, except George P. Poole, has violated the provisions of the Hatch Act. They wish to act contrary to its provisions and those of § 1 of the Civil Service Rules and desire a declaration of the legally permissible limits of regulation. . . . [The Court held that this amounted to asking for an advisory opinion, and refused to take jurisdiction.]

Third. The appellant Poole does present by the complaint and affidavit matters appropriate for judicial determination. The affidavits filed by appellees confirm that Poole has been charged by the Commission with political activity and a proposed order for his removal from his position adopted subject to his right under Commission procedure to reply to the charges and to present further evidence in refutation. We proceed to consider the controversy over constitutional power at issue between Poole and the Commission as defined by the charge and preliminary finding upon one side and the admissions of Poole's affidavit upon the other. Our determination is limited to those facts. This proceeding so limited meets the requirements of defined rights and a definite threat to interfere with a possessor of the menaced rights by a penalty for an act done in violation of the claimed restraint. . . .

Fourth. This brings us to consider the narrow but important point involved in Poole's situation. Poole's stated offense is taking an "active part in political management or in political campaigns." He was a ward executive committee man of a political party and was politically active on election day as a worker at the polls and a paymaster for the services of other party workers. The issue for decision and the only one we decide is whether such a breach of the Hatch Act and Rule 1 of the Commission can, without violating the Constitution, be made the basis for disciplinary action.

When the issue is thus narrowed, the interference with free expression is seen in better proportion as compared with the requirements of orderly management of administrative personnel. Only while the employee is politically active, in the sense of Rule 1, must he withhold expression of opinion on public subjects. We assume that Mr. Poole would be expected to comment publicly as committeeman on political matters, so that indirectly there is an attenuated interference. We accept appellant's contention that the nature of political rights reserved to the people by the Ninth and Tenth Amendments are involved. The right claimed as inviolate may be stated as the right of a citizen to act as a party official or worker to further his own political views. Thus we have a measure of interference by the Hatch Act and the Rules with what otherwise would be the freedom of the civil servant under the First, Ninth and Tenth Amendments. And, if we look upon due process as a guarantee of freedom in those fields, there is a corresponding impairment of that right under the Fifth Amendment. Appellants' objections under the Amendments are basically the same.

We do not find persuasion in appellants' arguments that such activities during free time are not subject to regulation even though admittedly political activities cannot be indulged in during working hours. The influence of political activity by government employees, if evil in its effects on the service, the employees or people dealing with them, is hardly less so because that activity takes place after hours. Of course, the question of the need for this regulation is for other branches of government rather than the courts. Our duty in this case ends if the Hatch Act provision under examination is constitutional.

Of course, it is accepted constitutional doctrine that these fundamental human rights are not absolutes. The requirements of residence and age must be met. The essential rights of the First Amendment in some instances are subject to the elemental need for order without which the guarantees of civil rights to others would be a mockery. The powers granted by the Constitution to the federal government are subtracted from the totality of sovereignty originally in the states and the people. Therefore, when objection is made that the exercise of a federal power infringes upon rights reserved by the Ninth and Tenth Amendments, the inquiry must be directed toward the granted power under which the action of the Union was taken. If granted power is found, necessarily the objection of invasion of those rights, reserved by the Ninth and Tenth Amendments, must fail. Again this Court must balance the extent of the guarantees of freedom against a congressional enactment to protect a democratic society against the supposed evil of political partisanship by classified employees of government.

As pointed out hereinbefore in this opinion, the practice of excluding classified employees from party offices and personal political activity at the polls has been in effect for several decades. Some incidents similar to those that are under examination here have been before this Court and the prohibition against certain types of political activity by office holders has been upheld. The leading case was decided in 1882. Ex parte Curtis, 106 U. S. 371. There a subordinate United States employee was indicted for violation of an act that forbade employees who were not appointed by the President and confirmed by the Senate from giving or receiving money for political purposes from or to other employees of the government on penalty of discharge and criminal punishment. Curtis urged that the statute was unconstitutional. This Court upheld the right of Congress to punish the infraction of this law. The decisive principle was the power of Congress, within reasonable limits, to regulate, so far as it might deem necessary, the political conduct of its employees. A list of prohibitions against acts by public officials that are permitted to other citizens was given. This Court said, 106 U. S. at page 373:

"The evident purpose of congress in all this class of enactments has been to promote efficiency and integrity in the discharge of official duties, and to maintain proper discipline in the public service. Clearly such a purpose is within the just scope of legislative power, and it is not easy to see why the act now under consideration does not come fairly within the legitimate means to such an end."

The right to contribute money through fellow employees to advance the contributor's political theories was held not to be protected by any constitutional provision. It was held subject to regulation. A dissent by Mr. Justice Bradley emphasized the broad basis of the Court's opinion. He contended that a citizen's right to promote his political views could not be so restricted merely because he was an official of government.

No other member of the Court joined in this dissent. The conclusion of the Court, that there was no constitutional bar to regulation of such financial contributions of public servants as distinguished from the exercise of political privileges such as the ballot, has found acceptance in the subsequent practice of Congress and the growth of the principle of required political neutrality for classified public servants as a sound element for efficiency. The conviction that an actively partisan governmental personnel threatens good administration has deepened since Ex parte Curtis. Congress recognizes danger to the service in that political rather than official effort may earn advancement and to the public in that governmental favor may be channeled through political connections.

In United States v. Wurzbach, 280 U. S. 396, the doctrine of legislative power over actions of governmental officials was held valid when extended to members of Congress. The members of Congress were prohibited from receiving contributions for "any political purpose whatever" from any other federal employees. Private citizens were not affected. The argument of unconstitutionality because of interference with the political rights of a citizen by that time was dismissed in a sentence. . . .

The provisions of § 9 of the Hatch Act and the Civil Service Rule 1 are not dissimilar in purpose from the statutes against political contributions of money. The prohibitions now under discussion are directed at political contributions of energy by government employees. These contributions, too, have a long background of disapproval. Congress and the President are responsible for an efficient public service. If, in their judgment, efficiency may be best obtained by prohibiting active participation by classified employees in politics as party officers or workers, we see no constitutional objection.

Another Congress may determine that on the whole, limitations on active political management by federal personnel are unwise. The teaching of experience has evidently led Congress to enact the Hatch Act provisions. To declare that the present supposed evils of political activity are beyond the power of Congress to redress would leave the nation impotent to deal with what many sincere men believe is a material threat to the democratic system. Congress is not politically naive or regardless of public welfare or that of the employees. It leaves untouched full participation by employees in political decisions at the ballot box and forbids only the partisan activity of federal personnel deemed offensive to efficiency. With that limitation only, employees may make their contributions to public affairs or protect their own interests, as before the passage of the act.

The argument that political neutrality is not indispensable to a merit system for federal employees may be accepted. But because it is not indispensable does not mean that it is not desirable or permissible. Modern American politics involves organized political parties. Many classifications of government employees have been accustomed to work in politics—national, state and local—as a matter of principle or to assure their tenure. Congress may reasonably desire to limit party activity of federal employees so as to avoid a tendency toward a one-party system. It may have considered that parties would be more truly devoted to the public welfare if public servants were not overactive politically.

Appellants urge that federal employees are protected by the Bill of Rights and that Congress may not "enact a regulation providing that no Republican, Jew or Negro shall be appointed to federal office, or that no federal employee shall attend Mass or take any active part in missionary work." None would deny such limitations on congressional power but because there are some limitations it does not follow that a prohibition against acting as ward leader or worker at the polls is invalid . . . It is only partisan political activity that is interdicted. It is active participation in political management and political campaigns. Expressions, public or private, on public affairs, personalities and matters of public interest, not an objective of party action, are unrestricted by law so long as the government employee does not direct his activities toward party success.

It is urged, however, that Congress has gone further than necessary in prohibiting political activity to all types of classified employees. It is pointed out by appellants "that the impartiality of many of these is a matter of complete indifference to the effective performance" of their duties. Mr. Poole would appear to be a good illustration for appellants' argument. The complaint states that he is a roller in the Mint. We take it this is a job calling for the qualities of a skilled mechanic and that it does not involve contact with the public. Nevertheless, if in free time he is engaged in political activity, Congress may have concluded that the activity may promote or retard his advancement or preferment with his superiors. Congress may have thought that government employees are handy elements for leaders in political policy to use in building a political machine. For regulation of employees it is not necessary that the act regulated be anything more than an act reasonably deemed by Congress to interfere with the efficiency of the public service. There are hundreds of thousands of United States employees with positions no more influential upon policy determination than that of Mr. Poole. Evidently what Congress feared was the cumulative effect on employee morale of political activity by all employees who could be induced to participate actively. It does not seem to us an unconstitutional basis for legislation.

There is a suggestion that administrative workers may be barred, constitutionally, from political management and political campaigns while the industrial workers may not be barred, constitutionally, without an act "narrowly drawn to define and punish specific conduct." A ready answer, it seems to us, lies in the fact that the prohibition of § 9(a) of the Hatch Act "applies without discrimination to all employees whether industrial or administrative" and that the Civil Service Rules, by § 15 made a part of the Hatch Act, makes clear that industrial workers are covered in the prohibition against political activity. Congress has determined that the presence of government employees, whether industrial or administrative, in the ranks of political party workers is bad. Whatever differences there may be between administrative employees of the government and industrial workers in its employ are differences in detail so far as the constitutional power under review is concerned. Whether there are such differences and what weight to attach to them, are all matters of detail for Congress. We do not know whether the number of federal employees will expand or contract; whether the need for regulation of their political activities will increase or diminish. The use of the constitutional power of regulation is for Congress, not for the courts.

We have said that Congress may regulate the political conduct of government employees "within reasonable limits," even though the regulation trenches to some extent upon unfettered political action. The determination of the extent to which political activities of governmental employees shall be regulated lies primarily with Congress. Courts will interfere only when such interference passes beyond the general existing conception of governmental power. That conception develops from practice, history, and changing educational, social and economic conditions. The regulation of such activities as Poole carried on has the approval of long practice by the Commission, court decisions upon similar problems and a large body of informed public opinion. Congress and the administrative agencies have authority over the discipline and efficiency of the public service. When actions of civil servants in the judgment of Congress menace the integrity and the competency of the service, legislation to forestall such danger and adequate to maintain its usefulness is required. The Hatch Act is the answer of Congress to this need. We cannot say with such a background that these restrictions are unconstitutional. . . .

The judgment of the District Court is accordingly affirmed.

Mr. Justice Frankfurter concurred. Mr. Justice Murphy and Mr. Justice Jackson took no part in the consideration or decision of this case. Messrs. Justices Rutledge, Black, and Douglas dissented.

YATES v. UNITED STATES
354 U. S. 298; 1 L. Ed. 2d 1356; 77 Sup. Ct. 1064. 1957.

In 1940 Congress passed the Smith Act (Alien Registration Act), which forbade the advocacy of the overthrow of government by force or violence, and conspiracies to bring this about. This was the first federal peacetime sedition act since the infamous Alien and Sedition Act of 1798. After eleven years the question of its validity reached the Supreme Court in Dennis v. United States, 341 U. S. 494 (1951). In 1948 the eleven top leaders of the American Communist party were indicted under the act for wilfully and knowingly conspiring to teach and advocate the overthrow of government by force and violence, and to organize the Communist party for the purpose of so doing. The trial in District Judge Medina's court in New York ran from January 20 to September 23, 1949, and resulted in conviction. Judge Medina charged the jury that their duty was to decide whether the evidence showed a violation of the statute, but that the question whether the evidence showed clear and present danger sufficient to justify the application of the statute under the First Amendment "is a matter of law with which you have no concern." Both the conviction and this charge to the jury were upheld by the Court of Appeals in an opinion by Judge Learned Hand. The Supreme Court limited the scope of its review to the constitutional questions raised, chief of which was the First Amendment question of free speech. It did not review the sufficiency of the evidence to support the verdict.

In the five opinions written in the Dennis case, there are four interpretations of the "clear and present danger" test, first stated by Mr. Justice Holmes in Schenck v. United States (p. 167). Chief Justice Vinson, speaking for the Court, paid allegiance to Holmes' statement and application of the test, but in reality adopted in its place Judge Hand's test of "clear and *probable* danger." Judge Hand had said: "In each case [courts] must ask whether the gravity of the 'evil,' discounted by its improbability, justifies such invasion of free speech as is necessary to avoid the danger." In short, the danger need not be imminent; it is enough that there is a group willing to attempt the overthrow of government if and when possible. The Chief Justice read the time element out of clear and present danger.

Mr. Justice Frankfurter had always rejected the idea that a law which on its face invades free speech must be presumed to be unconstitutional, or that the First Amendment occupies any "preferred position." (See Thomas v. Collins, p. 166). He felt that free speech cases call for the weighing of competing interests, and that the legislative judgment embodied in the Smith Act, that the Communist threat to the security of the country justifies punitive action, is amply supported by evidence.

In an incisive opinion Mr. Justice Jackson bluntly declared that the test of clear and present danger has no applicability to a criminal conspiracy such as that carried on by the Communist party. It was never intended to be applied in a case like this, and should be reserved for cases involving restrictions upon speeches and publications.

Justices Black and Douglas, dissenting, felt that the clear and present danger test had been destroyed. Mr. Justice Douglas emphasized that the defendants were charged with no overt acts, only with speeches and publications. He also felt that the question of clear and present danger should be decided by the jury and not by the court.

Those who greatly regretted what seemed to be the Court's abandonment in the Dennis case of the clear and present danger test could perhaps find some consolation in the fact that neither Justices Hughes nor Stone, both powerful defenders of the First Amendment, ever alluded to clear and present danger in a free speech case. They were content to rely upon due process of law, under which the Court balances according to its best judgment the restraint placed upon the freedom of the citizen over against the threat to the public security which is alleged to justify that restraint. Perhaps the results in the long run are much the same whatever the test is called.

The Court had occasion six years later in Yates v. United States, printed below, to re-examine the constitutional problems raised by the Smith Act. Here the government moved against the second-string Communist leaders, and later against some party members. At the time of the Yates decision 145 indictments and 80 convictions had been obtained for violation of the Smith Act. It may be noted that while in Dennis the Supreme Court did not review the evidence against the defendants, in Yates it examined the entire 14,000 page record and carefully weighed the facts.

In Scales v. United States, 367 U. S. 203 (1961), the Court held, five to four, that simple membership in the Communist party may be a violation of the Smith Act if it is "active membership in an organization engaged in illegal advocacy, by one having guilty knowledge and intent." The argument was strongly urged that the membership clause of the Smith Act had been repealed by the section of the Subversive Activities Control Act of 1950 (requiring registration of Communists), which provides that: "Neither the holding of office nor membership in any Communist organization by any person shall constitute per se a violation of subsection (a) or subsection (c) of this section or of any other criminal statute." Mr. Justice Frankfurter's opinion for the majority held that the section quoted from the Act of 1950 clarified, rather than repealed, the membership clause of the Smith Act; and he emphasized the difference between punishing a man for membership per se and punishing him for membership with guilty knowledge and with intent to aid in the violent overthrow of government. In the dissenting opinions it was urged that the Act of 1950 had repealed the Smith Act provision, and that the membership clause violated the First Amendment.

On the same day Noto v. United States, 367 U. S. 290 (1961), set aside Noto's conviction under the Smith Act for membership in the Communist party. The Court was unanimous. The evidence against Noto showed that the Communist organization to which he belonged had not advocated the violent overthrow of government but had merely engaged in the "abstract teaching of Communist theory." The decision rests upon the doctrine of the Yates case, and the facts distinguish it from the Scales case.

The Subversive Activities Control Act required, among other things, that "Communist action" organizations register with a Subversive Activities Control Board and list their officers and members. Failure of the organization to register made each member liable to register himself. In Communist Party v. S.A.C.B., 367 U. S. 1 (1961), the Court upheld the S.A.C.B. finding that the party was an "action" organization and had to register, and denied that the registration provision was a bill of attainder, violated the First Amendment, or denied due process of law. It held premature a claim of self-incrimination on the ground that no individual had yet been ordered to register. Upon continued refusal of the party to register, however, the board found that certain individuals were party members and ordered them to register. In Albertson v. S.A.C.B., 382 U. S. 70 (1965), this was held to be compulsory self-incrimination, since "admission of membership . . . may be used to prosecute the registrant under the membership clause of the Smith Act. . . ." (See Scales case above.) Nor did the provision, quoted above, that membership per se was not a crime amount to an adequate immunity statute under the doctrine of Counselman v. Hitchcock (see p. 122), since it did not preclude the use of information called for on the registration form "either as evidence or as an investigatory lead." The legal status of the Communist party is in sharp contrast to that of the National Association for the Advancement of Colored People. In N.A.A.C.P. v. Alabama, 357 U. S. 449 (1958), the Court held the N.A.A.C.P. could keep secret its membership lists. Forced disclosure, unjustified by a vital state interest, threatened the group's freedom of association in violation of the First and Fourteenth Amendments.

Mr. Justice Harlan delivered the opinion of the Court, saying in part:

We brought these cases here to consider certain questions arising under the Smith Act which have not heretofore been passed upon by this Court, and otherwise to review the convictions of these petitioners for conspiracy to violate that Act. Among other things, the convictions are claimed to rest upon an application of the Smith Act which is hostile to the principles upon which its constitutionality was upheld in Dennis v. United States, 341 U. S. 494.

These 14 petitioners stand convicted, after a jury trial in the United States District Court for the Southern District of California, upon a single count indictment charging them with conspiring (1) to advocate and teach the duty and necessity of overthrowing the Government of the United States by force and violence, and (2) to organize, as the Communist Party of the United States, a society of persons who so advocate and teach, all with the intent of causing the overthrow of the Government by force and violence as speedily as circumstances would permit. Act of June 28, 1940. The conspiracy is alleged to have originated in 1940 and continued down to the date of the indictment in 1951. . . .

Upon conviction each of the petitioners was sentenced to five years' imprisonment and a fine of $10,000. The Court of Appeals affirmed. 225 F2d 146. We granted certiorari for the reasons already indicated. . . .

In the view we take of this case, it is necessary for us to consider only the following of petitioners' contentions: (1) that the term "organize" as used in the Smith Act was erroneously construed by the two lower courts; (2) that the trial court's instructions to the jury erroneously excluded from the case the issue of "incitement to action"; (3) that the evidence was so insufficient as to require this Court to direct the acquittal of these petitioners; and (4) that petitioner Schneiderman's conviction was precluded by this Court's judgment in Schneiderman v. United States, 320 U. S. 118, under the doctrine of collateral estoppel. For reasons given hereafter, we conclude that these convictions must be reversed and the case remanded to the District Court with instructions to enter judgments of acquittal as to certain of the petitioners, and to grant a new trial as to the rest.

I. The Term "Organize"

One object of the conspiracy charged was to violate the third paragraph of 18 USC § 2385, which provides:

"Whoever organizes or helps or attempts to organize any society, group, or assembly of persons who teach, advocate, or encourage the overthrow or destruction of any [government in the United States] by force or violence . . . [s]hall be fined not more than $10,000 or imprisoned not more than ten years, or both . . . ."

Petitioners claim that "organize" means to "establish," "found," or "bring into existence," and that in this sense the Communist Party was organized by 1945 at the latest. On this basis petitioners contend that this part of the indictment, returned in 1951, was barred by the three-year statute of limitations. The Government, on the other hand, says that "organize" connotes a continuing process which goes on throughout the life of an organization, and that, in the words of the trial court's instructions to the jury, the term includes such things as "the recruiting of new members and the forming of new units, and the regrouping or expansion of existing clubs, classes and other units of any society, party, group or other organization." The two courts below accepted the Government's position. We think, however, that petitioners' position must prevail, upon principles stated by Chief Justice Marshall more than a century ago in United States v. Wiltberger, (U. S.) 5 Wheat. 76, 95, as follows:

"The rule that penal laws are to be construed strictly, is perhaps not much less old than construction itself. It is founded on the tenderness of the law for the rights of individuals; and on the plain principle that the power of punishment is vested in the legislative, not in the judicial department. It is the legislature, not the Court, which is to define a crime, and ordain its punishment. . . .

[The Court discusses the meaning of the word "organize" as used in the Smith Act. It finds nothing in the legislative history of the act to show that Congress intended to give to the word the broad meaning urged by the prosecution.]

We conclude, therefore, that since the Communist Party came into being in 1945, and the indictment was not returned until 1951, the three-year statute of limitations had run on the "organizing" charge, and required the withdrawal of that part of the indictment from the jury's consideration. . . .

II. *Instructions to the Jury*

Petitioners contend that the instructions to the jury were fatally defective in that the trial court refused to charge that, in order to convict, the jury must find that the advocacy which the defendants conspired to promote was of a kind calculated to "incite" persons to action for the forcible overthrow of the Government. It is argued that advocacy of forcible overthrow as mere *abstract doctrine* is within the free speech protection of the First Amendment; that the Smith Act, consistently with that constitutional provision, must be taken as proscribing only the sort of advocacy which incites to illegal *action;* and that the trial court's charge, by permitting conviction for mere advocacy, unrelated to its tendency to produce forcible action, resulted in an unconstitutional application of the Smith Act. The Government, which at the trial also requested the court to charge in terms of "incitement," now takes the position, however, that the true constitutional dividing line is not between inciting and abstract advocacy of forcible overthrow, but rather between advocacy as such, irrespective of its inciting qualities, and the mere discussion or exposition of violent overthrow as an abstract theory. . . .

There can be no doubt from the record that in so instructing the jury the court regarded as immaterial, and intended to withdraw from the jury's consideration, any issue as to the character of the advocacy in terms of its capacity to stir listeners to forcible action. Both the petitioners and the Government submitted proposed instructions which would have required the jury to find that the proscribed advocacy was not of a mere abstract doctrine of forcible overthrow, but of action to that end, by the use of language reasonably and ordinarily calculated to incite persons to such action. The trial court rejected these proposed instructions on the ground that any necessity for giving them which may have existed at the time the Dennis case was tried was removed by this Court's subsequent decision in that case. The court made it clear in colloquy with counsel that in its view the illegal advocacy was made out simply by showing that what was said dealt with forcible overthrow and that it was uttered with a specific intent to accomplish that purpose, insisting that all such advocacy was punishable "whether in language of incitement or not." . . .

We are thus faced with the question whether the Smith Act prohibits advocacy and teaching of forcible overthrow as an abstract principle, divorced from any effort to instigate action to that end, so long as such advocacy or teaching is engaged in with evil intent. We hold that it does not.

The distinction between advocacy of abstract doctrine and advocacy directed at promoting unlawful action is one that has been consistently recognized in the opinions of this Court, beginning with Fox v. Washington, 236 U. S. 273, and Schenck v. United States, 249 U. S. 47. This distinction was heavily underscored in Gitlow v. New York, 268 U. S 652, . . .

We need not, however, decide the issue before us in terms of constitutional compulsion, for our first duty is to construe this statute. In doing so we should not assume that Congress chose to disregard a constitutional danger zone so clearly marked, or that it used the words "advocate" and "teach" in their ordinary dictionary meanings when they had already been construed as terms of art carrying a special and limited connotation. . . . The legislative history of the Smith Act and related bills shows beyond all question that Congress was aware of the distinction between the advocacy or teaching of abstract doctrine and the advocacy or teaching of action, and that it did not intend to disregard it. The statute was aimed at the advocacy and teaching of concrete action for the forcible overthrow of the Government, and not of principles divorced from action.

The Government's reliance on this Court's decision in Dennis is misplaced. The jury instructions which were refused here were given there, and were referred to by this Court as requiring "the jury to find the facts *essential* to establish the substantive crime." 341 U. S. at 512 (emphasis added). It is true that at one point in the late Chief Justice's opinion it is stated that the Smith Act "is directed at advocacy, not discussion," but it is clear that the reference was to advocacy of action, not ideas, for in the very next sentence the opinion emphasizes that the jury was properly instructed that there could be no conviction for "advocacy in the realm of ideas." The two concurring opinions in that case likewise emphasize the distinction with which we are concerned.

In failing to distinguish between advocacy of forcible overthrow as an abstract doctrine and advocacy of action to that end, the District Court appears to have been led astray by the holding in Dennis that advocacy of violent action to be taken at some future time was enough. It seems to have considered that, since "inciting" speech is usually thought of as calculated to induce immediate action, and since Dennis held advocacy of action for future overthrow sufficient, this meant that advocacy, irrespective of its tendency to generate action, is punishable, provided only that it is uttered with a specific intent to accomplish overthrow. In other words, the District Court apparently thought that Dennis obliterated the traditional dividing line between advocacy of abstract doctrine and advocacy of action.

This misconceives the situation confronting the Court in Dennis and what was held there. Although the jury's verdict, interpreted in light of the trial court's instructions, did not justify the conclusion that the defendants' advocacy was directed at, or created any danger of, immediate overthrow, it did establish that the advocacy was aimed at building up a seditious group and maintaining it in readiness for action at a propitious time. . . . The essence of the Dennis holding was that indoctrination of a group in preparation for future violent action, as well as exhortation to immediate action, by advocacy found to be directed to "action for the accomplishment" of forcible overthrow, to violence "as a rule or principle of action," and employing "language of incitement," is not constitutionally protected when the group is of sufficient size and cohesiveness, is sufficiently oriented towards action, and other circumstances are such as reasonably to justify apprehension that action will occur. This is quite a different thing from the view of the District Court here that mere doctrinal justification of forcible overthrow, if engaged in with the intent to accomplish overthrow, is punishable per se under the Smith Act. That sort of advocacy, even though uttered with the hope that it may ultimately lead to violent revolution, is too remote from concrete action to be regarded as the kind of indoctrination preparatory to action which was condemned in Dennis. As one of the concurring opinions in Dennis put it: "Throughout our decisions there has recurred a distinction between the statement of an idea which may prompt its hearers to take unlawful action, and advocacy that such action be taken." There is nothing in Dennis which makes that historic distinction obsolete. . . .

In light of the foregoing we are unable to regard the District Court's charge upon this aspect of the case as adequate. The jury was never told that the Smith Act does not denounce advocacy in the sense of preaching abstractly the forcible overthrow of the Government. We think that the trial court's statement that the proscribed advocacy must include the "urging," "necessity," and "duty" of forcible overthrow, and not merely its "desirability" and "propriety," may not be regarded as a sufficient substitute for charging that the Smith Act reaches only advocacy of action for the overthrow of government by force and violence. The essential distinction is that those to whom the advocacy is addressed must be urged to *do* something, now or in the future, rather than merely to *believe* in something. At best the expressions used by the trial court were equivocal, since in the absence of any instructions differentiating advocacy of abstract doctrine from advocacy of action, they were as consistent with the former as they were with the latter. Nor do we regard their ambiguity as lessened by what the trial court had to say as to the right of the defendants to announce their beliefs as to the inevitability of violent revolution, or to advocate other unpopular opinions. Especially when it is unmistakable that the court did not consider the urging of action for forcible overthrow as being a necessary element of the proscribed advocacy, but rather considered the crucial question to be whether the advocacy was uttered with a specific intent to accomplish such overthrow, we would not be warranted in assuming that the jury drew from these instructions more than the court itself intended them to convey. . . .

We recognize that distinctions between advocacy or teaching of abstract doctrines, with evil intent, and that which is directed to stirring people to action, are often subtle and difficult to grasp, for in a broad sense, as Mr. Justice Holmes said in his dissenting opinion in Gitlow, supra: "Every idea is an incitement." But the very subtlety of these distinctions required the most clear and explicit instructions with reference to them, for they concerned an issue which went to the very heart of the charges against these petitioners. The need for precise and understandable instructions on this issue is further emphasized by the equivocal character of the evidence in this record, with which we deal in Part III of this opinion. Instances of speech that could be considered to amount to "advocacy of action" are so few and far between as to be almost completely overshadowed by the hundreds of instances in the record in which overthrow, if mentioned at all, occurs in the course of doctrinal disputation so remote from action as to be almost wholly lacking in probative value. Vague references to "revolutionary" or "militant" action of an unspecified character, which are found in the evidence, might in addition be given too great weight by the jury in the absence of more precise instructions. Particularly in light of this record, we must regard the trial court's charge in this respect as furnishing wholly inadequate guidance to the jury on this central point in the case. We cannot allow a conviction to stand on such "an equivocal direction to the jury on a basic issue." . . .

III. *The Evidence*

The determinations already made require a reversal of these convictions. Nevertheless, in the exercise of our power under 28 USC § 2106 to "direct the entry of such appropriate judgment . . . as may be just under the circumstances," we have conceived it to be our duty to scrutinize this lengthy record with care, in order to determine whether the way should be left open for a new trial of all or some of these petitioners. Such a judgment, we think, should, on the one hand, foreclose further proceedings against those of the petitioners as to whom the evidence in this record would be palpably insufficient upon a new trial, and should, on the other hand, leave the Government free to retry the other petitioners under proper legal standards, especially since it is by no means clear that certain aspects of the evidence against them could not have been clarified to the advantage of the Government had it not been under a misapprehension as to the burden cast upon it by the Smith Act. . . .

[Here follows an evaluation of the evidence against the fourteen defendants comprised in the 14,000-page record. On this basis the Court ordered the acquittal of five, and new trials for nine.]

IV. *Collateral Estoppel*

There remains to be dealt with petitioner Schneiderman's claim based on the doctrine of collateral estoppel by judgment. Petitioner urges that in Schneiderman v. United States, a denaturalization proceeding in which he was the prevailing party, this Court made determinations favorable to him which are conclusive in this proceeding under the doctrine of collateral estoppel. Specifically, petitioner contends that the Schneiderman decision determined, for purposes of this proceeding, (1) that the teaching of Marxism-Leninism by the Communist Party was not necessarily the advocacy of violent overthrow of government; (2) that at least one tenable conclusion to be drawn from the evidence was that the Communist Party desired to achieve its goal of socialism through peaceful means; (3) that it could not be presumed, merely because of his membership or officership in the Communist Party, that Schneiderman adopted an illegal interpretation of Marxist doctrine; and finally, (4) that absent proof of overt acts indicating that Schneiderman personally adopted a reprehensible interpretation, the Government had failed to establish its burden by the clear and unequivocal evidence necessary in a denaturalization case. In the courts below, petitioner urged unsuccessfully that these determinations were conclusive in this proceeding under the doctrine of collateral estoppel, and entitled him either to an acquittal or to special instructions to the jury. He makes the same contentions here. . . .

[The Court examines this argument in some detail, and concludes that the determinations made by the Court in the Schneiderman case in 1943 "could not operate as a complete bar to this proceeding." Schneiderman, therefore, was not acquitted, but granted a new trial.]

Since there must be a new trial, we have not found it necessary to deal with the contentions of the petitioners as to the fairness of the trial already held. The judgment of the Court of Appeals is reversed, and the case remanded to the District Court for further proceedings consistent with this opinion.

It is so ordered.

Justices Brennan and Whittaker took no part in the consideration or decision of this case.

Mr. Justice Burton concurred in the result.

Mr. Justice Black, with whom Mr. Justice Douglas joined, concurred in part and dissented in part. As in their dissents in the Dennis case, the two justices argued that the Smith Act violates the First Amendment.

Mr. Justice Clark wrote a dissenting opinion.

4

Restrictions on the States in Behalf of Civil and Political Rights

---

PALKO v. CONNECTICUT
302 U. S. 319; 82 L. Ed. 288; 58 Sup. Ct. 149. 1937.

In the note to Barron v. Baltimore (p. 74) it is stated that beginning about 1925 the Supreme Court began to expand the meaning of the term "liberty" in the due process clause of the Fourteenth Amendment to include some of the rights, i.e., freedom of speech and press, guaranteed by the federal Bill of Rights. On the other hand, as far back as 1884 in Hurtado v. California, 110 U. S. 516, the Court held that the due process clause of the Fourteenth Amendment did not require a grand jury indictment in a state court, even though the Fifth Amendment requires it in federal prosecutions. Thus the Court in case after case has been classifying the provisions of the Bill of Rights into those which are essential to due process of law and thus bind the states through the operation of the Fourteenth Amendment, and those which are not essential to due process and which the states may therefore ignore. The opinion in the present case is important since it gives an official summary of this classification up to 1937, and states clearly the principles upon which the classification rests.

With increasing impetus the Court has been adding to the list of Bill of Rights protections that apply to the states. In Wolf v. Colorado, 338 U. S. 25 (1949), the Court said: "The security of one's privacy against arbitrary intrusion by the police—which is at the core of the Fourth Amendment— is basic to a free society. It is therefore implicit in 'the concept of ordered liberty' and as such enforceable against the states through the Due Process Clause." It refused, however, to require a state court to exclude evidence which state officers had secured by unreasonable searches and seizures. In Mapp v. Ohio (p. 102) it reversed its stand on this and held that the state's use of such evidence denies due process of law. In Robinson v. California, 370 U. S. 660 (1962), the Court held that a California statute which made it a crime for a person to "be addicted to the use of narcotics" inflicted a cruel and unusual punishment "in violation of the Eighth and Fourteenth Amendments."

In Gideon v. Wainwright (p. 477), the Court made absolute the defendant's right to counsel in a state court, and in Escobedo v. Illinois (p. 515), it extended this protection to the period of pre-trial interrogation. In 1964, in Malloy v. Hogan, the Court overruled Twining v. New Jersey, 211 U. S. 78 (1908), and held the Fifth Amendment privilege against compulsory self-incrimination applicable to the states. In Pointer v. Texas, 380 U. S. 400 (1965), it held applicable to the states the Sixth Amendment right of a defendant to confront the witnesses against him.

Mr. Justice Cardozo delivered the opinion of the Court, saying in part:

. . . Appellant was indicted . . . for the crime of murder in the first degree. A jury found him guilty of murder in the second degree, and he was sentenced to confinement in the state prison for life. Thereafter the state of Connecticut, with the permission of the judge presiding at the trial, gave notice of appeal to the Supreme Court of Errors. This it did pursuant to an act adopted in 1886 which is printed in the margin. . . . ["Sec. 6494. *Appeals by the state in criminal cases.* Appeals from the rulings and decisions of the superior court or of any criminal court of common pleas, upon all questions of law arising on the trial of criminal cases, may be taken by the state, with the permission of the presiding judge, to the Supreme Court of Errors, in the same manner and to the same effect as if made by the accused."] Upon such appeal, the Supreme Court of Errors reversed the judgment and ordered a new trial. . . . It found that there had been error of law to the prejudice of the state. . . .

. . . [The] defendant was brought to trial again. Before a jury was impaneled and also at later stages of the case he made the objection that the effect of the new trial was to place him twice in jeopardy for the same offense, and in so doing to violate the Fourteenth Amendment of the Constitution of the United States. Upon the overruling of the objection the trial proceeded. The jury returned a verdict of murder in the first degree, and the court sentenced the defendant to the punishment of death. . . . The case is here upon appeal.

1. The execution of the sentence will not deprive appellant of his life without the process of law assured to him by the Fourteenth Amendment of the federal Constitution.

The argument for appellant is that whatever is forbidden by the Fifth Amendment is forbidden by the Fourteenth also. The Fifth Amendment, which is not directed to the states, but solely to the federal government, creates immunity from double jeopardy. No person shall be "subject for the same offense to be twice put in jeopardy of life or limb." The Fourteenth Amendment ordains, "nor shall any State deprive any person of life, liberty, or property, without due process of law." To retry a defendant, though under one indictment and only one, subjects him, it is said, to double jeopardy in violation of the Fifth Amendment, if the prosecution is one on behalf of the United States. From this the consequence is said to follow that there is a denial of life or liberty without due process of law, if the prosecution is one on behalf of the people of a state. . . .

We have said that in appellant's view the Fourteenth Amendment is to be taken as embodying the prohibitions of the Fifth. His thesis is even broader. Whatever would be a violation of the original Bill of Rights (Amendments 1 to 8) if done by the federal government is now equally unlawful by force of the Fourteenth Amendment if done by a state. There is no such general rule.

The Fifth Amendment provides, among other things, that no person shall be held to answer for a capital or otherwise infamous crime unless on presentment or indictment of a grand jury. This Court has held that, in prosecutions by a state, presentment or indictment by a grand jury may give way to informations at the instance of a public officer. Hurtado v. California, 110 U. S. 516. . . . The Fifth Amendment provides also that no person shall be compelled in any criminal case to be a witness against himself. This Court has said that, in prosecutions by a state, the exemption will fail if the state elects to end it. Twining v. New Jersey, 211 U. S. 78. . . . The Sixth Amendment calls for a jury trial in criminal cases and the Seventh for a jury trial in civil cases at common law where the value in controversy shall exceed twenty dollars. This Court has ruled that consistently with those amendments trial by jury may be modified by a state or abolished altogether. Walker v. Sauvinet, 92 U. S. 90; Maxwell v. Dow, 176 U. S. 581. . . . As to the Fourth Amendment, one should refer to Weeks v. United States, 232 U. S. 383, 398, and as to other provisions of the Sixth, to West v. Louisiana, 194 U. S. 258.

On the other hand, the due process clause of the Fourteenth Amendment may make it unlawful for a state to abridge by its statutes the freedom of speech which the First Amendment safeguards against encroachment by the Congress (De Jonge v. Oregon, 299 U. S. 353; Herndon v. Lowry, 301 U. S. 242) or the like freedom of the press (Grosjean v. American Press Co. 297 U. S. 233; Near v. Minnesota, 283 U. S. 697), or the free exercise of religion (Hamilton v. University of California, 293 U. S. 245; . . . Pierce v. Society of Sisters, 268 U. S. 510), or the right of peaceable assembly, without which speech would be unduly trammeled (De Jonge v. Oregon, 299 U. S. 353; Herndon v. Lowry, 301 U. S. 242), or the right of one accused of crime to the benefit of counsel (Powell v. Alabama, 287 U. S. 45). In these and other situations immunities that are valid as against the federal government by force of the specific pledges of particular amendments have been found to be implicit in the concept of ordered liberty, and thus, through the Fourteenth Amendment, become valid as against the states.

The line of division may seem to be wavering and broken if there is a hasty catalogue of the cases on the one side and the other. Reflection and analysis will induce a different view. There emerges the perception of a rationalizing principle which gives to discrete instances a proper order and coherence. The right to trial by jury and the immunity from prosecution except as the result of an indictment may have value and importance. Even so, they are not of the very essence of a scheme of ordered liberty. To abolish them is not to violate a "principle of justice so rooted in the traditions and conscience of our people as to be ranked as fundamental." . . . Few would be so narrow or provincial as to maintain that a fair and enlightened system of justice would be impossible without them. What is true of jury trials and indictments is true also, as the cases show, of the immunity from compulsory self-incrimination. . . . This too might be lost, and justice still be done. Indeed, today as in the past there are students of our penal system who look upon the immunity as a mischief rather than

a benefit, and who would limit its scope or destroy it altogether. . . .
The exclusion of these immunities and privileges from the privileges
and immunities protected against the action of the states has not been
arbitrary or casual. It has been dictated by a study and appreciation
of the meaning, the essential implications, of liberty itself.

We reach a different plane of social and moral values when we pass
to the privileges and immunities that have been taken over from the
earlier articles of the federal Bill of Rights and brought within the
Fourteenth Amendment by a process of absorption. These in their
origin were effective against the federal government alone. If the
Fourteenth Amendment has absorbed them, the process of absorption
has had its source in the belief that neither liberty nor justice would
exist if they were sacrificed. . . . This is true, for illustration, of freedom of thought and speech. Of that freedom one may say that it is
the matrix, the indispensable condition, of nearly every other form of
freedom. With rare aberrations a pervasive recognition of that truth
can be traced in our history, political and legal. So it has come about
that the domain of liberty, withdrawn by the Fourteenth Amendment from encroachment by the states, has been enlarged by latter-
day judgments to include liberty of the mind as well as liberty of
action. . . .

Our survey of the cases serves, we think, to justify the statement
that the dividing line between them, if not unfaltering throughout its
course, has been true for the most part to a unifying principle. On
which side of the line the case made out by the appellant has appropriate location must be the next inquiry and the final one. Is that
kind of double jeopardy to which the statute has subjected him a hardship so acute and shocking that our polity will not endure it? Does it
violate those "fundamental principles of liberty and justice which lie
at the base of all our civil and political institutions?" . . . The answer
surely must be "no." What the answer would have to be if the state
were permitted after a trial free from error to try the accused over
again or to bring another case against him, we have no occasion to
consider. We deal with the statute before us and no other. The state
is not attempting to wear the accused out by a multitude of cases with
accumulated trials. It asks no more than this, that the case against
him shall go on until there shall be a trial free from the corrosion of
substantial legal error. . . . This is not cruelty at all, nor even vexation
in any immoderate degree. If the trial had been infected with error
adverse to the accused, there might have been review at his instance,

and as often as necessary to purge the vicious taint. A reciprocal privilege, subject at all times to the discretion of the presiding judge . . . , has now been granted to the state. There is here no seismic innovation. The edifice of justice stands, in its symmetry, to many, greater than before.

2. The conviction of appellant is not in derogation of any privileges or immunities that belong to him as a citizen of the United States. . . .

Maxwell v. Dow, *supra*, gives all the answer that is necessary.

The judgment is affirmed.

Mr. Justice Butler dissents.

NEAR v. MINNESOTA
283 U. S. 697; 75 L. Ed. 1357; 51 Sup. Ct. 625. 1931.

The law in the present case was wholly novel. It was promptly dubbed the "Minnesota gag law." It provided for the "padlocking," by injunctive process, of a newspaper for printing matter which was scandalous, malicious, defamatory, or obscene. Such a "padlock" injunction, enforceable by the customary process of summary punishment for contempt of court, could be lifted only by convincing the judge who issued it that the publication would, in the future, be unobjectionable. This, in the judgment of the majority of the Court, amounted to previous censorship of publication and a violation of long-established canons of free speech and press.

The present case represents the climax of a striking evolution in our constitutional law whereby freedom of speech and press is at last effectively "nationalized" or confided to the protection of the federal courts against both national and state impairment. The steps in that evolution may be traced thus: (1) Before the Fourteenth Amendment there was no federal constitutional restraint upon state interference with free speech and press, since under the doctrine of Barron v. Baltimore (p. 74) the First Amendment does not apply to the states. (2) As late as 1922 the Supreme Court, in Prudential Insurance Co. v. Cheek, 259 U. S. 530, stated that "neither the Fourteenth Amendment nor any other provision of the Constitution of the United States imposes upon the states any restrictions about 'freedom of speech.'" (3) Even before this, however, the doctrine was being urged upon the Court that freedom of speech and press constituted an essential part of the "liberty" protected by the Fourteenth Amendment against deprivation without due process of law. In 1907, Mr. Justice Harlan, in a dissenting opinion in Patterson v. Colorado, 205 U. S. 454, declared: "I go further and hold that the privileges of free speech and a free press, belonging to every citizen of the United States, constitute essential parts of every man's liberty, and are protected against violation by that clause of the Fourteenth Amendment forbidding a state to deprive any person of his liberty without due process of law." (4) Beginning in 1923 the Court began to exhibit clear evidence of its conversion to this broadened conception of the term "liberty." In Meyer v. Nebraska, 262 U. S. 390 (1923), Mr. Justice McReynolds, in an opinion holding invalid a Nebraska statute forbidding the teaching of any subject in any language but English in any private, parochial, or public school, defined the "liberty" protected by the due process clause as follows: "Without doubt, it denotes not merely freedom from bodily restraint, but also the right of the individual to contract, to engage in any of the common occupations of life, to acquire useful knowledge, to marry, establish a home and bring up children, to worship God according to the dictates of his own conscience, and, generally, to enjoy those privileges long recognized at common law as essential to the orderly pursuit of happiness by free men." (5) In Gitlow v. New York, 268 U. S. 652 (1925), Gitlow, convicted of violating the New York Criminal Anarchy Act of 1902 by circulating communist literature, squarely urged on the Court that the New York statute, by unreasonably restricting freedom of press, deprived him of liberty without due process of law. In a truly remarkable judicial about-face the Court accepted this view declaring: "For present purposes we may and do assume that freedom of speech and of the press—which are protected by the First Amendment from abridgment by Congress—are among the fundamental personal rights and 'liberties' protected by the due process clause of the Fourteenth Amendment from impairment by the states." The Court held, however, that the New York act as applied in Gitlow's case did not unduly restrict freedom of press and was therefore valid. The present case of Near v. Minnesota was the first in which a state statute was held, by virtue of its general character, to deprive persons of liberty without due process of law because it unreasonably restricted freedom of speech and press.

This definition of liberty in the due process clause of the Fourteenth Amendment was an invitation to any one who thought that his basic civil liberties had been invaded by state action to go to the Supreme Court for relief. The Court has decided a number of important cases which have come to it in this way. In Grosjean v. American Press Co., 297 U. S. 233 (1936), the Court held void a Louisiana tax of two per cent on the gross receipts of newspapers having a circulation of more than 20,000 per week. This tax was aimed at the papers hostile to the late Senator Huey Long. It denied due process of law by abridging freedom of the press. In De Jonge v. Oregon, 299 U. S. 353 (1937), freedom of assembly was held to be part of the "liberty" protected by the due process clause against state impairment. The Oregon Criminal Syndicalism Act, under which De Jonge was convicted for attending and addressing a Communist meeting at which no unlawful conduct or utterances occurred, was held void as a denial of due process of law. Talley v. California, 362 U. S. 60 (1960), held that a Los Angeles ordinance violated freedom of speech and press in prohibiting the distribution of handbills which did not have printed on them the names and addresses of the persons who prepared, distributed, or sponsored them.

Mr. Chief Justice Hughes delivered the opinion of the Court, saying in part:

Chapter 285 of the Session Laws of Minnesota for the year 1925 provides for the abatement, as a public nuisance, of a "malicious, scandalous and defamatory newspaper, magazine or other periodical." Section one of the act is as follows:

"Section 1. Any person who, as an individual, or as a member or employee of a firm, or association or organization, or as an officer, director, member or employee of a corporation, shall be engaged in the business of regularly or customarily producing, publishing or circulating, having in possession, selling or giving away,

(a) an obscene, lewd and lascivious newspaper, magazine, or other periodical, or

(b) a malicious, scandalous and defamatory newspaper, magazine or other periodical,

is guilty of a nuisance, and all persons guilty of such nuisance may be enjoined, as hereinafter provided.

"Participation in such business shall constitute a commission of such nuisance and render the participant liable and subject to the proceedings, orders and judgments provided for in this act. Ownership, in whole or in part, directly or indirectly, of any such periodical, or of any stock or interest in any corporation or organization which owns the same in whole or in part, or which publishes the same, shall constitute such participation." . . .

Section two provides that whenever any such nuisance is committed or exists, the county attorney of any county where any such periodical is published or circulated, or, in case of his failure or refusal to proceed upon written request in good faith of a reputable citizen, the attorney general, or upon like failure or refusal of the latter, any citizen of the county, may maintain an action in the district court of the county in the name of the state to enjoin perpetually the persons committing or maintaining any such nuisance from further committing or maintaining it. Upon such evidence as the court shall deem sufficient, a temporary injunction may be granted. The defendants have the right to plead by demurrer or answer, and the plaintiff may demur or reply as in other cases.

The action, by section three, is to be "governed by the practice and procedure applicable to civil actions for injunctions," and after trial the court may enter judgment permanently enjoining the defendants found guilty of violating the act from continuing the violation and, "in and by such judgment, such nuisance may be wholly abated." The court is empowered, as in other cases of contempt, to punish disobedience to a temporary or permanent injunction by fine of not more than $1000 or by imprisonment in the county jail for not more than twelve months.

Under this statute, clause (b), the county attorney of Hennepin County brought this action to enjoin the publication of what was described as a "malicious, scandalous and defamatory newspaper, magazine and periodical," known as "The Saturday Press," published by the defendants in the city of Minneapolis. . . .

Without attempting to summarize the contents of the voluminous exhibits attached to the complaint, we deem it sufficient to say that the articles charged in substance that a Jewish gangster was in control of gambling, bootlegging and racketeering in Minneapolis, and that law enforcing officers and agencies were not energetically performing their duties. Most of the charges were directed against the chief of police; he was charged with gross neglect of duty, illicit relations with gangsters, and with participation in graft. The county attorney was charged with knowing the existing conditions and with failure to take adequate measures to remedy them. The mayor was accused of inefficiency and dereliction. One member of the grand jury was stated to be in sympathy with the gangsters. A special grand jury and a special prosecutor was demanded to deal with the situation in general, and, in particular to investigate an attempt to assassinate one Guilford, one of the original defendants, who, it appears from the articles, was shot by gangsters after the first issue of the periodical had been published. There is no question but that the articles made serious accusations against the public officers named and others in connection with the prevalence of crimes and the failure to expose and punish them. . . .

[Upon complaint the state court ordered Near to show cause why a temporary injunction should not be issued, and forbade meanwhile further publication of the periodical. Near demurred on constitutional grounds. The district court certified the question of the constitutionality of the statute to the state supreme court which held it valid. Near then answered the complaint but presented no evidence and a permanent injunction was issued.]

From the judgment as thus affirmed, the defendant Near appeals to this Court.

This statute, for the suppression as a public nuisance of a newspaper or periodical, is unusual, if not unique, and raises questions of grave importance transcending the local interests involved in the particular action. It is no longer open to doubt that the liberty of the press, and of speech, is within the liberty safeguarded by the due process clause of the Fourteenth Amendment from invasion by state action. . . . In maintaining this guaranty, the authority of the state to enact laws to promote the health, safety, morals and general welfare of its people is necessarily admitted. The limits of this sovereign power must always be determined with appropriate regard to the particular subject of its exercise. . . . Liberty of speech, and of the press, is also not an absolute right, and the state may punish its abuse. . . . Liberty, in each of its phases, has its history and connotation and, in the present instance, the inquiry is as to the historic conception of the liberty of the press and whether the statute under review violates the essential attributes of that liberty. . . .

. . . it is enough to say that in passing upon constitutional questions the Court has regard to substance and not to mere matters of form, and that, in accordance with familiar principles, the statute must be tested by its operation and effect. . . . That operation and effect we think is clearly shown by the record in this case. We are not concerned with mere errors of the trial court, if there be such, in going beyond the direction of the statute as construed by the supreme court of the state. It is thus important to note precisely the purpose and effect of the statute as the state court has construed it.

First. The statute is not aimed at the redress of individual or private wrongs. Remedies for libel remain available and unaffected. The statute, said the state court, "is not directed at threatened libel but at an existing business which, generally speaking, involves more than libel." It is aimed at the distribution of scandalous matter as "detrimental to public morals and to the general welfare," tending "to disturb the peace of the community" and "to provoke assaults and the commission of crime." In order to obtain an injunction to suppress the future publication of the newspaper or periodical, it is not necessary to prove the falsity of the charges that have been made in the publication condemned. In the present action there was no allegation that the matter published was not true. It is alleged, and the statute requires the allegation, that the publication was "malicious." But, as in prosecutions for libel, there is no requirement of proof by the state of malice in fact as distinguished from malice inferred from the mere publication of the defamatory matter. The judgment in this case proceeded upon the mere proof of publication. The statute permits the defense, not of the truth alone, but only that the truth was published with good motives and for justifiable ends. It is apparent that under the statute the publication is to be regarded as defamatory if it injures reputation, and that it is scandalous if it circulates charges of reprehensible conduct, whether criminal or otherwise, and the publication is thus deemed to invite public reprobation and to constitute a public scandal. The court sharply defined the purpose of the statute, bringing out the precise point, in these words: "There is no constitutional right to publish a fact merely because it is true. It is a matter of common knowledge that prosecutions under the criminal libel statutes do not result in efficient repression or suppression of the evils of scandal. Men who are the victims of such assaults seldom resort to the courts. This is especially true if their sins are exposed and the only question relates to whether it was done with good motives and for justifiable ends. This law is not for the protection of the person attacked nor to punish the wrongdoer. It is for the protection of the public welfare."

Second. The statute is directed not simply at the circulation of scandalous and defamatory statements with regard to private citizens, but at the continued publication by newspapers and periodicals of charges against public officers of corruption, malfeasance in office, or serious neglect of duty. Such charges by their very nature create a public scandal. They are scandalous and defamatory within the meaning of the statute, which has its normal operation in relation to publications dealing prominently and chiefly with the alleged dereliction of public officers.

Third. The object of the statute is not punishment, in the ordinary sense, but suppression of the offending newspaper or periodical. The reason for the enactment, as the state court said, is that prosecutions to enforce penal statutes for libel do not result in "efficient repression or suppression of the evils of scandal." Describing the business of publication as a public nuisance, does not obscure the substance of the proceeding which the statute authorizes. It is the continued publication of scandalous and defamatory matter that constitutes the business and the declared nuisance. In the case of public officers, it is the reiteration of charges of official misconduct, and the fact that the newspaper or periodical is principally devoted to that purpose, that exposes it to suppression. In the present instance, the proof was that nine editions of the newspaper or periodical in question were published on successive dates, and that they were chiefly devoted to charges against public officers and in relation to the prevalence and protection of crime. In such a case, these officers are not left to their ordinary remedy in a suit for libel, or the authorities to a prosecution for criminal libel. Under this statute, a publisher of a newspaper or periodical, undertaking to conduct a campaign to expose and to censure official derelictions, and devoting his publication principally to that purpose, must face not simply the possibility of a verdict against him in a suit or prosecution for libel, but a determination that his newspaper or periodical is a public nuisance to be abated, and that this abatement and suppression will follow unless he is prepared with legal evidence to prove the truth of the charges and also to satisfy the court that, in addition to being true, the matter was published with good motives and for justifiable ends.

This suppression is accomplished by enjoining publication and that restraint is the object and effect of the statute.

Fourth. The statute not only operates to suppress the offending newspaper or periodical but to put the publisher under an effective censorship. When a newspaper or periodical is found to be "malicious, scandalous and defamatory," and is suppressed as such, resumption of publication is punishable as a contempt of court by fine or imprisonment. Thus, where a newspaper or periodical has been suppressed because of the circulation of charges against public officers of official misconduct, it would seem to be clear that the renewal of the publication of such charges would constitute a contempt and that the judgment would lay a permanent restraint upon the publisher, to escape which he must satisfy the court as to the character of a new publication. Whether he would be permitted again to publish matter deemed to be derogatory to the same or other public officers would depend upon the court's ruling. In the present instance the judgment restrained the defendants from "publishing, circulating, having in their possession, selling or giving away any publication whatsoever which is a malicious, scandalous or defamatory newspaper, as defined by law." The law gives no definition except that covered by the words "scandalous and defamatory," and publications charging official misconduct are of that class. While the court, answering the objection that the judgment was too broad, saw no reason for construing it as restraining the defendants "from operating a newspaper in harmony with the public welfare to which all must yield," and said that the defendants had not indicated "any desire to conduct their business in the usual and legitimate manner," the manifest inference is that, at least with respect to a new publication directed against official misconduct, the defendant would be held, under penalty of punishment for contempt as provided in the statute, to a manner of publication which the court considered to be "usual and legitimate" and consistent with the public welfare.

If we cut through mere details of procedure, the operation and effect of the statute in substance is that public authorities may bring the owner or publisher of a newspaper or periodical before a judge upon a charge of conducting a business of publishing scandalous and defamatory matter—in particular that the matter consists of charges against public officers of official dereliction—and unless the owner or publisher is able and disposed to bring competent evidence to satisfy the judge that the charges are true and are published with good motives and for justifiable ends, his newspaper or periodical is suppressed and further publication is made punishable as a contempt. This is of the essence of censorship.

The question is whether a statute authorizing such proceedings in restraint of publication is consistent with the conception of the liberty of the press as historically conceived and guaranteed. In determining the extent of the constitutional protection, it has been generally, if not universally, considered that it is the chief purpose of the guaranty to prevent previous restraints upon publication. The struggle in England, directed against the legislative power of the licenser, resulted in renunciation of the censorship of the press. The liberty deemed to be established was thus described by Blackstone: "The liberty of the press is indeed essential to the nature of a free state; but this consists in laying no *previous* restraints upon publications, and not in freedom from censure for criminal matter when published. Every freeman has an undoubted right to lay what sentiments he pleases before the public; to forbid this, is to destroy the freedom of the press; but if he publishes what is improper, mischievous or illegal, he must take the consequence of his own temerity." 4 Bl. Com. 151, 152; see Story on the Constitution, §§ 1884, 1889. . . .

The criticism upon Blackstone's statement has not been because immunity from previous restraint upon publication has not been regarded as deserving of special emphasis, but chiefly because that immunity cannot be deemed to exhaust the conception of the liberty guaranteed by state and federal constitutions. The point of criticism has been "that the mere exemption from previous restraints cannot be all that is secured by the constitutional provisions;" and that "the liberty of the press might be rendered a mockery and a delusion, and the phrase itself a by-word, if, while every man was at liberty to publish what he pleased, the public authorities might nevertheless punish him for harmless publications." 2 Cooley, Const. Lim., 8th ed., p. 885. But it is recognized that punishment for the abuse of the liberty accorded to the press is essential to the protection of the public, and that the common law rules that subject the libeler to responsibility for the public offense, as well as for the private injury, are not abolished by the protection extended in our constitutions. . . . In the present case, we have no occasion to inquire as to the permissible scope of subsequent punishment. For whatever wrong the appellant has committed or may commit, by his publications, the state appropriately affords both public and private redress by its libel laws. As has been noted, the statute in question does not deal with punishments; it provides for no punishment, except in case of contempt for violation of the court's order, but for suppression and injunction, that is, for restraint upon publication.

The objection has also been made that the principle as to immunity from previous restraint is stated too broadly, if ever such restraint is deemed to be prohibited. That is undoubtedly true; the protection even as to previous restraint is not absolutely unlimited. But the limitation has been recognized only in exceptional cases: "When a nation is at war many things that might be said in time of peace are such a hindrance to its effort that their utterance will not be endured so long as men fight and that no court could regard them as protected by any constitutional right." Schenck v. United States, 249 U. S. 47, 52. . . .

The exceptional nature of its limitations places in a strong light the general conception that liberty of the press, historically considered and taken up by the federal Constitution, has meant, principally although not exclusively, immunity from previous restraints or censorship. The conception of the liberty of the press in this country had broadened with the exigencies of the colonial period and with the efforts to secure freedom from oppressive administration. That liberty was especially cherished for the immunity it afforded from previous restraint of the publication of censure of public officers and charges of official misconduct. . . .

The importance of this immunity has not lessened. While reckless assaults upon public men, and efforts to bring obloquy upon those who are endeavoring faithfully to discharge official duties, exert a baleful influence and deserve the severest condemnation in public opinion, it cannot be said that this abuse is greater, and it is believed to be less, than that which characterized the period in which our institutions took shape. Meanwhile, the administration of government has become more complex, the opportunities for malfeasance and corruption have multiplied, crime has grown to most serious proportions, and the danger of its protection by unfaithful officials and of the impairment of the fundamental security of life and property by criminal alliances and official neglect, emphasizes the primary need of a vigilant and courageous press, especially in great cities. The fact that the liberty of the press may be abused by miscreant purveyors of scandal does not make any the less necessary the immunity of the press from previous restraint in dealing with official misconduct. Subsequent punishment for such abuses as may exist is the appropriate remedy, consistent with constitutional privilege. . . .

The statute in question cannot be justified by reason of the fact that the publisher is permitted to show, before injunction issues, that the matter published is true and is published with good motives and for justifiable ends. If such a statute, authorizing suppression and injunction on such a basis, is constitutionally valid, it would be equally permissible for the legislature to provide that at any time the publisher of any newspaper could be brought before a court, or even an administrative officer (as the constitutional protection may not be regarded as resting on mere procedural details) and required to produce proof of the truth of his publication, or of what he intended to publish, and of his motives, or stand enjoined. If this can be done, the legislature may provide machinery for determining in the complete exercise of its discretion what are justifiable ends and restrain publication accordingly. And it would be but a step to a complete system of censorship. The recognition of authority to impose previous restraint upon publication in order to protect the community against the circulation of charges of misconduct, and especially of official misconduct, necessarily would carry with it the admission of the authority of the censor against which the constitutional barrier was erected. The preliminary freedom, by virtue of the very reason for its existence, does not depend, as this Court has said, on proof of truth. . . .

Equally unavailing is the insistence that the statute is designed to prevent the circulation of scandal which tends to disturb the public peace and to provoke assaults and the commission of crime. Charges of reprehensible conduct, and in particular of official malfeasance, unquestionably create a public scandal, but the theory of the constitutional guaranty is that even a more serious public evil would be caused by authority to prevent publication. . . . There is nothing new in the fact that charges of reprehensible conduct may create resentment and the disposition to resort to violent means of redress, but this well-understood tendency did not alter the determination to protect the press against censorship and restraint upon publication. . . . The danger of violent reactions becomes greater with effective organization of defiant groups resenting exposure, and if this consideration warranted legislative interference with the initial freedom of publication, the constitutional protection would be reduced to a mere form of words.

For these reasons we hold the statute, so far as it authorized the proceedings in this action under clause (b) of section one, to be an infringement of the liberty of the press guaranteed by the Fourteenth Amendment. We should add that this decision rests upon the operation and effect of the statute, without regard to the question of the truth of the charges contained in the particular periodical. The fact that the public officers named in this case, and those associated with the charges of official dereliction, may be deemed to be impeccable, cannot affect the conclusion that the statute imposes an unconstitutional restraint upon publication.

Judgment reversed.

Mr. Justice Butler dissented in an opinion in which Justices Van Devanter, McReynolds, and Sutherland concurred.

THOMAS v. COLLINS
323 U. S. 516; 89 L. Ed. 430; 65 Sup. Ct. 315. 1944.

Freedom of speech and press are not absolute rights. Restrictions upon public speeches and publications are necessary for the protection of the public safety and welfare. As Mr. Justice Holmes put it in the Schenck case mentioned below, "The most stringent protection of free speech would not protect a man in falsely shouting fire in a theatre and causing a panic." Free speech and press cases present to the courts difficult questions of degree, questions involving the balancing of the public and private interests. Are there standards or rules to guide the courts in striking this balance? The Supreme Court has evolved two such rules, one known as the "clear and present danger" test, the other as the "bad tendency" test.

The "clear and present danger" test was first stated by Mr. Justice Holmes in Schenck v. United States, 249 U. S. 47 (1919). Schenck was charged with circulating pamphlets urging resistance to the draft. He claimed he was merely exercising his constitutionally protected freedom of press. Admittedly Congress could punish obstruction of the draft. The Court applied to Schenck's pamphlets the test as to whether their circulation created a "clear and present danger" of obstruction of the draft, and found, in view of the facts, that it did. Schenck was punished, however, because his pamphlets were really dangerous; incendiary bombast, if futile and innocuous, remained innocent.

The "bad tendency" test was applied in Gitlow v. New York, 268 U. S. 652 (1925), elsewhere noted (p. 157). The New York Criminal Anarchy Act of 1902 forbade persons by speech or publication to advocate the overthrow of organized government by violence. Gitlow circulated Communist literature which, in lurid and fervent language, urged the workers of the country to engage in revolutionary mass action to bring about "a revolutionary dictatorship of the proletariat." He was convicted under the statute. There was no evidence that the circulation of his literature produced any results. It obviously created no "clear and present danger" of the overthrow of government. The Court pointed out, however, that the statute did not forbid merely the overthrow of government, but the "advocacy" of such overthrow. Under its police power the state may validly forbid speeches and publications which have a "tendency" to produce results dangerous to the public security, even though the speeches and publications themselves create no clear and present danger. The state need not wait for the danger to arise. The "bad tendency" test, while never repudiated by the Court, has not been applied in any case since Gitlow v. New York.

The vitality of the "clear and present danger" test of freedom of speech and press was shown by the Court's use of it in Herndon v. Lowry, 301 U. S. 242 (1937). A Negro organizer for the Communist party was sentenced by a Georgia court to twenty years in prison for violating a pre-Civil War statute forbidding "incitement to insurrection by violence." He was shown to have held three meetings, and to have had in his room when arrested some Communistic literature. The only printed matter, however, which he distributed were pamphlets urging unemployment and emergency relief. The Court held that none of Herndon's activities constituted any "clear and present danger" of incitement to insurrection or any other threat to the public security, and that therefore to punish him for holding meetings, making speeches, and distributing literature deprived him of his liberty without due process of law.

In Terminiello v. City of Chicago, 337 U. S. 1 (1949), the Court set aside the conviction for breach of the peace of a member of the Union of Christian Crusaders who had made an inflammatory racial speech in a crowded auditorium in which the police were unable to keep order, and outside which an angry and turbulent crowd of more than a thousand were protesting against the speech. By "clear and present danger," said the Court, is meant something more than public inconvenience, annoyance, or unrest. One of the functions of free speech is to invite dispute, and it may not be punished merely because it stirs people to anger and creates a condition of unrest.

In Bridges v. California, 314 U. S. 252 (1941), the issue of freedom of press arose in a new form. While a motion for a new trial was pending in a case involving a dispute between an A.F. of L. union and a C.I.O. union of which Harry Bridges was an officer, Bridges sent to the Secretary of Labor, and also released to the press, a telegram which described the judge's decision as "outrageous," and further stated: "Attempted enforcement of . . . decision will tie up port of Los Angeles and involve entire Pacific Coast. . . . [C.I.O. union] does not intend to allow state courts to override the majority vote of members in choosing its officers and representatives and to override the National Labor Relations Board." Bridges was cited for contempt of court on the ground that this telegram was an attempt to interfere by threats with the fair and orderly administration of justice. The Court reversed the contempt, holding there was no clear and present danger of influencing the court, since the telegram told the judge nothing he did not already know.

In New York Times v. Sullivan, 376 U. S. 254 (1964), new breadth was added to the right of public criticism. Following demonstrations in Montgomery, Alabama, the Times carried an advertisement describing mistreatment of Negroes by the police, whose commissioner promptly sued the Times for libel. A jury awarded him $500,000 damages. The Supreme Court reversed the judgment, holding that to constitute libel of a public official, a statement must be made with " 'actual malice'—that is, with a knowledge that it was false or with reckless disregard of whether it was false or not." Such malice must be proved in court, not merely presumed to exist, and the facts in this case did not support a finding of malice.

Later decisions make it clear that freedom of speech and freedom of press are not confined to the realm of political or intellectual discussion. If properly used they are legitimate and protected weapons in economic conflicts. Thus in Thornhill v. Alabama, 310 U. S. 88 (1940), the Supreme

Court held invalid a state statute so broadly drawn as to forbid any and all picketing by representatives of labor. Thornhill and others had engaged in picketing, but had resorted to no violence, disorder, or coercion. The Court said that "the dissemination of information concerning the facts of a labor dispute must be regarded as within that area of free discussion that is guaranteed by the Constitution," and peaceful and orderly picketing is merely a means of exercising one's right of free speech and free press. The same result was reached in Carlson v. California, 310 U. S. 106 (1940), as to a statute which forbade the public display of banners and placards in aid of picketing in a labor dispute. The Court made it clear, however, in these cases and in a number of later cases that this new doctrine gives no protection to picketing which is accompanied by violence or intimidation.

A number of states have sought by various statutory methods to curb the activities of labor unions and labor union organizers. Such a statute was the one passed in Texas and attacked on constitutional grounds in Thomas v. Collins, printed below. This act required every labor union organizer operating in the state to secure from the secretary of state an organizer's card before soliciting any members for his union. In order to get the card he had to give his name, his union affiliations, and show his credentials. The secretary of state had no discretion to refuse to register such an organizer if he met these requirements. When registered he was given a card which he was required to carry with him and show to any person whom he solicited for membership. R. J. Thomas, president of the United Automobile Workers, went to Texas after the passage of this act for the express purpose of contesting its validity. He announced his intention to address a labor union meeting, and this plan was widely advertised in advance. He did not apply for registration as a labor organizer as required by the statute. He addressed a meeting of union men and he specifically invited any non-union persons present to join the union. Prior to the meeting, a restraining order was served on Thomas, forbidding him to address the meeting in the capacity of an organizer since he had not registered, and he was later cited for contempt for a deliberate and wilful violation of the order.

One point in the opinion printed here merits special attention. This is the Court's insistence at the beginning of its discussion that the usual presumption in favor of the constitutionality of a law did not prevail in the case of a statute which appears to invade freedom of speech or press. This is an important exception to the principle which had governed the judicial review of the validity of legislation for more than a hundred years. Back in 1827, Mr. Justice Washington, in Ogden v. Saunders, 12 Wheaton (U. S.) 213, declared: "It is but a decent respect due to the wisdom, integrity, and patriotism of the legislative body, by which any law is passed, to presume in favor of its validity, until its violation of the Constitution is proved beyond all reasonable doubt." Mr. Justice Holmes spent his judicial lifetime insisting that if there was reasonable doubt about the validity of a statute the Court should hold it constitutional. In the present case, however, the Supreme Court stated that when a statute appears on its face to invade the basic liberties of the First Amendment the presumption is against the validity of the law, and the burden of proof will rest upon those who defend it to show that it is justified by some "clear and present danger" to the public security. Thus the rights protected by the First Amendment were given preferred status in our scheme of constitutional values. Justices Murphy and Rutledge were the chief spokesmen for this doctrine of the preferred status of First Amendment rights. Justice Frankfurter always believed it to be unsound. It is doubtful if the doctrine could command a majority of the present Court.

Mr. Justice Rutledge delivered the opinion of the Court, saying in part (beginning with section II):

The Supreme Court of Texas . . . sustained the act as a valid exercise of the state's police power, taken "for the protection of the general welfare of the public, and particularly the laboring class," with special reference to safeguarding laborers from imposture when approached by an alleged organizer. The provision, it was said, "affects only the right of one to engage in the business as a paid organizer, and not the mere right of an individual to express his views on the merits of the union.". . .

The court conceded however that the act "interferes to a certain extent with the right of the organizer to speak as the paid representative of the union." Nevertheless, it said, "such interferences are not necessarily prohibited by the Constitution. The state under its police power may enact laws which interfere indirectly and to a limited extent with the right of speech or the liberty of the people where they are reasonably necessary for the protection of the general public." Accordingly, it likened the instant prohibition to various other ones imposed by state or federal legislation upon "the right of one to operate or speak as the agent of another," including securities salesmen, insurance agents, real estate brokers, etc. And various decisions of this Court and others were thought to support the conclusion that the act "imposes no previous general restraint upon the right of free speech. . . . It merely requires paid organizers to register with the secretary of state before beginning to operate as such.". . .

Texas, on the other hand, asserts no issue of free speech or free assembly is presented. With the state court, it says the statute is directed at business practices, like selling insurance, dealing in securities, acting as commission merchant, pawnbroking, etc., and was adopted "in recognition of the fact that something more is done by a labor organizer than talking.". . .

The case confronts us again with the duty our system places on this Court to say where the individual's freedom ends and the state's power begins. Choice on that border, now as always delicate, is perhaps more so where the usual presumption supporting legislation is balanced by the preferred place given in our scheme to the great, the indispensable democratic freedoms secured by the First Amendment. That priority gives these liberties a sanctity and a sanction not permitting dubious intrusions. And it is the character of the right, not of the limitation, which determines what standard governs the choice.

For these reasons any attempt to restrict those liberties must be justified by clear public interest, threatened not doubtfully or remotely, but by clear and present danger. The rational connection between the remedy provided and the evil to be curbed, which in other contexts might support legislation against attack on due process grounds, will not suffice. These rights rest on firmer foundations. Accordingly, whatever occasion would restrain orderly discussion and persuasion, at appropriate time and place, must have clear support in public danger, actual or impending. Only the gravest abuses, endangering paramount interests, give occasion for permissible limitation. It is therefore in our tradition to allow the widest room for discussion, the narrowest range for its restriction, particularly when this right is exercised in conjunction with peaceable assembly. It was not by accident or coincidence that the rights to freedom in speech and press were coupled in a single guaranty with the rights of the people peaceably to assemble and to petition for redress of grievances. All these, though not identical, are inseparable. They are cognate rights, and therefore are united in the First Article's assurance.

This conjunction of liberties is not peculiar to religious activity and institutions alone. The First Amendment gives freedom of mind the same security as freedom of conscience. Great secular causes, with small ones, are guarded. The grievances for redress of which the right of petition was insured, and with it the right of assembly, are not solely religious or political ones. And the rights of free speech and a free press are not confined to any field of human interest.

The idea is not sound therefore that the First Amendment's safeguards are wholly inapplicable to business or economic activity. And it does not resolve where the line shall be drawn in a particular case merely to urge, as Texas does, that an organization for which the rights of free speech and free assembly are claimed is one "engaged in business activities" or that the individual who leads it in exercising these rights receives compensation for doing so. Nor, on the other hand, is the answer given, whether what is done is an exercise of those rights and the restriction a forbidden impairment, by ignoring the organization's economic function, because those interests of workingmen are involved or because they have the general liberties of the citizen, as appellant would do.

These comparisons are at once too simple, too general, and too inaccurate to be determinative. Where the line shall be placed in a particular application rests, not on such generalities, but on the concrete clash of particular interests and the community's relative evaluation both of them and of how the one will be affected by the specific restriction, the other by its absence. That judgment in the first instance is for the legislative body. But in our system where the line can constitutionally be placed presents a question this Court cannot escape answering independently, whatever the legislative judgment, in the light of our constitutional tradition. And the answer, under that tradition, can be affirmative, to support an intrusion upon this domain, only if grave and impending public danger requires this.

That the state has power to regulate labor unions with a view to protecting the public interest is, as the Texas court said, hardly to be doubted. They cannot claim special immunity from regulation. Such regulation however, whether aimed at fraud or other abuses, must not trespass upon the domain set apart for free speech and free assembly. This Court has recognized that "in the circumstances of our times the dissemination of information concerning the facts of a labor dispute must be regarded as within that area of free discussion that is guaranteed by the Constitution. . . . Free discussion concerning the conditions in industry and the causes of labor disputes appears to us indispensable to the effective and intelligent use of the processes of popular government to shape the destiny of modern industrial society." Thornhill v. Alabama, 310 U. S. 88. The right thus to discuss, and inform people concerning, the advantages and disadvantages of unions and joining them is protected not only as part of free speech, but as part of free assembly. The Texas court, in its disposition of the cause, did not give sufficient weight to this consideration, more particularly by its failure to take account of the blanketing effect of the prohibition's present application upon public discussion and also of the bearing of the clear and present danger test in these circumstances. . . .

Thomas went to Texas for one purpose and one only—to make the speech in question. Its whole object was publicly to proclaim the advantages of workers' organization and to persuade workmen to join Local No. 1002 as part of a campaign for members. These also were the sole objects of the meeting. The campaign, and the meeting, were incidents of an impending election for collective bargaining agent, previously ordered by national authority pursuant to the guaranties of national law. Those guaranties include the workers' right to organize freely for collective bargaining. And this comprehends whatever may be appropriate and lawful to accomplish and maintain such organization. It included, in this case, the right to designate Local No. 1002 or any other union or agency as the employees' representative. It included their right fully and freely to discuss and be informed concerning this choice, privately or in public assembly. Necessarily correlative was the right of the union, its members and officials, whether residents or nonresidents of Texas and, if the latter, whether there for a single occasion or sojourning longer, to discuss with and inform the employees concerning matters involved in their choice. These rights of assembly and discussion are protected by the First Amendment. Whatever would restrict them, without sufficient occasion, would infringe its safeguards. The occasion was clearly protected. The speech was an essential part of the occasion, unless all meaning and purpose were to be taken from it. And the invitations, both general and particular, were parts of the speech, inseparable incidents of the occasion and of all that was said or done.

That there was restriction upon Thomas' right to speak and the rights of the workers to hear what he had to say, there can be no doubt. The threat of the restraining order, backed by the power of contempt, and of arrest for crime, hung over every word. A speaker in such circumstances could avoid the words "solicit," "invite," "join." It would be impossible to avoid the idea. The statute requires no specific formula. It is not contended that only the use of the word "solicit" would violate the prohibition. Without such a limitation, the statute forbids any language which conveys, or reasonably could be found to convey, the meaning of invitation. That Thomas chose to meet the issue squarely, not to hide in ambiguous phrasing, does not counteract this fact. General words create different and often particular impressions on different minds. No speaker, however careful, can convey exactly his meaning, or the same meaning, to the different members of an audience. How one might "laud unionism," as the state and the state supreme court concede Thomas was free to do, yet in these circumstances not imply an invitation, is hard to conceive. This is the nub of the case, which the state fails to meet because it cannot do so. Workingmen do not lack capacity for making rational connections. They would understand, or some would, that the president of U.A.W. and vice president of C.I.O., addressing an organization meeting, was not urging merely a philosophic attachment to abstract principles of unionism, disconnected from the business immediately at hand. The feat would be incredible for a national leader, addressing such a meeting, lauding unions and their principles, urging adherence to union philosophy, not also and thereby to suggest attachment to the union by becoming a member.

Furthermore, whether words intended and designed to fall short of invitation would miss that mark is a question both of intent and of effect. No speaker, in such circumstances, safely could assume that anything he might say upon the general subject would not be understood by some as an invitation. In short, the supposedly clearcut distinction between discussion, laudation, general advocacy, and solicitation puts the speaker in these circumstances wholly at the mercy of the varied understanding of his hearers and consequently of whatever inference may be drawn as to his intent and meaning.

Such a distinction offers no security for free discussion. In these conditions it blankets with uncertainty whatever may be said. It compels the speaker to hedge and trim. He must take care in every word to create no impression that he means, in advocating unionism's most central principle, namely, that workingmen should unite for collective bargaining, to urge those present to do so. The vice is not merely that invitation; in the circumstances shown here, is speech. It is also that its prohibition forbids or restrains discussion which is not or may not be invitation. The sharp line cannot be drawn surely or securely. The effort to observe it could not be free speech, free press, or free assembly, in any sense of free advocacy of principle or cause. The restriction's effect, as applied, in a very practical sense was to prohibit Thomas not only to solicit members and memberships, but also to speak in advocacy of the cause of trade unionism in Texas, without having first procured the card. Thomas knew this and faced the alternatives it presented. When served with the order he had three choices: (1) to stand on his right and speak freely; (2) to quit, refusing entirely to speak; (3) to trim, and even thus to risk the penalty. He chose the first alternative. We think he was within his rights in doing so.

The assembly was entirely peaceable, and had no other than a wholly lawful purpose. The statements forbidden were not in themselves unlawful, had no tendency to incite to unlawful action, involved no element of clear and present, grave and immediate danger to the public welfare. Moreover, the state has shown no justification for placing restrictions on the use of the word "solicit." We have here nothing comparable to the case where use of the word "fire" in a crowded theater creates a clear and present danger which the state may undertake to avoid or against which it may protect. Schenck v. United States, 249 U. S. 47. We cannot say that "solicit" in this setting is such a dangerous word. So far as free speech alone is concerned, there can be no ban or restriction or burden placed on the use of such a word except on showing of exceptional circumstances where the public safety, morality or health is involved or some other substantial interest of the community is at stake.

If therefore use of the word or language equivalent in meaning was illegal here, it was so only because the statute and the order forbade the particular speaker to utter it. When legislation or its application can confine labor leaders on such occasions to innocuous and abstract discussion of the virtues of trade unions and so becloud even this with doubt, uncertainty and the risk of penalty, freedom of speech for them will be at an end. A restriction so destructive of the right of public discussion, without greater or more imminent danger to the public interest than existed in this case, is incompatible with the freedoms secured by the First Amendment. . . .

Apart from its "business practice" theory, the state contends that Section 5 is not inconsistent with freedom of speech and assembly, since this is merely a previous identification requirement which, according to the state court's decision, gives the secretary of state only "ministerial, not discretionary" authority.

How far the state can require previous identification by one who undertakes to exercise the rights secured by the First Amendment has been largely undetermined. . . .

As a matter of principle a requirement of registration in order to make a public speech would seem generally incompatible with an exercise of the rights of free speech and free assembly. Lawful public assemblies, involving no element of grave and immediate danger to an interest the state is entitled to protect, are not instruments of harm which require previous identification of the speakers. And the right either of workmen or of unions under these conditions to assemble and discuss their own affairs is as fully protected by the Constitution as the right of businessmen, farmers, educators, political party members or others to assemble and discuss their affairs and to enlist the support of others.

We think the controlling principle is stated in De Jonge v. Oregon, 299 U. S. 353. In that case this Court held that "consistently with the federal Constitution, peaceable assembly for lawful discussion cannot be made a crime.". . .

If the exercise of the rights of free speech and free assembly cannot be made a crime, we do not think this can be accomplished by the device of requiring previous registration as a condition for exercising them and making such a condition the foundation for restraining in advance their exercise and for imposing a penalty for violating such a restraining order. So long as no more is involved than exercise of the rights of free speech and free assembly, it is immune to such a restriction. If one who solicits support for the cause of labor may be required to register as a condition to the exercise of his right to make a public speech, so may he who seeks to rally support for any social, business, religious or political cause. We think a requirement that one must register before he undertakes to make a public speech to enlist support for a lawful movement is quite incompatible with the requirements of the First Amendment.

Once the speaker goes further, however, and engages in conduct which amounts to more than the right of free discussion comprehends, as when he undertakes the collection of funds or securing subscriptions, he enters a realm where a reasonable registration or identification requirement may be imposed. In that context such solicitation would be quite different from the solicitation involved here. . . .

As we think the requirement of registration, in the present circumstances, was in itself an invalid restriction, we have no occasion to consider whether the restraint as imposed goes beyond merely requiring previous identification or registration. . . .

The restraint is not small when it is considered what was restrained. The right is a national right, federally guaranteed. There is some modicum of freedom of thought, speech and assembly which all citizens of the Republic may exercise throughout its length and breadth, which no state, nor all together, nor the nation, itself, can prohibit, restrain or impede. If the restraint were smaller than it is, it is from petty tyrannies that large ones take root and grow. This fact can be no more plain than when they are imposed on the most basic rights of all. Seedlings planted in that soil grow great, and growing, break down the foundations of liberty. . . .

The judgment is reversed.

Mr. Justice Roberts dissented in an opinion in which Mr. Chief Justice Stone and Justices Reed and Frankfurter concurred.

BURSTYN v. WILSON
343 U. S. 495; 96 L. Ed. 1098; 72 Sup. Ct. 777. 1952.

Recent cases dealing with the censorship of motion pictures sharply illustrate the way in which law adjusts itself to the advance of mechanical and scientific progress in modern society. There was little in the "nickelodeon" of the early 1900's to suggest the modern motion picture palace with its dramatic productions and its documentary films. No one who can remember a motion picture as early as 1915, portraying mainly highway robberies, slapstick comedy, and bathing beauties, could quarrel with the Supreme Court's decision of that year (Mutual Film case, discussed in the opinion below) that these pictures did not form part of "the press of the country" or constitute "organs of public opinion." As the Court put it, "The judicial sense supporting the common sense of the country is against the contention." Motion pictures   e just shows, like a drama or a circus, and the censorship of them raised no question of the freedom of the press. Under the protection of this ruling, state and local censorship boards sprang up all over the country with power to forbid the showing of any film until it had been approved and licensed.

The constitutionality of motion picture censorship was attacked in the present case, which involved the highly controversial Italian film "The Miracle." The picture is built up around the final birth of a child to a poor, simple-minded girl, who while tending goats on a mountainside is seduced by a bearded stranger. The girl, in her religious ecstasy, believes the man to be her favorite saint. The film was licensed and shown in New York City. Bitter attacks upon it immediately ensued. The Vatican had condemned the film, and Catholic prelates in this country denounced it as blasphemous and sacrilegious. It had, however, important and respected defenders. The New York Board of Regents, who have the authority to censor motion pictures, reconsidered the film and withdrew its license on the ground that it was "sacrilegious" within the meaning of the New York censorship statute. The New York courts held that the statute was valid and that the Regents had acted within the proper range of their discretion under it.

Three points stand out in the unanimous opinion of the Supreme Court in the present case. First, the Court ruled that motion pictures are part of the press and are, as such, entitled to the protection of the First and Fourteenth Amendments. The conflicting statement in the Mutual Film case is overruled. Second, the Court held that due process was denied by the prior censorship of a film for the purpose of determining whether or not it was sacrilegious. It left open the question whether similar censorship could validly be employed to ban obscenity. In his concurring opinion, Mr. Justice Frankfurter held that the standard of censorship—sacrilege—denied due process because of vagueness. He lists in an appendix thirty-four English dictionaries published during the 17th and 18 centuries, upon which modern American dictionaries have depended, and gives their highly varied definitions of the words "sacrilege" and "blasphemy." Those definitions which are not too narrow to be applicable to the present case are so vague as to have no sharp edges.

Third, the Court did not rule out the possibility of the valid prior censorship of motion pictures, provided sufficiently definite standards can be drawn so that reasonable people can know what the law forbids. Such censorship is not precluded by Near v. Minnesota, for the opinion in that case states "the protection [of the press] even as to previous restraint is not absolutely unlimited."

The years following Burstyn saw the Court strike down, without opinion, a number of attempts at movie censorship, and in Kingsley Corp. v. Regents of the University of New York, 360 U. S. 684 (1959), it unanimously held void the ban on "Lady Chatterley's Lover" on the ground that the First Amendment "is not confined to the expression of ideas that are conventional or shared by a majority. It protects advocacy of the opinion that adultery may sometimes be proper, no less than advocacy of socialism or the single tax." But while the Court systematically invalidated the censorship brought before it, it would not say that all censorship was forbidden by the First Amendment. In Times Film Corp. v. Chicago, 365 U. S. 43 (1961), it refused to hold void on its face an ordinance requiring prior censorship of all films. The producer argued that *all* censorship was void and refused to submit the film, so the validity of the standards was not involved. Then, in Freedman v. Maryland, 380 U. S. 51 (1965), without actually overruling Times Film, the Court held that a film need not be submitted to censors where their procedure failed to protect First Amendment rights. Noting that any scheme of prior restraint carries a heavy presumption against its validity, the Court held that a decision to censor could not be enforced unless it was immediately reviewed and affirmed in a court of law. The Maryland machinery, like that in other states, forced the exhibitor to appeal from an adverse decision and withheld the license while he did so. Obscene material is that which "taken as a whole appeals to prurient interests" (Roth v. United States, 354 U. S. 476 (1957)), is "'utterly' without social importance" (Jacobellis v. Ohio, 378 U. S. 184 (1964)), or, in borderline cases, is so advertised as to pander to "the wide-spread weakness for titillation by pornography" (Ginsburg v. United States, 383 U. S. 463 (1966)).

Mr. Justice Clark delivered the opinion of the Court, saying in part:

The issue here is the constitutionality, under the First and Fourteenth Amendments, of a New York statute which permits the banning of motion picture films on the ground that they are "sacrilegious." That statute makes it unlawful "to exhibit, or to sell, lease or lend for exhibition at any place of amusement for pay or in connection with any business in the state of New York, any motion picture film or reel [with specified exceptions not relevant here], unless there is at the time in full force and effect a valid license or permit therefor of the education department. . . ." The statute further provides:

"The director of the [motion picture] division [of the education department] or, when authorized by the regents, the officers of a local office or bureau shall cause to be promptly examined every motion picture film submitted to them as herein required, and unless such film or a part thereof is obscene, indecent, immoral, inhuman, sacrilegious, or is of such a character that its exhibition would tend to corrupt morals or incite to crime, shall issue a license therefor. . . ."

As we view the case, we need consider only appellant's contention that the New York statute is an unconstitutional abridgment of free speech and a free press. In Mutual Film Corp. v. Industrial Comm. of Ohio, 1915, 236 U. S. 230, a distributor of motion pictures sought to enjoin the enforcement of an Ohio statute which required the prior approval of a board of censors before any motion picture could be publicly exhibited in the state, and which directed the board to approve only such films as it adjudged to be "of a moral, educational, or amusing and harmless character." The statute was assailed in part as an unconstitutional abridgment of the freedom of the press guaranteed by the First and Fourteenth Amendments. The District Court rejected this contention, stating that the first eight Amendments were not a restriction on state action. . . . On appeal to this Court, plaintiff in its brief abandoned this claim and contended merely that the statute in question violated the freedom of speech and publication guaranteed by the Constitution of Ohio. In affirming the decree of the District Court denying injunctive relief, this Court stated:

"It cannot be put out of view that the exhibition of moving pictures is a business, pure and simple, originated and conducted for profit, like other spectacles, not to be regarded, nor intended to be regarded by the Ohio Constitution, we think, as part of the press of the country, or as organs of public opinion.". . .

It cannot be doubted that motion pictures are a significant medium for the communication of ideas. They may affect public attitudes and behavior in a variety of ways, ranging from direct espousal of a political or social doctrine to the subtle shaping of thought which characterizes all artistic expression. The importance of motion pictures as an organ of public opinion is not lessened by the fact that they are designed to entertain as well as to inform. . . .

It is urged that motion pictures do not fall within the First Amendment's aegis because their production, distribution, and exhibition is a large-scale business conducted for private profit. We cannot agree. That books, newspapers, and magazines are published and sold for profit does not prevent them from being a form of expression whose liberty is safeguarded by the First Amendment. We fail to see why operation for profit should have any different effect in the case of motion pictures.

It is further urged that motion pictures possess a greater capacity for evil, particularly among the youth of a community, than other modes of expression. Even if one were to accept this hypothesis, it does not follow that motion pictures should be disqualified from First Amendment protection. If there be capacity for evil it may be relevant in determining the permissible scope of community control, but it does not authorize substantially unbridled censorship such as we have here.

For the foregoing reasons, we conclude that expression by means of motion pictures is included within the free speech and free press guaranty of the First and Fourteenth Amendments. To the extent that language in the opinion in Mutual Film Corp. v. Industrial Comm., supra, is out of harmony with the views here set forth, we no longer adhere to it.

To hold that liberty of expression by means of motion pictures is guaranteed by the First and Fourteenth Amendments, however, is not the end of our problem. It does not follow that the Constitution requires absolute freedom to exhibit every motion picture of every kind at all times and all places. That much is evident from the series of decisions of this Court with respect to other media of communication of ideas. Nor does it follow that motion pictures are necessarily subject to the precise rules governing any other particular method of expression. Each method tends to present its own peculiar problems. But the basic principles of freedom of speech and the press, like the First Amendment's command, do not vary. Those principles, as they have frequently been enunciated by this Court, make freedom of expression the rule. There is no justification in this case for making an exception to that rule.

The statute involved here does not seek to punish, as a past offense, speech or writing falling within the permissible scope of subsequent punishment. On the contrary, New York requires that permission to communicate ideas be obtained in advance from state officials who judge the content of the words and pictures sought to be communicated. This Court recognized many years ago that such a previous restraint is a form of infringement upon freedom of expression to be especially condemned. Near v. State of Minnesota ex rel. Olson, 1931, 283 U. S. 697. The Court there recounted the history which indicates that a major purpose of the First Amendment guaranty of a free press was to prevent prior restraints upon publication, although it was carefully pointed out that the liberty of the press is not limited to that protection. It was further stated that "the protection even as to previous restraint is not absolutely unlimited. But the limitation has been recognized only in exceptional cases.". . . In the light of the First Amendment's history and of the Near decision, the State has a heavy burden to demonstrate that the limitation challenged here presents such an exceptional case.

New York's highest court says there is "nothing mysterious" about the statutory provision applied in this case: "It is simply this: that no religion, as that word is understood by the ordinary, reasonable person, shall be treated with contempt, mockery, scorn and ridicule. . . ." This is far from the kind of narrow exception to freedom of expression which a state may carve out to satisfy the adverse demands of other interests of society. In seeking to apply the broad and all-inclusive definition of "sacrilegious" given by the New York courts, the censor is set adrift upon a boundless sea amid a myriad of conflicting currents of religious views, with no charts but those provided by the most vocal and powerful orthodoxies. New York cannot vest such unlimited restraining control over motion pictures in a censor. . . . Under such a standard the most careful and tolerant censor would find it virtually impossible to avoid favoring one religion over another, and he would be subject to an inevitable tendency to ban the expression of unpopular sentiments sacred to a religious minority. Application of the "sacrilegious" test, in these or other respects, might raise substantial questions under the First Amendment's guaranty of separate church and state with freedom of worship for all. However, from the standpoint of freedom of speech and the press, it is enough to point out that the state has no legitimate interest in protecting any or all religions from views distasteful to them which is sufficient to justify prior restraints upon the expression of those views. It is not the business of government in our nation to suppress real or imagined attacks upon a particular religious doctrine, whether they appear in publications, speeches, or motion pictures.

Since the term "sacrilegious" is the sole standard under attack here, it is not necessary for us to decide, for example, whether a state may censor motion pictures under a clearly-drawn statute designed and applied to prevent the showing of obscene films. That is a very different question from the one now before us. We hold only that under the First and Fourteenth Amendments a state may not ban a film on the basis of a censor's conclusion that it is "sacrilegious."

Reversed.

ENGEL v. VITALE
370 U. S. 421; 8 L. Ed. 2d 601; 82 Sup. Ct. 1261. 1962.

In its first one hundred and fifty years the Supreme Court decided but one important case which dealt with freedom of religion. In 1878 the case of Reynolds v. United States, 98 U. S. 145, reached the unavoidable conclusion that the religious liberty protected by the First Amendment does not include the right to commit immoral or criminal acts even though these are sanctioned by religious doctrine. Thus Reynolds, a Mormon in the Territory of Utah, was held properly convicted of the crime of polygamy in spite of the fact that the Mormon religion held polygamy to be proper and desirable. Supreme Court cases involving religious liberty were rare because the First Amendment, which protects freedom of religion, applied only to Congress and not to the states. See Barron v. Baltimore (p. 74). Congress had little opportunity and less inclination to violate the First Amendment, and what the states did by way of dealing with religious matters was their own business so far as the federal Constitution was concerned.

By the 1930's this situation began to change, and the Supreme Court has long held that freedom of religion in the First Amendment, like freedom of speech and press, is part of the liberty which the due process clause of the Fourteenth Amendment forbids the states to abridge. The first case decided on this theory was Hamilton v. Regents of University of California, 293 U. S. 245 (1934), which held that a student with religious scruples against bearing arms could be compelled, under penalty of expulsion from the university, to take military drill. The alleged invasion of his religious liberty did not deny him due process of law, since he was not compelled to attend the university and could assert no constitutional right to do so without complying with the state's requirement of military training.

In the early 1930's a religious group called Jehovah's Witnesses began a militant, nation-wide campaign to spread their religious tenets, which include virulent condemnation of all organized religions and churches, especially the Roman Catholic Church. They spread their teachings by personal appeals, by the sale or giving away of literature, and by going from house to house asking permission to play phonograph records, one of which, called "Enemies," is a bitter attack on religious organizations. Community resentment against the Witnesses and their methods was often intense; it expressed itself in a variety of legal measures designed to discourage the Witnesses and curb their more unpopular activities. With fanatical zeal the Witnesses fought every legal attempt to restrict their freedom of action. As a result they have brought to the Supreme Court many cases involving religious liberty issues. In a majority of these they were successful. These decisions have done much to clarify our constitutional law relating to freedom of religion.

Among these cases are Lovell v. Griffin, 303 U. S. 444 (1938), which held invalid, as an invasion of religious liberty, an ordinance which required a license for soliciting money for religious purposes. In Jones v. Opelika, 316 U. S. 584 (1942), the Court ruled in a five-to-four decision that nondiscriminatory license taxes or fees imposed on those who peddle, sell, or canvass, could be collected from the Jehovah's Witnesses who sell religious pamphlets and books. The following year the Court reversed the decision, again by a five-to-four vote, in Murdock v. Pennsylvania, 319 U. S. 105 (1943).

The most spectacular issue of religious liberty to be raised by the Jehovah's Witnesses was that of the compulsory flag salute. The Witnesses refuse to salute the flag or permit their children to do so, because they believe that this violates the First Commandment. This refusal caused bitter resentment, and some seventeen states passed statutes requiring all school children to salute the flag and providing for the expulsion of those who refused. The question whether these acts unconstitutionally restricted freedom of religion came to the Court in Minersville School District v. Gobitis, 310

U. S. 586 (1940). With one judge dissenting the Court held that it did not. In an opinion by Mr. Justice Frankfurter it was stated that freedom of religion is not absolute, and that some compromises may be necessary in order to secure the national unity which is the basis of national security. The flag salute contributes to that national unity, or at least the question whether it does or not is "an issue of educational policy for which the courtroom is not the proper arena." For the Court to hold the requirement void as abridging religious liberty "would amount to no less than the pronouncement of a pedagogical and psychological dogma in a field where courts possess no marked and certainly no controlling competence." The Court seemed content to assume that the Minersville school board was more competent to settle the flag salute issue than the Supreme Court, and it allowed the board's judgment to prevail. Mr. Justice Stone wrote a powerful dissenting opinion. The decision came as a shock and was widely and sharply criticized. Members of the Court who had participated in it began to have misgivings. When Jones v. Opelika, supra, was decided in 1942, Justices Black, Douglas, and Murphy dissented, and went further to state that they had become convinced that the Gobitis case was "wrongly decided." With Mr. Justice Stone, this made four members of the Court who no longer supported the Gobitis decision. When, in February, 1943, Mr. Justice Rutledge replaced Mr. Justice Byrnes on the bench, he joined with these four to overrule the Gobitis case by the decision in West Virginia State Board of Education v. Barnette, 319 U. S. 624 (1943).

While Article VI of the Constitution contains the provision that "no religious test shall ever be required as a qualification to any office or public trust under the United States," most of the early state constitutions did require such tests and some of those have survived. The constitution of Maryland provides that no religious test for public office shall be required "other than a declaration of belief in the existence of God." Torcaso was appointed to the office of notary public in Maryland but was refused his commission to the office because he would not declare his belief in God. In a unanimous decision the Court held that "this Maryland religious test for public office unconstitutionally invades the appellant's freedom of belief and religion and therefore cannot be enforced against him." See Torcaso v. Watkins, 367 U. S. 488 (1961).

It has long been customary in many public schools throughout the country to open the school session with some brief religious exercise such as reading from the Bible, recitation of the Lord's Prayer, etc. In the relatively few cases in which the constitutionality of this practice was challenged the state courts had decided both ways though most of them had held the practice valid. In Doremus v. Board of Education, 342 U. S. 429 (1952), a taxpayer challenged the validity of a New Jersey statute requiring the reading, without comment, of five verses from the Old Testament at the opening of each school day. He alleged that this involved the unconstitutional use of state funds and sought to enjoin its continuance. The state court upheld the act. The Supreme Court refused jurisdiction on the ground that the taxpayer was not shown to be out of pocket.

The Court's six-to-one decision in Engel v. Vitale, below, banning the recital in public schools of the so-called Regents' Prayer, is of far-reaching importance. It aroused a storm of protest, and members in both Houses of Congress began to work on a constitutional amendment which would nullify the decision.

Mr. Justice Black delivered the opinion of the Court, saying in part:

The respondent Board of Education of Union Free School District No. 9, New Hyde Park, New York, acting in its official capacity under state law, directed the School District's principal to cause the following prayer to be said aloud by each class in the presence of a teacher at the beginning of each school day:

Almighty God, we acknowledge our dependence upon Thee, and we beg Thy blessings upon us, our parents, our teachers and our country.

This daily procedure was adopted on the recommendation of the State Board of Regents, a governmental agency created by the State Constitution to which the New York Legislature has granted broad supervisory, executive, and legislative powers over the State's public school system. These state officials composed the prayer which they recommended and published as a part of their "Statement on Moral and Spiritual Training in the Schools," saying: "We believe that this Statement will be subscribed to by all men and women of good will, and we call upon all of them to aid in giving life to our program."

Shortly after the practice of reciting the Regents' prayer was adopted by the School District, the parents of ten pupils brought this action in a New York State Court insisting that use of this official prayer in the public schools was contrary to the beliefs, religions, or religious practices of both themselves and their children. Among other things, these parents challenged the constitutionality of both the state law authorizing the School District to direct the use of prayer in public schools and the School District's regulation ordering the recitation of this particular prayer on the ground that these actions of official governmental agencies violate that part of the First Amendment of the Federal Constitution which commands that "Congress shall make no law respecting an establishment of religion"—a command which was "made applicable to the State of New York by the Fourteenth Amendment of the said Constitution." The New York Court of Appeals . . . upheld the power of New York to use the Regents' prayer so long as the schools did not compel any pupil to join in the prayer over his or his parents' objection. . . .

We think that by using its public school system to encourage recitation of the Regents' prayer, the State of New York has adopted a practice wholly inconsistent with the Establishment Clause. There can, of course, be no doubt that New York's program of daily classroom invocation of God's blessings as prescribed in the Regents' prayer is a religious activity. It is a solemn avowal of divine faith and supplication for the blessings of the Almighty. The nature of such a prayer has always been religious, none of the respondents has denied this and the trial court expressly so found. . . .

The petitioners contend among other things that the state laws requiring or permitting use of the Regents' prayer must be struck down as a violation of the Establishment Clause because that prayer was composed by governmental officials as a part of a governmental program to further religious beliefs. For this reason, petitioners argue, the State's use of the Regents' prayer in its public school system breeches the constitutional wall of separation between Church and State. We agree with that contention since we think that the constitutional prohibition against laws respecting an establishment of religion must at least mean that in this country it is no part of the business of government to compose official prayers for any group of the American people to recite as a part of a religious program carried on by government.

It is a matter of history that this very practice of establishing governmentally composed prayers for religious services was one of the reasons which caused many of our early colonists to leave England and seek religious freedom in America. The Book of Common Prayer, which was created under governmental direction and which was approved by Acts of Parliament in 1548 and 1549, set out in minute detail the accepted form and content of prayer and other religious ceremonies to be used in the established, tax-supported Church of England. . . . [Controversies created by the use of the Book of Common Prayer are briefly summarized.]

It is an unfortunate fact of history that when some of the very groups which had most strenuously opposed the established Church of England found themselves sufficiently in control of colonial governments in this country to write their own prayers into law, they passed laws making their own religion the official religion of their respective colonies. Indeed, as late as the time of the Revolutionary War, there were established churches in at least eight of the thirteen former colonies and established religions in at least four of the other five. But the successful Revolution against English political domination was shortly followed by intense opposition to the practice of establishing religion by law. This opposition crystallized rapidly into an effective political force in Virginia where the minority religious groups such as Presbyterians, Lutherans, Quakers and Baptists had gained such strength that the adherents to the established Episcopal Church were actually a minority themselves. In 1785–1786, those opposed to the established Church, led by James Madison and Thomas Jefferson, who, though themselves not members of any of these dissenting religious groups, opposed all religious establishments by law on grounds of principle, obtained the enactment of the famous "Virginia Bill for Religious Liberty" by which all religious groups were placed on an equal footing so far as the State was concerned. Similar though less far-reaching legislation was being considered and passed in other States.

By the time of the adoption of the Constitution, our history shows that there was a widespread awareness among many Americans of the dangers of a union of Church and State. . . . The First Amendment was added to the Constitution to stand as a guarantee that neither the power nor the prestige of the Federal Government would be used to control, support or influence the kinds of prayer the American people can say—that the people's religions must not be subjected to the pressures of government for change each time a new political administration is elected to office. Under that Amendment's prohibition against governmental establishment of religion, as reinforced by the provisions of the Fourteenth Amendment, government in this country, be it state or federal, is without power to prescribe by law any particular form of prayer which is to be used as an official prayer in carrying on any program of governmentally sponsored religious activity.

There can be no doubt that New York's state prayer program officially establishes the religious beliefs embodied in the Regents' prayer. The respondents' argument to the contrary, which is largely based upon the contention that the Regents' prayer is "nondenominational" and the fact that the program, as modified and approved by state courts, does not require all pupils to recite the prayer but permits those who wish to do so to remain silent or be excused from the room, ignores the essential nature of the program's constitutional defects. Neither the fact that the prayer may be denominationally neutral, nor the fact that its observance on the part of the students is voluntary can serve to free it from the limitations of the Establishment Clause, as it might from the Free Exercise Clause, of the First Amendment, both of which are operative against the States by virtue of the Fourteenth Amendment. Although these two clauses may in certain instances overlap, they forbid two quite different kinds of governmental encroachment upon religious freedom. The Establishment Clause, unlike the Free Exercise Clause, does not depend upon any showing of direct governmental compulsion and is violated by the enactment of laws which establish an official religion whether those laws operate directly to coerce nonobserving individuals or not. This is not to say, of course, that laws officially prescribing a particular form of religious worship do not involve coercion of such individuals. When the power, prestige and financial support of government is placed behind a particular religious belief, the indirect coercive pressure upon religious minorities to conform to the prevailing officially approved religion is plain. But the purposes underlying the Establishment Clause go much further than that. Its first and most immediate purpose rested on the belief that a union of government and religion tends to destroy government and to degrade religion. The history of governmentally established religion, both in England and in this country, showed that whenever government had allied itself with one particular form of religion, the inevitable result had been that it had incurred the hatred, disrespect and even contempt of those who held contrary beliefs. That same history showed that many people had lost their respect for any religion that had relied upon the support of government to spread its faith. The Establishment Clause thus stands as an expression of principle on the part of the Founders of our Constitution that religion is too personal, too sacred, too holy, to permit its "unhallowed perversion" by a civil magistrate. Another purpose of the Establishment Clause rested upon an awareness of the historical fact that governmentally established religions and religious persecutions go hand in hand. . . . It was in large part to get completely away from this sort of systematic religious persecution that the Founders brought into being our Nation, our Constitution, and our Bill of Rights with its prohibition against any governmental establishment of religion. The New York laws officially prescribing the Regents' prayer are inconsistent with both the purposes of the Establishment Clause and with the Establishment Clause itself.

It has been argued that to apply the Constitution in such a way as to prohibit state laws respecting an establishment of religious services in public schools is to indicate a hostility toward religion or toward prayer. Nothing, of course, could be more wrong. The history of man is inseparable from the history of religion. And perhaps it is not too much to say that since the beginning of that history many people have devoutly believed that "More things are wrought by prayer than this world dreams of." It was doubtless largely due to men who believed this that there grew up a sentiment that caused men to leave the cross-currents of officially established state religions and religious persecution in Europe and come to this country filled with the hope that they could find a place in which they could pray when they pleased to the God of their faith in the language they chose. And there were men of this same faith in the power of prayer who led the fight for adoption of our Constitution and also for our Bill of Rights with the very guarantees of religious freedom that forbid the sort of governmental activity which New York has attempted here. These men knew that the First Amendment, which tried to put an end to governmental control of religion and of prayer, was not written to destroy either. They knew rather that it was written to quiet well-justified fears which nearly all of them felt arising out of an awareness that governments of the past had shackled men's tongues to make them speak only the religious thoughts that government wanted them to speak and to pray only to the God that government wanted them to pray to. It is neither sacrilegious nor antireligious to say that each separate government in this country should stay out of the business of writing or sanctioning official prayers and leave that purely religious function to the people themselves and to those the people choose to look to for religious guidance.

It is true that New York's establishment of its Regents' prayer as an officially approved religious doctrine of that State does not amount to a total establishment of one particular religious sect to the exclusion of all others—that, indeed, the governmental endorsement of that prayer seems relatively insignificant when compared to the governmental encroachments upon religion which were commonplace 200 years ago. To those who may subscribe to the view that because the

Regents' official prayer is so brief and general there can be no danger to religious freedom in its governmental establishment, however, it may be appropriate to say in the words of James Madison, the author of the First Amendment:

[I]t is proper to take alarm at the first experiment on our liberties. . . . Who does not see that the same authority which can establish Christianity, in exclusion of all other Religions, may establish with the same ease any particular sect of Christians, in exclusion of all other Sects? That the same authority which can force a citizen to contribute three pence only of his property for the support of any one establishment, may force him to conform to any other establishment in all cases whatsoever?

The judgment of the Court of Appeals of New York is reversed and the cause remanded for further proceedings not inconsistent with this opinion.

Reversed and remanded.

Mr. Justice Frankfurter took no part in the decision of this case.

Mr. Justice White took no part in the consideration or decision of this case.

Mr. Justice Douglas, concurring, said in part:

. . . The point for decision is whether the Government can constitutionally finance a religious exercise. Our system at the federal and state levels is presently honeycombed with such financing. Nevertheless, I think it is an unconstitutional undertaking whatever form it takes. . . .

The question presented by this case is . . . an extremely narrow one. It is whether New York oversteps the bounds when it finances a religious exercise.

What New York does on the opening of its public schools is what we do when we open court. Our Marshal has from the beginning announced the convening of the Court and then added "God save the United States and this honorable court." That utterance is a supplication, a prayer in which we, the judges, are free to join, but which we need not recite any more than the students need recite the New York prayer.

What New York does on the opening of its public schools is what each House of Congress does at the opening of each day's business. . . .

In New York the teacher who leads in prayer is on the public payroll; and the time she takes seems minuscule as compared with the salaries appropriated by state legislatures and Congress for chaplains to conduct prayers in the legislative halls. Only a bare fraction of the teacher's time is given to reciting this short 22-word prayer, about the same amount of time that our Marshal spends announcing the opening of our sessions and offering a prayer for this Court. Yet for me the principle is the same, no matter how briefly the prayer is said, for in each of the instances given the person praying is a public official on the public payroll, performing a religious exercise in a governmental institution. It is said that the element of coercion is inherent in the giving of this prayer. If that is true here, it is also true of the prayer with which this Court is convened, and with those that open the Congress. Few adults, let alone children, would leave our courtroom or the Senate or the House while those prayers are being given. Every such audience is in a sense a "captive" audience.

At the same time I cannot say that to authorize this prayer is to establish a religion in the strictly historic meaning of those words. A religion is not established in the usual sense merely by letting those who chose to do so say the prayer that the public school teacher leads. Yet once government finances a religious exercise it inserts a divisive influence into our communities. The New York court said that the prayer given does not conform to all of the tenets of the Jewish, Unitarian, and Ethical Culture groups. One of petitioners is an agnostic. . . .

. . . The First Amendment leaves the Government in a position not of hostility to religion but of neutrality. The philosophy is that the atheist or agnostic—the nonbeliever—is entitled to go his own way. The philosophy is that if government interferes in matters spiritual, it will be a divisive force. The First Amendment teaches that a government neutral in the field of religion better serves all religious interests.

My problem today would be uncomplicated but for Everson v. Board of Education, 330 U. S. 1, which allowed taxpayers' money to be used to pay "the bus fares of parochial school pupils as a part of a general program under which" the fares of pupils attending public and other schools were also paid. The Everson case seems in retrospect to be out of line with the First Amendment. Its result is appealing, as it allows aid to be given to needy children. Yet by the same token, public funds could be used to satisfy other needs of children in parochial schools—lunches, books, and tuition being obvious examples. . . .

Mr. Justice Stewart, dissenting, said in part:

. . . The Court today decides that in permitting this brief non-denominational prayer the school board has violated the Constitution of the United States. I think this decision is wrong.

The Court does not hold, nor could it, that New York has interfered with the free exercise of anybody's religion. For the state courts have made clear that those who object to reciting the prayer must be entirely free of any compulsion to do so, including any "embarrassments and pressures." But the Court says that in permitting school children to say this simple prayer, the New York authorities have established "an official religion."

With all respect, I think the Court has misapplied a great constitutional principle. I cannot see how an "official religion" is established by letting those who want to say a prayer say it. On the contrary, I think that to deny the wish of these school children to join in reciting this prayer is to deny them the opportunity of sharing in the spiritual heritage of our Nation.

The Court's historical review of the quarrels over the Book of Common Prayer in England throws no light for me on the issue before us in this case. . . . Moreover, I think that the Court's task, in this as in all areas of constitutional adjudication, is not responsibly aided by the uncritical invocation of metaphors like the "wall of separation," a phrase nowhere to be found in the Constitution. What is relevant to the issue here is not the history of an established church in sixteenth century England or in eighteenth century America, but the history of the religious traditions of our people, reflected in countless practices of the institutions and officials of our government. . . . [Here follows a summary of instances in which God has been, or is, mentioned in official ceremonies or speeches, concluding with the third stanza of "The Star-Spangled Banner."]

I do not believe that this Court, or the Congress, or the President has by the actions and practices I have mentioned established an "official religion" in violation of the Constitution. And I do not believe the State of New York has done so in this case. What each has done has been to recognize and to follow the deeply entrenched and highly cherished spiritual traditions of our Nation—traditions which come down to us from those who almost two hundred years ago avowed their "firm reliance on the Protection of Divine Providence" when they proclaimed the freedom and independence of this brave new world.

I dissent.

EVERSON v. BOARD OF EDUCATION
330 U. S. 1; 91 L. Ed. 711; 67 Sup. Ct. 504. 1947.

In the group of important cases which have arisen under the clause of the First Amendment forbidding any establishment of religion, most have concerned the problems of public aid to religion in connection with our nationwide system of compulsory education.

Early education in America was religious education, supported by the civil government in the Bible-commonwealth of Massachusetts, and by the various church groups in the middle and southern colonies. In the early nineteenth century the demand for free public education resulted in a system of public schools free from religious control and largely free from any sectarian influence, a situation wholly satisfactory to an overwhelmingly Protestant nation. Waves of Catholic immigration injected a new element into the picture. The Catholic Church regards the teaching of religion as a primary function of education. Unwilling to send their children to the public schools, which they regard as either devoid of all religious influence or tainted with Protestantism, the Catholics feel obliged to build and maintain a system of parochial schools at their own expense. When these parochial schools meet the state's educational standards they are accredited as schools in which the requirements of the compulsory education laws can be satisfied. In 1922 the state of Oregon passed a law requiring all parents to send their children to the public schools of the state. The Supreme Court, in Pierce v. Society of Sisters, 268 U. S. 510 (1925), held that the statute denied due process of law by taking from parents their freedom to "direct the upbringing and education" of their children by sending them either to parochial or to private non-sectarian schools of approved educational standards. It is not surprising that Catholic citizens, who pay taxes to support the public schools which they do not use, should try to secure some public aid for the parochial schools; and they exert a good deal of pressure to bring this about. Opposition to this, however, has been bitter and widespread, and by the end of the nineteenth century practically every state had adopted some kind of prohibition against the use of state funds for the support of religious education. In numerous cases the state courts held void attempts to extend direct or indirect aid to parochial schools. The extent to which such aid may be extended to parochial schools, particularly by the federal government, remains today a controversial issue.

Within the last twenty years new and varied services and benefits have been offered by the states to pupils in the public schools. These include free textbooks, free bus transportation, free lunches, and free medical service. Can the state, if it desires, also give these benefits to children attending parochial or private schools? It was argued on the one hand that to do so would not only violate the state constitutional clauses which forbid the use of public money in aid of religion or religious education, but violate also the clause of the First Amendment which forbids "an establishment of religion," a clause now carried over into the Fourteenth Amendment as a limitation on the states. It was argued on the other side that in providing these services and benefits the state was aiding the child and not the school which he attends. Most state courts accepted this latter reasoning, which came to be known as the "child benefit theory"; and the Supreme Court, in Cochran v. Louisiana State Board of Education, 281 U. S. 370 (1930), held valid a state law authorizing the use of public funds to supply "school books to the school children of the state," including not only public school children but also children in parochial and private non-sectarian schools. The Court agreed that "the school children and the state alone are beneficiaries" of these appropriations, and not the schools which the children attend. The majority opinion in the Everson case, below, proceeds on this same theory. In the five-to-four decision in the Everson case, Mr. Justice Douglas voted with the majority. It may be noted, however, that in his concurring opinion in Engel v. Vitale, above, he observed: "The Everson case seems in retrospect to be out of line with the First Amendment."

Illinois ex rel. McCollum v. Board of Education, 333 U. S. 203 (1948), involved the problem of religious instruction in the public schools. While it is recognized that the public schools cannot themselves give religious instruction, there is also a growing desire in many communities to provide organized religious instruction as an adjunct of the school system. To meet this desire the so-called "released time" arrangement was devised, one form of which, set up in Champaign, Illinois, was involved in the McCollum case. The plan was this. Public school pupils whose parents signed "request cards" attended religious-instruction classes conducted during regular school hours in the school building, but taught by outside teachers (chosen by a religious council representing the various faiths) who were subject to the approval and supervision of the superintendent of schools. These teachers were not paid from public funds. Records of attendance at these classes were kept and reported to the school authorities, and pupils who did not attend them spent their time on their ordinary studies. The Supreme Court held that this "released time" arrangement violated the constitutional principle of separation of church and state, as expressed in the First Amendment and made applicable to the states by the Fourteenth Amendment. Public school buildings were placed at the disposal of the religious instruction classes, and the whole arrangement was aided and in some measure supervised by public school officers and teachers. A New York City "released time" program, however, which authorized students to attend religious courses operated outside the school building by, and at the expense of, a duly constituted religious body, was held valid in Zorach v. Clauson, 343 U. S. 306 (1952).

In the Everson and McCollum cases all the justices on the Court agreed that the First Amendment sets up a complete separation of church and state, and that any government aid to religion violates this principle. They differed sharply in each case on whether aid to religion was in fact shown, but they did not question that had it been, it would be bad. Protestant and Catholic religious leaders alike have argued that the First Amendment does not forbid all aid to religion, but only aid that favors one religion over another. However, in Abington School District v. Schempp and Murray v. Curlett, 374 U. S. 203 (1963), the Court held void Pennsylvania and Baltimore requirements that the Bible be read at the opening of each school day.

In four cases decided on the same day the Court held valid the Sunday Closing Laws of Maryland, Massachusetts, and Pennsylvania. These laws were attacked on two grounds: (1) they were discriminatory because they allowed some things to be sold on Sunday but not others; (2) they discriminated against religious sects which do not observe the Christian Sabbath. The Court held that the classifications objected to under the first point were not arbitrary. On the second point the Court said: "That Sunday Closing Laws once held their genesis in religion does not preclude states from achieving secular goals by prescribing Sunday as a day of rest." See McGowan v. Maryland, 366 U. S. 420 (1961); Gallagher v. Crown Kosher Super Market of Massachusetts, 366 U. S. 617 (1961); Two Guys from Harrison-Allentown, Inc. v. McGinley, 366 U. S. 582 (1961). However, in Sherbert v. Verner, 374 U. S. 398 (1963), the "free exercise" clause was held violated where unemployment compensation was denied a Seventh Day Adventist who refused "suitable" work which required working on Saturday.

Mr. Justice Black delivered the opinion of the Court, saying in part:

A New Jersey statute authorizes its local school districts to make rules and contracts for the transportation of children to and from schools. The appellee, a township board of education, acting pursuant to this statute authorized reimbursement to parents of money expended by them for the bus transportation of their children on regular busses operated by the public transportation system. Part of this money was for the payment of transportation of some children in the community to Catholic parochial schools. These church schools give their students, in addition to secular education, regular religious instruction conforming to the religious tenets and modes of worship of the Catholic Faith. The superintendent of these schools is a Catholic priest.

The appellant, in his capacity as a district taxpayer, filed suit in a state court challenging the right of the board to reimburse parents of parochial school students. He contended that the statute and the resolution passed pursuant to it violated both the state and the federal Constitutions. . . .

Since there has been no attack on the statute on the ground that a part of its language excludes children attending private schools operated for profit from enjoying state payment for their transportation, we need not consider this exclusionary language; it has no relevancy to any constitutional question here presented. . . .

The only contention here is that the state statute and the resolution, in so far as they authorized reimbursement to parents of children attending parochial schools, violate the federal Constitution in these two respects, which to some extent, overlap. *First.* They authorize the State to take by taxation the private property of some and bestow it upon others, to be used for their own private purposes. This, it is alleged, violates the due process clause of the Fourteenth Amendment. *Second.* The statute and the resolution forced inhabitants to pay taxes to help support and maintain schools which are dedicated to, and which regularly teach, the Catholic Faith. This is alleged to be a use of state power to support church schools contrary to the prohibition of the First Amendment which the Fourteenth Amendment made applicable to the states. . . .

It is much too late to argue that legislation intended to facilitate the opportunity of children to get a secular education serves no public purpose. . . . The same thing is no less true of legislation to reimburse needy parents, or all parents, for payment of the fares of their children so that they can ride in public busses to and from schools rather than run the risk of traffic and other hazards incident to walking or "hitchhiking." . . . Nor does it follow that a law has a private rather than a public purpose because it provides that tax-raised funds will be paid to reimburse individuals on account of money spent by them in a way which furthers a public program. . . . Subsidies and loans to individuals such as farmers and home owners, and to privately owned transportation systems, as well as many other kinds of businesses, have been commonplace practice in our state and national history. . . .

Second. The New Jersey statute is challenged as a "law respecting the establishment of religion." The First Amendment, as made applicable to the states by the Fourteenth, . . . commands that a state "shall make no law respecting an establishment of religion, or prohibiting the free exercise thereof." These words of the First Amendment reflected in the minds of early Americans a vivid mental picture of conditions and practices which they fervently wished to stamp out in order to preserve liberty for themselves and for their posterity. Doubtless their goal has not been entirely reached; but so far has the nation moved toward it that the expression "law respecting the establishment of religion," probably does not so vividly remind present-day Americans of the evils, fears, and political problems that caused that expression to be written into our Bill of Rights. Whether this New Jersey law is one respecting the "establishment of religion" requires an understanding of the meaning of that language, particularly with respect to the imposition of taxes. Once again, therefore, it is not inappropriate briefly to review the background and environment of the period in which that constitutional language was fashioned and adopted.

A large proportion of the early settlers of this country came here from Europe to escape the bondage of laws which compelled them to support and attend government favored churches. The centuries immediately before and contemporaneous with the colonization of America had been filled with turmoil, civil strife, and persecutions, generated in large part by established sects determined to maintain their absolute political and religious supremacy. With the power of government supporting them, at various times and places, Catholics had persecuted Protestants, Protestants had persecuted Catholics, Protestant sects had persecuted other Protestant sects, Catholics of one shade of belief had persecuted Catholics of another shade of belief, and all of these had from time to time persecuted Jews. In efforts to force loyalty to whatever religious group happened to be on top and in league with the government of a particular time and place, men and women had been fined, cast in jail, cruelly tortured, and killed. Among the offenses for which these punishments had been inflicted were such things as speaking disrespectfully of the views of ministers of government-established churches, non-attendance at those churches, expressions of non-belief in their doctrines, and failure to pay taxes and tithes to support them.

These practices of the old world were transplanted to and began to thrive in the soil of the new America. The very charters granted by the English Crown to the individuals and companies designated to make the laws which would control the destinies of the colonials authorized these individuals and companies to erect religious establishments which all, whether believers or non-believers, would be required to support and attend. An exercise of this authority was accompanied by a repetition of many of the old world practices and persecutions. Catholics found themselves hounded and proscribed because of their faith; Quakers who followed their conscience went to jail; Baptists were peculiarly obnoxious to certain dominant Protestant sects; men and women of varied faiths who happened to be in a minority in a particular locality were persecuted because they steadfastly persisted in worshipping God only as their own consciences dictated. And all of these dissenters were compelled to pay tithes and taxes to support government-sponsored churches whose ministers preached inflammatory sermons designed to strengthen and consolidate the established faith by generating a burning hatred against dissenters.

These practices became so commonplace as to shock the freedom-loving colonials into a feeling of abhorrence. The imposition of taxes to pay ministers' salaries and to build and maintain churches and church property aroused their indignation. It was these feelings which found expression in the First Amendment. No one locality and no one group throughout the Colonies can rightly be given entire credit for having aroused the sentiment that culminated in adoption of the Bill of Rights' provisions embracing religious liberty. But Virginia, where the established church had achieved a dominant influence in political affairs and where many excesses attracted wide public attention, provided a great stimulus and able leadership for the movement. The people there, as elsewhere, reached the conviction that individual religious liberty could be achieved best under a government which was stripped of all power to tax, to support, or otherwise to assist any or all religions, or to interfere with the beliefs of any religious individual or group.

The movement toward this end reached its dramatic climax in Virginia in 1785–86 when the Virginia legislative body was about to renew Virginia's tax levy for the support of the established church. Thomas Jefferson and James Madison led the fight against this tax. Madison wrote his great Memorial and Remonstrance against the law. In it, he eloquently argued that a true religion did not need the support of law; that no person, either believer or non-believer, should be taxed to support a religious institution of any kind; that the best interest of a society required that the minds of men always be wholly free; and that cruel persecutions were the inevitable result of government-established religions. Madison's Remonstrance received strong support throughout Virginia, and the Assembly postponed consideration of the proposed tax measure until its next session. When the proposal came up for consideration at that session, it not only died in committee, but the Assembly enacted the famous "Virginia Bill for Religious Liberty" originally written by Thomas Jefferson. The preamble to that Bill stated among other things that

Almighty God hath created the mind free; that all attempts to influence it by temporal punishments, or burthens, or by civil incapacitations, tend only to beget habits of hypocrisy and meanness, and are a departure from the plan of the Holy author of our religion who being Lord both of body and mind, yet chose not to propagate it by coercions on either . . . ; that to compel a man to furnish contributions of money for the propagation of opinions which he disbelieves, is sinful and tyrannical; that even the forcing him to support this or that teacher of his own religious persuasion, is depriving him of the comfortable liberty of giving his contributions to the particular pastor, whose morals he would make his pattern. . . .

And the statute itself enacted

That no man shall be compelled to frequent or support any religious worship, place, or ministry whatsoever, nor shall be enforced, restrained, molested, or burthened, in his body or goods, nor shall otherwise suffer on account of his religious opinions or belief . . .

This Court has previously recognized that the provisions of the First Amendment, in the drafting and adoption of which Madison and Jefferson played such leading roles, had the same objective and were intended to provide the same protection against governmental intrusion on religious liberty as the Virginia statute. . . . Prior to the adoption of the Fourteenth Amendment, the First Amendment did not apply as a restraint against the states. Most of them did soon provide similar constitutional protections for religious liberty. But some states persisted for about half a century in imposing restraints upon the free exercise of religion and in discriminating against particular religious groups. In recent years, so far as the provision against the establishment of a religion is concerned, the question has most frequently arisen in connection with proposed state aid to church schools and efforts to carry on religious teachings in the public schools in accordance with the tenets of a particular sect. Some churches have either sought or accepted state financial support for their schools. Here again the efforts to obtain state aid or acceptance of it have not been limited to any one particular faith. The state courts, in the main, have remained faithful to the language of their own constitutional provisions designed to protect religious freedom and to separate religions and governments. Their decisions, however, show the difficulty in drawing the line between tax legislation which provides funds for the welfare of the general public and that which is designed to support institutions which teach religion. . . .

The "establishment of religion" clause of the First Amendment means at least this: Neither a state nor the federal government can set up a church. Neither can pass laws which aid one religion, aid all religions, or prefer one religion over another. Neither can force nor influence a person to go to or to remain away from church against his will or force him to profess a belief or disbelief in any religion. No person can be punished for entertaining or professing religious beliefs or disbeliefs, for church attendance or non-attendance. No tax in any amount, large or small, can be levied to support any religious activities or institutions, whatever they may be called, or whatever form they may adopt to teach or practice religion. Neither a state nor the federal government can, openly or secretly, participate in the affairs of any religious organizations or groups and *vice versa*. In the words of Jefferson, the clause against establishment of religion by law was intended to erect "a wall of separation between Church and State." . . .

Measured by these standards, we cannot say that the First Amendment prohibits New Jersey from spending tax-raised funds to pay the bus fares of parochial school pupils as a part of a general program under which it pays the fares of pupils attending public and other schools. It is undoubtedly true that children are helped to get to church schools. There is even a possibility that some of the children might not be sent to the church schools if the parents were compelled to pay their childrens' bus fares out of their own pockets when transporation to a public school would have been paid for by the state. The same possibility exists where the state requires a local transit company to provide reduced fares to school children including those attending parochial schools, or where a municipally owned transporation system undertakes to carry all school children free of charge. Moreover, state-paid policemen, detailed to protect children going to and from church schools from the very real hazards of traffic, would serve much the same purpose and accomplish much the same result as state provisions intended to guarantee free transporation of a kind which the state deems to be best for the school children's welfare. And parents might refuse to risk their children to the serious danger of traffic accidents going to and from parochial schools, the approaches to which were not protected by policemen. Similarly, parents might be reluctant to permit their children to attend schools which the state had cut off from such general government services as ordinary police and fire protection, connections for sewage disposal, public highways and sidewalks. Of course, cutting off church schools from these services, so separate and so indisputably marked off from the religious function, would make it far more difficult for the schools to operate. But such is obviously not the purpose of the First Amendment. That Amendment requires the state to be a neutral in its relations with groups of religious believers and non-believers; it does not require the state to be their adversary. State power is no more to be used so as to handicap religions than it is to favor them.

This Court has said that parents may, in the discharge of their duty under state compulsory education laws, send their children to a religious rather than a public school if the school meets the secular educational requirements which the state has power to impose. See Pierce v. Society of Sisters, 268 U. S. 510. It appears that these parochial schools meet New Jersey's requirements. The state contributes no money to the schools. It does not support them. Its legislation, as applied, does no more than provide a general program to help parents get their children, regardless of their religion, safely and expeditiously to and from accredited schools.

The First Amendment has erected a wall between church and state. That wall must be kept high and impregnable. We could not approve the slightest breach. New Jersey has not breached it here.

Affirmed.

Mr. Justice Jackson, dissenting, said in part:

It is of no importance in this situation whether the beneficiary of this expenditure of tax-raised funds is primarily the parochial school and incidentally the pupil, or whether the aid is directly bestowed on the pupil with indirect benefits to the school. The state cannot maintain a Church and it can no more tax its citizens to furnish free carriage to those who attend a Church. The prohibition against establishment of religion cannot be circumvented by a subsidy, bonus or reimbursement of expense to individuals for receiving religious instruction and indoctrination. . . .

The Court's holding is that this taxpayer has no grievance because the state has decided to make the reimbursement a public purpose and therefore we are bound to regard it as such. I agree that this Court has left, and always should leave to each state, great latitude in deciding for itself, in the light of its own conditions, what shall be public purposes in its scheme of things. It may socialize utilities and economic enterprises and make taxpayers' business out of what conventionally had been private business. It may make public business of individual welfare, health, education, entertainment or security. But it cannot make public business of religious worship or instruction, or of attendance at religious institutions of any character. There is no answer to the proposition more fully expounded by Mr. Justice Rutledge that the effect of the religious freedom Amendment to our Constitution was to take every form of propagation of religion out of the realm of things which could directly or indirectly be made public business and thereby be supported in whole or in part at taxpayers' expense. That is a difference which the Constitution sets up between religion and almost every other subject matter of legislation, a difference which goes to the very root of religious freedom and which the Court is overlooking today. This freedom was first in the Bill of Rights because it was first in the forefathers' minds; it was set forth in absolute terms, and its strength is its rigidity. It was intended not only to keep the states' hands out of religion, but to keep religion's hands off the state, and above all, to keep bitter religious controversy out of public life by denying to every denomination any advantage from getting control of public policy or the public purse. Those great ends I cannot but think are immeasurably compromised by today's decision. . . .

But we cannot have it both ways. Religious teaching cannot be a private affair when the state seeks to impose regulations which infringe on it indirectly, and a public affair when it comes to taxing citizens of one faith to aid another, or those of no faith to aid at all. If these principles seem harsh in prohibiting aid to Catholic education, it must not be forgotten that it is the same Constitution that alone assures Catholics the right to maintain these schools at all when predominant local sentiment would forbid them. Pierce v. Society of Sisters, 268 U. S. 510. Nor should I think that those who have done so well without this aid would want to see this separation between Church and State broken down. If the state may aid these religious schools, it may therefore regulate them. Many groups have sought aid from tax funds only to find that it carried political controls with it. Indeed this Court has declared that "It is hardly lack of due process for the government to regulate that which it subsidizes."

But in any event, the great purposes of the Constitution do not depend on the approval or convenience of those they restrain. I cannot read the history of the struggle to separate political from ecclesiastical affairs, well summarized in the opinion of Mr. Justice Rutledge in which I generally concur, without a conviction that the Court today is unconsciously giving the clock's hands a backward turn.

Mr. Justice Frankfurter joins in this opinion.

Mr. Justice Rutledge, with whom Mr. Justice Frankfurter, Mr. Justice Jackson and Mr. Justice Burton agree, dissenting, said in part:

"Congress shall make no law respecting an establishment of religion, or prohibiting the free exercise thereof. . . .

"Well aware that Almighty God hath created the mind free; . . . that to compel a man to furnish contributions of money for the propagation of opinions which he disbelieves, is sinful and tyrannical; . . .

"*We, the General Assembly, do enact,* That no man shall be compelled to frequent or support any religious worship, place, or ministry whatsoever, nor shall be enforced, restrained, molested, or burthened in his body or goods, nor shall otherwise suffer on account of his religious opinions or belief. . . ."[1]

I cannot believe that the great author of those words, or the men who made them law, could have joined in this decision. Neither so high nor so impregnable today as yesterday is the wall raised between church and state by Virginia's great statute of religious freedom and the First Amendment, now made applicable to all the states by the Fourteenth. New Jersey's statute sustained is the first, if indeed it is not the second breach to be made by this Court's action. That a third, and a fourth, and still others will be attempted, we may be sure. For just as Cochran v. Board of Education, 281 U. S. 370, has opened the way by oblique ruling for this decision, so will the two make wider

---

[1] "A Bill for Establishing Religious Freedom," enacted by the General Assembly of Virginia, January 19, 1786. See 1 Randall, The Life of Thomas Jefferson (1858) 219-220; XII Hening's Statutes of Virginia (1823) 84.

the breach for a third. Thus with time the most solid freedom steadily gives way before continuing corrosive decision.

This case forces us to determine squarely for the first time what was "an establishment of religion" in the First Amendment's conception; and by that measure to decide whether New Jersey's action violates its command. . . .

I.

Not simply an established church, but any law respecting an establishment of religion is forbidden. The Amendment was broadly but not loosely phrased. It is the compact and exact summation of its author's views formed during his long struggle for religious freedom. In Madison's own words characterizing Jefferson's Bill for Establishing Religious Freedom, the guaranty he put in our national charter, like the bill he piloted through the Virginia Assembly, was "a Model of technical precision, and perspicuous brevity." Madison could not have confused "church" and "religion," or "an established church" and "an establishment of religion."

The Amendment's purpose was not to strike merely at the official establishment of a single sect, creed or religion, outlawing only a formal relation such as had prevailed in England and some of the colonies. Necessarily it was to uproot all such relationships. But the object was broader than separating church and state in this narrow sense. It was to create a complete and permanent separation of the spheres of religious activity and civil authority by comprehensively forbidding every form of public aid or support for religion. In proof the Amendment's wording and history unite with this Court's consistent utterances whenever attention has been fixed directly upon the question.

No one would claim today that the Amendment is constricted, in "prohibiting the free exercise" of religion, to securing the free exercise of some formal or creedal observance, of one sect or of many. It secures all forms of religious expression, creedal, sectarian or non-sectarian wherever and however taking place, except conduct which trenches upon the like freedoms of others or clearly and presently endangers the community's good order and security. For the protective purposes of this phase of the basic freedom street preaching, oral or by distribution of literature, has been given "the same high estate under the First Amendment as . . . worship in the churches and preaching from the pulpits." And on this basis parents have been held entitled to send their children to private, religious schools. Pierce v. Society of Sisters, 268 U. S. 510. Accordingly, daily religious education commingled with secular is "religion" within the guaranty's comprehensive scope. So are religious training and teaching in whatever form. The word connotes the broadest content, determined not by the form or formality of the teaching or where it occurs, but by its essential nature regardless of those details.

"Religion" has the same broad significance in the twin prohibition concerning "an establishment." The Amendment was not duplicitous. "Religion" and "establishment" were not used in any formal or technical sense. The prohibition broadly forbids state support, financial or other, of religion in any guise, form or degree. It outlaws all use of public funds for religious purposes.

II.

No provision of the Constitution is more closely tied to or given content by its generating history than the religious clause of the First Amendment. It is at once the refined product and the terse summation of that history. The history includes not only Madison's authorship and the proceedings before the First Congress, but also the long and intensive struggle for religious freedom in America, more especially in Virginia, of which the Amendment was the direct culmination. In the documents of the times, particularly of Madison, who was leader in the Virginia struggle before he became the Amendment's sponsor, but also in the writings of Jefferson and others and in the issues which engendered them is to be found irrefutable confirmation of the Amendment's sweeping content. . . .

All the great instruments of the Virginia struggle for religious liberty thus became warp and woof of our constitutional tradition, not simply by the course of history, but by the common unifying force of Madison's life, thought and sponsorship. He epitomized the whole of that tradition in the Amendment's compact, but nonetheless comprehensive, phrasing.

As the Remonstrance discloses throughout, Madison opposed every form and degree of official relation between religion and civil authority. For him religion was a wholly private matter beyond the scope of civil power either to restrain or to support. Denial or abridgment of religious freedom was a violation of rights both of conscience and of natural equality. State aid was no less obnoxious or destructive to freedom and to religion itself than other forms of state interference. "Establishment" and "free exercise" were correlative and coextensive ideas, representing only different facets of the single great and fundamental freedom. The Remonstrance, following the Virginia statute's example, referred to the history of religious conflicts and the effects of all sorts of establishments, current and historical, to suppress religion's free exercise. With Jefferson, Madison believed that to tolerate any fragment of establishment would be by so much to perpetuate restraint upon that freedom. Hence he sought to tear out the institution not partially but root and branch, and to bar its return forever.

In no phase was he more unrelentingly absolute than in opposing state support or aid by taxation. Not even "three pence" contribution was thus to be exacted from any citizen for such a purpose. Remonstrance, Par. 3. Tithes had been the life blood of establishment before and after other compulsions disappeared. Madison and his coworkers made no exceptions or abridgments to the complete separation they created. Their objection was not to small tithes. It was to any tithes whatsoever. "If it were lawful to impose a small tax for religion the admission would pave the way for oppressive levies." Not the amount but "the principle of assessment was wrong." And the principle was as much to prevent "the interference of law in religion" as to restrain religious intervention in political matters. In this field the authors of our freedom would not tolerate "the first experiment on our liberties" or "wait till usurped power had strengthened itself by exercise, and entangled the question in precedents." Remonstrance, Par. 3. Nor should we.

In view of this history no further proof is needed that the Amendment forbids any appropriation, large or small, from public funds to aid or support any and all religious exercises. . . .

III.

Does New Jersey's action furnish support for religion by use of the taxing power? Certainly it does, if the test remains undiluted as Jefferson and Madison made it, that money taken by taxation from one is not to be used or given to support another's religious training or belief, or indeed one's own. Today as then the furnishing of "contributions of money for the propagation of opinions which he disbelieves" is the forbidden exaction; and the prohibition is absolute for whatever measure brings that consequence and whatever amount may be sought or given to that end.

The funds used here were raised by taxation. The Court does not dispute, nor could it, that their use does in fact give aid and encouragement to religious instruction. It only concludes that this aid is not "support" in law. But Madison and Jefferson were concerned with aid and support in fact, not as a legal conclusion "entangled in precedents." Remonstrance, Par. 3. Here parents pay money to send their children to parochial schools and funds raised by taxation are used to reimburse them. This not only helps the children to get to school and the parents to send them. It aids them in a substantial way to get the very thing which they are sent to the particular school to secure, namely, religious training and teaching.

Believers of all faiths, and others who do not express their feeling toward ultimate issues of existence in any creedal form, pay the New Jersey tax. When the money so raised is used to pay for transportation to religious schools, the Catholic taxpayer to the extent of his proportionate share pays for the transportation of Lutheran, Jewish and otherwise religiously affiliated children to receive their non-Catholic religious instruction. Their parents likewise pay proportionately for the transportation of Catholic children to receive Catholic instruction. Each thus contributes to "the propagation of opinions which he disbelieves" in so far as their religions differ, as do others who accept no creed without regard to those differences. Each thus pays taxes also to support the teaching of his own religion, an exaction equally forbidden since it denies "the comfortable liberty" of giving one's contribution to the particular agency of instruction he approves.

New Jersey's action therefore exactly fits the type of exaction and the kind of evil at which Madison and Jefferson struck. Under the test they framed it cannot be said that the cost of transportation is no part of the cost of education or of the religious instruction given. That it is a substantial and a necessary element is shown most plainly by the continuing and increasing demand for the state to assume it. Nor is there pretense that it relates only to the secular instruction given in religious schools or that any attempt is or could be made toward allocating proportional shares as between the secular and the religious instruction. It is precisely because the instruction is religious and relates to a particular faith, whether one or another, that parents send their children to religious schools under the Pierce doctrine. And the very purpose of the state's contribution is to defray the cost of conveying the pupil to the place where he will receive not simply secular, but also and primarily religious, teaching and guidance. . . .

Finally, transportation, where it is needed, is as essential to education as any other element. Its cost is as much a part of the total expense, except at times in amount, as the cost of textbooks, of school lunches, of athletic equipment, of writing and other materials; indeed of all other items composing the total burden. Now as always the core of the educational process is the teacher-pupil relationship. Without this the richest equipment and facilities would go for naught. . . . But the proverbial Mark Hopkins conception no longer suffices for the country's requirements. Without buildings, without equipment, without library, textbooks and other materials, and without transportation to bring teacher and pupil together in such an effective teaching environment, there can be not even the skeleton of what our times require. Hardly can it be maintained that transportation is the least essential of these items, or that it does not in fact aid, encourage, sustain and support, just as they do, the very process which is its purpose to accomplish. No less essential is it, or the payment of its cost, than the very teaching in the classroom or payment of the teacher's sustenance. Many types of equipment, now considered essential, better could be done without. . . .

IV.

But we are told that the New Jersey statute is valid in its present application because the appropriation is for a public, not a private purpose, namely, the promotion of education, and the majority accept this idea in the conclusion that all we have here is "public welfare legislation." If that is true and the Amendment's force can be thus destroyed, what has been said becomes all the more pertinent. For then there could be no possible objection to more extensive support of religious education by New Jersey.

If the fact alone be determinative that religious schools are engaged in education, thus promoting the general and individual welfare, together with the legislature's decision that the payment of public moneys for their aid makes their work a public function, then I can see no possible basis, except one of dubious legislative policy, for the state's refusal to make full appropriation for support of private, religious schools, just as is done for public instruction. There could not be, on that basis, valid constitutional objection.

We have here then one substantial issue, not two. To say that New Jersey's appropriation and her use of the power of taxation for raising the funds appropriated are not for public purposes but are for private ends, is to say that they are for the support of religion and religious teaching. Conversely, to say that they are for public purposes is to say that they are not for religious ones.

This is precisely for the reason that education which includes religious training and teaching, and its support, have been made matters of private right and function, not public, by the very terms of the First Amendment. That is the effect not only in its guaranty of religion's free exercise, but also in the prohibition of establishments. It was on this basis of the private character of the function of religious education that this Court held parents entitled to send their children to private, religious schools. Pierce v. Society of Sisters, *supra*. Now it declares in effect that the appropriation of public funds to defray part of the cost of attending those schools is for a public purpose. If so, I do not understand why the state cannot go farther or why this case approaches the verge of its power. . . .

Our constitutional policy is exactly the opposite. It does not deny the value or the necessity for religious training, teaching or observance. Rather it secures their free exercise. But to that end it does deny that the state can undertake or sustain them in any form or degree. For this reason the sphere of religious activity, as distinguished from the secular intellectual liberties, has been given the twofold protection and, as the state cannot forbid, neither can it perform or aid in performing the religious function. The dual prohibition makes that function altogether private. It cannot be made a public one by legislative act. This was the very heart of Madison's Remonstrance, as it is of the Amendment itself.

It is not because religious teaching does not promote the public or the individual's welfare, but because neither is furthered when the state promotes religious education, that the Constitution forbids it to do so. Both legislatures and courts are bound by that distinction. In failure to observe it lies the fallacy of the "public function"—"social legislation" argument, a fallacy facilitated by easy transference of the argument's basing from due process unrelated to any religious aspect to the First Amendment. . . .

The reasons underlying the Amendment's policy have not vanished with time or diminished in force. Now as when it was adopted the price of religious freedom is double. It is that the church and religion shall live both within and upon that freedom. There cannot be freedom of religion, safeguarded by the state, and intervention by the church or its agencies in the state's domain or dependency on its largesse. Madison's Remonstrance, Pars. 6, 8. The great condition of religious liberty is that it be maintained free from sustenance, as also from other interferences, by the state. For when it comes to rest upon that secular foundation it vanishes with the resting. Id., Pars. 7, 8. Public money devoted to payment of religious costs, educational or other, brings the quest for more. It brings too the struggle of sect against sect for the larger share or for any. Here one by numbers alone will benefit most, there another. That is precisely the history of societies which have had an established religion and dissident groups. It is the very thing Jefferson and Madison experienced and sought to guard against, whether in its blunt or in its more screened forms. The end of such strife cannot be other than to destroy the cherished liberty. The dominating group will achieve the dominant benefit; or all will embroil the state in their dissensions. . . .

This is not therefore just a little case over bus fares. In paraphrase of Madison, distant as it may be in its present form from a complete establishment of religion, it differs from it only in degree; and is the first step in that direction. . . .

The realm of religious training and belief remains, as the Amendment made it, the kingdom of the individual man and his God. It should be kept inviolately private, not "entangled . . . in precedents" or confounded with what legislatures legitimately may take over into the public domain.

V.

No one conscious of religious values can be unsympathetic toward the burden which our constitutional separation puts on parents who desire religious instruction mixed with secular for their children. They pay taxes for others' children's education, at the same time the added cost of instruction for their own. Nor can one happily see benefits denied to children which others receive, because in conscience they or their parents for them desire a different kind of training others do not demand.

But if those feelings should prevail, there would be an end to our historic constitutional policy and command. No more unjust or discriminatory in fact is it to deny attendants at religious schools the cost of their transportation than it is to deny them tuitions, sustenance for their teachers, or any other educational expense which others receive at public cost. Hardship in fact there is which none can blink. But, for assuring to those who undergo it the greater, the most comprehensive freedom, it is one written by design and firm intent into our basic law. . . .

That policy necessarily entails hardship upon persons who forego the right to educational advantages the state can supply in order to secure others it is precluded from giving. Indeed this may hamper the parent and the child forced by conscience to that choice. But it does not make the state unneutral to withhold what the Constitution forbids it to give. On the contrary it is only by observing the prohibition rigidly that the state can maintain its neutrality and avoid partisanship in the dissensions inevitable when sect opposes sect over demands for public moneys to further religious education, teaching or training in any form or degree, directly or indirectly. Like St. Paul's freedom, religious liberty with a great price must be bought. And for those who exercise it most fully, by insisting upon religious education for their children mixed with secular, by the terms of our Constitution the price is greater than for others.

The problem then cannot be cast in terms of legal discrimination or its absence. This would be true, even though the state in giving aid should treat all religious instruction alike. Thus, if the present statute and its application were shown to apply equally to all religious schools of whatever faith, yet in the light of our tradition it could not stand. For then the adherent of one creed still would pay for the support of another, the childless taxpayer with others more fortunate. Then too there would seem to be no bar to making appropriations for transportation and other expenses of children attending public or other secular schools, after hours in separate places and classes for their exclusively religious instruction. The person who embraces no creed also would be forced to pay for teaching what he does not believe. Again, it was the furnishing of "contributions of money for the propagation of opinions which he disbelieves" that the fathers outlawed. That consequence and effect are not removed by multiplying to all-inclusiveness the sects for which support is exacted. The Constitution requires, not comprehensive identification of state with religion, but complete separation. . . .

VI.

Two great drives are constantly in motion to abridge, in the name of education, the complete division of religion and civil authority which our forefathers made. One is to introduce religious education and observances into the public schools. The other, to obtain public funds for the aid and support of various private religious schools. . . . In my opinion both avenues were closed by the Constitution. Neither should be opened by this Court. The matter is not one of quantity, to be measured by the amount of money expended. Now as in Madison's day it is one of principle, to keep separate the separate spheres as the First Amendment drew them; to prevent the first experiment upon our liberties; and to keep the question from becoming entangled in corrosive precedents. We should not be less strict to keep strong and untarnished the one side of the shield of religious freedom than we have been of the other.

The judgment should be reversed.

SMITH v. ALLWRIGHT
321 U. S. 649; 88 L. Ed. 987; 64 Sup. Ct. 757. 1944.

The act of Congress of March 2, 1867, imposed Negro suffrage on the ten southern states as a part of the congressional policy of reconstruction, and three years later the Fifteenth Amendment undertook to establish, upon a permanent constitutional basis, the right of Negroes to vote. It was only natural that such a policy should meet with most bitter hostility from the southern white man, and for upwards of two decades the Negro was pretty effectively disfranchised throughout the south by intimidation, violence, and other irregular practices. Such methods, however, provided no permanent solution of the problem, and gradually means were perfected by which it was thought that the Negro could be disfranchised in a technically constitutional way. Mississippi proved a pioneer in this direction by requiring of the voter the payment of a poll tax and the display of the receipt therefor, and the ability to read the state constitution and to understand and interpret it reasonably when read to him. Fortressed behind clauses such as these the white election officials did not find it difficult to exclude the Negro without disturbing the white man. The Supreme Court of the United States held, in Williams v. Mississippi, 170 U. S. 213 (1898), that such provisions do not violate the Fifteenth Amendment since they do not deny to any one the right to vote because of his race or color. In Lassiter v.

Northampton County Board of Elections, 360 U. S. 45 (1959), the Court held unanimously that a North Carolina statute of 1957 was not unconstitutional "on its face" in requiring that "Every person presenting himself for registration shall be able to read and write any section of the Constitution of North Carolina in the English language." The case involved no direct racial discrimination since Lassiter had refused to submit to this literacy test.

A more interesting device for Negro disfranchisement, however, was the "grandfather clause." The essential features of this plan were two: first, the establishment of a rigorous educational qualification (in some states a property qualification) drastic enough to permit the disfranchisement of most Negroes; second, a provision that the qualification need not be met by those who were legal voters in 1866, or in 1867 (prior to the adoption of the act of March 2), or who were lineal descendants of such legal voters. In the case of Guinn v. United States, 238 U. S. 347 (1915), the Court held that the Oklahoma grandfather clause was a violation of the Fifteenth Amendment. The clause read as follows: "No person shall be registered as an elector of this state or be allowed to vote in any election held herein, unless he be able to read and write any section of the constitution of the State of Oklahoma; but no person who was, on January 1, 1866, or at any time prior thereto, entitled to vote under any form of government, or who at that time resided in some foreign nation, and no lineal descendant of such person, shall be denied the right to register and vote because of his inability to so read and write sections of such constitution." The Court emphasized that while the Fifteenth Amendment does not guarantee to any citizen the right to vote, since voting qualifications are fixed by state law, it does protect him against being denied the right to vote because of race or color. It held that while the grandfather clause did not mention race or color it was entirely clear that it set up a racial discrimination in the matter of voting since the only possible reason for picking out the date January 1, 1866, as a basis for classifying citizens was that before that date Negroes were not allowed to vote.

A sequel to the Guinn case is Lane v. Wilson, 307 U. S. 268 (1939). In 1916 the Oklahoma legislature passed a new suffrage law to replace the grandfather clause provisions held void the year before. The general election of 1914 had been held under the operation of the offending grandfather clause. The act of 1916 provided that those who had voted in the 1914 election automatically remained qualified to vote. All others were required to register between April 30 and May 11, 1916, with an extension to June 30 for those sick or out of the state during the earlier twelve-day period. The Court held that racial discrimination violating the Fifteenth Amendment resulted from thus granting voting privileges for life to white citizens originally sheltered by the grandfather clause, while subjecting colored citizens to the burden of a single twelve-day registration period as the only means of establishing voting privileges. "The amendment nullifies sophisticated as well as simple-minded modes of discrimination."

A novel attempt to disfranchise the southern Negro took the form of the so-called "white primary"—a scheme for preventing him from voting in primary elections. Since in most southern states nomination by the Democratic party is the equivalent of election, the denial of the right to vote in the primary really amounts to disfranchisement. In 1923 the Texas legislature passed a law providing that "in no event shall a negro be eligible to participate in a Democratic party primary election held in the state of Texas, and should a negro vote in a Democratic primary election, such ballot shall be void and election officials are herein directed to throw out such ballot, and not count the same." This appears to have been inspired by the supposed doctrine in Newberry v. United States, 256 U. S. 232 (1921), that a party primary is not an election within the meaning of the Constitution (see p. 64). In Nixon v. Herndon, 273 U. S. 536 (1927), the Court held the Texas statute void as a denial of the equal protection of the laws. The Court said: "We find it unnecessary to consider the Fifteenth Amendment, because it seems to us hard to imagine a more direct and obvious infringement of the Fourteenth." The Texas legislature then passed a new statute authorizing the state executive committee of any political party to determine who may vote in its primary. The Democratic state committee promptly passed a rule excluding Negroes from the Democratic primary of 1928. The Court again held, in Nixon v. Condon, 286 U. S. 73 (1932), that Negroes were denied the equal protection of the laws since the state law authorized the discrimination. But Texan ingenuity was equal to the occasion. The legislature took no further action, but the state Democratic convention adopted in 1932 a resolution declaring that "all white citizens of the state of Texas . . . shall be eligible to membership in the Democratic party and as such entitled to participate in its deliberations." A Negro who was denied the right to vote in the Democratic primary by this resolution was held, in Grovey v. Townsend, 295 U. S. 45 (1935), not to have been denied any constitutional rights under the Fourteenth Amendment since his exclusion was not the result, direct or indirect, of any state law or the act of any state official. The Democratic party is a private and not a governmental body, and private persons or groups cannot violate the Fourteenth Amendment.

When the Court decided United States v. Classic (p. 62), it did not mention Grovey v. Townsend. It was perfectly obvious that the two cases rested on conflicting principles. If, according to the Classic doctrine, a primary election is a vital part of the election machinery of the state, then clearly it is not the non-governmental and unofficial activity of a private voluntary association which Grovey v. Townsend held it to be. Accordingly steps were at once taken to bring before the Court for re-examination the question of the constitutionality of the Texas "white primary." In due course, Smith v. Allwright reached the Supreme Court and Grovey v. Townsend was overruled.

Smith v. Allwright did not end southern efforts to disfranchise the Negro. Alabama abandoned its white primary but adopted in 1946 the so-called "Boswell Amendment" which required voters to be able to "understand and explain" any Article of the Constitution of the United States to the satisfaction of local registration officers. The amendment did not by its language discriminate against Negroes, and it was widely assumed that this educational restriction upon the right to vote would be sustained by the Supreme Court upon the authority of the fifty-year-old decision in Williams v. Mississippi, mentioned above. In January, 1949, a three-judge federal district court held that the Boswell Amendment violated the Fifteenth Amendment. It did not even mention Williams v. Mississippi. It pointed out that the sole purpose of the amendment was to disfranchise the Negro, that it had been defended before the voters of the state as a measure that would do this, that evidence showed that it had been administered by Alabama election boards in such a way as to accomplish this result. The court said: "We cannot ignore the impact of the Boswell Amendment upon Negro citizens because it avoids mention of race or color, to do this would be to shut our eyes to what all others can see and understand." In March, 1949, the Supreme Court, without hearing argument in the case, affirmed the district court's opinion. See Schnell v. Davis, 336 U. S. 933.

South Carolina tried a different method of circumventing the decision in the Allwright case. It was believed that if the Democratic primary in the state could be converted into a purely "private club," Negroes could then be excluded from it without violating either the Fourteenth or the Fifteenth Amendments. Accordingly the state legislature repealed some 150 statutory provisions in which primaries were authorized, regulated, or just mentioned, and a special constitutional amendment was adopted deleting all mention of primaries from the state constitution. The Democratic party then proceeded to bar Negroes from its primary elections. The federal district court held that in spite of all the efforts which had been made, the South Carolina Democratic primary still remained in reality the only effective agency for selecting federal and other officials, and that since this was true Negroes could not constitutionally be barred from voting in it. This decision was affirmed by the circuit court of appeals, and on April 19, 1948, the Supreme Court let that decision stand by refusing certiorari. See Rice v. Elmore, 333 U. S. 875.

In some southern communities the effort to keep qualified Negroes from voting has taken the form of varied discriminatory acts on the part of local election officials. In United States v. Mississippi, 380 U. S. 128 (1965), the Court held that the United States could sue the state and its officials to protect voting rights, and in Louisiana v. United States, 380 U. S. 145 (1965), it struck down that state's "interpretation" test as "part of a successful plan to deprive Louisiana Negroes of their right to vote." With the adoption of the Civil Rights Acts of 1957, 1960, and 1964, and the Voting Rights Act of 1965, attention has turned to the meaning of these statutes and their effectiveness in halting voting discrimination. See South Carolina v. Katzenbach, p. 551. After the Twenty-fourth Amendment outlawed poll taxes in federal elections and the Civil Rights Act of 1965 waived them in certain state elections (see p. 558), the Court in 1966 held that state poll taxes violated the equal protection clause of the Fourteenth Amendment; see Harper v. Virginia Bd. of Education, 383 U. S. 663.

Mr. Justice Reed delivered the opinion of the Court, saying in part:

The State of Texas by its Constitution and statutes provides that every person, if certain other requirements are met which are not here in issue, qualified by residence in the district or county "shall be deemed a qualified elector." Primary elections for United States Senators, Congressmen and state officers are provided for by Chapters Twelve and Thirteen of the statutes. Under these chapters, the Democratic party was required to hold the primary which was the occasion of the alleged wrong to petitioner. These nominations are to be made by the qualified voters of the party. . . .

The Democratic party on May 24, 1932, in a State Convention adopted the following resolution, which has not since been "amended, abrogated, annulled or avoided":

"Be it resolved that all white citizens of the State of Texas who are qualified to vote under the Constitution and laws of the State shall be eligible to membership in the Democratic party and, as such, entitled to participate in its deliberations."

It was by virtue of this resolution that the respondents refused to permit the petitioner to vote.

Texas is free to conduct her elections and limit her electorate as she may deem wise, save only as her action may be affected by the prohibitions of the United States Constitution or in conflict with powers delegated to and exercised by the national government. The Fourteenth Amendment forbids a state from making or enforcing any law which abridges the privileges or immunities of citizens of the United States and the Fifteenth Amendment specifically interdicts any denial or abridgment by a state of the right of citizens to vote on account of color. Respondents appeared in the District Court and the Circuit Court of Appeals and defended on the ground that the Democratic party of Texas is a voluntary organization with members banded together for the purpose of selecting individuals of the group representing the common political beliefs as candidates in the general election. As such a voluntary organization, it was claimed, the Democratic party is free to select its own membership and limit to whites paticipation in the party primary. Such action, the answer asserted, does not violate the Fourteenth, Fifteenth or Seventeenth Amendment as officers of government cannot be chosen at primaries and the Amendments are applicable only to general elections where governmental officers are actually elected. Primaries, it is said, are political party affairs, handled by party, not governmental, officers. . . .

The right of a Negro to vote in the Texas primary has been considered heretofore by this Court. . . . [There follows a summary of the decisions in Nixon v. Herndon, and Nixon v. Condon, which are commented upon in the introductory note.]

In Grovey v. Townsend, 295 U. S. 45, this Court had before it another suit for damages for the refusal in a primary of a county clerk, a Texas officer with only public functions to perform, to furnish petitioner, a Negro, an absentee ballot. The refusal was solely on the ground of race. This case differed from Nixon v. Condon, in that a state convention of the Democratic party had passed the resolution of May 24, 1932, hereinbefore quoted. It was decided that the determination by the state convention of the membership of the Democratic party made a significant change from a determination by the Executive Committee. The former was party action, voluntary in character. The latter, as had been held in the Condon case, was action by authority of the state. The managers of the primary election were therefore declared not to be state officials in such sense that their action was state action. A state convention of a party was said not to be an organ of the state. This Court went on to announce that to deny a vote in a primary was a mere refusal of party membership with which "the state need have no concern," while for a state to deny a vote in a general election on the ground of race or color violated the Constitution. Consequently, there was found no ground for holding that the county clerk's refusal of a ballot because of racial ineligibility for party membership denied the petitioner any right under the Fourteenth or Fifteenth Amendment.

Since Grovey v. Townsend and prior to the present suit, no case from Texas involving primary elections has been before this Court. We did decide, however, United States v. Classic, 313 U. S. 299. We there held that section 4 of Article I of the Constitution authorized Congress to regulate primary as well as general elections, "where the primary is by law made an integral part of the election machinery." Consequently, in the Classic case, we upheld the applicability to frauds in a Louisiana primary of §§ 19 and 20 of the Criminal Code. Thereby corrupt acts of election officers were subjected to congressional sanctions because that body had power to protect rights of federal suffrage secured by the Constitution in primary as in general elections. This decision depended, too, on the determination that under the Louisiana statutes the primary was a part of the procedure for choice of federal officials. By this decision the doubt as to whether or not such primaries were a part of "elections" subject to federal control, which had remained unanswered since Newberry v. United States, 256 U. S. 232, was erased. The Nixon cases were decided under the equal protection clause of the Fourteenth Amendment without a determination of the status of the primary as a part of the electoral process. The exclusion of Negroes from the primaries by action of the state was held invalid under that Amendment. The fusing by the Classic case of the primary and general elections into a single instrumentality for choice of officers has a definite bearing on the permissibility under the Constitution of excluding Negroes from primaries. . . . Classic bears upon Grovey v. Townsend not because exclusion of Negroes from primaries is any more or less state action by reason of the unitary character of the electoral process but because the recognition of the place of the primary in the electoral scheme makes clear that state delegation to a party of the power to fix the qualifications of primary elections is delegation of a state function that may make the party's action the action of the State. When Grovey v. Townsend was written, the Court looked upon the denial of a vote in a primary, as a mere refusal by a party of party membership. As the Louisiana statutes for holding primaries are similar to those of Texas, our ruling in Classic as to the unitary character of the electoral process calls for a reexamination as to whether or not the exclusion of Negroes from a Texas party primary was state action. . . .

It may now be taken as a postulate that the right to vote in such a primary for the nomination of candidates without discrimination by the state, like the right to vote in a general election, is a right secured by the Constitution. By the terms of the Fifteenth Amendment that right may not be abridged by any state on account of race. Under our Constitution the great privilege of the ballot may not be denied a man by the state because of his color.

We are thus brought to an examination of the qualifications for Democratic primary electors in Texas, to determine whether state action or private action has excluded Negroes from participation. . . . [There follows a summary of the various ways in which Texas primaries are regulated by state statutes.]

We think that this statutory system for the selection of party nominees for inclusion on the general election ballot makes the party which is required to follow these legislative directions an agency of the state in so far as it determines the participants in a primary election. The party takes its character as a state agency from the duties imposed upon it by state statutes; the duties do not become matters of private law because they are performed by a political party. The plan of the Texas primary follows substantially that of Louisiana, with the exception that in Louisiana the state pays the cost of the primary while Texas assesses the cost against candidates. In numerous instances, the Texas statutes fix or limit the fees to be charged. Whether paid directly by the state or through state requirements, it is state action which compels. When primaries become a part of the machinery for choosing officials, state and national, as they have here, the same tests to determine the character of discrimination or abridgement should be applied to the primary as are applied to the general election. If the state requires a certain electoral procedure, prescribes a general election ballot made up of party nominees so chosen and limits the choice of the electorate in general elections for state offices, practically speaking, to those whose names appear on such a ballot, it endorses, adopts and enforces the discrimination against Negroes, practiced by a party entrusted by Texas law with the determination of the qualifications of participants in the primary. This is state action within the meaning of the Fifteenth Amendment.

The United States is a constitutional democracy. Its organic law grants to all citizens a right to participate in the choice of elected officials without restriction by any state because of race. This grant to the people of the opportunity for choice is not to be nullified by a state through casting its electoral process in a form which permits a private organization to practice racial discrimination in the election.

Constitutional rights would be of little value if they could be thus indirectly denied.

The privilege of membership in a party may be, as this Court said in Grovey v. Townsend, 295 U. S. 45, no concern of a state. But when, as here, that privilege is also the essential qualification for voting in a primary to select nominees for a general election, the state makes the action of the party the action of the state. In reaching this conclusion we are not unmindful of the desirability of continuity of decision in constitutional questions. However, when convinced of former error, this Court has never felt constrained to follow precedent. In constitutional questions, where correction depends upon amendment and not upon legislative action this Court throughout its history has freely exercised its power to reexamine the basis of its constitutional decisions. This has long been accepted practice, and this practice has continued to this day. This is particularly true when the decision believed erroneous is the application of a constitutional principle rather than an interpretation of the Constitution to extract the principle itself. Here we are applying, contrary to the recent decision in Grovey v. Townsend, the well-established principle of the Fifteenth Amendment, forbidding the abridgement by a state of a citizen's right to vote. Grovey v. Townsend is overruled.

Mr. Justice Frankfurter concurred in the result. Mr. Justice Roberts dissented.

BAKER v. CARR
369 U. S. 186; 7 L. Ed. 2d 663; 82 Sup. Ct. 691. 1962.

In Colegrove v. Green, 328 U. S. 549 (1946), judicial relief was sought from unjust congressional apportionment in Illinois. The Illinois constitution of 1870 provided that the state should be divided into fifty-one state senatorial districts, from each of which one state senator and three state representatives should be chosen. The legislature, after each census, was to redraw the lines of these districts to meet changes in population. By the turn of the century it was obvious that more than half the population of the state would shortly be concentrated in the metropolitan area of Chicago. Legislators from the down-state rural districts, enjoying a comfortable legislative majority, felt no inclination to yield their political control by reapportioning the state to give the growing metropolis the proportion of the fifty-one districts to which its population clearly entitled it. The political bitterness created by this inequitable situation had made it impossible for the Illinois legislature to agree upon a revision of its legislative districts since the apportionment of 1901. Attempts were made to invoke court action, but the supreme court of Illinois, itself applying the doctrine of "political questions," held that it had no power to compel the legislature to pass a new and fair redistricting law.

This all bears on the problem of congressional apportionment posed in Colegrove v. Green. When Congress after each census reapportions seats in the House of Representatives among the states, it becomes the duty of each state legislature to carve out such new congressional districts as the new allotments may require. But the Illinois legislature had been no more willing to give the Chicago metropolitan area its fair share of seats in Congress than in the state legislature itself. At the time the case arose it had not reapportioned congressional seats since 1901. Rank inequalities had resulted. One congressional district (in Chicago) had a population of 914,053, while another had a population of 112,116. The Court was asked to enjoin the Illinois state officials from conducting an election in November, 1946, to be held under the provisions of the old congressional apportionment act of 1901. Such an injunction would have compelled the state to elect all of its congressmen on one general ballot, instead of by districts; and this would have given full effect to the political strength of the populous urban areas.

The Court, four to three, refused to grant the relief asked, or to consider the validity of the Illinois apportionment on its merits. Mr. Justice Frankfurter, speaking for himself and Justices Reed and Burton, stated that the issue was "of a peculiarly political nature and therefore not meet for judicial determination." He went on further to say: "Nothing is clearer than that this controversy concerns matters that bring courts into immediate and active relations with party contests. From the determination of such issues this Court has traditionally held aloof. It is hostile to a democratic system to involve the judiciary in the politics of the people. And it is not less pernicious if such judicial intervention in an essentially political contest be dressed up in the abstract phrases of the law." This opinion was widely construed as stating the ruling of the case. Mr. Justice Rutledge, however, concurred in the decision on a different ground. Chief Justice Stone, who had died two months before, and Mr. Justice Jackson, did not participate in the decision. Justices Black, Douglas, and Murphy dissented. The Frankfurter doctrine did not, therefore, command majority support in the Court.

The Georgia "County Unit System" was challenged in South v. Peters, 339 U. S. 276 (1950). The scheme assigns to each county electoral votes which go to the candidate receiving the highest popular vote. The purpose and result has been the heavy disfranchisement of the urban Negro population. The Supreme Court held that "a state's geographical distribution of electoral strength among its political subdivisions" is a political question.

Since Baker v. Carr, however, the lower federal courts have held the Georgia system invalid, and ordered its modification.

The doctrine that the validity of a legislative apportionment can never be a subject for judicial review was unanimously rejected by the Court in Gomillion v. Lightfoot, 364 U. S. 399 (1960). The issue raised was unique. An Alabama statute of 1957 redefined the boundaries of the city of Tuskegee, within which is the well-known Tuskegee Institute. The city, which had been square in shape, was transformed "into a strangely irregular twenty-eight sided figure," with the intention and result of removing from the city "all save four or five of its 400 Negro voters while not removing a single white voter or resident." The Negroes thus excluded could not, of course, vote in municipal elections. The lower federal courts, relying in part upon Colegrove v. Green, had dismissed the complaint attacking the validity of the statute. In an opinion by Mr. Justice Frankfurter the Supreme Court, without passing on the truth of the allegations, held that the plaintiffs had a right to have a court decide whether the weird apportionment constituted discrimination against them in violation of the due process and equal protection clauses of the Fourteenth Amendment and denied them the right to vote in defiance of the Fifteenth Amendment.

Baker v. Carr is a landmark in constitutional law and in American government and politics. In a majority of states over the past few decades the rural counties have lost, and continue to lose, population to the cities and surrounding metropolitan areas. These rural counties in most states, however, have stubbornly refused to permit the change of the existing apportionment of legislative members which gives them a dominating overrepresentation at the expense of the growing urban centers. Reform could be achieved by constitutional amendment were it not for the fact that the existing legislatures control the amending process. Thus the holding in Colegrove v. Green seemed to make permanent the stranglehold of the rural and sparsely populated areas upon the political destinies of the state. Baker v. Carr holds that the courts may now scrutinize the fairness of legislative apportionments, and take steps to assure that serious inequalities are wiped out. A shift in the balance of political power throughout the entire country might result from this.

The Court did not itself pass on the validity of the legislative apportionment in Tennessee; it announced that such issues were justiciable and left to the lower courts the problem of deciding the actual cases. As these cases were appealed, in turn, the Supreme Court spelled out the doctrines that applied. In Wesberry v. Sanders, 376 U. S. 1 (1964), the Court held that Article I required that each man's vote weigh the same within a congressional district, and in Reynolds v. Sims (p. 487), the equal protection clause was held to require this of both houses in a state legislature.

The case treats in great length the historical evolution of apportionment, the Court's prior handling of "political" questions, and its basis for distinguishing Colegrove.

Mr. Justice Brennan delivered the opinion of the Court, saying in part:

This civil action was brought to redress the alleged deprivation of federal constitutional rights. The complaint, alleging that by means of a 1901 statute of Tennessee apportioning the members of the General Assembly among the State's 95 counties, "these plaintiffs and others similarly situated, are denied the equal protection of the laws accorded them by the Fourteenth Amendment to the Constitution of the United States by virtue of the debasement of their votes," was dismissed by a three-judge court. We hold that the dismissal was error, and remand the cause to the District Court for trial and further proceedings consistent with this opinion.

The General Assembly of Tennessee consists of the Senate with 33 members and the House of Representatives with 99 members. The Tennessee Constitution provides in Art. II as follows: . . . [The text of sections 3-6 follows.]

Thus, Tennessee's standard for allocating legislative representation among her counties is the total number of qualified voters resident in the respective counties, subject only to minor qualifications. . . . In 1901 the General Assembly abandoned separate enumeration in favor of reliance upon the Federal Census and passed the Apportionment Act here in controversy. In the more than 60 years since that action, all proposals in both Houses of the General Assembly for reapportionment have failed to pass.

Between 1901 and 1961, Tennessee has experienced substantial growth and redistribution of her population. In 1901 the population was 2,020,616, of whom 487,380 were eligible to vote. The 1960 Federal Census reports the State's population at 3,567,089, of whom 2,092,891 are eligible to vote. The relative standings of the counties in terms of qualified voters have changed significantly. It is primarily the continued application of the 1901 Apportionment Act to this shifted and enlarged voting population which gives rise to the present controversy.

Indeed, the complaint alleges that the 1901 statute, even as of the time of its passage, "made no apportionment of Representatives and Senators in accordance with the constitutional formula . . . , but instead arbitrarily and capriciously apportioned representatives in the

Senate and House without reference . . . to any logical or reasonable formula whatever." It is further alleged that "because of the population changes since 1900, and the failure of the legislature to reapportion itself since 1901," the 1901 statute became "unconstitutional and obsolete." Appellants also argue that, because of the composition of the legislature effected by the 1901 apportionment act, redress in the form of a state constitutional amendment to change the entire mechanism for reapportioning, or any other change short of that, is difficult or impossible. The complaint concludes that "these plaintiffs and others similarly situated, are denied the equal protection of the laws accorded them by the Fourteenth Amendment to the Constitution of the United States by virtue of the debasement of their votes." They seek a declaration that the 1901 statute is unconstitutional and an injunction restraining the appellees from acting to conduct any further elections under it. They also pray that unless and until the General Assembly enacts a valid reapportionment, the District Court should either decree a reapportionment by mathematical application of the Tennessee constitutional formulae to the most recent Federal Census figures, or direct the appellees to conduct legislative elections, primary and general, at large. They also pray for such other and further relief as may be appropriate.

I. THE DISTRICT COURT'S OPINION AND ORDER OF DISMISSAL.

[Here summarized.]

. . . In light of the District Court's treatment of the case, we hold today only (a) that the court possessed jurisdiction of the subject matter; (b) that a justiciable cause of action is stated upon which appellants would be entitled to appropriate relief; and (c) because appellees raise the issue before this Court, that the appellants have standing to challenge the Tennessee apportionment statutes. Beyond noting that we have no cause at this stage to doubt the District Court will be able to fashion relief if violations of constitutional rights are found, it is improper now to consider what remedy would be most appropriate if appellants prevail at the trial.

II. JURISDICTION OF THE SUBJECT MATTER.

The District Court was uncertain whether our cases withholding federal judicial relief rested upon a lack of federal jurisdiction or upon the inappropriateness of the subject matter for judicial consideration—what we have designated "nonjusticiability." The distinction between the two grounds is significant. In the instance of nonjusticiability, consideration of the cause is not wholly and immediately foreclosed; rather, the Court's inquiry necessarily proceeds to the point of deciding whether the duty asserted can be judicially identified and its breach judicially determined, and whether protection for the right asserted can be judicially molded. In the instance of lack of jurisdiction the cause either does not "arise under" the Federal Constitution, laws or treaties (or fall within one of the other enumerated categories of Art. III, § 2), or is not a "case or controversy" within the meaning of that section; or the cause is not one described by any jurisdictional statute. Our conclusion that this cause presents no nonjusticiable "political question" settles the only possible doubt that it is a case or controversy. Under the present heading of "Jurisdiction of the Subject Matter" we hold only that the matter set forth in the complaint does arise under the Constitution.

Article III, § 2 of the Federal Constitution provides that "the judicial Power shall extend to all Cases, in Law and Equity, arising under this Constitution, the Laws of the United States, and Treaties made, or which shall be made, under their Authority; . . . ." It is clear that the cause of action is one which "arises under" the Federal Constitution. The complaint alleges that the 1901 statute effects an apportionment that deprives the appellants of the equal protection of the laws in violation of the Fourteenth Amendment. Dismissal of the complaint upon the ground of lack of jurisdiction of the subject matter would, therefore, be justified only if that claim were "so attenuated and unsubstantial as to be absolutely devoid of merit." Since the District Court obviously and correctly did not deem the asserted federal constitutional claim unsubstantial and frivolous, it should not have dismissed the complaint for want of jurisdiction of the subject matter. And of course no further consideration of the merits of the claim is relevant to a determination of the court's jurisdiction of the subject matter. . . .

An unbroken line of our precedents sustains the federal courts' jurisdiction of the subject matter of federal constitutional claims of this nature. The first cases involved the redistricting of States for the purpose of electing Representatives to the Federal Congress. When the Ohio Supreme Court sustained Ohio legislation against an attack for repugnancy to Art. I, § 4, of the Federal Constitution, we affirmed on the merits and expressly refused to dismiss for want of jurisdiction "in view . . . of the subject-matter of the controversy and the Federal characteristics which inhere in it . . . ." Ohio ex rel. Davis v. Hildebrant, 241 U. S. 565. When the Minnesota Supreme Court affirmed the dismissal of a suit to enjoin the Secretary of State of Minnesota from acting under Minnesota redistricting legislation, we reviewed the constitutional merits of the legislation and reversed the State Supreme Court. Smiley v. Holm, 285 U. S. 355 [and other cases cited].

The appellees refer to Colegrove v. Green, 328 U. S. 549, as authority that the District Court lacked jurisdiction of the subject matter. Appellees misconceive the holding of that case. The holding was precisely contrary to their reading of it. Seven members of the Court participated in the decision. Unlike many other cases in this field which have assumed without discussion that there was jurisdiction, all three opinions filed in Colegrove discussed the question. Two of the opinions expressing the views of four of the Justices, a majority, flatly held that there was jurisdiction of that subject matter. . . .

We hold that the District Court has jurisdiction of the subject matter of the federal constitutional claim asserted in the complaint.

III. STANDING.

A federal court cannot "pronounce any statute, either of a state or of the United States, void, because irreconcilable with the constitution, except as it is called upon to adjudge the legal rights of litigants in actual controversies." Have the appellants alleged such a personal stake in the outcome of the controversy as to assure that concrete adverseness which sharpens the presentation of issues upon which the court so largely depends for illumination of difficult constitutional questions? This is the gist of the question of standing. It is, of course, a question of federal law.

The complaint was filed by residents of Davidson, Hamilton, Knox, Montgomery, and Shelby Counties. Each is a person allegedly qualified to vote for members of the General Assembly representing his county. These appellants sued "on their own behalf and on behalf of all qualified voters of their respective counties, and further, on behalf of all voters of the State of Tennessee who are similarly situated . . . ." The appellees are the Tennessee Secretary of State, Attorney General, Coordinator of Elections, and members of the State

Board of Elections; the members of the State Board are sued in their own right and also as representatives of the County Election Commissioners whom they appoint.

We hold that the appellants do have standing to maintain this suit. Our decisions plainly support this conclusion. Many of the cases have assumed rather than articulated the premise in deciding the merits of similar claims. . . .

These appellants seek relief in order to protect or vindicate an interest of their own, and of those similarly situated. Their constitutional claim is, in substance, that the 1901 statute constitutes arbitrary and capricious state action, offensive to the Fourteenth Amendment in its irrational disregard of the standard of apportionment prescribed by the State's Constitution or of any standard, effecting a gross disproportion of representation to voting population. The injury which appellants assert is that this classification disfavors the voters in the counties in which they reside, placing them in a position of constitutionally unjustifiable inequality *vis-à-vis* voters in irrationally favored counties. A citizen's right to a vote free of arbitrary impairment by state action has been judicially recognized as a right secured by the Constitution, when such impairment resulted from dilution by a false tally, or by a refusal to count votes from arbitrarily selected precincts, or by a stuffing of the ballot box.

It would not be necessary to decide whether appellants' allegations of impairment of their votes by the 1901 apportionment will, ultimately, entitle them to any relief, in order to hold that they have standing to seek it. If such impairment does produce a legally cognizable injury, they are among those who have sustained it. They are asserting "a plain, direct and adequate interest in maintaining the effectiveness of their votes," not merely a claim of "the right possessed by every citizen 'to require that the government be administered according to law . . .'." They are entitled to a hearing and to the District Court's decision on their claims. "The very essence of civil liberty certainly consists in the right of every individual to claim the protection of the laws, whenever he receives an injury."

IV. JUSTICIABILITY.

In holding that the subject matter of this suit was not justiciable, the District Court relied on Colegrove v. Green, supra, and subsequent *per curiam* cases. The court stated: "From a review of these decisions there can be no doubt that the federal rule . . . is that the federal courts . . . will not intervene in cases of this type to compel legislative reapportionment." We understand the District Court to have read the cited cases as compelling the conclusion that since the appellants sought to have a legislative apportionment held unconstitutional, their suit presented a "political question" and was therefore nonjusticiable. We hold that this challenge to an apportionment presents no nonjusticiable "political question." The cited cases do not hold the contrary.

Of course the mere fact that the suit seeks protection of a political right does not mean it presents a political question. Such an objection "is little more than a play upon words." Rather, it is argued that apportionment cases, whatever the actual wording of the complaint, can involve no federal constitutional right except one resting on the guaranty of a republican form of government, and that complaints based on that clause have been held to present political questions which are nonjusticiable.

We hold that the claim pleaded here neither rests upon nor implicates the Guaranty Clause and that its justiciability is therefore not foreclosed by our decisions of cases involving that clause. The District Court misinterpreted Colegrove v. Green and other decisions of this Court on which it relied. Appellants' claim that they are being denied equal protection is justiciable, and if "discrimination is sufficiently shown, the right to relief under the equal protection clause is not diminished by the fact that the discrimination relates to political rights." To show why we reject the argument based on the Guaranty Clause, we must examine the authorities under it. But because there appears to be some uncertainty as to why those cases did present political questions, and specifically as to whether this apportionment case is like those cases, we deem it necessary first to consider the contours of the "political question" doctrine.

Our discussion, even at the price of extending this opinion, requires review of a number of political question cases, in order to expose the attributes of the doctrine—attributes which, in various settings, diverge, combine, appear, and disappear in seeming disorderliness. Since that review is undertaken solely to demonstrate that neither singly nor collectively do these cases support a conclusion that this apportionment case is nonjusticiable, we of course do not explore their implications in other contexts. That review reveals that in the Guaranty Clause cases and in the other "political question" cases, it is the relationship between the judiciary and the coordinate branches of the Federal Government, and not the federal judiciary's relationship to the States, which gives rise to the "political question."

We have said that "in determining whether a question falls within [the political question] category, the appropriateness under our system of government of attributing finality to the action of the political departments and also the lack of satisfactory criteria for a judicial determination are dominant considerations." Coleman v. Miller, 307 U. S. 433. The nonjusticiability of a political question is primarily a function of the separation of powers. Much confusion results from the capacity of the "political question" label to obscure the need for case-by-case inquiry. Deciding whether a matter has in any measure been committed by the Constitution to another branch of government, or whether the action of that branch exceeds whatever authority has been committed, is itself a delicate exercise in constitutional interpretation, and is a responsibility of this Court as ultimate interpreter of the Constitution. To demonstrate this requires no less than to analyze representative cases and to infer from them the analytical threads that make up the political question doctrine. We shall then show that none of those threads catches this case. . . .

[Here follows a long summary of cases involving the political question doctrine as they have arisen in the fields of (1) foreign relations, (2) dates of duration of hostilities, (3) validity of enactments, (4) status of Indian tribes, and (5) republican form of government.]

We come, finally to the ultimate inquiry whether our precedents as to what constitutes a nonjusticiable "political question" bring the case before us under the umbrella of that doctrine. A natural beginning is to note whether any of the common characteristics which we have been able to identify and label descriptively are present. We find none: The question here is the consistency of state action with the Federal Constitution. We have no question decided, or to be decided, by a political branch of government coequal with this Court. Nor do we risk embarrassment of our government abroad, or grave disturbance at home if we take issue with Tennessee as to the constitutionality of her action here challenged. Nor need the appellants, in order to succeed in this action, ask the Court to enter upon policy determinations for which judicially manageable standards are lacking. Judicial standards under the Equal Protection Clause are well developed and familiar, and it has been open to courts since the enactment of the Fourteenth Amendment to determine, if on the particular facts they must, that a discrimination reflects *no* policy, but simply arbitrary and capricious action. . . .

We conclude that the complaint's allegations of a denial of equal protection present a justiciable constitutional cause of action upon which appellants are entitled to a trial and a decision. The right asserted is within the reach of judicial protection under the Fourteenth Amendment.

The judgment of the District Court is reversed and the cause is remanded for further proceedings consistent with this opinion.

Reversed and remanded.

Mr. Justice Whittaker did not participate in the decision of this case.

Mr. Justice Douglas, concurring, said in part:

While I join the opinion of the Court and, like the Court, do not reach the merits, a word of explanation is necessary. I put to one side the problems of "political" questions involving the distribution of power between this Court, the Congress, and the Chief Executive. We have here a phase of the recurring problem of the relation of the federal courts to state agencies. More particularly, the question is the extent to which a State may weight one person's vote more heavily than it does another's. . . .

I agree with my Brother Clark that if the allegations in the complaint can be sustained a case for relief is established. We are told that a single vote in Moore County, Tennessee, is worth 19 votes in Hamilton County, that one vote in Stewart or in Chester County is worth nearly eight times a single vote in Shelby or Knox County. The opportunity to prove that an "invidious discrimination" exists should therefore be given the appellants. . . .

With the exceptions of Colegrove v. Green, 328 U. S. 549, MacDougall v. Green, 335 U. S. 281, South v. Peters, 339 U. S. 276, and the decisions they spawned, the Court has never thought that protection of voting rights was beyond judicial cognizance. Today's treatment of those cases removes the only impediment to judicial cognizance of the claims stated in the present complaint. . . .

Mr. Justice Clark, concurring, said in part:

One emerging from the rash of opinions with their accompanying clashing of views may well find himself suffering a mental blindness.

The Court holds that the appellants have alleged a cause of action. However, it refuses to award relief here—although the facts are undisputed—and fails to give the District Court any guidance whatever. One dissenting opinion, bursting with words that go through so much and conclude with so little, contemns the majority action as "a massive repudiation of the experience of our whole past." Another describes the complaint as merely asserting conclusory allegations that Tennessee's apportionment is "incorrect," "arbitrary," "obsolete," and "unconstitutional." I believe it can be shown that this case is distinguishable from earlier cases dealing with the distribution of political power by a State, that a patent violation of the Equal Protection Clause of the United States Constitution has been shown, and that an appropriate remedy may be formulated.

. . . The widely heralded case of Colegrove v. Green was one not only in which the Court was bob-tailed but in which there was no majority opinion. Indeed, even the "political question" point in Mr. Justice Frankfurter's opinion was no more than an alternative ground. Moreover, the appellants did not present an equal protection argument. While it has served as a Mother Hubbard to most of the subsequent cases, I feel it was in that respect ill cast and for all of these reasons put it to one side. . . .

The controlling facts cannot be disputed.

. . . The frequency and magnitude of the inequalities in the present districting admit of no policy whatever. . . . It leaves but one conclusion, namely that Tennessee's apportionment is a crazy quilt without rational basis. . . .

[Examples are given of the inequalities in apportionment in Tennessee.]

The truth is that—although this case has been here for two years and has had over six hours' argument (three times the ordinary case) and has been most carefully considered over and over again by us in Conference and individually—no one, not even the State nor the dissenters, has come up with any rational basis for Tennessee's apportionment statute.

. . . Like the District Court, I conclude that appellants have met the burden of showing "Tennessee is guilty of a clear violation of the state constitution and of the [federal] rights of the plaintiffs. . . ."

Although I find the Tennessee apportionment statute offends the Equal Protection Clause, I would not consider intervention by this Court into so delicate a field if there were any other relief available to the people of Tennessee. But the majority of the people of Tennessee have no "practical opportunities for exerting their political weight at the polls" to correct the existing "invidious discrimination." Tennessee has no initiative and referendum. I have searched diligently for other "practical opportunities" present under the law. I find none other than through the federal courts. . . .

Finally, we must consider if there are any appropriate modes of effective judicial relief. The federal courts are, of course, not forums for political debate, nor should they resolve themselves into state constitutional conventions or legislative assemblies. Nor should their jurisdiction be exercised in the hope that such a declaration, as is made today, may have the direct effect of bringing on legislative action and relieving the courts of the problem of fashioning relief. To my mind this would be nothing less than blackjacking the Assembly into reapportioning the State. If judicial competence were lacking to fashion an effective decree, I would dismiss this appeal. However, like the Solicitor General of the United States, I see no such difficulty in the position of this case. One plan might be to start with the existing assembly districts, consolidate some of them, and award the seats thus released to those counties suffering the most egregious discrimination. Other possibilities are present and might be more effective. But the plan here suggested would at least release the stranglehold now on the Assembly and permit it to redistrict itself.

In this regard the appellants have proposed a plan based on the rationale of state-wide equal representation. Not believing that numerical equality of representation throughout a State is constitutionally required, I would not apply such a standard albeit a permissive one. Nevertheless, the dissenters attack it by the application of the Harlan "adjusted 'total representation'" formula. The result is that some isolated inequalities are shown, but this in itself does not make the proposed plan irrational or place it in the "crazy quilt" category. Such inequalities, as the dissenters point out in attempting to support the present apportionment as rational, are explainable. Moreover, there is no requirement that any plan have mathematical exactness in its application. Only where, as here, the total picture reveals incommensurables of both magnitude and frequency can it be said that there is present an invidious discrimination. . . .

As John Rutledge (later Chief Justice) said 175 years ago in the course of the Constitutional Convention, a chief function of the Court is to secure the national rights. Its decision today supports the proposition for which our forebears fought and many died, namely that "to be fully comformable to the principle of right, the form of government must be representative." That is the keystone upon which our government was founded and lacking which no republic can survive. It is well for this Court to practice self-restraint and discipline in constitutional adjudication, but never in its history have those principles received sanction where the national rights of so many have been so clearly infringed for so long a time. National respect for the courts is more enhanced through the forthright enforcement of those rights rather than by rendering them nugatory through the interposition of subterfuges. In my view the ultimate decision today is in the greatest tradition of this Court.

Mr. Justice Stewart, concurring, said in part:

. . . The Court today decides three things and no more: "(a) that the court possessed jurisdiction of the subject matter; (b) that a justiciable cause of action is stated upon which appellants would be entitled to appropriate relief; and (c) . . . that the appellants have standing to challenge the Tennessee apportionment statutes."

The complaint in this case asserts that Tennessee's system of apportionment is utterly arbitrary—without any possible justification in rationality. The District Court did not reach the merits of that claim, and this Court quite properly expresses no view on the subject. Contrary to the suggestion of my Brother Harlan, the Court does not say or imply that "state legislatures must be so structured as to reflect with approximate equality the voice of every voter." The Court does not say or imply that there is anything in the Federal Constitution "to prevent a State, acting not irrationally, from choosing any electoral legislative structure it thinks best suited to the interests, temper, and customs of its people." And contrary to the suggestion of my Brother Douglas, the Court most assuredly does not decide the question, "may a State weight the vote of one county or one district more heavily than it weights the vote in another?"

. . . My Brother Clark has made a convincing prima facie showing that Tennessee's system of apportionment is in fact utterly arbitrary —without any possible justification in rationality. My Brother Harlan has, with imagination and ingenuity, hypothesized possibly rational bases for Tennessee's system. But the merits of this case are not before us now. The defendants have not yet had an opportunity to be heard in defense of the State's system of apportionment; indeed, they have not yet even filed an answer to the complaint. As in other cases, the proper place for the trial is in the trial court, not here.

Mr. Justice Frankfurter, whom Mr. Justice Harlan joins, dissenting, said in part:

The Court today reverses a uniform course of decision established by a dozen cases, including one by which the very claim now sustained was unanimously rejected only five years ago. The impressive body of rulings thus cast aside reflected the equally uniform course of our political history regarding the relationship between population and legislative representation—a wholly different matter from denial of the franchise to individuals because of race, color, religion or sex. Such a massive repudiation of the experience of our whole past in asserting destructively novel judicial power demands a detailed analysis of the role of this Court in our constitutional scheme. Disregard of inherent limits in the effective exercise of the Court's "judicial Power" not only presages the futility of judicial intervention in the essentially political conflict of forces by which the relation between population and representation has time out of mind been and now is determined. It may well impair the Court's position as the ultimate organ of "the supreme Law of the Land" in that vast range of legal problems, often strongly entangled in popular feeling, on which this Court must pronounce. The Court's authority—possessed neither of the purse nor the sword—ultimately rests on sustained public confidence in its moral sanction. Such feeling must be nourished by the Court's complete detachment, in fact and in appearance, from political entanglements and by abstention from injecting itself into the clash of political forces in political settlements.

A hypothetical claim resting on abstract assumptions is now for the first time made the basis for affording illusory relief for a particular evil even though it foreshadows deeper and more pervasive difficulties in consequence. The claim is hypothetical and the assumptions are abstract because the Court does not vouchsafe the lower courts—state and federal—guide-lines for formulating specific, definite, wholly unprecedented remedies for the inevitable litigations that today's umbrageous disposition is bound to stimulate in connection with politically motivated reapportionments in so many States. In such a setting, to promulgate jurisdiction in the abstract is meaningless. It is devoid of reality as "a brooding omnipresence in the sky" for it conveys no intimation what relief, if any, a District Court is capable of affording that would not invite legislatures to play ducks and drakes with the judiciary. For this Court to direct the District Court to enforce a claim to which the Court has over the years consistently found itself required to deny legal enforcement and at the same time to find it necessary to withhold any guidance to the lower court how to enforce this turnabout, new legal claim, manifests an odd—indeed an esoteric—conception of judicial propriety. One of the Court's supporting opinions, as elucidated by commentary, unwittingly affords a disheartening preview of the mathematical quagmire (apart from divers judicially inappropriate and elusive determinants), into which this Court today catapults the lower courts of the country without so much as adumbrating the basis for a legal calculus as a means of extrication. Even assuming the indispensable intellectual disinterestedness on the part of judges in such matters, they do not have accepted legal standards or criteria or even reliable analogies to draw upon for making judicial judgments. To charge courts with the task of accommodating the incommensurable factors of policy that underlie these mathematical puzzles is to attribute, however flatteringly, omnicompetence to judges. The Framers of the Constitution persistently rejected a proposal that embodied this assumption and Thomas Jefferson never entertained it.

Recent legislation, creating a district appropriately described as "an atrocity of ingenuity," is not unique. Considering the gross inequality among legislative electoral units within almost every State, the Court naturally shrinks from asserting that in districting at least substantial equality is a constitutional requirement enforceable by courts. Room continues to be allowed for weighting. This of course implies that geography, economics, urban-rural conflict, and all the other non-legal factors which have throughout our history entered into political districting are to some extent not to be ruled out in the undefined vista now opened up by review in the federal courts of state reapportionments. To some extent—aye, there's the rub. In effect, today's decision empowers the courts of the country to devise what should constitute the proper composition of the legislatures of the fifty States. If state courts should for one reason or another find themselves unable to discharge this task, the duty of doing so is put on the federal courts or on this Court, if State views do not satisfy this Court's notion of what is proper districting.

We were soothingly told at the bar of this Court that we need not worry about the kind of remedy a court could effectively fashion once the abstract constitutional right to have courts pass on a state-wide system of electoral districting is recognized as a matter of judicial rhetoric, because legislatures would heed the Court's admonition. This is not only an euphoric hope. It implies a sorry confession of judicial impotence in place of a frank acknowledgment that there is not under our Constitution a judicial remedy for every political mischief, for every undesirable exercise of legislative power. The Framers carefully and with deliberate forethought refused so to enthrone the judiciary. In this situation, as in others of like nature, appeal for relief does not belong here. Appeal must be to an informed, civically militant electorate. In a democratic society like ours, relief must come through an aroused popular conscience that sears the conscience of the people's representatives. In any event there is nothing judicially more unseemly nor more self-defeating than for this Court to make *in terrorem* pronouncements, to indulge in merely empty rhetoric, sounding a word of promise to the ear, sure to be disappointing to the hope. . . .

[Mr. Justice Frankfurter continued in a long and heavily documented opinion to support the position he had taken in Colegrove *v.* Green.]

Dissenting opinion of Mr. Justice Harlan, whom Mr. Justice Frankfurter joins. The opinion says in part:

The dissenting opinion of Mr. Justice Frankfurter, in which I join, demonstrates the abrupt departure the majority makes from judicial history by putting the federal courts into this area of state concerns— an area which, in this instance, the Tennessee state courts themselves have refused to enter. . . .

Once one cuts through the thicket of discussion devoted to "jurisdiction," "standing," "justiciability," and "political question," there emerges a straightforward issue which, in my view, is determinative of this case. Does the complaint disclose a violation of a federal constitutional right, in other words, a claim over which a United States District Court would have jurisdiction . . . .

It is at once essential to recognize this case for what it is. The issue here relates not to a method of state electoral apportionment by which seats in the *federal* House of Representatives are allocated, but solely to the right of a State to fix the basis of representation in its *own* legislature. . . .

I can find nothing in the Equal Protection Clause or elsewhere in the Federal Constitution which expressly or impliedly supports the view that state legislatures must be so structured as to reflect with approximate equality the voice of every voter. Not only is that proposition refuted by history, as shown by my Brother Frankfurter, but it strikes deep into the heart of our federal system. Its acceptance would require us to turn our backs on the regard which this Court has always shown for the judgment of state legislatures and courts on matters of basically local concern.

In the last analysis, what lies at the core of this controversy is a difference of opinion as to the function of representative government. It is surely beyond argument that those who have the responsibility for devising a system of representation may permissibly consider that factors other than bare numbers should be taken into account. The existence of the United States Senate is proof enough of that. To consider that we may ignore the Tennessee Legislature's judgment in this instance because that body was the product of an asymmetrical electoral apportionment would in effect be to assume the very conclusion here disputed. Hence we must accept the present form of the Tennessee Legislature as the embodiment of the State's choice, or, more realistically, its compromise, between competing political philosophies. The federal courts have not been empowered by the Equal Protection Clause to judge whether this resolution of the State's internal political conflict is desirable or undesirable, wise or unwise. . . .

In short, there is nothing in the Federal Constitution to prevent a State, acting not irrationally, from choosing any electoral legislative structure it thinks best suited to the interests, temper, and customs of its people. . . .

The claim that Tennessee's system of apportionment is so unreasonable as to amount to a capricious classification of voting strength stands up no better under dispassionate analysis.

The Court has said time and again that the Equal Protection Clause does not demand of state enactments either mathematical identity or rigid equality. It is not inequality alone that calls for a holding of unconstitutionality; only if the inequality is based on an impermissible standard may this Court condemn it.

What then is the basis for the claim made in this case that the distribution of state senators and representatives is the product of capriciousness or of some constitutionally prohibited policy? It is not that Tennessee has arranged its electoral districts with a deliberate purpose to dilute the voting strength of one race, or that some religious group is intentionally underrepresented. Nor is it a charge that the legislature has indulged in sheer caprice by allotting representatives to each county on the basis of a throw of the dice, or of some other determinant bearing no rational relation to the question of apportionment. Rather, the claim is that the State Legislature has unreasonably retained substantially the same allocation of senators and representatives as was established by statute in 1901, refusing to recognize the great shift in the population balance between urban and rural communities that has occurred in the meantime. . . .

Thus reduced to its essentials, the charge of arbitrariness and capriciousness rests entirely on the consistent refusal of the Tennessee Legislature over the past 60 years to alter a pattern of apportionment that was reasonable when conceived.

A Federal District Court is asked to say that the passage of time has rendered the 1901 apportionment obsolete to the point where its continuance becomes vulnerable under the Fourteenth Amendment. But is not this matter one that involves a classic legislative judgment? Surely it lies within the province of a state legislature to conclude that an existing allocation of senators and representatives constitutes a desirable balance of geographical and demographical representation, or that in the interest of stability of government it would be best to defer for some further time the redistribution of seats in the state legislature.

Indeed, I would hardly think it unconstitutional if a state legislature's expressed reason for establishing or maintaining an electoral imbalance between its rural and urban population were to protect the State's agricultural interests from the sheer weight of numbers of those residing in its cities. . . .

In conclusion, it is appropriate to say that one need not agree, as a citizen, with what Tennessee has done or failed to do, in order to deprecate, as a judge, what the majority is doing today. Those observers of the Court who see it primarily as the last refuge for the correction of all inequality or injustice, no matter what its nature or source, will no doubt applaud this decision and its break with the past. Those who consider that continuing national respect for the

Court's authority depends in large measure upon its wise exercise of self-restraint and discipline in constitutional adjudication, will view the decision with deep concern.

I would affirm.

CHAMBERS v. FLORIDA
309 U. S. 227; 84 L. Ed. 716; 60 Sup. Ct. 472. 1940.

While the due process clause of the Fourteenth Amendment does not require a state to accord a man a grand jury indictment or even a jury trial, it does require that he be given an essentially fair trial. The Court has never listed in one place all of the elements indispensable to such a fair trial. Separate cases, however, indicate what some of these elements are.

In Powell v. Alabama, 287 U. S. 45 (1932), the first "Scottsboro case," seven Negroes convicted of rape and sentenced to death were held to be deprived of life and liberty without due process of law by being denied adequate assistance of counsel before and during trial. The vague and ineffective suggestion of the trial judge that he "appointed all the members of the bar to represent them" was found to fall far short of insuring adequate legal defense.

In 1962 a national scandal broke involving Texas millionaire Billie Sol Estes, accused of influence and fraud in grain-storage and cotton-acreage dealings. Against a backdrop of a dead Department of Agriculture official, two congressional inquiries, and four fraud indictments, Estes was convicted before a national TV audience of swindling a farmer. In Estes v. Texas, 381 U. S. 532 (1965), the Court reversed for lack of due process. A day in court is not a day in a "stadium . . . or nationwide arena."

In Moore v. Dempsey, 261 U. S. 86 (1923), five Negroes were convicted in an Arkansas court of the murder of a white man and sentenced to death. The Court described the trial in these words: "The court and the neighborhood were thronged with an adverse crowd that threatened the most dangerous consequences to any one interfering with the desired result. The counsel did not venture to demand delay or a change of venue, to challenge a juryman, or to ask for separate trials. He had had no preliminary consultation with the accused, called no witnesses for the defense, although they could have been produced, and did not put the defendants on the stand. The trial lasted about three quarters of an hour, and in less than five minutes the jury brought in a verdict of murder in the first degree. According to the allegations and affidavits there never was a chance for the petitioners to be acquitted; no juryman could have voted for an acquittal and continued to live in Phillips County, and if any prisoner, by any chance, had been acquitted by a jury, he could not have escaped the mob." Under these conditions no trial in the true sense was possible and the defendants were denied due process of law.

There have been other "third degree" cases in the Supreme Court besides the Chambers case printed below. In Brown v. Mississippi, 297 U. S. 278 (1936), the conviction of three Negroes for murder solely upon the basis of confessions obtained by brutality and physical torture was held to deny them due process of law. The same result was reached in Ashcraft v. Tennessee, 322 U. S. 143 (1944), where the prisoner confessed to a murder after thirty-six hours of continuous questioning under powerful electric lights, not physical abuse. In Breithaupt v. Abram, 352 U. S. 432 (1957), however, the Court upheld a manslaughter conviction arising from a fatal accident caused by defendant's drunken driving. The evidence of drunkenness was a blood test taken at police request while the defendant was unconscious. A sharply divided Court found no denial of due process. In Rochin v. California, 342 U. S. 165 (1952), the defendant, about to be arrested on a narcotics charge, swallowed two capsules of morphine. By police orders he was forcibly given an emetic through a stomach tube. The use against him as evidence of the morphine thus recovered was held to deny due process of the law.

Mr. Justice Black delivered the opinion of the Court, saying in part:

The grave question presented . . . is whether proceedings in which confessions were utilized, and which culminated in sentences of death upon four young negro men in the state of Florida, failed to afford the safeguard of that due process of law guaranteed by the Fourteenth Amendment. . . .

After one week's constant denial of all guilt, petitioners "broke."

Just before sunrise, the state officials got something "worthwhile" from petitioners which the state's attorney would "want"; again he was called; he came; in the presence of those who had carried on and witnessed the all night questioning, he caused his questions and petitioners' answers to be stenographically reported. These are the confessions utilized by the state to obtain the judgments upon which petitioners were sentenced to death. . . . When Chambers was tried, his conviction rested upon his confession and testimony of the other three confessors. The convict guard and the sheriff "were in the court room sitting down in a seat." And from arrest until sentenced to death, petitioners were never—either in jail or in court—wholly removed from the constant observation, influence, custody and control of those whose persistent pressure brought about the sunrise confessions.

. . . The scope and operation of the Fourteenth Amendment have been fruitful sources of controversy in our constitutional history. However, in view of its historical setting and the wrongs which called it into being, the due process provision of the Fourteenth Amendment—just as that in the Fifth—has led few to doubt that it was intended to guarantee procedural standards adequate and appropriate, then and thereafter, to protect, at all times, people charged with or suspected of crime by those holding positions of power and authority. . . .

The determination to preserve an accused's right to procedural due process sprang in large part from knowledge of the historical truth that the rights and liberties of people accused of crime could not be safely entrusted to secret inquisitorial process. The testimony of centuries, in governments of varying kinds over populations of different races and beliefs, stood as proof that physical and mental torture and coercion had brought about the tragically unjust sacrifices of some who were the noblest and most useful of their generations. The rack, the thumbscrew, the wheel, solitary confinement, protracted questioning and cross questioning, and other ingenious forms of entrapment of the helpless or unpopular had left their wake of mutilated bodies and shattered minds along the way to the cross, the guillotine, the stake and the hangman's noose. And they who have suffered most from secret and dictatorial proceedings have almost always been the poor, the ignorant, the numerically weak, the friendless, and the powerless.

This requirement—of conforming to fundamental standards of procedure in criminal trials—was made operative against the states by the Fourteenth Amendment. Where one of several accused had limped into the trial court as a result of admitted physical mistreatment inflicted to obtain confessions upon which a jury had returned a verdict of guilty of murder, this Court recently declared, Brown v. Mississippi [297 U. S. 278], that "It would be difficult to conceive of methods more revolting to the sense of justice than those taken to procure the confessions of these petitioners, and the use of the confessions thus obtained as the basis for conviction and sentence was a clear denial of due process."

Here, the record develops a sharp conflict upon the issue of physical violence and mistreatment, but shows, without conflict, the dragnet methods of arrest on suspicion without warrant, and the protracted questioning and cross questioning of these ignorant young colored tenant farmers by state officers and other white citizens, in a fourth floor jail room, where as prisoners they were without friends, advisers or counselors, and under circumstances calculated to break the strongest nerves and the stoutest resistance. Just as our decision in Brown v. Mississippi was based upon the fact that the confessions were the result of compulsion, so in the present case, the admitted practices were such as to justify the statement that "The undisputed facts showed that compulsion was applied."

For five days petitioners were subjected to interrogations culminating in Saturday's (May 20th) all night examination. Over a period of five days they steadily refused to confess and disclaimed any guilt. The very circumstances surrounding their confinement and their questioning without any formal charges having been brought, were such as to fill petitioners with terror and frightful misgivings. Some were practically strangers in the community; three were arrested in a one-room farm tenant house which was their home; the haunting fear of mob violence was around them in an atmosphere charged with excitement and public indignation. From virtually the moment of their arrest until their eventual confessions, they never knew just when anyone would be called back to the fourth floor room, and there, surrounded by his accusers and others, interrogated by men who held their very lives—so far as these ignorant petitioners could know—in the balance. . . . To permit human lives to be forfeited upon confessions thus obtained would make of the constitutional requirement of due process of law a meaningless symbol.

We are not impressed by the argument that law enforcement methods such as those under review are necessary to uphold our laws. The Constitution proscribes such lawless means irrespective of the end. And this argument flouts the basic principle that all people must stand on an equality before the bar of justice in every American court. Today, as in ages past, we are not without tragic proof that the exalted power of some governments to punish manufactured crime dictatorially is the handmaid of tyranny. Under our constitutional system, courts stand against any winds that blow as havens of refuge for those who might otherwise suffer because they are helpless, weak, outnumbered, or because they are non-conforming victims of prejudice and public excitement. Due process of law, preserved for all by our Constitution, commands that no such practice as that disclosed by this record shall send any accused to his death. No higher duty, no more solemn responsibility, rests upon this Court, than that of translating into living law and maintaining this constitutional shield deliberately planned and inscribed for the benefit of every human being subject to our Constitution—of whatever race, creed or persuasion.

The supreme court of Florida was in error and its judgment is reversed.

NORRIS v. ALABAMA
294 U. S. 587; 79 L. Ed. 1074; 55 Sup. Ct. 579. 1935.

While the Fourteenth Amendment does not mention any race or class, it is well known that the primary, though probably not the exclusive, purpose of its framers was to secure to the newly freed Negro full protection and equality in the enjoyment of civil and political rights.

By an interesting series of judicial decisions, however, the Negro has found the Fourteenth Amendment a very much less ample and effective guarantee of equality than the legislative leaders of the reconstruction period intended it to be. For example, by its decision in the Civil Rights Cases, 109 U. S. 3 (1883), holding void the Civil Rights Act of 1875, the Supreme Court made it clear that Congress in enforcing the provisions of the Fourteenth Amendment could not penalize race discrimination directed against the Negro by private persons. The act in question had forbidden the proprietors of public conveyances, hotels, restaurants, and places of amusement to refuse accommodations to any person on account of his race, color, or previous condition of servitude. The Fourteenth Amendment forbids only undue racial discrimination when practiced by the state itself.

On the other hand the Fourteenth Amendment has protected the Negro against discrimination in the actual administration of justice. As far back as 1880 the Court held that a Negro was entitled to be tried by a jury from which Negroes had not been excluded because of their race; Strauder v. West Virginia, 100 U. S. 303. At the same time it was decided that the Negro was not entitled to have any Negroes on the jury. See Virginia v. Rives, 100 U. S. 313 (1880). The southern commonwealths adjusted themselves to these two judicial rules by the simple process of avoiding any open discrimination against Negroes in the calling of grand or petit juries; and yet no names of Negroes found their way on to the jury lists and none were ever called for jury service. This situation was tacitly acquiesced in until Norris v. Alabama (the second "Scottsboro case") came to the Supreme Court. The Court examined with care the procedure by which the juries which had indicted and tried the Negroes had been chosen, found that Negroes had been excluded from them because of their race, and held that their rights under the Fourteenth Amendment had been violated. In Akins v. Texas, 325 U. S. 398 (1944), the Court said that no race is entitled to proportional representation on a jury. On the other hand, in Cassell v. Texas, 339 U. S. 282 (1950), it found discrimination despite the presence of Negroes on the jury list. In Swain v. Alabama, 380 U. S. 202 (1965), the Court refused to upset the system of peremptory challenges used in the state, even though it was used by the prosecutor to strike Negroes from the jury.

The Bill of Rights forbids the federal government to invade the civil liberties of the citizen; the Fourteenth Amendment forbids the state governments to do so. A private citizen cannot violate either the Bill of Rights or the Fourteenth Amendment, because neither forbids him to do anything. This rule was sharply emphasized in decisions holding that private landowners may lawfully agree with one another not to sell or lease their land to Negroes. Such agreements, known as restrictive covenants, became increasingly important after the Supreme Court in Buchanan v. Warley, 245 U. S. 60 (1917), held that an ordinance of Louisville, Kentucky, establishing exclusive residential zones for whites and blacks violated the due process clause of the Fourteenth Amendment. What the city had tried unsuccessfully to do by law could still be done on a limited scale by private contract. In thousands of communities land in residential areas was sold by deeds which contained "covenants running with the land" by which the successive purchasers bound themselves not to sell or lease the property to Negroes. The validity of such a covenant was challenged in the Supreme Court in 1926 in Corrigan v. Buckley, 271 U. S. 323. Here thirty white persons, owning twenty-five parcels of land in the District of Columbia, had entered into a mutually restrictive covenant barring the sale or use of the land by Negroes for a period of twenty-one years. Buckley, one of the owners, sought to enjoin Corrigan, another owner, from breaching the covenant by selling one of the parcels of land to a Negro. It was argued that the covenant violated the due process clause of the Fifth Amendment since it discriminated against Negroes. (Had the case arisen in a state, the argument would have been grounded on the Fourteenth Amendment.) The Court unanimously held the covenant valid. In a brief opinion it declared: "The Fifth Amendment is a limitation only upon the powers of the general government, and is not directed against the action of individuals."

In Shelley v. Kraemer, 334 U. S. 1 (1948), the Court laid down a new rule with respect to these covenants. It held that while a contract between private parties to discriminate against Negroes is entirely valid, as Corrigan v. Buckley had held, the judicial enforcement against Negroes of such a contract by a state court makes the state a guilty partner in the racial discrimination and thereby violates the Fourteenth Amendment. In Hurd v. Hodge, 334 U. S. 24 (1948), decided the same day, the Court held that under the Fifth Amendment the federal courts could not validly enforce against Negroes a racially restrictive covenant in the District of Columbia. Thus racially restrictive covenants have become mere "gentlemen's agreements" unenforceable in any court of law.

While it was settled that the Bill of Rights and the Fourteenth Amendment are not "directed against the action of individuals," it must not be assumed that the citizen enjoys no protection against the invasion of his civil rights by private persons. As far back as 1884 in the case of Ex parte Yarbrough, 110 U. S. 651 (p. 62), the Court had upheld the power of Congress to punish as a crime the private invasion of the rights and immunities of citizens of the United States, in that case the right to vote in a federal election. The scope of federal power in this respect is limited, however, by the narrow ruling of the Slaughterhouse Cases (p. 52) upon what are the privileges and immunities of citizens of the United States. The states, on the other hand, enjoy broad police powers, and there is a growing body of state legislation punishing individuals who practice racial discrimination in the employment of labor, the operating of hotels and restaurants, and many other fields.

Mr. Chief Justice Hughes delivered the opinion of the Court, saying in part:

Petitioner, Clarence Norris, is one of nine negro boys who were indicted in March, 1931, in Jackson County, Alabama, for the crime of rape. On being brought to trial in that county eight were convicted. This Court reversed the judgments of conviction upon the ground that the defendants had been denied due process of law in that the trial court had failed in the light of the circumstances disclosed, and of the inability of the defendants at that time to obtain counsel, to make an effective appointment of counsel to aid them in preparing and presenting their defense. Powell v. Alabama, 287 U. S. 45. . . .

After the remand, a motion for change of venue was granted and the cases were transferred to Morgan County. Norris was brought to trial in November, 1933. At the outset, a motion was made on his behalf to quash the indictment upon the ground of the exclusion of negroes from juries in Jackson County where the indictment was found. A motion was also made to quash the trial venire in Morgan County upon the ground of the exclusion of negroes from juries in that county. In relation to each county, the charge was of long continued, systematic and arbitrary exclusion of qualified negro citizens from service on juries, solely because of their race and color, in violation of the Constitution of the United States. . . . The trial . . . proceeded and resulted in the conviction of Norris who was sentenced to death. On appeal, the supreme court of the state considered and decided the federal question which Norris had raised and affirmed the judgment. . . . We granted a writ of certiorari.

First. There is no controversy as to the constitutional principle involved . . . this Court thus stated the principle in Carter v. Texas, 177 U. S. 442, 447, in relation to exclusion from service on grand juries: "Whenever by any action of a state, whether through its legislature, through its courts, or through its executive or administrative officers, all persons of the African race are excluded, solely because of their race or color, from serving as grand jurors in the criminal prosecution of a person of the African race, the equal protection of the laws is denied to him, contrary to the Fourteenth Amendment. . . . The principle is equally applicable to a similar exclusion of negroes from service on petit juries. . . . And although the state statute defining the qualifications of jurors may be fair on its face, the constitutional provision affords protection against action of the state through its administrative officers in effecting the prohibited discrimination. . . .

The question is of the application of this established principle to the facts disclosed by the record. That the question is one of fact does not relieve us of the duty to determine whether in truth a federal right has been denied. When a federal right has been specially set up and claimed in a state court, it is our province to inquire not merely whether it was denied in express terms but also whether it was denied in substance and effect. . . .

Second. The evidence on the motion to quash the indictment. In 1930, the total population of Jackson County, where the indictment was found, was 36,881, of whom 2688 were negroes. The male population over twenty-one years of age numbered 8801, and of these 666 were negroes.

The qualifications of jurors were thus prescribed by the state statute . . . : "The jury commission shall place on the jury roll and in the jury box the names of all male citizens of the county who are generally reputed to be honest and intelligent men, and are esteemed in the community for their integrity, good character and sound judgment, but no person must be selected who is under twenty-one or over sixty-five years of age, or who is an habitual drunkard, or who, being afflicted with a permanent disease or physical weakness is unfit to discharge the duties of a juror, or who cannot read English, or who has ever been convicted of any offense involving moral turpitude. If a person cannot read English and has all the other qualifications prescribed herein and is a freeholder or householder, his name may be placed on the jury roll and in the jury box." . . .

Defendant adduced evidence to support the charge of unconstitutional discrimination in the actual administration of the statute in

Jackson County. The testimony, as the state court said, tended to show that "in a long number of years no negro had been called for jury service in that county." It appeared that no negro had served on any grand or petit jury in that county within the memory of witnesses who had lived there all their lives. Testimony to that effect was given by men whose ages ran from fifty to seventy-six years. Their testimony was uncontradicted. It was supported by the testimony of officials. The clerk of the jury commission and the clerk of the circuit court had never known of a negro serving on a grand jury in Jackson County. The court reporter, who had not missed a session in that county in twenty-four years, and two jury commissioners testified to the same effect. One of the latter, who was a member of the commission which made up the jury roll for the grand jury which found the indictment, testified that he had "never known of a single instance where any negro sat on any grand or petit jury in the entire history of that county."

That testimony in itself made out a *prima facie* case of the denial of the equal protection which the Constitution guarantees. . . . The case thus made was supplemented by direct testimony that specified negroes, thirty or more in number, were qualified for jury service. Among these were negroes who were members of school boards, or trustees, of colored schools, and property owners and householders. It also appeared that negroes from that county had been called for jury service in the federal court. Several of those who were thus described as qualified were witnesses. While there was testimony which cast doubt upon the qualifications of some of the negroes who had been named, and there was also general testimony by the editor of a local newspaper who gave his opinion as to the lack of "sound judgment" of the "good negroes" in Jackson County, we think that the definite testimony as to the actual qualifications of individual negroes, which was not met by any testimony equally direct, showed that there were negroes in Jackson County qualified for jury service. . . .

The state court rested its decision upon the ground that even if it were assumed that there was no name of a negro on the jury roll, it was not established that race or color caused the omission. The court pointed out that the statute fixed a high standard of qualifications for jurors . . . and that the jury commission was vested with a wide discretion. The court adverted to the fact that more white citizens possessing age qualifications had been omitted from the jury roll than the entire negro population of the county, and regarded the testimony as being to the effect that "the matter of race, color, politics, religion or fraternal affiliations" had not been discussed by the commission and had not entered into their consideration, and that no one had been excluded because of race or color. . . .

We are of the opinion that the evidence required a different result from that reached in the state court. We think that the evidence that for a generation or longer no negro had been called for service on any jury in Jackson County, that there were negroes qualified for jury service, that according to the practice of the jury commission their names would normally appear on the preliminary list of male citizens of the requisite age but that no names of negroes were placed on the jury roll, and the testimony with respect to the lack of appropriate consideration of the qualifications of negroes, established the discrimination which the Constitution forbids. The motion to quash the indictment upon that ground should have been granted.

Third. The evidence on the motion to quash the trial venire. The population of Morgan County, where the trial was had, was larger than that of Jackson County, and the proportion of negroes was much greater. The total population of Morgan County in 1930 was 46,176, and of this number 8311 were negroes.

Within the memory of witnesses, long resident there, no negro had ever served on a jury in that county or had been called for such service. Some of these witnesses were over fifty years of age and had always lived in Morgan County. Their testimony was not contradicted. A clerk of the circuit court, who had resided in the county for thirty years, and who had been in office for over four years, testified that during his official term approximately 2500 persons had been called for jury service and that not one of them was a negro; that he did not recall "ever seeing any single person of the colored race serve on any jury in Morgan County."

There was abundant evidence that there were a large number of negroes in the county who were qualified for jury service. Men of intelligence, some of whom were college graduates, testified to long lists (said to contain nearly 200 names) of such qualified negroes, including many business men, owners of real property and householders. When defendant's counsel proposed to call many additional witnesses in order to adduce further proof of qualifications of negroes for jury service, the trial judge limited the testimony, holding that the evidence was cumulative.

We find no warrant for a conclusion that the names of any of the negroes as to whom this testimony was given, or of any other negroes, were placed on the jury rolls. No such names were identified. The evidence that for many years no negro had been called for jury service itself tended to show the absence of the names of negroes from the jury rolls, and the state made no effort to prove their presence. . . .

For this long-continued, unvarying, and wholesale exclusion of negroes from jury service we find no justification consistent with the constitutional mandate.

. . . That showing as to the long-continued exclusion of negroes from jury service, and as to the many negroes qualified for that service, could not be met by mere generalities. If, in the presence of such testimony as defendant adduced, the mere general assertions by officials of their performance of duty were to be accepted as an adequate justification for the complete exclusion of negroes from jury service, the constitutional provision—adopted with special reference to their protection—would be but a vain and illusory requirement. . . .

We are concerned only with the federal question which we have discussed, and in view of the denial of the federal right suitably asserted, the judgment must be reversed and the cause remanded for further proceedings not inconsistent with this opinion. . . .

BROWN v. BOARD OF EDUCATION OF TOPEKA
347 U. S. 483; 98 L. Ed. 873; 74 Sup. Ct. 686. 1954.

BOLLING v. SHARPE
347 U. S. 497; 98 L. Ed. 884; 74 Sup. Ct. 693. 1954.

It has been the settled policy of the southern states to segregate by compulsion the Negroes and whites in the use of the facilities of common carriers, hotels, restaurants, parks, places of amusement, and the like. Whatever the framers of the Fourteenth Amendment would have thought of this segregation, the Supreme Court for many years sustained its validity. In Plessy v. Ferguson, 163 U. S. 537 (1896), it held that a Louisiana statute requiring railroads to "provide equal but separate accommodations for the white and colored races" did not constitute a denial of the equal protection of the laws in violation of the Fourteenth Amendment. Such a law is a proper exercise of the state's police power aimed at the maintenance of peace and order. The Court dismissed the contention that "the enforced separation of the two races stamps the colored race with a badge of inferiority," and observed: "If this be so, it is not by reason of anything found in the act, but solely because the colored race chooses to put that construction upon it." In a stinging dissent, Mr. Justice Harlan declared: "Our Constitution is color-blind, and neither knows nor tolerates classes among citizens. In respect of civil rights, all citizens are equal before the law." In Berea College v. Kentucky, 211 U. S. 45 (1908), it was similarly held that the state could validly forbid a college, even though a private corporation, to teach whites and blacks at the same time and place, and this left no doubt of the validity of the southern laws requiring the education of white and black children in separate tax-supported schools.

While the Plessy rule made the segregation of whites and blacks valid, it also required that the "separate" accommodations provided for the two races be "equal." At first, however, the Supreme Court was extremely lenient in construing what this "equality" required. It held that the term meant, not exact or mathematical equality, but only "substantial" equality. In Cumming v. County Board of Education, 175 U. S. 528 (1899), it found no denial of equal protection of the laws in the failure of a southern county to provide a high school for sixty colored children, although it maintained a high school for white children. The Court seemed satisfied with the county's defense that it could not afford to build a high school for Negro children. In Gong Lum v. Rice, 275 U. S. 78 (1927), the Court held that a Chinese girl could validly be required to attend a school for colored children in a neighboring school district, rather than be allowed to attend the nearby school for white children. It looked as though the Negro was not only to be segregated, but must also be content with very inferior accommodations and services under that segregation.

In 1914 the Supreme Court began to show signs of requiring a much stricter standard of equality under segregation. In McCabe v. Atchison, T. & S. F. Ry. Co., 235 U. S. 151 (1914), an Oklahoma law was held not to accord equal accommodations to Negroes and whites when it allowed railroads to haul sleeping, dining, and chair cars for the exclusive use of whites without providing them on demand for the use of Negroes.

In Missouri ex rel. Gaines v. Canada, 305 U. S. 337 (1938), the Court invalidated a Missouri statute dealing with segregation in law schools. Negroes were barred from the law school at the state university; but in order to give them "equal" treatment, the state would pay their tuition in any out-of-state law school (Illinois, Indiana, etc.) which would admit them. Gaines, a Negro, refused to accept this compromise, and Chief Justice Hughes, in a strong opinion, held that Gaines was "entitled to be admitted to the law school of the state university in the absence of other and proper provision for his legal training within the state . . . ."

In Sweatt v. Painter, 339 U. S. 629 (1950), the state of Texas claimed that its new law school for Negroes afforded educational opportunities essentially equal to those at the University of Texas Law School. The Court rejected this claim of equality on very significant grounds. The law school for white students, it said, "possesses to a far greater degree those qualities which are incapable of objective measurement but which make for greatness in a law school. . . . The law school, the proving ground for legal learning and practice, cannot be effective in isolation from the individuals and institutions with which the law interacts. . . . The [Negro] law school . . . excludes from its student body members of racial groups which number 85% of the population of the State and include most of the lawyers, judges and other officials with whom petitioner will inevitably be dealing when he becomes a member of the Texas bar. With such a substantial and significant segment of society excluded, we cannot conclude that the education offered petitioner is substantially equal to that which he would receive if admitted to the University of Texas Law School." This strongly suggests that no Negro law school could ever be "equal" under segregation.

While Congress had full power to regulate interstate commerce it had never abolished racial segregation on interstate trains. All it had done was to forbid any interstate common carrier to give any person or group any "unreasonable preference or advantage," or subject them to "any undue or unreasonable prejudice or disadvantage." In practice these restrictions had been interpreted in the light of the "separate but equal" doctrine of Plessy v. Ferguson. The Southern Railway Company segregated Negroes in dining cars by reserving ten tables exclusively for white passengers, and one table exclusively for Negroes. A curtain or partition cut the Negro table off from the others. In Henderson v. United States, 339 U. S. 816 (1950), the Court held that such segregation subjected Negro passengers to undue prejudice and disadvantage.

In the cases dealing with Negro segregation that reached the Supreme Court after Plessy v. Ferguson (p. 249), the doctrine of that case was followed, and never re-examined. The Court seemed content with the "separate but equal" rule of that case, which, as someone aptly put it, guarantees to the Negro "the equal, but different, protection of the laws." During the forty-year period beginning with the McCabe case (p. 250) in 1914, the Court, applying ever more rigid standards of equality under segregation, found that Negro plaintiffs in each case had in fact been denied equality of treatment. And so the Court, following the rule that it will not decide constitutional issues if it can avoid doing so, continued to grant relief to Negroes, not because they were segregated, but because they were unequally treated under segregation. While in the Texas law school case and the dining car case (p. 250) the Court virtually states that there are circumstances in which segregation in itself results in inequality of treatment, the rule of Plessy v. Ferguson remained intact.

In the fall of 1952, however, the Supreme Court had on its docket cases from four states (Kansas, South Carolina, Virginia, and Delaware) and from the District of Columbia, challenging the constitutionality of racial segregation in public schools. In all of these cases the facts showed that "the Negro and white schools involved have been equalized, or are being equalized, with respect to buildings, curricula, qualifications and salaries of teachers, and other 'tangible' factors." After nearly sixty years the Court again had squarely before it the question of the constitutionality of segregation per se—the question whether the doctrine of Plessy v. Ferguson should be affirmed or reversed.

The five cases were argued together in December, 1952, and the country waited with tense interest for the Court's decision. On June 8, 1953, the Court restored the cases to the docket for reargument in the fall, and issued a list of questions upon which it wished that argument to turn. The Court asked for enlightenment on two main points. First, is there historical evidence which shows the intentions of those who framed and ratified the Fourteenth Amendment with respect to the impact of that amendment upon racial segregation in the public schools? Second, if the Court finds racial segregation violates the Fourteenth Amendment, what kind of decree could and should be issued to bring about an end of segregation?

The cases were reargued in December, 1953. Elaborate briefs set forth in great detail the background of the Fourteenth Amendment and the intentions of its framers and ratifiers. The negative result of this historical research is commented on in the opinion below. Some of the briefs, including the one filed by the Attorney General, presented suggestions on the form of the court decree by which segregation might best be ended should the Court hold it to be invalid. Counsel for the National Association for the Advancement of Colored People, who had played a major part in the instigation of these cases, declined to deal with this point. In their view segregation, if held invalid, should be abolished completely and without delay.

Following the rehearing of the present case ordered in the opinion below, the Court directed the various district courts to see that desegregation plans were formulated and put into effect "with all deliberate speed." Of course southern school boards that were not parties to the present case were not affected by the Court's order and generally refused to desegregate voluntarily, waiting instead for suits to be brought to compel them, and in parts of the South "legal" measures were adopted to thwart the Court's decision, the best known being those of Prince Edward County, Virginia. See p. 526. Threats to withhold federal aid to segregated schools under the Civil Rights Act of 1964 resulted in widespread token compliance, largely by offering Negroes "freedom of choice" among schools. Yet with the start of the 1965–66 school year fewer than 10% of the South's Negroes were attending desegregated schools. In March of 1966 the Office of Education announced new guidelines designed to desegregate all 12 grades by the fall of 1967, but their effectiveness has yet to be demonstrated.

A separate opinion was necessary to invalidate segregation in the schools of the District of Columbia which is under congressional authority. The Bolling case below holds that the due process clause of the Fifth Amendment forbids racial segregation by the federal government.

The Supreme Court decision in the Brown case rests upon principles which apply equally to racial segregation by any governmental body in any area. It is unnecessary to mention the cases, many of them decided without opinion, in which the rule has been applied to publicly owned parks, housing projects, golf courses, airports, etc.

Mr. Chief Justice Warren, delivering the opinion of the Court in the Brown case, said in part:

These cases come to us from the States of Kansas, South Carolina, Virginia, and Delaware. They are premised on different facts and different local conditions, but a common legal question justifies their consideration together in this consolidated opinion.

In each of the cases, minors of the Negro race, through their legal representatives, seek the aid of the courts in obtaining admission to the public schools of their community on a nonsegregated basis. In each instance, they have been denied admission to schools attended by white children under laws requiring or permitting segregation according to race. This segregation was alleged to deprive the plaintiffs of the equal protection of the laws under the Fourteenth Amendment. . . .

The plaintiffs contend that segregated public schools are not "equal" and cannot be made "equal," and that hence they are deprived of the equal protection of the laws. Because of the obvious importance of the question presented, the Court took jurisdiction. Argument was heard in the 1952 Term, and reargument was heard this Term on certain questions propounded by the Court.

Reargument was largely devoted to the circumstances surrounding the adoption of the Fourteenth Amendment in 1868. It covered exhaustively consideration of the Amendment in Congress, ratification by the states, then existing practices in racial segregation, and the views of proponents and opponents of the Amendment. This discussion and our own investigation convince us that, although these sources cast some light, it is not enough to resolve the problem with which we are faced. At best, they are inconclusive. The most avid proponents of the post-War Amendments undoubtedly intended them to remove all legal distinctions among "all persons born or naturalized in the United States." Their opponents, just as certainly, were antagonistic to both the letter and the spirit of the Amendments and wished them to have the most limited effect. What others in Congress and the state legislatures had in mind cannot be determined with any degree of certainty.

An additional reason for the inconclusive nature of the Amendment's history, with respect to segregated schools, is the status of public education at that time. In the South, the movement toward free common schools, supported by general taxation, had not yet taken hold. Education of white children was largely in the hands of private groups. Education of Negroes was almost nonexistent, and practically all of the race were illiterate. In fact, any education of Negroes was forbidden by law in some states. Today, in contrast, many Negroes have achieved outstanding success in the arts and sciences as well as in the business and professional world. It is true that public education had already advanced further in the North, but the effect of the Amendment on Northern States was generally ignored in the congressional debates. Even in the North, the conditions of public education did not approximate those existing today. The curriculum was usually rudimentary; ungraded schools were common in rural areas; the school term was but three months a year in many states; and compulsory school attendance was virtually unknown. As a consequence, it is not surprising that there should be so little in the history of the Fourteenth Amendment relating to its intended effect on public education.

In the first cases in this Court construing the Fourteenth Amendment, decided shortly after its adoption, the Court interpreted it as proscribing all state-imposed discriminations against the Negro race. The doctrine of "separate but equal" did not make its appearance in this Court until 1896 in the case of Plessy v. Ferguson, supra, involving not education but transportation. American courts have since labored with the doctrine for over half a century. In this Court, there have been six cases involving the "separate but equal" doctrine in the field of public education. In Cumming v. Board of Education of Richmond County, 175 U. S. 528, and Gong Lum v. Rice, 275 U. S. 78, the validity of the doctrine itself was not challenged. In more recent cases, all on the graduate school level, inequality was found in that specific benefits enjoyed by white students were denied to Negro students of the same educational qualifications. State of Missouri ex rel. Gaines v. Canada, 305 U. S. 337; Sipuel v. Board of Regents of University of Oklahoma, 332 U. S. 631; Sweatt v. Painter, 339 U. S. 629; McLaurin v. Oklahoma State Regents, 339 U. S. 637. In none of these cases was it necessary to re-examine the doctrine to grant relief to the Negro plaintiff. And in Sweatt v. Painter, supra, the Court expressly reserved decision on the question whether Plessy v. Ferguson should be held inapplicable to public education.

In the instant cases, that question is directly presented. Here, unlike Sweatt v. Painter, there are findings below that the Negro and white schools involved have been equalized, or are being equalized, with respect to buildings, curricula, qualifications and salaries of teachers, and other "tangible" factors. Our decision, therefore, cannot turn on merely a comparison of these tangible factors in the Negro and white schools involved in each of the cases. We must look instead to the effect of segregation itself on public education.

In approaching this problem, we cannot turn the clock back to 1868 when the Amendment was adopted, or even to 1896 when Plessy v. Ferguson was written. We must consider public education in the light of its full development and its present place in American life throughout the Nation. Only in this way can it be determined if segregation in public schools deprives these plaintiffs of the equal protection of the laws.

Today, education is perhaps the most important function of state and local governments. Compulsory school attendance laws and the great expenditures for education both demonstrate our recognition of the importance of education to our democratic society. It is required in the performance of our most basic public responsibilities, even service in the armed forces. It is the very foundation of good citizenship. Today it is a principal instrument in awakening the child to cultural values, in preparing him for later professional training, and in helping him to adjust normally to his environment. In these days, it is doubtful that any child may reasonably be expected to succeed in life if he is denied the opportunity of an education. Such an opportunity, where the state has undertaken to provide it, is a right which must be made available to all on equal terms.

We come then to the question presented: Does segregation of children in public schools solely on the basis of race, even though the physical facilities and other "tangible" factors may be equal, deprive the children of the minority group of equal educational opportunities? We believe that it does.

In Sweatt v. Painter, supra, in finding that a segregated law school for Negroes could not provide them equal educational opportunities, this Court relied in large part on "those qualities which are incapable of objective measurement but which make for greatness in a law school." In McLaurin v. Oklahoma State Regents, supra, the Court, in requiring that a Negro admitted to a white graduate school be treated like all other students, again resorted to intangible considerations: ". . . his ability to study, to engage in discussions and exchange views with other students, and, in general, to learn his profession." Such considerations apply with added force to children in grade and high schools. To separate them from others of similar age and qualifications solely because of their race generates a feeling of inferiority as to their status in the community that may affect their hearts and minds in a way unlikely ever to be undone. The effect of this separation on their educational opportunities was well stated by a finding in the Kansas case by a court which nevertheless felt compelled to rule against the Negro plaintiffs:

"Segregation of white and colored children in public schools has a detrimental effect upon the colored children. The impact is greater when it has the sanction of the law; for the policy of separating the races is usually interpreted as denoting the inferiority of the Negro group. A sense of inferiority affects the motivation of a child to learn. Segregation with the sanction of law, therefore, has a tendency to retard the educational and mental development of Negro children and to deprive them of some of the benefits they would receive in a racially integrated school system." Whatever may have been the extent of psychological knowledge at the time of Plessy v. Ferguson, this finding is amply supported by modern authority. Any language in Plessy v. Ferguson contrary to this finding is rejected.

We conclude that in the field of public education the doctrine of "separate but equal" has no place. Separate educational facilities are inherently unequal. Therefore, we hold that the plaintiffs and others similarly situated for whom the actions have been brought are, by reason of the segregation complained of, deprived of the equal protection of the laws guaranteed by the Fourteenth Amendment. This disposition makes unnecessary any discussion whether such segregation also violates the Due Process Clause of the Fourteenth Amendment.

Because these are class actions, because of the wide applicability of this decision, and because of the great variety of local conditions, the formulation of decrees in these cases presents problems of considerable complexity. On reargument, the consideration of appropriate relief was necessarily subordinated to the primary question—the constitutionality of segregation in public education. We have now announced that such segregation is a denial of the equal protection of the laws. In order that we may have the full assistance of the parties in formulating decrees, the cases will be restored to the docket, and the parties are requested to present further argument on Questions 4 and 5 previously propounded by the Court for the reargument this Term.[1] The Attorney General of the United States is again invited to participate. The Attorneys General of the states requiring or permitting segregation in public education will also be permitted to appear as *amici curiae* upon request to do so by September 15, 1954, and submission of briefs by October 1, 1954.

It is so ordered.

Mr. Chief Justice Warren delivered the opinion of the Court in the Bolling case:

This case challenges the validity of segregation in the public schools of the District of Columbia. The petitioners, minors of the Negro race, allege that such segregation deprives them of due process of law under the Fifth Amendment. They were refused admission to a public school attended by white children solely because of their race. They sought the aid of the District Court for the District of Columbia in obtaining admission. That court dismissed their complaint. We granted a writ of certiorari before judgment in the Court of Appeals because of the importance of the constitutional question presented.

We have this day held that the Equal Protection Clause of the Fourteenth Amendment prohibits the states from maintaining racially

---

[1] "4. Assuming it is decided that segregation in public schools violates the Fourteenth Amendment

"(a) would a decree necessarily follow providing that, within the limits set by normal geographic school districting, Negro children should forthwith be admitted to schools of their choice, or

"(b) may this Court, in the exercise of its equity powers, permit an effective gradual adjustment to be brought about from existing segregated systems to a system not based on color distinctions?

"5. On the assumption on which questions 4(a) and (b) are based, and assuming further that this Court will exercise its equity powers to the end described in question 4(b),

"(a) should this Court formulate detailed decrees in these cases;

"(b) if so, what specific issues should the decrees reach;

"(c) should this Court appoint a special master to hear evidence with a view to recommending specific terms for such decrees;

"(d) should this Court remand to the courts of first instance with directions to frame decrees in these cases, and if so, what general directions should the decrees of this Court include and what procedures should the courts of first instance follow in arriving at the specific terms of more detailed decrees?"

segregated public schools. The legal problem in the District of Columbia is somewhat different, however. The Fifth Amendment, which is applicable in the District of Columbia, does not contain an equal protection clause as does the Fourteenth Amendment which applies only to the states. But the concepts of equal protection and due process, both stemming from our American ideal of fairness, are not mutually exclusive. The "equal protection of the laws" is a more explicit safeguard of prohibited unfairness than "due process of law," and, therefore, we do not imply that the two are always interchangeable phrases. But, as this Court has recognized, discrimination may be so unjustifiable as to be violative of due process.

Classifications based solely upon race must be scrutinized with particular care, since they are contrary to our traditions and hence constitutionally suspect. As long ago as 1896, this Court declared the principle "that the Constitution of the United States, in its present form, forbids, so far as civil and political rights are concerned, discrimination by the general government, or by the states, against any citizen because of his race." And in Buchanan v. Warley, 245 U. S. 60, the Court held that a statute which limited the right of a property owner to convey his property to a person of another race was, as an unreasonable discrimination, a denial of due process of law.

Although the Court has not assumed to define "liberty" with any great precision, that term is not confined to mere freedom from bodily restraint. Liberty under law extends to the full range of conduct which the individual is free to pursue, and it cannot be restricted except for a proper governmental objective. Segregation in public education is not reasonably related to any proper governmental objective, and thus it imposes on Negro children of the District of Columbia a burden that constitutes an arbitrary deprivation of their liberty in violation of the Due Process Clause.

In view of our decision that the Constitution prohibits the states from maintaining racially segregated public schools, it would be unthinkable that the same Constitution would impose a lesser duty on the Federal Government. We hold that racial segregation in the public schools of the District of Columbia is a denial of the due process of law guaranteed by the Fifth Amendment to the Constitution.

For the reasons set out in Brown v. Board of Education, this case will be restored to the docket for reargument on Questions 4 and 5 previously propounded by the Court.

It is so ordered.

Case restored to docket for reargument on question of appropriate decree.

NEBBIA v. NEW YORK
291 U. S. 502; 78 L. Ed. 940; 54 Sup. Ct. 505. 1934.

Munn v. Illinois, 94 U. S. 113 (1877), was the first of a famous group of cases usually called the "Granger Cases." They were decided during the seventies and eighties and involved the new and important problem of the extent of the power of state legislatures to regulate the rates and service of railroads and other businesses affected with a public interest. The close of the Civil War ushered in a period of rapid railroad expansion. In the east, where industrial development tended to keep pace with the multiplication of transportation facilities, railroad building proved satisfactorily profitable. In the west, however, where new country was being opened up and population was sparse, the railroads had difficulty in paying dividends and frequently yielded to the temptation to indulge in stock-watering, questionable manipulation of credits, doubtful practices in respect to grants of lands, rebating, discrimination, and other objectionable practices. As against the desperate efforts of the railroads to make profits there existed a desire upon the part of the western farmer to enjoy adequate railroad facilities at reasonable rates in order to facilitate the movement of crops in sparsely settled communities, together with fierce resentment against the unfair or dishonest methods of which some of the roads were known to be guilty. Out of this conflict of interests grew the Granger Movement, an organized effort upon the part of the western farmers to secure through state legislation the remedies which they felt the evils of the existing transportation system demanded. Granger legislation began in Illinois in 1871 with the enactment of a statute, authorized by the new state constitution of 1870, which created a railroad and warehouse commission with supervisory power over the roads, forbade discrimination under severe penalties, and established maximum passenger and freight rates. Other states followed the lead taken by Illinois; and soon the railroads found themselves subjected to a wide variety of restrictive and more or less burdensome laws, some of them vitally affecting their earning capacity. In the Granger cases the validity of these laws was presented to the Supreme Court.

Munn v. Illinois did not relate to railroad rate legislation but dealt rather with the question of the validity of an Illinois statute providing for the fixing of maximum charges for the storage of grain, in Chicago and other places having not less than one hundred thousand population, in warehouses "in which grain is stored in bulk, and in which the grain of different owners is mixed together, or in which grain is stored in such a manner that the identity of different lots or parcels cannot be accurately preserved." The case was argued before the Supreme Court by eminent lawyers, and the decision was awaited with wide-spread interest not only by the granges but by all those who had money invested in businesses which the states were seeking to regulate. Here, as in the Slaughterhouse Cases, an attempt was made to convince the Court that the legislation in question was in violation of the Fourteenth Amendment. It was urged that it involved a deprivation of property without due process of law and a denial of the equal protection of the laws. But here again the attempt failed. The Court decided that terminal grain elevators were businesses sufficiently affected with a public interest to enable the legislature to regulate the charges which they made. It then went on to point out that the Fourteenth Amendment provided no restriction upon burdensome or confiscatory rates; in cases where the legislature could regulate rates at all the degree of regulation was a matter of legislative discretion, and "for protection against abuses by legislatures the people must resort to the polls, not to the courts." This somewhat startling proposition was not strictly called for by the facts of the Munn case and was in the nature of obiter dictum, because it had not been the limits imposed upon grain elevator charges that had been attacked but the right of the legislature to establish any rate at all.

It would have been wholly out of keeping with the judicial development of the Fourteenth Amendment if the Court had not retreated from the position taken in this dictum in Munn v. Illinois. As in the case of the police power of the state the Court, step by step, came to look upon the due process clause as imposing a judicially enforceable check upon unreasonable or arbitrary exercise of the power of public utility regulation. In the case of C. M. & St. P. Ry. Co. v. Minnesota, 134 U. S. 418 (1890), the Court held that a railroad rate established by a state railroad and warehouse commission could not be regarded as conclusively reasonable and that unless a way was provided whereby the question of reasonableness might be judicially determined there was a denial of due process of law. This doctrine was reaffirmed and extended in the case of Reagan v. Farmers' Loan and Trust Co., 154 U. S. 362 (1894). A still further advance in the direction of complete judicial review of rate regulation was made in the celebrated case of Smyth v. Ames, 169 U. S. 466, decided in 1898. The railroad rate under review in this case had been established directly by the legislature itself and not by a commission, and it was strongly defended as being not unreasonable. The Supreme Court, in invalidating the rate, laid down in this decision the important principle that due process of law requires not merely a judicial review of the reasonableness of rates, as had been established in the earlier cases, but requires also that the rate established shall be such as will allow the railroad a fair return on a fair valuation of its investment. Whether the return from a particular rate is fair or not is therefore a judicial question, although the Court did not in this case define what it meant concretely by "fair." It did so, however, in several later cases.

From Munn v. Illinois and cases following it, arose the doctrine that the government could regulate prices or control terms of service only of businesses which are "affected with a public interest." To impose these regulations upon a business not affected with a public interest was to deprive it of its liberty and property without due process of law. This doctrine seemed fair on its face and comported with the tradition of American individualism. But what is a business "affected with a public interest?" This question the Court found great difficulty in answering, and with the passage of time it became clear that there was no single characteristic which would invariably distinguish a business affected with a public interest. In Wolff Packing Co. v. Industrial Court, 262 U. S. 522 (1923), in an opinion holding that a meat-packing establishment is not a business affected with a public interest, Chief Justice Taft went on to say that such businesses fall into three categories. These are as follows: "(1) Those which are carried on under the authority of a public grant of privileges which either expressly or impliedly imposes the affirmative duty of rendering a public service demanded by any member of the public. Such are the railroads, other common carriers and public utilities. (2) Certain occupations, regarded as exceptional, the public interest attaching to which, recognized from earliest times, has survived the period of arbitrary laws by Parliament or colonial legislatures for regulating all trades and callings. Such are those of the keepers of inns, cabs, and gristmills. . . . (3) Businesses which though not public at their inception may be fairly said to have risen to be such and have become subject in consequence to some government regulation. They have come to hold such a peculiar relation to the public that this is superimposed upon them. In the language of the cases, the owner by devoting his business to the public use, in effect grants the public an interest in that use and subjects himself to public regulation to the extent of that interest although the property continues to belong to the private owner and to be entitled to protection accordingly."

The concept of a business "affected with a public interest" was applied by the Court in later cases to invalidate laws fixing the prices of theatre tickets, of gasoline, of ice, and of the services of an employment agency.

The continued application of so vague a judicial test did not fail to produce criticism, some of the sharpest of which came from the members of the Court itself. In his dissenting opinion in New State Ice Company v. Liebmann, 285 U. S. 262 (1932),—the case involving the price of ice,— Mr. Justice Brandeis struck out boldly with the assertion: "The notion of a distinct category of business 'affected with a public interest' employing property 'devoted to a public use' rests upon historical error. In my opinion, the true principle is that the state's power extends to every regulation of any business reasonably required and appropriate for the public protection. I find in the due process clause no other limitation upon the character or the scope of regulation permissible." This minority view has finally prevailed. The Nebbia case printed below abandons entirely the concept of a business affected with a public interest as the constitutional criterion of price control. The milk business is admitted to be not so affected with a public interest. Price control is merely a phase of the police power of the state subject only to the limitations of due process of law upon arbitrary interference with liberty and property.

Mr. Justice Roberts delivered the opinion of the Court, saying in part:

The legislature of New York established, by Chapter 158 of the Laws of 1933, a Milk Control Board with power, among other things, to "fix minimum and maximum . . . retail prices to be charged by . . . stores to consumers for consumption off the premises where sold." The board fixed nine cents as the price to be charged by a store for a quart of milk. Nebbia, the proprietor of a grocery store in Rochester, sold two quarts and a five cent loaf of bread for eighteen cents; and was convicted for violating the board's order. At his trial he asserted the statute and order contravene the equal protection clause and the due process clause. . . .

The question for decision is whether the federal Constitution prohibits a state from so fixing the selling price of milk. We first inquire as to the occasion for the legislation and its history.

During 1932 the prices received by farmers for milk were much below the cost of production. The decline in prices during 1931 and 1932 was much greater than that of prices generally. The situation of the families of dairy producers had become desperate and called for state aid similar to that afforded the unemployed, if conditions should not improve.

On March 10, 1932, the senate and assembly resolved "That a joint legislative committee is hereby created . . . to investigate the causes of the decline of the price of milk to producers and the resultant effect of the low prices upon the dairy industry. . . ."

In part those conclusions [of the committee] are:

Milk is an essential item of diet. It cannot long be stored. It is an excellent medium for growth of bacteria. These facts necessitate safeguards in its production and handling for human consumption which greatly increase the cost of the business. Failure of producers to receive a reasonable return for their labor and investment over an extended period threatens a relaxation of vigilance against contamination.

The production and distribution of milk is a paramount industry of the state, and largely affects the health and prosperity of its people. Dairying yields fully one half of the total income from all farm products. Dairy farm investment amounts to approximately $1,000,-000,000. Curtailment or destruction of the dairy industry would cause a serious economic loss to the people of the state.

In addition to the general price decline, other causes for the low price of milk include: a periodic increase in the number of cows and in milk production; the prevalence of unfair and destructive trade practices in the distribution of milk, leading to a demoralization of prices in the metropolitan area and other markets; and the failure of transportation and distribution charges to be reduced in proportion to the reduction in retail prices for milk and cream.

The fluid milk industry is affected by factors of instability peculiar to itself which call for special methods of control. Under the best practicable adjustment of supply to demand the industry must carry a surplus of about 20 per cent, because milk, an essential food, must be available as demanded by consumers every day in the year, and demand and supply vary from day to day and according to the season; but milk is perishable and cannot be stored. Close adjustment of supply to demand is hindered by several factors difficult to control. Thus surplus milk presents a serious problem, as the prices which can be realized for it for other uses are much less than those obtainable for milk sold for consumption in fluid form or as cream. A satisfactory stabilization of prices for fluid milk requires that the burden of surplus milk be shared equally by all producers and all distributors in the milk-shed. So long as the surplus burden is unequally distributed the pressure to market surplus milk in fluid form will be a serious disturbing factor. The fact that the larger distributors find it necessary to carry large quantities of surplus milk, while the smaller distributors do not, leads to price-cutting and other forms of destructive competition. Smaller distributors, who take no responsibility for the surplus, by purchasing their milk at the blended prices (i.e., an average between the price paid the producer for milk for sale as fluid milk, and the lower surplus milk price paid by the larger organizations) can undersell the larger distributors. Indulgence in this price-cutting often compels the larger dealer to cut the price, to his own and the producer's detriment.

Various remedies were suggested, amongst them united action by producers, the fixing of minimum prices for milk and cream by state authority, and the imposition of certain graded taxes on milk dealers proportioned so as to equalize the cost of milk and cream to all dealers and so remove the cause of price-cutting.

The legislature adopted Chapter 158 [creating a Milk Control Board with power to fix prices] as a method of correcting the evils, which the report of the committee showed could not be expected to right themselves through the ordinary play of the forces of supply and demand, owing to the peculiar and uncontrollable factors affecting the industry. . . .

First. The appellant urges that the order of the Milk Control Board denies him the equal protection of the laws. It is shown that the order requires him, if he purchases his supply from a dealer, to pay eight cents per quart and five cents per pint, and to resell at not less than nine and six, whereas the same dealer may buy his supply from a farmer at lower prices and deliver milk to consumers at ten cents the quart and six cents the pint. We think the contention that the discrimination deprives the appellant of equal protection is not well founded. For aught that appears, the appellant purchased his supply of milk from a farmer as do distributors, or could have procured it from a farmer if he so desired. There is therefore no showing that the order placed him at a disadvantage, or in fact affected him adversely, and this alone is fatal to the claim of denial of equal protection. But if it were shown that the appellant is compelled to buy from a distributor, the difference in the retail price he is required to charge his customers, from that prescribed for sales by distributors, is not on its face arbitrary or unreasonable, for there are obvious distinctions between the two sorts of merchants which may well justify a difference of treatment, if the legislature possesses the power to control the prices to be charged for fluid milk. . . .

Second. The more serious question is whether in the light of the conditions disclosed, [the price-regulation] denied the appellant the due process secured to him by the Fourteenth Amendment. . . .

Under our form of government the use of property and the making of contracts are normally matters of private and not of public concern. The general rule is that both shall be free of governmental interference. But neither property rights nor contract rights are absolute; for government cannot exist if the citizen may at will use his property to the detriment of his fellows, or exercise his freedom of contract to work them harm. Equally fundamental with the private right is that of the public to regulate it in the common interest. . . .

The milk industry in New York has been the subject of long-standing and drastic regulation in the public interest. The legislative investigation of 1932 was persuasive of the fact that for this and other reasons unrestricted competition aggravated existing evils, and the normal law of supply and demand was insufficient to correct maladjustments detrimental to the community. The inquiry disclosed destructive and demoralizing competitive conditions and unfair trade practices which resulted in retail price-cutting and reduced the income of the farmer below the cost of production. We do not understand the appellant to deny that in these circumstances the legislature might reasonably consider further regulation and control desirable for protection of the industry and the consuming public. That body believed conditions could be improved by preventing destructive price-cutting by stores which, due to the flood of surplus milk, were able to buy at much lower prices than the larger distributors and to sell without incurring the delivery costs of the latter. In the order of which complaint is made the Milk Control Board fixed a price of ten cents per quart for sales by a distributor to a consumer, and nine cents by a store to a consumer, thus recognizing the lower costs of the store, and endeavoring to establish a differential which would be just to both. In the light of the facts the order appears not to be unreasonable or arbitrary, or without relation to the purpose to prevent ruthless competition from destroying the wholesale price structure on which the farmer depends for his livelihood, and the community for an assured supply of milk.

But we are told that because the law essays to control prices it denies due process. Notwithstanding the admitted power to correct existing economic ills by appropriate regulation of business, even though an indirect result may be a restriction of the freedom of contract or a modification of charges for services or the price of commodities, the appellant urges that direct fixation of prices is a type of regulation absolutely forbidden. His position is that the Fourteenth Amendment requires us to hold the challenged statute void for this reason alone. The argument runs that the public control of rates or prices is *per se* unreasonable and unconstitutional, save as applied to businesses affected with a public interest; that a business so affected is one in which property is devoted to an enterprise of a sort which the public itself might appropriately undertake, or one whose owner relies on a public grant or franchise for the right to conduct the business, or in which he is bound to serve all who apply; in short, such as is commonly called a public utility; or a business in its nature a monopoly. The milk industry, it is said, possesses none of these characteristics, and, therefore, not being affected with a public interest, its charges may not be controlled by the state. Upon the soundness of this contention the appellant's case against the statute depends.

We may as well say at once that the dairy industry is not, in the accepted sense of the phrase, a public utility. We think the appellant is also right in asserting that there is in this case no suggestion of any monopoly or monopolistic practice. It goes without saying that those engaged in the business are in no way dependent upon public grants or franchises for the privilege of conducting their activities. But if, as must be conceded, the industry is subject to regulation in the public interest, what constitutional principle bars the state from correcting existing maladjustments by legislation touching prices? We think there is no such principle. The due process clause makes no mention of sales or of prices any more than it speaks of business or contracts or buildings or other incidents of property. The thought seems nevertheless to have persisted that there is something peculiarly sacrosanct about the price one may charge for what he makes or sells, and that, however able to regulate other elements of manufacture or trade, with incidental effect upon price, the state is incapable of directly controlling the price itself. This view was negatived many years ago. Munn v. Illinois, 94 U. S. 113. . . . [Here follows an analysis of the Munn case in which it is pointed out that the Court therein regarded the term "affected with a public interest" as the equivalent of "subject to the exercise of the police power."]

It is clear that there is no closed class or category of businesses affected with a public interest, and the function of courts in the application of the Fifth and Fourteenth Amendments is to determine in each case whether circumstances vindicate the challenged regulation as a reasonable exertion of governmental authority or condemn it as arbitrary or discriminatory. . . . The phrase "affected with a public interest" can, in the nature of things, mean no more than that an industry, for adequate reason, is subject to control for the public good. In several of the decisions of this Court wherein the expressions "affected with a public interest," and "clothed with a public use," have been brought forward as the criteria of the validity of price control, it has been admitted that they are not susceptible of definition and form an unsatisfactory test of the constitutionality of legislation directed at business practices or prices. These decisions must rest, finally, upon the basis that the requirements of due process were not met because the laws were found arbitrary in their operation and effect. But there can be no doubt that upon proper occasion and by appropriate measures the state may regulate a business in any of its aspects, including the prices to be charged for the products or commodities it sells.

So far as the requirement of due process is concerned, and in the absence of other constitutional restriction, a state is free to adopt whatever economic policy may reasonably be deemed to promote public welfare, and to enforce that policy by legislation adapted to its purpose. The courts are without authority either to declare such policy, or, when it is declared by the legislature, to override it. . . .

. . . The Constitution does not secure to anyone liberty to conduct his business in such fashion as to inflict injury upon the public at large, or upon any substantial group of the people. Price control, like any other form of regulation, is unconstitutional only if arbitrary, discriminatory, or demonstrably irrelevant to the policy the legislature is free to adopt, and hence an unnecessary and unwarranted interference with individual liberty.

Tested by these considerations we find no basis in the due process clause of the Fourteenth Amendment for condemning the provisions of the Agriculture and Markets Law here drawn into question. . . .

Mr. Justice McReynolds dissented in an opinion concurred in by Justices Van Devanter, Sutherland, and Butler.

LOCHNER v. NEW YORK
198 U. S. 45; 49 L. Ed. 937; 25 Sup. Ct. 539. 1905.

Due process of law was not a new concept in our constitutional law; however, it was not until the period before the Civil War that due process clauses of the state constitutions had come tentatively to be construed as limitations upon the substance or content of legislation; and when, in the Slaughterhouse Cases, Mr. Justice Miller stated that the due process clause of the Fourteenth Amendment did not restrict the police power of the state, he was merely giving it a long-standing and orthodox interpretation.

This construction of the due process clause, however, was not destined to persist. The close of the Civil War ushered in an industrial and economic revolution marked by the enormous expansion of the interstate market through increased railroad facilities, the development of large-scale production carried on by huge accumulations of capital, and the development of a fairly well-defined labor class. Social and economic conditions of a new and complex nature sprang up, and these the legislatures of the various states attempted to deal with by statutes passed in the exercise of their police power. Some of these related to the control of the railroads and the establishment of the charges made by public utilities, others to the relations between laborer and employer, the latter now collectively designated as "capital." Naturally, organized industry looked upon any legislative effort to ameliorate such things as factory conditions and hours of labor as intolerable interferences with the employer's private affairs.

During the development of the situation just described the courts had been continuously besieged to depart, chiefly on behalf of capital, from the narrow construction of due process of law set forth in the Slaughterhouse Cases and to apply that clause as a broad and general restraint upon the state police power. In a case argued before the Supreme Court in 1885, San Mateo County v. Southern Pacific R. R. Co., 116 U. S. 138, Mr. Roscoe Conkling, who had been a member of the Committee of Fifteen on Reconstruction which had drafted the Fourteenth Amendment, produced in court the unpublished journal of the committee in support of his contention that the amendment had not been originally intended by its framers for the exclusive protection of the Negro race. As a result of the subtle pressure of such influences as these, together with the changes in personnel in the Supreme Court itself, that tribunal ultimately came to assume the position which many had felt it ought originally to have taken, and stood openly for the doctrine that the Fourteenth Amendment does impose judicially enforceable restrictions upon social legislation passed by the states.

But what constitutes deprivation of life, liberty, or property without due process of law in such a connection? This question the Court wisely declared it would not attempt to settle by the enunciation of any general doctrine but it would dispose separately of each case which came before it for decision. It is not possible, therefore, to define due process of law authoritatively beyond saying that it operates to prevent the enactment by the states of such measures as may be arbitrary and unreasonable in character, with what constitutes the test of "arbitrary" and "unreasonable" depending largely upon the opinion of the tribunal applying it. Every exercise of police power necessarily imposes restraint in some measure upon individual liberty or the free use of individual property; and if it is to be justified it must be upon the ground that it is necessary for the protection of the public health, morals, safety, good order, or general welfare. In other words, the due process test concretely means this: if the court believes that the infringement of individual rights involved in the statute is warranted by the pressing nature of the social need it is established to promote, then the law does not violate due process of law; but if it is not so warranted, then the due process clause is held to be contravened.

It was entirely natural that in its early application of these principles the courts should react to the problems which arose in the light of the background of their training and the legal and economic philosophy prevalent at the time that training was received. This philosophy was individualistic in character; and regulations of labor and other social conditions based upon the assumption that the state ought to intervene at the expense of the individual for the benefit of a particular group or class in economic society were looked upon with horror by the courts.

This early individualistic interpretation by the courts of due process of law found finally a definite basis in the development during the eighties of the doctrine of "liberty of contract." The first case turning upon this doctrine was decided by the supreme court of Pennsylvania in 1886, Godcharles v. Wigeman, 113 Pa. State 431, but the theory was soon incorporated into the doctrine of due process of law as applied by both state and federal courts. The concept of "liberty of contract" was both plausible and alluring. It asserted in substance that when two parties, neither of whom was under any legal disability, came together to make a contract which was not contrary to public policy, the legislature had no right to interfere and dictate the terms of the agreement. Of course such liberty of contract was not absolute, but the weight of opinion was that only the strongest public necessity afforded justification for its violation. The application of this doctrine to the problem of protective labor legislation produced, however, some very startling results, due in large measure to the naïve assumption by the courts that the individual employee of a great industrial corporation possessed full liberty of contract and could dicker with his employer upon equal terms. Naturally, as time went on the courts found frequently that this vaunted liberty of contract was infringed by the laws regulating hours of labor, method and time of wage payment, employer's liability, factory conditions, and similar matters. In Holden v. Hardy, 169 U. S. 366 (1898), however, the Supreme Court had sustained a state statute providing an eight-hour law for miners (referred to by Mr. Justice Holmes, p. 279).

If in these early cases the concept of "liberty of contract" resulted in placing a heavy burden of proof on those who defended the constitutionality of labor and social welfare legislation, that burden of proof was ultimately assumed in a novel and telling way. When Muller v. Oregon, 208 U. S. 412 (1908), involving the validity of the Oregon ten-hour law for women, was argued in the Supreme Court, the justices had before them the first of the famous "Brandeis briefs." This brief, prepared by Mr. Louis D. Brandeis (later Mr. Justice Brandeis) set out very little in the way of strictly legal argument, but at great length presented documentary evidence of the social and economic facts and conditions which had led the legislature to pass the law. The Court was impressed, and it held the Oregon statute valid. After Mr. Brandeis' appointment to the Supreme Court the same kind of brief was filed by Professor Felix Frankfurter (later Mr. Justice Frankfurter) in a series of similar cases.

The change in the Supreme Court's attitude with respect to the validity under due process of law of what seemed increasingly drastic social legislation may be traced in the cases involving minimum-wage legislation.

In 1913 the state of Washington passed a law to provide minimum wages for women and children in industry. The act was twice upheld by the supreme court of the state. In 1913 Oregon likewise passed a similar statute which was held valid by the supreme court of Oregon. This time, attack on the act was carried to the Supreme Court of the United States. Mr. Brandeis helped prepare the brief in defense of the act and when, in 1916, he was appointed to the Supreme Court, Professor Frankfurter took his place and argued the case. With Mr. Justice Brandeis disqualified because of his earlier connection with the case, the Court, in Stettler v. O'Hara, 243 U. S. 629 (1917), divided four to four and the decision of the Oregon court upholding the minimum wage law was accordingly affirmed. It was confidently assumed that the full Court would in due course follow the doctrines announced in the cases upholding restrictions upon the hours of labor of women and declare the minimum wage legislation constitutional. In 1923, however, the Court, now substantially changed in personnel, held invalid as a denial of due process of law the minimum wage law passed by Congress in 1918 for the District of Columbia. This was the case of Adkins v. Children's Hospital, 261 U. S. 525 (1923). The Court divided five to three. Again Mr. Justice Brandeis did not sit, this time because his daughter was a member of the minimum wage commission. The majority opinion of Mr. Justice Sutherland reads like the opinion of the Court in the Lochner case, which it quotes at length with approval. There is no such connection between the wages women receive and their health, morals, or welfare as to justify destroying by law the freedom of contract of employers and the women who work for them. Furthermore, the act does not guarantee that the minimum wage fixed shall not exceed the fair value of the service for which it is paid. In 1925 and in 1927, the Court without opinion ruled that the Adkins case rendered invalid the state minimum wage laws of Arizona and Arkansas respectively.

In 1933 New York passed a minimum wage law for women and children. Its framers sought to escape the ban of the Adkins decision by providing that the wages fixed should be based on the fair value of the labor paid for. The attempt failed. In Morehead v. New York ex rel. Tipaldo, 298 U. S. 587 (1936), the Supreme Court in a five-to-four decision held the New York statute invalid. In the majority opinion Mr. Justice Butler held that the statute was like the one held void in the Adkins case, but said in substance that any minimum wage law, regardless of its provisions, would be invalid as a denial of due process of law. In a separate dissenting opinion Mr. Justice Stone observed: "It is difficult to imagine any grounds, other than our own personal economic predilections, for saying that the contract of employment is any the less an appropriate subject of legislation than are scores of others, in dealing with which this Court has held that legislatures may curtail individual freedom in the public interest."

During all this time, the Washington statute of 1913 had been in force; and a case involving its validity was on the Court's docket when the New York case was decided. The case was argued on its merits. Five justices, Mr. Justice Roberts crossing over, overruled the Adkins case and upheld the Washington statute in West Coast Hotel Co. v. Parrish, 300 U. S. 379 (1937). Four justices dissented.

The police power of the state is often used, not to control the conduct of individuals, but to regulate or restrict the uses to which property may be put. A striking example is to be found in the modern legislation establishing municipal zoning. In Euclid v. Ambler Reality Co., 272 U. S. 365 (1926), the Court in a notable opinion held valid the zoning ordinance of the village of Euclid, a suburb of Cleveland. The ordinance divided the village into six classes of districts according to the use made of land or buildings, three classes according to heights of buildings permitted, and four classes according to the percentage of the land which could be built upon. This is now, of course, a very common type of zoning regulation throughout the country, but it was startling in 1926. The Supreme Court held the ordinance to be a reasonable exercise of the state's police power, under which the state has always had the authority to abate nuisances. A nuisance need not be rigidly defined to include only things which jeopardize public health, safety, or morals. "A nuisance," said the Court, "may merely be a right thing in the wrong place—like a pig in the parlor instead of the barnyard."

The Lochner case is printed here because it is, in a sense, a museum piece. The archaic opinion of Mr. Justice Peckham for the majority expresses with accuracy the dominant judicial doctrine of that period, with its reliance upon the concept of "liberty of contract," a doctrine which was widely believed to be essential to stability and good order in our economic and social life. The classic dissenting opinion of Mr. Justice Holmes, however, laid down the challenge which was to revolutionize judicial thinking with respect to the state's power to legislate in behalf of the economic and social welfare of its citizens.

Lochner was convicted of violating a New York statute called the Labor Law, which provided that no employee should be "required or permitted to work in a biscuit, bread or cake bakery or confectionery establishment more than sixty hours in any one week, or more than ten hours in any one day unless for the purpose of making a shorter day on the last day of the week." The legislature had proceeded upon the assumption that the conditions in the baking industry were such as to demand the intervention of the state in behalf of the employees. The majority of the Supreme Court did not agree that such protection was reasonably necessary and accordingly held that there was no adequate justification for this infringement of the private rights of the employer.

Mr. Justice Peckham delivered the opinion of the Court, saying in part:

. . . The statute necessarily interferes with the right of contract between the employer and employees, concerning the number of hours in which the latter may labor in the bakery of the employer. The general right to make a contract in relation to his business is part of the liberty of the individual protected by the Fourteenth Amendment of the federal Constitution. . . . Under that provision no state can deprive any person of life, liberty, or property without due process of law. The right to purchase or to sell labor is part of the liberty protected by this amendment, unless there are circumstances which exclude the right. There are, however, certain powers, existing in the sovereignty of each state in the Union, somewhat vaguely termed police powers, the exact description and limitation of which have not been attempted by the courts. Those powers, broadly stated, and without, at present, any attempt at a more specific limitation, relate to the safety, health, morals, and general welfare of the public. Both property and liberty are held on such reasonable conditions as may be imposed by the governing power of the state in the exercise of those powers, and with such conditions the Fourteenth Amendment was not designed to interfere. . . .

The state, therefore, has power to prevent the individual from making certain kinds of contracts, and in regard to them the federal Constitution offers no protection. If the contract be one which the state, in the legitimate exercise of its police power, has the right to prohibit, it is not prevented from prohibiting it by the Fourteenth Amendment. Contracts in violation of a statute, either of the federal or state government, or a contract to let one's property for immoral purposes, or to do any other unlawful act, could obtain no protection from the federal Constitution, as coming under the liberty of person or of free contract. Therefore, when the state, by its legislature, in the assumed exercise of its police powers, has passed an act which seriously limits the right to labor or the right of contract in regard to their means of livelihood between persons who are sui juris (both employer and employee), it becomes of great importance to determine which shall prevail,—the right of the individual to labor for such time as he may choose, or the right of the state to prevent the individual from laboring, or from entering into any contract to labor, beyond a certain time prescribed by the state. . . .

It must, of course, be conceded that there is a limit to the valid exercise of the police power by the state. There is no dispute concerning this general proposition. Otherwise the Fourteenth Amendment would have no efficacy and the legislatures of the states would have unbounded power, and it would be enough to say that any piece of legislation was enacted to conserve the morals, the health, or the safety of the people; such legislation would be valid, no matter how absolutely without foundation the claim might be. The claim of the police power would be a mere pretext,—become another and delusive name for the supreme sovereignty of the state to be exercised free from constitutional restraint. This is not contended for. In every case that comes before this Court, therefore, where legislation of this character is concerned, and where the protection of the federal Constitution is sought, the question necessarily arises: Is this a fair, reasonable, and appropriate exercise of the police power of the state, or is it an unreasonable, unnecessary, and arbitrary interference with the right of the individual to his personal liberty, or to enter into those contracts in relation to labor which may seem to him appropriate or necessary for the support of himself and his family? Of course the liberty of contract relating to labor includes both parties to it. The one has as much right to purchase as the other to sell labor.

This is not a question of substituting the judgment of the court for that of the legislature. If the act be within the power of the state it is valid, although the judgment of the court might be totally opposed to the enactment of such a law. But the question would still remain: Is it within the police power of the state? and that question must be answered by the court.

The question whether this act is valid as a labor law, pure and simple, may be dismissed in a few words. There is no reasonable ground for interfering with the liberty of person or the right of free contract, by determining the hours of labor, in the occupation of a baker. There is no contention that bakers as a class are not equal in intelligence and capacity to men in other trades or manual occupations, or that they are not able to assert their rights and care for themselves without the protecting arm of the state, interfering with their independence of judgment and of action. They are in no sense wards of the state. Viewed in the light of a purely labor law, with no reference whatever to the question of health, we think that a law like the one before us involves neither the safety, the morals, nor the welfare of the public, and that the interest of the public is not in the slightest degree affected by such an act. The law must be upheld, if at all, as a law pertaining to the health of the individual engaged in the occupation of a baker. It does not affect any other portion of the public than those who are engaged in that occupation. Clean and wholesome bread does not depend upon whether the baker works but ten hours per day or only sixty hours a week. The limitation of the hours of labor does not come within the police power on that ground.

It is a question of which of two powers or rights shall prevail,—the power of the state to legislate or the right of the individual to liberty of person and freedom of contract. The mere assertion that the subject relates, though but in a remote degree, to the public health, does not necessarily render the enactment valid. The act must have a more direct relation, as a means to an end, and the end itself must be appropriate and legitimate, before an act can be held to be valid which interferes with the general right of an individual to be free in his person and in his power to contract in relation to his own labor. . . .

We think the limit of the police power has been reached and passed in this case. There is, in our judgment, no reasonable foundation for holding this to be necessary or appropriate as a health law to safeguard the public health, or the health of the individuals who are following the trade of a baker. If this statute be valid, and if, therefore, a proper case is made out in which to deny the right of an individual, sui juris, as employer or employee, to make contracts for the labor of the latter under the protection of the provisions of the federal Constitution, there would seem to be no length to which legislation of this nature might not go. . . .

We think that there can be no fair doubt that the trade of a baker, in and of itself, is not an unhealthy one to that degree which would authorize the legislature to interfere with the right to labor, and with the right of free contract on the part of the individual, either as employer or employee. In looking through statistics regarding all trades and occupations, it may be true that the trade of a baker does not appear to be as healthy as some other trades, and is also vastly more healthy than still others. To the common understanding the trade of a baker has never been regarded as an unhealthy one. Very likely physicians would not recommend the exercise of that or of any other trade as a remedy for ill health. Some occupations are more healthy than others, but we think there are none which might not come under the power of the legislature to supervise and control the hours of working therein, if the mere fact that the occupation is not absolutely and perfectly healthy is to confer that right upon the legislative department of the government. It might be safely affirmed that almost all occupations more or less affect the health. There must be more than the mere fact of the possible existence of some small amount of unhealthiness to warrant legislative interference with liberty. It is unfortunately true that labor, even in any department, may possibly carry with it the seeds of unhealthiness. But are we all, on that account, at the mercy of legislative majorities? A printer, a tinsmith, a locksmith, a carpenter, a cabinetmaker, a dry goods clerk, a bank's, a lawyer's, or a physician's clerk, or a clerk in almost any kind of business, would all come under the power of the legislature, on this assumption. No trade, no occupation, no mode of earning one's living, could escape this all-pervading power, and the acts of the legislature in limiting the hours of labor in all employments would be valid, although such limitation might seriously cripple the ability of the laborer to support himself and his family.

In our large cities there are many buildings into which the sun penetrates for but a short time in each day, and these buildings are occupied by people carrying on the business of bankers, brokers, lawyers, real estate, and many other kinds of business, aided by many clerks, messengers, and other employees. Upon the assumption of the validity of this act under review, it is not possible to say that an act, prohibiting lawyers' or bank clerks, or others, from contracting to labor for their employers more than eight hours a day would be invalid. It might be said that it is unhealthy to work more than that number of hours in an apartment lighted by artificial light during the working hours of the day; that the occupation of the bank clerk, the lawyer's clerk, the real-estate clerk, or the broker's clerk, in such offices is therefore unhealthy, and the legislature in its paternal wisdom must, therefore, have the right to legislate on the subject of and to limit the hours for such labor, and, if it exercises that power, and its validity be questioned, it is sufficient to say, it has reference to the public health; it has reference to the health of the employees condemned to labor day after day in buildings where the sun never shines; it is a health law, and therefore it is valid, and cannot be questioned by the courts.

It is also urged, pursuing the same line of argument, that it is to the interest of the state that its population should be strong and robust, and therefore any legislation which may be said to tend to make people healthy must be valid as health laws, enacted under the police power. If this be a valid argument and a justification for this kind of legislation, it follows that the protection of the federal Constitution from undue interference with liberty of person and freedom of contract is visionary, wherever the law is sought to be justified as a valid exercise of the police power. Scarcely any law but might find shelter under such assumptions, and conduct, properly so called, as well as contract, would come under the restrictive sway of the legislature. Not only the hours of employees, but the hours of employers, could be regulated, and doctors, lawyers, scientists, all professional men, as well as athletes and artisans, could be forbidden to fatigue their brains and bodies by prolonged hours of exercise, lest the fighting strength of the state be impaired. We mention these extreme cases because the contention is extreme.

We do not believe in the soundness of the views which uphold this law. On the contrary, we think that such a law as this, although passed in the assumed exercise of the police power, and as relating to the public health, or the health of the employees named, is not within that power, and is invalid. The act is not, within any fair meaning of the term, a health law, but is an illegal interference with the rights of individuals, both employers and employees, to make contracts regarding labor upon such terms as they may think best, or which they may agree upon with the other parties to such contracts. Statutes of the nature of that under review, limiting the hours in which grown and intelligent men may labor to earn their living, are mere meddlesome interferences with the rights of the individual, and they are not saved from condemnation by the claim that they are passed in the exercise of the police power and upon the subject of the health of the individual whose rights are interfered with, unless there be some fair ground, reasonable in and of itself, to say that there is material danger to the public health, or to the health of the employees, if the hours of labor are not curtailed. . . .

It was further urged on the argument that restricting the hours of labor in the case of bakers was valid because it tended to cleanliness on the part of the workers, as a man was more apt to be cleanly when not overworked, and if cleanly then his "output" was also more likely to be so. . . . The connection, if any exist, is too shadowy and thin to build any argument for the interference of the legislature. If the man works ten hours a day it is all right, but if ten and a half or eleven his health is in danger and his bread may be unhealthful, and, therefore, he shall not be permitted to do it. This, we think, is unreasonable and entirely arbitrary.

. . . It seems to us that the real object and purpose were simply to regulate the hours of labor between the master and his employees (all being men, sui juris), in a private business, not dangerous in any degree to morals, or in any real and substantial degree to the health of the employees. Under such circumstances the freedom of master and employee to contract with each other in relation to their employment, and in defining the same, cannot be prohibited or interfered with, without violating the federal Constitution. . . .

Mr. Justice Harlan, with whom concurred Mr. Justice White and Mr. Justice Day, in dissenting said in part:

. . . I find it impossible, in view of common experience, to say that there is here no real or substantial relation between the means employed by the state and the end sought to be accomplished by its legislation. . . .

We judicially know that the question of the number of hours during which a workman should continuously labor has been, for a long period, and is yet, a subject of serious consideration among civilized peoples, and by those having special knowledge of the laws of health. Suppose the statute prohibited labor in bakery and confectionery establishments in excess of eighteen hours each day. No one, I take it, could dispute the power of the state to enact such a statute. But the statute before us does not embrace extreme or exceptional cases. It may be said to occupy a middle ground in respect of the hours of labor. What is the true ground for the state to take between legitimate protection, by legislation, of the public health and liberty of contract is not a question easily solved, nor one in respect of which there is or can be absolute certainty. There are very few, if any, questions in political economy about which entire certainty may be predicated. . . .

I do not stop to consider whether any particular view of this economic question presents the sounder theory. What the precise facts are it may be difficult to say. It is enough for the determination of this case, and it is enough for this Court to know, that the question is one about which there is room for debate and for an honest difference of opinion. There are many reasons of a weighty, substantial character, based upon the experience of mankind, in support of the theory that, all things considered, more than ten hours steady work each day, from week to week, in a bakery or confectionery establishment, may endanger the health and shorten the lives of the workmen, thereby diminishing their physical and mental capacity to serve the state and to provide for those dependent upon them.

If such reasons exist that ought to be the end of this case, for the state is not amenable to the judiciary, in respect of its legislative enactments, unless such enactments are plainly, palpably, beyond all question, inconsistent with the Constitution of the United States. . . .

Mr. Justice Holmes in dissenting said:

I regret sincerely that I am unable to agree with the judgment in this case, and I think it my duty to express my dissent.

This case is decided upon an economic theory which a large part of the country does not entertain. If it were a question whether I agreed with that theory, I should desire to study it further and long before making up my mind. But I do not conceive that to be my duty, because I strongly believe that my agreement or disagreement has nothing to do with the right of a majority to embody their opinions in law. It is settled by various decisions of this Court that state constitutions and state laws may regulate life in many ways which we as legislators might think as injudicious or if you like as tyrannical as this, and which equally with this interfere with the liberty to contract. Sunday laws and usury laws are ancient examples. A more modern one is the prohibition of lotteries. The liberty of the citizen to do as he likes so long as he does not interfere with the liberty of others to do the same, which has been a shibboleth for some well-known writers, is interfered with by school laws, by the postoffice, by every state or municipal institution which takes his money for purposes thought desirable, whether he likes it or not.

The Fourteenth Amendment does not enact Mr. Herbert Spencer's Social Statics. The other day we sustained the Massachusetts vaccination law. Jacobson v. Massachusetts, 197 U. S. 11. United States and state statutes and decisions cutting down the liberty to contract by way of combination are familiar to this court. Northern Securities Co. v. United States, 193 U. S. 197. Two years ago we upheld the prohibition of sales of stock on margins or for future delivery in the constitu-

tion of California. Otis v. Parker, 187 U. S. 606. The decision
sustaining an eight-hour law for miners is still recent. Holden v.
Hardy, 169 U. S. 366. Some of these laws embody convictions or
prejudices which judges are likely to share. Some may not. But a constitution is not intended to embody a particular economic theory,
whether of paternalism and the organic relation of the citizen to the
state or of laissez faire. It is made for people of fundamentally differing views, and the accident of our finding certain opinions natural and
familiar or novel and even shocking ought not to conclude our judgment upon the question whether statutes embodying them conflict
with the Constitution of the United States.

General propositions do not decide concrete cases. The decision will
depend on a judgment or intuition more subtle than any articulate
major premise. But I think that the proposition just stated, if it is accepted, will carry us far toward the end. Every opinion tends to become a law. I think that the word "liberty" in the Fourteenth
Amendment is perverted when it is held to prevent the natural outcome of a dominant opinion, unless it can be said that a rational and
fair man necessarily would admit that the statute proposed would
infringe fundamental principles as they have been understood by the
traditions of our people and our law. It does not need research to
show that no such sweeping condemnation can be passed upon the
statute before us. A reasonable man might think it a proper measure
on the score of health. Men whom I certainly could not pronounce
unreasonable would uphold it as a first instalment of a general regulation of the hours of work. Whether in the latter aspect it would be
open to the charge of inequality I think it unnecessary to discuss.

DARTMOUTH COLLEGE CASE:
THE TRUSTEES OF DARTMOUTH COLLEGE
v. WOODWARD
4 Wheaton 518; 4 L. Ed. 629. 1819.

When the framers of the Constitution forbade the states to pass laws
impairing the obligation of contracts they had in mind the ordinary execu-
tory contracts between man and man, which during the "critical period"
had so frequently been interfered with by the enactment of "stay laws,"
legal tender laws, and other legislation for the benefit of insolvent debtors.
The first interpretation of the contract clause by the Supreme Court was
given in the case of Fletcher v. Peck, 6 Cranch 87 (1810), which did not

relate to this sort of contract at all, but which involved the question whether an executed contract in the form of a legislative grant of land made by the state itself through its legislature could be later rescinded by the state. The Court held here that the grant of land, even though made under circumstances of the most scandalous corruption, is a contract within the meaning of the constitutional provision and cannot be rescinded by the state after the land in question has passed into the hands of innocent purchasers. It is interesting to note that at the very end of his opinion in this case Chief Justice Marshall left the legal profession in some doubt as to the precise ground upon which he held the rescinding act to be void by saying: "The state of Georgia was restrained, either by general principles which are common to our free institutions, or by particular provisions of the Constitution of the United States, from passing a law," etc. This plainly suggests that the rescinding act might have been held void as an interference with vested rights.

Of far greater significance was the Dartmouth College Case, in which the contract clause was given an even wider application. In 1769 Dartmouth College was chartered by the English Crown. The charter created a board of trustees with power to choose a president and to fill vacancies in its own membership. In 1779 the first president, dying, was succeeded by his son John Wheelock, who seems to have lacked the tact necessary for a good administrator. Difficulties between Wheelock and his trustees grew apace, at first personal, then sectarian, and finally political. The Wheelock faction came to comprise the Presbyterian Republicans throughout the state, while the board of trustees drew their support from the Congregationalist Federalist group. In 1815 Wheelock was removed from the presidency of the college by the board. In 1816 the Republicans carried the state, electing the governor and a majority in the legislature, and forthwith passed a law entirely reorganizing the government of the college. The name of the institution was changed to Dartmouth University; the trustees were increased from twelve to twenty-one and were to be appointed by the governor and council; a body of twenty-five overseers was created, twenty-one of whom were to be appointed by the governor and council with a veto power on the acts of the trustees. The president was required to report annually to the governor on the management of the college, and the governor and council were empowered to "inspect" the college every five years and report to the legislature. Promptly the old trustees refused to be governed by the provisions of the law; whereupon the new trustees ousted the old trustees from the college buildings, called themselves the new university, and elected Wheelock as the new university president. The old trustees, nothing daunted, gathered about them their sympathizers among the professors, hired rooms nearby, and continued to operate as the "college," most of the students remaining loyal to the old regime. Woodward, who was the secretary and treasurer of the original college, sided with the Wheelock faction and the new university and now refused to allow the old "college" to have possession of the seal, records, and account books which were in his possession. The trustees of the old "college" thereupon brought an action of trover (a proceeding to recover the value of property wrongfully withheld) against Woodward, thus raising the general question of the constitutionality of the statute of 1816 reorganizing the college.

The case was argued before the supreme court of New Hampshire in 1817. Little reference was made to the contract clause. The state court decided against the college on the ground that the institution had become public in character and as such was subject to state control. The case was taken to the United States Supreme Court on a writ of error and was argued in 1818. Webster, who was not yet at the height of his fame, represented the college and made an argument which has long been celebrated. He laid much more emphasis on the necessity of protecting vested rights than upon the contract clause. Rumor has it that the Court was divided in its opinion on the case at the close of the argument and that Marshall, who favored the college, postponed the decision until the next term and in the meantime won over his colleagues to his own position. At the opening of the next term of court the decision was handed down in favor of the college.

The doctrine of this case, that a corporate charter is a contract which may not be impaired by legislative enactment, has been most bitterly criticized as making it possible for corrupt and ignorant legislatures irrevocably to grant away privileges and rights contrary to the public interest and welfare. There can be no doubt that it did create opportunities for legislative corruption. At the same time it put the public upon its guard with reference to corporate grants and it emphasized the importance of good faith at a time when public opinion seemed willing to sponsor interference with promises. In an economic sense the decision was of great importance in giving to those who invested money in corporate enterprises assurance that the corporations would be free from legislative interference, and it thus encouraged the expansion of business enterprise in the fields of railroad construction, insurance, commerce, and industry.

The doctrine of the Dartmouth College Case was somewhat softened by succeeding decisions of the Supreme Court. In the case of Charles River Bridge v. Warren Bridge, 11 Peters 420 (1837), it was held that the terms of a charter contract must be strictly construed and that no rights or privileges can be held granted away by the public by mere implication. In the case of Ogden v. Saunders, 12 Wheaton 213 (1827), the Court decided that the obligation of a contract within the meaning of the contract clause consists not merely in the promise or agreement between the parties but also in the law applicable to the subject which is in existence when the contract is made. This rule makes it possible for the states to pass general laws reserving the right to amend or repeal corporate charters under certain circumstances.

In the exercise of what may be called the essential or "paramount" powers of government the states are not limited by the contract clause. Thus a state may not, even if it desires to, contract away its police power. In Stone v. Mississippi, 101 U. S. 814 (1880), the state legislature chartered a corporation to operate a lottery for twenty-five years upon the payment of $5,000 and further annual payments. In 1868 and 1870 a new state constitution and statute forbade all lotteries. The Court upheld the new legislation, stating that the state had not bargained away its police power by which it could abolish the evils of gambling. The same result was reached with respect to the power of eminent domain in Pennsylvania Hospital v. Philadelphia, 245 U. S. 20 (1917). Here the hospital, in 1845, secured an agreement with the state that no streets or alleys should ever be opened through its grounds, and in return the hospital granted some land and paid some money to the state. In 1913 the city, under authority from the state, condemned a street through the hospital grounds in plain violation of the 1845 contract. The Court held that the power of eminent domain overrode the contract and that the condemnation was valid.

A startling application of this doctrine of "paramount" state power with reference to private contracts occurred during the depression, and was upheld in Home Building and Loan Association v. Blaisdell, 290 U. S. 398 (1934). One of the most pressing problems of that grim period was the dire situation of the land- or home-owner facing a foreclosure of his mortgage. With rising taxes and falling income he faced complete financial ruin. To meet this acute emergency the Minnesota Mortgage Moratorium Act of 1933, typical of others, was passed. The act provided that "during the emergency declared to exist, relief may be had through authorized judicial proceedings with respect to foreclosures of mortgages, and execution sales, of real estate; that sales may be postponed and periods of redemption may be extended." During this period of grace the mortgagor was to pay "all or a reasonable part of such income or rental value, in or toward the payment of taxes, insurance, interest, mortgage . . . indebtedness at such times and in such manner" as the court should determine. Thus the owner received income from the property, but he had to wait before he could foreclose the mortgage. In a five-to-four decision the Court, speaking through Chief Justice Hughes, held the statute valid. An emergency existed in Minnesota which the state, through its police power, might validly seek to alleviate. This temporary and reasonable legislation overrode, therefore, the contract obligations embodied in the mortgages.

Mr. Chief Justice Marshall, in delivering the opinion of the Court, said in part:

. . . This Court can be insensible neither to the magnitude nor delicacy of this question. The validity of a legislative act is to be examined; and the opinion of the highest law tribunal of a state is to be revised: an opinion which carries with it intrinsic evidence of the diligence, of the ability, and the integrity with which it was formed. On more than one occasion this Court has expressed the cautious circumspection with which it approaches the consideration of such questions; and has declared that, in no doubtful case, would it pronounce a legislative act to be contrary to the Constitution. But the American people have said, in the Constitution of the United States, that "no State shall pass any bill of attainder, ex post facto law, or law impairing the obligation of contracts." In the same instrument they have also said, "that the judicial power shall extend to all cases in law and equity arising under the Constitution." On the judges of this Court, then, is imposed the high and solemn duty of protecting, from even legislative violation, those contracts which the Constitution of our country has placed beyond legislative control; and, however irksome the task may be, this is a duty from which we dare not shrink. . . .

It can require no argument to prove that the circumstances of this case constitute a contract. An application is made to the Crown for a charter to incorporate a religious and literary institution. In the application it is stated that large contributions have been made for the object, which will be conferred on the corporation as soon as it shall be created. The charter is granted, and on its faith the property is conveyed. Surely in this transaction every ingredient of a complete and legitimate contract is to be found.

The points for consideration are,

1. Is this contract protected by the Constitution of the United States?

2. Is it impaired by the acts under which the defendant holds?

1. On the first point it has been argued that the word "contract," in its broadest sense, would comprehend the political relations between the government and its citizens, would extend to offices held within a state for state purposes, and to many of those laws concerning civil institutions, which must change with circumstances, and be modified by ordinary legislation; which deeply concern the public, and which, to preserve good government, the public judgment must control. That even marriage is a contract, and its obligations are affected by the laws respecting divorces. That the clause in the Constitution, if construed in its greatest latitude, would prohibit these laws. Taken in its

broad, unlimited sense, the clause would be an unprofitable and vexatious interference with the internal concerns of a state, would unnecessarily and unwisely embarrass its legislation, and render immutable those civil institutions which are established for purposes of internal government, and which, to subserve those purposes, ought to vary with varying circumstances. That as the framers of the Constitution could never have intended to insert in that instrument a provision so unnecessary, so mischievous, and so repugnant to its general spirit, the term "contract" must be understood in a more limited sense. That it must be understood as intended to guard against a power of at least doubtful utility, the abuse of which had been extensively felt, and to restrain the legislature in future from violating the right to property. That anterior to the formation of the Constitution, a course of legislation had prevailed in many, if not in all, of the states, which weakened the confidence of man in man, and embarrassed all transactions between individuals, by dispensing with a faithful performance of engagements. To correct this mischief, by restraining the power which produced it, the state legislatures were forbidden "to pass any law impairing the obligation of contracts," that is, of contracts respecting property, under which some individual could claim a right to something beneficial to himself; and that since the clause in the Constitution must in construction receive some limitation, it may be confined, and ought to be confined, to cases of this description; to cases within the mischief it was intended to remedy.

The general correctness of these observations cannot be controverted. That the framers of the Constitution did not intend to restrain the states in the regulation of their civil institutions, adopted for internal government, and that the instrument they have given us is not to be so construed, may be admitted. The provision of the Constitution never has been understood to embrace other contracts than those which respect property or some object of value, and confer rights which may be asserted in a court of justice. It never has been understood to restrict the general right of the legislature to legislate on the subject of divorces. Those acts enable some tribunal, not to impair a marriage contract, but to liberate one of the parties because it has been broken by the other. When any state legislature shall pass an act annulling all marriage contracts, or allowing either party to annul it without the consent of the other, it will be time enough to inquire whether such an act be constitutional.

The parties in this case differ less on general principles, less on the true construction of the Constitution in the abstract, than on the application of those principles to this case, and on the true construction of the charter of 1769. This is the point on which the cause essentially depends. If the act of incorporation be a grant of political power, if it create a civil institution to be employed in the administration of the government, or if the funds of the college be public property, or if the state of New Hampshire, as a government, be alone interested in its transactions, the subject is one in which the legislature of the state may act according to its own judgment, unrestrained by any limitation of its power imposed by the Constitution of the United States.

But if this be a private eleemosynary institution, endowed with a capacity to take property for objects unconnected with government, whose funds are bestowed by individuals on the faith of the charter; if the donors have stipulated for the future disposition and management of those funds in the manner prescribed by themselves; there may be more difficulty in the case, although neither the persons who have made these stipulations, nor those for whose benefit they were made, should be parties to the cause. Those who are no longer interested in the property may yet retain such an interest in the preservation of their own arrangements as to have a right to insist that those arrangements shall be held sacred. Or, if they have themselves disappeared, it becomes a subject of serious and anxious inquiry whether those whom they have legally empowered to represent them forever may not assert all the rights which they possessed while in being; whether, if they be without personal representatives who may feel injured by a violation of the compact, the trustees be not so completely their representatives in the eye of the law as to stand in their place, not only as respects the government of the college, but also as respects the maintenance of the college charter.

It becomes then the duty of the Court most seriously to examine this charter, and to ascertain its true character. . . .

[In the course of his comment upon the charitable objects of the donors of Dartmouth College occurs Marshall's classic description of a corporation]:

A corporation is an artificial being, invisible, intangible, and existing only in contemplation of law. Being the mere creature of law, it possesses only those properties which the charter of its creation confers upon it, either expressly or as incidental to its very existence. These are such as are supposed best calculated to effect the object for which it was created. Among the most important are immortality, and, if the expression may be allowed, individuality; properties, by which a perpetual succession of many persons are considered as the same, and may act as a single individual. They enable a corporation to manage its own affairs, and to hold property without the perplexing intricacies, the hazardous and endless necessity, of perpetual conveyances for the purpose of transmitting it from hand to hand. It is chiefly for the purpose of clothing bodies of men in succession with these qualities and capacities that corporations were invented and are in use. By these means, a perpetual succession of individuals are capable of acting for the promotion of the particular object, like one immortal being. . . .

From this review of the charter, it appears that Dartmouth College is an eleemosynary institution, incorporated for the purpose of perpetuating the application of the bounty of the donors to the specified objects of that bounty; that its trustees or governors were originally named by the founder, and invested with the power of perpetuating themselves; that they are not public officers, nor is it a civil institution, participating in the administration of government; but a charity school, or a seminary of education, incorporated for the preservation of its property, and the perpetual application of that property to the objects of its creation. . . .

According to the theory of the British constitution, their Parliament is omnipotent. To annul corporate rights might give a shock to public opinion, which that government has chosen to avoid; but its power is not questioned. Had Parliament, immediately after the emanation of this charter and the execution of those conveyances which followed it, annulled the instrument, so that the living donors would have witnessed the disappointment of their hopes, the perfidy of the transaction would have been universally acknowledged. Yet then, as now, the donors would have had no interest in the property; then, as now, those who might be students would have had no rights to be violated; then, as now, it might be said that the trustees, in whom the rights of all were combined, possessed no private, individual, beneficial interest in the property confided to their protection. Yet the contract would at that time have been deemed sacred by all. What has since occurred to strip it of its inviolability? Circumstances have not changed it. In reason, in justice, and in law, it is now what it was in 1769.

This is plainly a contract to which the donors, the trustees, and the Crown (to whose rights and obligations New Hampshire succeeds) were the original parties. It is a contract made on a valuable consideration. It is a contract for the security and disposition of property. It is a contract on the faith of which real and personal estate has been conveyed to the corporation. It is then a contract within the letter of the Constitution, and within its spirit also, unless the fact that the property is invested by the donors in trustees for the promotion of religion and education, for the benefit of persons who are perpetually changing, though the objects remain the same, shall create a particular exception, taking this case out of the prohibition contained in the Constitution.

It is more than possible that the preservation of rights of this description was not particularly in view of the framers of the Constitution when the clause under consideration was introduced into that instrument. It is probable that interferences of more frequent recurrence, to which the temptation was stronger and of which the mischief was more extensive, constituted the great motive for imposing this restriction on the state legislatures. But although a particular and a rare case may not in itself be of sufficient magnitude to induce a rule, yet it must be governed by the rule, when established, unless some plain and strong reason for excluding it can be given. It is not enough to say that this particular case was not in the mind of the convention when the article was framed, nor of the American people when it was adopted. It is necessary to go farther, and to say that, had this particular case been suggested, the language would have been so varied as to exclude it, or it would have been made a special exception. The case, being within the words of the rule, must be within its operation likewise, unless there be something in the literal construction so obviously absurd, or mischievous, or repugnant to the general spirit of the instrument as to justify those who expound the Constitution in making it an exception.

On what safe and intelligible ground can this exception stand? There is no expression in the Constitution, no sentiment delivered by its contemporaneous expounders, which would justify us in making it. In the absence of all authority of this kind, is there, in the nature and reason of the case itself, that which would sustain a construction of the Constitution, not warranted by its words? Are contracts of this description of a character to excite so little interest that we must exclude them from the provisions of the Constitution, as being unworthy of the attention of those who framed the instrument? Or does public policy so imperiously demand their remaining exposed to legislative alteration, as to compel us, or rather permit us to say, that these words, which were introduced to give stability to contracts, and which in their plain import comprehend this contract, must yet be so construed, as to exclude it?

Almost all eleemosynary corporations, those which are created for the promotion of religion, of charity, or of education, are of the same character. The law of this case is the law of all. . . .

The opinion of the Court, after mature deliberation, is, that this is a contract, the obligation of which cannot be impaired without violating the Constitution of the United States. This opinion appears to us to be equally supported by reason and by the former decisions of this Court.

2. We next proceed to the inquiry whether its obligation has been impaired by those acts of the legislature of New Hampshire to which the special verdict refers.

From the review of this charter which has been taken it appears that the whole power of governing the college, of appointing and removing tutors, of fixing their salaries, of directing the course of study to be pursued by the students, and of filling up vacancies created in their own body, was vested in the trustees. On the part of the Crown it was expressly stipulated that this corporation, thus constituted, should continue forever; and that the number of trustees should forever consist of twelve, and no more. By this contract the Crown was bound, and could have made no violent alteration in its essential terms without impairing its obligation.

By the Revolution the duties as well as the powers of government devolved on the people of New Hampshire. It is admitted that among the latter was comprehended the transcendent power of Parliament, as well as that of the executive department. It is too clear to require the support of argument that all contracts and rights respecting property remained unchanged by the Revolution. The obligations, then, which were created by the charter to Dartmouth College were the same in the new that they had been in the old government. The power of the government was also the same. A repeal of this charter at any time prior to the adoption of the present Constitution of the United States would have been an extraordinary and unprecedented act of power, but one which could have been contested only by the restrictions upon the legislature to be found in the constitution of the state. But the Constitution of the United States has imposed this additional limitation, that the legislature of a state shall pass no act "impairing the obligation of contracts."

It has been already stated that the act "to amend the charter and enlarge and improve the corporation of Dartmouth College" increases the number of trustees to twenty-one, gives the appointment of the additional members to the executive of the state, and creates a board of overseers, to consist of twenty-five persons, of whom twenty-one are also appointed by the executive of New Hampshire, who have power to inspect and control the most important acts of the trustees.

On the effect of this law two opinions cannot be entertained. Between acting directly and acting through the agency of trustees and overseers no essential difference is perceived. The whole power of governing the college is transformed from trustees appointed according to the will of the founder, expressed in the charter, to the executive of New Hampshire. The management and application of the funds of this eleemosynary institution, which are placed by the donors in the hands of trustees named in the charter, and empowered to perpetuate themselves, are placed by this act under the control of the government of the state. The will of the state is substituted for the will of the donors in every essential operation of the college. This is not an immaterial change. The founders of the college contracted, not merely for the perpetual application of the funds which they gave to the objects for which those funds were given; they contracted also to secure that application by the constitution of the corporation. They contracted for a system which should, as far as human foresight can provide, retain forever the government of the literary institution they had formed, in the hands of persons approved by themselves. This system is totally changed. The charter of 1769 exists no longer. It is reorganized; and reorganized in such a manner as to convert a literary institution, molded according to the will of its founders and placed under the control of private literary men, into a machine entirely subservient to the will of government. This may be for the advantage of this college in particular, and may be for the advantage of literature in general; but it is not according to the will of the donors, and is subversive of that contract on the faith of which their property was given.

In the view which has been taken of this interesting case, the Court has confined itself to the rights possessed by the trustees, as the assignees and representatives of the donors and founders, for the benefit of religion and literature. Yet it is not clear that the trustees ought to be considered as destitute of such beneficial interest in themselves as the law may respect. In addition to their being the legal owners of the property, and to their having a freehold right in the powers confided to them, the charter itself countenances the idea that trustees may also be tutors with salaries. The first president was one of the original trustees; and the charter provides, that in case of vacancy in that office, "the senior professor or tutor, being one of the trustees, shall exercise the office of president, until the trustees shall make choice of, and appoint a president." According to the tenor of the charter, then, the trustees might, without impropriety, appoint a president and other professors from their own body. This is a power not entirely unconnected with an interest. Even if the proposition of the counsel for the defendant were sustained; if it were admitted, that those contracts only are protected by the Constitution, a beneficial interest in which is vested in the party who appears in court to assert that interest; yet it is by no means clear that the trustees of Dartmouth College have no beneficial interest in themselves.

But the Court has deemed it unnecessary to investigate this particular point, being of opinion, on general principles that in these private eleemosynary institutions, the body corporate, as possessing the whole legal and equitable interest, and completely representing the donors, for the purpose of executing the trust, has rights which are protected by the Constitution.

It results from this opinion, that the acts of the legislature of New Hampshire, which are stated in the special verdict found in this cause, are repugnant to the Constitution of the United States; and that the judgment on this special verdict ought to have been for the plaintiffs. The judgment of the state court must, therefore, be reversed.

Mr. Justice Washington and Mr. Justice Story rendered separate concurring opinions. Mr. Justice Duvall dissented.

ADLER v. BOARD OF EDUCATION
342 U. S. 485; 96 L. Ed. 517; 72 Sup. Ct. 380. 1952.

A loyalty oath which requires a teacher or public officer to swear to support the Constitution or make some similar statement of present loyalty to the government raises no constitutional question. Such oaths are required of all federal and state officers in Article VI of the Constitution. But a loyalty oath of the old "test oath" variety is very different. It requires a sworn statement with regard to both past and present loyalty and imposes various liabilities upon those who cannot or will not take the oath. In recent years many states and local governments have required such loyalty oaths.

The Los Angeles loyalty oath came before the Court in Garner v. Board of Public Works of Los Angeles, 341 U. S. 716. In a five-to-four decision in

1951 it was held constitutional. An ordinance of 1948 required every employee of the city to take an oath that he does not, and for the preceding five years has not, advised, advocated, or taught the overthrow of government by force and violence or other unlawful means; that he is not, and for the past five years has not been, a member of any party or organization which does so; and that he will not engage in any such activities while in the public employ. In addition he must submit an affidavit setting out in full detail past or present membership, if any, in the Communist party. The majority rejected the view that the oath constituted either an ex post facto law or a bill of attainder. It is a reasonable measure for determining present fitness to hold public office, rather than a punishment for past crimes or misconduct. In holding the ordinance valid the Court so construed it as to bar from public employment only those who "knowingly" belonged to the proscribed organizations.

The importance of this last point in the Garner case became clear in the case of Wieman v. Updegraff, 344 U. S. 183 (1952). Here a unanimous Court held invalid a loyalty oath statute passed by Oklahoma in 1951. This barred from public employment all state officers and employees who could not swear that they had not been members of any subversive organization for five years. The blacklisted organizations included any which advocated the overthrow of government by force and violence, including the Communist party and any group listed as subversive by the Attorney General or other authorized agency of the federal government. This was held to deny due process of law because it made simple membership in one of the listed organizations conclusive evidence of disloyalty and unfitness for public employment. "Membership," said the Court, "may be innocent." It pointed out that persons of undoubted loyalty have belonged to some of the listed organizations without knowing them to be subversive, and have left them upon learning their true character. Also, some of these organizations were innocent when formed, and only later became infiltrated and dominated by subversive elements. An irrebuttable presumption of crime or misconduct denies due process of law.

In 1954 California denied any tax exemption to all persons unless they first signed an oath declaring that they did not advocate the overthrow of government by force or violence. The requirement was challenged by two churches and by two war veterans. The Court held that the oath requirement was a punishment of those who advocated subversion the net effect of which was to place on them the burden of proving their innocence. This, the Court held, was a denial of due process of law. The cases are Speiser v. Randall, 357 U. S. 513 (1958), and First Unitarian Church v. Los Angeles, 357 U. S. 545 (1958).

The Feinberg Law, a more carefully drawn statute passed in New York in 1949, was held valid in the Adler case, below. This statute did not itself require an oath. After an elaborate finding in the preamble that Communists are known to have been infiltrating the public school system of the state with harmful and menacing results, it provides for the disqualification and removal of all superintendents, teachers, and employees in the public schools of the state who advocate the overthrow of government by unlawful means, or who belong to organizations that do. The Board of Regents is directed to list, after full notice and hearing, the organizations which advocate the overthrow of government by force and violence, and to keep this list revised. In making the list, the Regents may utilize similar lists drawn up by any federal officer or agency. Membership in any organization thus listed is made prima facie evidence of disqualification to hold any office or position in the public school system. But any person thus presumed to be disqualified must be given a full hearing, with the privilege of being represented by counsel, and he enjoys the right of judicial review. Adler and others sought to have the statute declared unconstitutional and its enforcement enjoined.

Mr. Justice Minton delivered the opinion of the Court, saying in part:

. . . It is first argued that the Feinberg Law and the rules promulgated thereunder constitute an abridgment of speech and assembly of persons employed or seeking employment in the public schools of the State of New York.

It is clear that such persons have the right under our law to assemble, speak, think and believe as they will. . . . It is equally clear that they have no right to work for the State in the school system on their own terms. United Public Workers v. Mitchell, 330 U. S. 75. They may work for the school system upon the reasonable terms laid down by the proper authorities of New York. If they do not choose to work on such terms, they are at liberty to retain their beliefs and associations and go elsewhere. Has the State thus deprived them of any right to free speech or assembly? We think not. Such persons are or may be denied, under the statutes in question, the privilege of working for the school system of the State of New York because first, of their advocacy of the overthrow of the government by force or violence, or secondly, by unexplained membership in an organization found by the school authorities, after notice and hearing, to teach and advocate the overthrow of the government by force or violence, and known by such persons to have such purpose.

The constitutionality of the first proposition is not questioned here. . . .

As to the second, it is rather subtly suggested that we should not follow our recent decision in Garner v. Board of Public Works of Los Angeles, 341 U. S. 716. We there said: "We think that a municipal employer is not disabled because it is an agency of the State from inquiring of its employees as to matters that may prove relevant to their fitness and suitability for the public service. Past conduct may well relate to present fitness; past loyalty may have a reasonable relationship to present and future trust. Both are commonly inquired into in determining fitness for both high and low positions in private industry and are not less relevant in public employment." . . .

We adhere to that case. A teacher works in a sensitive area in a schoolroom. There he shapes the attitude of young minds towards the society in which they live. In this, the state has a vital concern. It must preserve the integrity of the schools. That the school authorities have the right and the duty to screen the officials, teachers, and employees as to their fitness to maintain the integrity of the schools as a part of ordered society, cannot be doubted. One's associates, past and present, as well as one's conduct, may properly be considered in determining fitness and loyalty. From time immemorial, one's reputation has been determined in part by the company he keeps. In the employment of officials and teachers of the school system, the state may very properly inquire into the company they keep, and we know of no rule, constitutional or otherwise, that prevents the state, when determining the fitness and loyalty of such persons, from considering the organizations and persons with whom they associate.

If, under the procedure set up in the New York law, a person is found to be unfit and is disqualified from employment in the public school system because of membership in a listed organization, he is not thereby denied the right of free speech and assembly. His freedom of choice between membership in the organization and employment in the school system might be limited, but not his freedom of speech or assembly, except in the remote sense that limitation is inherent in every choice. Certainly such limitation is not one the state may not make in the exercise of its police power to protect the schools from pollution and thereby to defend its own existence.

It is next argued by appellants that the provision in § 3022 directing the Board of Regents to provide in rules and regulations that membership in any organization listed by the Board after notice and hearing, with provision for review in accordance with the statute, shall constitute prima facie evidence of disqualification, denies due process, because the fact found bears no relation to the fact presumed. In other words, from the fact found that the organization was one that advocated the overthrow of government by unlawful means and that the person employed or to be employed was a member of the organization and knew of its purpose, to presume that such member is disqualified for employment is so unreasonable as to be a denial of due process of law. We do not agree.

"The law of evidence is full of presumptions either of fact or law. The former are, of course, disputable, and the strength of any inference of one fact from proof of another depends upon the generality of the experience upon which it is founded. . . .

"Legislation providing that proof of one fact shall constitute *prima facie* evidence of the main fact in issue is but to enact a rule of evidence, and quite within the general power of government. Statutes, national and state, dealing with such methods of proof in both civil and criminal cases, abound, and the decisions upholding them are numerous." Mobile, J. & K. C. R. Co. v. Turnipseed, 219 U. S. 35 at page 42.

Membership in a listed organization found to be within the statute and known by the member to be within the statute is a legislative finding that the member by his membership supports the thing the organization stands for, namely, the overthrow of government by unlawful means. We cannot say that such a finding is contrary to fact or that "generality of experience" points to a different conclusion. Disqualification follows therefore as a reasonable presumption from such membership and support. Nor is there here a problem of procedural due process. The presumption is not conclusive but arises only in a hearing where the person against whom it may arise has full opportunity to rebut it. . . .

Where, as here, the relation between the fact found and the presumption is clear and direct and is not conclusive, the requirements of due process are satisfied. . . .

We find no constitutional infirmity in § 12-a of the Civil Service Law of New York or in the Feinberg Law which implemented it, and the judgment is affirmed.

Affirmed.

Mr. Justice Black, dissenting, said:

While I fully agree with the dissent of Mr. Justice Douglas, the importance of this holding prompts me to add these thoughts.

This is another of those rapidly multiplying legislative enactments which make it dangerous—this time for school teachers—to think or say anything except what a transient majority happen to approve at the moment. Basically these laws rest on the belief that government should supervise and limit the flow of ideas into the minds of men. The tendency of such governmental policy is to mould people into a common intellectual pattern. Quite a different governmental policy rests on the belief that government should leave the mind and spirit of man absolutely free. Such a governmental policy encourages varied intellectual outlooks in the belief that the best views will prevail. This policy of freedom is in my judgment embodied in the First Amendment and made applicable to the states by the Fourteenth. Because of this policy public officials cannot be constitutionally vested with powers to select the ideas people can think about, censor the public views they can express, or choose the persons or groups people can associate with. Public officials with such powers are not public servants; they are public masters.

I dissent from the Court's judgment sustaining this law which effectively penalizes school teachers for their thoughts and their associates.

Mr. Justice Douglas, with whom Mr. Justice Black concurs, in dissenting said:

I have not been able to accept the recent doctrine that a citizen who enters the public service can be forced to sacrifice his civil rights. I cannot for example find in our constitutional scheme the power of a state to place its employees in the category of second class citizens by denying them freedom of thought and expression. The Constitution guarantees freedom of thought and expression to everyone in our society. All are entitled to it; and none needs it more than the teacher.

The public school is in most respects the cradle of our democracy. The increasing role of the public school is seized upon by proponents of the type of legislation represented by New York's Feinberg Law as proof of the importance and need for keeping the school free of "subversive influences." But that is to misconceive the effect of this type of legislation. Indeed the impact of this kind of censorship on the public school system illustrates the high purpose of the First Amendment in freeing speech and thought from censorship.

The present law proceeds on a principle repugnant to our society— guilt by association. A teacher is disqualified because of her membership in an organization found to be "subversive." The finding as to the "subversive" character of the organization is made in a proceeding to which the teacher is not a party and in which it is not clear that she may even be heard. To be sure she may have a hearing when charges of disloyalty are leveled against her. But in that hearing the finding as to the "subversive" character of the organization apparently may not be reopened in order to allow her to show the truth of the matter. The irrebuttable charge that the organization is "subversive" therefore hangs as an ominous cloud over her own hearing. The mere fact of membership in the organization raises a prima facie case of her own guilt. She may, it is said, show her innocence. But innocence in this case turns on knowledge; and when the witch hunt is on, one who must rely on ignorance leans on a feeble reed.

The very threat of such a procedure is certain to raise havoc with academic freedom. Youthful indiscretions, mistaken causes, misguided enthusiasms—all long forgotten—become the ghosts of a harrowing present. Any organization committed to a liberal cause, any group organized to revolt against an hysterical trend, any committee launched to sponsor an unpopular program becomes suspect. These are the organizations into which Communists often infiltrate. Their presence infects the whole, even though the project was not conceived in sin. A teacher caught in that mesh is almost certain to stand condemned. Fearing condemnation, she will tend to shrink from any association that stirs controversy. In that manner freedom of expression will be stifled.

But that is only part of it. Once a teacher's connection with a listed organization is shown, her views become subject to scrutiny to determine whether her membership in the organization is innocent or, if she was formerly a member, whether she has *bona fide* abandoned her membership.

The law inevitably turns the school system into a spying project. Regular loyalty reports on the teachers must be made out. The principals become detectives; the students, the parents, the community become informers. Ears are cocked for tell-tale signs of disloyalty. The prejudices of the community come into play in searching out the disloyal. This is not the usual type of supervision which checks a teacher's competency; it is a system which searches for hidden meanings in a teacher's utterances.

What was the significance of the reference of the art teacher to socialism? Why was the history teacher so openly hostile to Franco Spain? Who heard overtones of revolution in the English teacher's discussion of the Grapes of Wrath? What was behind the praise of

Soviet progress in metallurgy in the chemistry class? Was it not "subversive" for the teacher to cast doubt on the wisdom of the venture in Korea?

What happens under this law is typical of what happens in a police state. Teachers are under constant surveillance; their pasts are combed for signs of disloyalty; their utterances are watched for clues to dangerous thoughts. A pall is cast over the classrooms. There can be no real academic freedom in that environment. Where suspicion fills the air and holds scholars in line for fear of their jobs, there can be no exercise of the free intellect. Supineness and dogmatism take the place of inquiry. A "party line"—as dangerous as the "party line" of the Communists—lays hold. It is the "party line" of the orthodox view, of the conventional thought, of the accepted approach. A problem can no longer be pursued with impunity to its edges. Fear stalks the classroom. The teacher is no longer a stimulant to adventurous thinking; she becomes instead a pipe line for safe and sound information. A deadening dogma takes the place of free inquiry. Instruction tends to become sterile; pursuit of knowledge is discouraged; discussion often leaves off where it should begin.

This, I think, is what happens when a censor looks over a teacher's shoulder. This system of spying and surveillance with its accompanying reports and trials cannot go hand in hand with academic freedom. It produces standardized thought, not the pursuit of truth. Yet it was the pursuit of truth which the First Amendment was designed to protect. A system which directly or inevitably has that effect is alien to our system and should be struck down. Its survival is a real threat to our way of life. We need be bold and adventuresome in our thinking to survive. A school system producing students trained as robots threatens to rob a generation of the versatility that has been perhaps our greatest distinction. The Framers knew the danger of dogmatism; they also knew the strength that comes when the mind is free, when ideas may be pursued wherever they lead. We forget these teachings of the First Amendment when we sustain this law.

Of course the school systems of the country need not become cells for Communist activities; and the classrooms need not become forums for propagandizing the Marxist creed. But the guilt of the teacher should turn on overt acts. So long as she is a law abiding citizen, so long as her performance within the public school system meets professional standards, her private life, her political philosophy, her social creed should not be the cause of reprisals against her.

5

The President
and Executive Power

MISSISSIPPI v. JOHNSON
4 Wallace 475; 18 L. Ed. 437. 1867.

It would have been surprising indeed if, after the decision in the Milligan case (p. 79), an attempt had not been made to bring before the Supreme Court the question of the constitutionality of the military government established by Congress in the southern states. The attempt was boldly made in the form of a bill of equity which the state of Mississippi sought to file to enjoin President Johnson and the general in command of the military district of Mississippi and Arkansas from enforcing the acts of March 2 and March 25, 1867, commonly known as the Reconstruction Acts, upon the ground of their unconstitutionality. There was a good deal of popular criticism of the proceedings, which were looked upon as an effort upon the part of the defeated rebels to recover in the courtroom what they had lost on the battlefield, and the leaders in Congress awaited the decision of the Court with a good deal of anxiety in view of the well-founded rumor that at least five members of the Court regarded the Reconstruction Acts as unconstitutional.

The Court avoided a dangerous clash with Congress, however, by deciding that it had no jurisdiction to control the acts of the President. This rule unquestionably embodies sound law and sound common sense. The Court may well have been aided in reaching its conclusions not only by the considerations set forth in the opinion but by the recollection that Chief Justice Marshall had subpœnaed President Jefferson at the time of the trial of Aaron Burr for treason, only to have his subpœna ignored; and that in any actual conflict between a strong-minded chief executive and the Court the former occupies a highly strategic position which may well enable him to defy decrees of the latter with impunity. This immunity of the President from judicial control, however, is carefully safeguarded in the interests of private rights. It does not extend to any subordinate executive officers. It may be recalled that in the case of Marbury v. Madison it was stated by the Court that the Secretary of State could be held subject to mandamus if the case was brought in a court having jurisdiction; and in Kendall v. United States, 12 Peters 524 (1838), the Postmaster General was mandamused to perform a duty imposed upon him by statute. Furthermore, while the President is himself immune from judicial control even with respect to the doing of unlawful acts, no agent or subordinate who attempts to carry out the President's unlawful orders is protected. The court may not punish the chief executive who issues the order but it may punish the underling who obeys the order. In Little v. Barreme, 2 Cranch 170 (1804), a naval commander was held liable in damages for injury to property which he inflicted in carrying out the provisions of a proclamation of President Adams which the Supreme Court held to be in excess of the President's power.   . .

With the failure to get a decision from the Court on the validity of the Reconstruction Acts in the case of Mississippi v. Johnson, those interested immediately filed another bill to restrain Secretary of War Stanton and General Grant from enforcing the acts. In this way it was thought that the obstacle of the personal and official immunity of the President could be avoided. The Court, however, held that the issues involved were political rather than judicial in character and that the Court could not undertake to control the exercise by an executive officer of discretionary power. Georgia v. Stanton, 6 Wallace 50 (1867).

Mr. Chief Justice Chase delivered the opinion of the Court, saying in part:

. . . We shall limit our inquiry to the question . . . whether, in any case, the President of the United States may be required, by the process of this Court, to perform a purely ministerial act under a positive law, or may be held amenable, in any case, otherwise than by impeachment for crime.

The single point which requires consideration is this: Can the President be restrained by injunction from carrying into effect an act of Congress alleged to be unconstitutional?

It is assumed by the counsel for the state of Mississippi, that the President, in the execution of the Reconstruction Acts, is required to perform a mere ministerial duty. In this assumption there is, we think, a confounding of the terms ministerial and executive, which are by no means equivalent in import.

A ministerial duty, the performance of which may, in proper cases, be required of the head of a department, by judicial process, is one in respect to which nothing is left to discretion. It is a simple, definite duty, arising under conditions admitted or proved to exist, and imposed by law. . . .

Very different is the duty of the President in the exercise of the power to see that the laws are faithfully executed, and among these laws the acts named in the bill. By the first of these acts he is required to assign generals to command in the several military districts, and to detail sufficient military force to enable such officers to discharge their duties under the law. By the supplementary act, other duties are imposed on the several commanding generals, and these duties must necessarily be performed under the supervision of the President as commander-in-chief. The duty thus imposed on the President is in no just sense ministerial. It is purely executive and political.

An attempt on the part of the judicial department of the government to enforce the performance of such duties by the President might be justly characterized, in the language of Chief Justice Marshall, as "an absurd and excessive extravagance."

It is true that in the instance before us the interposition of the Court is not sought to enforce action by the Executive under constitutional legislation, but to restrain such action under legislation alleged to be unconstitutional. But we are unable to perceive that this circumstance takes the case out of the general principles which forbid judicial interference with the exercise of executive discretion.

It was admitted in the argument that the application now made to us is without a precedent; and this is of much weight against it.

Had it been supposed at the bar that this Court would, in any case, interpose, by injunction, to prevent the execution of an unconstitutional act of Congress, it can hardly be doubted that applications with that object would have been heretofore addressed to it.

Occasions have not been wanting.

The constitutionality of the act for the annexation of Texas was vehemently denied. It made important and permanent changes in the relative importance of states and sections, and was by many supposed to be pregnant with disastrous results to large interests in particular states. But no one seems to have thought of an application for an injunction against the execution of the act by the President.

And yet it is difficult to perceive upon what principle the application now before us can be allowed and similar applications in that and other cases have been denied.

The fact that no such application was ever before made in any case indicates the general judgment of the profession that no such application should be entertained.

It will hardly be contended that Congress [the courts?] can interpose, in any case, to restrain the enactment of an unconstitutional law; and yet how can the right to judicial interposition to prevent such an enactment, when the purpose is evident and the execution of that purpose certain, be distinguished, in principle, from the right to such interposition against the execution of such a law by the President?

The Congress is the legislative department of the government; the President is the executive department. Neither can be restrained in its action by the judicial department; though the acts of both, when performed, are, in proper cases, subject to its cognizance.

The impropriety of such interference will be clearly seen upon consideration of its possible consequences.

Suppose the bill filed and the injunction prayed for allowed. If the President refuse obedience, it is needless to observe that the Court is without power to enforce its process. If, on the other hand, the President complies with the order of the Court and refuses to execute the acts of Congress, is it not clear that a collision may occur between the executive and legislative departments of the government? May not the House of Representatives impeach the President for such refusal? And in that case could this Court interfere, in behalf of the President, thus endangered by compliance with its mandate, and restrain by injunction the Senate of the United States from sitting as a court of impeachment? Would the strange spectacle be offered to the public world of an attempt by this Court to arrest proceedings in that court?

These questions answer themselves.

It is true that a state may file an original bill in this Court. And it may be true, in some cases, that such a bill may be filed against the United States. But we are fully satisfied that this Court has no jurisdiction of a bill to enjoin the President in the performance of his official duties; and that no such bill ought to be received by us.

It has been suggested that the bill contains a prayer that, if the relief sought cannot be had against Andrew Johnson, as President, it may be granted against Andrew Johnson as a citizen of Tennessee. But it is plain that relief as against the execution of an act of Congress by Andrew Johnson, is relief against its execution by the President. A bill praying an injunction against the execution of an act of Congress by the incumbent of the presidential office cannot be received, whether it describes him as President or as a citizen of a state.

The motion for leave to file the bill is, therefore, denied.

HUMPHREY'S EXECUTOR (RATHBUN) v. UNITED STATES
295 U. S. 602; 79 L. Ed. 1611; 55 Sup. Ct. 869. 1935.

While the Constitution indicates how federal executive officers shall be appointed, it is entirely silent as to their removal save by impeachment, a clumsy process applicable only to cases of grave misconduct. May the President remove his subordinates at will? Or may Congress deny or limit his power to do so? These are questions of great practical importance. Congresses and Presidents, from 1789 on, have guessed at the answers, and those guesses have often conflicted. The Supreme Court does not answer constitutional questions, however important, unless they squarely arise in actual litigation; and one hundred and thirty-seven years elapsed before a case came up which clearly involved the question of the President's power of removal. It arose then only because a Mr. Myers saw fit to sue the government in the Court of Claims for his salary. See Myers v. United States, 272 U. S. 52 (1926). The facts in the case are as follows: In 1917 President Wilson appointed Myers to a first-class postmastership at Portland, Oregon, for a term of four years. He removed him from office in 1920. A statute of 1876, still in force, provided that "postmasters of the first, second, and third classes shall be appointed and may be removed by the President by and with the advice and consent of the Senate and shall hold their offices for four years unless sooner removed or suspended according to law." The removal of Myers was not referred to the Senate for its consent. The President did not nominate a successor to Myers but made a recess appointment which the Senate never confirmed. This fact is important because such confirmation of Myers' successor would have amounted to senatorial consent to Myers' removal. He protested against his removal, refrained from accepting other remunerative employment, and when the four-year period for which he had been appointed expired he sued in the Court of Claims for the salary for about eighteen months of which his removal had deprived him. This amounted to $8,838.72.

The decision of the Court that Congress may not restrict the President's power to remove officers appointed by him with senatorial consent is supported in Chief Justice Taft's long opinion upon two main grounds. One of these is historical, the other is constitutional. The historical argument is built chiefly upon what the Chief Justice called the "decision of 1789." This "decision" took the form of a vote or a series of votes in the First Congress upon the establishment of a department of foreign affairs. It was originally voted in the House that such a department be created under a secretary appointed by the President with the advice and consent of the Senate and removable by the President. After debate this was amended in two ways. First, a clause was added clearly implying unrestricted removal power in the President alone by alluding to vacancies created in that way. Second, the clause granting the power of removal to the President was stricken out, on the ground that such a grant implied that without it the President would not have the power. The Senate concurred in these actions. By this "decision," declares the Chief Justice, Congress recognized and established the exclusive and untrammeled power of the President to remove executive officers whom he appoints. There follows a mass of historical material, including the opinions of statesmen, tending to show that this has been the accepted theory of the removal power throughout our history, save in one or two instances when "heated political difference of opinion between the then President and the majority leaders of Congress" led to a different result, as in passage of the Tenure of Office Act of 1867. These exceptions, however, are deemed to be outweighed by the force of almost continuous governmental practice.

The constitutional argument advanced by the Chief Justice is much more important than the historical evidence just reviewed. It is clear that such power of removal as the President enjoys is an implied power. Implied from what? Implied from the general grant of executive power in Article II, and the further injunction in the same Article that the President "shall take care that the laws be faithfully executed." By placing it on this broad ground the Court avoids the difficulties which would result from implying the removal power solely from the President's power of appointment, although it is admitted that the power of appointing provides a supplementary and supporting basis for implying the power of removal. It is clear that this argument rests upon the conviction, which Mr. Taft's presidential experience undoubtedly confirmed and emphasized, that the President cannot effectively and responsibly administer his office unless he can control his subordinates through an unrestricted power of removal. By thus holding that the removal power is a necessary and inherent part of the broad executive power granted by the Constitution to the President it naturally follows that any attempt upon the part of Congress to limit or interfere with the removal power is a violation of the doctrine of the separation of powers. The decision in the Myers case was rightly viewed as of very great importance, although the immediate point involved, the removal of a postmaster, was of no broad interest. What did arouse much controversy and rather general concern was the sweeping dictum of the Chief Justice that the President's unrestricted removal power extended not merely to his immediate executive subordinates but also to the members of the great independent commissions, such as the Interstate Commerce Commission, the Federal Trade Commission, and presumably also to the Comptroller General. These officers are appointed under the provisions of statutes conferring upon them duties with respect to which a high degree of independence and freedom from political control is deemed desirable. Congress has carefully specified the causes for which they may be removed with the intention that they be free from removals of a "political" nature. If the Taft theory with respect to them were to prevail, however, their independence from presidential control would be broken down. It was to be expected, therefore, that sooner or later the question whether the President's unlimited removal power did actually extend to these independent commissions and officers would be presented to the Court on facts requiring a specific answer. This was done in the Rathbun case. It is interesting to note that in overruling Chief Justice Taft's dictum and holding that the President's removal power extends only to executive officers the Court invokes the same doctrine of the separation of powers which lies at the basis of the Myers decision. The separation of powers protects the President in the exercise of his power to remove executive officers appointed by him, but it also prevents him from removing officers who are not essentially executive and whose removal has been restricted by Congress.

In 1938 the President removed Dr. A. E. Morgan, chairman of the Tennessee Valley Authority, for reasons of policy. The T.V.A. is not, however, a quasi-judicial or quasi-legislative agency like the Federal Trade Commission. It is primarily a business enterprise. Furthermore, the statute creating it gives the President important executive authority over it. When Dr. Morgan contested his removal on constitutional grounds the Circuit Court of Appeals upheld the removal, and the Supreme Court refused to review the decision. See Morgan v. T.V.A., 312 U. S. 701 (1941).

An important unsolved problem remained concerning the status of the members of the quasi-judicial agencies with respect to which Congress has said nothing about removal. The FPC, the SEC, and the FCC are in this category. The problem was settled by the Court in Wiener v. United States, 357 U. S. 349 (1958). Wiener was a member of the War Claims Commission, a strictly adjudicatory agency. Congress had said nothing about the removal of the members. President Eisenhower removed Wiener for political reasons, and Wiener challenged his right to do so. The Court held the removal invalid because of the nature of the office involved. "We are compelled to conclude that no such power is given to the President directly by the Constitution, and none is impliedly conferred upon him by statute simply because Congress said nothing about it."

Mr. Justice Sutherland delivered the Court's opinion, saying in part:

Plaintiff brought suit in the Court of Claims against the United States to recover a sum of money alleged to be due the deceased for salary as a federal trade commissioner from October 8, 1933, when the President undertook to remove him from office, to the time of his death on February 14, 1934. The court below has certified to this Court two questions . . . in respect of the power of the President to make the removal. The material facts which give rise to the question are as follows:

William E. Humphrey, the decedent, on December 10, 1931, was nominated by President Hoover to succeed himself as a member of the Federal Trade Commission and was confirmed by the United States Senate. He was duly commissioned for a term of seven years expiring September 25, 1938; and, after taking the required oath of office, entered upon his duties. On July 25, 1933, President Roosevelt addressed a letter to the commissioner asking for his resignation, on the ground "that the aims and purposes of the Administration with respect to the work of the commission can be carried out most effectively with personnel of my own selection," but disclaiming any reflection upon the commissioner personally or upon his services. The commissioner replied, asking time to consult his friends. After some further correspondence upon the subject, the President, on August 31, 1933, wrote the commissioner expressing the hope that the resignation would be forthcoming and saying:

"You will, I know, realize that your mind and my mind do not go along together on either the policies or the administering of the Federal Trade Commission, and, frankly, I think it is best for the people of this country that I should have a full confidence."

The commissioner declined to resign, and on October 7, 1933, the President wrote him:

"Effective as of this date, you are hereby removed from the office of Commissioner of the Federal Trade Commission."

Humphrey never acquiesced in this action, but continued thereafter to insist that he was still a member of the commission, entitled to perform its duties and receive the compensation provided by law at the rate of $10,000 per annum. Upon these and other facts set forth in the certificate which we deem it unnecessary to recite, the following questions are certified:

"1. Do the provisions of § 1 of the Federal Trade Commission Act, stating that 'any commissioner may be removed by the President for inefficiency, neglect of duty or malfeasance in office,' restrict or limit the power of the President to remove a commissioner except upon one or more of the causes named?

"If the foregoing question is answered in the affirmative, then—

"2. If the power of the President to remove a commissioner is restricted or limited as shown by the foregoing interrogatory and the answer made thereto, is such a restriction or limitation valid under the Constitution of the United States?"

The Federal Trade Commission Act . . . creates a commission of five members to be appointed by the President by and with the advice and consent of the Senate, and Section 1 provides:

"Not more than three of the commissioners shall be members of the same political party. The first commissioners appointed shall continue in office for terms of three, four, five, six and seven years, respectively, from the date of the taking effect of this act, the term of each to be designated by the President, but their successors shall be appointed for terms of seven years, except that any person chosen to fill a vacancy shall be appointed only for the unexpired term of the commissioner whom he shall succeed. The commission shall choose a chairman from its own membership. No commissioner shall engage in any other business, vocation, or employment. Any commissioner may be removed by the President for inefficiency, neglect of duty, or malfeasance in office."

Section 5 of the act in part provides:

"Unfair methods of competition in commerce are hereby declared unlawful.

"The commission is hereby empowered and directed to prevent persons, partnerships or corporations, except banks and common carriers subject to the acts to regulate commerce, from using unfair methods of competition in commerce."

In exercising this power the commission must issue a complaint stating its charges and giving notice of hearing upon a day to be fixed.

A person, partnership or corporation proceeded against is given the right to appear at the time and place fixed and show cause why an order to cease and desist should not be issued. There is provision for intervention by others interested. If the commission finds the method of competition is one prohibited by the act it is directed to make a report in writing stating its findings as to the facts, and to issue and cause to be served a cease and desist order. If the order is disobeyed the commission may apply to the appropriate circuit court of appeals for its enforcement. This party subject to the order may seek and obtain a review in the circuit court of appeals in a manner provided by the act.

Section 6, among other things, gives the commission wide powers of investigation in respect of certain corporations subject to the act, and in respect of other matters, upon which it must report to Congress with recommendations. Many such investigations have been made, and some have served as the basis of congressional legislation.

Section 7 provides:

"That in any suit in equity brought by or under the direction of the Attorney General, as provided in the anti-trust acts, the court may, upon the conclusion of the testimony therein if it shall be then of opinion that the complainant is entitled to relief, refer said suit to the commission, as a master in chancery, to ascertain and report an appropriate form of decree therein. The commission shall proceed upon such notice to the parties and under such rules of procedure as the court may prescribe and upon the coming in of such report such exceptions may be filed and such proceedings had in relation thereto as upon the report of a master in other equity causes, but the court may adopt or reject such report, in whole or in part, and enter such decree as the nature of the case may in its judgment require."

1. The question first to be considered is whether, by the provisions of paragraph 1 of the Federal Trade Commission Act already quoted, the President's power is limited to removal for the specific causes enumerated therein.

. . . The statute fixes a term of office in accordance with many precedents. The first commissioners appointed are to continue in office for terms of three, four, five, six and seven years, respectively; and their successors are to be appointed for terms of seven years— any commissioner being subject to removal by the President for inefficiency, neglect of duty or malfeasance in office. The words of the act are definite and unambiguous.

The government says the phrase "continue in office" is of no legal significance, and moreover, applies only to the first commissioners. We think it has significance. It may be that, literally, its application is restricted as suggested; but it, nevertheless, lends support to a view contrary to that of the government as to the meaning of the entire requirement in respect of tenure; for it is not easy to suppose that Congress intended to secure the first commissioners against removal except for the causes specified and deny like security to their successors. Putting this phrase aside, however, the fixing of a definite term subject to removal for cause, unless there be some countervailing provision or circumstance indicating the contrary, which here we are unable to find, is enough to establish the legislative intent that the term is not to be curtailed in the absence of such cause.

But if the intention of Congress that no removal should be made during the specified term except for one or more of the enumerated causes were not clear it would be made clear by a consideration of the character of the commission and the legislative history which accompanied and preceded the passage of the act. The commission is to be non-partisan; and it must, from the very nature of its duties, act with entire impartiality. It is charged with the enforcement of no policy except the policy of the law. Its duties are neither political nor executive, but predominantly quasi-legislative. Like the Interstate Commerce Commission, its members are called upon to exercise the trained judgment of a body of experts "appointed by law and enforced by experience." . . .

The legislative reports in both houses of Congress clearly reflect the view that a fixed term was necessary to the effective and fair administration of the law. . . .

The debates in both houses demonstrate that the prevailing view was that the commission was not to be "subject to anybody in the government but only to the people of the United States," free from "political domination or control," or the "probability or possibility of such a thing," to be "separate and apart from any existing department of the government—not subject to the orders of the President." . . .

Thus the language of the act, the legislative reports and the general purposes of the legislation as reflected by the debates, all combine to demonstrate the congressional intent to create a body of experts who shall gain experience by length of service—a body which shall be independent of executive authority, except in its selection, and free to exercise its judgment without the leave or hindrance of any other official or any department of the government. To the accomplishment of these purposes it is clear that Congress was of opinion that length and certainty of tenure would vitally contribute. And to hold that, nevertheless, the members of the commission continue in office at the mere will of the President, might be to thwart, in large measure, the very ends which Congress sought to realize by definitely fixing the term of office.

We conclude that the intent of the act is to limit the executive power of removal to the causes enumerated, the existence of none of which is claimed here; and we pass to the second question.

Second. To support its contention that the removal provision of § 1, as we have just construed it, is an unconstitutional interference with the executive powers of the President, the government's chief reliance is Myers v. United States, 272 U. S. 52. . . . Nevertheless, the narrow point actually decided was only that the President had power to remove a postmaster of the first class, without the advice and consent of the Senate, as required by act of Congress. In the course of the opinion of the Court, expressions occur which tend to sustain the government's contention, but these are beyond the point involved, and therefore, do not come within the rule of stare decisis. In so far as they are out of harmony with the views here set forth, these expressions are disapproved. . . .

The office of a postmaster is so essentially unlike the office now involved that the decision in the Myers case cannot be accepted as controlling our decision here. A postmaster is an executive officer restricted to the performance of executive functions. He is charged with no duty at all related to either the legislative or judical power. The actual decision in the Myers case finds support in the theory that such an officer is merely one of the units in the executive department and hence inherently subject to the exclusive and illimitable power of removal by the chief executive, whose subordinate and aid he is. Putting aside dicta, which may be followed if sufficiently persuasive but which are not controlling, the necessary reach of the decision goes far enough to include all purely executive officers. It goes no farther—must less does it include an officer who occupies no place in the executive department and who exercises no part of the executive power vested by the Constitution in the President.

The Federal Trade Commission is an administrative body created by Congress to carry into effect legislative policies embodied in the statute, in accordance with the legislative standard therein prescribed, and to perform other specified duties as a legislative or as a judicial aid. Such a body cannot in any proper sense be characterized as an arm or an eye of the executive. Its duties are performed without executive leave and, in the contemplation of the statute, must be free from executive control. In administrating the provisions of the statute in respect of "unfair methods of competition"—that is to say in filling in and administering the details embodied by the general standard—the commission acts in part quasi-legislatively and in part quasi-judicially. In making investigations and reports thereon for the information of Congress in aid of the legislative power it acts as a legislative agency. Under 7, which authorizes the commission to act as a master in chancery under rules prescribed by the court, it acts as an agency of the judiciary. To the extent that it exercises any executive function— as distinguished from executive power in the constitutional sense—it does so in the discharge and effectuation of its quasi-legislative or quasi-judicial powers, or as an agency of the legislative or judicial departments of the government.

If Congress is without authority to prescribe causes for removal of members of the Trade Commission and limit executive power of removal accordingly, that power at once becomes practically all inclusive in respect of civil officers, with the exception of the judiciary provided for by the Constitution. The Solicitor General at the bar, apparently recognizing this to be true, with commendable candor agreed that his view in respect of the removability of members of the Federal Trade Commission necessitated a like view in respect of the Interstate Commerce Commission and the Court of Claims. We are thus confronted with the serious question whether not only the members of these quasi-legislative and quasi-judicial bodies, but the judges of the legislative Court of Claims, exercising judicial power . . . continue in office only at the pleasure of the President.

We think it plain under the Constitution that illimitable power of removal is not possessed by the President in respect of officers of the character of those just named. The authority of Congress, in creating quasi-legislative or quasi-judicial agencies, to require them to act in discharge of their duties independently of executive control, cannot well be doubted; and that authority includes, as an appropriate incident, power to fix the period during which they shall continue, and to forbid their removal except for cause in the meantime. For it is quite evident that one who holds his office only during the pleasure of another cannot be depended upon to maintain an attitude of independence against the latter's will.

The fundamental necessity of maintaining each of the three general departments of government entirely free from the control of coercive influence, direct or indirect, of either of the others, has often been stressed and is hardly open to serious question. So much is implied in the very fact of the separation of the powers of these departments by the Constitution, and in the rule which recognizes their essential co-equality. The sound application of a principle that makes one master in his own house precludes him from imposing his control in the house of another who is master there. . . .

The power of removal here claimed for the President falls within this principle, since its coercive influence threatens the independence of a commission, which is not only wholly disconnected from the executive department, but which, as already fully appears, was created by Congress as a means of carrying into operation legislative and judicial powers, and as an agency of the legislative and judicial departments.

In the light of the question now under consideration, we have re-examined the precedents referred to in the Myers case, and find nothing in them to justify a conclusion contrary to that which we have reached. . . .

The result of what we now have said is this: Whether the power of the President to remove an officer shall prevail over the authority of Congress to condition the power by fixing a definite term and precluding a removal except for cause will depend upon the character of the office. The Myers decision, affirming the power of the President alone to make the removal, is confined to purely executive officers. And as to officers of the kind here under consideration, we hold that no removal can be made during the prescribed term for which the officer is appointed, except for one or more of the causes named in the applicable statute.

To the extent that, between the decision in the Myers case, which sustains the unrestrictable power of the President to remove purely executive officers and our present decision that such power does not extend to an office such as that here involved there shall remain a field of doubt, we leave such cases as may fall within it for future consideration and determination as they arise.

In accordance with the foregoing the questions submitted are answered.

Question No. 1, Yes.

Question No. 2, Yes.

YOUNGSTOWN SHEET & TUBE COMPANY v. SAWYER
343 U. S. 579; 96 L. Ed. 1153; 72 Sup. Ct. 863. 1952.

The abnormal problems created by an economic depression followed by a world war called for the use of governmental powers clearly invalid save in time of crisis. Woods v. Miller (p. 372) held that the war power of Congress could be employed after hostilities had ended to deal with problems generated by the war. From 1933 on, Congress had from time to time granted to the President "emergency powers" in a variety of fields, and parallel to this trend there grew up the theory, sometimes put into practice, that the President enjoys powers to deal with national emergencies which come, not from congressional grants, but from his constitutional position as President and as commander in chief. It is this theory that was challenged in the "Steel Seizure Case" printed below.

This case climaxed a long dispute between the steel companies and the steel workers. On December 18, 1951, the United Steel Workers of America, C.I.O., gave notice that it would strike on December 31. The Federal Mediation and Conciliation Service failed to effect a settlement. The Federal Wage Stabilization Board, to which President Truman referred the dispute on December 22, also failed. He did not invoke the provisions of the Taft-Hartley Act, which would have set up a "period of waiting" before a strike. On April 4, 1952, the union announced that it would call a nationwide strike on April 9. A few hours before the strike was to begin the President directed Secretary of Commerce Sawyer to seize and operate most of the country's steel mills. The Secretary issued the appropriate orders. The President reported the seizure to Congress on April 9, and again on April 21, but Congress took no action. The steel companies complied under protest with the seizure order, but sought a temporary injunction to restrain the government's action. On April 30, the District Court of the District of Columbia issued a preliminary injunction, which was stayed on the same day by the Court of Appeals.

On May 3, the Supreme Court, by-passing the Court of Appeals, brought the case to its docket by certiorari. It heard argument on May 12, and decided the case on June 2. These dates indicate the celerity with which the Supreme Court can act when the national interest requires speed.

The difficulty and complexity of the case is shown by the fact that the Court divided six to three, and that seven justices wrote separate opinions totalling 128 pages. The Court did not face here the naked question of the President's power to seize the steel plants in the absence of any congressional enactments or expressions of policy. Congress had provided limited powers of seizure in the Selective Service Act of 1948 and in the Defense Production Act of 1950. Furthermore, in its debates on the Taft-Hartley Act of 1947 Congress had considered an amendment authorizing seizure of plants by the President in case of strike, and had rejected it. In fact, over a period of years, Congress had made it clear that the seizure of private property in time of emergency was a problem to be controlled by congressional policy. For a variety of reasons, the majority of the Court found that this legislative occupation of the field made untenable the President's claim of authority to seize the plants as an exercise of inherent executive power or as commander in chief. Congress had set up various procedures for the President to follow in such cases, and he had not followed them.

Chief Justice Vinson presents a novel concept of presidential power in his dissenting opinion. He states that the broad grant of executive power in Article II, coupled with the mandate to "take care that the laws be faithfully executed," confers upon the President not merely the narrow power to execute specific statutes but a broad discretionary power to implement general legislative programs, such as those for the national defense and economic stability. Since these legislative programs would be paralyzed by a nationwide steel strike, the President may properly use his executive power to prevent such a strike.

While it is hard to state a succinct rule of law established in this case, the force of the decision re-emphasizes the checks and balances which exist between the legislative and executive departments of the government, and it placed a curb upon presidential powers which had been steadily growing over twenty years of "emergency" conditions.

Mr. Justice Black delivered the opinion of the Court, saying in part:

We are asked to decide whether the President was acting within his constitutional power when he issued an order directing the Secretary of Commerce to take possession of and operate most of the Nation's steel mills. The mill owners argue that the President's order amounts to lawmaking, a legislative function which the Constitution has expressly confided to the Congress and not to the President. The Government's position is that the order was made on findings of the President that his action was necessary to avert a national catastrophe which would inevitably result from a stoppage of steel production, and that in meeting this grave emergency the President was acting within the aggregate of his constitutional powers as the Nation's

Chief Executive and the Commander in Chief of the Armed Forces of the United States. . . .

The President's power, if any, to issue the order must stem either from an act of Congress or from the Constitution itself. There is no statute that expressly authorizes the President to take possession of property as he did here. Nor is there any act of Congress to which our attention has been directed from which such a power can fairly be implied. Indeed, we do not understand the Government to rely on statutory authorization for this seizure. There are two statutes which do authorize the President to take both personal and real property under certain conditions. (The Selective Service Act of 1948 and the Defense Production Act of 1950). However, the Government admits that these conditions were not met and that the President's order was not rooted in either of them. The Government refers to the seizure provisions of one of these statutes (§ 201 (b) of the Defense Production Act) as "much too cumbersome, involved, and time-consuming for the crisis which was at hand."

Moreover, the use of the seizure technique to solve labor disputes in order to prevent work stoppages was not only unauthorized by any congressional enactment; prior to this controversy, Congress had refused to adopt that method of settling labor disputes. When the Taft-Hartley Act was under consideration in 1947, Congress rejected an amendment which would have authorized such governmental seizures in cases of emergency. Apparently it was thought that the technique of seizure, like that of compulsory arbitration, would interfere with the process of collective bargaining. Consequently, the plan Congress adopted in that Act did not provide for seizure under any circumstances. Instead, the plan sought to bring about settlements by use of the customary devices of mediation, conciliation, investigation by boards of inquiry, and public reports. In some instances temporary injunctions were authorized to provide cooling-off periods. All this failing, the unions were left free to strike if the majority of the employees, by secret ballot, expressed a desire to do so.

It is clear that if the President had authority to issue the order he did, it must be found in some provisions of the Constitution. And it is not claimed that express constitutional language grants this power to the President. The contention is that presidential power should be implied from the aggregate of his powers under Article II of the Constitution. Particular reliance is placed on the provisions which say that "the executive Power shall be vested in a President . . ."; that "he shall take Care that the Laws be faithfully executed"; and that he "shall be Commander in Chief of the Army and Navy of the United States."

The order cannot properly be sustained as an exercise of the President's military power as Commander in Chief of the Armed Forces. The Government attempts to do so by citing a number of cases upholding broad powers in military commanders engaged in day-to-day fighting in a theater of war. Such cases need not concern us here. Even though "theater of war" be an expanding concept, we cannot with faithfulness to our constitutional system hold that the Commander in Chief of the Armed Forces has the ultimate power as such to take possession of private property in order to keep labor disputes from stopping production. This is a job for the Nation's lawmakers, not for its military authorities.

Nor can the seizure order be sustained because of the several constitutional provisions that grant executive power to the President. In the framework of our Constitution the President's power to see that the laws are faithfully executed refutes the idea that he is to be a lawmaker. The Constitution limits his functions in the lawmaking process to the recommending of laws he thinks wise and the vetoing of laws he thinks bad. And the Constitution is neither silent nor equivocal about who shall make laws which the President is to execute. The first section of the first article says that "All legislative Powers herein granted shall be vested in a Congress of the United States.". . .

The President's order does not direct that a congressional policy be executed in a manner prescribed by Congress—it directs that a presidential policy be executed in a manner prescribed by the President. The preamble of the order itself, like that of many statutes, sets out reasons why the President believes certain policies should be adopted, proclaims these policies as rules of conduct to be followed, and again, like a statute, authorizes a government official to promulgate additional rules and regulations consistent with the policy proclaimed and needed to carry that policy into execution. The power of Congress to adopt such public policies as those proclaimed by the order is beyond question. It can authorize the taking of private property for public use. It can make laws regulating the relationships between employers and employees, prescribing rules designed to settle labor disputes, and fixing wages and working conditions in certain fields of our economy. The Constitution did not subject this law-making power of Congress to presidential or military supervision or control.

It is said that other Presidents without congressional authority have taken possession of private business enterprises in order to settle labor disputes. But even if this be true, Congress has not thereby lost its exclusive constitutional authority to make laws necessary and proper to carry out the powers vested by the Constitution "in the Government of the United States, or any Department or Officer thereof."

The Founders of this Nation entrusted the law-making power to the Congress alone in both good and bad times. It would do no good to recall the historical events, the fears of power and the hopes for freedom that lay behind their choice. Such a review would but confirm our holding that this seizure order cannot stand.

The judgment of the District Court is affirmed.

Affirmed.

Mr. Justice Burton, concurring, said in part:

. . . In the case before us, Congress authorized a procedure which the President declined to follow. Instead, he followed another procedure which he hoped might eliminate the need for the first. Upon its failure, he issued an executive order to seize the steel properties in the face of the reserved right of Congress to adopt or reject that course as a matter of legislative policy.

This brings us to a further crucial question. Does the President, in such a situation, have inherent constitutional power to seize private property which makes congressional action in relation thereto unnecessary? We find no such power available to him under the present circumstances. The present situation is not comparable to that of an imminent invasion or threatened attack. We do not face the issue of what might be the President's constitutional power to meet such catastrophic situations. Nor is it claimed that the current seizure is the nature of a military command addressed by the President, as Commander in Chief, to a mobilized nation waging, or imminently threatened with, total war.

The controlling fact here is that Congress, within its constitutionally delegated power, has prescribed for the President specific procedures, exclusive of seizure, for his use in meeting the present type of emergency. Congress has reserved to itself the right to determine where and when to authorize the seizure of property in meeting such an emergency. Under these circumstances, the President's order of April 8 invaded the jurisdiction of Congress. It violated the essence of the principle of the separation of governmental powers. Accordingly, the injunction against its effectiveness should be sustained.

Mr. Justice Frankfurter, concurring, said in part:

. . . Apart from his vast share of responsibility for the conduct of our foreign relations, the embracing function of the President is that "he shall take Care that the Laws be faithfully executed. . . ." Art. II, § 3. The nature of that authority has for me been comprehensively indicated by Mr. Justice Holmes. "The duty of the President to see that the laws be executed is a duty that does not go beyond the laws or require him to achieve more than Congress sees fits to leave within his power." Myers v. United States, 272 U. S. 52, 177. The powers of the President are not as particularized as are those of Congress. But unenumerated powers do not mean undefined powers. The separation of powers built into our Constitution gives essential content to undefined provisions in the frame of our government. . . .

A scheme of government like ours no doubt at times feels the lack of power to act with complete, all-embracing, swiftly-moving authority. No doubt a government with distributed authority, subject to be challenged in the courts of law, at least long enough to consider and adjudicate the challenge, labors under restrictions from which other governments are free. It has not been our tradition to envy such governments. In any event our government was designed to have such restrictions. The price was deemed not too high in view of the safeguards which these restrictions afford. . . .

Mr. Justice Clark, concurring, said in part:

. . . In my view . . . the Constitution does grant to the President extensive authority in times of grave and imperative national emergency. In fact, to my thinking, such a grant may well be necessary to the very existence of the Constitution itself. As Lincoln aptly said, "[is] it possible to lose the nation and yet preserve the Constitution?" In describing this authority I care not whether one calls it "residual," "inherent," "moral," "implied," "aggregate," "emergency," or otherwise. . . .

I conclude that where Congress has laid down specific procedures to deal with the type of crisis confronting the President, he must follow those procedures in meeting the crisis; but that in the absence of such action by Congress, the President's independent power to act depends upon the gravity of the situation confronting the nation. I cannot sustain the seizure in question because here, . . . Congress had prescribed methods to be followed by the President in meeting the emergency at hand. . . .

. . . the Government made no effort to comply with the procedures established by the Selective Service Act of 1948, a statute which expressly authorizes seizures when producers fail to supply necessary defense matériel. . . .

Mr. Justice Jackson, concurring, said in part:

That seems to be the logic of an argument tendered at our bar—that the President having, on his own responsibility, sent American troops abroad derives from that act "affirmative power" to seize the means of producing a supply of steel for them. . . .

I cannot foresee all that it might entail if the Court should indorse this argument. Nothing in our Constitution is plainer than that declaration of a war is entrusted only to Congress. Of course, a state of war may in fact exist without a formal declaration. But no doctrine that the Court could promulgate would seem to me more sinister and alarming than that a President whose conduct of foreign affairs is so largely uncontrolled, and often even is unknown, can vastly enlarge his mastery over the internal affairs of the country by his own commitment of the Nation's armed forces to some foreign venture. . . .

The Solicitor General lastly grounds support of the seizure upon nebulous, inherent powers never expressly granted but said to have accrued to the office from the customs and claims of preceding administrations. The plea is for a resulting power to deal with a crisis or an emergency according to the necessities of the case, the unarticulated assumption being that necessity knows no law. . . .

The appeal, however, that we declare the existence of inherent powers *ex necessitate* to meet an emergency asks us to do what many think would be wise, although it is something the forefathers omitted. They knew what emergencies were, knew the pressures they engender for authoritative action, knew, too, how they afford a ready pretext for usurpation. We may also suspect that they suspected that emergency powers would tend to kindle emergencies. . . .

In the practical working of our Government we already have evolved a technique within the framework of the Constitution by which normal executive powers may be considerably expanded to meet an emergency. Congress may and has granted extraordinary authorities which lie dormant in normal times but may be called into play by the Executive in war or upon proclamation of a national emergency. In 1939, upon congressional request, the Attorney General listed ninety-nine such separate statutory grants by Congress of emergency or war-time executive powers. They were invoked from time to time as need appeared. Under this procedure we retain Government by law—special, temporary law, perhaps, but law nonetheless. The public may know the extent and limitations of the powers that can be asserted, and persons affected may be informed from the statute of their rights and duties.

In view of the ease, expedition and safety with which Congress can grant and has granted large emergency powers, certainly ample to embrace this crisis, I am quite unimpressed with the argument that we should affirm possession of them without statute. Such power either has no beginning or it has no end. If it exists, it need submit to no legal restraint. I am not alarmed that it would plunge us straightway into dictatorship, but it is at least a step in that wrong direction. . . .

But I have no illusion that any decision by this Court can keep power in the hands of Congress if it is not wise and timely in meeting its problems. A crisis that challenges the President equally, or perhaps primarily, challenges Congress. If not good law, there was worldly wisdom in the maxim attributed to Napolean that "The tools belong to the man who can use them." We may say that power to legislate for emergencies belongs in the hands of Congress, but only Congress itself can prevent power from slipping through its fingers.

The essence of our free Government is "leave to live by no man's leave, underneath the law"—to be governed by those impersonal forces which we call law. Our Government is fashioned to fulfill this concept so far as humanly possible. The Executive, except for recommendation and veto, has no legislative power. The executive action we have here originates in the individual will of the President and represents an exercise of authority without law. No one, perhaps not even the President, knows the limits of the power he may seek to exert in this instance and the parties affected cannot learn the limit of their rights. We do not know today what powers over labor or property would be claimed to flow from Government possession if we should legalize it, what rights to compensation would be claimed or recognized, or on what contingency it would end. With all its defects, delays and inconveniences, men have discovered no technique for long preserving free government except that the Executive be under the law, and that the law be made by parliamentary deliberations.

Such institutions may be destined to pass away. But it is the duty of the Court to be last, not first, to give them up.

Mr. Justice Douglas, concurring, said in part:

There can be no doubt that the emergency which caused the President to seize these steel plants was one that bore heavily on the country. But the emergency did not create power; it merely marked an occasion when power should be exercised. And the fact that it was necessary that measures be taken to keep steel in production does not mean that the President, rather than the Congress, had the constitutional authority to act. The Congress, as well as the President, is trustee of the national welfare. The President can act more quickly than the Congress. The President with the armed services at his disposal can move with force as well as with speed. All executive power—from the reign of ancient kings to the rule of modern dictators—has the outward appearance of efficiency.

Legislative power, by contrast, is slower to exercise. There must be delay while the ponderous machinery of committees, hearings, and debates is put into motion. That takes time; and while the Congress slowly moves into action, the emergency may take its toll in wages, consumer goods, war production, the standard of living of the people, and perhaps even lives. Legislative action may indeed often be cumbersome, time-consuming, and apparently inefficient. But as Mr. Justice Brandeis stated in his dissent in Myers v. United States, 272 U. S. 52, 293:

"The doctrine of the separation of powers was adopted by the Convention of 1787, not to promote efficiency but to preclude the exercise of arbitrary power. The purpose was, not to avoid friction, but, by means of the inevitable friction incident to the distribution of the governmental powers among three departments, to save the people from autocracy."

We therefore cannot decide this case by determining which branch of government can deal most expeditiously with the present crisis. The answer must depend on the allocation of powers under the Constitution. That in turn requires an analysis of the conditions giving rise to the seizure and of the seizure itself. . . .

The great office of President is not a weak and powerless one. The President represents the people and is their spokesman in domestic and foreign affairs. The office is respected more than any other in the land. It gives a position of leadership that is unique. The power to formulate policies and mould opinion inheres in the Presidency and conditions our national life. The impact of the man and the philosophy he represents may at times be thwarted by the Congress. Stalemates may occur when emergencies mount and the Nation suffers for lack of harmonious, reciprocal action between the White House and Capitol Hill. That is a risk inherent in our system of separation of powers. The tragedy of such stalemates might be avoided by allowing the President the use of some legislative authority. The Framers with memories of the tyrannies produced by a blending of executive and legislative power rejected that political arrangement. Some future generation may, however, deem it so urgent that the President have legislative authority that the Constitution will be amended. We could not sanction the seizures and condemnations of the steel plants in this case without reading Article II as giving the President not only the power to execute the laws but to make some. Such a step would most assuredly alter the pattern of the Constitutiton.

We pay a price for our system of checks and balances, for the distribution of power among the three branches of government. It is a price that today may seem exorbitant to many. Today a kindly President uses the seizure power to effect a wage increase and to keep the steel furnaces in production. Yet tomorrow another President might use the same power to prevent a wage increase, to curb trade unionists, to regiment labor as oppressively as industry thinks it has been regimented by this seizure.

Mr. Chief Justice Vinson, with whom Justices Reed and Minton joined, dissented, saying in part:

. . . Focusing now on the situation confronting the President on the night of April 8, 1952, we cannot but conclude that the President was performing his duty under the Constitution "to take care that the laws be faithfully executed"—a duty described by President Benjamin Harrison as "the central idea of the office."

The President reported to Congress the morning after the seizure that he acted because a work stoppage in steel production would immediately imperil the safety of the Nation by preventing execution of the legislative programs for procurement of military equipment. And, while a shutdown could be averted by granting the price concessions requested by plaintiffs, granting such concessions would disrupt the price stabilization program also enacted by Congress. Rather than fail to execute either legislative program, the President acted to execute both.

Much of the argument in this case has been directed at straw men. We do not now have before us the case of a President acting solely on the basis of his own notions of the public welfare. Nor is there any question of unlimited executive power in this case. The President himself closed the door to any such claim when he sent his Message to Congress stating his purpose to abide by any action of Congress, whether approving or disapproving his seizure action. Here, the President immediately made sure that Congress was fully informed of the temporary action he had taken only to preserve the legislative programs from destruction until Congress could act.

The absence of a specific statute authorizing seizure of the steel mills as a mode of executing the laws—both the military procurement program and the anti-inflation program—has not until today been thought to prevent the President from executing the laws. Unlike an administrative commission confined to the enforcement of the statute under which it was created, or the head of a department when administering a particular statute, the President is a constitutional officer charged with taking care that a "mass of legislation" be executed. Flexibility as to mode of execution to meet critical situations is a matter of practical necessity. . . .

As the District Judge stated, this is no time for "timorous" judicial action. But neither is this a time for timorous executive action. Faced with the duty of executing the defense programs which Congress had enacted and the disastrous effects that any stoppage in steel production would have on those programs, the President acted to preserve those programs by seizing the steel mills. There is no question that the possession was other than temporary in character and subject to congressional direction—either approving, disapproving or regulating the manner in which the mills were to be administered and returned to the owners. The President immediately informed Congress of his action and clearly stated his intention to abide by the legislative will. No basis for claims of arbitrary action, unlimited powers or dictatorial usurpation of congressional power appears from the facts of this case. On the contrary, judicial, legislative and executive precedents throughout our history demonstrate that in this case the President acted in full conformity with his duties under the Constitution. Accordingly, we would reverse the order of the District Court.

6

The Judiciary

MARBURY v. MADISON
1 Cranch 137; 2 L. Ed. 60. 1803.

Although the election in the autumn of 1800 brought to the Federalist party a defeat which they never retrieved, President Adams and his Federalist associates did not retire from office until March, 1801. While the Federalists had been for some time considering plans to reform the federal courts by remodeling the Judiciary Act of 1789, yet now in the eleventh hour they boldly set themselves to the task with renewed energy in order to make sure that the needed changes should be made by themselves rather than by the triumphant incoming Republicans and in order, undoubtedly, to insure a fortress for Federalist principles not easily to be broken down. Accordingly they passed the Judiciary Act of February 13, 1801, which relieved the Supreme Court justices of circuit court duty, increased the number of circuit court judges, and created a considerable number of minor judicial positions. President Adams proceeded during the last sixteen days of his administration to fill these newly created vacancies, sixty-seven in all, with loyal Federalists, and the task of signing their commissions occupied him until well into the night before the inauguration of Jefferson.

The federal courts had already incurred the bitter animosity of the Jeffersonian party, largely because of the vigor with which they had enforced the obnoxious Alien and Sedition Acts of 1798; and the Republicans were enraged beyond measure at what they deemed the effrontery of the Federalists in enacting the statute just mentioned. The judiciary was caustically referred to by Randolph as a "hospital for decayed politicians," while Jefferson wrote to a friend, "The Federalists have retired into the judiciary as a stronghold . . . and from that battery all the works of republicanism are to be beaten down and erased." One of the first Republican efforts, therefore, was to repeal the Judiciary Act of 1801, and after a long and acrimonious debate this was accomplished, March 8, 1802. This repealing act restored the Supreme Court judges to circuit court duty and abolished the new judgeships which had been created. The Federalists in Congress had bitterly assailed the repealing statute as unconstitutional, and Marshall himself always adhered to that view and probably would have held the law void if it had come before him in his judicial capacity. In order to prevent this, however, the repealing act had so altered the sessions of the Supreme Court that it did not convene again for fourteen months, by which time acquiescence in the act by the judges affected made an attack upon its validity impracticable.

However, when the Court convened in February, 1803, the case of Marbury v. Madison was on the docket. Marbury was one of those whom President Adams had appointed to a justiceship of the peace in the District of Columbia under an act of 1801, and whose commission, signed and sealed on March 3, had not been delivered when Jefferson, with Madison as his Secretary of State, had taken office on March 4. Ironically, the Secretary of State who should have given Marbury his commission before the Adams administration expired was none other than John Marshall who, although he was Chief Justice of the United States, was also serving without salary as Secretary of State. Needless to say the commission was not delivered by the two Republican statesmen, and Marbury filed a suit asking the Supreme Court in the exercise of its original jurisdiction to issue a writ of mandamus to compel Madison to deliver the commission. The right to issue such a writ had been conferred upon the Court by a provision of the Judiciary Act of 1789 and jurisdiction thereunder had been exercised by the Court twice before Marshall's accession to the bench. When the case came on for argument it assumed very largely the aspect of a quarrel between the President and the judiciary. Marbury's own interest in it was small, since it was fairly clear that Jefferson had no intention of giving him his commission even if the Court ordered it to be given. The Republicans seem to have expected that the Court would issue the mandamus asked for and there were open threats that Marshall would be impeached if that occurred.

The decision in Marbury v. Madison was therefore received with some astonishment, for while Marshall held that the case was one in which a writ of mandamus afforded a proper remedy and took occasion to scold the Republican administration for not having delivered the commission, he went on to hold that the section of the Judiciary Act of 1789 purporting to add to the original jurisdiction of the Supreme Court the power to issue such a writ exceeded the power of Congress under the Constitution. This being the case he announced that it became the duty of the Court to declare the section in question void. Thus was established the great doctrine of judicial review, or the power of the Supreme Court to declare acts of Congress unconstitutional.

It is worth noting that this important doctrine was by no means an innovation. Most of the arguments which Marshall used in his famous opinion had been presented again and again in the debates in Congress on the Repeal Act of 1802. Moreover, the power of invalidating legislation had been exercised by the lower federal courts without opposition, and there seems to be evidence that public opinion looked upon the practice as one of the normal incidents of judicial power. Criticism of the decision was at the moment directed at the Court not because of its enunciation of this important doctrine but because Marshall had held that a cabinet officer was subject to control by mandamus if issued by a court having jurisdiction. It was only as the doctrine of judicial review came eventually to appear to the Republicans as a menace to their party program that they opposed it.

The case of Marbury v. Madison has a certain strategic significance which should not be left out of account. The next case in which an act of Congress was invalidated by the Supreme Court was the famous Dred Scott case decided in 1857. By that time nearly seventy years had elapsed from the time of the formation of our constitutional system, and the Court was composed of men holding nationalistic views far less strong than those of Marshall and his associates. If the power of judicial review had not been exercised and the doctrine established in the case of Marbury v. Madison, one may well conjecture whether our constitutional development would have been the same.

Since, according to Marshall's reasoning below, the courts derive their power of judicial review from the language of Article III which extends federal judicial power to "cases and controversies," the Supreme Court from the beginning has refused to pass upon the validity of a statute unless it was involved in an actual case or controversy presented to it for decision. The Court, in short, will not render "advisory opinions" upon constitutional questions. In 1793 President Washington sent to the Court twenty-nine questions relating to the construction of a pending treaty. Chief Justice Jay returned them with the explanation that the Court could not answer them, since to do so would be to exercise non-judicial power, because no case or controversy was before the Court for decision. This rule has been rigidly followed ever since. As a result, some constitutional questions never come to the Court for decision and many others come only after long delay, since they must wait until lawsuits arise in which they are squarely presented for decision. Thus the long and hotly debated issue whether a protective tariff is constitutional did not come before the Court for decision until 1928 in the case of Hampton & Co. v. United States, 276 U. S. 394. See also the comment on Myers v. United States, p. 302.

What is the legal effect of a court decision holding a statute to be unconstitutional? Mr. Justice Field gave one answer to this question years ago when he said: "An unconstitutional act is not a law, it confers no rights, it imposes no duties, it affords no protection, it creates no office; it is, in legal contemplation, as inoperative as though it had never been passed." See Norton v. Shelby County, 118 U. S. 425 (1886). The court's decision does not change a valid statute into a void one; the statute has always been void. The court has merely discovered and announced that invalidity, much as a jeweller may state, after examining it, that what was supposed to be a diamond is in reality paste. He does not make it paste, he merely finds out that it is. In most cases the courts have followed this "principle of absolute retroactive invalidity." In Schechter v. United States, 295 U. S. 495 (1935), the Schechters were convicted of violating a code of fair competition set up under the National Industrial Recovery Act (see p. 355). The Supreme Court held the statute and the code to be unconstitutional, and the Schechters were instantly free of any taint of criminality. They had violated a law which legally had never existed.

In some cases the rigid application of this principle of invalidity works serious injustice. This fact has led the Court in some instances to soften and compromise the strict rule, and to hold, in the words of Chief Justice Hughes: "The actual existence of a statute, prior to such a determination [of unconstitutionality] is an operative fact and may have consequences which cannot justly be ignored. The past cannot always be erased by a new judicial declaration. The effect of the subsequent ruling as to invalidity may have to be considered in various aspects—with respect to particular relations, individual and corporate, and particular conduct, private or official." See Chicot County Drainage District v. Baxter State Bank, 308 U. S. 371 (1940).

The Supreme Court, furthermore, has held that "a statute may be invalid as applied to one state of facts, and yet valid as applied to another." See Dahnke-Walker Milling Co. v. Bondurant, 257 U. S. 282 (1921). In this case a state statute regulating corporations was valid when applied to corporations doing local business within the state, but invalid when applied to those engaged in interstate commerce.

Sometimes the Court finds that part of a statute is valid and part invalid. In such a case, if the invalid part is so clearly separable from the rest that when it is deleted there still remains a complete and self-executing statute which the legislature might reasonably wish to have left in operation, then the Court will hold void only the invalid section. But if the void portion is so interwoven with the valid parts that it cannot be struck out without leaving an incomplete and more or less mangled remainder, then the Court will hold the entire act void. Thus the Child Labor Tax section of the Revenue Act of 1919 was held invalid (see Bailey v. Drexel Furniture Co., p. 462) without disturbing the other provisions of the statute. On the other hand, in Carter v. Carter Coal Co., 298 U. S. 238 (1936), the Court held unconstitutional the sections of the Guffey Coal Act which related to labor relations, and held further that as the price-control sections of the act were not separable from the labor sections the entire statute was therefore invalid.

The portion of Marshall's opinion here printed deals only with the question of the power of the courts to invalidate an act of Congress.

. . . The authority, therefore, given to the Supreme Court, by the act establishing the judicial courts of the United States, to issue writs of mandamus to public officers, appears not to be warranted by the Constitution; and it becomes necessary to inquire whether a jurisdiction so conferred can be exercised.

The question whether an act repugnant to the Constitution can become the law of the land, is a question deeply interesting to the United States; but, happily, not of an intricacy proportioned to its interest. It seems only necessary to recognize certain principles, supposed to have been long and well established to decide it.

That the people have an original right to establish, for their future government, such principles as, in their opinion, shall most conduce to their own happiness, is the basis on which the whole American fabric has been erected. The exercise of this original right is a very great exertion; nor can it nor ought it to be frequently repeated. The principles, therefore, so established, are deemed fundamental. And as the authority from which they proceed is supreme, and can seldom act, they are designed to be permanent.

This original and supreme will organizes the government, and assigns to different departments their respective powers. It may either stop here, or establish certain limits not to be transcended by those departments.

The government of the United States is of the latter description. The powers of the legislature are defined and limited; and that those limits may not be mistaken, or forgotten, the Constitution is written. To what purpose are powers limited, and to what purpose is that limitation committed to writing, if these limits may, at any time, be passed by those intended to be restrained? The distinction between a government with limited and unlimited powers is abolished, if those limits do not confine the persons on whom they are imposed, and if acts prohibited and acts allowed are of equal obligation. It is a proposition too plain to be contested, that the Constitution controls any legislative act repugnant to it; or, that the legislature may alter the Constitution by an ordinary act.

Between these alternatives there is no middle ground. The Constitution is either a superior paramount law, unchangeable by ordinary means, or it is on a level with ordinary legislative acts, and, like other acts, is alterable when the legislature shall please to alter it.

If the former part of the alternative be true, then a legislative act contrary to the Constitution is not law; if the latter part be true, then written constitutions are absurd attempts, on the part of the people, to limit a power in its own nature illimitable.

Certainly all those who have framed written constitutions contemplate them as forming the fundamental and paramount law of the nation, and, consequently, the theory of every such government must be, that an act of the legislature, repugnant to the constitution, is void.

This theory is essentially attached to a written constitution, and is consequently to be considered, by this Court, as one of the fundamental principles of our society. It is not, therefore, to be lost sight of in the further consideration of this subject.

If an act of the legislature, repugnant to the Constitution, is void, does it, notwithstanding its invalidity, bind the courts, and oblige them to give it effect? Or, in other words, though it be not law, does it constitute a rule as operative as if it was a law? This would be to overthrow in fact what was established in theory; and would seem, at first view, an absurdity too gross to be insisted on. It shall, however, receive a more attentive consideration.

It is emphatically the province and duty of the judicial department to say what the law is. Those who apply the rule to particular cases, must of necessity expound and interpret that rule. If two laws conflict with each other, the courts must decide on the operation of each.

So if a law be in opposition to the Constitution; if both the law and the Constitution apply to a particular case, so that the court must either decide that case conformably to the law, disregarding the Constitution, or conformably to the Constitution, disregarding the law, the court must determine which of these conflicting rules governs the case. This is of the very essence of judicial duty.

If, then, the courts are to regard the Constitution, and the Constitution is superior to any ordinary act of the legislature, the Constitution, and not such ordinary act, must govern the case to which they both apply.

Those, then, who controvert the principle that the Constitution is to be considered, in court, as a paramount law, are reduced to the necessity of maintaining that courts must close their eyes on the Constitution, and see only the law.

This doctrine would subvert the very foundation of all written constitutions. It would declare that an act which, according to the principles and theory of our government, is entirely void, is yet, in practice, completely obligatory. It would declare that if the legislature shall do what is expressly forbidden, such act, notwithstanding the express prohibition, is in reality effectual. It would be giving to the legislature a practical and real omnipotence, with the same breath which professes to restrict their powers within narrow limits. It is prescribing limits, and declaring that those limits may be passed at pleasure.

That it thus reduces to nothing what we have deemed the greatest improvement on political institutions, a written constitution, would of itself be sufficient, in America, where written constitutions have been viewed with so much reverence, for rejecting the construction. But the peculiar expressions of the Constitution of the United States furnish additional arguments in favor of its rejection.

The judicial power of the United States is extended to all cases arising under the Constitution.

Could it be the intention of those who gave this power, to say that in using it the Constitution should not be looked into? That a case arising under the Constitution should be decided without examining the instrument under which it arises?

This is too extravagant to be maintained.

In some cases, then, the Constitution must be looked into by the judges. And if they can open it at all, what part of it are they forbidden to read or to obey?

There are many other parts of the Constitution which serve to illustrate this subject.

It is declared that "no tax or duty shall be laid on articles exported from any State." Suppose a duty on the export of cotton, of tobacco, or of flour; and a suit instituted to recover it. Ought judgment to be rendered in such a case? ought the judges to close their eyes on the Constitution, and only see the law?

The Constitution declares "that no bill of attainder or ex post facto law shall be passed."

If, however, such a bill should be passed, and a person should be prosecuted under it, must the court condemn to death those victims whom the Constitution endeavors to preserve?

"No person," says the Constitution, "shall be convicted of treason unless on the testimony of two witnesses to the same overt act, or on confession in open court."

Here the language of the Constitution is addressed especially to the courts. It prescribes, directly for them, a rule of evidence not to be departed from. If the legislature should change that rule, and declare one witness, or a confession out of court, sufficient for conviction, must the constitutional principle yield to the legislative act?

From these, and many other selections which might be made, it is apparent that the framers of the Constitution contemplated that instrument as a rule for the government of courts, as well as of the legislature.

Why otherwise does it direct the judges to take an oath to support it? This oath certainly applies in an especial manner to their conduct in their official character. How immoral to impose it on them, if they were to be used as the instruments, and the knowing instruments, for violating what they swear to support!

The oath of office, too, imposed by the legislature, is completely demonstrative of the legislative opinion on this subject. It is in these words: "I do solemnly swear that I will administer justice without respect to persons, and do equal right to the poor and to the rich; and that I will faithfully and impartially discharge all the duties incumbent on me as ———, according to the best of my abilities and understanding, agreeably to the Constitution and laws of the United States."

Why does a judge swear to discharge his duties agreeably to the Constitution of the United States, if that Constitution forms no rule for his government? if it closed upon him, and cannot be inspected by him?

If such be the real state of things, this is worse than solemn mockery. To prescribe, or to take this oath, becomes equally a crime.

It is also not entirely unworthy of observation, that in declaring what shall be the supreme law of the land, the Constitution itself is first mentioned; and not the laws of the United States generally, but those only which shall be made in pursuance of the Constitution, have that rank.

Thus, the particular phraseology of the Constitution of the United States confirms and strengthens the principle, supposed to be essential to all written constitutions, that a law repugnant to the Constitution is void; and that courts, as well as other departments, are bound by that instrument.

The rule must be discharged.

EAKIN v. RAUB
12 Sergeant and Rawle (Pennsylvania Supreme Court) 330. 1825.

The power of the Supreme Court to declare acts of Congress unconstitutional has so long been an integral part of our constitutional system, and Marshall's reasoning in the case of Marbury v. Madison is so impressive, that it is easy to lose sight of the fact that a most cogent argument may be made against the establishment of the power, and that had the Supreme Court never enjoyed it no very calamitous results would have ensued. Jefferson, Marshall's most bitter personal and political adversary, never admitted the authority of the Supreme Court to determine the validity of an act of Congress, but held that each of the three departments of the national government being equal and separate was equally empowered "to decide on the validity of an act according to its own judgment and uncontrolled by the opinions of any other department." This view was shared by many other thoughtful men of the day. In the exercise of its power of judicial review the Court will not pass upon what it terms "political questions" (see Luther v. Borden p. 335), questions the final determination of which has been confided by the Constitution to the discretion of the political departments, that is, the legislative or the executive. According to the view of Jefferson and his followers all questions involving the constitutionality of acts of Congress which might come before the Court would be "political questions." The statute might conflict with the Constitution, but that fact would not of itself endow the Court with any power to invalidate it; rather it would be the duty of the Court to enforce the statute without questioning its validity. That such a system would not have been followed by any strikingly disastrous results may be inferred from the fact that in most of the constitutional governments of the world the courts do not enjoy the power of judicial review, and that in this country less than eighty statutes of Congress have been held unconstitutional (through the 1961 term of the Court), of which only a very few involved problems of any vital or lasting importance. As Mr. Justice Holmes declared, "The United States would not come to an end if we lost our power to declare an act of Congress void." In fact, the power to declare an act of Congress invalid is a power very much less important to the Supreme Court than the power to pass upon the validity of state legislation. This last authority may well be regarded as vital to the preservation of our federal system by providing a necessary method of preventing the state governments from encroaching upon the domain of federal authority or impairing the federal rights and immunities of the individual.

Perhaps the most lucid and carefully reasoned answer to Marshall's argument in Marbury v. Madison is to be found in the following excerpts from a dissenting opinion written by Mr. Justice Gibson of the supreme court of Pennsylvania in 1825. The case itself is of no intrinsic interest or importance, but it raised the question of the power of the state supreme court to invalidate a statute, and Judge Gibson took occasion to express his views upon this point although a majority of his brethren did not agree with him. It is interesting to note that twenty years later a lawyer in pleading his case cited to the court this opinion, whereupon Judge Gibson replied to the lawyer: "I have changed that opinion, for two reasons. The late convention [which had framed the Pennsylvania constitution of 1838], by their silence, sanctioned the pretensions of the courts to deal freely with the acts of the legislature; and from experience of the necessity of the case" (Norris v. Clymer, 2 Pa. St. 277, 281, 1845).

Mr. Justice Gibson said:

. . . I am aware, that a right to declare all unconstitutional acts void, without distinction as to either constitution, is generally held as a professional dogma; but, I apprehend, rather as a matter of faith than of reason. I admit that I once embraced the same doctrine, but without examination, and I shall therefore state the arguments that impelled me to abandon it, with great respect for those by whom it is still maintained. But I may premise, that it is not a little remarkable, that although the right in question has all along been claimed by the judiciary, no judge has ventured to discuss it, except Chief Justice Marshall (in Marbury v. Madison, 1 Cranch, 176), and if the argument of a jurist so distinguished for the strength of his ratiocinative powers be found inconclusive, it may fairly be set down to the weakness of the position which he attempts to defend. . . .

The Constitution and the right of the legislature to pass the act, may be in collison. But is that a legitimate subject for judicial determination? If it be, the judiciary must be a peculiar organ, to revise the proceedings of the legislature, and to correct its mistakes; and in what part of the Constitution are we to look for this proud pre-eminence? Viewing the matter in the opposite direction, what would be thought of an act of assembly in which it should be declared that the Supreme Court had, in a particular case, put a wrong construc-tion on the Constitution of the United States, and that the judgment should therefore be reversed? It would doubtless be thought a usurpa-tion of judicial power. But it is by no means clear, that to declare a law void which has been enacted according to the forms prescribed in the Constitution, is not a usurpation of legislative power. It is an act of sovereignty; and sovereignty and legislative power are said by Sir William Blackstone to be convertible terms. It is the business of the judiciary to interpret the laws, not scan the authority of the law-giver; and without the latter, it cannot take cognizance of a collision between a law and the Constitution. So that to affirm that the judiciary has a right to judge of the existence of such collision, is to take for granted the very thing to be proved. And, that a very cogent argument may be made in this way, I am not disposed to deny; for no conclusions are so strong as those that are drawn from the petitio principii.

But it has been said to be emphatically the business of the judiciary, to ascertain and pronounce what the law is; and that this necessarily involves a consideration of the Constitution. It does so: but how far? If the judiciary will inquire into anything besides the form of enact-ment, where shall it stop? There must be some point of limitation to such an inquiry; for no one will pretend that a judge would be justi-fiable in calling for the election returns, or scrutinizing the qualifica-tions of those who composed the legislature. . . .

Everyone knows how seldom men think exactly alike on ordinary subjects; and a government constructed on the principle of assent by all its parts, would be inadequate to the most simple operations. The notion of a complication of counter checks has been carried to an extent in theory, of which the framers of the Constitution never dreamt. When the entire sovereignty was separated into its elementary parts, and distributed to the appropriate branches, all things incident to the exercise of its powers were committed to each branch ex-clusively. The negative which each part of the legislature may exercise, in regard to the acts of the other, was thought sufficient to prevent material infractions of the restraints which were put on the power of the whole; for, had it been intended to interpose the judiciary as an additional barrier, the matter would surely not have been left in doubt. The judges would not have been left to stand on the insecure and ever shifting ground of public opinion as to constructive powers; they would have been placed on the impregnable ground of an express grant. . . .

But the judges are sworn to support the Constitution, and are they not bound by it as the law of the land? In some respects they are. In the very few cases in which the judiciary, and not the legislature, is the immediate organ to execute its provisions, they are bound by it in preference to any act of assembly to the contrary. In such cases, the Constitution is a rule to the courts. But what I have in view in this inquiry, is the supposed right of the judiciary to interfere, in cases where the Constitution is to be carried into effect through the instrumentality of the legislature, and where that organ must necessarily first decide on the constitutionality of its own act. The oath to support the Constitution is not peculiar to the judges, but is taken indiscriminately by every officer of the government, and is designed rather as a test of the political principles of the man, than to bind the officer in the discharge of his duty: otherwise it were difficult to determine what operation it is to have in the case of a recorder of deeds, for instance, who, in the execution of his office, has nothing to do with the Constitution. But granting it to relate to the official conduct of the judge, as well as every other officer, and not to his political principles, still it must be understood in reference to supporting the Constitution, only as far as that may be involved in his official duty; and, consequently, if his official duty does not comprehend an inquiry into the authority of the legislature, neither does his oath. It is worthy of remark here, that the foundation of every argument in favor of the right of the judiciary, is found at last to be an assumption of the whole ground in dispute. Granting that the object of the oath is to secure a support of the Constitution in the discharge of official duty, its terms may be satisfied by restraining it to official duty in the exercise of the ordinary judicial powers. Thus, the Constitution may furnish a rule of construction, where a particular interpretation of a law would conflict with some constitutional principle; and such interpretation, where it may, is always to be avoided. But the oath was more probably designed to secure the powers of each of the different branches from being usurped by any of the rest: for instance, to prevent the House of Representatives from erecting itself into a court of judicature, or the Supreme Court from attempting to control the legislature; and, in this view, the oath furnishes an argument equally plausible against the right of the judiciary. But if it require a support of the Constitution in anything beside official duty, it is in fact an oath of allegiance to a particular form of government; and, considered as such, it is not easy to see why it should not be taken by the citizens at large, as well as by the officers of the government. It has never been thought that an officer is under greater restraint as to measures which have for their avowed end a total change of the Constitution, than a citizen who has taken no oath at all. The official oath, then, relates only to the official conduct of the officer, and does not prove that he ought to stray from the path of his ordinary business to search for violations of duty in the business of others; nor does it, as supposed, define the powers of the officer.

But do not the judges do a positive act in violation of the Constitution, when they give effect to an unconstitutional law? Not if the law has been passed according to the forms established in the Constitution. The fallacy of the question is, in supposing that the judiciary adopts the acts of the legislature as its own; whereas the enactment of a law and the interpretation of it are not concurrent acts, and as the judiciary is not required to concur in the enactment, neither is it in the breach of the Constitution which may be the consequence of the enactment. The fault is imputable to the legislature, and on it the responsibility exclusively rests. In this respect, the judges are in the predicament of jurors who are bound to serve in capital cases, although unable, under any circumstances, to reconcile it to their duty to deprive a human being of life. To one of these, who applied to be discharged from the panel, I once heard it remarked, by an eminent and humane judge: "You do not deprive a prisoner of life by finding him guilty of a capital crime; you but pronounce his case to be within the law, and it is therefore those who declare the law, and not you, who deprive him of life."

LUTHER v. BORDEN
7 Howard (U. S.) 1; 12 L. Ed. 581. 1849.

Not all questions which arise under the Constitution of the United States are questions which the Supreme Court will undertake to answer. Very early in the exercise of its power of judicial review the Court pointed out that certain powers are vested in the legislative or executive departments of the government to be exercised in a purely discretionary manner, and that whether they have been constitutionally exercised or not is a "political question" which the Court will not decide. One of the early and very striking instances of this type of question was that which was raised in the famous case of Luther v. Borden.

This case arose out of the following facts: The original constitution of Rhode Island, which was merely the colonial charter with a few minor adaptations, provided for a very restricted suffrage based upon the possession of property; and the right to vote continued to be thus limited long after universal manhood suffrage had been generally adopted throughout the country. Many efforts were made to have the constitution amended so as to put the franchise upon a more democratic basis, but they were all defeated by the relatively small group of legal voters. In 1841 the popular feeling regarding the situation ran even higher than before; mass meetings were held throughout the state, and without any semblance of constitutional sanction the citizens were directed to choose by universal manhood suffrage delegates to a constitutional convention. This convention met and drafted a new state constitution which established adult manhood suffrage and made many other changes. A popular referendum was conducted in which all the adult male citizens of the state were permitted to vote, and the new constitution was approved by a majority of the votes cast. The leader of the whole movement was a young lawyer, Thomas W. Dorr, who was elected governor under the new constitution and immediately attempted to put the new government into operation. The regular charter government did not, of course, recognize the validity of any of these acts. It called out the state militia and declared martial law and finally appealed to President Tyler to send federal troops to aid in putting down the "insurrection." The President took steps to comply with this request and the "Dorr Rebellion" collapsed. Dorr himself was captured, tried for treason, and finally sentenced to life imprisonment. He was later pardoned. He naturally had managed to arouse a good deal of sympathy for his cause outside the state, particularly amongst the Democrats, and it was felt that it would be desirable to present to the Supreme Court of the United States the question of the legality of the new constitution and the acts done under it. This was tried first by Dorr himself, who attempted to sue out a writ of habeas corpus in the Supreme Court; but that tribunal dismissed the petition for want of jurisdiction. See Ex Parte Dorr, 3 Howard 103 (1845). Upon the assumption that the same issue could be raised collaterally, the civil controversy between Luther and Borden, relatively unimportant in itself, was pushed through to the Supreme Court. Luther had been a supporter of the Dorr movement, and in an effort to arrest him, Borden and others who were enrolled as members of the militia under the charter government broke into Luther's house. This act they justified upon the ground that martial law had been declared and that they were acting under the orders of their superior officers. Luther sued Borden for trespass, claiming that the act of the legislature establishing martial law was void inasmuch as the Dorr government, elected by the people of the state, was the lawful government. (It should be noted that in January, 1842, the charter government had called a constitutional convention and drafted a new constitution which was ratified by the people in due form and went into effect in 1843. Thus the Dorr movement did not entirely fail in its purposes.)

By the facts as presented in this case, the Court was invited to decide which of the two governments struggling for supremacy in Rhode Island in the year 1842 was the lawful one. But this question, replied the Supreme Court, was a "political question." The President in exercising the power conferred on him by Congress to send federal troops to aid states in suppressing insurrection had indicated that he regarded the charter government as the lawful government, and this decision was binding upon the Court. The Court intimated that Congress itself would also share the power of deciding between the competing governments by deciding which group of rival Senators and Representatives it would seat in Congress, but Congress was not asked to make such a decision. The Court declined to decide whether Rhode Island had a republican form of government within the meaning of the guaranty in the United States Constitution, Article IV, section 4, but held that the enforcement of that guaranty was confided to the political departments of the government.

There are other questions which have been held by the Supreme Court to be "political" in character. Such is the question whether there is a sufficient emergency to justify the President, acting under the authority of an act of Congress, in calling out the militia to repel invasion or to put down insurrection. See Martin v. Mott, 12 Wheaton 19 (1827). Many such questions arise for determination in the course of the conduct of foreign relations; as, for instance, the recognition of a foreign government, the acquisition of territory, the determination of boundaries, the existence or termination of a treaty, and the like. The early case of Foster v. Neilson, 2 Peters 253 (1829), raising the question as to the title to certain territory which was the subject of international dispute, emphasized the unwillingness of the Court to attempt to settle this type of question. The question whether or not a state of the Union has a republican form of government within the meaning of that clause of the Constitution guaranteeing such form of government was squarely raised in 1912 in the case of Pacific States Telephone & Telegraph Co. v. Oregon, 223 U. S. 118. In 1902 Oregon had amended her state constitution so as to establish the initiative and referendum. In 1906 a law was proposed by popular initiative and duly enacted by the people which imposed certain taxes on corporations. The plaintiff corporation resisted the payment of the tax on the ground that the incorporation of the initiative and referendum into the constitutional system of the state destroyed the republican character of its government and thus robbed it of lawful authority. The argument was that republican government means representative government and that representative government is destroyed by the system of direct legislation. The Supreme Court refused to pass on the question whether Oregon had a republican form of government or not, and pointed out that that question was political in character and had been determined by Congress in admitting Senators and Representatives of the state to their seats in Congress.

In Coleman v. Miller (p. 1), the Court makes clear that many of the questions relating to the adoption of federal amendments are "political" in nature, and beyond the reach of the courts.

Colegrove v. Green, 328 U. S. 549 (1946), has previously been included in this chapter. It was generally viewed as holding, in an elaborate opinion by Mr. Justice Frankfurter, that questions relating to legislative apportionment are political questions which the courts cannot properly decide. Actually, the justices divided three to three on this point; the other majority justice (Rutledge) relied on another point. Baker v. Carr (p. 220) discarded this view and held that the Court must decide whether a legislative apportionment was so inequitable as to deny the equal protection of the laws. In the opinions in both of these cases are elaborate discussions of the history and nature of political questions.

Mr. Chief Justice Taney delivered the opinion of the Court, saying in part:

. . . The fourth section of the fourth article of the Constitution of the United States provides that the United States shall guarantee to every state in the Union a republican form of government, and shall protect each of them against invasion; and on the application of the legislature or of the executive (when the legislature cannot be convened) against domestic violence.

Under this article of the Constitution it rests with Congress to decide what government is the established one in a state. For as the United States guarantee to each state a republican government, Congress must necessarily decide what government is established in the state before it can determine whether it is republican or not. And when the Senators and Representatives of a state are admitted into the councils of the Union, the authority of the government under which they are appointed, as well as its republican character, is recognized by the proper constitutional authority. And its decision is binding on every other department of the government, and could not be ques-

tioned in a judicial tribunal. It is true that the contest in this case
did not last long enough to bring the matter to this issue; and as no
Senators or Representatives were elected under the authority of the
government of which Mr. Dorr was the head, Congress was not called
upon to decide the controversy. Yet the right to decide is placed there,
and not in the courts.

So, too, as relates to the clause in the above-mentioned article of the
Constitution, providing for cases of domestic violence. It rested with
Congress, too, to determine upon the means proper to be adopted to
fulfill this guarantee. They might, if they had deemed it most advis-
able to do so, have placed it in the power of a court to decide when
the contingency had happened which required the federal government
to interfere. But Congress thought otherwise, and no doubt wisely;
and by the act of February 28, 1795, provided that, "in case of any
insurrection in any state against the government thereof, it shall be
lawful for the President of the United States, on application of the
legislature of such state or of the executive (when the legislature
cannot be convened) to call forth such number of militia of any other
state or states, as may be applied for, as he may judge sufficient to
suppress such insurrection."

By this act, the power of deciding whether the exigency had arisen
upon which the government of the United States is bound to interfere, is given to the President. He is to act upon the application of
the legislature or of the executive, and consequently he must determine what body of men constitute the legislature, and who is the
governor, before he can act. The fact that both parties claim the
right to the government cannot alter the case, for both cannot be entitled to it. If there is an armed conflict, like the one of which we
are speaking, it is a case of domestic violence, and one of the parties
must be in insurrection against the lawful government. And the
President must, of necessity, decide which is the government, and
which party is unlawfully arrayed against it, before he can perform
the duty imposed upon him by the act of Congress.

After the President has acted and called out the militia, is a circuit
court of the United States authorized to inquire whether his decision
was right? Could the court, while the parties were actually contend-
ing in arms for the possession of the government, call witnesses before
it and inquire which party represented a majority of the people?
If it could, then it would become the duty of the court (provided it
came to the conclusion that the President had decided incorrectly)

to discharge those who were arrested or detained by the troops in the service of the United States or the government which the President was endeavoring to maintain. If the judicial power extends so far, the guarantee contained in the Constitution of the United States is a guarantee of anarchy, and not of order. Yet if this right does not reside in the courts when the conflict is raging, if the judicial power is, at that time, bound to follow the decision of the political, it must be equally bound when the contest is over. It cannot, when peace is restored, punish as offenses and crimes the acts which it before recognized, and was bound to recognize, as lawful.

It is true that in this case the militia were not called out by the President. But upon the application of the governor under the charter government, the President recognized him as the executive power of the state, and took measures to call out the militia to support his authority, if it should be found necessary for the general government to interfere; and it is admitted in the argument that it was the knowledge of this decision that put an end to the armed opposition to the charter government, and prevented any further efforts to establish by force the proposed constitution. The interference of the President, therefore, by announcing his determination, was as effectual as if the militia had been assembled under his orders. And it should be equally authoritative. For certainly no court of the United States, with a knowledge of this decision, would have been justified in recognizing the opposing party as the lawful government, or in treating as wrong-doers or insurgents the officers of the government which the President had recognized, and was prepared to support by an armed force. In the case of foreign nations, the government acknowledged by the President is always recognized in the courts of justice. And this principle has been applied by the act of Congress to the sovereign states of the Union.

It is said that this power in the President is dangerous to liberty, and may be abused. All power may be abused if placed in unworthy hands. But it would be difficult, we think, to point out any other hands in which this power would be more safe, and at the same time equally effectual. When citizens of the same state are in arms against each other, and the constituted authorities unable to execute the laws, the interposition of the United States must be prompt, or it is of little value. The ordinary course of proceedings in courts of justice would be utterly unfit for the crisis. And the elevated office of the President, chosen as he is by the people of the United States, and the high responsibility he could not fail to feel when acting in a case of so much moment, appear to furnish as strong safeguards against a wilful abuse of power as human prudence and foresight could well provide. At all events, it is conferred upon him by the Constitution and laws of the United States, and must, therefore, be respected and enforced in its judicial tribunals.

. . . Undoubtedly, if the President, in exercising this power, shall fall into error, or invade the rights of the people of the state, it would be in the power of Congress to apply the proper remedy. But the courts must administer the law as they find it. . . .

Much of the argument on the part of the plaintiff turned upon political rights and political questions, upon which the court has been urged to express an opinion. We decline doing so. The high power has been conferred on this court of passing judgment upon the acts of the state sovereignties, and of the legislative and executive branches of the federal government, and of determining whether they are beyond the limits of power marked out for them respectively by the Constitution of the United States. This tribunal, therefore, should be the last to overstep the boundaries which limit its own jurisdiction. And while it should always be ready to meet any question confided to it by the Constitution, it is equally its duty not to pass beyond its appropriate sphere of action, and to take care not to involve itself in discussions which properly belong to other forums. No one, we believe, has ever doubted the proposition, that, according to the institutions of this country, the sovereignty in every state resides in the people of the state, and that they may alter and change their form of government at their own pleasure. But whether they have changed it or not by abolishing an old government, and establishing a new one in its place, is a question to be settled by the political power. And when that power has decided, the courts are bound to take notice of its decision, and to follow it.

The judgment of the circuit court must, therefore, be affirmed.

NEW HAMPSHIRE v. LOUISIANA
108 U. S. 76; 27 L. Ed. 656; 2 Sup. Ct. 176. 1883.

When the Constitution was before the states for ratification, its opponents raised the objection that the clause which provided that the judicial power of the United States should extend to controversies "between a State and citizens of another State" (Article III, section 2) would subject the states to suits brought by individual creditors and others who might feel that they had grievances. This idea was particularly obnoxious because the states had neither the intention nor the desire to repay money which was owing to loyalists or British subjects or to restore the property which had been confiscated during the war. That the clause in question would authorize suits by citizens against the states was denied by Hamilton in The Federalist (No. 81) and was also vigorously repudiated by Madison and Marshall in the Virginia ratifying convention of 1788 (Elliot's Debates, 2d Ed. III, 533, 555). That the fears which had been aroused were not ill-founded, however, was evidenced by the fact that within two years after the organization of the Supreme Court four cases were instituted before that tribunal against states of the Union by individuals. The first case which came on for decision was that of Chisholm v. Georgia, 2 Dallas 419 (1793), which involved a suit brought by Chisholm and another, citizens of South Carolina, as executors of an English creditor of the state of Georgia. Georgia hotly declined to appear to defend the suit, denying the jurisdiction of the Supreme Court to entertain such an action. The Court, however, to the general surprise, held that the suit was properly brought and that a state could be sued in the Supreme Court by an individual. Construing the clause of the judiciary article above quoted, the Court observed that surely a controversy between A and B was also a controversy between B and A and under the wording of the clause it had no choice but to assume jurisdiction. Since the state of Georgia still refused to appear as a defendant a judgment by default was entered against the state.

The decision aroused immediate and bitter opposition. The lower house of the Georgia legislature passed a bill to punish by hanging any person who should attempt to aid in enforcing the decree of the Court. Other states also protested, for upon the authority of the Court's decision suits were soon instituted against several other states. Within two days of the handing down of the decision in Chisholm v. Georgia, a constitutional amendment was introduced into Congress depriving the federal courts of all jurisdiction in cases brought against a state by the citizens of other states or of any foreign country. This was ratified in 1798 and became the Eleventh Amendment. In Hans v. Louisiana, 134 U. S. 1 (1890), the Supreme Court held that a state could not be sued by one of its own citizens; and in Monaco v. Mississippi, 292 U. S. 313 (1934), it held that a state may not be sued by a foreign state. These two cases rest on the doctrine that the right to sue a state without its consent exists only in those cases in which the Constitution plainly creates that right. Thus the Eleventh Amendment made it possible for any state of the Union, with perfect impunity so far as judicial interference was concerned, to repudiate its debts to individuals. A number of states have availed themselves of this dubious right, although none in recent years.

In the case of New Hampshire v. Louisiana (combined with New York

v. Louisiana) the two plaintiff states sought by appropriate bills in equity to compel the state of Louisiana to pay the interest on certain of its bonds —bonds which had been assigned by their owners to the states of New Hampshire and New York for collection. Under acts in New Hampshire in 1879 and in New York in 1880, any citizen of the state holding a valid claim against any other state of the Union, which claim was past due and unpaid, might assign in writing the claim in question to the state, the attorney general being thereupon authorized to bring suit against the defaulting state upon the bonds or claims and carry the case through to final judgment. The money thus recovered was then to be paid to the assignors after the expenses of the litigation had been deducted. In short, the state merely served as a collecting agency for the individual creditors. It was an attempt to defeat the purpose of the Eleventh Amendment by allowing the state to sue the defaulting state inasmuch as the individual creditor could not himself seek relief in court. It was upon the ground that the plan violated the spirit and purpose of the Eleventh Amendment that the Supreme Court dismissed these suits.

An interesting sequel to this case is that of South Dakota v. North Carolina, 192 U. S. 286, decided in 1904. In 1867 North Carolina had issued bonds to complete a railroad within the state, these bonds secured by mortgages of equivalent amounts on the stock owned by the state in another railway corporation. These bonds matured in 1897 and a substantial number of them remained unpaid. In 1901 ten of these were presented to the state of South Dakota as a gift by their owners. South Dakota thereupon brought suit in the Supreme Court against North Carolina, asking that North Carolina be required to pay the amounts due, or in case of default that the shares of railway stock upon the security of which the bonds had been issued be sold to satisfy the debt. Was this forbidden by the Eleventh Amendment as the earlier suits in New Hampshire and New York against Louisiana had been? The Court held that it was not. Here the plaintiff state was the actual owner of the bonds and was as much entitled to sue upon them as it would have been had South Dakota herself originally loaned the money in question. The fact that the bonds were donated to the state did not diminish the state's title to them. South Dakota was here suing in her own behalf and not, as had been true in the earlier cases discussed, merely on behalf of private creditors to whose claims the jurisdiction of the Court did not extend. The Supreme Court issued a decree ordering North Carolina to pay the amount due, and in the event of her failure to do so, ordered the sale of the shares of stock held as security. North Carolina after some delay paid the money due so that a forced sale of the bonds was not resorted to.

A later action brought by North Dakota against Minnesota sought the recovery of damages for injuries resulting from the overflow of certain streams caused by the straightening of certain rivers in Minnesota, and also an injunction against the continuance of the injury. The damages sought were in the amount of $5,000 for injury to the public property of the state and $1,000,000 in behalf of the inhabitants of the region affected. These injured persons had joined together and subscribed money to a fund to pay the expenses of the suit and the assurance had been given that they would share in the benefits of a judgment in proportion to the losses they had sustained. This action in behalf of its citizens the Supreme Court held could not properly be brought by the state of North Dakota, under the doctrine of New Hampshire v. Louisiana. See North Dakota v. Minnesota, 263 U. S. 365 (1923).

One of the most spectacular interstate disputes to reach the Supreme Court was the debt controversy between Virginia and West Virginia. When Virginia seceded from the Union at the outbreak of the Civil War the western counties of the state remained loyal, and in 1863 were admitted to the Union as the new State of West Virginia. At this time West Virginia agreed to "take upon itself a just proportion of the public debt of the Commonwealth of Virginia, prior to January 1, 1861." Beginning in 1865 Virginia sought by negotiation to secure from West Virginia the sums due, but West Virginia showed no disposition to pay. In 1906 Virginia filed in the Supreme Court the first of nine successive actions against West Virginia which comprise the judicial history of this dispute. In the more important of these the Supreme Court held that it had jurisdiction to settle the case, and that West Virginia, by 1915, owed Virginia some $12,000,000. West Virginia, defying the Supreme Court, still refused to pay the debt; and in 1918, in Virginia v. West Virginia, 246 U. S. 565, the Supreme Court had before it the demand of Virginia that the Court should enter an order directing the legislature of West Virginia to levy a tax to pay the judgment. The Court was obviously at a loss regarding how to proceed. It expressed the hope that West Virginia might without further legal action pay the debt. It suggested that Congress might possibly pass a law for the enforcement of the judgment. It concluded by setting the case for further argument at the next term of Court, with instructions that the argument deal with the specific means which could be used to enforce the judgment against West Virginia. At this juncture West Virginia saved the Court further embarrassment by providing, in 1919, for a bond issue whereby the debt would be paid off by 1939. The whole case exposes the fact that the Constitution provides no procedure for compelling a state to perform its legal obligations in a case of this kind.

Mr. Chief Justice Waite, in delivering the opinion of the Court, said in part:

. . . The first question we have to settle is whether, upon the facts shown, these suits can be maintained in this Court. . . .

[Here follows an account of the case of Chisholm v. Georgia and the subsequent adoption of the Eleventh Amendment.] That amendment is as follows: "The judicial power of the United States shall not be construed to extend to any suit in law or equity, commenced or prosecuted against one of the United States by citizens of another State, or by citizens and subjects of any foreign state."

Under the operation of this amendment the actual owners of the bonds and coupons held by New Hampshire and New York are precluded from prosecuting these suits in their own names. The real question, therefore, is whether they can sue in the name of their respective states after getting the consent of the state, or, to put it in another way, whether a state can allow the use of its name in such a suit for the benefit of one of its citizens.

The language of the amendment is, in effect, that the judicial power of the United States shall not extend to any suit commenced or prosecuted *by* citizens of one state against another state. No one can look at the pleadings and testimony in these cases without being satisfied, beyond all doubt, that they were in legal effect commenced and are now prosecuted solely by the owners of the bonds and coupons. In New Hampshire, before the attorney general is authorized to begin a suit, the owner of the bond must deposit with him a sum of money sufficient to pay all costs and expenses. No compromise can be effected except with the consent of the owner of the claim. No money of the state can be expended in the proceeding, but all expenses must be borne by the owner, who may associate with the attorney general such counsel as he chooses, the state being in no way responsible for fees. All moneys collected are to be kept by the attorney general, as special trustee, separate and apart from the other moneys of the state, and paid over by him to the owner of the claim, after deducting all expenses incurred, not before that time paid by the owner. The bill, although signed by the attorney general is also signed, and was evidently drawn, by the same counsel who prosecuted the suits for the bondholders in Louisiana, and it is manifested in many ways that both the state and the attorney general are only nominal actors in the proceeding. The bond-owner, whoever he may be, was the promoter and is the manager of the suit. He pays the expenses, is the only one authorized to conclude a compromise, and, if any money is ever collected, it must be paid to him without even passing through the form of getting into the treasury of the state.

In New York no special provision is made for compromise or the employment of additional counsel, but the bondholder is required to secure and pay all expenses and gets all the money that is recovered. This state as well as New Hampshire is nothing more nor less than a mere collecting agent of the owners of the bonds and coupons, and while the suits are in the names of the states, they are under the actual control of individual citizens, and are prosecuted and carried on altogether by and for them.

It is contended, however, that, notwithstanding the prohibition of the amendment, the states may prosecute the suits, because, as the "sovereign and trustee of its citizens," a state is "clothed with the right and faculty of making an imperative demand upon another independent state for the payment of debts which it owes to citizens of the former." There is no doubt but one nation may, if it sees fit, demand of another nation the payment of a debt owing by the latter to a citizen of the former. Such power is well recognized as an incident of national sovereignty, but it involves also the national powers of levying war and making treaties. As was said in U. S. v. Diekelman, 92 U. S. 524, if a sovereign assumes the responsibility of presenting the claim of one of his subjects against another sovereign, the prosecution will be "as one nation proceeds against another, not by suit in the courts, as of right, but by diplomatic negotiation, or, if need be, by war."

All the rights of the states, as independent nations, were surrendered to the United States. The states are not nations, either as between themselves or towards foreign nations. They are sovereign within their spheres, but their sovereignty stops short of nationality. Their political status at home and abroad is that of states in the United States. They can neither make war nor peace without the consent of the national government. Neither can they, except with like consent, "enter into any agreement or compact with another State." Article 1, section 10, clause 3.

But it is said that even if a state, as sovereign trustee for its citizens, did surrender to the national government its power of prosecuting the claims of its citizens against another state by force, it got in lieu the constitutional right of suit in the national courts. There is no principle of international law which makes it the duty of one nation to assume the collection of the claims of its citizens against another nation, if the citizens themselves have ample means of redress without the intervention of their government. Indeed, Sir Robert Phillimore says, in his Commentaries on International Law, vol. 2, (2d Ed.) p. 12: "As a general rule, the proposition of Martens seems to be correct, that the foreigner can only claim to be put on the same footing as the native creditor of the state." Whether this be in all respects true or not, it is clear that no nation ought to interfere, except under very extraordinary circumstances, if the citizens can themselves employ the identical and only remedy open to the government if it takes on itself the burden of the prosecution. Under the Constitution, as it was originally construed, a citizen of one state could sue another state in the courts of the United States for himself, and obtain the same relief his state could get for him if it should sue. Certainly, when he can sue for himself, there is no necessity for power in his state to sue in his behalf, and we cannot believe it was the intention of the framers of the Constitution to allow both remedies in such a case. Therefore, the special remedy, granted to the citizen himself, must be deemed to have been the only remedy the citizen of one state could have under the Constitution against another state for the redress of his grievances, except such as the delinquent state saw fit itself to grant. In other words, the giving of the direct remedy to the citizen himself was equivalent to taking away any indirect remedy he might otherwise have claimed, through the intervention of his state, upon any principle of the law of nations. It follows that when the amendment took away the special remedy there was no other left. Nothing was added to the Constitution by what was thus done. No power, taken away by the grant of the special remedy, was restored by the amendment. The effect of the amendment was simply to revoke the new right that had been given, and leave the limitations to stand as they were. In the argument of the opinions filed by the several justices in the Chisholm case, there is not even an intimation that if the citizen could not sue, his state could sue for him. The evident purpose of the amendment, so promptly proposed and finally adopted, was to prohibit all suits against a state by or for citizens of other states, or aliens, without the consent of the state to be sued, and, in our opinion, the one state cannot create a controversy with another state, within the meaning of that term as used in the judicial clauses of the Constitution, by assuming the prosecution of debts owing by the other state to its citizens. Such being the case, we are satisfied that we are prohibited, both by the letter and the spirit of the Constitution, from entertaining these suits and the bill in each of them is dismissed.

7

Powers of Congress—
Nature and Construction

UNITED STATES v. CURTISS-WRIGHT EXPORT CORPORATION
299 U. S. 304; 81 L. Ed. 255; 57 Sup. Ct. 216. 1936.

Throughout our constitutional history the courts have given the broadest and most liberal construction to the powers of Congress. Thus Congress has been held to possess not only those powers which are expressly delegated to it by the Constitution but such further authority as may be reasonably implied from those specific grants, with the term "reasonably" most generously interpreted. Congress derives power also from the grants of authority to the other departments of the government, as will be seen in the case of Missouri v. Holland (p. 369). Another group of cases holds that an "implied" power of Congress does not have to be derived from a single power specifically delegated by the Constitution, but may rest upon any combination of such powers taken together. Thus the power to condemn by eminent domain the land for the national cemetery at Gettysburg was sustained upon the theory that it could be implied from a group of federal powers combined. This has sometimes been called the theory of "resulting powers."

In what has been said so far there has been no suggestion that Congress could exercise any power which could not in some reasonable way be derived from the grants of authority enumerated in the Constitution. "Implied" and "resulting" powers must be implied, or must result, from something in the Constitution. Those who favor a powerful national government have occasionally advanced the doctrine that the federal government possesses not merely the delegated powers and those derived from them, but in addition such powers as are necessary to cope with any truly national problem, whether those powers are delegated or not. This is sometimes called the doctrine of inherent federal power. It has been attributed, somewhat dubiously, to James Wilson; but it received rebirth and wide publicity through the sponsorship of Theodore Roosevelt, who labeled it the "New Nationalism." He deplored the existence of a "twilight zone" between federal and state authority, within which large corporations might operate to the detriment of the general welfare free from the control of either government. During his second term this doctrine was urged upon the Supreme Court by the Attorney General in the case of Kansas v. Colorado, 206 U. S. 46 (1907), in which the federal government sought to intervene in the suit between the two states on the ground that since the reclamation project in controversy overlapped the jurisdiction of each state it must automatically fall within the scope of federal power. The Attorney General's theory was that the Constitution must be presumed to divide up all possible governmental power between the states and the national government. If, therefore, the states were unable because of limited jurisdiction to deal with a problem calling for public control, then the federal government must necessarily have power over it. Mr. Justice Brewer effectively repudiated the whole theory of inherent federal powers in the following paragraph:

"But the proposition that there are legislative powers affecting the nation as a whole which belong to, although not expressed in, the grant of powers, is in direct conflict with the doctrine that this is a government of enumerated powers. That this is such a government clearly appears from the Constitution, independently of the amendments, for otherwise there would be an instrument granting certain specified things made operative to grant other and distinct things. This natural construction of the original body of the Constitution is made absolutely certain by the Tenth Amendment. This amendment, which was seemingly adopted with prescience of just such contention as the present, disclosed the widespread fear that the national government might, under the pressure of a supposed general welfare, attempt to exercise powers which had not been granted. With equal determination the framers intended that no such assumption should ever find justification in the organic act, and that if in the future further powers seemed necessary they should be granted by the people in the manner they had provided for amending that act. It reads: 'The powers not delegated to the United States by the Constitution, nor prohibited by it to the states, are reserved to the states respectively, or to the people.' " In short, if a national problem emerges with which Congress under the Constitution has not delegated power to deal, the only way to meet the situation is to amend the Constitution and delegate the necessary power to Congress.

There is, however, one important exception to the basic principle just discussed. In a long line of decisions the Supreme Court has held that in conducting its relations with foreign nations the United States is a sovereign nation and must be held to possess with respect to foreign relations all the powers that other sovereign nations enjoy, and these powers are not limited to those which are delegated by the clauses of the Constitution. Thus, while the Constitution mentions none of these powers, Congress has been held to have the power to punish the counterfeiting in this country of foreign money or securities, to annex unoccupied territory, to set up judicial tribunals in foreign countries, and to exclude, deport, or regulate the admission of aliens.

This broad power of Congress in the field of foreign relations was upheld in the case of Fong Yue Ting v. United States, 149 U. S. 698 (1893), upholding the power of Congress to exclude or deport aliens. Fong Yue Ting was born in China and came to the United States prior to 1879, during a period when the United States and China had a treaty according the rights of domicile in this country to Chinese. In 1892 Congress passed a statute prohibiting further Chinese immigration and providing that all Chinese laborers who were entitled to remain in the country should apply to the proper authorities for a certificate of residence; if they failed to do this they were to be deemed unlawfully in the country and deported. Fong Yue Ting's failure to comply with the statute resulted in deportation proceedings against him, and in resisting such action he set up the unconstitutionality of the statute. The opinion of the Court sustaining the act is a clear exposition of the doctrine of the sovereign authority of Congress with respect to international affairs. The theory as laid down forms the constitutional basis of all our immigration legislation not resting upon treaty provisions.

In 1856 Congress passed an act authorizing the annexation of any unoccupied guano islands which might be discovered by any American citizen. Such an island was discovered in the Caribbean Sea in 1859, was annexed by proclamation, and criminal jurisdiction was extended over it by federal statute. In Jones v. United States, 137 U. S. 202 (1890), Jones, who had been convicted of the crime of murder committed on this island, contended that the statute authorizing the acquisition of the island was invalid and that the court therefore had no jurisdiction to try him. The Supreme Court upheld the statute on the ground that under the law of nations recognized by all civilized states, new territory may be acquired by discovery and occupation. This fact fully justified the legislation under which the island was annexed.

In the case printed below the Court re-examines and reaffirms the doctrine. In 1934 Congress passed a joint resolution providing that if the President finds that an embargo on the sale of arms and munitions in the United States to countries at war in the Chaco (Bolivia and Paraguay) "may contribute to the re-establishment of peace between those countries," he may, after consultation with other American republics, establish such an embargo by proclamation. Violation of such an embargo was made a crime. The President set up the embargo, and the defendant company was convicted of violating it by selling machine guns to Bolivia. The joint resolution clearly delegated legislative power to the President. In Schechter v. United States (p. 356), the Court had held the National Industrial Recovery Act void partly because it delegated legislative power to the President without a sufficiently clear and definite statement of legislative policy to guide the exercise of his discretion. The joint resolution did not restrict or direct the President's discretion in setting up the embargo. Was it also an unconstitutional delegation of legislative power? Does the rule against such delegation apply in the field of foreign affairs in the same way it applies to internal legislative policy?

Mr. Justice Sutherland delivered the opinion of the Court, saying in part:

. . . *First.* It is contended that by the joint resolution, the going into effect and continued operation of the resolution was conditioned (a) upon the President's judgment as to its beneficial effect upon the reestablishment of peace between the countries engaged in armed conflict in the Chaco; (b) upon the making of a proclamation, which was left to his unfettered discretion, thus constituting an attempted substitution of the President's will for that of Congress; (c) upon the making of a proclamation putting an end to the operation of the resolution, which again was left to the President's unfettered discretion; and (d) further, that the extent of its operation in particular cases was subject to limitation and exception by the President, controlled by no standard. In each of these particulars, appellees urge that Congress abdicated its essential functions and delegated them to the Executive.

Whether, if the joint resolution had related solely to internal affairs it would be open to the challenge that it constituted an unlawful delegation of legislative power to the Executive, we find it unnecessary to determine. The whole aim of the resolution is to affect a situation entirely external to the United States, and falling within the category of foreign affairs. The determination which we are called to make, therefore, is whether the joint resolution, as applied to that situation, is vulnerable to attack under the rule that forbids a delegation of the law-making power. In other words, assuming (but not deciding) that the challenged delegation, if it were confined to internal affairs, would be invalid, may it nevertheless be sustained on the ground that its exclusive aim is to afford a remedy for a hurtful condition within foreign territory?

It will contribute to the elucidation of the question if we first consider the differences between the powers of the federal government in respect of foreign or external affairs and those in respect of domestic or internal affairs. That there are differences between them, and that these differences are fundamental, may not be doubted.

The two classes of powers are different, both in respect of their origin and their nature. The broad statement that the federal government can exercise no powers except those specifically enumerated in the Constitution, and such implied powers as are necessary and proper to carry into effect the enumerated powers, is categorically true only in respect of our internal affairs. In that field, the primary purpose of the Constitution was to carve from the general mass of legislative powers *then possessed by the states* such portions as it was thought desirable to vest in the federal government, leaving those not included in the enumeration still in the states. . . . That this doctrine applies only to powers which the states had, is self evident. And since the states severally never possessed international powers, such powers could not have been carved from the mass of state powers but obviously were transmitted to the United States from some other source. . . .

It results that the investment of the federal government with the powers of external sovereignty did not depend upon the affirmative grants of the Constitution. The powers to declare and wage war, to conclude peace, to make treaties, to maintain diplomatic relations with other sovereignties, if they had never been mentioned in the Constitution, would have vested in the federal government as necessary concomitants of nationality. . . . As a member of the family of nations, the right and power of the United States in that field are equal to the right and power of the other members of the international family. Otherwise, the United States is not completely sovereign. The power to acquire territory by discovery and occupation (Jones v. United States, 137 U. S. 202), the power to expel undesirable aliens (Fong Yue Ting v. United States, 149 U. S. 698), the power to make such international agreements as do not constitute treaties in the constitutional sense (B. Altman & Co. v. United States, 224 U. S. 583), none of which is expressly affirmed by the Constitution, nevertheless exist as inherently inseparable from the conception of nationality. This the Court recognized, and in each of the cases cited found the warrant for its conclusions not in the provisions of the Constitution, but in the law of nations. . . .

Not only, as we have shown, is the federal power over external affairs in origin and essential character different from that over internal affairs, but participation in the exercise of the power is significantly limited. In this vast external realm, with its important, complicated, delicate and manifold problems, the President alone has the power to speak or listen as a representative of the nation. He *makes* treaties with the advice and consent of the Senate; but he alone negotiates. Into the field of negotiation the Senate cannot intrude; and Congress itself is powerless to invade it. As Marshall said in his great argument of March 7, 1800, in the House of Representatives, "The President is the sole organ of the nation in its external relations, and its sole representative with foreign nations." Annals, 6th Cong., col. 613. . . .

It is important to bear in mind that we are here dealing not alone with an authority vested in the President by an exertion of legislative power, but with such an authority plus the very delicate, plenary and exclusive power of the President as the sole organ of the federal government in the field of international relations—a power which does not require as a basis for its exercise an act of Congress, but which, of course, like every other governmental power, must be exercised in subordination to the applicable provisions of the Constitution. It is quite apparent that if, in the maintenance of our international relations, embarrassment—perhaps serious embarrassment—is to be avoided and success for our aims achieved, congressional legislation which is to be made effective through negotiation and inquiry within the international field must often accord to the President a degree of discretion and freedom from statutory restriction which would not be admissible were domestic affairs alone involved. Moreover, he, not Congress, has the better opportunity of knowing the conditions which prevail in foreign countries, and especially is this true in time of war. He has his confidential sources of information. He has his agents in the form of diplomatic, consular and other officials. Secrecy in respect of information gathered by them may be highly necessary, and the premature disclosure of it productive of harmful results. Indeed, so clearly is this true that the first President refused to accede to a request to lay before the House of Representatives the instructions, correspondence and documents relating to the negotiation of the Jay Treaty—a refusal the wisdom of which was recognized by the House itself and has never since been doubted. . . .

In the light of the foregoing observations, it is evident that this Court should not be in haste to apply a general rule which will have the effect of condemning legislation like that under review as constituting an unlawful delegation of legislative power. The principles which justify such legislation find overwhelming support in the unbroken legislative practice which has prevailed almost from the inception of the national government to the present day. . . .

The result of holding that the joint resolution here under attack is void and unenforceable as constituting an unlawful delegation of legislative power would be to stamp this multitude of comparable acts and resolutions as likewise invalid. And while this Court may not, and should not, hesitate to declare acts of Congress, however many times repeated, to be unconstitutional if beyond all rational doubt it finds them to be so, an impressive array of legislation such as we have just set forth, enacted by nearly every Congress from the beginning of our national existence to the present day, must be given unusual weight in the process of reaching a correct determination of the problem. A legislative practice such as we have here, evidenced not by only occasional instances, but marked by the movement of a steady stream for a century and a half of time, goes a long way in the direction of proving the presence of unassailable ground for the constitutionality of the practice, to be found in the origin and history of the power involved, or in its nature, or in both combined. . . .

The uniform, long-continued and undisputed legislative practice just disclosed rests upon an admissible view of the Constitution which, even if the practice found far less support in principle than we think it does, we should not feel at liberty at this late day to disturb.

We deem it unnecessary to consider, seriatim, the several clauses which are said to evidence the unconstitutionality of the joint resolution as involving an unlawful delegation of legislative power. It is enough to summarize by saying that, both upon principle and in accordance with precedent, we conclude there is sufficient warrant for the broad discretion vested in the President to determine whether the enforcement of the statute will have a beneficial effect upon the reestablishment of peace in the affected countries; whether he shall make proclamation to bring the resolution into operation; whether and when the resolution shall cease to operate and to make proclamation accordingly; and to prescribe limitations and exceptions to which the enforcement of the resolution shall be subject. . . .

Mr. Justice McReynolds dissented.

THE SOCIAL SECURITY ACT CASES: CHARLES C. STEWARD MACHINE CO. v. DAVIS
301 U. S. 548; 81 L. Ed. 1279; 57 Sup. Ct. 883. 1937.

Most of the decisions of the Supreme Court which held unconstitutional important segments of the early New Deal program, while they made first-page headlines at the time, are remembered now, if at all, chiefly as providing the impetus for President Roosevelt's ill-fated proposal in 1937 to enlarge the Supreme Court. Some of the New Deal problems have disappeared or have been dealt with in other ways; in some instances the Court, without outright reversals, has retreated from the doctrines it relied upon in those cases. These decisions, however, should not be entirely ignored.

An extremely important part of the Roosevelt recovery program was the "N.R.A.," the enormous administrative organization set up under the authority of the National Industrial Recovery Act. It sought to stimulate the volume of business and improve working conditions by raising wages, reducing hours, and eliminating child labor; to drive out unfair and destructive competitive practices; to conserve natural resources in certain basic commodities; and to relieve unemployment. This was to be accomplished by the establishment of "codes of fair competition" in the industries brought under the act. These codes were to be drawn up by representatives of the industries acting in close co-operation with government officials, and were to receive the final approval of the President who was charged by the law with seeing that certain minimum standards with respect to working conditions and freedom from monopoly were observed. Should an industry be unable to formulate a code for itself, the President might impose a code upon it. Within eighteen months codes were established in more than seven hundred industries. These codes were mandatory upon all those engaged in the industry, whether they had participated in their formation or not, and the provisions were enforceable both by criminal prosecution and by civil process. It was not until the National Industrial Recovery Act was almost on the point of expiring by limitation on June 16, 1935, that a decision on the validity of the statute was handed down by the Supreme Court. The government finally selected the Schechter case, arising under the poultry code, as the one on which to stake the constitutional fortunes of the

N.R.A. The act was held invalid in Schechter v. United States, 295 U. S. 495 (1935).

The first ground upon which the National Industrial Recovery Act was held void was that it delegated legislative power to the President and thereby violated the fundamental doctrine of the separation of powers. The Court had taken a very liberal attitude in the past with respect to this matter. Presidential or administrative rules and regulations designed to carry into effect the broad and general provisions of various statutes had been held valid on the ground that they were administrative measures for the effectuation of legislative policy. The President, in short, had been allowed very wide freedom in "filling in the details of legislation." Prior to the N.R.A. cases there had been no instance in which a delegation to the President of the power to issue administrative rules and regulations had been held void by the Court as an improper delegation of legislative power. But in January, 1935, the Court in Panama Refining Company v. Ryan, 293 U. S. 388, invalidated the oil control provisions of the National Industrial Recovery Act on the ground that they delegated legislative power to the President. This section of the N.I.R.A. had given to the President the power to forbid the transportation in interstate commerce of "hot oil" (oil produced or withdrawn from storage in violation of state law) but, as the Court pointed out, the statute did not contain any definition of the circumstances or conditions in which the transportation was to be permitted or prohibited. In other words, the power given to the President was purely discretionary. He was not merely filling in the details of a legislative policy, since no legislative policy was outlined to guide or control him.

In two later cases of importance the Court returned again to a much more liberal view as to how sharp and definite must be the legislative standards or criteria under which Congress may delegate legislative power to executive officers. These are United States v. Rock Royal Co-operative, 307 U. S. 533 (1939), and Hood & Sons v. United States, 307 U. S. 588 (1939), in which the Court upheld the Agricultural Marketing Agreement Act of 1937 against the charge, amongst others, that it invalidly delegated legislative power to the Secretary of Agriculture. The cases involved the Secretary's acts under the statute regulating the marketing of milk in the metropolitan areas of New York and Boston respectively. The broad powers given to the Secretary are restricted only by the following declaration of policy set out in the act: "to establish and maintain such orderly marketing conditions for agricultural commodities in interstate commerce as will establish prices to farmers at a level that will give agricultural commodities a purchasing power with respect to articles that farmers buy, equivalent to the purchasing power of agricultural commodities in the base period [1909 to 1914]." To effectuate this policy the Secretary is authorized to enter into marketing agreements with producers and handlers of agricultural products, to establish uniform prices to be paid by handlers of milk to producers, to set up equalization pools to stabilize prices received by producers, etc. A majority of the Court held that the basic policy of restoring "parity prices" was a definite enough guide to the Secretary's discretion to meet the charge of invalid delegation.

Similarly the Emergency Price Control Act of 1942 conferred broad powers upon the Office of Price Administration. It stated in detail the purposes of the act and directed the O.P.A. to fix prices which would tend to achieve those purposes, and which would be "fair and equitable." Also it was ordered "so far as practicable" to "give due consideration to the prices prevailing between October 1 and October 15, 1941." In Yakus v. United States, 321 U. S. 414 (1944), the Court, besides finding the act valid on other grounds, held that it did not invalidly delegate legislative power to the O.P.A.

The National Industrial Recovery Act was found invalid on the additional ground that it exceeded the proper range of the delegated powers of Congress by extending its requirements and prohibitions, through its codes, to business transactions essentially local in character and not, therefore, a part of interstate commerce. Without repudiating its previously broad interpretations of the commerce power, the Court held that since practically every business transaction may in some way or other affect interstate commerce the line must in concrete cases be drawn between those which "directly" and those which "indirectly" impinge upon such commerce. The power of Congress extends to the former but not to the latter, and most of the transactions covered by the N.R.A. codes fall in the "indirect" category.

It became clear, as the depression of the 30's continued, that the acute problems of unemployment and old-age relief could be adequately met, not by casual or emergency measures, but only by a permanent, constructive, and self-respecting policy grounded on the principles of insurance. Furthermore, national action was imperative. The whole problem received careful study. In 1935 the Social Security Act was passed. The act is an elaborate one. It lays a federal excise tax upon employers to secure funds for unemployment compensation. It lays federal taxes upon both employers and employees to finance a system of old-age benefits. It encourages state cooperation and participation in the social security program by an elaborate system of subsidies and credits (set out in the opinion below). It provides federal aid to dependent children, for maternal and child welfare, and public health. It creates an independent agency, the Social Security Board, to administer the act.

A few months after the act was passed the Supreme Court handed down a decision which appeared to jeopardize the social security program. This was the case of United States v. Butler, 297 U. S. 1 (1936), which held unconstitutional the Agricultural Adjustment Act of 1933 on grounds of far-reaching significance. The A.A.A. was one of the major parts of the New Deal recovery program. It undertook to restore the level of farm prices, and thus the purchasing power of the farmer. This was to be done by persuading the farmers to reduce their production of certain basic agricultural commodities enough to restore the pre-war market prices. Farmers who thus reduced their production were paid by the government enough to make up the difference. The money for these crop-reduction payments was raised by levying processing taxes on the industries which prepared farm products for the market. The program was voluntary in the sense that no farmer was compelled by law to reduce his crops. He was merely well paid if he did so. Butler and others paid the processing taxes under protest, and sued to get them back again on the ground that the A.A.A. was unconstitutional. The Court, with three justices dissenting, held the statute invalid. Three novel and important points were made in the majority opinion written by Mr. Justice Roberts. (1) For the first time the Court construed the "general welfare" clause of the Constitution and passed upon the scope of the power of Congress to spend money. The first of the powers granted to Congress by the Constitution (Art. I, sec. 8) is the power "to lay and collect taxes, duties, imposts and excises, to pay the debts and provide for the common defense and general welfare of the United States . . ." The Court declared that the phrase "general welfare" states the purpose for which money raised by federal taxation may be spent; and that to "provide for the general welfare" is not an independent grant of power, unconnected with taxation. However, the "general welfare" is not to be narrowly construed as including only objects or purposes falling squarely within the delegated powers of Congress; on the contrary, Congress may tax in order to raise money to be used in promoting a broad national public welfare. (2) Without deciding whether money appropriated for the purpose of aiding agriculture is used for this national general welfare, the Court held that the processing taxes were void because the money raised from them was to be used to finance a system of federal regulation of agriculture which lay outside the delegated powers of Congress. It will be seen that the invalidity of the processing taxes is sharply contrasted with the invalidity of the child labor tax. See Bailey v. Drexel Furniture Co. (p. 462). The child labor tax was a destructive levy designed to drive out of existence the thing taxed. It sought no revenue and was held to be not a tax but a penalty upon the employment of children. The processing taxes, on the other hand, were not destructive, nor even regulatory, in effect. Their sole purpose was to raise money, and lots of it. They brought in, as a matter of fact, over a billion dollars. But this money was to be used by Congress for a purpose which lay within the reserved powers of the states: namely, the regulation of agriculture. The statute therefore violated the Tenth Amendment. Thus the Court laid down the important doctrine that the purpose and scope of the delegated powers of Congress are impliedly limited by the existence of the reserved powers of the states, or, Congress may not use its delegated powers to accomplish legislative ends which fall within the reserved powers of the states. Professor E. S. Corwin has labeled this the doctrine of "dual federalism" (see his *Twilight of the Supreme Court*, Chapter I). (3) But did the A.A.A. "regulate" agriculture in any mandatory way? Did it not merely pay money to farmers who voluntarily agreed to reduce their crops? The Court held that the program was "coercive" in character because it offered to the farmer benefits so attractive that he could not afford to pass them up. It was clearly necessary to establish this point of "coercion" unless the Court's decision was to invalidate by inference most of the federal grant-in-aid legislation of the last seventy-five years. Congress has spent billions of dollars for the widest variety of purposes, and has frequently made its grant of money contingent upon the recipient's doing things which the federal government had no direct authority to command. However, these other federal subsidies were held by the Court not to be coercive.

It is difficult to see why the Social Security Act, held valid in the opinion printed below, is not just as vulnerable under the doctrine of "dual federalism" as was the A.A.A. The dissenting justices protested that it was, that federal money was spent under the act for purposes which lay outside the range of federal delegated powers. But in holding the act valid the Court neither applied the doctrine of "dual federalism" nor repudiated it. It merely ignored it, and rested its decision on the ground that the purposes of social security legislation fall well within the scope of the general national welfare. It should be noted that this change in judicial attitude on so important a point took place without any change in the membership of the Court.

The doctrine of "dual federalism" was, in fact, destined to be short-lived. Although the Court did not mention the Butler case by name it squarely overruled the doctrine of "dual federalism" in the Darby case (p. 413), in which it held the Fair Labor Standards Act valid, by declaring that the Tenth Amendment imposes no limitation upon the federal government in the exercise of its delegated powers. In 1945, the Court held in Cleveland v. United States, 323 U. S. 329, that Congress could validly condemn land and build low-cost housing under the United States Housing Act, since the purpose of the act was declared to be "to promote the general welfare of the nation by employing . . . funds and credit to assist the states and their political subdivisions to relieve unemployment and safeguard the health, safety and morals of the Nation's citizens by improving housing conditions."

Helvering v. Davis, 301 U. S. 619 (1937), upheld the old-age benefits provisions of the Social Security Act. Mr. Justice Cardozo emphasized that Congress may validly spend money "in aid of the general welfare," and that to provide economic security for the aged is to promote such welfare. The opinion relied in the main upon that in the Steward Machine Company case, below. Justices McReynolds and Butler dissented, alleging that the old-age benefits provisions violate the Tenth Amendment.

Mr. Justice Cardozo delivered the Court's opinion, saying in part:

. . . The Social Security Act (Act of August 14, 1935) is divided into eleven separate titles, of which only titles IX and III are so related to this case as to stand in need of summary.

The caption of title IX is "Tax on Employers of Eight or More." Every employer (with stated exceptions) is to pay for each calendar year "an excise tax, with respect to having individuals in his employ," the tax to be measured by prescribed percentages of the total wages payable by the employer during the calendar year with respect to such employment. One is not, however, an "employer" within the meaning of the act unless he employs eight persons or more. There are also other limitations of minor importance. The term "employment" too has its special definition, excluding agricultural labor, domestic service in a private home and some other smaller classes. The tax begins with the year 1936, and is payable for the first time on January 31, 1937. During the calendar year 1936 the rate is to be one per cent, during 1937 two per cent, and three per cent thereafter. The proceeds, when collected, go into the Treasury of the United States like internal-revenue collections generally. They are not earmarked in any way. In certain circumstances, however, credits are allowable. If the taxpayer has made contributions to an unemployment fund under a state law, he may credit such contributions against the federal tax, provided, however, that the total credit allowed to any taxpayer shall not exceed 90 per centum of the tax against which it is credited, and provided also that the state law shall have been certified to the Secretary of the Treasury by the Social Security Board as satisfying certain minimum criteria. . . . Some of the conditions thus attached to the allowance of a credit are designed to give assurance that the state unemployment compensation law shall be one in substance as well as name. Others are designed to give assurance that the contributions shall be protected against loss after payment to the state. To this last end there are provisions that before a state law shall have the approval of the board it must direct that the contributions to the state fund be paid over immediately to the Secretary of the Treasury to the credit of the "Unemployment Trust Fund." For the moment it is enough to say that the fund is to be held by the Secretary of the Treasury, who is to invest in government securities any portion not required in his judgment to meet current withdrawals. He is authorized and directed to pay out of the fund to any competent state agency such sums as it may duly requisition from the amount standing to its credit.

Title III, which is also challenged as invalid, has the caption "Grants to States for Unemployment Compensation Administration." Under this title, certain sums of money are "authorized to be appropriated" for the purpose of assisting the states in the administration of their unemployment compensation laws, the maximum for the fiscal year ending June 30, 1936 to be $4,000,000, and $49,000,000 for each fiscal year thereafter. No present appropriation is made to the extent of a single dollar. All that the title does is to authorize future appropriations. The appropriations when made were not specifically out of the proceeds of the employment tax, but out of any moneys in the Treasury. Other sections of the title . . . are designed to give assurance to the federal government that the moneys granted by it will not be expended for purposes alien to the grant, and will be used in the administration of genuine unemployment compensation laws.

The assault on the statute proceeds on an extended front. Its assailants take the ground that the tax is not an excise; that it is not uniform throughout the United States as excises are required to be; that its exceptions are so many and arbitrary as to violate the Fifth Amendment; that its purpose was not revenue, but an unlawful invasion of the reserved powers of the states; and that the states in submitting to it have yielded to coercion and have abandoned governmental functions which they are not permitted to surrender.

The objections will be considered seriatim with such further explanation as may be necessary to make their meaning clear.

First: The tax, which is described in the statute as an excise, is laid with uniformity throughout the United States as a duty, an impost or an excise upon the relation of employment.

1. We are told that the relation of employment is one so essential to the pursuit of happiness that it may not be burdened with a tax. Appeal is made to history. From the precedents of colonial days we are supplied with illustrations of excises common in the colonies. They are said to have been bound up with the enjoyment of particular commodities. Appeal is also made to principle or the analysis of concepts. An excise, we are told, imports a tax upon a privilege; employment, it is said, is a right, not a privilege, from which it follows that employment is not subject to an excise. Neither the one appeal nor the other leads to the desired goal.

As to the argument from history: Doubtless there were many excises in colonial days and later that were associated, more or less intimately, with the enjoyment or the use of property. This would not prove, even if no others were then known, that the forms then accepted were not subject to enlargement. . . . But in truth other excises *were* known, and known since early times. . . . [Here follow examples of colonial taxes upon the employment of servants, workmen, and the like.]

The historical prop failing, the prop or fancied prop of principle remains. We learn that employment for lawful gain is a "natural" or "inherent" or "inalienable" right, and not a "privilege" at all. But natural rights, so called, are as much subject to taxation as rights of less importance. An excise is not limited to vocations or activities that may be prohibited altogether. It is not limited to those that are the outcome of a franchise. It extends to vocations or activities pursued as of common right. What the individual does in the operation of a business is amenable to taxation just as much as what he owns, at all events if the classification is not tyrannical or arbitrary. "Business is as legitimate an object of the taxing powers as property." . . .

. . . The statute books of the states are strewn with illustrations of taxes laid on occupations pursued of common right. We find no basis for a holding that the power in that regard which belongs by accepted practice to the legislatures of the states, has been denied by the Constitution to the Congress of the nation.

2. The tax being an excise, its imposition must conform to the canon of uniformity. There has been no departure from this requirement. According to the settled doctrine the uniformity exacted is geographical, not intrinsic. . . .

Second: The excise is not invalid under the provisions of the Fifth Amendment by force of its exemptions.

The statute does not apply, as we have seen, to employers of less than eight. It does not apply to agricultural labor, or domestic service in a private home or to some other classes of less importance. Petitioner contends that the effect of these restrictions is an arbitrary discrimination vitiating the tax.

The Fifth Amendment unlike the Fourteenth has no equal protection clause. . . . But even the states, though subject to such a clause, are not confined to a formula of rigid uniformity in framing measures of taxation. . . . They may tax some kinds of property at one rate, and others at another, and exempt others altogether. . . . They may lay an excise on the operations of a particular kind of business, and exempt some other kind of business closely akin thereto. . . . If this latitude of judgment is lawful for the states, it is lawful, a fortiori, in legislation by the Congress, which is subject to restraints less narrow and confining. . . .

The classifications and exemptions directed by the statute now in controversy have support in considerations of policy and practical convenience that cannot be condemned as arbitrary. The classifications and exemptions would therefore be upheld if they had been adopted by a state and the provisions of the Fourteenth Amendment were invoked to annul them. . . . The act of Congress is therefore valid, so far at least as its system of exemptions is concerned, and this though we assume that discrimination, if gross enough, is equivalent to confiscation and subject under the Fifth Amendment to challenge and annulment.

Third: The excise is not void as involving the coercion of the states in contravention of the Tenth Amendment or of restrictions implicit in our federal form of government.

The proceeds of the excise when collected are paid into the Treasury at Washington, and thereafter are subject to appropriation like public moneys generally. . . . No presumption can be indulged that they will be misapplied or wasted. Even if they were collected in the hope or expectation that some other and collateral good would be furthered as an incident, that without more would not make the act invalid. . . . This indeed is hardly questioned. The case for the petitioner is built on the contention that here an ulterior aim is wrought into the very structure of the act, and what is even more important that the aim is not wholly ulterior, but essentially unlawful. In particular, the 90 per cent credit is relied upon as supporting that conclusion. But before the statute succumbs to an assault upon these lines, two propositions must be made out by the assailant. . . . There must be a showing in the first place that separated from the credit the revenue provisions are incapable of standing by themselves. There must be a showing in the second place that the tax and the credit in combination are weapons of coercion, destroying or impairing the autonomy of the states. The truth of each proposition being essential to the success of the assault, we pass for convenience to a consideration of the second, without pausing to inquire whether there has been a demonstration of the first.

To draw the line intelligently between duress and inducement there is need to remind ourselves of facts as to the problem of unemployment that are now matters of common knowledge. . . . The relevant statistics are gathered in the brief of counsel for the government. Of the many available figures a few only will be mentioned. During the years 1929 to 1936, when the country was passing through a cyclical depression, the number of the unemployed mounted to unprecedented heights. Often the average was more than 10 million; at times a peak was attained of 16 million or more. Disaster to the breadwinner meant disaster to dependents. Accordingly the roll of the unemployed, itself formidable enough, was only a partial roll of the destitute or needy. The fact developed quickly that the states were unable to give the requisite relief. The problem had become national in area and dimensions. There was need of help from the nation if the people were not to starve. It is too late today for the argument to be heard with tolerance that in a crisis so extreme the use of the moneys of the nation to relieve the unemployed and their dependents is a use for any purpose narrower than the promotion of the general welfare. . . . [Federal appropriations for unemployment relief are here summarized.]

In the presence of this urgent need for some remedial expedient, the question is to be answered whether the expedient adopted has overleapt the bounds of power. The assailants of the statute say that its dominant end and aim is to drive the state legislatures under the whip of economic pressure into the enactment of unemployment compensation laws at the bidding of the central government. Supporters of the statute say that its operation is not constraint, but the creation of a larger freedom, the states and the nation joining in a cooperative endeavor to avert a common evil. . . .

The Social Security Act is an attempt to find a method by which all these public agencies may work together to a common end. Every dollar of the new taxes will continue in all likelihood to be used and needed by the nation as long as states are unwilling, whether through timidity or for other motives, to do what can be done at home. At least the inference is permissible that Congress so believed, though retaining undiminished freedom to spend the money as it pleased. On the other hand fulfillment of the home duty will be lightened and encouraged by crediting the taxpayer upon his account with the Treasury of the nation to the extent that his contributions under the laws of the locality have simplified or diminished the problem of relief and the probable demand upon the resources of the fisc. Duplicated taxes, or burdens that approach them, are recognized hardships that government, state or national, may properly avoid. . . . If Congress believed that the general welfare would better be promoted by relief through local units than by the system then in vogue, the cooperating localities ought not in all fairness to pay a second time.

Who then is coerced through the operation of this statute? Not the taxpayer. He pays in fulfillment of the mandate of the local legislature. Not the state. Even now she does not offer a suggestion that in passing the unemployment law she was affected by duress. . . . For all that appears she is satisfied with her choice, and would be sorely disappointed if it were now to be annulled. The difficulty with the petitioner's contention is that it confuses motive with coercion. "Every tax is in some measure regulatory. To some extent it interposes an economic impediment to the activity taxed as compared with others not taxed." . . . In like manner every rebate from a tax when conditioned upon conduct is in some measure a temptation. But to hold that motive or temptation is equivalent to coercion is to plunge the law in endless difficulties. The outcome of such a doctrine is the acceptance of a philosophical determinism by which choice becomes impossible. Till now the law has been guided by a robust common sense which assumes the freedom of the will as a working hypothesis in the solution of its problems. The wisdom of the hypothesis has illustration in this case. Nothing in the case suggests the exertion of a power akin to undue influence, if we assume that such a concept can ever be applied with fitness to the relations between state and nation. Even on that assumption the location of the point at which pressure turns into compulsion, and ceases to be inducement, would be a question of degree, —at times, perhaps, of fact. The point had not been reached when Alabama made her choice. We cannot say that she was acting, not of her unfettered will, but under the strain of a persuasion equivalent to undue influence, when she chose to have relief administered under laws of her own making, by agents of her own selection, instead of under federal laws, administered by federal officers, with all the ensuing evils, at least to many minds, of federal patronage and power. There would be a strange irony, indeed, if her choice were now to be annulled on the basis of an assumed duress in the enactment of a statute which her courts have accepted as a true expression of her will. . . . We think the choice must stand.

In ruling as we do, we leave many questions open. We do not say that a tax is valid, when imposed by an act of Congress, if it is laid upon the condition that a state may escape its operation through the adoption of a statute unrelated in subject matter to activities fairly within the scope of national policy and power. No such question is before us. In the tender of this credit Congress does not intrude upon fields foreign to its function. . . .

United States v. Butler, 297 U. S. 1, is cited by petitioner as a decision to the contrary. There a tax was imposed on processors of farm products, the proceeds to be paid to farmers who would reduce their acreage and crops under agreements with the Secretary of Agriculture, the plan of the act being to increase the prices of certain farm products by decreasing the quantities produced. The Court held (1) that the so-called tax was not a true one, the proceeds being earmarked for the benefit of farmers complying with the prescribed conditions, (2) that there was an attempt to regulate production without the consent of the state in which production was affected, and (3) that the payments to farmers were coupled with coercive contracts, unlawful in their aim and oppressive in their consequences. The decision was by a divided Court, a minority taking the view that the objections were untenable. None of them is applicable to the situation here developed.

(a) The proceeds of the tax in controversy are not earmarked for a special group.

(b) The unemployment compensation law which is a condition of the credit has had the approval of the state and could not be a law without it.

(c) The condition is not linked to an irrevocable agreement, for the state at its pleasure may repeal its unemployment law, terminate the credit, and place itself where it was before the credit was accepted.

(d) The condition is not directed to the attainment of an unlawful end, but to an end, the relief of unemployment, for which nation and state may lawfully cooperate.

Fourth: The statute does not call for a surrender by the states of powers essential to their quasi-sovereign existence.

Argument to the contrary has its source in two sections of the act. One section defines the minimum criteria to which a state compensation system is required to conform if it is to be accepted by the [Social Security] Board as the basis for a credit. The other section rounds out the requirement with complementary rights and duties. Not all the criteria or their incidents are challenged as unlawful. We will speak of them first generally, and then more specifically in so far as they are questioned.

A credit to taxpayers for payments made to a state under a state unemployment law will be manifestly futile in the absence of some assurance that the law leading to the credit is in truth what it professes to be. An unemployment law framed in such a way that the unemployed who look to it will be deprived of reasonable protection is one in name and nothing more. What is basic and essential may be assured by suitable conditions. The terms embodied in these sections are directed to that end. A wide range of judgment is given to the several states as to the particular type of statute to be spread upon their books. . . . What they may not do, if they would earn the credit, is to depart from those standards which in the judgment of Congress are to be ranked as fundamental. Even if opinion may differ as to the fundamental quality of one or more of the conditions, the difference will not avail to vitiate the statute. In determining essentials Congress must have the benefit of a fair margin of discretion. One cannot say with reason that this margin has been exceeded, or that the basic standards have been determined in any arbitrary fashion. In the event that some particular condition shall be found to be too uncertain to be capable of enforcement, it may be severed from the others, and what is left will still be valid.

We are to keep in mind steadily that the conditions to be approved by the board as the basis for a credit are not provisions of a contract, but terms of a statute, which may be altered or repealed. The state does not bind itself to keep the law in force. It does not even bind itself that the moneys paid into the federal fund will be kept there indefinitely or for any stated time. On the contrary, the Secretary of the Treasury will honor a requisition for the whole or any part of the deposit in the fund whenever one is made by the appropriate officials. The only consequence of the repeal or excessive amendment of the statute, or the expenditure of the money, when requisitioned, for other than compensation uses or administrative expenses, is that approval of the law will end, and with it the allowance of a credit, upon notice to the state agency and an opportunity for hearing.

These basic considerations are in truth a solvent of the problem. Subjected to their test, the several objections on the score of abdication are found to be unreal.

Thus, the argument is made that by force of an agreement the moneys when withdrawn must be "paid through public employment offices in the state or through such other agencies as the board may approve." But in truth there is no agreement as to the method of disbursement. There is only a condition which the state is free at pleasure to disregard or to fulfill. Moreover, approval is not requisite if public employment offices are made the disbursing instruments. Approval is to be a check upon resort to "other agencies" that may, perchance, be irresponsible. A state looking for a credit must give assurance that her system has been organized upon a base of rationality.

There is argument again that the moneys when withdrawn are to be devoted to specific uses, the relief of unemployment, and that by agreement for such payment the quasi-sovereign position of the state has been impaired, if not abandoned. But again there is confusion between promise and condition. Alabama is still free, without breach of an agreement, to change her system over night. No officer or agency of the national government can force a compensation law upon her or keep it in existence. No officer or agency of that government, either by suit or other means, can supervise or control the application of the payments.

Finally and chiefly, abdication is supposed to follow from § 904 of the statute and the parts of § 903 that are complementary thereto. By these the Secretary of the Treasury is authorized and directed to receive and hold in the Unemployment Trust Fund all moneys deposited therein by a state agency for a state unemployment fund and to invest in obligations of the United States such portion of the fund as is not in his judgment required to meet current withdrawals. We are told that Alabama in consenting to that deposit has renounced the plenitude of power inherent in her statehood.

The same pervasive misconception is in evidence again. All that the state has done is to say in effect through the enactment of a statute that her agents shall be authorized to deposit the unemployment tax receipts in the Treasury at Washington. . . . The statute may be repealed. The consent may be revoked. The deposits may be withdrawn. The moment the state commission gives notice to the depositary that it would like the moneys back, the Treasurer will return them. To find state destruction there is to find it almost anywhere. With nearly as much reason one might say that a state abdicates its functions when it places the state moneys on deposit in a national bank. . . .

The inference of abdication thus dissolves in thinnest air when the deposit is conceived of as dependent upon a statutory consent, and not upon a contract effective to create a duty. By this we do not intimate that the conclusion would be different if a contract were discovered. Even sovereigns may contract without derogating from their sovereignty. . . . The states are at liberty, upon obtaining the consent of Congress, to make agreements with one another. . . . We find no room for doubt that they may do the like with Congress if the essence of their statehood is maintained without impairment. Alabama is seeking and obtaining a credit of many millions in favor of her citizens out of the Treasury of the nation. Nowhere in our scheme of government— in the limitations express or implied of our federal Constitution—do we find that she is prohibited from assenting to conditions that will assure a fair and just requital for benefits received. . . .

The judgment is affirmed.

Justices McReynolds, Sutherland, Van Devanter, and Butler dissented.

MISSOURI v. HOLLAND
252 U. S. 416; 64 L. Ed. 641; 40 Sup. Ct. 382. 1920.

In discussing the implied powers of Congress it is important to bear in mind that they may be derived not merely from the specific grants of power to Congress but also from the clause of the Constitution which authorizes Congress "to make all laws which shall be necessary and proper for carrying into execution the foregoing powers, *and all other powers vested by this Constitution in the government of the United States, or in any department or officer thereof.*" Among these "other powers" vested in the departments or officers of the government is the treaty-making power, which resides in the President and Senate. Thus Congress may derive legislative authority from the power to carry out the provisions of a treaty when it could not derive it from any of the specific grants of legislative power enumerated in Article. 1.

This point is clearly emphasized by the judicial history of the two migratory birds acts passed by Congress. In 1913 Congress passed an act forbidding save under strict regulations the killing of migratory birds. The control of bird life is not one of the powers which the Constitution grants to Congress, and two lower federal courts held the law unconstitutional: United States v. Shauver, 214 Fed. 154 (1914), and United States v. McCullagh, 221 Fed. 288 (1915). These cases have been generally regarded as correct.

In 1916 we entered into a treaty with Great Britain by the terms of which the United States and Canada agreed to protect migratory birds, and propose legislation for that purpose. In 1918 Congress passed such a law, much more elaborate than the act of 1913, forbidding the killing, capturing, or selling of the birds included within the provisions of the treaty except in accordance with regulations set by the Secretary of Agriculture. The Secretary of Agriculture promulgated suitable regulations, and the state of Missouri, on the ground that her reserved powers were invaded by the act, brought action to enjoin a game warden of the United States from enforcing the provisions of the act and the rules established by the Secretary of Agriculture. The decision of the Court makes it clear that Congress may regulate bird life as a means of carrying into effect the provisions of a treaty when it could not regulate it as an independent exercise of legislative power.

A treaty or executive agreement may not, however, violate a provision of the Constitution. The Reid v. Covert decision of 1957 (p. 91) held that our Status of Forces Agreements (executive agreements) could not validly authorize the trial by court-martial of civilian dependents of American soldiers overseas, since the Constitution guarantees them trial by jury.

Mr. Justice Holmes delivered the opinion of the Court, saying in part:

. . . as we have said, the question raised is the general one whether the treaty and statute are void as an interference with the rights reserved to the states.

To answer this question it is not enough to refer to the Tenth Amendment, reserving the powers not delegated to the United States, because by Article II, section 2, the power to make treaties is delegated expressly, and by Article VI, treaties made under the authority of the United States, along with the Constitution and laws of the United States, made in pursuance thereof, are declared the supreme law of the land. If the treaty is valid, there can be no dispute about the validity of the statute under Article I, section 8, as a necessary and proper means to execute the powers of the government. The language of the Constitution as to the supremacy of treaties being general, the question before us is narrowed to an inquiry into the ground upon which the present supposed exception is placed.

It is said that a treaty cannot be valid if it infringes the Constitution, that there are limits, therefore, to the treaty-making power, and that one such limit is that what an act of Congress could not do unaided, in derogation of the powers reserved to the states, a treaty cannot do. An earlier act of Congress that attempted by itself and not in pursuance of a treaty to regulate the killing of migratory birds within the states had been held bad in the district court.

United States v. Shauver, 214 Fed. 154; United States v. McCullagh, 221 Fed. 288. Those decisions were supported by arguments that migratory birds were owned by the states in their sovereign capacity for the benefit of their people, and that under cases like Geer v. Connecticut, 161 U. S. 519, this control was one that Congress had no power to displace. The same argument is supposed to apply now with equal force.

Whether the two cases cited were decided rightly or not, they cannot be accepted as a test of the treaty power. Acts of Congress are the supreme law of the land only when made in pursuance of the Constitution, while treaties are declared to be so when made under the authority of the United States. It is open to question whether the authority of the United States means more than the formal acts prescribed to make the convention. We do not mean to imply that there are no qualifications to the treaty-making power; but they must be ascertained in a different way. It is obvious that there may be matters of the sharpest exigency for the national well-being that an act of Congress could not deal with, but that a treaty followed by such an act could, and it is not lightly to be assumed that, in matters requiring national action, "a power which must belong to and somewhere reside in every civilized government" is not to be found. . . . We are not yet discussing the particular case before us, but only are considering the validity of the test proposed. With regard to that, we may add that when we are dealing with words that also are a constituent act, like the Constitution of the United States, we must realize that they have called into life a being the development of which could not have been foreseen completely by the most gifted of its begetters. It was enough for them to realize or to hope that they had created an organism; it has taken a century and has cost their successors much sweat and blood to prove that they created a nation. The case before us must be considered in the light of our whole experience, and not merely in that of what was said a hundred years ago. The treaty in question does not contravene any prohibitory words to be found in the Constitution. The only question is whether it is forbidden by some invisible radiation from the general terms of the Tenth Amendment. We must consider what this country has become in deciding what that amendment has reserved.

The state, as we have intimated, founds its claim of exclusive authority upon an assertion of title to migratory birds,—an assertion that is embodied in statute. No doubt it is true that, as between a state and its inhabitants, the state may regulate the killing and sale of such birds, but it does not follow that its authority is exclusive of paramount powers. To put the claim of the state upon title is to lean upon a slender reed. Wild birds are not in the possession of anyone; and possession is the beginning of ownership. The whole foundation of the state's rights is the presence within their jurisdiction of birds that yesterday had not arrived, to-morrow may be in another state, and in a week a thousand miles away. If we are to be accurate, we cannot put the case of the state upon higher ground than that the treaty deals with creatures that for the moment are within the state borders, that it must be carried out by officers of the United States within the same territory, and that, but for the treaty, the state would be free to regulate this subject itself.

As most of the laws of the United States are carried out within the states, and as many of them deal with matters which, in the silence of such laws, the state might regulate, such general grounds are not enough to support Missouri's claim. Valid treaties, of course, "are as binding within the territorial limits of the states as they are elsewhere throughout the dominion of the United States.". . . No doubt the great body of private relations usually fall within the control of the state, but a treaty may override its power. . . .

Here a national interest of very nearly the first magnitude is involved. It can be protected only by national action in concert with that of another power. The subject-matter is only transitorily within the state, and has no permanent habitat therein. But for the treaty and the statute, there soon might be no birds for any powers to deal with. We see nothing in the Constitution that compels the government to sit by while a food supply is cut off and the protectors of our forests and our crops are destroyed. It is not sufficient to rely upon the states. The reliance is vain, and were it otherwise, the question is whether the United States is forbidden to act. We are of the opinion that the treaty and statute must be upheld. . . .

Mr. Justice Van Devanter and Mr. Justice Pitney dissent.

WOODS v. MILLER

333 U. S. 138; 92 L. Ed. 596; 68 Sup. Ct. 421. 1948.

The Constitution gives Congress the power to declare war, and to raise and support armies. The war power which has developed from these simple grants staggers the imagination by its scope and variety. This is because, as the late Chief Justice Hughes once said, "the power to wage war is the power to wage war successfully." In short, what is necessary to win the war Congress may do, and the Supreme Court has shown no inclination to hold void new and drastic war measures. In World War II the war power was invoked to fix price ceilings, to ration food and fuel, to commandeer factories, and to direct the production, distribution, and consumption of commodities. Our entire economy was mobilized for the war effort. A number of specific war powers exercised by Congress have been challenged in the courts, but in every case unsuccessfully.

The power of Congress to draft men into the armed services was attacked during World War I, although the draft had been resorted to sporadically and inefficiently during the Civil War. In 1917 Congress passed the Selective Draft Act which made all male citizens between the ages of 21 and 30 subject to national military service. Public officers, ministers of religion, and theological students were exempt from the draft, while conscientious objectors on religious grounds were permitted to engage in non-combatant duty. In Selective Draft Law Cases (Arver v. United States, 245 U. S. 366, 1918), the Supreme Court unanimously held the act valid. The power to compel men to serve in the armed forces is reasonably implied from the power to raise and support armies, for a grant of power with no compulsion behind it is no power at all. The exemption of ministers and theological students is not an "establishment of religion" forbidden by the First Amendment; nor does compulsory military service constitute "involuntary servitude" forbidden by the Thirteenth Amendment.

During World War I, Congress passed a limited type of rent control act applicable to the District of Columbia. It forbade a landlord to evict a tenant at the expiration of his lease if the latter wished to remain and continued to pay the former rent and observed the other conditions of the lease. In Block v. Hirsh, 256 U. S. 135 (1921), the Supreme Court held that the housing emergency growing out of the war justified the exercise of this power. In World War II, Congress resorted to rent and price controls in earnest. The Emergency Price Control Act of 1942 gave the Administrator of the Office of Price Administration (OPA) broad authority to fix maximum prices on most commodities and on residential rents. The act created a special Emergency Court of Appeals, manned by federal judges designated by the Chief Justice of the United States, to pass upon the validity of OPA regulations. In Yakus v. United States, 321 U. S. 414 (1944), the Court held valid the price-fixing provisions of the statute, while in Bowles v. Willingham, 321 U. S. 503 (1944), it upheld the rent-control sections of the act. It is interesting to note that in these two cases there was no frontal attack upon the power of Congress to control rents and prices under its war power. The act was challenged upon the ground that it invalidly delegated legislative power to the OPA Administrator, and that it did not provide fair procedure for the review of the rights of those subject to the act. In Steuart & Bros. Inc. v. Bowles, 322 U. S. 398 (1944), the Court held that the Second War Powers Act of 1942, which authorized the rationing of materials and commodities, empowered the President through the OPA to withhold rationed goods from those who acquired or distributed them in violation of ration regulations. Here again the power of Congress to authorize rationing was taken for granted.

In Woods v. Miller, below, the issue is not whether the war power of Congress validly supports rent control, but whether it can keep on supporting it after hostilities have ended. On December 31, 1946, President Truman issued a proclamation declaring the termination of hostilities. Congress itself, however, had passed no act or resolution declaring the war to be ended. On June 30, 1947, Congress enacted the Housing and Rent Act, effective on July 1, 1947, continuing in force the rent-control provisions of the Emergency Price Control Act of 1942. Does the war power continue after the fighting is over? More important still, does it continue, as the Court intimates, as long as problems generated by the war still face us?

Mr. Justice Douglas delivered the opinion of the Court, saying in part:

The case is here on a direct appeal . . . from a judgment of the District Court holding unconstitutional Title II of the Housing and Rent Act of 1947.

The act became effective on July 1, 1947, and the following day the appellee demanded of its tenants increases of 40% and 60% for rental accommodations in the Cleveland Defense-Rental Area, an admitted violation of the act and regulations adopted pursuant thereto. . . .

The District Court was of the view that the authority of Congress to regulate rents by virtue of the war power . . . ended with the Presidential Proclamation terminating hostilities on December 31, 1946, since that proclamation inaugurated "peace-in-fact" though it did not mark termination of the war. It also concluded that, even if the war power continues, Congress did not act under it because it did not say so, and only if Congress says so, or enacts provisions so implying, can it be held that Congress intended to exercise such power. That Congress did not so intend, said the District Court, follows from the provision that the Housing Expediter can end controls in any area without regard to the official termination of the war, and from the fact that the preceding federal rent control laws (which were concededly exercises of the war power) were neither amended nor extended. The District Court expressed the further view that rent control is not within the war power because "the emergency created by housing shortage came into existence long before the war.". . .

We conclude, in the first place, that the war power sustains this legislation. The Court said in Hamilton v. Kentucky Distilleries Co., 251 U. S. 146, that the war power includes the power "to remedy the evils which have arisen from its rise and progress" and continues for the duration of that emergency. Whatever may be the consequences when war is officially terminated, the war power does not necessarily end with the cessation of hostilities. We recently held that it is adequate to support the preservation of rights created by wartime legislation, Fleming v. Mohawk Wrecking & Lumber Co., 331 U. S. 111. But it has a broader sweep. In Hamilton v. Kentucky Distilleries Co., and Ruppert v. Caffey, 251 U. S. 264, prohibition laws which were enacted after the Armistice in World War I were sustained as exercises of the war power because they conserved manpower and increased efficiency of production in the critical days during the period of demobilization, and helped to husband the supply of grains and cereals depleted by the war effort. . . .

The constitutional validity of the present legislation follows *a fortiori* from those cases. The legislative history of the present Act makes abundantly clear that there has not yet been eliminated the deficit in housing which in considerable measure was caused by the heavy demobilization of veterans and by the cessation or reduction in residential construction during the period of hostilities due to the allocation of building materials to military projects. Since the war effort contributed heavily to that deficit, Congress has the power even after the cessation of hostilities to act to control the forces that a short supply of the needed article created. If that were not true, the Necessary and Proper Clause, Art. I, sec. 8, cl. 18, would be drastically limited in its application to the several war powers. The Court has declined to follow that course in the past. . . . We decline to take it today. The result would be paralyzing. It would render Congress powerless to remedy conditions the creation of which necessarily followed from the mobilization of men and materials for successful prosecution of the war. So to read the Constitution would be to make it self-defeating.

We recognize the force of the argument that the effects of war under modern conditions may be felt in the economy for years and years, and that if the war power can be used in days of peace to treat all the wounds which war inflicts on our society, it may not only swallow up all other powers of Congress but largely obliterate the Ninth and Tenth Amendments as well. There are no such implications in today's decision. We deal here with the consequences of a housing deficit greatly intensified during the period of hostilities by the war effort. Any power, of course, can be abused. But we cannot assume that Congress is not alert to its constitutional responsibilities. And the question whether the war power has been properly employed in cases such as this is open to judicial inquiry. . . .

The question of the constitutionality of action taken by Congress does not depend on recitals of the power which it undertakes to exercise. Here it is plain from the legislative history that Congress was invoking its war power to cope with a current condition of which the war was a direct and immediate cause. Its judgment on that score is entitled to the respect granted like legislation enacted pursuant to the police power. . . .

Reversed.

Mr. Justice Jackson, concurring; said:

I agree with the result in this case, but the arguments that have been addressed to us lead me to utter more explicit misgivings about war powers than the Court has done. The government asserts no constitutional basis for this legislation other than this vague, undefined and undefinable "war power."

No one will question that this power is the most dangerous one to free government in the whole catalogue of powers. It usually is invoked in haste and excitement when calm legislative consideration of constitutional limitation is difficult. It is executed in a time of patriotic fervor that makes moderation unpopular. And, worst of all, it is interpreted by judges under the influence of the same passions and pressures. Always, as in this case, the government urges hasty decision to forestall some emergency or serve some purpose and pleads that paralysis will result if its claims to power are denied or their confirmation delayed.

Particularly when the war power is invoked to do things to the liberties of people, or to their property or economy that only indirectly affect conduct of the war and do not relate to the management of the war itself, the constitutional basis should be scrutinized with care.

I think we can hardly deny that the war power is as valid a ground for federal rent control now as it has been at any time. We still are technically in a state of war. I would not be willing to hold that war powers may be indefinitely prolonged merely by keeping legally alive a state of war that had in fact ended. I cannot accept the argument that war powers last as long as the effects and consequences of war, for if so they are permanent—as permanent as the war debts. But I find no reason to conclude that we could find fairly that the present state of war is merely technical. We have armies abroad exercising our war power and have made no peace terms with our allies, not to mention our principal enemies. I think the conclusion that the war power has been applicable during the lifetime of this legislation is unavoidable.

WATKINS v. UNITED STATES
354 U. S. 178; 1 L. Ed. 2d 1273; 77 Sup. Ct. 1173. 1957.

One of the basic principles of the American constitutional system is that of the separation of the three powers of government: legislative, executive, and judicial. The doctrine is nowhere stated in so many words but is embodied in the so-called distributing clauses of the Constitution which declare: (1) "All legislative powers herein granted shall be vested in a Congress of the United States . . ." (2) "The executive power shall be vested in a President . . ." (3) "The judicial power . . . shall be vested in one Supreme Court [etc.] . . .". But an absolute separation of powers is impossible if the government is to function. A considerable amount of overlapping amongst the three departments is provided for in the Constitution itself, and the practical necessities of administration have occasioned a good deal more.

And yet in spite of these relaxations the doctrine retains its vitality. It is still true that a department may neither interfere with the work of another nor wantonly assume the functions of another. May it, however, use a power normally belonging to another department as a means of exercising its own proper powers? The power to subpœna witnesses and punish them for contempt if they do not come and testify is a vital and inherent judicial power. No court is really a court without it. Can a house of Congress borrow this judicial power as a means of performing its own delegated functions without violating the doctrine of the separation of powers?

This question was effectively dealt with in McGrain v. Daugherty, 273 U. S. 135 (1927). Early in the Harding administration scandals were uncovered in the federal government, with the result that the Senate created a special committee to investigate the Department of Justice and the possible misconduct in office of Attorney General Harry M. Daugherty.

In the course of the investigation the committee subpœnaed Mally S. Daugherty, brother of the Attorney General, to appear before it and testify. This he refused to do. The Senate then issued a warrant ordering McGrain, a deputy sergeant-at-arms, to arrest Mally S. Daugherty and bring him before the Senate to testify. Daugherty challenged the Senate's power to compel him to do this.

The Court upheld the Senate action. Its opinion mentioned that in 1792 the House of Representatives had appointed a select committee to inquire into the ill-fated St. Clair expedition against the Indians; and it then reviewed the legislative practice, congressional enactments, and court decisions bearing on the power of Congress to conduct inquiries and to punish for contempt. The Court concluded "that the power of inquiry—with process to enforce it—is an essential and appropriate auxiliary to the legislative function." However, it is a power which may validly be used only "in aid of the legislative function." Daugherty had alleged, and the lower court had agreed, that the committee was not seeking information to help it in legislation, but was in reality putting the Attorney General on trial. The Supreme Court disagreed. It said, "The only legitimate object the Senate could have in ordering the investigation was to aid it in legislating; and we think the subject-matter was such that the presumption should be indulged that this was the object. An express avowal of the object would have been better; but . . . was not indispensable."

McGrain v. Daugherty gave Congress and its committees a sense of security from judicial interference with their power to compel testimony. The Court had generously declared that if there was a possible legislative purpose which could be served by a congressional demand for evidence and facts, the Court would presume that this was the purpose of the investigation whether it was or not. But the McGrain case did not give congressional committees carte blanche. There were two reservations: the investigation must be in aid of a valid congressional duty or power, and the questions asked of witnesses must be relevant to the purpose of the inquiry. These points were dealt with in later cases.

The House Committee on Lobbying cited for contempt the secretary of an organization engaged in the nationwide distribution of political propaganda. He had refused to disclose the names of those who had purchased these materials in bulk. In United States v. Rumely, 345 U. S. 41 (1953), the Supreme Court reversed his conviction for contempt. It held that the committee was authorized by Congress to investigate lobbying only. Lobbying comprises the activities of those who seek to persuade Congress to pass or not to pass legislation. It does not include the effort to influence public opinion.

From the time of their origin congressional committees which were set up to investigate subversive or "un-American" activities were in a number of respects sui generis. They were given by Congress roving commissions to find out what they could about persons, organizations, or movements which were believed to be subversive or unorthodox, and to suggest ways and means of defeating these undermining influences. Very early in the game these committees convinced themselves that their most useful function was the public "exposure" of persons of dubious loyalty. This had been explicitly stated by Congressman Martin Dies when his resolution calling for the creation of the House Committee on Un-American Activities was being debated in the House. He said, "I am not in a position to say whether we can legislate effectively in reference to this matter, but I do know that exposure in a democracy of subversive activities is the most effective weapon that we have in our possession." During the Second World War and the subsequent cold war, House and Senate committees investigating subversion were dominated by this zeal to "expose" persons or groups whose loyalty was open to question, in the well-grounded belief that an aroused public opinion would inflict its own non-legal punishments or reprisals. The "exposure" of disloyalty or crime came to be generally accepted as the controlling purpose of such legislative investigating committees. The idea that committee investigations were justifiable only if they aided Congress in its wise consideration of legislation was almost wholly forgotten.

The Court's decision in the Watkins case indicated that our congressional committees on subversive activities do not enjoy unrestricted authority in their investigations. They can no longer conduct those investigations solely for the purpose of "exposing" subversive activity, and their inquiries must be relevant to a valid and clearly defined legislative purpose. Sweezy v. New Hampshire, 354 U. S. 234 (1957), dealt in the same way with a state investigation of subversive activities conducted under the authority of the state legislature by the state's attorney general. Sweezy, a university professor, when summoned before the attorney general refused to answer questions regarding the content of a lecture he had given at the state university, and also questions concerning the Progressive party and its adherents. The Supreme Court held that Sweezy's conviction for contempt denied him due process of law because the legislature had not indicated in its authorizing resolution that it desired the information to which the questions asked by the attorney general related, and that he was, therefore, without authority to ask them.

In a series of later cases, decided five to four, the Court has limited the supposed scope and impact of the Watkins case. In Barenblatt v. United States, 360 U. S. 109 (1959), the Court upheld a conviction for contempt of the House Committee on Un-American Activities. In doing so it ruled that the committee was authorized to inquire into Communist activities in the field of education. The inquiry was not unlawful on the ground that its purpose was "exposure," since "so long as Congress acts in pursuance of its constitutional power, the judiciary lacks authority to intervene on the basis of the motives which spurred the exercise of that power." And finally it concluded that "the balance between the individual and the government interests here at stake must be struck in favor of the latter, and that therefore the provisions of the First Amendment have not been offended." On somewhat similar facts, and by similar reasoning, the Court held in Uphaus v. Wyman, 360 U. S. 72 (1959), that the conviction of Uphaus for contempt for refusing to give to the attorney general of New Hampshire the names of those attending a "World Fellowship" camp, alleged to be a Communist front organization, did not deny him due process of law under the Fourteenth Amendment.

However, the Court has set aside convictions for contempt of the House Committee on Un-American Activities in two cases, in each by a five-to-four decision. In Russell v. United States, 369 U. S. 749 (1962), it did so on the ground that the committee had not clearly identified the subject which was under inquiry when it asked its questions, and in Deutch v. United States, 367 U. S. 456 (1961), on the ground that the committee had required answers to questions which were not shown to be pertinent to its inquiry. However, in Braden v. United States, 365 U. S. 431 (1961), Braden's conviction for contempt was upheld, also five to four, because of his refusal to answer questions in the belief that the Court's decision in the Watkins case excused him from doing so. His refusal occurred before Barenblatt was decided.

In the present case Watkins, a union officer, appeared as a witness before the House Committee on Un-American Activities. He testified with complete candor about his own earlier associations and activities. He also answered questions about persons known by him to have been members of the Communist party. He said, "I will not, however, answer questions with respect to others with whom I associated in the past. I do not believe that any law in this country requires me to testify about persons who may in the past have been Communist Party members or otherwise engaged in Communist Party activity but who to the best of my knowledge and belief have long since removed themselves from the Communist movement.

"I do not believe that such questions are relevant to the work of this committee nor do I believe that this committee has the right to undertake the public exposure of persons because of their past activities. I may be wrong, and the committee may have this power, but until and unless a court of law so holds and directs me to answer, I most firmly refuse to discuss the political activities of my past associates."

Mr. Chief Justice Warren delivered the opinion of the Court, saying in part:

. . . We start with several basic premises on which there is general agreement. The power of the Congress to conduct investigations is inherent in the legislative process. That power is broad. It encompasses inquiries concerning the administration of existing laws as well as proposed or possibly needed statutes. It includes surveys of defects in our social, economic or political system for the purpose of enabling the Congress to remedy them. It comprehends probes into departments of the Federal Government to expose corruption, inefficiency or waste. But broad as is this power of inquiry, it is not unlimited. There is no general authority to expose the private affairs of individuals without justification in terms of the functions of the Congress. This was freely conceded by the Solicitor General in his argument of this case. Nor is the Congress a law enforcement or trial agency. These are functions of the executive and judicial departments of government. No inquiry is an end in itself; it must be related to and in furtherance of a legitimate task of the Congress. Investigations conducted solely for the personal aggrandizement of the investigators or to "punish" those investigated are indefensible.

It is unquestionably the duty of all citizens to cooperate with the Congress in its efforts to obtain the facts needed for intelligent legislative action. It is their unremitting obligation to respond to subpoenas, to respect the dignity of the Congress and its committees and to testify fully with respect to matters within the province of proper investigation. This, of course, assumes that the constitutional rights of witnesses will be respected by the Congress as they are in a court of justice. The Bill of Rights is applicable to investigations as to all forms of governmental action. Witnesses cannot be compelled to give evidence against themselves. They cannot be subjected to unreasonable search and seizure. Nor can the First Amendment freedoms of speech, press, religion, or political belief and association be abridged. . . .

[Here follows a résumé of the evolution of the power of legislative bodies to punish for contempt, from its early origin in English tradition and practice down through the American cases culminating in McGrain v. Daugherty.]

In the decade following World War II, there appeared a new kind of congressional inquiry unknown in prior periods of American history. Principally this was the result of the various investigations into the threat of subversion of the United States Government, but other subjects of congressional interest also contributed to the changed scene. This new phase of legislative inquiry involved a broad-scale intrusion into the lives and affairs of private citizens. It brought before the courts novel questions of the appropriate limits of congressional inquiry. . . . In the more recent cases, the emphasis shifted to problems of accommodating the interest of the Government with the rights and privileges of individuals. The central theme was the application of the Bill of Rights as a restraint upon the assertion of governmental power in this form.

It was during this period that the Fifth Amendment privilege against self-incrimination was frequently invoked and recognized as a legal limit upon the authority of a committee to require that a witness answer its questions. Some early doubts as to the applicability of that privilege before a legislative committee never matured. When the matter reached this Court, the Government did not challenge in any way that the Fifth Amendment protection was available to the witness, and such a challenge could not have prevailed. It confined its argument to the character of the answers sought and to the adequacy of the claim of privilege. . . .

A far more difficult task evolved from the claim by witnesses that the committees' interrogations were infringements upon the freedoms of the First Amendment. Clearly, an investigation is subject to the command that the Congress shall make no law abridging freedom of speech or press or assembly. While it is true that there is no statute to be reviewed, and that an investigation is not a law, nevertheless an investigation is part of law-making. It is justified solely as an adjunct to the legislative process. The First Amendment may be invoked against infringement of the protected freedoms by law or by law-making.

Abuses of the investigative process may imperceptibly lead to abridgment of protected freedoms. The mere summoning of a witness and compelling him to testify, against his will, about his beliefs, expressions or associations is a measure of governmental interference. And when those forced revelations concern matters that are unorthodox, unpopular, or even hateful to the general public, the reaction in the life of the witness may be disastrous. This effect is even more harsh when it is past beliefs, expressions or associations that are disclosed and judged by current standards rather than those contemporary with the matters exposed. Nor does the witness alone suffer the consequences. Those who are identified by witnesses and thereby placed in the same glare of publicity are equally subject to public stigma, scorn and obloquy. Beyond that, there is the more subtle and immeasurable effect upon those who tend to adhere to the most orthodox and uncontroversial views and associations in order to avoid a similar fate at some future time. That this impact is partly the result of non-governmental activity by private persons cannot relieve the investigators of their responsibility for initiating the reaction. . . .

Accommodation of the congressional need for particular information with the individual and personal interest in privacy is an arduous and delicate task for any court. We do not underestimate the difficulties that would attend such an undertaking. It is manifest that despite the adverse effects which follow upon compelled disclosure of private matters, not all such inquiries are barred. . . . The critical element is the existence of, and the weight to be ascribed to, the interest of the Congress in demanding disclosures from an unwilling witness. We cannot simply assume, however, that every congressional investigation is justified by a public need that overbalances any private rights affected. To do so would be to abdicate the responsibility placed by the Constitution upon the judiciary to insure that the Congress does not unjustifiably encroach upon an individual's right to privacy nor abridge his liberty of speech, press, religion or assembly.

Petitioner has earnestly suggested that the difficult questions of protecting these rights from infringement by legislative inquiries can be surmounted in this case because there was no public purpose served in his interrogation. His conclusion is based upon the thesis that the Subcommittee was engaged in a program of exposure for the sake of exposure. . . .

We have no doubt that there is no congressional power to expose for the sake of exposure. The public is, of course, entitled to be informed concerning the workings of its government. That cannot be inflated into a general power to expose where the predominant result can only be an invasion of the private rights of individuals. But a solution to our problem is not to be found in testing the motives of committee members for this purpose. Such is not our function. Their motives alone would not vitiate an investigation which had been instituted by a House of Congress if that assembly's legislative purpose is being served.

. . . The theory of a committee inquiry is that the committee members are serving as the representatives of the parent assembly in collecting information for a legislative purpose. Their function is to act as the eyes and ears of the Congress in obtaining facts upon which the full legislature can act. . . .

An essential premise in this situation is that the House or Senate shall have instructed the committee members on what they are to do with the power delegated to them. It is the responsibility of the Congress, in the first instance, to insure that compulsory process is used only in furtherance of a legislative purpose. That requires that the instructions to an investigating committee spell out that group's jurisdiction and purpose with sufficient particularity. Those instructions are embodied in the authorizing resolution. That document is the committee's charter. Broadly drafted and loosely worded, however, such resolutions can leave tremendous latitude to the discretion of the investigators. The more vague the committee's charter is, the greater becomes the possibility that the committee's specific actions are not in conformity with the will of the parent House of Congress.

The authorizing resolution of the Un-American Activities Committee was adopted in 1938 when a select committee, under the chairmanship of Representative Dies, was created. Several years later, the Committee was made a standing organ of the House with the same mandate. It defines the Committee's authority as follows:

"The Committee on Un-American Activities, as a whole or by subcommittee, is authorized to make from time to time investigations of (i) the extent, character, and objects of un-American propaganda activities in the United States, (ii) the diffusion within the United States of subversive and un-American propaganda that is instigated from foreign countries or of a domestic origin and attacks the principle of the form of government as guaranteed by our Constitution, and (iii) all other questions in relation thereto that would aid Congress in any necessary remedial legislation."

It would be difficult to imagine a less explicit authorizing resolution. Who can define the meaning of "un-American"? What is that single, solitary "principle of the form of government as guaranteed by our Constitution"? There is no need to dwell upon the language, however. At one time, perhaps, the resolution might have been read narrowly to confine the Committee to the subject of propaganda. The events that have transpired in the fifteen years before the interrogation of petitioner make such a construction impossible at this date.

The members of the Committee have clearly demonstrated that they did not feel themselves restricted in any way to propaganda in the narrow sense of the word. Unquestionably the Committee conceived of its task in the grand view of its name. Un-American activities were its target, no matter how or where manifested. Notwithstanding the broad purview of the Committee's experience, the House of Representatives repeatedly approved its continuation. . . .

Combining the language of the resolution with the construction it has been given, it is evident that the preliminary control of the Committee exercised by the House of Representatives is slight or non-existent. No one could reasonably deduce from the charter the kind of investigation that the Committee was directed to make. As a result, we are asked to engage in a process of retroactive rationalization. Looking backward from the events that transpired, we are asked to uphold the Committee's actions unless it appears that they were clearly not authorized by the charter. As a corollary to this inverse approach, the Government urges that we must view the matter hospitably to the power of the Congress—that if there is any legislative purpose which might have been furthered by the kind of disclosure sought, the witness must be punished for withholding it. No doubt every reasonable indulgence of legality must be accorded to the actions of a coordinate branch of our Government. But such deference cannot yield to an unnecessary and unreasonable dissipation of precious constitutional freedoms.

The Government contends that the public interest at the core of the investigations of the Un-American Activities Committee is the need by the Congress to be informed of efforts to overthrow the Government by force and violence so that adequate legislative safeguards can be erected. From this core, however, the Committee can radiate outward infinitely to any topic thought to be related in some way to armed insurrection. The outer reaches of this domain are known only by the content of "un-American activities." . . .

The consequences that flow from this situation are manifold. In the first place, a reviewing court is unable to make the kind of judgment made by the Court in United States v. Rumely. The Committee is allowed, in essence, to define its own authority, to choose the direction and focus of its activities. In deciding what to do with the power that has been conferred upon them, members of the Committee may act pursuant to motives that seem to them to be the highest. Their decisions, nevertheless, can lead to ruthless exposure of private lives in order to gather data that is neither desired by the Congress nor useful to it. Yet it is impossible in this circumstance, with constitutional freedoms in jeopardy, to declare that the Committee has ranged beyond the area committed to it by its parent assembly because the boundaries are so nebulous.

More important and more fundamental than that, however, it insulates the House that has authorized the investigation from the witnesses who are subjected to the sanctions of compulsory process. There is a wide gulf between the responsibility for the use of investigative power and the actual exercise of that power. This is an especially vital consideration in assuring respect for constitutional liberties. Protected freedoms should not be placed in danger in the absence of a clear determination by the House or the Senate that a particular inquiry is justified by a specific legislative need.

. . . An excessively broad charter, like that of the House Un-American Activities Committee, places the courts in an untenable position if they are to strike a balance between the public need for a particular interrogation and the right of citizens to carry on their affairs free from unnecessary governmental interference. It is impossible in such a situation to ascertain whether any legislative purpose justifies the disclosures sought and, if so, the importance of that information to the Congress in furtherance of its legislative function. The reason no court can make this critical judgment is that the House of Representatives itself has never made it. Only the legislative assembly initiating an investigation can assay the relative necessity of specific disclosures.

Absence of the qualitative consideration of petitioner's questioning by the House of Representatives aggravates a serious problem, revealed in this case, in the relationship of congressional investigating committees and the witnesses who appear before them. Plainly these committees are restricted to the missions delegated to them, i.e., to acquire certain data to be used by the House or the Senate in coping with a problem that falls within its legislative sphere. No witness can be compelled to make disclosures on matters outside that area. This is a jurisdictional concept of pertinency drawn from the nature of a congressional committee's source of authority. It is not wholly different from nor unrelated to the element of pertinency embodied in the criminal statute under which petitioner was prosecuted. When the definition of jurisdictional pertinency is as uncertain and wavering as in the case of the Un-American Activities Committee, it becomes extremely difficult for the Committee to limit its inquiries to statutory pertinency.

Since World War II, the Congress has practically abandoned its original practice of utilizing the coercive sanction of contempt proceedings at the bar of the House. The sanction there imposed is imprisonment by the House until the recalcitrant witness agrees to testify or disclose the matters sought, provided that the incarceration does not extend beyond adjournment. The Congress has instead invoked the aid of the federal judicial system in protecting itself against contumacious conduct. It has become customary to refer these matters to the United States Attorneys for prosecution under criminal law.

The appropriate statute is found in 2 USC § 192. It provides:

"Every person who having been summoned as a witness by the authority of either House of Congress to give testimony or to produce papers upon any matter under inquiry before either House, or any joint committee established by a joint or concurrent resolution of the two Houses of Congress, or any committee of either House of Congress, willfully makes default, or who, having appeared, refuses to answer any question pertinent to the question under inquiry, shall be deemed guilty of a misdemeanor, punishable by a fine of not more than $1,000 nor less than $100 and imprisonment in a common jail for not less than one month nor more than twelve months."

In fulfillment of their obligation under this statute, the courts must accord to the defendants every right which is guaranteed to defendants in all other criminal cases. Among these is the right to have available, through a sufficiently precise statute, information revealing the standard of criminality before the commission of the alleged offense. Applied to persons prosecuted under § 192, this raises a special problem in that the statute defines the crime as refusal to answer "any question pertinent to the question under inquiry." Part of the standard of criminality, therefore, is the pertinency of the questions propounded to the witness.

The problem attains proportion when viewed from the standpoint of the witness who appears before a congressional committee. He must decide at the time the questions are propounded whether or not to answer. As the Court said in Sinclair v. United States, 279 U. S. 263, the witness acts at his peril. He is ". . . bound rightly to construe the statute." An erroneous determination on his part, even if made in the utmost good faith, does not exculpate him if the court should later rule that the questions were pertinent to the question under inquiry.

It is obvious that a person compelled to make this choice is entitled to have knowledge of the subject to which the interrogation is deemed pertinent. That knowledge must be available with the same degree of explicitness and clarity that the Due Process Clause requires in the expression of any element of a criminal offense. The "vice of vagueness" must be avoided here as in all other crimes. There are several sources that can outline the "question under inquiry" in such a way that the rules against vagueness are satisfied. The authorizing resolution, the remarks of the chairman or members of the committee, or even the nature of the proceedings themselves might sometimes make the topic clear. This case demonstrates, however, that these sources often leave the matter in grave doubt.

The first possibility is that the authorizing resolution itself will so clearly declare the "question under inquiry" that a witness can understand the pertinency of questions asked him. The Government does not contend that the authorizing resolution of the Un-American Activities Committee could serve such a purpose. Its confusing breadth is amply illustrated by the innumerable and diverse questions into which the Committee has inquired under this charter since 1938. If the "question under inquiry" were stated with such sweeping and uncertain scope, we doubt that it would withstand an attack on the ground of vagueness. . . .

No aid is given as to the "question under inquiry" in the action of the full Committee that authorized the creation of the Subcommittee before which petitioner appeared. The Committee adopted a formal resolution giving the Chairman the power to appoint subcommittees ". . . for the purpose of performing any and all acts which the Committee as a whole is authorized to do." . . .

The Government believes that the topic of inquiry before the Subcommittee concerned Communist infiltration in labor. In his introductory remarks, the Chairman made reference to a bill, then pending before the Committee, which would have penalized labor unions controlled or dominated by persons who were, or had been, members of a "Communist-action" organization, as defined in the Internal Security Act of 1950. The Subcommittee, it is contended, might have been endeavoring to determine the extent of such a problem. . . .

[The Court examines the record of the hearings conducted by the subcommittee and concludes that "the subject before the Subcommittee was not defined in terms of Communism in labor."]

Having exhausted the several possible indicia of the "question under inquiry," we remain unenlightened as to the subject to which the questions asked petitioner were pertinent. Certainly, if the point is that obscure after trial and appeal, it was not adequately revealed to petitioner when he had to decide at his peril whether or not to answer. Fundamental fairness demands that no witness be compelled to make such a determination with so little guidance. Unless the subject matter has been made to appear with undisputable clarity, it is the duty of the investigative body, upon objection of the witness on grounds of pertinency, to state for the record the subject under inquiry at that time and the manner in which the propounded questions are pertinent thereto. To be meaningful, the explanation must describe what the topic under inquiry is and the connective reasoning whereby the precise questions asked relate to it.

The statement of the Committee Chairman in this case, in response to petitioner's protest, was woefully inadequate to convey sufficient information as to the pertinency of the questions to the subject under inquiry. Petitioner was thus not accorded a fair opportunity to determine whether he was within his rights in refusing to answer, and his conviction is necessarily invalid under the Due Process Clause of the Fifth Amendment.

. . . The conclusions we have reached in this case will not prevent the Congress, through its committees, from obtaining any information it needs for the proper fulfillment of its role in our scheme of government. The legislature is free to determine the kinds of data that should be collected. It is only those investigations that are conducted by use of compulsory process that give rise to a need to protect the rights of individuals against illegal encroachment. That protection can be readily achieved through procedures which prevent the separation of power from responsibility and which provide the constitutional requisites of fairness for witnesses. A measure of added care on the part of the House and the Senate in authorizing the use of compulsory process and by their committees in exercising that power would suffice. That is a small price to pay if it serves to uphold the principles of limited, constitutional government without restricting the power of the Congress to inform itself.

The judgment of the Court of Appeals is reversed, and the case is remanded to the District Court with instructions to dismiss the indictment.

It is so ordered.

Mr. Justice Burton and Mr. Justice Whittaker took no part in the consideration or decision of this case.

Mr. Justice Frankfurter concurred in a separate opinion.

Mr. Justice Clark wrote a vigorous dissenting opinion.

8

Commerce

GIBBONS v. OGDEN
9 Wheaton 1; 6 L. Ed. 23. 1824.

In 1798 Robert R. Livingston secured from the New York legislature an exclusive twenty-year grant to navigate by steam the rivers and other waters of the state, provided that within two years he should build a boat which would make four miles an hour against the current of the Hudson River. The grant was made amidst the ribald jeers of the legislators, who had no faith whatever in the project. The terms of the grant were not met, however, and it was renewed in 1803—this time to Livingston together with his partner, Robert Fulton,—and again for two years in 1807. In August, 1807, Fulton's steamboat made its first successful trip from New York to Albany, and steamboat navigation became a reality. The following year the legislature, now fully aware of the practical significance of Fulton's achievement, passed a law providing that for each new boat placed on New York waters by Fulton and Livingston they should be entitled to a five-year extension of their monopoly, which should, however, not exceed thirty years. The monopoly was made effective by further providing that no one should be allowed to navigate New York waters by steam without a license from Fulton and Livingston, and any unlicensed vessel should be forfeited to them. The business of steamboat navigation developed rapidly. Boats were put in operation between New York and Albany and intervening points, and steam ferries ran between Fulton Street, New York

City, and points in New Jersey. Naturally the monopolistic nature of the Fulton-Livingston rights worked hardship on their would-be competitors, and neighboring states began to pass retaliatory laws directed against the New York partners. The New Jersey legislature in 1811 authorized the owner of any boat seized under the forfeiture clause of the Fulton-Livingston charter to capture and hold in retaliation any boat belonging to any New York citizen. Connecticut in 1822 forbade any vessel licensed by Fulton and Livingston to enter the waters of that state, and Ohio passed a somewhat similar law in the same year. Granting such exclusive franchises was a game at which more than one state could play, and such grants were made by the Territory of Orleans (later Louisiana), Georgia, Massachusetts, Pennsylvania, Tennessee, New Hampshire, and Vermont; and with the inevitable increase of feeling created by such policies retaliatory acts became common. In short, an achievement of science which had seemed destined to enlarge the means of communication and develop the commerce of the nation appeared rather to be embroiling the states in such bitter antagonisms and commercial warfare as prevailed during the dismal period of the Confederation. It is against the background of this intensely acute economic situation that the case of Gibbons v. Ogden must be read.

Ogden had secured a license for steam navigation from Fulton and Livingston. Gibbons had originally been his partner but was now his rival and was operating steamboats between New York and New Jersey under the authority of a coasting license obtained from the United States government. Upon Ogden's petition the New York court had enjoined Gibbons from continuing in business. The great jurist Chancellor James Kent wrote the opinion in this case, upholding the validity of the New York statute establishing the monopoly and repudiating the idea that there was any conflict involved between federal and state authority. An appeal was taken by Gibbons to the Supreme Court of the United States, thus presenting to that tribunal its first case under the commerce clause of the Constitution. It involved the momentous questions: What constitutes commerce? What commerce is interstate? What authority, if any, may the states exercise over interstate commerce when Congress has acted with respect to the same subject-matter?

Just what is interstate commerce remains a troublesome question. In 1869, the Court held in Paul v. Virginia, 8 Wallace (U. S.) 168, that "the business of insurance is not interstate commerce." Here an insurance company doing business across state lines tried unsuccessfully to escape state controls on the ground that it was engaged in interstate commerce. In United States v. South-Eastern Underwriters Association, 322 U. S. 533 (1944), some two hundred fire insurance companies were prosecuted under the Sherman Act for monopolistic practices. The Court held that the insurance business as a whole as carried on by the companies comprises elements and transactions which are interstate commerce, and the business is therefore subject to federal control under the commerce clause.

The Court has taken an amusingly paradoxical position on the question whether our nationally organized professional sports, which depend upon the moving of teams or individual athletes around the country, are so engaged in and dependent upon interstate commerce as to be subject to the Antitrust Act. In Federal Baseball Club v. National League, 259 U. S. 200 (1922), Mr. Justice Holmes held that major league baseball games were local activities and thus beyond congressional power under the Commerce Clause. He said: "The business is giving exhibitions of baseball, which are purely state affairs." In Toolson v. New York Yankees, Inc., 346 U. S. 356 (1953), the Court reaffirmed the Federal Baseball Club decision, and it still stands. But in United States v. International Boxing Club of New York, 348 U. S. 236 (1955), and Radovich v. National Football League, 352 U. S. 445 (1957), the Court refused to exempt boxing and football from the Antitrust Act. In Radovich, the Court, seemingly somewhat embarrassed, observed: "If this ruling is unrealistic, inconsistent, or illogical, it is sufficient to answer . . . that were we considering the question of baseball for the first time upon a clean slate we would have no doubts. But Federal Baseball held the business of baseball outside the scope of the Act. No other business claiming the coverage of those cases has such an adjudication."

The efforts of the states to ward off unwelcome competition moving against them across state lines did not end with Gibbons v. Ogden. In Baldwin v. Seelig, 294 U. S. 511 (1935), the state of New York, which had fixed by law the prices at which milk could be bought and sold in the state, sought to prevent Seelig from buying milk in Vermont at lower than New York prices and selling it in New York. The Court held that the state could not restrict interstate commerce in milk for the purpose of escaping the competition of cheaper milk brought in from outside the state. In H. P. Hood & Sons v. Du Mond, 336 U. S. 525 (1949), the state of New York denied the Hood company, which bought milk in New York for resale in the Boston area, a license to open a new plant in New York on the ground that this would create destructive competition for the local milk supply. The Court held that the state may not, for the purpose of protecting local business from competition, restrict the shipment of milk out of the state.

Mr. Chief Justice Marshall delivered the opinion of the Court, saying in part:

The appellant contends that this decree is erroneous, because the laws which purport to give the exclusive privilege it sustains are repugnant to the Constitution and laws of the United States.

They are said to be repugnant—

1. To that clause in the Constitution which authorizes Congress to regulate commerce.

2. To that which authorizes Congress to promote the progress of science and useful arts. . . .

As preliminary to the very able discussions of the Constitution which we have heard from the bar, and as having some influence on its construction, reference has been made to the political situation of these states, anterior to its formation. It has been said that they were sovereign, were completely independent, and were connected with each other only by a league. This is true. But, when these allied sovereigns converted their league into a government, when they converted their congress of ambassadors, deputed to deliberate on their common concerns, and to recommend measures of general utility, into a legislature, empowered to enact laws on the most interesting subjects, the whole character in which the states appear underwent a change, the extent of which must be determined by a fair consideration of the instrument by which that change was effected.

This instrument contains an enumeration of powers expressly granted by the people to their government. It has been said that these powers ought to be construed strictly. But why ought they to be so construed? Is there one sentence in the Constitution which gives countenance to this rule? In the last of the enumerated powers, that which grants, expressly, the means for carrying all others into execution, Congress is authorized "to make all laws which shall be necessary and proper" for the purpose. But this limitation on the means which may be used is not extended to the powers which are conferred; nor is there one sentence in the Constitution, which has been pointed out by the gentlemen of the bar, or which we have been able to discern, that prescribes this rule. We do not, therefore, think ourselves justified in adopting it. What do gentlemen mean by a strict construction? If they contend only against that enlarged construction, which would extend words beyond their natural and obvious import, we might question the application of the term, but should not controvert the principle. If they contend for that narrow construction which, in support of some theory not to be found in the Constitution, would deny to the government those powers which the words of the grant, as usually understood, import, and which are consistent with the general views and objects of the instrument; for that narrow construction, which would cripple the government, and render it unequal to the objects for which it is declared to be instituted, and to which the powers given, as fairly understood, render it competent; then we cannot perceive the propriety of this strict construction, nor adopt it as the rule by which the Constitution is to be expounded. As men whose intentions require no concealment generally employ the words which most directly and aptly express the ideas they intend to convey, the enlighted patriots who framed our Constitution, and the people who adopted it, must be understood to have employed words in their natural sense, and to have intended what they have said. If, from the imperfection of human language, there should be serious doubts respecting the extent of any given power, it is a well settled rule that the objects for which it was given, especially when those objects are expressed in the instrument itself, should have great influence in the construction. We know of no reason for excluding this rule from the present case. The grant does not convey power which might be beneficial to the grantor, if retained by himself, or which can enure solely to the benefit of the grantee; but is an investment of power for the general advantage, in the hands of agents selected for that purpose; which power can never be exercised by the people themselves, but must be placed in the hands of agents, or lie dormant. We know of no rule for construing the extent of such powers, other than is given by the language of the instrument which confers them, taken in connection with the purposes for which they were conferred.

The words are: "Congress shall have power to regulate commerce with foreign nations, and among the several States, and with the Indian tribes." The subject to be regulated is commerce; and our Constitution being, as was aptly said at the bar, one of enumeration, and not of definition, to ascertain the extent of the power, it becomes necessary to settle the meaning of the word. The counsel for the appellee would limit it to traffic, to buying and selling, or the interchange of commodities, and do not admit that it comprehends navigation. This would restrict a general term, applicable to many objects, to one of its significations. Commerce, undoubtedly, is traffic, but it is something more; it is intercourse. It describes the commercial intercourse between nations, and parts of nations, in all its branches, and is regulated by prescribing rules for carrying on that intercourse. The mind can scarcely conceive a system for regulating commerce between nations which shall exclude all laws concerning navigation, which shall be silent on the admission of the vessels of the one nation into the ports of the other, and be confined to prescribing rules for the conduct of individuals, in the actual employment of buying and selling, or of barter.

If commerce does not include navigation, the government of the Union has no direct power over that subject, and can make no law prescribing what shall constitute American vessels, or requiring that they shall be navigated by American seamen. Yet this power has been exercised from the commencement of the government, has been exercised with the consent of all, and has been understood by all to be a commercial regulation. All America understands, and has uniformly understood, the word "commerce" to comprehend navigation. It was so understood, and must have been so understood, when the Constitution was framed. The power over commerce, including navigation, was one of the primary objects for which the people of America adopted their government, and must have been contemplated in forming it. The Convention must have used the word in that sense, because all have understood it in that sense; and the attempt to restrict it comes too late. . . .

The word used in the Constitution, then, comprehends, and has been always understood to comprehend, navigation within its meaning; and a power to regulate navigation is as expressly granted as if that term had been added to the word "commerce."

To what commerce does this power extend? The Constitution informs us, to commerce "with foreign nations, and among the several States, and with the Indian tribes." It has, we believe, been universally admitted that these words comprehend every species of commercial intercourse between the United States and foreign nations. No sort of trade can be carried on between this country and any other to which this power does not extend. It has been truly said that commerce, as the word is used in the Constitution, is a unit, every part of which is indicated by the term. If this be the admitted meaning of the word, in its application to foreign nations, it must carry the same meaning throughout the sentence, and remain a unit, unless there be some plain intelligible cause which alters it.

The subject to which the power is next applied is to commerce "among the several States." The word "among" means intermingled with. A thing which is among others is intermingled with them. Commerce among the states cannot stop at the external boundary line of each state, but may be introduced into the interior.

It is not intended to say that these words comprehend that commerce which is completely internal, which is carried on between man and man in a state, or between different parts of the same state, and which does not extend to or affect other states. Such a power would be inconvenient and is certainly unnecessary.

Comprehensive as the word "among" is, it may very properly be restricted to that commerce which concerns more states than one. . . . The completely internal commerce of a state, then, may be considered as reserved for the state itself.

But, in regulating commerce with foreign nations, the power of Congress does not stop at the jurisdictional lines of the several states. It would be a very useless power if it could not pass those lines. The commerce of the United States with foreign nations is that of the whole United States. Every district has a right to participate in it. The deep streams which penetrate our country in every direction pass through the interior of almost every state in the Union, and furnish the means of exercising this right. If Congress has the power to regulate it, that power must be exercised whenever the subject exists. If it exists within the states, if a foreign voyage may commence or terminate at a port within a state, then the power of Congress may be exercised within a state.

This principle is, if possible, still more clear when applied to commerce "among the several States." They either join each other, in which case they are separated by a mathematical line, or they are remote from each other, in which case other states lie between them. What is commerce "among" them; and how is it to be conducted? Can a trading expedition between two adjoining states commence and terminate outside of each? And if the trading intercourse be between two states remote from each other, must it not commence in one, terminate in the other, and probably pass through a third? Commerce among the states must, of necessity, be commerce with the states. In the regulation of trade with the Indian tribes, the action of the law, especially when the Constitution was made, was chiefly within a state. The power of Congress, then, whatever it may be, must be exercised within the territorial jurisdiction of the several states. . . .

We are now arrived at the inquiry, what is this power?

It is the power to regulate; that is, to prescribe the rule by which commerce is to be governed. This power, like all others vested in Congress, is complete in itself, may be exercised to its utmost extent, and acknowledges no limitations other than are prescribed in the Constitution. These are expressed in plain terms, and do not affect the questions which arise in this case, or which have been discussed at the bar. . . .

The power of Congress, then, comprehends navigation within the limits of every state in the Union, so far as that navigation may be, in any manner, connected with "commerce with foreign nations, or among the several States, or with the Indian tribes." It may, of consequence, pass the jurisdictional line of New York, and act upon the very waters to which the prohibition now under consideration applies.

But it has been urged with great earnestness that, although the power of Congress to regulate commerce with foreign nations, and among the several states, be co-extensive with the subject itself, and have no other limits than are prescribed in the Constitution, yet the states may severally exercise the same power within their respective jurisdictions. In support of this argument, it is said that they possessed it as an inseparable attribute of sovereignty before the formation of the Constitution, and still retain it, except so far as they have surrendered it by that instrument; that this principle results from the nature of the government, and is secured by the Tenth Amendment; that an affirmative grant of power is not exclusive, unless in its own nature it be such that the continued exercise of it by the former possessor is inconsistent with the grant, and that this is not of that description.

The appellant, conceding these postulates, except the last, contends that full power to regulate a particular subject implies the whole power, and leaves no residuum; that a grant of the whole is incompatible with the existence of a right in another to any part of it. . . .

In discussing the question whether this power is still in the states, in the case under consideration, we may dismiss from it the inquiry, whether it is surrendered by the mere grant to Congress, or is retained until Congress shall exercise the power. We may dismiss that inquiry because it has been exercised, and the regulations which Congress deemed it proper to make are now in full operation. The sole question is, can a state regulate commerce with foreign nations and among the states while Congress is regulating it? . . .

The act passed in 1803, prohibiting the importation of slaves into any state which shall itself prohibit their importation, implies, it is said, an admission that the states possessed the power to exclude or admit them; from which it is inferred that they possess the same power with respect to other articles.

If this inference were correct; if this power was exercised, not under any particular clause in the Constitution, but in virtue of a general right over the subject of commerce, to exist as long as the Constitution itself, it might now be exercised. Any state might now import African slaves into its own territory. But it is obvious that the power of the states over this subject, previous to the year 1808, constitutes an exception to the power of Congress to regulate commerce, and the exception is expressed in such words as to manifest clearly the intention to continue the preexisting right of the states to admit or exclude for a limited period. The words are, "the migration or importation of such persons as any of the States now existing shall think proper to admit, shall not be prohibited by the Congress prior to the year 1808." The whole object of the exception is, to preserve the power to those states which might be disposed to exercise it; and its language seems to the Court to convey this idea unequivocally. The possession of this particular power, then, during the time limited in the Constitution, cannot be admitted to prove the possession of any other similar power.

It has been said that the act of August 7, 1789, acknowledges a concurrent power in the states to regulate the conduct of pilots, and hence is inferred an admission of their concurrent right with Congress to regulate commerce with foreign nations and amongst the states. But this inference is not, we think, justified by the fact. Although Congress cannot enable a state to legislate, Congress may adopt the provisions of a state on any subject. When the government of the Union was brought into existence, it found a system for the regulation of its pilots in full force in every state. The act which has been mentioned adopts this system, and gives it the same validity as if its provisions had been specially made by Congress. But the act, it may be said, is prospective also, and the adoption of laws to be made in future presupposes the right in the maker to legislate on the subject.

The act unquestionably manifests an intention to leave this subject entirely to the states until Congress should think proper to interpose; but the very enactment of such a law indicates an opinion that it was necessary; that the existing system would not be applicable to the new state of things unless expressly applied to it by Congress. . . .

These acts were cited at the bar for the purpose of showing an opinion in Congress that the states possess, concurrently with the legislature of the Union, the power to regulate commerce with foreign nations and among the states. Upon reviewing them, we think they do not establish the proposition they were intended to prove. They show the opinion that the states retain powers enabling them to pass the laws to which allusion has been made, not that those laws proceed from the particular power which has been delegated to Congress.

It has been contended by the counsel for the appellant that, as the word to "regulate" implies in its nature full power over the thing to be regulated, it excludes, necessarily, the action of all others that would perform the same operation on the same thing. That regulation is designed for the entire result, applying to those parts which remain as they were, as well as to those which are altered. It produces a uniform whole, which is as much disturbed and deranged by changing what the regulating power designs to leave untouched, as that on which it has operated.

There is great force in this argument, and the Court is not satisfied that it has been refuted.

Since, however, in exercising the power of regulating their own purely internal affairs, whether of trading or police, the states may sometimes enact laws, the validity of which depends on their interfering with, and being contrary to, an act of Congress passed in pursuance of the Constitution, the Court will enter upon the inquiry whether the laws of New York, as expounded by the highest tribunal of that state, have, in their application to this case, come into collision with an act of Congress, and deprived a citizen of a right to which that act entitles him. Should this collision exist, it will be immaterial whether those laws were passed in virtue of a concurrent power "to regulate commerce with foreign nations and among the several States," or, in virtue of a power to regulate their domestic trade and police. In one case and the other, the acts of New York must yield to the law of Congress, and the decision sustaining the privileges they confer, against a right given by a law of the Union, must be erroneous. . . .

The questions . . . whether the conveyance of passengers be a part of the coasting trade, and whether a vessel can be protected in that occupation by a coasting license, are not, and cannot be, raised in this case. The real and sole question seems to be, whether a steam machine, in actual use, deprives a vessel of the privileges conferred by a license.

In considering this question, the first idea which presents itself, is that the laws of Congress for the regulation of commerce, do not look to the principle by which vessels are moved. That subject is left entirely to individual discretion; and in that vast and complex system of legislative enactment concerning it, which embraces everything which the legislature thought it necessary to notice, there is not, we believe, one word respecting the peculiar principle by which vessels are propelled through the water, except what may be found in a single act, granting a particular privilege to steamboats. With this exception, every act, either prescribing duties, or granting privileges, applies to every vessel, whether navigated by the instrumentality of wind or fire, of sails or machinery. The whole weight of proof, then, is thrown upon him who would introduce a distinction to which the words of the law give no countenance.

If a real difference could be admitted to exist between vessels carrying passengers and others, it has already been observed that there is no fact in this case which can bring up that question. And, if the occupation of steamboats be a matter of such general notoriety that the Court may be presumed to know it, although not specially informed by the record, then we deny that the transportation of passengers is their exclusive occupation. It is a matter of general history, that, in our western waters, their principal employment is the transportation of merchandise; and all know, that in the waters of the Atlantic they are frequently so employed.

But all inquiry into this subject seems to the Court to be put completely at rest, by the act already mentioned, entitled, "An act for the enrolling and licensing of steamboats."

This act authorizes a steamboat employed, or intended to be employed, only in a river or bay of the United States, owned wholly or in part by an alien, resident within the United States, to be enrolled and licensed as if the same belonged to a citizen of the United States.

This act demonstrates the opinion of Congress, that steamboats may be enrolled and licensed, in common with vessels using sails. They are, of course, entitled to the same privileges, and can no more be restrained from navigating waters, and entering ports which are free to such vessels, than if they were wafted on their voyage by the winds, instead of being propelled by the agency of fire. The one element may be as legitimately used as the other, for every commercial purpose authorized by the laws of the Union; and the act of a state inhibiting the use of either to any vessel having a license under the act of Congress, comes, we think, in direct collision with that act.

As this decides the cause, it is unnecessary to enter in an examination of that part of the Constitution which empowers Congress to promote the progress of science and the useful arts. . . .

COOLEY v. THE BOARD OF WARDENS OF THE PORT OF PHILADELPHIA
12 Howard 299; 13 L. Ed. 996. 1852.

In the early judicial construction of the commerce clause of the Constitution, one important and difficult question remained long unanswered: namely, whether the power of Congress to regulate foreign and interstate commerce was absolutely exclusive, or could be shared in part by the states. Gibbons v. Ogden, above, had held that state action affecting commerce which is in conflict with congressional regulation is invalid, but it had left unsettled the question whether a state may lawfully legislate regarding subjects pertaining to interstate commerce upon which Congress has passed no law. It was this issue which came before the Court in the case of Cooley v. The Board of Wardens of the Port of Philadelphia.

The legislature of Pennsylvania in 1803 had passed a statute establishing an elaborate system of regulations affecting pilotage in the port of Philadelphia and imposing certain penalties of money in case of the failure of a master, owner, or consignee to comply with these rules. Cooley had rendered himself liable to the enforcement of these penalties against him but alleged in appealing his case to the Supreme Court that the state statute was unconstitutional as an invasion of the exclusive authority of Congress over foreign and interstate commerce. In holding the state statute valid because Congress had not legislated independently with respect to pilotage and in view of the local nature of the problems of pilotage, the Court laid down a rule for determining the exclusive or nonexclusive character of federal commercial regulations which has been of utmost importance and value. It is interesting to note that two justices dissented vigorously on the ground that the power of Congress over commerce should be held absolutely exclusive.

The doctrine of the Cooley case, while simple enough to state, is by no means so simple to apply. Involving as it does the determination by the Court of the question whether a particular subject of commercial regulation admits of and requires uniform and national control or whether it is sufficiently local in character to make state regulation permissible, it imposes upon the Court the solution of many complicated and difficult questions. The doctrine has been criticized on the ground that the determination of such a question properly belongs to Congress rather than to the courts; but aside from that the rule has generally been regarded as a wise one, sufficiently protecting federal commercial interests on the one hand while permitting the local control of local commercial problems on the other.

The aspects of interstate commerce which may still be regulated by the states on the ground that "uniform national control" is unnecessary are becoming fewer. A clear example is provided by ferries, bridges, and tunnels which span the boundaries between states. To regulate the rates or tolls charged for the use of these facilities is clearly to regulate interstate commerce, but the states are permitted to do this under the doctrine of the Cooley case. See Port Richmond & Bergen Point Ferry Co. v. Board of Chosen Freeholders of Hudson County, 234 U. S. 317 (1914).

On the other hand the policy of segregating or not segregating Negroes and whites on interstate carriers was held to be not a local matter with which the states might deal. In Hall v. De Cuir, 95 U. S. 485 (1878), the Court held invalid as a burden on interstate commerce a state statute forbidding the segregation of the races on public carriers, in this case a steamboat on the Mississippi River. In Morgan v. Commonwealth of Virginia, 328 U. S. 373 (1946), a state statute was held invalid which required segregation on all buses, including interstate ones. In each case the Court, referring to the Cooley case, stated that the problem of segregation or nonsegregation must be dealt with, if at all, by national uniform legislation. In 1961, the Interstate Commerce Commission issued a regulation forbidding interstate motor carriers of passengers to discriminate on grounds of race, color, creed, or national origin in the seating of such passengers, or in the terminal facilities provided for them, such as "waiting room, restroom, eating, drinking, and ticket sales facilities," or to display signs indicating such discrimination.

Mr. Justice Curtis delivered the opinion of the Court, saying in part:

. . . That the power to regulate commerce includes the regulation of navigation, we consider settled. And when we look to the nature of the service performed by pilots, to the relations which that service and its compensations bear to navigation between the several states, and between the ports of the United States and foreign countries, we are brought to the conclusion, that the regulation of the qualifications of pilots, of the modes and times of offering and rendering their services, of the responsibilities which shall rest upon them, of the powers they shall possess, of the compensation they may demand, and of the penalties by which their rights and duties may be enforced, do constitute regulations of navigation, and consequently of commerce, within the just meaning of this clause of the Constitution.

The power to regulate navigation is the power to prescribe rules in conformity with which navigation must be carried on. It extends to the persons who conduct it, as well as to the instruments used. Accordingly, the first Congress assembled under the Constitution passed laws, requiring the masters of ships and vessels of the United States to be citizens of the United States, and established many rules for the government and regulation of officers and seamen. I Stats. at Large, 55, 131. These have been from time to time added to and changed, and we are not aware that their validity has been questioned.

Now, a pilot, so far as respects the navigation of the vessel in that part of the voyage which is his pilotage-ground, is the temporary master charged with the safety of the vessel and cargo, and of the lives of those on board, and intrusted with the command of the crew. He is not only one of the persons engaged in navigation, but he occupies a most important and responsible place among those thus engaged. And if Congress has power to regulate the seamen who assist the pilot in the management of the vessel, a power never denied, we can perceive no valid reason why the pilot should be beyond the reach of the same power. It is true that, according to the usages of modern commerce on the ocean, the pilot is on board only during a part of the voyage between ports of different states, or between ports of the United States and foreign countries; but if he is on board for such a purpose and during so much of the voyage as to be engaged in navigation, the power to regulate navigation extends to him while thus engaged, as clearly as it would if he were to remain on board throughout the whole passage, from port to port. For it is a power which extends to every part of the voyage, and may regulate those who conduct or assist in conducting navigation in one part of a voyage as much as in another part, or during the whole voyage.

Nor should it be lost sight of, that this subject of the regulation of pilots and pilotage has an intimate connection with, and an important relation to, the general subject of commerce with foreign nations and among the several states, over which it was one main object of the Constitution to create a national control.

. . . And a majority of the Court are of opinion, that a regulation of pilots is a regulation of commerce, within the grant to Congress of the commercial power, contained in the third clause of the eighth section of the first Article of the Constitution.

It becomes necessary, therefore, to consider whether this law of Pennsylvania, being a regulation of commerce, is valid.

The act of Congress of the 7th of August, 1789, section 4, is as follows:

"That all pilots in the bays, inlets, rivers, harbors, and ports of the United States shall continue to be regulated in conformity with the existing laws of the states, respectively, wherein such pilots may be, or with such laws as the states may respectively hereafter enact for the purpose, until further legislative provision shall be made by Congress."

. . . we are brought directly and unavoidably to the consideration of the question, whether the grant of the commercial power to Congress did per se deprive the states of all power to regulate pilots. This question has never been decided by this Court, nor, in our judgment, has any case depending upon all the considerations which must govern this one, come before this Court. The grant of commercial power to Congress does not contain any terms which expressly exclude the states from exercising an authority over its subject-matter. If they are excluded, it must be because the nature of the power thus granted to Congress requires that a similar authority should not exist in the states. If it were conceded on the one side that the nature of this power, like that to legislate for the District of Columbia, is absolutely and totally repugnant to the existence of similar power in the states, probably no one would deny that the grant of the power to Congress, as effectually and perfectly excludes the states from all future legislation on the subject, as if express words had been used to exclude them. And on the other hand, if it were admitted that the existence of this power in Congress, like the power of taxation, is compatible with the existence of a similar power in the states, then it would be in conformity with the contemporary exposition of the Constitution (Federalist, No. 32), and with the judicial construction given from time to time by this Court, after the most deliberate consideration, to hold that the mere grant of such a power to Congress, did not imply a prohibition on the states to exercise the same power; that it is not the mere existence of such a power, but its exercise by Congress, which may be incompatible with the exercise of the same power by the states, and that the states may legislate in the absence of congressional regulations. . . .

The diversities of opinion, therefore, which have existed on this subject have arisen from the different views taken of the nature of this power. But when the nature of a power like this is spoken of, when it is said that the nature of the power requires that it should be exercised exclusively by Congress, it must be intended to refer to the subjects of that power, and to say they are of such a nature as to require exclusive legislation by Congress. Now the power to regulate commerce embraces a vast field, containing not only many, but exceedingly various subjects, quite unlike in their nature; some imperatively demanding a single uniform rule, operating equally on the commerce of the United States in every port; and some, like the subject now in question, as imperatively demanding that diversity, which alone can meet the local necessities of navigation.

Either absolutely to affirm, or deny that the nature of this power requires exclusive legislation by Congress, is to lose sight of the nature of the subjects of this power, and to assert concerning all of them, what is really applicable but to a part. Whatever subjects of this power are in their nature national, or admit only of one uniform system, or plan of regulation, may justly be said to be of such a nature as to require exclusive legislation by Congress. That this cannot be affirmed of laws for the regulation of pilots and pilotage, is plain. The act of 1789 contains a clear and authoritative declaration by the first Congress, that the nature of this subject is such that until Congress should find it necessary to exert its power, it should be left to the legislation of the states; that it is local and not national; that it is likely to be the best provided for, not by one system, or plan of regulation, but by as many as the legislative discretion of the several states should deem applicable to the local peculiarities of the ports within their limits. . . .

It is the opinion of a majority of the Court that the mere grant to Congress of the power to regulate commerce, did not deprive the states of power to regulate pilots, and that although Congress has legislated on this subject, its legislation manifests an intention, with a single exception, not to regulate this subject, but to leave its regulation to the several states. To these precise questions, which are all we are called on to decide, this opinion must be understood to be confined. It does not extend to the question what other subjects, under the commercial power, are within the exclusive control of Congress, or may be regulated by the states in the absence of all congressional legislation; nor to the general question, how far any regulation of a subject by Congress may be deemed to operate as an exclusion of all legislation by the states upon the same subject. We decide the precise questions before us, upon what we deem sound principles, applicable to this particular subject in the state in which the legislation of Congress has left it. We go no further. . . .

Mr. Justice McLean, with Mr. Justice Wayne concurring, rendered a dissenting opinion. Mr. Justice Daniel rendered an opinion which differed in reasoning but concurred in the judgment of the Court.

KENTUCKY WHIP & COLLAR COMPANY v. ILLINOIS CENTRAL RAILROAD COMPANY
299 U. S. 334; 81 L. Ed. 270; 57 Sup. Ct. 277. 1937.

In determining in concrete cases the extent to which the power of Congress over interstate commerce is exclusive, under the rule laid down in the case of Cooley v. The Board of Wardens of the Port of Philadelphia above, many difficult problems have arisen out of the exercise by the states of their police power in such a way as to affect either directly or incidentally interstate commerce. Under what circumstances can a state law designed to protect the local health, morals, and safety be enforced against interstate carriers or those engaged in interstate commerce? No more interesting illustration of the complexity of this problem can be found than in the history of the attempts made by various states from time to time to regulate or prohibit interstate shipments of intoxicating liquor.

Prohibition sentiment in the states was slow in making itself effective, and it was not until the License Cases, 5 Howard 504 (1847), that the Supreme Court was asked to consider the relation of local regulations of the liquor traffic to interstate commerce. These cases involved the validity of statutes of New Hampshire, Rhode Island, and Massachusetts forbidding the sale of liquor in small quantities and without licenses. In the Rhode Island and Massachusetts cases the liquor in question was imported from abroad; in the New Hampshire case it was brought in from Boston and was sold in the original barrel. The cases presented considerable difficulty. Twenty years before, in the case of Brown v. Maryland, 12 Wheaton 419 (1827), the Court had held that goods imported from abroad could not be subjected to license tax requirements by the state as long as they remained unsold or in the original packages. Should a similar rule apply to a barrel of gin shipped from Boston to New Hampshire and there offered for sale in the same barrel? Six justices wrote separate opinions in the case, but the state statutes were sustained. The leading opinion was written by Chief Justice Taney, who took the position that the power of Congress over interstate commerce was not exclusive, and that the license requirements in question were legitimate as long as they conflicted with no federal legislation.

General abatement of interest in the prohibition movement prevented further judicial scrutiny of this problem until 1888. In that year, in Bowman v. C. & N. W. Ry. Co., 125 U. S. 465, the Supreme Court held invalid an Iowa statute of 1886 imposing a fine of $100 upon any railroad which should knowingly bring into the state intoxicating liquor without first obtaining a certificate that the consignee could lawfully sell it, as an attempt on the part of the state to exercise jurisdiction beyond its own territorial limits and a direct interference with interstate commerce. Two years later the case of Leisy v. Hardin, 135 U. S. 100 (1890), was decided.

Leisy, a brewer in Peoria, Illinois, had shipped certain barrels and cases of beer to a consignee in Keokuk, Iowa. There the beer was seized while still in the original packages by Hardin, the city marshal, acting under authority of an Iowa statute forbidding the manufacture and sale of intoxicating liquor except for medicinal, sacramental, etc. purposes. Leisy brought an action (replevin) against Hardin to recover possession of the beer, alleging the unconstitutionality of the statute because it authorized state confiscation while still in the original packages of goods shipped in interstate commerce. The Court sustained Leisy's contention, and applied its famous "original package rule" that until the original packages had been broken or the goods had been sold, commodities shipped in interstate commerce were not subject to the police power of the state. It emphasized that the transportation of products across state lines is a subject calling for uniform and national regulation within the principle enunciated in the Cooley case. Apparently conscious, however, of the devastating results of its decision upon the practical enforcement of state prohibition laws the Court suggested, or implied, in several parts of its opinion that Congress might consent to the exercise of the police power by the states over articles of interstate commerce at an earlier point in their passage than was possible without such consent. In short, the Court seemed to invite Congress to provide a legislative remedy for the difficulty which its decision created.

This invitation was acted upon by Congress with promptness and within a few months the Wilson Act was placed upon the statute book. This provided that liquor shipped through the channels of interstate commerce into any state should "upon arrival in such state" be subject immediately to the police power of the state regardless of whether or not it remained in the original packages. This statute was held constitutional by the Supreme Court in the case of In re Rahrer, 140 U. S. 545 (1891), against the contention, among others, that it involved a delegation to the states of the power over interstate commerce. The beneficial results intended by the enactment of the Wilson Act were, however, of short duration. In 1898 a box labeled "groceries" and consigned to one Horn was received by the station agent at Brighton, Iowa, and placed by him in the station warehouse, where a few hours later it was seized under a search warrant by a constable on what proved to be the correct suspicion that it contained liquor. The question of the validity of this seizure was finally brought to the Supreme Court of the United States, which held that the words "upon arrival in such state" used in the Wilson Act meant arrival actually in the hands of the consignee, and that until such arrival the exclusive jurisdiction of Congress over goods shipped in interstate commerce protected them from state interference. Rhodes v. Iowa, 170 U. S. 412 (1898).

The difficult problem of devising a plan whereby the states could adequately protect themselves from liquor brought in through interstate commerce without encroaching upon the domain of federal control over such commerce was at last solved by the enactment in 1913 of an ingenious piece of federal legislation, the Webb-Kenyon Act. This was in some ways a most remarkable law. It merely provided that the shipment of intoxicating liquors into any state or territory, when such liquors were intended by any persons interested in them to be used or sold in violation of the law of such state or territory, should be prohibited. No federal penalty was attached to the statute; it merely outlawed from interstate commerce shipments of liquor to be used in violation of state law, and the state, therefore, was at liberty to seize and confiscate them as soon as it could get its hands on them. There were grave doubts in many minds as to the validity of this act, which, it was alleged, amounted to an abdication by Congress of a portion of its authority over interstate commerce. President Taft, upon the advice of Attorney General Wickersham, vetoed the bill upon this ground, but it was passed over his veto. The Supreme Court, however, upheld the validity of the law in the case of Clark Distilling Co. v. Western Maryland Railway Co., 242 U. S. 311 (1917), pointing out that after all it was the will of Congress which made the prohibitions in question effective and that the rule established was uniform even though the conditions calling its provisions into play might vary from state to state. In 1917 Congress went still further in the passage of the Reed "Bone-Dry" Amendment, and forbade under federal penalty the shipping even for personal use of intoxicating liquor into any state which forbade its manufacture or sale. This act was sustained by the Supreme Court in the case of United States v. Hill, 248 U. S. 420 (1919).

The net result of all this is that Congress may forbid the use of the facilities of interstate commerce for the purpose of violating the valid police laws of the states. Clearly the method may be used in dealing with other things besides liquor. It was subsequently applied to the problem of the marketing of convict-made goods in open competition with goods made by free labor. A number of states require prisoners in penal institutions to be employed in the making of saleable goods, or permit them to be hired out under contract to concerns which use them in the making of such goods. Since convicts are paid only nominal wages if any, the goods which they make can be sold at prices far below those which the ordinary manufacturer must charge to keep his business going. The competition of convict labor tends inevitably to pull down the wage scale of the ordinary workman and for years organized labor sought legislative protection for free wage earners from the disastrous results of this competition. In 1929 Congress passed the Hawes-Cooper Act, modeled on the Wilson Act of 1890. This was held valid in Whitfield v. Ohio, 297 U. S. 431 (1936).

The Ashurst-Sumners Act of 1935 was patterned after the Webb-Kenyon Act. It makes it unlawful to ship in interstate or foreign commerce goods made by convict labor into any state where the goods are intended to be received, possessed, sold, or used in violation of its laws. Packages containing convict-made goods must be plainly labeled as such. Unlike the Webb-Kenyon Act, this statute provides penalties of fine and forfeiture for its violation. In the present case the plaintiff company manufactured, with convict labor, horse collars, harness, etc., which it sold in various states. It tendered to the railroad company shipments of convict-made goods, not labeled as such, some of which were consigned to customers in states whose laws forbade the sale of convict-made goods within their borders. The railroad, in obedience to the statute, refused the shipments and the company sought a mandatory injunction to compel it to accept them, alleging the unconstitutionality of the act.

In 1902 Congress provided, after the pattern of the Wilson Act of 1890, that oleomargarine and other imitations of butter should be subject to the police power of the states upon "arrival within the limits of the state." In 1940 it changed a statute of 1912, which had forbidden entirely the interstate shipment of prize-fight films, so that such films are now subject to the police power of any state "upon crossing the boundary of such state."

Mr. Chief Justice Hughes delivered the opinion of the Court, saying in part:

. . . Petitioner contends (1) that the Congress is without constitutional authority to prohibit the movement in interstate commerce of useful and harmless articles made by convict labor and (2) that the Congress has no power to exclude from interstate commerce convict-made goods which are not labeled as such.

First.—The commerce clause confers upon the Congress "the power to regulate, that is, to prescribe the rule by which commerce is to be governed." This power "is complete in itself, may be exercised to its utmost extent, and acknowledges no limitations, other than are prescribed in the Constitution," Gibbons v. Ogden, 9 Wheat. 1, 196. By the act now before us, the Congress purports to establish a rule governing interstate transportation, which is unquestionably interstate commerce. The question is whether this rule goes beyond the authority to "regulate."

Petitioner's argument necessarily recognizes that in certain circumstances an absolute prohibition of interstate transportation is constitutional regulation. The power to prohibit interstate transportation has been upheld by this Court in relation to diseased livestock, lottery tickets, commodities owned by the interstate carrier transporting them, except such as may be required in the conduct of its business as a common carrier, adulterated and misbranded articles, under the Pure Food and Drugs Act, women, for immoral purposes, intoxicating liquors, diseased plants, stolen motor vehicles, and kidnaped persons.

The decisions sustaining this variety of statutes disclose the principles deemed to be applicable. We have frequently said that in the exercise of its control over interstate commerce, the means employed by the Congress may have the quality of police regulations. . . . The power was defined in broad terms in Brooks v. United States, 267 U. S. 432. "Congress can certainly regulate interstate commerce to the extent of forbidding and punishing the use of such commerce as an agency to promote immorality, dishonesty or the spread of any evil or harm to the people of other states from the state of origin. In doing this it is merely exercising the police power for the benefit of the public, within the field of interstate commerce."

The anticipated evil or harm may proceed from something inherent in the subject of transportation as in the case of diseased or noxious articles, which are unfit for commerce. . . . Or the evil may lie in the purpose of the transportation, as in the case of lottery tickets, or the transportation of women for immoral purposes. . . . The prohibition may be designed to give effect to the policies of the Congress in relation to the instrumentalities of interstate commerce, as in the case of commodities owned by interstate carriers. . . . And, while the power to regulate interstate commerce resides in the Congress, which must determine its own policy, the Congress may shape that policy in the light of the fact that the transportation in interstate commerce, if permitted, would aid in the frustration of valid state laws for the protection of persons and property. . . .

The contention is inadmissible that the act of Congress is invalid merely because the horse collars and harness which petitioner manufactures and sells are useful and harmless articles. The motor vehicles, which are the subject of the transportation prohibited in the National Motor Vehicle Theft Act, are in themselves useful and proper subjects of commerce, but their transportation by one who knows they have been stolen is "a gross misuse of interstate commerce" and the Congress may properly punish it "because of its harmful result and its defeat of the property rights of those whose machines against their will are taken into other jurisdictions." . . . Similarly, the object of the

Federal Kidnaping Act is to aid in the protection of the personal liberty of one who has been unlawfully seized or carried away. . . .

On the same general principle, the Congress may prevent interstate transportation from being used to bring into a state articles the traffic in which the state has constitutional authority to forbid, and has forbidden, in its internal commerce. In that view, we sustained the acts of Congress designed to prevent the use of interstate transportation to hamper the execution of state policy with respect to traffic in intoxicating liquors. This was not because intoxicating liquors were not otherwise legitimate articles of commerce. On the contrary they were recognized as such "by the usages of the commercial world, the laws of Congress and the decisions of courts." Leisy v. Hardin, 135 U. S. 100. . . . It was because intoxicating liquors were legitimate subjects of commercial intercourse that the states were powerless to interfere with their transportation in interstate commerce. . . . But because of the effects ascribed to the traffic in intoxicating liquors, the states in the exercise of their police power in relation to their internal commerce could restrict or interdict that traffic without violating the federal Constitution. . . . To aid the states in securing the full protection they desired, Congress brought into play its power to regulate interstate commerce. . . . [The Court here reviews the federal statutes and the cases upholding them which are discussed in the note above.]

The ruling in Hammer v. Dagenhart, 247 U. S. 251, upon which petitioner relies, in no way contravenes or limits the principle of these decisions. In the Hammer case, the Court concluded that the act of Congress there under consideration had as its aim the placing of local production under federal control. Far from disapproving the decisions we have cited, the Court expressly recognized their authority. "In each of these instances," the Court said, "the use of interstate transportation was necessary to the accomplishment of harmful results. In other words, although the power over interstate transportation was to regulate, that could only be accomplished by prohibiting the use of the facilities of interstate commerce to effect the evil intended." . . .

The course of congressional legislation with respect to convict-made goods has followed closely the precedents as to intoxicating liquors. By the Hawes-Cooper Act of January 19, 1929, the Congress provided that convict-made goods (with certain exceptions) transported into any state should be subject upon arrival, whether in the original packages or otherwise, to the operation of state laws as if produced within the state. In Whitfield v. Ohio, 297 U. S. 431, petitioner was charged in the state court in Ohio with selling convict-made goods in violation of the state law. It appeared that the goods had been sold in the original packages as shipped in interstate commerce and that there was "nothing harmful, injurious or deleterious" about them. But this Court said that the view of the state of Ohio, that the sale of convict-made goods in competition with the products of free labor was an evil, found ample support in fact and in the similar legislation of a preponderant number of other states. The Court observed that the Congress had prohibited the importation of the products of convict labor. All such legislation, state and federal, proceeded upon the view "that free labor, properly compensated, cannot compete successfully with the enforced and unpaid or underpaid convict labor of the prison." The Court upheld the power of the state, so far as the federal Constitution is concerned, to base nondiscriminatory legislation upon that conception, and as it appeared that the Ohio statute would be unassailable if made to take effect after sale in the original package, the statute was held to be equally unassailable in the light of the provisions of the Hawes-Cooper Act. As to the validity of the latter act, the Court followed the decision In Re Rahrer, 140 U. S. 545, in relation to the Wilson Act.

The Ashurst-Sumners Act as to interstate transportation of convict-made goods has substantially the same provisions as the Webb-Kenyon Act as to intoxicating liquors and finds support in similar considerations. The subject of the prohibited traffic is different, the effects of the traffic are different, but the underlying principle is the same. The pertinent point is that where the subject of commerce is one as to which the power of the state may constitutionally be exerted by restriction or prohibition in order to prevent harmful consequences, the Congress may, if it sees fit, put forth its power to regulate interstate commerce so as to prevent that commerce from being used to impede the carrying out of the state policy.

In the congressional action there is nothing arbitrary or capricious bringing the statute into collision with the requirements of due process of law. The Congress in exercising the power confided to it by the Constitution is as free as the states to recognize the fundamental interests of free labor. Nor has the Congress attempted to delegate its authority to the states. The Congress has not sought to exercise a power not granted or to usurp the police powers of the states. It has not acted on any assumption of a power enlarged by virtue of state action. The Congress has exercised its plenary power which is subject to no limitation other than that which is found in the Constitution itself. The Congress has formulated its own policy and established its own rule. The fact that it has adopted its rule in order to aid the enforcement of valid state laws affords no ground for constitutional objection.

Second.—As the Congress could prohibit the interstate transportation of convict-made goods as provided in section one of the act, the Congress could require packages containing convict-made goods to be labeled as required by section two. The requirement of labels, disclosing the nature of the contents, the name and location of the penal institution where the goods were produced, and the names and addresses of shippers and consignees, was manifestly reasonable and appropriate for the carrying out of the prohibition. . . . The fact that the labeling was required in all shipments of convict-made goods, regardless of the law of the state of destination, does not invalidate the provision as its scope could reasonably be deemed to be necessary to accomplish the legitimate purpose of the act. . . .

The decree is affirmed.

UNITED STATES v. DARBY
312 U. S. 100; 85 L. Ed. 609; 61 Sup. Ct. 451. 1941.

It used to be said that the federal government has no police power. In a narrow sense this is true, for the police power is defined as the general power to pass regulatory laws for the protection of the health, morals, safety, good order, and general welfare of the community. The Constitution grants no such broad power to Congress, and so, by the operation of the Tenth Amendment, it is reserved to the states. In recent years, however, what may be fairly called a federal police power has come into existence through the use by Congress of certain of its delegated powers to achieve some of the same social objectives which the states achieve through the state police power. Thus Congress has no delegated power to forbid the production of impure food products; but it does have power to forbid the shipping of impure food in interstate commerce. It cannot punish ordinary business swindles; but it may make it a crime to use the mails for purposes of fraud. In this way Congress has been able to use its power to regulate interstate commerce, to operate the postal service, and to tax, as "constitutional pegs" upon which to hang policies for the national welfare which it has no direct authority to promulgate. By this somewhat indirect method Congress has come to exercise control over an ever-increasing number of social and economic problems. By far the largest part of this growing federal police power is based upon the commerce clause.

This penetration of federal power into new areas aroused plenty of protest on constitutional grounds, and the Supreme Court jogged cautiously along step by step in dealing with the new forms of federal social legislation. It found little difficulty, however, in sustaining the validity of the federal safety appliance acts, laws regulating the transportation of explosives, restrictions upon the hours of labor of trainmen and telegraphers, the federal employers' liability statute applicable to railroads, the federal antitrust laws, and many similar statutes. While Congress in passing these acts was often seeking to control social and economic problems, the Court held the statutes valid on the rather narrow ground that they all tended to keep interstate commerce safe, efficient, and unobstructed. If the power to regulate commerce means anything it means the power to protect that commerce and promote its efficiency. See B. & O. R. Co. v. Interstate Commerce Commission, 221 U. S. 612 (1911), sustaining the Hours of Service Act, and Second Employers' Liability Cases, 223 U. S. 1 (1912), upholding the Federal Employers' Liability Act of 1908.

Much more important was the doctrine announced in the Lottery Case (Champion v. Ames, 188 U. S. 321, 1903), that Congress could validly bar from interstate commerce commodities which are dangerous or otherwise objectionable. In 1895 Congress forbade the sending of lottery tickets through interstate commerce or the mails. After holding that lottery tickets are articles of commerce, the Court decided that Congress had the power to guard the people of the United States from the "widespread pestilence of lotteries" by keeping lottery tickets out of the channels of interstate commerce over which Congress has undisputed control. Congress was not slow to exercise the kind of power sustained in the Lottery Case. It has excluded from interstate commerce impure or misbranded food and drugs, meat not properly inspected, obscene literature, and prize fight films (later modified in part), and other injurious or fraudulent commodities. Under a federal statute, if fabrics shipped in interstate commerce are marked "all wool" they must be in fact all wool. It may be noted in passing that the power of Congress over the postal system has enabled it to exercise a wide police power by excluding objectionable articles from the mails, and by forbidding the use of the mails for purposes of fraud.

There is no difference in principle between barring objectionable articles from interstate commerce and forbidding the use of the facilities of interstate commerce to aid immoral or criminal activities. The Court, at least, found no such difference. In Hoke v. United States, 227 U. S. 308 (1913), it held valid the Mann Act of 1910 which makes it a crime to transport women across a state line for immoral purposes. The act was not aimed at localized prostitution, but at the organized gangs of white slavers who carried on the interstate traffic in girls and women upon which commercialized vice depends. In 1925 Congress made it a crime knowingly to drive a stolen automobile across a state line, and this was upheld in Brooks v. United States, 267 U. S. 432 (1925). Under the recent "antifence" laws, the same ban was put upon the interstate shipment of stolen goods in general. The so-called Lindbergh Act makes kidnapping a federal crime if the kidnapped person is carried across a state line (held valid in Gooch v. United States, 297 U. S. 124 (1936), and it is also a federal crime to use the mails, telephone, telegraph, or any system of interstate communication for purposes of extortion or blackmail. The theory in all these cases is clear and convincing. Congress, which is responsible for interstate commerce, may punish those who use the facilities of that commerce for immoral or criminal purposes.

The federal police power development reviewed thus far had fairly plain sailing constitutionally. All the articles barred from commerce had been "bad" articles, and all the forbidden uses of the facilities of that commerce had been "bad" uses. In 1916, however, Congress pushed the police power theory somewhat further in passing the Child Labor Act of 1916. Congress was well aware that it lacked the power to forbid child labor throughout the country. What it did, therefore, was to forbid the transportation in interstate commerce of the products of mines or factories in which children were employed in violation of the standards set up in this act. In other words, any employer who wished to market his goods through interstate commerce would have to stop employing children. It could not be claimed that the commodities produced in establishments using child labor were "bad" commodities, but merely that the conditions under which they were produced were "bad" conditions. The Supreme Court, split five to four, held the statute invalid in Hammer v. Dagenhart, 247 U. S. 251 (1918). The majority opinion emphasized that the goods barred from interstate commerce by the act were harmless; that the effect of the act was to regulate, not interstate commerce, but the conditions under which goods entering that commerce were produced, and that it was, therefore, not a bona fide exercise of the commerce power. The Court rejected the argument that Congress could validly prevent those who produce goods under unsatisfactory labor conditions from using the channels of interstate commerce in order to compete with producers in other states who maintain decent labor conditions. It said: "Many causes may cooperate to give one state, by reason of local laws or conditions, an economic advantage over others. The commerce clause was not intended to give Congress a general authority to equalize such conditions." Finally, the act was void under the Tenth Amendment because Congress was using its delegated power over commerce for the purpose of regulating child labor, a power which lies within the range of the powers reserved to the states. This was the "dual federalism" argument later developed in the Butler case discussed above (p. 357).

Mr. Justice Holmes dissented in Hammer v. Dagenhart in a strong opinion in which he declared that the Child Labor Act was a clear and direct exercise of the commerce power, that it did "not meddle with anything belonging to the states," and that it should not be held void because of its indirect effects upon state authority. He said: "It does not matter whether the supposed evil precedes or follows the transportation. It is enough that, in the opinion of Congress, the transportation encourages the evil. The notion that prohibition is any less prohibition when applied to things now thought evil I do not understand. But if there is any matter upon which civilized countries have agreed,—far more unanimously than they have with regard to intoxicants and some other matters over which this country is now emotionally aroused,—it is the evil of premature and excessive child labor. I should have thought that if we were to introduce our own moral conceptions where, in my opinion, they do not belong, this was preeminently a case for upholding the exercise of all its powers by the United States. But I had thought that the propriety of the exercise of a power admitted to exist in some cases was for the consideration of Congress alone, and that this Court always had disavowed the right to intrude its judgment upon questions of policy or morals. It is not for this Court to pronounce when prohibition is necessary to regulation if it ever may be necessary—to say that it is permissible as against strong drink, but not as against the product of ruined lives. The act does not meddle with anything belonging to the states. They may regulate their internal affairs and their domestic commerce as they like. But when they seek to send their products across the state line they are no longer within their rights."

Seldom has judicial and professional opinion been more sharply divided than on the issues presented in Hammer v. Dagenhart. It is therefore both interesting and important that in the Darby case printed below the Court overruled Hammer v. Dagenhart. It is equally significant that this reversal met with virtually universal approval. In the twenty-three years which had intervened we had reached a clearer and surer understanding of the responsibility which the commerce clause places upon Congress. The early and not uncommon idea that the use by Congress of its commerce power to deal with broad social problems was not quite honest, that it amounted to "covert" or "backstairs" legislation, was largely forgotten. We had come to realize that serious evils which menace the health, safety, and welfare of the nation are spread and even generated by our vast national system of transportation and communication, and by our continent-wide network of interstate markets. It was clear that interstate commerce could be used for the public injury as well as for the public welfare. The commerce clause makes Congress the guardian of interstate commerce—and the only guardian. It is therefore not only the right of Congress, but its clear duty, to see to it that the facilities of interstate commerce are not used by any one, in any manner, to do any kind of harm. This is the basic doctrine on which the Darby case rests.

Mr. Justice Stone delivered the opinion of the Court, saying in part:

The two principal questions raised by the record in this case are, first, whether Congress has constitutional power to prohibit the shipment in interstate commerce of lumber manufactured by employees whose wages are less than a prescribed minimum or whose weekly hours of labor at that wage are greater than a prescribed maximum, and, second, whether it has power to prohibit the employment of workmen in the production of goods "for interstate commerce" at other than prescribed wages and hours. A subsidiary question is whether in connection with such prohibitions Congress can require the employer subject to them to keep records showing the hours worked each day and week by each of his employees including those engaged "in the production and manufacture of goods to wit, lumber, for 'interstate commerce.'" . . .

The Fair Labor Standards Act set up a comprehensive legislative scheme for preventing the shipment in interstate commerce of certain products and commodities produced in the United States under labor conditions as respects wages and hours which fail to conform to standards set up by the act. Its purpose, as we judicially know from the declaration of policy in § 2(a) of the act, and the reports of congressional committees proposing the legislation, is to exclude from interstate commerce goods produced for the commerce and to prevent their production for interstate commerce, under conditions detrimental to the maintenance of the minimum standards of living necessary for health and general well-being; and to prevent the use of interstate commerce as the means of competition in the distribution of goods so produced, and as the means of spreading and perpetuating such substandard labor conditions among the workers of the several states. The act also sets up an administrative procedure whereby those standards may from time to time be modified generally as to industries subject to the act or within an industry in accordance with specified standards, by an administrator acting in collaboration with "Industry Committees" appointed by him. . . .

The indictment charges that appellee is engaged, in the state of Georgia, in the business of acquiring raw materials, which he manufactures into finished lumber with the intent, when manufactured, to ship it in interstate commerce to customers outside the state, and that he does in fact so ship a large part of the lumber so produced. There are numerous counts charging appellee with the shipment in interstate commerce from Georgia to points outside the state of lumber in the production of which, for interstate commerce, appellee has employed workmen at less than the prescribed minimum wage or more than the prescribed maximum hours without payment to them of any wage for overtime. Other counts charge the employment by appellee of workmen in the production of lumber for interstate commerce at wages of less than 25 cents an hour or for more than the maximum hours per week without payment to them of the prescribed overtime wage. Still another count charges appellee with failure to keep records showing the hours worked each day a week by each of his employees as required by § 11(c) and the regulation of the administrator, and also that appellee unlawfully failed to keep such records of employees engaged "in the production and manufacture of goods, to wit lumber, for interstate commerce." . . .

The case comes here on assignments by the government that the district court erred in so far as it held that Congress was without constitutional power to penalize the acts set forth in the indictment, and appellee seeks to sustain the decision below on the grounds that the prohibition by Congress of those acts is unauthorized by the commerce clause and is prohibited by the Fifth Amendment. . . . We . . . confine our decision to the validity and construction of the statute.

The prohibition of shipment of the proscribed goods in interstate commerce. Section 15(a) (1) prohibits, and the indictment charges, the shipment in interstate commerce, of goods produced for interstate commerce by employees whose wages and hours of employment do not conform to the requirements of the act. Since this section is not violated unless the commodity shipped has been produced under labor conditions prohibited by § 6 and § 7, the only question arising under the commerce clause with respect to such shipments is whether Congress has the constitutional power to prohibit them.

While manufacture is not of itself interstate commerce the shipment of manufactured goods interstate is such commerce and the prohibition of such shipment by Congress is indubitably a regulation of the commerce. The power to regulate commerce is the power "to prescribe the rule by which commerce is governed." Gibbons v. Ogden, 9 Wheaton (U. S.) 1. It extends not only to those regulations which aid, foster and protect the commerce, but embraces those which prohibit it. It is conceded that the power of Congress to prohibit transportation in interstate commerce includes noxious articles, Lottery Case (Champion v. Ames) 188 U. S. 321; stolen articles, Brooks v. United States, 267 U. S. 432; kidnapped persons, Gooch v. United States, 297 U. S. 124; and articles such as intoxicating liquor or convict made goods, traffic in which is forbidden or restricted by the laws of the state of destination. Kentucky Whip & Collar Co. v. Illinois C. R. Co., 299 U. S. 334.

But it is said that the present prohibition falls within the scope of none of these categories; that while the prohibition is nominally a regulation of the commerce its motive or purpose is regulation of wages and hours of persons engaged in manufacture, the control of which has been reserved to the states and upon which Georgia and some of the states of destination have placed no restriction; that the effect of the present statute is not to exclude the prescribed articles from interstate commerce in aid of state regulation as in Kentucky Whip & Collar Co. v. Illinois C. R. Co. *supra*, but instead, under the guise of a regulation of interstate commerce, it undertakes to regulate wages and hours within the state contrary to the policy of the state which has elected to leave them unregulated.

The power of Congress over interstate commerce "is complete in itself, may be exercised to its utmost extent, and acknowledges no limitations other than are prescribed in the Constitution." That power can neither be enlarged nor diminished by the exercise or non-exercise of state power. Congress, following its own conception of public policy concerning the restrictions which may appropriately be imposed on interstate commerce, is free to exclude from the commerce articles whose use in the states for which they are destined it may conceive to be injurious to the public health, morals or welfare, even though the state has not sought to regulate their use.

Such regulation is not a forbidden invasion of state power merely because either its motive or its consequence is to restrict the use of articles of commerce within the states of destination and is not prohibited unless by other constitutional provisions. It is no objection to the assertion of the power to regulate interstate commerce that its exercise is attended by the same incidents which attend the exercise of the police power of the states.

The motive and purpose of the present regulation are plainly to make effective the congressional conception of public policy that interstate commerce should not be made the instrument of competition in the distribution of goods produced under substandard labor conditions, which competition is injurious to the commerce and to the states from and to which the commerce flows. The motive and purpose of a regulation of interstate commerce are matters for the legislative judgment upon the exercise of which the Constitution places no restriction and over which the courts are given no control. "The judicial cannot prescribe to the legislative department of the government limitations upon the exercise of its acknowledged power." Veazie Bank v. Fenno, 8 Wallace (U. S.) 533. Whatever their motive and purpose, regulations of commerce which do not infringe some constitutional prohibition are within the plenary power conferred on Congress by the commerce clause. Subject only to that limitation, presently to be considered, we conclude that the prohibition of the shipment interstate of goods produced under the forbidden substandard labor conditions is within the constitutional authority of Congress.

In the more than a century which has elapsed since the decision of Gibbons v. Ogden, these principles of constitutional interpretation have been so long and repeatedly recognized by this Court as applicable to the commerce clause, that there would be little occasion for repeating them now were it not for the decision of this Court twenty-two years ago in Hammer v. Dagenhart, 247 U. S. 251. In that case it was held by a bare majority of the Court over the powerful and now classic dissent of Mr. Justice Holmes setting forth the fundamental issues involved, that Congress was without power to exclude the products of child labor from interstate commerce. The reasoning and conclusion of the Court's opinion there cannot be reconciled with the conclusion which we have reached, that the power of Congress under the commerce clause is plenary to exclude any article from interstate commerce subject only to the specific prohibitions of the Constitution.

Hammer v. Dagenhart has not been followed. The distinction on which the decision was rested that congressional power to prohibit interstate commerce is limited to articles which in themselves have some harmful or deleterious property—a distinction which was novel when made and unsupported by any provision of the Constitution— has long since been abandoned. Brooks v. United States, 267 U. S. 432; Kentucky Whip & Collar Co. v. Illinois C. R. Co., 299 U. S. 334; Mulford v. Smith, 307 U. S. 38. The thesis of the opinion that the motive of the prohibition or its effect to control in some measure the use or production within the states of the article thus excluded from the commerce can operate to deprive the regulation of its constitutional authority has long since ceased to have force. And finally we have declared "The authority of the federal government over interstate commerce does not differ in extent or character from that retained by the states over intrastate commerce." United States v. Rock Royal Co-operative, 307 U. S. 533.

The conclusion is inescapable that Hammer v. Dagenhart was a departure from the principles which have prevailed in the interpretation of the commerce clause both before and since the decision and that such vitality, as a precedent, as it then had has long since been exhausted. It should be and now is overruled.

Validity of the wage and hour requirements. Section 15(a) (2), 29 USCA § 215 and §§ 6 and 7, 29 USCA §§ 206, 207, require employers to conform to the wage and hour provisions with respect to all employees engaged in the production of goods for interstate commerce. As appellee's employees are not alleged to be "engaged in interstate commerce" the validity of the prohibition turns on the question whether the employment, under other than the prescribed labor standards, of employees engaged in the production of goods for interstate commerce is so related to the commerce and so affects it as to be within the reach of the power of Congress to regulate it.

To answer this question we must at the outset determine whether the particular acts charged in the counts which are laid under § 15(a) (2) as they were construed below, constitute "production for commerce" within the meaning of the statute. As the government seeks to apply the statute in the indictment, and as the court below construed the phrase "produced for interstate commerce," it embraces at least the case where an employer engaged, as is appellee, in the manufacture and shipment of goods in filling orders of extrastate customers, manufactures his product with the intent or expectation that according to the normal course of his business all or some part of it will be selected for shipment to those customers.

Without attempting to define the precise limits of the phrase, we think the acts alleged in the indictment are within the sweep of the statute. The obvious purpose of the act was not only to prevent the interstate transportation of the proscribed product, but to stop the initial step toward transportation, production with the purpose of so transporting it. Congress was not unaware that most manufacturing businesses shipping their product in interstate commerce make it in their shops without reference to its ultimate destination and then after manufacture select some of it for shipment interstate and some intrastate according to the daily demands of their business, and that it would be practically impossible, without disrupting manufacturing businesses, to restrict the prohibited kind of production to the particular pieces of lumber, cloth, furniture or the like which later move in interstate rather than intrastate commerce.

The recognized need of drafting a workable statute and the well known circumstances in which it was to be applied are persuasive of the conclusion, which the legislative history supports, that the "production for commerce" intended includes at least production of goods, which, at the time of production, the employer, according to the normal course of his business, intends or expects to move in interstate commerce although, through the exigencies of the business, all of the goods may not thereafter actually enter interstate commerce.

There remains the question whether such restriction on the production of goods for commerce is a permissible exercise of the commerce power. The power of Congress over interstate commerce is not confined to the regulation of commerce among the states. It extends to those activities intrastate which so affect interstate commerce or the exercise of the power of Congress over it as to make regulation of them appropriate means to the attainment of a legitimate end, the exercise of the granted power of Congress to regulate interstate commerce.

While this Court has many times found state regulation of interstate commerce, when uniformity of its regulation is of national concern, to be incompatible with the commerce clause even though Congress has not legislated on the subject, the Court has never implied such restraint on state control over matters intrastate not deemed to be regulations of interstate commerce or its instrumentalities even though they affect the commerce. In the absence of congressional legislation on the subject state laws which are not regulations of the commerce itself or its instrumentalities are not forbidden even though they affect interstate commerce.

But it does not follow that Congress may not by appropriate legislation regulate intrastate activities where they have a substantial effect on interstate commerce. A recent example is the National Labor Relations Act for the regulation of employer and employee relations in industries in which strikes, induced by unfair labor practices named in the Act, tend to disturb or obstruct interstate commerce. See National Labor Relations Bd. v. Jones & L. Steel Corp., 301 U. S. 1. But long before the adoption of the National Labor Relations Act this Court had many times held that the power of Congress to regulate interstate commerce extends to the regulation through legislative action of activities intrastate which have a substantial effect on the commerce or the exercise of the congressional power over it.

In such legislation Congress has sometimes left it to the courts to determine whether the intrastate activities have the prohibited effect on the commerce, as in the Sherman Act. It has sometimes left it to an administrative board or agency to determine whether the activities sought to be regulated or prohibited have such effect, as in the case of the Interstate Commerce Act, and the National Labor Relations Act or whether they come within the statutory definition of the prohibited act as in the Federal Trade Commission Act. And sometimes Congress itself has said that a particular activity affects the commerce as it did in the present act, the Safety Appliance Act and the Railway Labor Act. In passing on the validity of legislation of the class last mentioned the only function of courts is to determine whether the particular activity regulated or prohibited is within the reach of the federal power.

Congress, having by the present act adopted the policy of excluding from interstate commerce all goods produced for the commerce which do not conform to the specified labor standards, it may choose the means reasonably adapted to the attainment of the permitted end, even though they involve control of intrastate activities. . . . A familiar like exercise of power is the regulation of intrastate transactions which are so commingled with or related to interstate commerce that all must be regulated if the interstate commerce is to be effectively controlled. Shreveport Case, 234 U. S. 342. Similarly Congress may require inspection and preventive treatment of all cattle in a disease infected area in order to prevent shipment in interstate commerce of some of the cattle without the treatment. Thornton v. United States, 271 U. S. 414. It may prohibit the removal, at destination, of labels required by the Pure Food & Drugs Act to be affixed to articles transported in interstate commerce. McDermott v. Wisconsin, 228 U. S. 115. And we have recently held that Congress in the exercise of its power to require inspection and grading of tobacco shipped in interstate commerce may compel such inspection and grading of all tobacco sold at local auction rooms from which a substantial part but not all of the tobacco sold is shipped in interstate commerce. Currin v. Wallace, 306 U. S. 11.

We think also that § 15(a) (2), 29 USCA § 215 (a) (2), now under consideration, is sustainable independently of § 15(a) (1), which prohibits shipment or transportation of the proscribed goods. As we have said the evils aimed at by the act are the spread of substandard labor conditions through the use of the facilities of interstate commerce for competition by the goods so produced with those produced under the prescribed or better labor conditions; and the consequent dislocation of the commerce itself caused by the impairment or destruction of local businesses by competition made effective through interstate commerce. The act is thus directed at the suppression of a method or kind of competition in interstate commerce which it has in effect condemned as "unfair," as the Clayton Act has condemned other "unfair methods of competition" made effective through interstate commerce.

The Sherman Act and the National Labor Relations Act are familiar examples of the exertion of the commerce power to prohibit or control activities wholly intrastate because of their effect on interstate commerce.

The means adopted by § 15(a) (2) for the protection of interstate commerce by the suppression of the production of the condemned goods for interstate commerce is so related to the commerce and so affects it as to be within the reach of the commerce power. Congress, to attain its objective in the suppression of nation-wide competition in interstate commerce by goods produced under substandard labor conditions, has made no distinction as to the volume or amount of shipments in the commerce or of production for commerce by any particular shipper or producer. It recognized that in present day industry, competition by a small part may affect the whole and that the total effect of the competition of many small producers may be great. The legislation aimed at a whole embraces all its parts.

So far as Carter v. Carter Coal Co. 298 U. S. 238, is inconsistent with this conclusion, its doctrine is limited in principle by the decisions under the Sherman Act and the National Labor Relations Act, which we have cited and which we follow.

Our conclusion is unaffected by the Tenth Amendment which provides: "The powers not delegated to the United States by the Constitution nor prohibited by it to the states are reserved to the states respectively or to the people." The amendment states but a truism that all is retained which has not been surrendered. There is nothing in the history of its adoption to suggest that it was more than declaratory of the relationship between the national and state governments as it had been established by the Constitution before the amendment or that its purpose was other than to allay fears that the new national government might seek to exercise powers not granted, and that the states might not be able to exercise fully their reserved powers.

From the beginning and for many years the amendment has been construed as not depriving the national government of authority to resort to all means for the exercise of a granted power which are appropriate and plainly adapted to the permitted end. Whatever doubts may have arisen of the soundness of that conclusion they have been put at rest by the decisions under the Sherman Act and the National Labor Relations Act which we have cited.

Validity of the requirement of records of wages and hours. Section 15(a) (5) and § 11(c), 29 USCA §§ 215(a) (5) and 211 (c). These requirements are incidental to those for the prescribed wages and hours, and hence validity of the former turns on validity of the latter. Since, as we have held, Congress may require production for interstate commerce to conform to those conditions, it may require the employer, as a means of enforcing the valid law, to keep a record showing whether he has in fact complied with it. The requirement for records even of the intrastate transaction is an appropriate means to the legitimate end.

Validity of the wage and hour provisions under the Fifth Amendment. Both provisions are minimum wage requirements compelling the payment of a minimum standard wage with a prescribed increased wage for overtime. . . . Since our decision in West Hotel Co. v. Parrish, 300 U. S. 379, it is no longer open to question that the fixing of a minimum wage is within the legislative power and that the bare fact of its exercise is not a denial of due process under the Fifth more than under the Fourteenth Amendment. Nor is it any longer open to question that it is within the legislative power to fix maximum hours. Similarly the statute is not objectionable because applied alike to both men and women.

The act is sufficiently definite to meet constitutional demands. One who employs persons, without conforming to the prescribed wage and hour conditions, to work on goods which he ships or expects to ship across state lines, is warned that he may be subject to the criminal penalties of the act. No more is required. . . .

Reversed.

NATIONAL LABOR RELATIONS BOARD v. JONES & LAUGHLIN STEEL CORPORATION
301 U. S. 1; 81 L. Ed. 893; 57 Sup. Ct. 615. 1937.

Until the advent of the New Deal federal control of labor relations was confined to interstate railroads or common carriers, a field pretty obviously within the scope of the commerce power. The National Industrial Recovery Act of 1933 required, among other things, the establishment of reasonable hours and wages, and forbade "yellow dog contracts" and child labor, on the theory that unsatisfactory labor conditions, even when existing locally, adversely affect interstate commerce. At the same time the President created by executive order in 1933 the National Labor Board to deal with the rising tide of labor difficulties. This was followed by the National Labor Relations Board of 1934, also created by executive order authorized by statute. These agencies were not wisely organized, were endowed with insufficient authority, and were in the main unsuccessful.

Accordingly in July, 1935, after the N.I.R.A. had been held void in the Schechter case, 295 U. S. 495, Congress passed the Wagner Labor Relations Act, the first thoroughgoing and genuinely regulatory federal act to deal with the relations between labor and capital. The act is unique both in scope and in method. Its scope includes all labor disputes which burden or obstruct interstate commerce. Such burden or obstruction may take the form (a) of impairing the efficiency or safety of the instrumentalities of commerce, (b) of restraining the flow of raw materials or manufactured goods through interstate commerce, or controlling the prices thereof, (c) of reducing employment and wages sufficiently to reduce substantially the market for goods moving in interstate commerce, (d) of obstructing directly the actual current of commerce. The method employed by the act is that of defining carefully seven or eight "unfair labor practices" which are forbidden, and of creating a new National Labor Relations Board with power upon investigation to issue "cease and desist orders," enforceable in the courts, against those guilty of these practices. This is the technique employed in the Federal Trade Commission Act under which the commission issues "cease and desist orders" against those found to be engaging in unfair competitive trade practices. The National Labor Relations Board is, therefore, a very powerful body.

In dealing with labor relations Congress is circumscribed by the constitutional limitation that it can regulate such labor relations only through a bona fide exercise of its commerce power. What this constitutional limitation means concretely must be learned from the decisions of the Supreme Court. And here there has been as interesting and startling an evolution of judicial doctrines as of legislative policy. In the case of Adair v. United States, 208

U. S. 161 (1908), the Court held void an act penalizing an interstate carrier for discharging a workman because he belonged to a labor union. The relations between the railroad and its men were held to have nothing to do with the interstate commerce in which the railroad was engaged, and the restriction was also held to abridge the liberty of contract essential to due process of law. The Court in 1930, however, upheld the act of 1926 which forbade railroad interference with the integrity of labor union organization (see Texas & N.O.R. Co. v. Brotherhood of R. & S. S. Clerks, 281 U. S. 548). And in 1937 it sustained the mandatory provisions of the Railway Labor Act of 1934 (see Virginian Ry. Co. v. System Federation No. 40, 300 U. S. 515). These two cases are especially significant because in each of them the men involved in the labor controversy were not directly engaged in the processes of interstate commerce, being in the first case office clerks, and in the later case repair men. The Court appeared to have reached the conclusion that labor disputes occurring in any part of an interstate railroad system are likely to burden and obstruct interstate commerce and that Congress may, therefore, take reasonable means to regulate labor relations in the entire railroad field.

The Wagner Labor Relations Act appeared in the beginning to rest upon precarious footing, since its provisions extended to labor relations in the processes of manufacturing goods which were to be moved in interstate commerce. From the time the question first arose the Court had insisted upon the existence of a sharp constitutional line between manufacturing and the interstate commerce which follows it. Congress could control the latter but not the former. This was one of the principal grounds for the Court's decision in the first Child Labor Case (p. 415f.). In the Schechter case invalidating the N.I.R.A. the Court insisted that the conditions and processes of manufacturing, or of conducting a local business, were only "indirectly" connected with interstate commerce and were, therefore, outside the reach of federal power. The Court might very consistently have held the Wagner Act void in its application to labor relations in the field of manufacturing.

The Wagner Act came before the Court in five cases, decided on the same day. In three of these the act was invoked against unfair labor practices upon the part of employers of men who were engaged in manufacturing goods for the interstate market. The first of these, the Jones & Laughlin Steel Corporation case, involved one of the largest steel companies in the country. In the second case, National Labor Relations Board v. Fruehauf Trailer Company, 301 U. S. 49 (1937), the trailer company, a large manufacturing concern which ships its product all over the country, had discharged some of its men because of their membership and activity in a labor union. The act was held validly enforceable against them. Similarly the third case, National Labor Relations Board v. Friedman-Harry Marks Clothing Company, 301 U. S. 58 (1937), involved the discharge for union membership of men engaged in manufacturing men's clothing. It was emphasized in this case that the raw materials used were shipped in through interstate commerce and the manufactured product was widely distributed the country over. The opinions in these two later cases consist merely in a careful analysis of the facts to show the interstate character of the business and the obstruction which would result from disturbed labor conditions therein. The argument in the Jones & Laughlin Company case is referred to but not repeated.

In Washington, Virginia & Maryland Coach Company v. National Labor Relations Board, 301 U. S. 142 (1937), the facts were much the same as in the three cases just mentioned. Since there was no dispute as to the fact that the coach company was clearly and exclusively engaged in interstate commerce in the actual carrying on of which the employees involved were engaged, the act was held validly applicable by a unanimous Court.

In Associated Press v. N.L.R.B., 301 U. S. 103 (1937), in which an editor had been dismissed because of labor union activity, the Court found that the man had been engaged in work which was a part of interstate commerce. It held further that there was no invalid abridgment of freedom of press in thus preventing the Associated Press from discharging an editor because of his labor union associations.

It is important to note that in these cases the Court does not commit itself to the broad doctrine that any and all labor relations in industries producing goods for the interstate market are *ipso facto* directly connected with interstate commerce so as to fall automatically within the range of the Wagner Act. In each case there is a careful scrutiny of the scope and organization of the business and the probable results upon interstate commerce of a disruption through strikes or other labor disturbances of the continuity of the particular employments involved. In later cases, however, the Court has continued to apply the act broadly. In Santa Cruz Fruit Packing Co. v. N.L.R.B., 303 U. S. 453 (1938), it was held applicable to labor disputes in a California establishment which shipped only thirty-seven per cent of its product out of the state. In Consolidated Edison Co. v. N.L.R.B., 305 U. S. 197 (1938), the power company's labor relations were held to fall within the scope of the act although it did not sell power for resale outside the state, and although nearly all of its business was the production of electric energy consumed in the state. The Court held that the facilities by which interstate commerce is carried on in and around New York City are dependent upon the company for power. A disruption of its labor relations would therefore directly affect interstate commerce.

In the present case the National Labor Relations Board found that the Jones & Laughlin Steel Corporation had discharged some of its men because of their labor union activities. The board ordered the company to reinstate them and to cease such discrimination. The company was the fourth largest producer of steel in the country. It had nineteen subsidiaries which comprised an integrated system. It owned mines, ships, railroads, furnaces, and mills. The board found that the plants in which the labor troubles occurred "might be likened to the heart of a self-contained, highly integrated body. They draw in the raw materials from Michigan, Minnesota, West Virginia, Pennsylvania in part through arteries and by means controlled by the respondent; they transform the materials and then pump them out to all parts of the nation through the vast mechanism which the respondent has elaborated." Can the National Labor Relations Act be validly applied to such an organization?

Mr. Chief Justice Hughes delivered the opinion of the Court, saying in part:

. . . *First. The scope of the act.*—The act is challenged in its entirety as an attempt to regulate all industry, thus invading the reserved powers of the states over their local concerns. It is asserted that the references in the act to interstate and foreign commerce are colorable at best; that the act is not a true regulation of such commerce or of matters which directly affect it but on the contrary has the fundamental object of placing under the compulsory supervision of the federal government all industrial labor relations within the nation. The argument seeks support in the broad words of the preamble (section one) and in the sweep of the provisions of the act, and it is further insisted that its legislative history shows an essential universal purpose in the light of which its scope cannot be limited by either construction or by the application of the separability clause.

If this conception of terms, intent and consequent inseparability were sound, the act would necessarily fall by reason of the limitation upon the federal power which inheres in the constitutional grant, as well as because of the explicit reservation of the Tenth Amendment. . . . The authority of the federal government may not be pushed to such an extreme as to destroy the distinction, which the commerce clause itself establishes, between commerce "among the several states" and the internal concerns of a state. That distinction between what is national and what is local in the activities of commerce is vital to the maintainance of our federal system. . . .

We think it clear that the National Labor Relations Act may be construed so as to operate within the sphere of constitutional authority. The jurisdiction conferred upon the board, and invoked in this instance, is found in § 10(a), which provides:

"Sec. 10(a). The board is empowered, as hereinafter provided, to prevent any person from engaging in any unfair labor practice (listed in § 8) affecting commerce."

The critical words of this provision, prescribing the limits of the board's authority in dealing with the labor practices, are "affecting commerce." The act specifically defines the "commerce" to which it refers (§ 2(6)):

"The term 'commerce' means trade, traffic, commerce, transportation, or communication among the several states, or between the District of Columbia or any territory of the United States and any state or other territory, or between any foreign country and any state, territory, or the District of Columbia, or within the District of Columbia or any territory, or between points in the same state but through any other state or any territory or the District of Columbia or any foreign country."

There can be no question that the commerce thus contemplated by the act (aside from that within a territory or the District of Columbia) is interstate and foreign commerce in the constitutional sense. The act also defines the term "affecting commerce" (§ 2(7)):

"The term 'affecting commerce' means in commerce, or burdening or obstructing commerce or the free flow of commerce, or having led or tending to lead to a labor dispute burdening or obstructing commerce or the free flow of commerce."

This definition is one of exclusion as well as inclusion. The grant of authority to the board does not purport to extend to the relationship between all industrial employees and employers. Its terms do not impose collective bargaining upon all industry regardless of effects upon interstate or foreign commerce. It purports to reach only what may be deemed to burden or obstruct that commerce and, thus qualified, it must be construed as contemplating the exercise of control within constitutional bounds. It is a familiar principle that acts which directly burden or obstruct interstate or foreign commerce, or its free flow, are within the reach of the congressional power. Acts having that effect are not rendered immune because they grow out of labor disputes. . . . It is the effect upon commerce, not the source of the inquiry, which is the criterion. . . . Whether or not particular action does affect commerce in such a close and intimate fashion as to be subject to federal control, and hence to lie within the authority conferred upon the board, is left by the statute to be determined as individual cases arise. We are thus to inquire whether in the instant case the constitutional boundary has been passed.

Second. The unfair labor practices in question.—The unfair labor practices found by the board are those defined in § 8, subdivisions (1) and (3). These provide:

"Sec. 8. It shall be an unfair labor practice for an employer—

"(1) To interfere with, restrain, or coerce employees in the exercise of the rights guaranteed in § 7."

"(3) By discrimination in regard to hire or tenure of employment or any term or condition of employment to encourage or discourage membership in any labor organization: . . ."

Section 8, subdivision (1), refers to § 7, which is as follows:

"Sec. 7. Employees shall have the right to self-organization, to form, join, or assist labor organizations, to bargain collectively through representatives of their own choosing, and to engage in concerted activities, for the purpose of collective bargaining or other mutual aid or protection."

Thus, in its present application, the statute goes no further than to safeguard the right of employees to self-organization and to select representatives of their own choosing for collective bargaining or other mutual protection without restraint or coercion by their employer.

That is a fundamental right. Employees have as clear a right to organize and select their representatives for lawful purposes as the respondent has to organize its business and select its own officers and agents. Discrimination and coercion to prevent the free exercise of the right of employees to self-organization and representation is a proper subject for condemnation by competent legislative authority. Long ago we stated the reason for labor organizations. We said that they were organized out of the necessities of the situation; that a single employee was helpless in dealing with an employer; that he was dependent ordinarily on his daily wage for the maintenance of himself and family; that if the employer refused to pay him the wages that he thought fair, he was nevertheless unable to leave the employ and resist arbitrary and unfair treatment; that union was essential to give laborers opportunity to deal on an equality with their employer. . . . Fully recognizing the legality of collective action on the part of employees in order to safeguard their proper interests, we said that Congress was not required to ignore this right but could safeguard it. Congress could seek to make appropriate collective action of employees an instrument of peace rather than of strife. We said that such collective action would be a mockery if representation were made futile by interference with freedom of choice. Hence the prohibition by Congress of interference with the selection of representatives for the purpose of negotiation and conference between employers and employees, "instead of being an invasion of the constitutional right of either, was based on the recognition of the rights of both." . . .

Third. The application of the act to employees engaged in production.—The principle involved.—Respondent says that whatever may be said of employees engaged in interstate commerce, the industrial relations and activities in the manufacturing department of respondent's enterprise are not subject to federal regulation. The argument rests upon the proposition that manufacturing in itself is not commerce. Kidd v. Pearson, 128 U. S. 1; . . . A. L. A. Schechter Poultry Corp. v. United States, 295 U. S. 495; Carter v. Carter Coal Co., 298 U. S. 238.

The government distinguishes these cases. The various parts of respondent's enterprise are described as interdependent and as thus involving "a great movement of iron ore, coal and limestone along well-defined paths to the steel mills, thence through them, and thence in the form of steel products into the consuming centers of the country—a definite and well-understood course of business." It is urged that these activities constitute a "stream" or "flow" of commerce, of which the Aliquippa manufacturing plant is the focal point, and that industrial strife at that point would cripple the entire movement. Reference is made to our decision sustaining the Packers and Stockyards Act. Stafford v. Wallace, 258 U. S. 495. The Court found that the stockyards were but a "throat" through which the current of commerce flowed and the transactions which there occurred could not be separated from that movement. Hence the sales at the stockyards were not regarded as merely local transactions, for while they created "a local change of title" they did not "stop the flow," but merely changed the private interests in the subject of the current. . . . Applying the doctrine of Stafford v. Wallace, *supra,* the Court sustained the Grain Futures Act of [September 11] 1922 with respect to transactions on the Chicago Board of Trade, although these transactions were "not in and of themselves interstate commerce." Congress had found that they had become "a constantly recurring burden and obstruction to that commerce." Board of Trade v. Olsen, 262 U. S. 1. . . .

Respondent contends that the instant case presents material distinctions. Respondent says that the Aliquippa plant is extensive in size and represents a large investment in buildings, machinery and equipment. The raw materials which are brought to the plant are delayed for long periods and, after being subjected to manufacturing processes "are changed substantially as to character, utility and value." The finished products which emerge "are to a large extent manufactured without reference to pre-existing orders and contracts and are entirely different from the raw materials which enter at the other end." Hence respondent argues that "If importation and exportation in interstate commerce do not singly transfer purely local activities into the field of congressional regulation, it should follow that their combination would not alter the local situation." . . .

We do not find it necessary to determine whether these features of defendant's business dispose of the asserted analogy to the "stream of commerce" cases. The instances in which that metaphor has been used are but particular, and not exclusive, illustrations of the protective power which the government invokes in support of the present act. The congressional authority to protect interstate commerce from burdens and obstructions is not limited to transactions which can be deemed to be an essential part of a "flow" of interstate or foreign commerce. Burdens and obstructions may be due to injurious action springing from other sources. The fundamental principle is that the power to regulate commerce is the power to enact "all appropriate legislation" for "its protection and advancement" . . . ; to adopt measures "to promote its growth and insure its safety" . . . ; "to foster, protect, control and restrain." . . . That power is plenary and may be exerted to protect interstate commerce "no matter what the source of the dangers which threaten it." . . . Although activities may be intrastate in character when separately considered, if they have such a close and substantial relation to interstate commerce that their control is essential or appropriate to protect that commerce from burdens and obstructions, Congress cannot be denied the power to exercise that control. . . . Undoubtedly the scope of this power must be considered in the light of our dual system of government and may not be extended so as to embrace effects upon interstate commerce so indirect and remote that to embrace them, in view of our complex society, would effectually obliterate the distinction between what is national and what is local and create a completely centralized government. The question is necessarily one of degree. . . .

That intrastate activities, by reason of close and intimate relation to interstate commerce, may fall within federal control is demonstrated in the case of carriers who are engaged in both interstate and intrastate transportation. There federal control has been found essential to secure the freedom of interstate traffic from interference or unjust discrimination and to promote the efficiency of the interstate service. Shreveport Case (Houston, E. & W.T.R. Co. v. United States) 234 U. S. 342; Railroad Commission v. Chicago, B. & Q. R. Co., 257 U. S. 563. It is manifest that intrastate rates deal *primarily* with a local activity. But in rate-making they bear such a close relation to interstate rates that effective control of the one must embrace some control over the other. Under the Transportation Act [February 28] 1920, Congress went so far as to authorize the Interstate Commerce Commission to establish a state-wide level of intrastate rates in order to prevent an unjust discrimination against interstate commerce. . . .

The close and intimate effect which brings the subject within the reach of federal power may be due to activities in relation to productive industry although the industry when separately viewed is local. This has been abundantly illustrated in the application of the Federal Anti-Trust Act. In the Standard Oil Co. case, 221 U. S. 1, and American Tobacco Co. case, 221 U. S. 106, that statute was applied to combinations of employers engaged in productive industry. . . .

Upon the same principle, the Anti-Trust Act has been applied to the conduct of employees engaged in production. . . .

It is thus apparent that the fact that the employees here concerned were engaged in production is not determinative. The question remains as to the effect upon interstate commerce of the labor practice involved. In the A. L. A. Schechter Poultry Corp. case, 295 U. S. 495, *supra,* we found that the effect there was so remote as to be beyond the federal power. To find "immediacy or directness" there was to find it "almost everywhere," a result inconsistent with the maintenance of our federal system. . . .

Fourth. Effects of the unfair labor practice in respondent's enterprise.—Giving full weight to respondent's contention with respect to a break in the complete continuity of the "stream of commerce" by reason of respondent's manufacturing operations, the fact remains that the stoppage of those operations by industrial strife would have a most serious effect upon interstate commerce. In view of respondent's far-flung activities, it is idle to say that the effect would be indirect or remote. It is obvious that it would be immediate and might be catastrophic. We are asked to shut our eyes to the plainest facts of our national life and to deal with the question of direct and indirect effects in an intellectual vacuum. Because there may be but indirect and remote effects upon interstate commerce in connection with a host of local enterprises throughout the country, it does not follow that other industrial activities do not have such a close and intimate relation to interstate commerce as to make the presence of industrial strife a matter of the most urgent national concern. When industries organize themselves on a national scale, making their relation to interstate commerce the dominant factor in their activities, how can it be maintained that their industral labor relations constitute a forbidden field into which Congress may not enter when it is necessary to protect interstate commerce from the paralyzing consequences of industrial war? We have often said that interstate commerce itself is a practical conception. It is equally true that interferences with that commerce must be appraised by a judgment that does not ignore actual experience.

Experience has abundantly demonstrated that the recognition of the right of employees to self-organization and to have representatives of their own choosing for the purpose of collective bargaining is often an essential condition of industrial peace. Refusal to confer and negotiate has been one of the most prolific causes of strife. This is such an outstanding fact in the history of labor disturbances that it is a proper subject of judicial notice and requires no citation of instances. The opinion in the case of Virginian Railway Co. v. System Federation No. 40, points out that, in the case of carriers, experience has shown that before the amendment, of 1934, of the Railway Labor Act "when there was no dispute as to the organizations authorized to represent the employees, and when there was a willingness of the employer to meet such representative for a discussion of their grievances, amicable adjustment of differences had generally followed and strikes had been avoided." That, on the other hand, "a prolific source of dispute had been the maintenance by the railroads of company unions and the denial by railway management of the authority of representatives chosen by their employees." The opinion in that case also points to the large measure of success of the labor policy embodied in the Railway Labor Act. But with respect to the appropriateness of the recognition of self-organization and representation in the promotion of peace, the question is not essentially different in the case of employees in industries of such a character that interstate commerce is put in jeopardy from the case of employees of transportation companies. And of what avail is it to protect the facility of transportation, if interstate commerce is throttled with respect to the commodities to be transported!

These questions have frequently engaged the attention of Congress and have been the subject of many inquiries. The steel industry is one of the great basic industries of the United States, with ramifying activities affecting interstate commerce at every point. The government aptly refers to the steel strike of 1919–1920 with its far-reaching consequences. The fact that there appears to have been no major disturbance in that industry in the more recent period did not dispose of the possibilities of future and like dangers to interstate commerce which Congress was entitled to foresee and to exercise its protective power to forestall. It is not necessary again to detail the facts as to respondent's enterprise. Instead of being beyond the pale, we think that it presents in a most striking way the close and intimate relation which a manufacturing industry may have to interstate commerce and we have no doubt that Congress had constitutional authority to safeguard the right of respondent's employees to self-organization and freedom in the choice of representatives for collective bargaining.

Fifth. The means which the act employs.—Questions under the due process clause and other constitutional restrictions.—Respondent asserts its right to conduct its business in an orderly manner without being subjected to arbitrary restraints. What we have said points to the fallacy in the argument. Employees have their correlative right to organize for the purpose of securing the redress of grievances and to promote agreements with employers relating to rate of pay and conditions of work. . . . Restraint for the purpose of preventing an unjust interference with that right cannot be considered arbitrary or capricious. . . .

The act does not compel agreements between employers and employees. It does not compel any agreement whatever. It does not prevent the employer "from refusing to make a collective contract and hiring individuals on whatever terms" the employer "may by unilateral action determine." The act expressly provides in § 9(a) that any individual employee or a group of employees shall have the right at any time to present grievances to their employer. The theory of the act is that free opportunity for negotiation with accredited representatives of employees is likely to promote industrial peace and may bring about the adjustments and agreements which the act in itself does not attempt to compel. . . . The act does not interfere with the normal exercise of the right of the employer to select its employees or to discharge them. The employer may not, under cover of that right, intimidate or coerce its employees with respect to their self-organization and representation, and, on the other hand, the board is not entitled to make its authority a pretext for interference with the right of discharge when that right is exercised for other reasons than such intimidation and coercion. The true purpose is the subject of investigation with full opportunity to show the facts. It would seem that when employers freely recognize the right of their employees to their own organizations and their unrestricted right of representation there will be much less occasion for controversy in respect to the free and appropriate exercise of the right of selection and discharge.

The act has been criticized as one-sided in its application; that it subjects the employer to supervision and restraint and leaves untouched the abuses for which employees may be responsible. That it fails to provide a more comprehensive plan,—with better assurances of fairness to both sides and with increased chances of success in bringing about, if not compelling, equitable solutions of industrial disputes affecting interstate commerce. But we are dealing with the power of Congress, not with a particular policy, or with the extent to which policy should go. We have frequently said that the legislative authority, exerted within its proper field, need not embrace all the evils within its reach. The Constitution does not forbid "cautious advance, step by step," in dealing with the evils which are exhibited in activities within the range of legislative power. . . . The question in such cases is whether the legislature, in what it does prescribe, has gone beyond constitutional limits.

The procedural provisions of the act are assailed. But these provisions, as we construe them, do not offend against the constitutional requirements governing the creation and action of administrative bodies. . . .

Respondent complains that the board not only ordered reinstatement but directed the payment of wages for the time lost by the discharge, less amounts earned by the employee during that period. . . . It is argued that the requirement is equivalent to a money judgment and hence contravenes the Seventh Amendment with respect to trial by jury. The Seventh Amendment provides that "In suits at common law, where the value in controversy shall exceed twenty dollars, the right of trial by jury shall be preserved." . . .

The instant case is not a suit at common law or in the nature of such a suit. The proceeding is one unknown to the common law. It is a statutory proceeding. Reinstatement of the employee and payment for time lost are requirements imposed for violation of the statute and are remedies appropriate to its enforcement. The contention under the Seventh Amendment is without merit.

Our conclusion is that the order of the board was within its competency and that the act is valid as here applied. . . .

Mr. Justice McReynolds delivered the following dissenting opinion, saying in part:

Mr. Justice Van Devanter, Mr. Justice Sutherland, Mr. Justice Butler and I are unable to agree with the decisions just announced. . . .

The Court, as we think, departs from well-established principles followed in A. L. A. Schechter Poultry Corp. v. United States, 295 U. S. 495, and Carter v. Carter Coal Co., 298 U. S. 238. Upon the authority of those decisions . . . the power of Congress under the commerce clause does not extend to relations between employers and their employees engaged in manufacture, and therefore the act conferred upon the National Labor Relations Board no authority in respect of matters covered by the questioned orders. . . . No decision or judicial opinion to the contrary has been cited, and we find none. Every consideration brought forward to uphold the act before us was applicable to support the acts held unconstitutional in causes decided within two years. And the lower courts rightly deemed them controlling. . . .

Any effect on interstate commerce by the discharge of employees shown here, would be indirect and remote in the highest degree, as consideration of the facts will show. In No. 419 [The Jones & Laughlin case] ten men out of ten thousand were discharged; in the other cases only a few. The immediate effect in the factory may be to create discontent among all those employed and a strike may follow, which, in turn, may result in reducing production, which ultimately may reduce the volume of goods moving in interstate commerce. By this chain of indirect and progressively remote events we finally reach the evil with which it is said the legislation under consideration undertakes to deal. A more remote and indirect interference with

interstate commerce or a more definite invasion of the powers reserved to the states is difficult, if not impossible, to imagine.

The Constitution still recognizes the existence of states with indestructible powers; the Tenth Amendment was supposed to put them
beyond controversy. . . .

MULFORD v. SMITH
307 U. S. 38; 83 L. Ed. 1092; 59 Sup. Ct. 648. 1939.

The Agricultural Adjustment Act of 1933, which was held void in United
States v. Butler (p. 357), had relied for its constitutional underpinning upon
the delegated powers of Congress to tax and to spend money. The Agricultural Adjustment Act of 1938, which aimed at similar objectives, was based
on commerce power. The act declared that its policy (in part) is: "to regulate interstate and foreign commerce in cotton, wheat, corn, tobacco and
rice to the extent necessary to provide an orderly, adequate, and balanced
flow of such commodities in interstate and foreign commerce through storage of reserve supplies, loans, marketing, quotas, assisting farmers to obtain,
in so far as practicable, parity prices for such commodities and parity of
income, and assisting consumers to obtain an adequate and steady supply of
such commodities at fair prices."

The attack upon the validity of the statute arose under the sections
providing for the establishment of marketing quotas for flue-cured tobacco.
There are similar sections dealing with cotton, wheat, corn, and rice. The
relevant provisions were as follows: When the Secretary of Agriculture finds
that the total supply of tobacco exceeds the "reserve supply level" defined in
the act, he is authorized to proclaim the total supply and to put into effect a
national marketing quota. This quota is to be the amount which will make
available during the following year a supply of tobacco equal to the reserve
supply level. Within thirty days after such proclamation, the Secretary is to
conduct a referendum of the producers of the preceding year's crop to determine whether they favor the imposition of a quota. If more than one-third
oppose, the quota shall not be effective. If established, the quota is to be
first apportioned among the states according to the amount of tobacco
produced in each state during the preceding five years. There is a limit
below which the quota of the state may not be reduced. The state quota is
then allocated among the farms which produce tobacco. The farm quotas
are based on past marketing, with a minimum at the bottom. They are to
be worked out by local committees of farmers according to standards prescribed in the act. A dissatisfied farmer may have his quota reviewed by a
local reviewing committee and ultimately by a court. If tobacco in excess of

the quota for the farm on which it is produced is marketed through a warehouse man, the latter must pay to the Secretary a penalty equal to fifty per cent of the market price of the excess, and may deduct this amount from the prices paid to the producer. In the present case, quotas were established in accordance with the statute. Producers who exceeded their quotas sought by injunction to restrain local warehouse men from deducting the fifty per cent penalties under the act from the sale of the tobacco in excess of the quota; this was on the ground that the statute was unconstitutional.

A more extreme application of the 1938 statute was upheld in Wickard v. Filburn, 317 U. S. 111 (1942). Quotas were established for the production of wheat in order to prevent surpluses and maintain prices. Filburn raised 23 acres of wheat, none of which was intended for interstate commerce, and all of which he consumed or fed to his stock. The quota allotted to him, however, was 11.1 acres, and the Court held him validly liable to the statutory penalties on the wheat produced in excess of this quota. His production of this wheat affected interstate commerce "directly" just as much as though he had farmed 23,000 acres instead of 23.

These cases, along with those upholding the National Labor Relations Act, indicate that the Court has abandoned the old distinction between manufacturing and interstate commerce, and between agricultural production and interstate commerce, as the line which divides the things which Congress may constitutionally regulate under the commerce clause from those which it may not.

Mr. Justice Roberts delivered the opinion of the Court, saying in part:

. . . The appellants plant themselves upon three propositions: (1) that the act is a statutory plan to control agricultural production and, therefore, beyond the powers delegated to Congress; (2) that the standard for calculating farm quotas is uncertain, vague, and indefinite, resulting in an unconstitutional delegation of legislative power to the Secretary; (3) that, as applied to appellants' 1938 crop, the act takes their property without due process of law.

First. The statute does not purport to control production. It sets no limit upon the acreage which may be planted or produced and imposes no penalty for the planting and producing of tobacco in excess of the marketing quota. It purports to be solely a regulation of interstate commerce, which it reaches and affects at the throat where tobacco enters the stream of commerce,—the marketing warehouse. The record discloses that at least two-thirds of all flue-cured tobacco sold at auction warehouses is sold for immediate shipment to an interstate or foreign destination. In Georgia nearly one hundred per cent of the tobacco so sold is purchased by extrastate purchasers. In markets where tobacco is sold to both interstate and intrastate purchasers it is not known, when the grower places his tobacco on the warehouse floor for sale, whether it is destined for interstate or intrastate commerce. Regulation to be effective, must, and therefore may constitutionally, apply to all sales. This Court has recently declared that sales of tobacco by growers through warehousemen to purchasers for removal outside the state constitute interstate commerce. Any rule, such as that embodied in the act, which is intended to foster, protect and conserve that commerce, or to prevent the flow of commerce from working harm to the people of the nation, is within the competence of Congress. Within these limits the exercise of the power, the grant being unlimited in its terms, may lawfully extend to the absolute prohibition of such commerce, and a fortiori to limitation of the amount of a given commodity which may be transported in such commerce. The motive of Congress in exerting the power is irrelevant to the validity of the legislation.

The provisions of the act under review constitute a regulation of interstate and foreign commerce within the competency of Congress under the power delegated to it by the Constitution.

Second. The appellants urge that the standard for allotting farm quotas is so uncertain, vague, and indefinite that it amounts to a delegation of legislative power to an executive officer and thus violates the Constitutional requirement that laws shall be enacted by the Congress.

What has been said in summarizing the provisions of the act sufficiently discloses that definite standards are laid down for the government of the Secretary, first, in fixing the quota and, second, in its allotment amongst states and farms. He is directed to adjust the allotments so as to allow for specified factors which have abnormally affected the production of the state or the farm in question in the test years. Certainly fairness requires that some such adjustment shall be made. The Congress has indicated in detail the considerations which are to be held in view in making these adjustments, and, in order to protect against arbitrary action, has afforded both administrative and judicial review to correct errors. This is not to confer unrestrained arbitrary power on an executive officer. In this aspect the act is valid within the decisions of this Court respecting delegation to administrative officers.

Third. In support of their contention that the act, as applied to the crop year 1938, deprives them of their property without due process of law in violation of the Fifth Amendment, the appellants rely on the following undisputed facts.

Tobacco growers in southern Georgia and northern Florida began to arrange for the planting of their 1938 crop in December, 1937, when it was necessary for them to prepare beds for the planting of the seeds. Thereafter it was necessary to cultivate the seed beds, sow and water the seed, cover the beds with cloth, and otherwise care for the plants until they were large enough to be transplanted. At the date of approval of the act each of the plaintiffs had planted his seed beds and, about the middle of March, began transplanting into the fields, which were prepared and fertilized at large expense. The plants were thereafter cultivated and sprayed, and harvesting began during June and continued during July, followed by the curing and grading of the tobacco.

All of these activities involved labor and expense. The production of flue-cured tobacco requires, at prevailing price levels, a cash outlay of between thirty and forty dollars per acre for fertilizer, plant bed covering, twine, poison, etc. The use of animals and permanent and semi-permanent equipment demands an average expenditure, over a period of years, ranging from twenty to thirty dollars an acre. The labor expended per acre is between three hundred and four hundred man-hours. The total cost per pound varies from ten cents to twenty cents.

The marketing season for flue-cured tobacco in Georgia and Florida commences about August 1st of each year. Each of the appellants was notified of the quota of his farm shortly before the opening of the auction markets. Prior to the receipt of notice each of them had largely, if not wholly, completed planting, cultivating, harvesting, curing and grading his tobacco. Until receipt of notice none knew, or could have known, the exact amount of his quota, although, at the time of filing the bill, each had concluded from available information that he would probably market tobacco in excess of any quota for his farm.

The act was approved February 16, 1938. The Secretary proclaimed a quota for flue-cured tobacco on February 18th and, on the same date, issued instructions for holding a referendum on March 12th. March 25th the Secretary proclaimed the result of the referendum which was favorable to the imposition of a national marketing quota. In June he issued regulations governing the fixing of farm quotas within the states.

July 22nd he determined the apportionment as between states and issued regulations relative to the records to be kept by warehousemen and others. Shortly before the markets opened each appellant received notice of the allotment to his farm.

On the basis of these facts it is argued that the statute operated retroactively and therefore amounted to a taking of appellants' property without due process. The argument overlooks the circumstance that the statute operates not on farm production, as the appellants insist, but upon the marketing of their tobacco in interstate commerce. The law, enacted in February, affected the marketing which was to take place about August 1st following, and so was prospective in its operation upon the activity it regulated. The act did not prevent any producer from holding over the excess tobacco produced, or processing and storing it for sale in a later year; and the circumstance that the producers in Georgia and Florida had not provided facilities for these purposes is not of legal significance.

The decree is affirmed.

Justices Butler and McReynolds dissented.

EDWARDS v. CALIFORNIA
314 U. S. 160; 86 L. Ed. 119; 62 Sup. Ct. 164. 1941.

It was held in the Cooley case (p. 401) that when Congress has not acted, the states may validly regulate such aspects of interstate commerce as do not require national uniform control. As a matter of fact there is relatively little state legislation directed at interstate commerce as such; but there is a vast body of state police legislation which, if applied uniformly within the state's borders, will strike persons engaged in, or transactions comprising, interstate commerce. These laws are not aimed at interstate commerce, but they are bound to hit it unless, for constitutional reasons, they are required to sidestep it. The states may not burden or obstruct interstate commerce. But the Court has long held that a state police regulation may be validly enforced if it "affects" interstate commerce only indirectly or incidentally. To decide whether a new form of state police legislation may constitutionally be applied to interstate commerce is one of the Court's most continual and perplexing tasks. Here, as in many other situations, the line between the valid and the invalid is a matter of degree.

A common type of state police regulation affecting interstate commerce is that which regulates railroads and motor vehicles for the protection of the public safety. In passing upon the validity of these regulations the Court balances the local need for such protection over against the amount of inconvenience or burden placed on the common carrier. Thus in Southern Railway Co. v. King, 217 U. S. 524 (1910), a Georgia statute limiting the speed of trains was held applicable to interstate trains since there was no showing of unreasonable obstruction or delay. But in Seaboard Air Line R. Co. v. Blackwell, 244 U. S. 310 (1917), a later Georgia statute which, as applied to an interstate train, would have required it to slow down for 124 grade crossings in 123 miles, thereby losing three minutes at each and more than doubling its running time, was held to burden interstate commerce and was therefore void. In South Carolina State Highway Department v. Barnwell Bros., 303 U. S. 177 (1938), a state statute forbade the use on state highways of motor trucks whose width exceeds 90″ and whose weight, including load, exceeds 20,000 pounds. Although the Court admitted that the act burdened interstate commerce, it held the act valid as applied to interstate trucks, since in the absence of federal regulations of the size and weight of trucks the state could validly pass reasonable rules to insure the safety of motor traffic and prevent undue wear and tear on its roads. An Arizona statute forbade the operation within the state of a railroad train of more than 14 passenger cars or 70 freight cars. This was held void in Southern Pacific Co. v. Arizona, 325 U. S. 761 (1945); Congress has not dealt with the length of trains, but the state regulation was unduly burdensome because it is standard practice on the main line railroads of the country to run trains much longer than this.

Some state police regulations seek to require licenses of those engaged in interstate commerce. A Washington statute required bus and truck lines to secure from the state authorities "certificates of convenience and necessity" before using the state highways. A bus line operating between Seattle, Washington, and Portland, Oregon, was denied such a certificate on the ground that there were already enough buses in operation. In Buck v. Kuykendall, 267 U. S. 307 (1925), the Court held that the state could not validly deny the right to carry on interstate commerce within its borders. A different result was reached in Bradley v. Public Utilities Commission, 289 U. S. 92 (1933). Bradley was denied a certificate of convenience and necessity to operate a commercial trucking line over Route 20 between Cleveland, Ohio, and Flint, Michigan. The reason for the denial was that the congestion of traffic on Route 20 was so great that the addition of a new fleet of trucks would increase the risk of traffic accidents. The Court upheld the state's action, both because it was a reasonable safety regulation and because there were alternate routes which Bradley could travel. A California statute of 1933 regulated the business of agents who sell "transportation over the public highways of the state": namely, bus transportation. Such an agent must secure a license, pay a dollar fee, and file a thousand dollar bond as a guarantee of the faithful performance of the transportation contracts which he negotiates. In California v. Thompson, 313 U. S. 109 (1941), this act was held valid as applied to agents selling tickets for interstate bus travel. The Court held that it did not obstruct or burden interstate commerce, but was a reasonable regulation designed to prevent fraud. The decision overruled the case of Di Santo v. Pennsylvania, 273 U. S. 34 (1927), in which an almost identical Pennsylvania statute applicable to agents selling ocean steamship transportation was held invalid.

Many states have set up quarantine regulations and applied them to persons or goods entering the state. These are valid if they do not cut off legitimate interstate commerce, or compete with existing federal controls. In an early case, Hannibal & St. J. R. Co. v. Husen, 95 U. S. 465 (1877), a Missouri statute, in order to keep out of the state any cattle which might be infected with Texas fever, forbade the bringing into the state of any "Texas, Mexican or Indian" cattle between March 1 and November 1 of each year. This was held void since it imposed a complete embargo upon all interstate shipments of cattle from the areas specified instead of confining itself to barring diseased animals. However, in Mintz v. Baldwin, 289 U. S. 346 (1933), the state of New York was upheld in forbidding the bringing into the state for dairy or breeding purposes any cattle unless such cattle, and the herds from which they came, were certified by the chief sanitary officer of the state of origin to be free from Bang's disease. This requirement was held to be not an invalid burden upon interstate commerce.

The statute of California at issue in Edwards v. California, printed below, was known popularly as the "anti-Okie" law. Along with similar statutes passed by more than twenty other states it penalized the bringing into the state of indigent persons. The importance and sweep of the social problem involved in this legislation lifted the Edwards case out of the usual category of conflicts between state police power and interstate commerce, and, in fact, led four members of the Court to conclude that the invalidity of the statute ought not to rest on the commerce clause but on the more basic ground that the act abridged the privileges and immunities of citizens of the United States in violation of the Fourteenth Amendment. To make this minority position amply clear the concurring opinion of Mr. Justice Jackson is printed below. It is interesting to recall that in Crandall v. Nevada, 6 Wallace (U. S.) 35 (1868), the Court had held invalid a state statute which imposed on common carriers a charge of one dollar for each passenger transported out of the state. This was held to abridge the privilege of national citizenship to move freely about the country. Two justices concurred in the result, but stated that the act should have been held void as unconstitutional obstruction of interstate commerce. In the Edwards case the majority of the Court preferred to invalidate the California statute as an obstruction of commerce, leaving the concurring justices to defend the position taken by the majority in the Crandall case.

Mr. Justice Byrnes delivered the opinion of the Court, saying in part:

The facts of this case are simple and are not disputed. Appellant is a citizen of the United States and a resident of California. In December, 1939, he left his home in Marysville, California, for Spur, Texas, with the intention of bringing back to Marysville his wife's brother, Frank Duncan, a citizen of the United States and a resident of Texas. When he arrived in Texas, appellant learned that Duncan had last been employed by the Works Progress Administration. Appellant thus became aware of the fact that Duncan was an indigent person and he continued to be aware of it throughout the period involved in this case. The two men agreed that appellant should transport Duncan from Texas to Marysville in appellant's automobile. Accordingly, they left Spur on January 1, 1940, entered California by way of Arizona on January 3, and reached Marysville on January 5. When he left Texas, Duncan had about $20. It had all been spent by the time he reached Marysville. He lived with appellant for about ten days until he obtained financial assistance from the Farm Security Administration. During the ten day interval, he had no employment.

In Justice Court a complaint was filed against appellant under § 2615 of the Welfare and Institutions Code of California, which provides: "Every person, firm or corporation or officer or agent thereof that brings or assists in bringing into the State any indigent person who is not a resident of the State, knowing him to be an indigent person, is guilty of a misdemeanor." . . . The appellant was convicted and sentenced to six months imprisonment in the county jail, and sentence was suspended. . . .

Article 1, section 8 of the Constitution delegates to the Congress the authority to regulate interstate commerce. And it is settled beyond question that the transportation of persons is "commerce," within the meaning of that provision. It is nevertheless true that the states are not wholly precluded from exercising their police power in matters of local concern even though they may thereby affect interstate commerce. The issue presented in this case, therefore, is whether the prohibition embodied in § 2615 against the "bringing" or transportation of indigent persons into California is within the police power of that state. We think that it is not, and hold that it is an unconstitutional barrier to interstate commerce.

The grave and perplexing social and economic dislocation which this statute reflects is a matter of common knowledge and concern. We are not unmindful of it. We appreciate that the spectacle of large segments of our population constantly on the move has given rise to urgent demands upon the ingenuity of government. Both the brief of the Attorney General of California and that of the Chairman of the Select Committee of the House of Representatives of the United States, as *amicus curiae,* have sharpened this appreciation. The state asserts that the huge influx of migrants into California in recent years has resulted in problems of health, morals, and especially finance, the proportions of which are staggering. It is not for us to say that this is not true. We have repeatedly and recently affirmed, and we now reaffirm, that we do not conceive it our function to pass upon "the wisdom, need, or appropriateness" of the legislative efforts of the states to solve such difficulties.

But this does not mean that there are no boundaries to the permissible area of state legislative activity. There are. And none is more certain than the prohibition against attempts on the part of any single state to isolate itself from difficulties common to all of them by restraining the transportation of persons and property across its borders. It is frequently the case that a state might gain a momentary respite from the pressure of events by the simple expedient of shutting its gates to the outside world. But, in the words of Mr. Justice Cardozo: "The Constitution was framed under the dominion of a political philosophy less parochial in range. It was framed upon the theory that the peoples of the several states must sink or swim together, and that in the long run prosperity and salvation are in union and not division." Baldwin v. Seelig, 294 U. S. 511.

It is difficult to conceive of a statute more squarely in conflict with this theory than the section challenged here. Its express purpose and inevitable effect is to prohibit the transportation of indigent persons across the California border. The burden upon interstate commerce is intended and immediate; it is the plain and sole function of the statute. Moreover, the indigent non-residents who are the real victims of the statute are deprived of the opportunity to exert political pressure upon the California legislature in order to obtain a change in policy. We think this statute must fail under any known test of the validity of state interference with interstate commerce.

It is urged, however, that the concept which underlies § 2615 enjoys a firm basis in English and American history. This is the notion that each community should care for its own indigent, that relief is solely the responsibility of local government. Of this it must first be said that we are not now called upon to determine anything other than the propriety of an attempt by a state to prohibit the transportation of indigent non-residents into its territory. The nature and extent of its obligation to afford relief to newcomers is not here involved. We do, however, suggest that the theory of the Elizabethan poor laws no longer fits the facts. Recent years, and particularly the past decade, have been marked by a growing recognition that in an industrial society the task of providing assistance to the needy has ceased to be local in character. The duty to share the burden, if not wholly to assume it, has been recognized not only by state governments, but by the federal government as well. The changed attitude is reflected in the social security laws under which the federal and state governments cooperate for the care of the aged, the blind and dependent children. It is reflected in the works programs under which work is furnished the unemployed, with the states supplying approximately 25% and the federal government approximately 75% of the cost. It is further reflected in the farm security laws, under which the entire cost of the relief provisions is borne by the federal government.

Indeed, the record in this case illustrates the inadequate basis in fact for the theory that relief is presently a local matter. Before leaving Texas, Duncan had received assistance from the Works Progress Administration. After arriving in California he was aided by the Farm Security Administration, which, as we have said, is wholly financed by the federal government. This is not to say that our judgment would be different if Duncan had received relief from local agencies in Texas and California. Nor is it to suggest that the financial burden of assistance to indigent persons does not continue to fall heavily upon local and state governments. It is only to illustrate that in not inconsiderable measure the relief of the needy has become the common responsibility and concern of the whole nation.

What has been said with respect to financing relief is not without its bearing upon the regulation of the transportation of indigent persons. For the social phenomenon of large-scale interstate migration is as certainly a matter of national concern as the provision of assistance to those who have found a permanent or temporary abode. Moreover, and unlike the relief problem, this phenomenon does not admit of diverse treatment by the several states. The prohibition against transporting indigent non-residents into one state is an open invitation to retaliatory measures, and the burdens upon the transportation of such persons become cumulative. Moreover, it would be a virtual impossibility for migrants and those who transport them to acquaint themselves with the peculiar rules of admission of many states. "This Court has repeatedly declared that the grant [the commerce clause] established the immunity of interstate commerce from the control of the states respecting all those subjects embraced within the grant which are of such a nature as to demand that, if regulated at all, their regulation must be prescribed by a single authority." Milk Control Board v. Eisenberg Farm Products, 306 U. S. 346. We are of the opinion that the transportation of indigent persons from state to state clearly falls within this class of subjects. The scope of congressional power to deal with this problem we are not now called upon to decide.

There remains to be noticed only the contention that the limitation upon state power to interfere with the interstate transportation of persons is subject to an exception in the case of "paupers." It is true that support for this contention may be found in early decisions of this Court. In New York v. Miln, 11 Pet. 102, it was said that it is "as competent and as necessary for a state to provide precautionary measures against the moral pestilence of paupers, vagabonds, and possibly convicts, as it is to guard against the physical pestilence which may arise from unsound and infectious articles imported. . . ." This language has been casually repeated in numerous later cases up to the turn of the century. In none of these cases, however, was the power of a state to exclude "paupers" actually involved.

Whether an able-bodied but unemployed person like Duncan is a "pauper" within the historical meaning of the term is open to considerable doubt. But assuming that the term is applicable to him and to persons similarly situated, we do not consider ourselves bound by the language referred to. City of New York v. Miln was decided in 1837. Whatever may have been the notion then prevailing, we do not think that it will now be seriously contended that because a person is without employment and without funds he constitutes a "moral pestilence." Poverty and immorality are not synonymous.

We are of the opinion that § 2615 is not a valid exercise of the police power of California, that it imposes an unconstitutional burden upon interstate commerce, and that the conviction under it cannot be sustained. In the view we have taken it is unnecessary to decide whether the section is repugnant to other provisions of the Constitution.

Reversed.

Mr. Justice Douglas wrote a concurring opinion, in which Justices Black and Murphy joined. He contended that the statute was void because "The right to move freely from state to state is an incident of *national* citizenship protected by the privileges and immunities clause of the Fourteenth Amendment against state interference."

Mr. Justice Jackson, concurring, said in part:

I concur in the result reached by the Court, and I agree that the grounds of its decision are permissible ones under applicable authorities. But the migrations of a human being, of whom it is charged that he possesses nothing that can be sold and has no wherewithal to buy, do not fit easily into my notions as to what is commerce. To hold that the measure of his rights is the commerce clause is likely to result eventually either in distorting the commercial law or in denaturing human rights. I turn, therefore, away from principles by which commerce is regulated to that clause of the Constitution by virtue of which Duncan is a citizen of the United States and which forbids any state to abridge his privileges or immunities as such.

This clause was adopted to make United States citizenship the dominant and paramount allegiance among us. The return which the law had long associated with allegiance was protection. The power of citizenship as a shield against oppression was widely known from the example of Paul's Roman citizenship, which sent the centurion scurrying to his higher-ups with the message: "Take heed what thou doest: for this man is a Roman." I suppose none of us doubts that the hope of imparting to American citizenship some of this vitality was the purpose of declaring in the Fourteenth Amendment: "All persons born or naturalized in the United States, and subject to the jurisdiction thereof, are citizens of the United States and of the State wherein they reside. No State shall make or enforce any law which shall abridge the privileges or immunities of citizens of the United States . . ."

But the hope proclaimed in such generality soon shriveled in the process of judicial interpretation. For nearly three-quarters of a century this Court rejected every plea to the privileges and immunities clause. The judicial history of this clause and the very real difficulties in the way of its practical application to specific cases have been too well and recently reviewed to warrant repetition.

While instances of valid "privileges or immunities" must be but few,

I am convinced that this is one. I do not ignore or belittle the difficulties of what has been characterized by this Court as an "almost forgotten" clause. But the difficulty of the task does not excuse us from giving these general and abstract words whatever of specific content and concreteness they will bear as we mark out their application, case by case. That is the method of the common law, and it has been the method of this Court with other no less general statements in our fundamental law. This Court has not been timorous about giving concrete meaning to such obscure and vagrant phrases as "due process," "general welfare," "equal protection," or even "commerce among the several States." But it has always hesitated to give any real meaning to the privileges and immunities clause lest it improvidently give too much.

This Court should, however, hold squarely that it is a privilege of citizenship of the United States, protected from state abridgment, to enter any state of the Union, either for temporary sojourn or for the establishment of permanent residence therein and for gaining resultant citizenship thereof. If national citizenship means less than this, it means nothing.

The language of the Fourteenth Amendment declaring two kinds of citizenship is discriminating. It is: "All persons born or naturalized in the United States, and subject to the jurisdiction thereof, are citizens of the United States and of the State wherein they reside." While it thus establishes national citizenship from the mere circumstance of birth within the territory and jurisdiction of the United States, birth within a state does not establish citizenship thereof. State citizenship is ephemeral. It results only from residence and is gained or lost therewith. That choice of residence was subject to local approval is contrary to the inescapable implications of the westward movement of our civilization.

Even as to an alien who had "been admitted to the United States under the federal law," this Court, through Mr. Justice Hughes, declared that "He was thus admitted with the privilege of entering and abiding in the United States, and hence of entering and abiding in any state in the Union." Truax v. Raich, 239 U. S. 33. Why we should hesitate to hold that federal citizenship implies rights to enter and abide in any state of the Union at least equal to those possessed by aliens passes my understanding. The world is even more upside down than I had supposed it to be, if California must accept aliens in deference to their federal privileges but is free to turn back citizens of the United States unless we treat them as subjects of commerce.

The right of the citizen to migrate from state to state which, I agree with Mr. Justice Douglas, is shown by our precedents to be one of national citizenship, is not, however, an unlimited one. In addition to being subject to all constitutional limitations imposed by the federal government, such citizen is subject to some control by state governments. He may not, if a fugitive from justice, claim freedom to migrate unmolested, nor may he endanger others by carrying contagion about. These causes, and perhaps others that do not occur to me now, warrant any public authority in stopping a man where it finds him and arresting his progress across a state line quite as much as from place to place within the state.

It is here that we meet the real crux of this case. Does "indigence" as defined by the application of the California statute constitute a basis for restricting the freedom of a citizen, as crime or contagion warrants its restriction? We should say now, and in no uncertain terms, that a man's mere property status, without more, cannot be used by a state to test, qualify, or limit his rights as a citizen of the United States. "Indigence" in itself is neither a source of rights nor a basis for denying them. The mere state of being without funds is a neutral fact—constitutionally an irrelevance, like race, creed, or color. I agree with what I understand to be the holding of the Court that cases which may indicate the contrary are overruled.

Any measure which would divide our citizenry on the basis of property into one class free to move from state to state and another class that is poverty-bound to the place where it has suffered misfortune is not only at war with the habit and custom by which our country has expanded, but is also a short-sighted blow at the security of property itself. Property can have no more dangerous, even if unwitting, enemy than one who would make its possession a pretext for unequal or exclusive civil rights. Where those rights are derived from national citizenship no state may impose such a test, and whether the Congress could do so we are not called upon to inquire.

I think California had no right to make the condition of Duncan's purse, with no evidence of violation by him of any law or social policy which caused it, the basis of excluding him or of punishing one who extended him aid.

If I doubted whether his federal citizenship alone were enough to open the gates of California to Duncan, my doubt would disappear on consideration of the obligations of such citizenship. Duncan owes a duty to render military service, and this Court has said that this duty is the result of his citizenship. Mr. Chief Justice White declared in the Selective Draft Law Cases, 245 U. S. 366: "It may not be doubted that the very conception of a just government and its duty to the citizen includes the reciprocal obligation of the citizen to render military service in case of need and the right to compel it." A contention that a citizen's duty to render military service is suspended by "indigence" would meet with little favor. Rich or penniless, Duncan's citizenship under the Constitution pledges his strength to the defense of California as a part of the United States, and his right to migrate to any part of the land he must defend is something she must respect under the same instrument. Unless this Court is willing to say that citizenship of the United States means at least this much to the citizen, then our heritage of constitutional privileges and immunities is only a promise to the ear to be broken to the hope, a teasing illusion like a munificent bequest in a pauper's will.

9

Taxation

GRAVES v. NEW YORK ex rel. O'KEEFE
306 U. S. 466; 83 L. Ed. 927; 59 Sup. Ct. 595. 1939.

Under our federal system in which the national and state government each has its separate power of taxation, to what extent may each tax the other, or affect the other by taxation? In other words, is intergovernmental taxation between state and nation constitutional? This important and difficult question was first pressed upon the Supreme Court in McCulloch v. Maryland (p. 10). It was there held that a state could not validly levy a discriminatory tax which burdened an important federal agency, the Bank of the United States, since the doctrine of the supremacy of federal law, embodied in the very words of the Constitution, protected such a federal agency from hostile state taxation. It is worth noting that in this case Marshall plainly states that this federal immunity from state taxation, an immunity of the "whole" from taxation by one of its "parts," does not imply a converse immunity of the states from federal taxation. A little later, in Weston v. Charleston, 2 Peters 449 (1829), a state tax on United States stock was held void even when the tax was non-discriminatory.

This rule of tax immunity came later to be applied to state and nation alike. Marshall's epigram in the McCulloch case, that "the power to tax involves the power to destroy," pointed logically to the need for protecting the states from federal taxation. Such a rule was announced in Collector v. Day, 11 Wallace, 113 (1871), in which the Court held the salary of a state judge immune from federal income taxation on the ground that such immunity was necessarily implied from the very nature of our federal system in which the state and the federal government is each independent within its respective sphere.

This doctrine of intergovernmental tax immunity was elaborated in case after case. In the main the area of immunity tended to grow; but at the same time certain judicial rules emerged which limited its scope. The Court's position took shape in the form of three fairly clear doctrines. The first of these may be stated thus: The government of state or nation, together with its functions, property, instrumentalities, and processes, is absolutely immune from any tax levied by the other government. Anything which seemed reasonably to be an attribute of the sovereignty of the government falls into this group. To hold the tax bad it is not necessary to show that it imposes a burden; it is merely necessary to show that the tax hits something which, by its nature, ought not to be hit. Originally this absolute immunity from taxation covered the salaries of all government officers and employees, on the ground that the official relationship is the object of the tax. Dobbins v. Commissioners of Erie County, 16 Peters 435 (1842), held federal salaries immune from state taxation, while Collector v. Day, supra, held state salaries free from federal taxation. The immunity covers government bonds and the interest on them, since to tax these would strike at the government's borrowing power. Weston v. Charleston, supra, held federal securities free from state taxation; while Mercantile Bank v. New York, 121 U. S. 138 (1887), and Pollock v. Farmers' Loan & Trust Company, 158 U. S. 601 (1895), held state and municipal bonds, and the interest on them, immune from federal taxation. The immunity also covers sales of goods to the government, on the theory that the government is one of the parties to the contract of sale, and is thus directly hit by a sales tax on the transaction. Thus in Panhandle Oil Co. v. Mississippi, 277 U. S. 218 (1928), a state tax on the sale of gasoline to the federal government was held void; while a federal tax on the sale of a motorcycle to a municipal police department was held bad in Indian Motocycle Co. v. United States, 283 U. S. 570 (1931). It may be noted that by a statute of April 12, 1939, Congress withdrew the immunity of all federal salaries from state taxation, and authorized the federal taxation of all state salaries.

The second doctrine limits the immunity rule by holding that when a state engages in a business enterprise, in contrast to a function traditionally governmental in nature, it loses its tax immunity on that undertaking. This rule was announced in South Carolina v. United States, 199 U. S. 437 (1905), in which the state was required to pay the regular federal excise taxes on the liquor sold by state dispensaries set up for the wholesale and retail sale of such liquor. Selling liquor was held not to be a governmental function and a state engaging in the business was taxable as was any other liquor dealer. In Ohio v. Helvering, 292 U. S. 360 (1934), the rule was re-affirmed and applied to the liquor monopolies set up in a dozen or more states after the repeal of national prohibition. On the same theory the state-appointed officers of the Boston Elevated Railway were held liable to federal income taxation in Helvering v. Powers, 293 U. S. 214 (1934); and in Allen v. Regents of University System of Georgia, 304 U. S. 439 (1938), the receipts from state university athletic contests were held subject to federal taxation. In New York v. United States, 326 U. S. 572 (1946), the Court held that the federal excise tax on mineral waters could be collected from the state of New York on the sale of mineral waters taken from Saratoga Springs which the state owns. While admitting that the South Carolina case was a clear precedent, the majority justices engaged in a spirited de-bate on whether the distinction on which that case rested—the distinction between state functions which are "governmental" and those which are "business or proprietary"—provided a satisfactory working principle. It was suggested that the rule should be that Congress could "include the states in levying a tax exacted equally from private persons upon the same subject matter." This, however, did not command majority acceptance. Two justices strongly dissented.

The third doctrine holds that those who merely have business or other relations with the government, but are not themselves officers, can claim tax immunity only by showing that to tax them is to impose a direct and sub-stantial burden on the government itself. This rule was clearly stated in Met-calf & Eddy v. Mitchell, 269 U. S. 514 (1926), in which two consulting engineers who advised states and municipalities in regard to water supply and sewage disposal systems were held liable to federal income taxation. They were not public officers; they rendered their services under contract; and to tax their income was not to burden the governments which they served.

Beginning in the 1920's there were signs of a judicial tendency to narrow the scope of the immunity from intergovernmental taxation. In Long v. Rockwood, 277 U. S. 142 (1928), the Court held in a five-to-four decision that a state could not tax income in the form of royalties received from pat-ents issued by the United States, since a patent is a federal instrumentality. Four years later the Court reversed this decision in Fox Film Corporation v. Doyal, 286 U. S. 123 (1932), holding that copyrights (and patents) are not federal instrumentalities after they are issued, and that to exempt them from state taxation benefits only the patentee and not the federal govern-ment. Mr. Justice Holmes dissented strongly in Panhandle Oil Co. v. Mississippi, supra, which held the sale of gasoline to the federal government immune from state sales taxation. He declared that tax immunity ought to rest only on a showing of real and substantial burden on the government; and referring to Marshall's famous dictum, "the power to tax involves the power to destroy," he observed, "the power to tax is not the power to destroy while this Court sits." In Alabama v. King & Boozer, 314 U. S. 1 (1941), the Court held that the state could validly collect a sales tax on the purchases by a contractor of materials for use in building an army camp for the United States on a cost plus basis. At the same time, however, it held void a state sales tax imposed upon the purchase of materials by a federal land bank for use in repairing farm property acquired by the bank through a foreclosure of a mortgage. The bank was created by Congress to function as a government agency. See Federal Land Bank v. Bismark Lumber Co., 314 U. S. 95 (1941).

Further relaxation of the tax immunity rule appears in Wilmette Park District v. Campbell, 338 U. S. 411 (1949). Here the Court upheld the collection by the United States of a tax on the fees charged for admission to a bathing beach operated by a subdivision (local park district) of a state. The decision did not rest on the nature of the function performed, but on the fact that the tax was paid by patrons to the beach, leaving the burden on the state only "speculative and uncertain" at best.

Mr. Justice Stone delivered the opinion of the Court, saying in part:

We are asked to decide whether the imposition by the state of New York of an income tax on the salary of an employee of the Home Owners' Loan Corporation places an unconstitutional burden upon the federal government.

Respondent, a resident of New York, was employed during 1934 as an examining attorney for the Home Owners' Loan Corporation at an annual salary of $2,400. In his income tax return for that year he included his salary as subject to the New York state income tax . . . [and sought tax refund on the ground of his federal employment]. Petitioners, New York State Tax Commissioners, rejected respondent's claim for a refund of the tax . . .

For the purposes of this case we may assume that the creation of the Home Owners' Loan Corporation was a constitutional exercise of the powers of the federal government. . . . As that government derives its authority wholly from powers delegated to it by the Constitution, its every action within its constitutional power is governmental action, and since Congress is made the sole judge of what powers within the constitutional grant are to be exercised, all activities of government constitutionally authorized by Congress must stand on a parity with respect to their constitutional immunity from taxation. . . . And when the national government lawfully acts through a corporation which it owns and controls, those activities are governmental functions entitled to whatever tax immunity attaches to those functions when carried on by the government itself through its departments. . . .

The single question with which we are now concerned is whether the tax laid by the state upon the salary of respondent, employed by a corporate instrumentality of the federal government, imposes an unconstitutional burden upon that government. The theory of the tax immunity of either government, state or national, and its instrumentalities, from taxation by the other, has been rested upon an implied limitation on the taxing power of each, such as to forestall undue interference, through the exercise of that power, with the governmental activities of the other. That the two types of immunity may not, in all respects, stand on a parity has been recognized from the beginning, M'Culloch v. Maryland (4 Wheat. 435, 436), and possible differences in application, deriving from differences in the source, nature and extent of the immunity of the governments and their agencies, were pointed out and discussed by this Court in detail during the last term. Helvering v. Gerhardt (304 U. S. 405).

So far as now relevant, those differences have been thought to be traceable to the fact that the federal government is one of delegated powers in the exercise of which Congress is supreme; so that every agency which Congress can constitutionally create is a governmental agency. And since the power to create the agency includes the implied power to do whatever is needful or appropriate, if not expressly prohibited, to protect the agency, there has been attributed to Congress some scope, the limits of which it is not now necessary to define, for granting or withholding immunity of federal agencies from state taxation. . . . Whether its power to grant tax exemptions as an incident to the exercise of powers specifically granted by the Constitution can ever, in any circumstances, extend beyond the constitutional immunity of federal agencies which courts have implied, is a question which need not now be determined.

Congress has declared in § 4 of the act that the Home Owners' Loan Corporation is an instrumentality of the United States and that its bonds are exempt, as to principal and interest, from federal and state taxation, except surtaxes, estate, inheritance and gift taxes. The corporation itself, "including its franchise, its capital, reserves and surplus, and its loans and income," is likewise exempted from taxation; its real property is subject to tax to the same extent as other real property. But Congress has given no intimation of any purpose either to grant or withhold immunity from state taxation of the salary of the corporation's employees, and the congressional intention is not to be gathered from the statute by implication. . . .

It is true that the silence of Congress, when it has authority to speak, may sometimes give rise to an implication as to the congressional purpose. The nature and extent of that implication depend upon the nature of the congressional power and the effect of its exercise. But there is little scope for the application of that doctrine to the tax immunity of governmental instrumentalities. The constitutional immunity of either government from taxation by the other, where Congress is silent, has its source in an implied restriction upon the powers of the taxing government. So far as the implication rests upon the purpose to avoid interference with the functions of the taxed government or the imposition upon it of the economic burden of the tax, it is plain that there is no basis for implying a purpose of Congress to exempt the federal government or its agencies from tax burdens which are unsubstantial or which courts are unable to discern. Silence of Congress implies immunity no more than does the silence of the Constitution. It follows that when exemption from state taxation is claimed on the ground that the federal government is burdened by the tax, and Congress has disclosed no intention with respect to the claimed immunity, it is in order to consider the nature and effect of the alleged burden, and if it appears that there is no ground for implying a constitutional immunity, there is equally a want of any ground for assuming any purpose on the part of Congress to create an immunity.

The present tax is a non-discriminatory tax on income applied to salaries at a specified rate. It is not in form or substance a tax upon the Home Owners' Loan Corporation or its property or income, nor is it paid by the corporation or the government from their funds. It is laid upon income which becomes the property of the taxpayer when received as compensation for his services; and the tax laid upon the privilege of receiving it is paid from his private funds and not from the funds of the government, either directly or indirectly. The theory, which once won a qualified approval, that a tax on income is legally or economically a tax on its source, is no longer tenable, . . . and the only possible basis for implying a constitutional immunity from state income tax of the salary of an employee of the national government or of a governmental agency is that the economic burden of the tax is in some way passed on so as to impose a burden on the national government tantamount to an interference by one government with the other in the performance of its functions.

In the four cases in which this Court has held that the salary of an officer or employee of one government or its instrumentality was immune from taxation by the other, it was assumed, without discussion, that the immunity of a government or its instrumentality extends to the salaries of its officers and employees. . . . It was further pointed out that, as applied to the taxation of salaries of the employees of one government, the purpose of the immunity was not to confer benefits on the employees by relieving them from contributing their share of the financial support of the other government, whose benefits they enjoy, or to give an advantage to that government by enabling it to engage employees at salaries lower than those paid for like services by other employers, public or private, but to prevent undue interference with the one government by imposing on it the tax burdens of the other.

In applying these controlling principles in the Gerhardt case the Court held that the salaries of employees of the New York Port Authority, a state instrumentality created by New York and New Jersey, were not immune from federal income tax, even though the Authority be regarded as not subject to federal taxation. It was said that the taxpayers enjoyed the benefit and protection of the laws of the United States and were under a duty, common to all citizens, to contribute financial support to the government; that the tax laid on their salaries and paid by them could be said to affect or burden their employer, the Port Authority, or the states creating it, only so far as the burden of the tax was economically passed on to the employer; that a nondiscriminatory tax laid on the income of all members of the community could not be assumed to obstruct the function which New York and New Jersey had undertaken to perform, or to cast an economic burden upon them, more than does the general taxation of property and income which, to some extent, incapable of measurement by economists, may tend to raise the price level of labor and materials. The Court concluded that the claimed immunity would do no more than relieve the taxpayers from the duty of financial support to the national government in order to secure to the state a theoretical advantage, speculative in character and measurement and too unsubstantial to form the basis of an implied constitutional immunity from taxation.

The conclusion reached in the Gerhardt case that in terms of constitutional tax immunity a federal income tax on the salary of an employee is not a prohibited burden on the employer makes it imperative that we should consider anew the immunity here claimed for the salary of an employee of a federal instrumentality. As already indicated, such differences as there may be between the implied tax immunity of a state and the corresponding immunity of the national government and its instrumentalities may be traced to the fact that the national government is one of delegated powers, in the exercise of which it is supreme. Whatever scope this may give to the national government to claim immunity from state taxation of all instrumentalities which it may constitutionally create, and whatever authority Congress may possess as incidental to the exercise of its delegated powers to grant or withhold immunity from state taxation, Congress has not sought in this case to exercise such power. Hence these distinctions between the two types of immunity cannot affect the question with which we are now concerned. The burden on government of a nondiscriminatory income tax applied to the salary of the employee of a government or its instrumentality is the same, whether a state or national government is concerned. The determination in the Gerhardt case that the federal income tax imposed on the employees of the Port Authority was not a burden on the Port Authority made it unnecessary to consider whether the Authority itself was immune from federal taxation; the claimed immunity failed because even if the Port Authority were itself immune from federal income tax, the tax upon the income of its employees cast upon it no unconstitutional burden.

Assuming, as we do, that the Home Owners' Loan Corporation is clothed with the same immunity from a state taxation as the government itself, we cannot say that the present tax on the income of its employees lays any unconstitutional burden upon it. All the reasons for refusing to imply a constitutional prohibition of federal income taxation of salaries of state employees, stated at length in the Gerhardt case, are of equal force when immunity is claimed from state income tax on salaries paid by the national government or its agencies. In this respect we perceive no basis for a difference in result whether the taxed income be salary or some other form of compensation, or whether the taxpayer be an employee or an officer of either a state or the national government, or of its instrumentalities. In no case is there basis for the assumption that any such tangible or certain economic burden is imposed on the government concerned as would justify a court's declaring that the taxpayer is clothed with the implied constitutional tax immunity of the government by which he is employed. That assumption, made in Collector v. Day (Buffington v. Day) 11 Wall. 113, and New York ex rel. Rogers v. Graves, 299 U. S. 401, is contrary to the reasoning and to the conclusions reached in the Gerhardt case and in Metcalf & Eddy v. Mitchell, 269 U. S. 514 [other cases cited]. . . . In their light the assumption can no longer be made. Collector v. Day (Buffington v. Day) 11 Wall. 113, and New York ex rel. Rogers v. Graves, 299 U. S. 401, are overruled so far as they recognize an implied constitutional immunity from income taxation of the salaries of officers or employees of the national or a state government or their instrumentalities.

So much of the burden of a non-discriminatory general tax upon the incomes of employees of a government, state or national, as may be passed on economically to that government, through the effect of the tax on the price level of labor or materials, is but the normal incident of the organization within the same territory of two governments, each possessing the taxing power. The burden, so fas as it can be said to exist or to affect the government in any indirect or incidental way, is one which the Constitution presupposes, and hence it cannot rightly be deemed to be within an implied restriction upon the taxing power of the national and state governments which the Constitution has expressly granted to one and has confirmed to the other. The immunity is not one to be implied from the Constitution, because if allowed it would impose to an inadmissible extent a restriction on the taxing power which the Constitution has reserved to the state governments.

Reversed.

Mr. Chief Justice Hughes concurred in the result.
Mr. Justice Frankfurter concurred in a separate opinion.
Justices Butler and McReynolds dissented.

THE CHILD LABOR TAX CASE
BAILEY v. DREXEL FURNITURE COMPANY
259 U. S. 20; 66 L. Ed. 817; 42 Sup. Ct. 449. 1922.

It is well established in the law of taxation that if the power to tax exists at all with reference to a person or commodity, the tax actually imposed is not unconstitutional merely because it is deemed too high. A tax of 100%

is no more invalid than a tax of 1%. The only checks upon the rate of taxation are political checks. An actual fiscal need will justify even very burdensome levies. This is apparently what Chief Justice Marshall meant when, in his opinion in the case of McCulloch v. Maryland (p. 10), he said, "the power to tax involves the power to destroy." This maxim, however, has been given a somewhat different interpretation by some writers and has been assumed to mean that the power of taxation might be used independently as a means of driving out of existence commodities or practices regarded as obnoxious by the taxing authority. This theory has been used to support the exercise by Congress of a wide police power through the use of destructive taxes. The questions involved in the federal child labor tax case represent the culmination of a long controversy regarding the purposes for which Congress may legitimately levy taxes, and some aspects of that controversy should be thoroughly understood.

There could never be any doubt as to the propriety of using the taxing power of Congress as a means of raising revenue, since that is the obvious and primary reason for establishing the power. But almost immediately after the organization of the national government Congress, over the protest of the strict constructionist school, passed a protective tariff; and during most of our subsequent history we have had similar legislation on our statute books. Some of the tariff schedules have been so high as to prevent entirely the importation of certain commodities, and in such cases it would seem that Congress had used its power of taxation for the purpose of destroying the thing taxed. A still more striking instance of the same thing is to be found in the federal tax upon state bank notes levied by Congress in 1866. This imposed a tax of 10% upon all bank notes issued by state banks and had the desired result of preventing the further issue of such notes. The validity of this tax came before the Court in the case of Veazie Bank v. Fenno, 8 Wallace 533 (1869), and that decision states the principle upon which this type of taxation is upheld. It was pointed out by the Court that while the 10% tax was undoubtedly destructive, it was merely a use by Congress of its power to tax as a means of doing indirectly what it might have done directly: namely, protect the note issue of the newly established national banks from the competition of state bank notes. Congress has full delegated authority over the federal currency, and could have prohibited the further issuance of state bank notes by a simple prohibition. It chose to use the indirect method of taxation, but in so doing the power of taxation was being used as a means of exercising the power over the currency.

But Congress has gone farther than this and has from time to time levied destructive or regulatory taxes for the purpose of exercising authority not within the scope of its delegated power. In 1902 it imposed a tax of ten cent per pound upon all oleomargarine colored to look like butter. In 1890 a tax of $10 per pound was placed upon smoking opium and in 1914 this tax was increased to $300 per pound. In 1912 Congress made impossible the manufacture of matches in which poisonous phosphorous was used by placing upon such matches a tax of two cents per hundred. The oleomargarine tax came before the Supreme Court in the case of McCray v. United States, 195 U. S. 27 (1904). This opinion will bear careful study. In it Mr. Justice White, who as United States Senator from Louisiana in the early nineties had vigorously attacked the constitutionality of a similar taxing statute then pending before Congress, held that since the tax imposed had all the external appearances of an ordinary revenue act the Court could not invalidate it because it was destructive in its effect or because Congress in imposing it had sought to exercise a police power which was beyond the scope of its delegated authority. In short, if the tax is "on its face" a revenue act the courts are not permitted to question further into the motives which may have led to its enactment. While the language used in the opinion was guarded, it seemed on the whole to lend support to those who were advocating the use of the taxing power of Congress as a means of exercising a general police power.

It was natural, therefore, that when, after the disappointment resulting from the Supreme Court's decision in the case of Hammer v. Dagenhart (p. 415), the opponents of child labor turned their attention to the problem of finding a constitutional basis for the enactment of a new federal child labor law, they should turn to the taxing clause with some assurance that here they would be on safer ground. Accordingly there emerged after some debate the child labor tax provision of the general Revenue Act of February 24, 1919. This imposed a 10% excise tax upon the annual net profits of mines, quarries, factories, and other establishments which during any portion of the taxable year employed children contrary to the regulations established. These regulations as to age, hours, and days of labor, etc., were identical with those in the first Child Labor Act. The Drexel Furniture Company permitted a boy under the age of fourteen years to work in its factory during the taxable year 1919. It received notice from Bailey, who was United States collector of internal revenue for the district, that the firm would be assessed 10% of its net profits for the year, or $6,312.79, under the provisions of the child labor tax act. It paid the tax under protest and brought suit to recover the amount of the tax upon the ground that the law imposing it was unconstitutional. It will be recalled that in 1941, in the Darby case, supra, the federal prohibition of child labor was finally accomplished under the commerce clause.

The Bailey case established an important check upon the exercise by Congress of its taxing power for police power purposes. When Congress levies taxes which appear to the Court to be penalties rather than taxes they can be held void. This was the fate of the special federal excise tax of

$1,000 imposed annually upon those who carry on the liquor business in violation of state law. See United States v. Constantine, 296 U. S. 287 (1935). But if Congress can make a regulatory or destructive tax look like a revenue statute, the Court, following the McCray case, will uphold it. Thus in Sonzinsky v. United States, 300 U. S. 506 (1937), the Court upheld the National Firearms Act of 1934 which not only imposed a $200 annual license tax on dealers in firearms but also laid a tax of $200 on each transfer of a machine gun, sawed-off shot gun, and silencer. "On its face," said the Court, "it is only a taxing measure." In 1953, the Court held valid a 1951 federal excise tax on gambling. See United States v. Kahriger, 345 U. S. 22.

Mr. Chief Justice Taft delivered the opinion of the Court, saying in part:

. . . The law is attacked on the ground that it is a regulation of the employment of child labor in the states,—an exclusively state function under the federal Constitution and within the reservations of the Tenth Amendment. It is defended on the ground that it is a mere excise tax levied by the Congress of the United States under its broad power of taxation conferred by section 8, Article I, of the federal Constitution. We must construe the law and interpret the intent and meaning of Congress from the language of the act. The words are to be given their ordinary meaning unless the context shows that they are differently used. Does this law impose a tax with only that incidental restraint and regulation which a tax must inevitably involve? Or does it regulate by the use of the so-called tax as a penalty? If a tax, it is clearly an excise. If it were an excise on a commodity or other thing of value we might not be permitted under previous decisions of this Court to infer solely from its heavy burden that the act intends a prohibition instead of a tax. But this act is more. It provides a heavy exaction for a departure from a detailed and specified course of conduct in business. That course of business is that employers shall employ in mines and quarries, children of an age greater than sixteen years; in mills and factories, children of an age greater than fourteen years; and shall prevent children of less than sixteen years in mills and factories from working more than eight hours a day or six days in the week. If an employer departs from this prescribed course of business, he is to pay to the government one tenth of his entire net income in the business for a full year. The amount is not to be proportioned in any degree to the extent or frequency of the departures, but is to be paid by the employer in full measure whether he employs five hundred children for a year, or employs only one for a day. Moreover, if he does not know the child is within the named age limit, he is not to pay; that is to say, it is only where he knowingly departs from the prescribed course that payment is to be exacted. Scienter is associated with penalties, not with taxes. The employer's factory is to be subject to inspection at any time not only by the taxing officers of the Treasury, the department normally charged with the collection of taxes, but also by the Secretary of Labor and his subordinates, whose normal function is the advancement and protection of the welfare of the workers. In the light of these features of the act, a court must be blind not to see that the so-called tax is imposed to stop the employment of children within the age limits prescribed. Its prohibitory and regulatory effect and purpose are palpable. All others can see and understand this. How can we properly shut our minds to it?

It is the high duty and function of this Court in cases regularly brought to its bar to decline to recognize or enforce seeming laws of Congress, dealing with subjects not intrusted to Congress, but left or committed by the supreme law of the land to the control of the states. We cannot avoid the duty even though it requires us to refuse to give effect to legislation designed to promote the highest good. The good sought in unconstitutional legislation is an insidious feature because it leads citizens and legislators of good purpose to promote it without thought of the serious breach it will make in the ark of our covenant or the harm which will come from breaking down recognized standards. In the maintenance of local self-government, on the one hand, and the national power, on the other, our country has been able to endure and prosper for near a century and a half.

Out of a proper respect for the acts of a coordinate branch of the government, this Court has gone far to sustain taxing acts as such, even though there has been ground for suspecting, from the weight of the tax, it was intended to destroy its subject. But in the act before us, the presumption of validity cannot prevail, because the proof of the contrary is found on the very face of its provisions. Grant the validity of this law, and all that Congress would need to do hereafter, in seeking to take over to its control any one of the great number of subjects of public interest, jurisdiction of which the states have never parted with, and which are reserved to them by the Tenth Amendment, would be to enact a detailed measure of complete regulation of the subject and enforce it by a so-called tax upon departures from it. To give such magic to the word "tax" would be to break down all constitutional limitation of the powers of Congress and completely wipe out the sovereignty of the states.

The difference between a tax and a penalty is sometimes difficult to define, and yet the consequences of the distinction in the required method of their collection often are important. Where the sovereign enacting the law has power to impose both tax and penalty, the difference between revenue production and mere regulation may be immaterial; but not so when one sovereign can impose a tax only, and the power of regulation rests in another. Taxes are occasionally imposed in the discretion of the legislature on proper subjects with the primary motive of obtaining revenue from them, and with the incidental motive of discouraging them by making their continuance onerous. They do not lose their character as taxes because of the incidental motive. But there comes a time in the extension of the penalizing features of the so-called tax when it loses its character as such and becomes a mere penalty, with the characteristics of regulation and punishment. Such is the case in the law before us. Although Congress does not invalidate the contract of employment, or expressly declare that the employment within the mentioned ages is illegal, it does exhibit its intent practically to achieve the latter result by adopting the criteria of wrongdoing, and imposing its principal consequence on those who transgress its standard. . . .

The case before us cannot be distinguished from that of Hammer v. Dagenhart. . . .

In the case at the bar, Congress, in the name of a tax which, on the face of the act, is a penalty, seeks to do the same thing, and the effort must be equally futile.

The analogy of the Dagenhart case is clear. The congressional power over interstate commerce is, within its proper scope, just as complete and unlimited as the congressional power to tax; and the legislative motive in its exercise is just as free from judicial suspicion and inquiry. Yet when Congress threatened to stop interstate commerce in ordinary and necessary commodities, unobjectionable as subjects of transportation, and to deny the same to the people of a state, in order to coerce them into compliance with Congress's regulation of state concerns, the Court said this was not in fact regulation of interstate commerce, but rather that of state concerns, and was invalid. So here the so-called tax is a penalty to coerce people of a state to act as Congress wishes them to act in respect of a matter completely the business of the state government under the federal Constitution. This case requires, as did the Dagenhart case, the application of the principle announced by Chief Justice Marshall in McCulloch v. Maryland, 4 Wheaton 316, 423, in a much-quoted passage:

"should Congress, in the execution of its powers, adopt measures which are prohibited by the Constitution, or should Congress, under the pretext of executing its powers, pass laws for the accomplishment of objects not intrusted to the government, it would become the painful duty of this tribunal, should a case requiring such a decision come before it, to say that such an act was not the law of the land." . . .

For the reasons given, we must hold the Child Labor Tax Law invalid, and the judgment of the district court is affirmed.

Mr. Justice Clarke dissented.

10

Territories

BALZAC v. PORTO RICO
258 U. S. 298; 66 L. Ed. 627; 42 Sup. Ct. 343. 1922.

The problem of the status and government of territories antedates the Constitution itself. Questions arising out of the possession of western lands by the states had some influence in the movement toward national union, and the federal government established in 1789 found itself possessed of large tracts of fertile and sparsely settled territory. The Constitution empowered Congress to make needful rules and regulations regarding territories; and it was the question whether that power extended to the exclusion of slavery from the territories that separated the various parties upon the eve of the Civil War. The problem as to the form of government by which territories should be ruled and the character of the constitutional rights which territorial inhabitants should enjoy did not become acute during the early period. Alaska, acquired in 1867, was the first of the non-contiguous territories which the United States came to possess; and it presented few problems by reason of its sparse population made up in the main of Americans.

When, however, we acquired by treaty with Spain in 1898 the islands of Porto Rico (now Puerto Rico) and the Philippines and annexed the islands of Hawaii, the United States found itself exercising sovereign authority over several million inhabitants of alien races, unaccustomed to Anglo-Saxon laws or institutions, many of them as yet incapable of full self-government. Thus arose for the first time the important question whether territory annexed to the United States immediately became an integral part of the United States, or could be held merely as a dependency. The constitutional questions involved were among the most difficult which the Supreme Court has ever faced, calling as they did for the application of constitutional principles to conditions entirely unforeseen by the framers of the Constitution. These were dealt with by the Supreme Court in a series of decisions known as the Insular Cases.

The first problem to arise was whether the island of Porto Rico, after its annexation to the United States, was to be regarded as foreign territory to the extent that tariff duties could still be imposed upon goods imported from it into this country. In DeLima v. Bidwell, 182 U. S. 1 (1901), the Court held that while Porto Rico did not become an integral part of the federal Union by the mere fact of annexation it did nevertheless cease to be foreign territory, and that the duties in question could not without further congressional action be collected upon goods imported therefrom. Congress thereupon modified the tariff statutes in such a way as to retain certain duties upon goods brought in from Porto Rico and the Philippines. The validity of this legislation came before the Court in the case of Downes v. Bidwell, 182 U. S. 244 (1901), the argument against it being grounded upon the clause of the Constitution which requires that "all duties, imposts, and excises shall be uniform throughout the United States." Did Porto Rico become part of the United States within the meaning of this provision? The Court held that it did not. It held this by a five-to-four decision in which there was difference of opinion as to reasons even among those judges who agreed with each other as to result. The result seemed to be, however, that territories could be classified into two categories, incorporated and unincorporated; that incorporated territory became an integral part of the country as a result of the action or implied intention of Congress to make it such; that annexed territory remained unincorporated until such congressional intention was made manifest; that Porto Rico was not thus incorporated, so that while it was not foreign territory in an international sense it was still foreign territory in a domestic sense, was merely an appurtenant possession, and not entitled to equality of treatment under the tariff laws unless Congress chose to extend such treatment.

In the meantime a similar important question had been brewing: namely, the measure of civil liberty and constitutional rights which must be extended to the inhabitants of the new insular possessions, a question which was broadcast by newspapers and political leaders under the spectacular caption, "Does the Constitution Follow the Flag?" This meant concretely: is Congress in governing these islands bound by the provisions of the federal Bill of Rights and other similar guarantees of civil liberty just as it would be bound by them were it passing laws applicable to the nation at large? This seemed to present an even more awkward dilemma than had been involved in the tariff cases. If the Constitution does not limit Congress in governing these unincorporated territories, then the inhabitants thereof have no protection against arbitrary and tyrannical legislation. If, on the other hand, all of the constitutional guarantees must be observed, the problems of governmental administration over the semi-civilized portions of the territories would be practically impossible of solution. This was the problem which the Court faced in the case of Hawaii v. Mankichi in the concrete question whether the requirements of indictment by grand jury and trial by jury as guaranteed in the Fifth and Sixth Amendments applied of their own force in the then unincorporated territory of Hawaii. Mankichi was tried for manslaughter upon an indictment not presented by a grand jury and was convicted by a verdict rendered by nine of the twelve jurors instead of by a unanimous verdict held uniformly to be required in federal courts by the constitutional provision for jury trial. He petitioned for a writ of habeas corpus alleging the violation of his rights under the federal Constitution. The Court's answer to the question, "Does the Constitution Follow the Flag," was both ingenious and bold: The guarantees of civil liberty in the Constitution are not all of the same force and authority. Some of them embody fundamental or "natural" rights, and these Congress may not transgress in the government of any territory be it incorporated or unincorporated. Others, however, are the statements of rights which are "formal" or procedural or remedial in character, arising out of the peculiar customs of Anglo-Saxon jurisprudence, and these Congress is not obliged to extend to unincorporated territories unless it wishes to do so. In the light of this classification the rights of jury trial and grand jury indictment are "formal" rather than fundamental. Hawaii v. Mankichi, 190 U. S. 197 (1903). Hawaii became incorporated by act of Congress in 1900, but after Mankichi had been indicted.

In Rassmussen v. United States, 197 U. S. 516 (1905), the Court held that Alaska was an incorporated territory and that the jury trial provision of the Sixth Amendment applied there of its own force and could not be abrogated by any congressional or territorial enactment.

One question which the Insular Cases left unanswered was how a territory actually becomes incorporated. What is the precise nature of the metamorphosis which it undergoes? Obviously Congress could pass an act declaring a particular territory to be thereby incorporated, but this Congress has never done. In 1905 in the case of Rassmussen v. United States, the Court declared the territory of Alaska to be incorporated as the result of a series of congressional acts relating to it beginning as far back as 1868, which in the judgment of the Court indicated the intention of Congress to regard it as incorporated. The same process of incorporation would doubtless have been recognized as operating in the case of Oklahoma,

Arizona, or New Mexico during the period prior to their admission to statehood. The status of incorporation was recognized only as a result of the intention of Congress with reference thereto. So much was established. Whether such intention could be inferred from the Organic Act of Porto Rico passed by Congress in 1917 was the question presented by the case of Balzac v. Porto Rico.

The organic act in question had conferred United States citizenship upon the inhabitants of the island, had established territorial courts, and had extended to Porto Rico the operation of numerous federal laws. It had, however, not mentioned the matter of incorporation, and it had included a bill of rights containing most of the provisions of the federal Bill of Rights except those relating to jury trial. After the passage of the act, Balzac, the editor of a Porto Rican newspaper, was convicted of criminal libel in the territorial court without a jury. He appealed to the United States Supreme Court upon the ground that Porto Rico had become an incorporated territory by virtue of the Organic Act of 1917 and that consequently the Sixth Amendment guaranteeing jury trial was made applicable to the island and should have governed the procedure followed in his own trial. This contention the Supreme Court rejected, thus holding that the granting of United States citizenship to the inhabitants of an unincorporated territory does not in and of itself incorporate it. Just what does incorporate such a territory is a question which the Court has never answered. In 1952 Porto Rico was set up by Congress as a "commonwealth" with power to elect its own governor and legislature. Since Alaska (1958) and Hawaii (1959) are now states, the United States has no incorporated territories.

Mr. Chief Justice Taft delivered the opinion of the Court, saying in part:

. . . We have now to inquire whether that part of the Sixth Amendment to the Constitution which requires that, in all criminal prosecutions, the accused shall enjoy the right to a speedy and public trial by an impartial jury of the state and district wherein the crime shall have been committed, which district shall have been previously ascertained by law, applies to Porto Rico. Another provision on the subject is in Article III of the Constitution providing that the trial of all crimes, except in cases of impeachment, shall be by jury; and such trial shall be held in the state where the said crimes shall have been committed; but when not committed within any state, the trial shall be at such place or places as the Congress may by law have directed. The Seventh Amendment of the Constitution provides that in suits at common law, when the value in controversy shall exceed $20, the right of trial by jury shall be preserved. It is well settled that these provisions for jury trial in criminal and civil cases apply to the territories of the United States. . . . But it is just as clearly settled that they do not apply to territory belonging to the United States which has not been incorporated into the Union. Hawaii v. Mankichi, 190 U. S. 197. . . . It was further settled in Downes v. Bidwell, 182 U. S. 244, and confirmed by Dorr v. United States, 195 U. S. 138, that neither the Philippines nor Porto Rico was territory which has been incorporated in the Union or become a part of the United States, as distinguished from merely belonging to it; and that the acts giving temporary governments to the Philippines . . . had no such effect. . . .

The question before us, therefore, is: Has Congress, since the Foraker Act of April 12, 1900, enacted legislation incorporating Porto Rico into the Union? Counsel for the plaintiff in error give, in their brief, an extended list of acts, to which we shall refer later, which they urge as indicating a purpose to make the island a part of the United States, but they chiefly rely on the Organic Act of Porto Rico of March 2, 1917 . . . known as the Jones Act.

The act is entitled, "An Act to Provide a Civil Government for Porto Rico, and for Other Purposes." It does not indicate by its title that it has a purpose to incorporate the island into the Union. It does not contain any clause which declares such purpose or effect. While this is not conclusive, it strongly tends to show that Congress did not have such an intention. Few questions have been the subject of such discussion and dispute in our country as the status of our territory acquired from Spain in 1899. The division between the political parties in respect to it, the diversity of the views of the members of this Court in regard to its constitutional aspects, and the constant recurrence of the subject in the houses of Congress, fixed the attention of all on the future relation of this acquired territory to the United States. Had Congress intended to take the important step of changing the treaty status of Porto Rico by incorporating it into the Union, it is reasonable to suppose that it would have done so by the plain declaration, and would not have left it to mere inference. Before the question became acute at the close of the Spanish War, the distinction between acquisition and incorporation was not regarded as important; or at least it was not fully understood and had not aroused great controversy. Before that, the purpose of Congress might well be a matter of mere inference from various legislative acts; but in these latter days, incorporation is not to be assumed without express declaration, or an implication so strong as to exclude any other view.

Again, the second section of the act is called a "bill of rights," and included therein is substantially every one of the guaranties of the federal Constitution, except those relating to indictment by a grand jury in the case of infamous crimes and the right of trial by jury in civil and criminal cases. If it was intended to incorporate Porto Rico into the Union by this act, which would, ex proprio vigore, make applicable the whole Bill of Rights of the Constitution to the island, why was it thought necessary to create for it a bill of rights and carefully exclude trial by jury? In the very forefront of the act is this substitute for incorporation and application of the Bill of Rights of the Constitution. This seems to us a conclusive argument against the contention of counsel for the plaintiff in error.

The section of the Jones Act which counsel press on us is section 5. This in effect declares that all persons who, under the Foraker Act, were made citizens of Porto Rico, and certain other residents, shall become citizens of the United States, unless they prefer not to become such, in which case they are to declare such preference within six months, and thereafter they lose certain political rights under the new government. In the same section the United States district court is given power separately to naturalize individuals of some other classes of residents. . . . Unaffected by the considerations already suggested, perhaps the declaration of section 5 would furnish ground for an inference such as counsel for plaintiff in error contend; but, under the circumstances, we find it entirely consistent with non-incorporation. When Porto Ricans passed from under the government of Spain, they, lost the protection of that government as subjects of the king of Spain, a title by which they had been known for centuries. They had a right to expect, in passing under the dominion of the United States, a status entitling them to the protection of their new sovereign. In theory and in law, they had it as citizens of Porto Rico, but it was an anomalous status, or seemed to be so, in view of the fact that those who owed and rendered allegiance to the other great world powers were given the same designation and status as those living in their respective home countries, so far as protection against foreign injustice went. It became a yearning of the Porto Ricans to be American citizens, therefore, and this act gave them the boon. What additional rights did it give them? It enabled them to move into the continental United States and becoming residents of any state there to enjoy every right of any other citizen of the United States, civil, social, and political. A citizen of the Philippines must be naturalized before he can settle and vote in this country. . . . Not so the Porto Rican under the Organic Act of 1917.

In Porto Rico, however, the Porto Rican cannot insist upon the right of trial by jury, except as his own representatives in his legislature shall confer it on him. The citizen of the United States living in Porto Rico cannot there enjoy a right of trial by jury under the federal Constitution, any more than the Porto Rican. It is locality that is determinative of the application of the Constitution in such matters as judicial procedure, and not the status of the people who live in it.

It is true that in the absence of other and countervailing evidence, a law of Congress or a provision in a treaty acquiring territory, declaring an intention to confer political and civil rights on the inhabitants of the new lands as American citizens, may be properly interpreted to mean an incorporation of it into the Union, as in the case of Louisiana and Alaska. This was one of the chief grounds upon which this Court placed its conclusion that Alaska had been incorporated in the Union, in Rassmussen v. United States, 197 U. S. 516. But Alaska was a very different case from that of Porto Rico. It was an enormous territory, very sparsely settled, and offering opportunity for immigration and settlement by American citizens. It was on the American continent and within easy reach of the then United States. It involved none of the difficulties which incorporation of the Philippines and Porto Rico presents, and one of them is in the very matter of trial by jury. . . .

The jury system needs citizens trained to the exercise of the responsibilities of jurors. In common-law countries centuries of tradition have prepared a conception of the impartial attitudes jurors must assume. The jury system postulates a conscious duty of participation in the machinery of justice which it is hard for people not brought up in fundamentally popular government at once to acquire. One of its greatest benefits is in the security it gives the people that they, as jurors actual or possible, being part of the judicial system of the country, can prevent its arbitrary use or abuse. Congress has thought that a people like the Filipinos or the Porto Ricans, trained to a complete judicial system which knows no juries, living in compact and ancient communities, with definitely formed customs and political conceptions, should be permitted themselves to determine how far they wish to adopt this institution of Anglo-Saxon origin, and when. . . .

We need not dwell on another consideration which requires us not lightly to infer, from acts thus easily explained on other grounds, an intention to incorporate in the Union these distant ocean communities of a different origin and language from those of our continental people. Incorporation has always been a step, and an important one, leading to statehood. Without, in the slightest degree, intimating an opinion as to the wisdom of such a policy, for that is not our province, it is reasonable to assume that when such a step is taken it will be begun and taken by Congress deliberately and with a clear declaration of purpose, and not left a matter of mere inference or construction.

Counsel for the plaintiff in error also rely on the organization of a United States district court in Porto Rico, on the allowance of review of the Porto Rican supreme court in cases when the Constitution of the United States is involved, on the statutory permission that Porto Rican youth can attend West Point and Annapolis academies, on the authorized sale of United States stamps in the island, on the extension of revenue, navigation, immigration, national banking, bankruptcy, federal employers' liability, safety appliance, extradition, and census laws in one way or another to Porto Rico. With the background of the considerations already stated, none of these, nor all of them put together, furnish ground for the conclusion pressed on us. . . .

On the whole, therefore, we find no features in the Organic Act of Porto Rico of 1917 from which we can infer the purpose of Congress to incorporate Porto Rico into the United States, with the consequences which would follow. . . .

The judgments of the supreme court of Porto Rico are affirmed.

Mr. Justice Holmes concurred in the result.

11

Cases Added, 1966

GIDEON v. WAINWRIGHT
372 U. S. 335; 9 L. Ed. 2d 799; 83 Sup. Ct. 792. 1963.

Probably no more difficult task confronts a democratic people than that of reconciling and compromising the conflicting claims of the individual and his society. Each person as a member of society looks to the government to insure him a maximum amount of security for his life and property; each as an individual wants that government to guarantee him rights and liberties *against* that society. To achieve the former the political branches of the government are authorized to make and enforce laws for the public good; to achieve the latter a bill of rights is written into the constitution, and to the judiciary primarily falls the job of seeing that the other branches of the government do not go too far. But how far is "too far"? There is no general answer to this, and public officials in all branches of government tend to make on-the-spot decisions based upon their own ideas of where the line should be drawn.

During the past decade the Supreme Court has moved haltingly, but with increasing speed, in the direction of greater protection for the rights of individuals against the society of which they are a part. Wide public attention has been attracted by such moves in the areas of racial equality and equal representation in the legislature. Less spectacular, but no less significant, has been the increased protection afforded to individuals in their uneven struggle with those charged with enforcing the criminal law. This latter move has taken two rather different forms. One involves interpreting the guarantees of the Bill of Rights and Fourteenth Amendment so as to increase the protection they afford. This is discussed in the note to Escobedo v. Illinois, p. 515. The other is to broaden the applicability of the Bill of Rights so that the states, which have long set their own standards of fairness, will be made to meet the more stringent standards applicable to the federal government.

Prior to 1960 the process of making the provisions of the Bill of Rights applicable to the states had encompassed very little beyond the First Amendment. See discussion pp. 151, 156. Efforts had been made to include others, but a majority of the Court had shied away from "incorporation," or "absorption," a process in which the clauses of the Bill of Rights, *as interpreted against the federal government,* are applied to the states so that state and federal cases serve interchangeably as precedent. Rights not incorporated were protected by the more flexible rule that any state conduct which is shockingly unfair denies due process of law. It was generally assumed, for example, both from the language of the case and from its being listed with First Amendment cases in Palko v. Connecticut (p. 151), that Powell v. Alabama, 287 U. S. 45 (1932), had incorporated the right to counsel into the due process clause of the Fourteenth Amendment. In 1942, however, the Supreme Court made it clear that this was not the case. In Betts v. Brady, 316 U. S. 455, summarized in the opinion below, it emphasized that "the due process clause of the Fourteenth Amendment does not incorporate, as such, the specific guarantees found in the Sixth Amendment although a denial by a state of rights or privileges specifically embodied in that and others of the first eight amendments may, in certain circumstances, or in connection with other elements, operate, in a given case, to deprive a litigant of due process of law. . . . That which may, in one setting, constitute a denial of fundamental fairness, shocking to the universal sense of justice, may, in other circumstances, and in the light of other considerations, fall short of such denial."

The importance of this distinction was emphasized in Louisiana ex rel. Francis v. Resweber, 329 U. S. 459 (1947), a case holding it was not a cruel and unusual punishment to try a second time to electrocute a person after the first attempt had failed to kill him. While four members of the majority stated somewhat ambiguously that the "Fourteenth [Amendment] would prohibit by its due process clause execution by a state in a cruel manner," Mr. Justice Frankfurter wrote a concurring opinion to explain that in his view "the penology of a state is not to be tested by the scope of the Eighth Amendment."

In 1949 the Court in Wolf v. Colorado, 338 U. S. 25, held that the right to privacy, which was the "core of the Fourth Amendment," was made applicable to the states by the Fourteenth, and while Mr. Justice Frankfurter denied that this entailed incorporation (see his dissent in Mapp v. Ohio, p. 111), it was generally assumed that incorporation had in fact taken place. Whatever the merits of this, the Court in Wolf effectively nullified such protection as it had extended by refusing to apply to the states the Weeks rule excluding unreasonably seized evidence from court— admittedly the only real deterrent to unlawful police searches. See discussion p. 104.

The attitude of judicial self-restraint under which the states had been shaping their own standards of fair criminal procedure came to an abrupt halt in 1961. In Mapp v. Ohio (p. 102), the Court overruled Wolf and clearly made the Fourth Amendment, together with its exclusionary rule, applicable to the states. Then in 1962 it removed all doubt about the "incorporation" of cruel and unusual punishments when it used the formula, made familiar by First Amendment cases, that the state had violated the "Eighth and Fourteenth Amendments"; see Robinson v. California, 370 U. S. 660. The following year any lingering doubts about the meaning of "incorporation" were dispelled when eight members of the Court in Ker v. California, 374 U. S. 23, agreed that federal constitutional standards of reasonableness of searches "is the same under the Fourth and Fourteenth Amendments." Only Mr. Justice Harlan clung to the view that "the more flexible concept of 'fundamental' fairness" should apply to the states. In 1964, following the decision in the present case, the Court in Malloy v. Hogan, 378 U. S. 1, incorporated the Fifth Amendment privilege against compulsory self-incrimination, and in Griffin v. California, 381 U. S. 957 (1965), it held applicable the federal standards and reversed a state conviction in which the judge and prosecutor had commented unfavorably upon the defendant's failure to testify. In Pointer v. Texas, 380 U. S. 400 (1965), the Court held that "the confrontation guarantee of the Sixth Amendment . . . is 'to be enforced against the States under the Fourteenth Amendment according to the same standards that protect those personal rights against federal encroachment.' "

Following the reversal of his conviction in the present case, Gideon was retried by the state of Florida in the same courtroom, before the same judge, with the same witnesses, but with a lawyer appointed by the court at Gideon's request. This time he was acquitted.

Mr. Justice Black delivered the opinion of the Court, saying in part:

Petitioner was charged in a Florida state court with having broken and entered a poolroom with intent to commit a misdemeanor. This offense is a felony under Florida law. Appearing in court without funds and without a lawyer, petitioner asked the court to appoint counsel for him, whereupon the following colloquy took place:

"The Court: Mr. Gideon, I am sorry, but I cannot appoint Counsel to represent you in this case. Under the laws of the State of Florida, the only time the Court can appoint Counsel to represent a Defendant is when that person is charged with a capital offense. I am sorry, but I will have to deny your request to appoint Counsel to defend you in this case.

"The Defendant: The United States Supreme Court says I am entitled to be represented by Counsel."

Put to trial before a jury, Gideon conducted his defense about as well as could be expected from a layman. He made an opening statement to the jury, cross-examined the State's witnesses, presented witnesses in his own defense, declined to testify himself, and made a short argument "emphasizing his innocence to the charge contained in the Information filed in this case." The jury returned a verdict of guilty, and petitioner was sentenced to serve five years in the state prison. . . . Since 1942, when Betts v. Brady, 316 U. S. 455, was decided by a divided Court, the problem of a defendant's federal constitutional right to counsel in a state court has been a continuing source of controversy and litigation in both state and federal courts. To give this problem another review here, we granted certiorari. Since Gideon was proceeding in forma pauperis, we appointed counsel to represent him and requested both sides to discuss in their briefs and oral arguments the following: "Should this Court's holding in Betts v. Brady be reconsidered?"

I.

The facts upon which Betts claimed that he had been unconstitutionally denied the right to have counsel appointed to assist him are strikingly like the facts upon which Gideon here bases his federal constitutional claim. Betts was indicted for robbery in a Maryland state court. On arraignment, he told the trial judge of his lack of funds to hire a lawyer and asked the court to appoint one for him. Betts was advised that it was not the practice in that county to appoint counsel for indigent defendants except in murder and rape cases. He then pleaded not guilty, had witnesses summoned, cross-examined the State's witnesses, examined his own, and chose not to testify himself. He was found guilty by the judge, sitting without a jury, and sentenced to eight years in prison. Like Gideon, Betts sought release by habeas corpus, alleging that he had been denied the right to assistance of counsel in violation of the Fourteenth Amendment. Betts was denied any relief, and on review this Court affirmed. It was held that a refusal to appoint counsel for an indigent defendant charged with a felony did not necessarily violate the Due Process Clause of the Fourteenth Amendment, which for reasons given the Court deemed to be the only applicable federal constitutional provision. The Court said:

"Asserted denial [of due process] is to be tested by an appraisal of the totality of facts in a given case. That which may, in one setting, constitute a denial of fundamental fairness, shocking to the universal sense of justice, may, in other circumstances, and in the light of other considerations, fall short of such denial."

Treating due process as "a concept less rigid and more fluid than those envisaged in other specific and particular provisions of the Bill of Rights," the Court held that refusal to appoint counsel under the particular facts and circumstances in the Betts Case was not so "offensive to the common and fundamental ideas of fairness" as to amount to a denial of due process. Since the facts and circumstances of the two cases are so nearly indistinguishable, we think the Betts v. Brady holding if left standing would require us to reject Gideon's claim that the Constitution guarantees him the assistance of counsel. Upon full reconsideration we conclude that Betts v. Brady should be overruled.

II.

The Sixth Amendment provides, "In all criminal prosecutions, the accused shall enjoy the right . . . to have the Assistance of Counsel for his defence." We have construed this to mean that in federal courts counsel must be provided for defendants unable to employ counsel unless the right is competently and intelligently waived. Betts argued that this right is extended to indigent defendants in state courts by the Fourteenth Amendment. In response the Court stated that, while the Sixth Amendment laid down "no rule for the conduct of the States, the question recurs whether the constraint laid by the Amendment upon the national courts expresses a rule so fundamental and essential to a fair trial, and so, to due process of law, that it is made obligatory upon the States by the Fourteenth Amendment." In order to decide whether the Sixth Amendment's guarantee of counsel is of this fundamental nature, the Court in Betts set out and considered "relevant data on the subject . . . afforded by constitutional and statutory provisions subsisting in the colonies and the States prior to the inclusion of the Bill of Rights in the national Constitution, and in the constitutional, legislative, and judicial history of the States to the present date." On the basis of this historical data the Court concluded that "appointment of counsel is not a fundamental right, essential to a fair trial." It was for this reason the Betts Court refused to accept the contention that the Sixth Amendment's guarantee of counsel for indigent federal defendants was extended to or, in the words of that Court, "made obligatory upon the States by the Fourteenth Amendment." Plainly, had the Court concluded that appointment of counsel for an indigent criminal defendant was "a fundamental right, essential to a fair trial," it would have held that the Fourteenth Amendment requires appointment of counsel in a state court, just as the Sixth Amendment requires in a federal court.

We think the Court in Betts had ample precedent for acknowledging that those guarantees of the Bill of Rights which are fundamental safeguards of liberty immune from federal abridgment are equally protected against state invasion by the Due Process Clause of the Fourteenth Amendment. This same principle was recognized, explained and applied in Powell v. Alabama, 287 U. S. 45 (1932), a case upholding the right of counsel, where the Court held that despite sweeping language to the contrary in Hurtado v. California, 110 U. S. 516 (1884), the Fourteenth Amendment "embraced" those " 'fundamental principles of liberty and justice which lie at the base of all our civil and political institutions,' " even though they had been "specifically dealt with in another part of the federal constitution." In many cases other than Powell and Betts, this Court has looked to the fundamental nature of original Bill of Rights guarantees to decide whether the Fourteenth Amendment makes them obligatory on the States. Explicitly recognized to be of this "fundamental nature" and therefore made immune from state invasion by the Fourteenth, or some part of it, are the First Amendment's freedoms of speech, press, religion, assembly, association, and petition for redress of grievances. For the same reason, though not always in precisely the same terminology, the Court has made obligatory on the States the Fifth Amendment's command that private property shall not be taken for public use without just compensation, the Fourth Amendment's prohibition of unreasonable searches and seizures, and the Eighth's ban on cruel and unusual punishment. On the other hand, this Court in Palko v. Connecticut [p. 151] refused to hold that the Fourteenth Amendment

made the double jeopardy provision of the Fifth Amendment obligatory on the States. In so refusing, however, the Court, speaking
through Mr. Justice Cardozo, was careful to emphasize that "immunities that are valid as against the federal government by force of the
specific pledges of particular amendments have been found to be implicit in the concept of ordered liberty, and thus, through the Fourteenth Amendment, become valid as against the states" and that
guarantees "in their origin . . . effective against the federal government alone" had by prior cases "been taken over from the
earlier articles of the federal bill of rights and brought within the
Fourteenth Amendment by a process of absorption."

We accept Betts v. Brady's assumption, based as it was on our
prior cases, that a provision of the Bill of Rights which is "fundamental and essential to a fair trial" is made obligatory upon the
States by the Fourteenth Amendment. We think the Court in Betts
was wrong, however, in concluding that the Sixth Amendment's guarantee of counsel is not one of these fundamental rights. Ten years
before Betts v. Brady, this Court, after full consideration of all the
historical data examined in Betts, had unequivocally declared that
"the right to the aid of counsel is of this fundamental character." . . .
While the Court at the close of its Powell opinion did by its language,
as this Court frequently does, limit its holding to the particular facts
and circumstances of that case, its conclusions about the fundamental
nature of the right to counsel are unmistakable. Several years later, in
1936, the Court reemphasized what it had said about the fundamental
nature of the right to counsel in this language:

"We concluded that certain fundamental rights, safeguarded by the
first eight amendments against federal action, were also safeguarded
against state action by the due process clause of the Fourteenth
Amendment, and among them the fundamental right of the accused
to the aid of counsel in a criminal prosecution." Grosjean v. American
Press Co., 297 U. S. 233 (1936).

And again in 1938 this Court said:

"[The assistance of counsel] is one of the safeguards of the Sixth
Amendment deemed necessary to insure fundamental human rights of
life and liberty. . . . The Sixth Amendment stands as a constant
admonition that if the constitutional safeguards it provides be lost,
justice will not 'still be done.'" Johnson v. Zerbst, 304 U. S. 458
(1938). . . .

In light of these and many other prior decisions of this Court, it is not surprising that the Betts Court, when faced with the contention that "one charged with crime, who is unable to obtain counsel, must be furnished counsel by the State," conceded that "expressions in the opinions of this court lend color to the argument. . . ." The fact is that in deciding as it did—that "appointment of counsel is not a fundamental right, essential to a fair trial"—the Court in Betts v. Brady made an abrupt break with its own well-considered precedents. In returning to these old precedents, sounder we believe than the new, we but restore constitutional principles established to achieve a fair system of justice. Not only these precedents but also reason and reflection require us to recognize that in our adversary system of criminal justice, any person haled into court, who is too poor to hire a lawyer, cannot be assured a fair trial unless counsel is provided for him. This seems to us to be an obvious truth. Governments, both state and federal, quite properly spend vast sums of money to establish machinery to try defendants accused of crime. Lawyers to prosecute are everywhere deemed essential to protect the public's interest in an orderly society. Similarly, there are few defendants charged with crime, few indeed, who fail to hire the best lawyers they can get to prepare and present their defenses. That government hires lawyers to prosecute and defendants who have the money hire lawyers to defend are the strongest indications of the widespread belief that lawyers in criminal courts are necessities, not luxuries. The right of one charged with crime to counsel may not be deemed fundamental and essential to fair trials in some countries, but it is in ours. From the very beginning, our state and national constitutions and laws have laid great emphasis on procedural and substantive safeguards designed to assure fair trials before impartial tribunals in which every defendant stands equal before the law. This noble ideal cannot be realized if the poor man charged with crime has to face his accusers without a lawyer to assist him. A defendant's need for a lawyer is nowhere better stated than in the moving words of Mr. Justice Sutherland in Powell v. Alabama:

"The right to be heard would be, in many cases, of little avail if it did not comprehend the right to be heard by counsel. Even the intelligent and educated layman has small and sometimes no skill in the science of law. If charged with crime, he is incapable, generally, of determining for himself whether the indictment is good or bad. He is unfamiliar with the rules of evidence. Left without the aid of counsel he may be put on trial without a proper charge, and convicted upon incompetent evidence, or evidence irrelevant to the issue or otherwise inadmissible. He lacks both the skill and knowledge adequately to prepare his defense, even though he have a perfect one. He requires the guiding hand of counsel at every step in the proceedings against him. Without it, though he be not guilty, he faces the danger of conviction because he does not know how to establish his innocence."

The Court in Betts v. Brady departed from the sound wisdom upon which the Court's holding in Powell v. Alabama rested. Florida, supported by two other States, has asked that Betts v. Brady be left intact. Twenty-two States, as friends of the Court, argue that Betts was "an anachronism when handed down" and that it should now be overruled. We agree.

The judgment is reversed and the cause is remanded to the Supreme Court of Florida for further action not inconsistent with this opinion.

Reversed.

Mr. Justice Douglas, while joining the opinion of the Court, wrote a separate opinion, saying in part:

My Brother Harlan is of the view that a guarantee of the Bill of Rights that is made applicable to the States by reason of the Fourteenth Amendment is a lesser version of that same guarantee as applied to the Federal Government. Mr. Justice Jackson shared that view. But that view has not prevailed and rights protected against state invasion by the Due Process Clause of the Fourteenth Amendment are not watered-down versions of what the Bill of Rights guarantees.

Mr. Justice Clark, concurring in the result, wrote a separate opinion.

Mr. Justice Harlan, concurring, said in part:

I agree that Betts v. Brady should be overruled, but consider it entitled to a more respectful burial than has been accorded, at least on the part of those of us who were not on the Court when that case was decided.

I cannot subscribe to the view that Betts v. Brady represented "an abrupt break with its own well-considered precedents." In 1932, in

Powell v. Alabama, a capital case, this Court declared that under the particular facts there presented—"the ignorance and illiteracy of the defendants, their youth, the circumstances of public hostility . . . and above all that they stood in deadly peril of their lives"—the state court had a duty to assign counsel for the trial as a necessary requisite of due process of law. It is evident that these limiting facts were not added to the opinion as an afterthought; they were repeatedly emphasized, and were clearly regarded as important to the result.

Thus when this Court, a decade later, decided Betts v. Brady, it did no more than to admit of the possible existence of special circumstances in noncapital as well as capital trials, while at the same time to insist that such circumstances be shown in order to establish a denial of due process. . . .

[Mr. Justice Harlan here notes the "troubled journey" of the Powell and Betts doctrines and concedes that since 1950 no "special circumstances" have been found to justify the absence of counsel.]

. . . The Court has come to recognize, in other words, that the mere existence of a serious criminal charge constituted in itself special circumstances requiring the services of counsel at trial. In truth the Betts v. Brady rule is no longer a reality.

This evolution, however, appears not to have been fully recognized by many state courts, in this instance charged with the front-line responsibility for the enforcement of constitutional rights. To continue a rule which is honored by this Court only with lip service is not a healthy thing and in the long run will do disservice to the federal system. . . .

In agreeing with the Court that the right to counsel in a case such as this should now be expressly recognized as a fundamental right embraced in the Fourteenth Amendment, I wish to make a further observation. When we hold a right or immunity, valid against the Federal Government, to be "implicit in the concept of ordered liberty" and thus valid against the States, I do not read our past decisions to suggest that by so holding, we automatically carry over an entire body of federal law and apply it in full sweep to the States. Any such concept would disregard the frequently wide disparity between the legitimate interests of the States and of the Federal Government, the divergent problems that they face, and the significantly different consequences of their actions. . . . In what is done today I do not understand the Court to depart from the principles laid down in Palko v.

Connecticut, or to embrace the concept that the Fourteenth Amendment "incorporates" the Sixth Amendment as such.

On these premises I join in the judgment of the Court.

REYNOLDS v. SIMS
377 U. S. 533; 12 L. Ed. 2d 506; 84 Sup. Ct. 1362. 1964.

While in Baker v. Carr (p. 220), the Court had held the fairness of a state legislative apportionment subject to challenge in the courts, it had provided almost no guides as to what standards such districting had to meet. The farthest it had gone was to say, in striking down Georgia's County Unit System, that "once the geographical unit for which a representative is to be chosen is designated, all who participate in the election are to have an equal vote—whatever their race, whatever their sex, whatever their occupation, whatever their income, and wherever their home may be in that geographical unit. This is required by the Equal Protection Clause of the Fourteenth Amendment." See Gray v. Sanders, 372 U. S. 368 (1963). Significant as it was, this directive left unanswered a number of far-reaching questions. Does fairness require that all legislative districts within the state be equal in population, and if so, how much deviation from absolute equality is permissible? Can a state, if it wishes, apportion one of its two houses on some basis other than population, as is done with Congress? If so, what bases are permissible? In the event a state fails to provide a fair apportionment scheme, can a United States district court draw the district lines, or is the judicial function limited to forbidding the use of non-reapportioned districts for election purposes?

The first of these questions was answered for congressional districts in Wesberry v. Sanders, 376 U. S. 1 (1964), a case involving the fairness of legislative districts in the state of Georgia. Speaking for six members of the Court, Mr. Justice Black concluded from historical evidence that "the command of Art. I, § 2, that Representatives be chosen 'by the People of the several States' means that as nearly as is practicable one man's vote in a congressional election is to be worth as much as another's." It would, he said, "defeat the principle solemnly embodied in the Great Compromise—equal representation in the House for equal numbers of people—for us to hold that, within the States, legislatures may draw the lines of congressional districts in such a way as to give some voters a greater voice in choosing a Congressman than others. The House of Representatives, the Convention agreed, was to represent the people as individuals, and on a basis of complete equality for each voter." Inasmuch as the Georgia apportionment "grossly discriminates against voters in the Fifth Congressional District," the apportionment statute is void.

In a long and impassioned dissent, Mr. Justice Harlan, joined by Mr. Justice Stewart, rejected the majority's contention that the framers intended one man's vote to be worth as much as another's. First, in speaking of the allocation of representatives according to "the number of the State's inhabitants," the Constitution clearly refers to apportionment of representatives *among* the states, rather than *within* the states. Second, both the three-fifths compromise regarding representation for slaves and the provision that each state, no matter how small, have one representative show the framers intended "weighted" votes to some extent. Third, the Court, in deciding the issue at all, is derogating the authority given Congress and the states in Article I to set the "Times, Places and Manner" of holding congressional elections.

Four cases decided at the same time as the present case held void state legislative apportionment in New York, Maryland, Virginia, and Delaware. See WMCA v. Lomenzo, 377 U. S. 633; Maryland Committee v. Tawes, 377 U. S. 656; Davis v. Mann, 377 U. S. 678; and Roman v. Sincock, 377 U. S. 695. In each case the Court examined the actual workings of the apportionment scheme, finding that the share of the population represented by a majority in a legislative house ranged from a high of about 41% in the New York and Virginia senates to a low of 18.5% in the Delaware house. Moreover, in none of these states was there the kind of political machinery that would afford an adequate political remedy to the disadvantaged majority. In 1965, however, the Court upheld a Georgia scheme where some state senators were elected in single-member districts and some at large in multimember districts. There was no evidence that one man's vote was not approximately equal to another's or that the scheme attempted to cancel out a particular group's voting strength. See Fortson v. Dorsey, 379 U. S. 433.

A fifth case, Lucas v. Colorado General Assembly, 377 U. S. 713 (1964), presented a somewhat different problem. Not only did the majority have the power to remedy malapportionment, but as recently as 1962 the people had rejected by a two-to-one vote a system that could have provided equal popular representation in both houses and adopted instead one which took into account "other factors" in apportioning the senate. A majority of the house, under the plan, represented 45.1% of the population—a figure so close to equality that both parties in the lower court had conceded its validity. A majority of the senate, however, represented only 33.2% of the people. Without passing upon the house apportionment separately, the Supreme Court held that the "overall legislative representation in the two houses" was not "sufficiently grounded on population to be constitutionally sustainable." The Court also rejected the contention that the plan was made valid by the fact that it was the choice of the people, who could change it if they did not like it. "Except as an interim remedial procedure justifying a court in staying its hand temporarily, we find no significance in the fact that a nonjudicial, political remedy may be available for the effectuation of asserted rights to equal representation in a state legislature. . . . An individual's constitutionally protected right to cast an equally weighted vote cannot be denied even by a vote of a majority of the State's electorate. . . . A citizen's constitutional rights can hardly be infringed simply because a majority of the people choose to do so." Justices Clark and Stewart dissented in the Colorado and New York cases on the ground that a state should be able to choose any system of representation it wants as long as it is not "arbitrary and capricious" and does not systematically prevent "effective majority rule." Mr. Justice Harlan dissented in all the cases on the basis of his dissent in the present case.

In two cases in 1964 the Court dealt with problems of race discrimination in the electoral process. The first involved a 1960 amendment to the Louisiana election law providing that a candidate's race should be placed in parentheses after his name on the ballot. In Anderson v. Martin, 375 U. S. 399, the Supreme Court unanimously held the provision void on the ground that its effect was to "influence the citizen to cast his ballot along racial lines." In the second case, it rejected a claim that the lines of two New York congressional districts had been drawn so as to exclude Negroes and Puerto Ricans from the first and concentrate them in the second. Despite the fact that the seventeenth ("silk stocking") district was 94.9% white, that the eighteenth was 86.3% Negro and Puerto Rican, and that all recent changes had tended to maintain these ratios, the Court rejected the argument that a prima facie case of discrimination had been made and held the "difficult burden" of proving the apportionment racially motivated had not been met. See Wright v. Rockefeller, 376 U. S. 52 (1964).

In Reynolds v. Sims, printed below, the United States district court had held void the sixty-year-old apportionment of Alabama under which the 35 counties, ranging in size from 635,000 to 15,000, each elected one senator. This "population-variance ratio" of about 41-to-1 was matched by a ratio of about 16-to-1 in the house. The Alabama legislature had met in special session and provided two alternative apportionment schemes. The first, known as the "67-Senator Amendment," provided for 67 counties and would have put control into the hands of senators representing 19.4% of the people and house members representing about 43%. While this reduced the population-variance ratio to 4.7-to-1 in the house, it increased it to about 59-to-1 in the senate. The second scheme, the Crawford-Webb Act, was a legislative stop-gap to be used if the amendment failed to pass or to satisfy the courts. Control of the house rested in representatives of 37% of the population and control of the senate in senators representing 27.6%.

None of these schemes in its entirety met district court approval, so for 1962 it ordered the house elected under the 67-Senator Amendment and the senate under the Crawford-Webb Act. Although it was hoped that this temporary arrangement would break the stranglehold of the small counties and permit the legislature to produce a fair apportionment scheme of its own, the court retained jurisdiction of the case against the chance that this might not be accomplished. The legislature elected under the plan did nothing in 1963. Meanwhile, an appeal from the district court's decision reached the Supreme Court.

Chief Justice Warren delivered the opinion of the Court, saying in part:

III.

A predominant consideration in determining whether a State's legislative apportionment scheme constitutes an invidious discrimination violative of rights asserted under the Equal Protection Clause is that the rights allegedly impaired are individual and personal in nature. . . .

Legislators represent people, not trees or acres. Legislators are elected by voters, not farms or cities or economic interests. As long as ours is a representative form of government, and our legislatures are those instruments of government elected directly by and directly representative of the people, the right to elect legislators in a free and unimpaired fashion is a bedrock of our political system. It could hardly be gainsaid that a constitutional claim had been asserted by an allegation that certain otherwise qualified voters had been entirely prohibited from voting for members of their state legislature. And, if a State should provide that the votes of citizens in one part of the State should be given two times, or five times, or 10 times the weight of votes of citizens in another part of the State, it could hardly be contended that the right to vote of those residing in the disfavored areas had not been effectively diluted. It would appear extraordinary to suggest that a State could be constitutionally permitted to enact a law providing that certain of the State's voters could vote two, five, or 10 times for their legislative representatives, while voters living elsewhere could vote only once. And is it inconceivable that a state law to the effect that, in counting votes for legislators, the votes of citizens in one part of the State would be multiplied by two, five or 10, while the votes of persons in another area would be counted only at face value, could be constitutionally sustainable. Of course, the effect of state legislative districting schemes which give the same number of representatives to unequal numbers of constituents is identical. Overweighting and overvaluation of the votes of those living here has the certain effect of dilution and undervaluation of the votes of those living there. The resulting discrimination against those individual voters living in disfavored areas is easily demonstrable mathematically. Their right to vote is simply not the same right to vote as that of those living in a favored part of the State. Two, five, or 10 of them must vote before the effect of their voting is equivalent to that of their favored neighbor. Weighting the votes of citizens differently, by any method or means, merely because of where they happen to reside, hardly seems justifiable. One must be ever aware that the Constitution forbids "sophisticated as well as simple-minded modes of discrimination." Lane v. Wilson [p. 213]. . . . As we stated in Wesberry v. Sanders [376 U. S. 1 (1964)]:

"We do not believe that the Framers of the Constitution intended to permit the same vote-diluting discrimination to be accomplished through the device of districts containing widely varied numbers of inhabitants. To say that a vote is worth more in one district than in another would . . . run counter to our fundamental ideas of democratic government. . . . "

State legislatures are, historically, the fountainhead of representative government in this country. A number of them have their roots in colonial times, and substantially antedate the creation of our Nation and our Federal Government. In fact, the first formal stirrings of American political independence are to be found, in large part, in the views and actions of several of the colonial legislative bodies. With the birth of our National Government, and the adoption and ratification of the Federal Constitution, state legislatures retained a most important place in our Nation's governmental structure. But representative government is in essence self-government through the medium of elected representatives of the people, and each and every citizen has an inalienable right to full and effective participation in the political processes of his State's legislative bodies. Most citizens can achieve this participation only as qualified voters through the election of legislators to represent them. Full and effective participation by all citizens in state government requires, therefore, that each citizen have an equally effective voice in the election of members of his state legislature. Modern and viable state government needs, and the Constitution demands, no less.

Logically, in a society ostensibly grounded on representative government, it would seem reasonable that a majority of the people of a State could elect a majority of that State's legislators. To conclude differently, and to sanction minority control of state legislative bodies, would appear to deny majority rights in a way that far surpasses any possible denial of minority rights that might otherwise be thought to result. Since legislatures are responsible for enacting laws by which all citizens are to be governed, they should be bodies which are collectively responsive to the popular will. . . . Our constitutional system amply provides for the protection of minorities by means other than giving them majority control of state legislatures. And the democratic ideals of equality and majority rule, which have served this Nation so well in the past, are hardly of any less significance for the present and the future. . . .

To the extent that a citizen's right to vote is debased, he is that much less a citizen. The fact that an individual lives here or there is not a legitimate reason for overweighting or diluting the efficacy of his vote. The complexions of societies and civilizations change, often with amazing rapidity. A nation once primarily rural in character becomes predominantly urban. Representation schemes once fair and equitable become archaic and outdated. But the basic principle of representative government remains, and must remain, unchanged— the weight of a citizen's vote cannot be made to depend on where he lives. Population is, of necessity, the starting point for consideration and the controlling criterion for judgment in legislative apportionment controversies. A citizen, a qualified voter, is no more nor no less so because he lives in the city or on the farm. This is the clear and strong command of our Constitution's Equal Protection Clause. This is an essential part of the concept of a government of laws and not men. This is at the heart of Lincoln's vision of "government of the people, by the people, [and] for the people." The Equal Protection Clause demands no less than substantially equal state legislative representation for all citizens, of all places as well as of all races.

IV.

We hold that, as a basic constitutional standard, the Equal Protection Clause requires that the seats in both houses of a bicameral state legislature must be apportioned on a population basis. Simply stated, an individual's right to vote for state legislators is unconstitutionally impaired when its weight is in a substantial fashion diluted when compared with votes of citizens living in other parts of the State. Since, under neither the existing apportionment provisions nor either of the proposed plans was either of the houses of the Alabama Legislature apportioned on a population basis, the District Court correctly held that all three of these schemes were constitutionally invalid. Furthermore, the existing apportionment, and also to a lesser extent the apportionment under the Crawford-Webb Act, presented little more than crazy quilts, completely lacking in rationality, and could be found invalid on that basis alone. . . .

[The Court here reviews the three apportionment schemes and finds that even under the best of them, the 67-Senator Amendment, the deviation from a population basis is "too egregious" to be constitutional.]

V.

Since neither of the houses of the Alabama Legislature, under any of the three plans considered by the District Court, was apportioned on a population basis, we would be justified in proceeding no further. However, one of the proposed plans, that contained in the so-called 67-Senator Amendment, at least superficially resembles the scheme of legislative representation followed in the Federal Congress. Under this plan, each of Alabama's 67 counties is allotted one senator, and no counties are given more than one Senate seat. Arguably, this is analogous to the allocation of two Senate seats, in the Federal Congress, to each of the 50 States, regardless of population. Seats in the Alabama House, under the proposed constitutional amendment, are distributed by giving each of the 67 counties at least one, with the remaining 39 seats being allotted among the more populous counties on a population basis. This scheme, at least at first glance, appears to resemble that prescribed for the Federal House of Representatives, where the 435 seats are distributed among the States on a population basis, although each State, regardless of its population, is given at least one Congressman. Thus, although there are substantial differences in underlying rationale and result, the 67-Senator Amendment, as proposed by the Alabama Legislature, at least arguably presents for consideration a scheme analogous to that used for apportioning seats in Congress.

Much has been written since our decision in Baker v. Carr about the applicability of the so-called federal analogy to state legislative apportionment arrangements. After considering the matter, the court below concluded that no conceivable analogy could be drawn between the federal scheme and the apportionment of seats in the Alabama Legislature under the proposed constitutional amendment. We agree with the District Court, and find the federal analogy inapposite and irrelevant to state legislative districting schemes. Attempted reliance on the federal analogy appears often to be little more than an after-the-fact rationalization offered in defense of maladjusted state apportionment arrangements. The original constitutions of 36 of our States provided that representation in both houses of the state legislatures would be based completely, or predominantly, on population. And the Founding Fathers clearly had no intention of establishing a pattern or model for the apportionment of seats in state legislatures when the system of representation in the Federal Congress was adopted. Demonstrative of this is the fact that the Northwest Ordinance, adopted in the same year, 1787, as the Federal Constitution, provided for the apportionment of seats in territorial legislatures solely on the basis of population.

The system of representation in the two Houses of the Federal Congress is one ingrained in our Constitution, as part of the law of the land. It is one conceived out of compromise and concession indispensable to the establishment of our federal republic. Arising from unique historical circumstances, it is based on the consideration that in establishing our type of federalism a group of formerly independent States bound themselves together under one national government. . . . The fact that almost three-fourths of our present States were never in fact independently sovereign does not detract from our view that the so-called federal analogy is inapplicable as a sustaining precedent for state legislative apportionments. The developing history and growth of our republic cannot cloud the fact that, at the time of the inception of the system of representation in the Federal Congress, a compromise between the larger and smaller States on this matter averted a deadlock in the Constitutional Convention which had threatened to abort the birth of our Nation. . . .

Political subdivisions of States—counties, cities, or whatever—never were and never have been considered as sovereign entities. Rather, they have been traditionally regarded as subordinate governmental instrumentalities created by the State to assist in the carrying out of state governmental functions. . . .

Thus, we conclude that the plan contained in the 67-Senator

Amendment for apportioning seats in the Alabama Legislature cannot be sustained by recourse to the so-called federal analogy. Nor can any other inequitable state legislative apportionment scheme be justified on such an asserted basis. . . .

Since we find the so-called federal analogy inapposite to a consideration of the constitutional validity of state legislative apportionment schemes, we necessarily hold that the Equal Protection Clause requires both houses of a state legislature to be apportioned on a population basis. Tne right of a citizen to equal representation and to have his vote weighted equally with those of all other citizens in the election of members of one house of a bicameral state legislature would amount to little if States could effectively submerge the equal-population principle in the apportionment of seats in the other house. . . . Deadlock between the two bodies might result in compromise and concession on some issues. But in all too many cases the more probable result would be frustration of the majority will through minority veto in the house not apportioned on a population basis. . . .

We do not believe that the concept of bicameralism is rendered anachronistic and meaningless when the predominant basis of representation in the two state legislative bodies is required to be the same—population. A prime reason for bicameralism, modernly considered, is to insure mature and deliberate consideration of, and to prevent precipitate action on, proposed legislative measures. Simply because the controlling criterion for apportioning representation is required to be the same in both houses does not mean that there will be no differences in the composition and complexion of the two bodies. Different constituencies can be represented in the two houses. One body could be composed of single-member districts while the other could have at least some multimember districts. The length of terms of the legislators in the separate bodies could differ. The numerical size of the two bodies could be made to differ, even significantly, and the geographical size of districts from which legislators are elected could also be made to differ. . . .

VI.

By holding that as a federal constitutional requisite both houses of a state legislature must be apportioned on a population basis, we mean that the Equal Protection Clause requires that a State make an honest and good faith effort to construct districts, in both houses of its legislature, as nearly of equal population as is practicable. We realize that it is a practical impossibility to arrange legislative districts so that each one has an identical number of residents, or citizens, or voters. Mathematical exactness or precision is hardly a workable constitutional requirement.

In Wesberry v. Sanders, supra, the Court stated that congressional representation must be based on population as nearly as is practicable. In implementing the basic constitutional principle of representative government as enunciated by the Court in Wesberry—equality of population among districts—some distinctions may well be made between congressional and state legislative representation. . . . Somewhat more flexibility may . . . be constitutionally permissible with respect to state legislative apportionment than in congressional districting. . . . For the present, we deem it expedient not to attempt to spell out any precise constitutional tests.

History indicates, however, that many States have deviated, to a greater or lesser degree, from the equal-population principle in the apportionment of seats in at least one house of their legislatures. So long as the divergences from a strict population standard are based on legitimate considerations incident to the effectuation of a rational state policy, some deviations from the equal-population principle are constitutionally permissible with respect to the apportionment of seats in either or both of the two houses of a bicameral state legislature. But neither history alone, nor economic or other sorts of group interests, are permissible factors in attempting to justify disparities from population-based representation. Citizens, not history or economic interests, cast votes. Considerations of area alone provide an insufficient justification for deviations from the equal-population principle. Again, people, not land or trees or pastures, vote. Modern developments and improvements in transportation and communications make rather hollow, in the mid-1960's, most claims that deviations from population-based representation can validly be based solely on geographical considerations. Arguments for allowing such deviations in order to insure effective representation for sparsely settled areas and to prevent legislative districts from becoming so large that the availability of access of citizens to their representatives is impaired are today, for the most part, unconvincing.

A consideration that appears to be of more substance in justifying some deviations from population-based representation in state legislatures is that of insuring some voice to political subdivisions, as political subdivisions. . . . In many States much of the legislature's activity involves the enactment of so-called local legislation, directed only to the concerns of particular political subdivisions. And a State may legitimately desire to construct districts along political subdivision lines to deter the possibilities of gerrymandering. However, permitting deviations from population-based representation does not mean that each local governmental unit or political subdivision can be given separate representation, regardless of population. . . . If, even as a result of a clearly rational state policy of according some legislative representation to political subdivisions, population is submerged as the controlling consideration in the apportionment of seats in the particular legislative body, then the right of all of the State's citizens to cast an effective and adequately weighted vote would be unconstitutionally impaired.

VII.

One of the arguments frequently offered as a basis for upholding a State's legislative apportionment arrangement, despite substantial disparities from a population basis in either or both houses, is grounded on congressional approval, incident to admitting States into the Union, of state apportionment plans containing deviations from the equal-population principle. Proponents of this argument contend that congressional approval of such schemes, despite their disparities from population-based representation, indicate that such arrangements are plainly sufficient as establishing a "republican form of government." As we stated in Baker v. Carr, some questions raised under the Guaranty Clause are nonjusticiable, where "political" in nature and where there is a clear absence of judicially manageable standards. Nevertheless, it is not inconsistent with this view to hold that, . . . the Equal Protection Clause can and does require more. And an apportionment scheme in which both houses are based on population can hardly be considered as failing to satisfy the Guaranty Clause requirement. . . . In any event, congressional approval, however well-considered, could hardly validate an unconstitutional state legislative apportionment. Congress simply lacks the constitutional power to insulate States from attack with respect to alleged deprivations of individual constitutional rights.

VIII.

That the Equal Protection Clause requires that both houses of a state legislature be apportioned on a population basis does not mean that States cannot adopt some reasonable plan for periodic revision of their apportionment schemes. Decennial reapportionment appears to be a rational approach to readjustment of legislative representation in order to take into account population shifts and growth. . . . While we do not intend to indicate that decennial reapportionment is a constitutional requisite, compliance with such an approach would clearly meet the minimal requirements for maintaining a reasonably current scheme of legislative representation. And we do not mean to intimate that more frequent reapportionment would not be constitutionally permissible or practicably desirable. But if reapportionment were accomplished with less frequency, it would assuredly be constitutionally suspect. . . .

X.

We do not consider here the difficult question of the proper remedial devices which federal courts should utilize in state legislative apportionment cases. . . . It is enough to say now that, once a State's legislative apportionment scheme has been found to be unconstitutional, it would be the unusual case in which a court would be justified in not taking appropriate action to insure that no further elections are conducted under the invalid plan. However, . . . a court is entitled to and should consider the proximity of a forthcoming election and the mechanics and complexities of state election laws, and should act and rely upon general equitable principles. With respect to the timing of relief, a court can reasonably endeavor to avoid a disruption of the election process which might result from requiring precipitate changes . . . .

We feel that the District Court in this case acted in a most proper and commendable manner. . . . We affirm the judgment below and remand the cases for further proceedings consistent with the views stated in this opinion.

It is so ordered.

Mr. Justice Clark, concurring in the affirmance, said in part:

It seems to me that all that the Court need say in this case is that each plan considered by the trial court is "a crazy quilt," clearly revealing invidious discrimination in each house of the Legislature and therefore violative of the Equal Protection Clause.

Mr. Justice Stewart, concurring, said in part:

I would affirm the judgment of the District Court holding that this apportionment violated the Equal Protection Clause.

Mr. Justice Harlan dissented, saying in part:

Preliminary Statement.

Today's holding is that the Equal Protection Clause of the Fourteenth Amendment requires every State to structure its legislature so that all the members of each house represent substantially the same number of people; other factors may be given play only to the extent that they do not significantly encroach on this basic "population" principle. Whatever may be thought of this holding as a piece of political ideology—and even on that score the political history and practices of this country from its earliest beginnings leave wide room for debate (see the dissenting opinion of Frankfurter, J., in Baker v. Carr)—I think it demonstrable that the Fourteenth Amendment does not impose this political tenet on the States or authorize this Court to do so. . . . Stripped of aphorisms, the Court's argument boils down to the assertion that appellees' right to vote has been individiously "debased" or "diluted" by systems of apportionment which entitle them to vote for fewer legislators than other voters, an assertion which is tied to the Equal Protection Clause only by the constitutionally frail tautology that "equal" means "equal."

Had the Court paused to probe more deeply into the matter, it would have found that the Equal Protection Clause was never intended to inhibit the States in choosing any democratic method they pleased for the apportionment of their legislatures. This is shown by the language of the Fourteenth Amendment taken as a whole, by the understanding of those who proposed and ratified it, and by the political practices of the States at the time the Amendment was adopted. It is confirmed by numerous state and congressional actions since the adoption of the Fourteenth Amendment, and by the common under-

standing of the Amendment as evidenced by subsequent constitutional amendments and decisions of this Court before Baker v. Carr
made an abrupt break with the past in 1962.

The failure of the Court to consider any of these matters cannot be
excused or explained by any concept of "developing" constitutional-
ism. It is meaningless to speak of constitutional "development" when
both the language and history of the controlling provisions of the
Constitution are wholly ignored. Since it can, I think, be shown beyond doubt that state legislative apportionments, as such, are wholly
free of constitutional limitations, save such as may be imposed by the
Republican Form of Government Clause (Const. Art. IV, § 4), the
Court's action now bringing them within the purview of the Fourteenth Amendment amounts to nothing less than an exercise of the
amending power by this Court.

[There follows an exhaustive analysis of the equal protection clause
and the intent of those ratifying it, showing that not only the "loyal"
states, but in those which had to conform to the clause in order to be
readmitted had legislatures deviating from the principle of equal
representation. Also discussed is the status of apportionment in the
states at present, the problems faced by the courts in actually applying
the equality rule, and a list of things the states cannot consider for
purposes of representation.]

Although the Court—necessarily, as I believe—provides only generalities in elaboration of its main thesis, its opinion nevertheless fully
demonstrates how far removed these problems are from fields of
judicial competence. Recognizing that "indiscriminate districting" is
an invitation to "partisan gerrymandering," the Court nevertheless
excludes virtually every basis for the formation of electoral districts
other than "indiscriminate districting." In one or another of today's
opinions, the Court declares it unconstitutional for a State to give
effective consideration to any of the following in establishing legislative districts:

(1) history; (2) "economic or other sorts of group interests"; (3)
area; (4) geographical considerations; (5) a desire "to insure effective
representation for sparsely settled areas"; (6) "availability of access
of citizens to their representatives"; (7) theories of bicameralism (except those approved by the Court); (8) occupation; (9) "an attempt
to balance urban and rural power"; (10) the preference of a majority
of voters in the State.

So far as presently appears, the *only* factor which a State may consider, apart from numbers, is political subdivisions. But even "a clearly rational state policy" recognizing this factor is unconstitutional if "population is submerged as the controlling consideration. . . ."

I know of no principle of logic or practical or theoretical politics, still less any constitutional principle, which establishes all or any of these exclusions. Certain it is that the Court's opinion does not establish them. So far as the Court says anything at all on this score, it says only that "legislators represent people, not trees or acres"; that "citizens, not history or economic interests, cast votes"; that "people, not land or trees or pastures, vote." All this may be conceded. But it is surely equally obvious, and, in the context of elections, more meaningful to note that people are not ciphers and that legislators can represent their electors only by speaking for their interests—economic, social, political—many of which do reflect the place where the electors live. The Court does not establish, or indeed even attempt to make a case for the proposition that conflicting interests within a State can only be adjusted by disregarding them when voters are grouped for purposes of representation.

MURPHY v. WATERFRONT COMMISSION OF NEW YORK
378 U. S. 52; 12 L. Ed. 2d 678; 84 Sup. Ct. 1594. 1964.

Despite the fact that ours is a federal system and most of us are subject to both state and federal criminal law, the absence of a single set of constitutional guarantees and uniform criminal procedures usually does not result in any serious unfairness, either for the defendants or for the governments involved. That a state may not provide you a grand jury indictment, a jury trial, or a court-appointed lawyer does not ordinarily affect your claim to these rights in a federal trial. In some areas of civil rights, however, the existence of the two sovereign governments with two sets of rules has a very marked impact indeed.

One of these areas, recently eliminated by the Supreme Court, was the right against unreasonable search and seizure. Despite the guarantee in the Fourth Amendment, a defendant sometimes found the substance of the right effectively denied him. A state, free to seize what information it could, regardless of rights of privacy, was also free under the "silver platter" doctrine to turn it over to the United States courts where it could be used against the defendant. Conversely, if a federal officer obtained information illegally, while he might not be able to use it in a federal trial, he could make it available to state officers for use in state courts. State-federal cooperation thus enabled the federal government to benefit from unreasonable searches and seizures, although technically the Fourth Amendment remained intact. See discussion on p. 104. The Supreme Court has now closed off this avenue of evasion. Starting with Rea v. United States, 350 U. S. 214 (1956), through its control over the administration of federal justice, it forbade a federal officer to turn narcotics over to a state court for use against the defendant. The narcotics had been obtained by an unreasonable search and a federal case against the defendant had already been dismissed for this reason. Then, in Benanti v. United States, 355 U. S. 96 (1957), and Elkins v. United States, 364 U. S. 206 (1960), the Court banned from the federal courts information got by state officers either illegally or unconstitutionally, thus putting an end to the silver platter doctrine. Finally, in Mapp v. Ohio (p. 102), it banned the use of unconstitutional evidence in state courts as well.

A second area where federalism has caused troublesome conflicts is in the protection against double jeopardy. In United States v. Lanza (p. 99), the Court in 1922 held that a person who had committed a single act which was both a state and federal crime could be tried by both sovereignties without violating the double jeopardy clause of the Constitution. It reaffirmed this ruling as recently as 1959 in the Abbate and Bartkus cases discussed on p. 99.

While the Lanza rule is logically persuasive, and the Court still adheres to it, it has not been given wide application. It is not, for example, followed in international law. As early as 1820 the Supreme Court recognized that while all states could try a person for piracy, "there can be no doubt that the plea of *autrefois acquit* would be good, in any civilized state, though resting on a prosecution in the courts of any other civilized state." See United States v. Furlong, 5 Wheaton 86. Nor has the Court felt the rule should apply where two states have concurrent jurisdiction, as on the Columbia River where Washington and Oregon both have jurisdiction over the entire river "to avoid any nice question as to whether a criminal act sought to be prosecuted was committed on one side or the other of the exact boundary in the channel." "Where an act is . . . prohibited and punishable by the laws of both states," the Court commented, "the one first acquiring jurisdiction of the person may prosecute the offense, and its judgment is a finality in both states, so that one convicted or acquitted in the courts of the one state cannot be prosecuted for the same offense in the courts of the other." See Nielson v. Oregon, 212 U. S. 315 (1909).

The remaining area in which the existence of two sovereignties has raised serious questions of fairness is in the area of compulsory self-incrimination. If a person could simply plead the privilege and remain silent, no problem would, of course, arise. But once one government undertakes to compel testimony in exchange for freedom from prosecution, the question arises as to the right of the other government to make use of his testimony or of the person to remain silent for *fear* the other government will use it. In the present case the Court overrules the long-standing rule of United States v. Murdock, 284 U. S. 141 (1931), and Feldman v. United States, 322 U. S. 487 (1944), that an immunity statute protects a person only in the jurisdiction which grants it. See discussion p. 123.

Mr. Justice Goldberg delivered the opinion of the Court, saying in part:

We have held today that the Fifth Amendment privilege against self-incrimination must be deemed fully applicable to the States through the Fourteenth Amendment. Malloy v. Hogan, 378 U. S. 1. This case presents a related issue: whether one jurisdiction within our federal structure may compel a witness, whom it has immunized from prosecution under its laws, to give testimony which might then be used to convict him of a crime against another such jurisdiction.

Petitioners were subpoenaed to testify at a hearing conducted by the Waterfront Commission of New York Harbor concerning a work stoppage at the Hoboken, New Jersey, piers. After refusing to respond to certain questions about the stoppage on the ground that the answers might tend to incriminate them, petitioners were granted immunity from prosecution under the laws of New Jersey and New York. Notwithstanding this grant of immunity, they still refused to respond to the questions on the ground that the answers might tend to incriminate them under *federal* law, to which the grant of immunity did not purport to extend. Petitioners were thereupon held in civil and criminal contempt of court. The New Jersey Supreme Court . . . , relying on this Court's decisions in Knapp v. Schweitzer, 357 U. S. 371; Feldman v. United States, 322 U. S. 487; and United States v. Murdock, 284 U. S. 141, affirmed the civil contempt judgments on the merits. The court held that a State may constitutionally compel a witness to give testimony which might be used in a federal prosecution against him.

Since a grant of immunity is valid only if it is coextensive with the scope of the privilege against self-incrimination, Counselman v. Hitchcock, 142 U. S. 547, we must now decide the fundamental constitutional question of whether, absent an immunity provision, one jurisdiction in our federal structure may compel a witness to give testimony which might incriminate him under the laws of another jurisdiction. The answer to this question must depend, of course, on whether such an application of the privilege promotes or defeats its policies and purposes.

I. The Policies of the Privilege.

The privilege against self-incrimination "registers an important advance in the development of our liberty—'one of the great landmarks in man's struggle to make himself civilized.'" Ullmann v. United States [p. 122]. It reflects many of our fundamental values and most noble aspirations: our unwillingness to subject those suspected of crime to the cruel trilemma of self-accusation, perjury or contempt; our preference for an accusatorial rather than an inquisitorial system of criminal justice; our fear that self-incriminating statements will be elicited by inhumane treatment and abuses; our sense of fair play which dictates "a fair state-individual balance by requiring the government to leave the individual alone until good cause is shown for disturbing him and by requiring the government in its contest with the individual to shoulder the entire load" . . . ; our respect for the inviolability of the human personality and of the right of each individual "to a private enclave where he may lead a private life" . . . ; our distrust of self-deprecatory statements; and our realization that the privilege, while sometimes "a shelter to the guilty," is often "a protection to the innocent." . . .

Most, if not all, of these policies and purposes are defeated when a witness "can be whipsawed into incriminating himself under both state and federal law even though" the constitutional privilege against self-incrimination is applicable to each. . . . This has become especially true in our age of "cooperative federalism," where the federal and state governments are waging a united front against many types of criminal activity.

Respondent contends, however, that we should adhere to the "established rule" that the constitutional privilege against self-incrimination does not protect a witness in one jurisdiction against being compelled to give testimony which could be used to convict him in another jurisdiction. This "rule" has three decisional facets: United States v. Murdock held that the Federal Government could compel a witness to give testimony which might incriminate him under state law; Knapp v. Schweitzer held that a State could compel a witness to give testimony which might incriminate him under federal law; and Feldman v. United States held that testimony thus compelled by a State could be introduced into evidence in the federal courts.

Our decision today in Malloy v. Hogan necessitates a reconsideration of this rule.* Our review of the pertinent cases in this Court and of their English antecedents reveals that Murdock did not adequately consider the relevant authorities and has been significantly weakened by subsequent decisions of this Court, and, further, that the legal premises underlying Feldman and Knapp have since been rejected.

[The Court here reviews in detail the early English and American cases and concludes that they have not been interpreted properly in the past and hence do not serve as a sound foundation of precedent for the Murdock case. The results of that analysis are summarized below.]

III. The Recent Supreme Court Cases.

In 1931, the Court decided United States v. Murdock, the case principally relied on by respondent here. Appellee had been indicted for failing to supply certain information to federal revenue agents. He claimed that his refusal had been justified because it rested on the fear of federal and state incrimination. The Government argued that the record supported only a claim of state, not federal, incrimination, and that the Fifth Amendment does not protect against a claim of state incrimination. Appellee did not respond to the latter argument, but instead rested his entire case on the claim that his refusals had in each instance been based on federal as well as state incrimination. . . .

This Court decided that appellee's refusal to answer rested solely on a fear of state prosecution, and then concluded, in one brief paragraph, that such a fear did not justify a refusal to answer questions put by federal officers.

The Court gave three reasons for this conclusion. The first was that:

---

* The constitutional privilege against self-incrimination has two primary interrelated facets: The Government may not use compulsion to elicit self-incriminating statements, see, e. g., Counselman v. Hitchcock; and the Government may not permit the use in a criminal trial of self-incriminating statements elicited by compulsion. . . . In every "whipsaw" case, either the "compelling" government or the "using" government is a State, and, until today, the States were not deemed fully bound by the privilege against self-incrimination. Now that both governments are fully bound by the privilege, the conceptual difficulty of pinpointing the alleged violation of the privilege on "compulsion" or "use" need no longer concern us.

"Investigations for federal purposes may not be prevented by matters depending upon state law. Constitution, Art. VI, § 2."

This argument, however, begs the critical question. No one would suggest that state law could prevent a proper federal investigation; the Court had already held that the Federal Government could, under the Supremacy Clause, grant immunity from state prosecution, and that, accordingly, state law could not prevent a proper federal investigation. The critical issue was whether the Federal Government, *without granting immunity from state prosecution,* could compel testimony which would incriminate under state law. The Court's first "reason" was not responsive to this issue.

The second reason given by the Court was that:

"The English rule of evidence against compulsory self-incrimination, on which historically that contained in the Fifth Amendment rests, does not protect witnesses against disclosing offenses in violation of the laws of another country. . . ."

As has been demonstrated, the cases cited were in one instance overruled and in the other inapposite, and the English rule was the opposite from that stated in this Court's opinion: The rule did "protect witnesses against disclosing offenses in violation of the laws of another country." . . .

The third reason given by the Court in Murdock was that:

"This court has held that immunity against state prosecution is not essential to the validity of federal statutes declaring that a witness shall not be excused from giving evidence on the ground that it will incriminate him, and also that the lack of state power to give witnesses protection against federal prosecution does not defeat a state immunity statute. The principle established is that full and complete immunity against prosecution by the government compelling the witness to answer is equivalent to the protection furnished by the rule against compulsory self-incrimination. Counselman v. Hitchcock. Brown v. Walker, 161 U. S. 591. Jack v. Kansas, 199 U. S. 372. Hale v. Henkel, 201 U. S. 43. . . ."

This argument—that the rule in question had already been "established" by the past decisions of the Court—is not accurate. The first case cited by the Court—Counselman v. Hitchcock—said nothing about the problem of incrimination under the law of another sovereign. The second case—Brown v. Walker—merely held that the federal immunity statute there involved did protect against state prosecution. The third case—Jack v. Kansas—held that the Due Process Clause of the Fourteenth Amendment did not prevent a State from compelling an answer to a question which presented no "real danger of a Federal prosecution." The final case—Hale v. Henkel—contained dictum in support of the rule announced which was without real authority and which had been questioned by a unanimous Court in Vajtauer v. Commissioner of Immigration [273 U. S. 103 (1927)]. Moreover, the Court subsequently said, in no uncertain terms, that the rule announced in Murdock had not been previously "established" by the decisions of the Court. When Murdock appealed his subsequent conviction on the ground, inter alia, that an instruction on willfulness should have been given, the Court affirmed the Court of Appeals' reversal of his conviction and said that:

"Not until this court pronounced judgment in United States v. Murdock had it been definitely settled that one under examination in a federal tribunal could not refuse to answer on account of probable incrimination under state law. . . ." United States v. Murdock, 290 U. S. 389 [1933].

Thus, neither the reasoning nor the authority relied on by the Court in United States v. Murdock supports its conclusion that the Fifth Amendment permits the Federal Government to compel answers to questions which might incriminate under state law.

In 1944 the Court, in Feldman v. United States, was confronted with the situation where evidence compelled by a State under a grant of state immunity was "availed of by the [Federal] Government" and introduced in a federal prosecution. Jack v. Kansas. This was the situation which the Court had earlier said it did "not believe" would occur. Nevertheless, the Court, in a 4-to-3 decision, upheld this practice, but did so on the authority of a principle which is no longer accepted by this Court. The Feldman reasoning was essentially as follows:

"[T]he Fourth and Fifth Amendments, intertwined as they are, [express] supplementing phases of the same constitutional purpose. . . ."

"[O]ne of the settled principles of our Constitution has been that these Amendments protect only against invasion of civil liberties by the [Federal] Government whose conduct they alone limit."

"And so, while evidence secured through unreasonable search and seizure by federal officials is inadmissible in a federal prosecution, Weeks v. United States [232 U. S. 383]; . . . incriminating documents so secured by state officials without participation by federal officials but turned over for their use are admissible in a federal prosecution. Burdeau v. McDowell, 256 U. S. 465."

The Court concluded, therefore, by analogy to the then extant search and seizure rule, that evidence compelled by a state grant of immunity could be used by the Federal Government. But the legal foundation upon which that 4-to-3 decision rested no longer stands. Evidence illegally seized by state officials may not now be received in federal courts. In Elkins v. United States, 364 U. S. 206, the Court held, over the dissent of the writer of the Feldman decision, that "evidence obtained by state officers during a search which, if conducted by federal officers, would have violated the defendant's immunity from unreasonable searches and seizures under the Fourth Amendment is inadmissible over the defendant's timely objection in a federal criminal trial." Thus, since the fundamental assumption underlying Feldman is no longer valid, the constitutional question there decided must now be regarded as an open one.

The relevant cases decided by this Court since Feldman fall into two categories. Those involving a federal immunity statute—exemplified by Adams v. Maryland, 347 U. S. 179—in which the Court suggested that the Fifth Amendment bars use by the States of evidence obtained by the Federal Government under the threat of contempt. And those involving a state immunity statute—exemplified by Knapp v. Schweitzer—where the Court, applying a rule today rejected, held the Fifth Amendment inapplicable to the States.

In Adams v. Maryland, petitioner had testified before a United States Senate Committee investigating crime, and his testimony had later been used to convict him of a state crime. A federal statute at that time provided that no testimony given by a witness in congressional inquiries "shall be used as evidence in any criminal proceeding against him in any court. . . ." 62 Stat. 833. The State questioned the application of the statute to petitioner's testimony and the constitutionality of the statute if construed to apply to state courts. The Court, in an opinion joined by seven members, made the following significant statement: "a witness does not need any statute to protect him from the use of self-incriminating testimony he is compelled to give over his objection. The Fifth Amendment takes care of that without a statute." This statement suggests that any testimony elicited under threat of contempt by a government to whom the constitutional privilege against self-incrimination is applicable (at the time of that decision it was deemed applicable only to the Federal Government) may not constitutionally be admitted into evidence against him in any criminal trial conducted by a government to whom the privilege is also applicable. This statement, read in light of today's decision in Malloy v. Hogan, draws into question the continuing authority of the statements to the contrary in United States v. Murdock and Feldman v. United States.

Knapp v. Schweitzer involved a state contempt conviction for a witness' refusal to answer questions, under a grant of state immunity, on the ground that his answers might subject him to prosecution under federal law. Petitioner claimed that "the Fifth Amendment gives him the privilege, which he can assert against either a State or the National Government, against giving testimony that might tend to implicate him in a violation" of federal law. The Court, applying the rule then in existence, denied petitioner's claim and declared that:

"It is plain that the [Fifth Amendment] can no more be thought of as restricting action by the States than as restricting the conduct of private citizens. The sole—although deeply valuable—purpose of the Fifth Amendment privilege against self-incrimination is the security of the individual against the exertion of the power of the Federal Government to compel incriminating testimony with a view to enabling that same Government to convict a man out of his own mouth."

The Court has today rejected that rule, and with it, all the earlier cases resting on that rule.

The foregoing makes it clear that there is no continuing legal vitality to, or historical justification for, the rule that one jurisdiction within our federal structure may compel a witness to give testimony which could be used to convict him of a crime in another jurisdiction.

IV. Conclusions.

In light of the history, policies and purposes of the privilege against self-incrimination, we now accept as correct the construction given the privilege by the English courts. . . . [The Court also relies on language in two early American cases which touched on, but did not decide, self-incrimination questions.] We reject—as unsupported by history or policy—the deviation from that construction only recently adopted by this Court in United States v. Murdock and Feldman v. United States. We hold that the constitutional privilege against self-incrimination protects a state witness against incrimination under federal as well as state law and a federal witness against incrimination under state as well as federal law.

We must now decide what effect this holding has on existing state immunity legislation. In Counselman v. Hitchcock this Court considered a federal statute which provided that no "evidence obtained from a party or witness by means of a judicial proceeding . . . shall be given in evidence, or in any manner used against him . . . in any court of the United States. . . ." Not withstanding this statute, appellant, claiming his privilege against self-incrimination, refused to answer certain questions before a federal grand jury. The Court said "that legislation cannot abridge a constitutional privilege, and that it cannot replace or supply one, at least unless it is so broad as to have the same extent in scope and effect." Applying this principle to the facts of that case, the Court upheld appellant's refusal to answer on the ground that the statute: "could not, and would not, prevent the use of this testimony to search out other testimony to be used in evidence against him or his property, in a criminal proceeding in such court . . . ," that it: "could not prevent the obtaining and the use of witnesses and evidence which should be attributable directly to the testimony he might give under compulsion, and on which he might be convicted, when otherwise, and if he had refused to answer, he could not possibly have been convicted . . . ," and that: "affords no protection against that use of compelled testimony which consists in gaining therefrom a knowledge of the details of a crime, and of sources of information which may supply other means of convicting the witness or party."

Applying the holding of that case to our holdings today that the privilege against self-incrimination protects a state witness against federal prosecution, and that "the same standards must determine whether [a witness'] silence in either a federal or state proceeding is justified," Malloy v. Hogan, we hold the constitutional rule to be that a state witness may not be compelled to give testimony which may be incriminating under federal law unless the compelled testimony and its fruits cannot be used in any manner by federal officials in connection with a criminal prosecution against him. We conclude, moreover, that in order to implement this constitutional rule and accommodate the interests of the State and Federal Governments in investigating and prosecuting crime, the Federal Government must be prohibited from making any such use of compelled testimony and its fruits.* This exclusionary rule, while permitting the States to secure information necessary for effective law enforcement, leaves the witness and the Federal Government in substantially the same position as if the witness had claimed his privilege in the absence of a state grant of immunity.

It follows that petitioners here may now be compelled to answer the questions propounded to them. At the time they refused to answer, however, petitioners had a reasonable fear, based on this Court's decision in Feldman v. United States, supra, that the federal authorities might use the answers against them in connection with a federal prosecution. We have now overruled Feldman and held that the Federal Government may make no such use of the answers. Fairness dictates that petitioners should now be afforded an opportunity, in light of this development, to answer the questions. . . . Accordingly, the judgment of the New Jersey courts ordering petitioners to answer the questions may remain undisturbed. But the judgment of contempt is vacated and the cause remanded to the New Jersey Supreme Court for proceedings not inconsistent with this opinion.

It is so ordered.

Mr. Justice Black concurs in the judgment and opinion of the Court for the reasons stated in that opinion and for the reasons stated in Feldman v. United States (dissenting opinion) . . . .

Mr. Justice Harlan, whom Mr. Justice Clark joins, concurring in the judgment, saying in part:

Unless I wholly misapprehend the Court's opinion, its holding that testimony compelled in a state proceeding over a witness' claim that such testimony will incriminate him may not be used against the witness in a federal criminal prosecution rests on *constitutional* grounds. On that basis, the contrary conclusion of Feldman v. United States is overruled.

I believe that the constitutional holding of Feldman was correct, and would not overrule it. To the extent, however, that the decision

---

* Once a defendant demonstrates that he has testified, under a state grant of immunity, to matters related to the federal prosecution, the federal authorities have the burden of showing that their evidence is not tainted by establishing that they had an independent, legitimate source for the disputed evidence.

in that case may have rested also on a refusal to exercise this Court's "supervisory power" over the administration of justice in federal courts, I think that it can no longer be considered good law, in light of this Court's subsequent decision in Elkins v. United States. In Elkins, this Court, exercising its supervisory power, did away with the "silver platter" doctrine and prohibited the use of evidence unconstitutionally seized by state authorities in a federal criminal trial involving the person suffering such a seizure. I believe that a similar supervisory rule of exclusion should follow in a case of the kind now before us, and solely on that basis concur in this judgment.

I.

The Court's constitutional conclusions are thought by it to follow from what it terms the "policies" of the privilege against self-incrimination and a re-examination of various cases in this Court, particularly in the context of early English law. Almost entirely absent from the statement of "policies" is any reference to the particular problem of this case; at best, the statement suggests the set of values which are on one side of the issue. The discussion of precedent is scarcely more helpful. It intertwines decisions of this Court with decisions in English courts, which *perhaps* follow a different rule, and casts doubt for one reason or another on every American case which does not accord with the result now reached. When the skein is untangled, however, and the line of cases is spread out, two facts clearly emerge:

(1) With two early and somewhat doubtful exceptions, this Court has consistently rejected the proposition that the danger of incrimination in the court of another jurisdiction is a sufficient basis for invoking a privilege against self-incrimination;

(2) Without any exception, in every case involving an immunity statute in which the Court has treated the question now before us, it has rejected the present majority's views.

[Mr. Justice Harlan here reviews the same cases examined by the Court and reaches the opposite conclusion regarding their holding.]

II.

Part I of this opinion shows, I believe, that the Court's analysis of prior cases hardly furnishes an adequate basis for a new departure in constitutional law. Even if the Court's analysis were sound, however, it would not support reversal of the Feldman rule on *constitutional* grounds.

If the Court were correct in asserting that the "separate sovereignty" theory of self-incrimination should be discarded, that would, as the Court says, lead to the conclusion that "a state witness [is protected] against incrimination under federal as well as state law and a federal witness against incrimination under state as well as federal law." However, dealing strictly with the situation presented by this case, that conclusion does *not* in turn lead to a constitutional rule that the testimony of a state witness (or evidence to which his testimony leads) who is compelled to testify in state proceedings may not be used against him in a federal prosecution. Protection which the Due Process Clause affords against the *States* is quite obviously not any basis for a constitutional rule regulating the conduct of *federal* authorities in *federal* proceedings.

The Court avoids this problem by mixing together the Fifth Amendment and the Fourteenth and talking about "the constitutional privilege against self-incrimination." Such an approach, which deals with "constitutional" rights at large, unrelated either to particular provisions of the Constitution or to relevant differences between the States and the Federal Government warns of the dangers for our federalism to which the "incorporation" theory of the Fourteenth Amendment leads. . . .

The Court's reasons for overruling Feldman thus rest on an entirely new conception of the *Fifth Amendment*, namely that it applies to federal use of state compelled incriminating testimony. The opinion, however, contains nothing at all to contradict the traditional, well-understood conception of the Fifth Amendment, to which, therefore, I continue to adhere:

"The sole—although deeply valuable—purpose of the Fifth Amendment privilege against self-incrimination is the security of the individual against the exertion of the power of the Federal Government to compel incriminating testimony with a view to enabling that same Government to convict a man out of his own mouth." Knapp v. Schweitzer.

It is no service to our constitutional liberties to encumber the particular provisions which safeguard them with a gloss for which neither the text nor history provides any support.

Accordingly, I cannot accept the majority's conclusion that a rule prohibiting federal authorities from using in aid of a federal prosecution incriminating testimony compelled in state proceedings is constitutionally required.

III.

I would, however, adopt such a rule in the exercise of our supervisory power over the administration of federal criminal justice. . . . The rule seems to me to follow from the Court's rejection, in the exercise of its supervisory power, of the "silver platter" doctrine as applied to the use in federal courts of evidence unconstitutionally seized by state officers. Elkins v. United States. . . .

On this basis, I concur in the judgment of the Court.

Mr. Justice White, with whom Mr. Justice Stewart joins, concurring, said in part:

In reaching its result the Court does not accept the far-reaching and in my view wholly unnecessary constitutional principle that the privilege requires not only complete protection against any use of compelled testimony in any manner in other jurisdictions but also absolute immunity in these jurisdictions from any prosecution pertaining to any of the testimony given. . . .

The Constitution does not require that immunity go so far as to protect against all prosecutions to which the testimony relates, including prosecutions of another government, whether or not there is any causal connection between the disclosure and the prosecution or evidence offered at trial. In my view it is possible for a federal prosecution to be based on untainted evidence after a grant of federal immunity in exchange for testimony in a federal criminal investigation. Likewise it is possible that information gathered by a state government which has an important but wholly separate purpose in conducting the investigation and no interest in any federal prosecution will not in any manner be used in subsequent federal proceedings, at least "while this Court sits" to review invalid convictions. Panhandle Oil Co. v. [Mississippi], 277 U. S. 218 (Holmes, J., dissenting). It is precisely this possibility of a prosecution based on untainted evidence that we must recognize. For if it is meaningful to say that the Federal Government may not use compelled testimony to convict a witness of a federal crime, then, of course, the Constitution permits the State to compel such testimony.

"The real evil aimed at by the Fifth Amendment's flat prohibition

against the compulsion of self-incriminatory testimony was that
thought to inhere in using a man's compelled testimony to punish
him." . . . I believe the State may compel testimony incriminating
under federal law, but the Federal Government may not use such
testimony or its fruits in a federal criminal proceeding. Immunity
must be as broad as, but not harmfully and wastefully broader than,
the privilege against self-incrimination.

ESCOBEDO v. ILLINOIS
378 U. S. 478; 12 L. Ed. 2d 977; 84 Sup. Ct. 1758. 1964.

The right to be represented by counsel in a criminal case has been
recognized in this country since its earliest days. It rests on an appreciation
of the fact that trial procedure is complex and confusing and that its rules
are highly technical. A layman's ignorance of such procedure may cause a
mistrial, a loss of rights to which he is entitled, and hopelessly frustrate
his efforts to get his story into the record. There is much truth in the
aphorism that one who defends himself has a fool for a lawyer.

The Sixth Amendment expressly guarantees that in "all criminal prosecutions the accused shall . . . have the assistance of counsel for his defense," and in Johnson v. Zerbst, 304 U. S. 458 (1942), the Supreme Court
held that the federal government must furnish a lawyer if necessary. This
right to appointed counsel has gradually been extended to the states under
the Fourteenth Amendment. In Powell v. Alabama, 287 U. S. 45 (1932),
a state was required to furnish counsel to a person in a capital case,
although not in a non-capital case unless an unfair trial would result without one; see Betts v. Brady, 316 U. S. 455 (1942). In Gideon v. Wainwright (p. 477), this distinction was finally rejected, and a person became
entitled to appointed counsel in any criminal trial—state or federal, capital
or non-capital.

Beginning in the 1960's the Court, recognizing that counsel is necessary
in certain pre-trial formalities if valuable rights are to be saved, began
extending the scope of the right to counsel beyond the period of trial. In
Hamilton v. Alabama, 368 U. S. 52 (1961), the right was extended to the
arraignment, since certain defenses such as insanity had to be pleaded at
that time or completely forfeited; and in White v. Maryland, 373 U. S. 59
(1963), it was pushed back to the preliminary hearing stage because a
guilty plea made at that point became a permanent part of the record. In
both cases the Court noted that these were "critical stages" at which a
lack of procedural knowledge could cost the defendant his life or liberty.

While these changes were taking place, the Court was also struggling with the somewhat unrelated problem of coerced confessions. Although it had held in 1936 (see Brown v. Mississippi, 297 U. S. 278) that a state could not use a coerced confession, it was continually plagued by the problem of what constitutes coercion. It conceded that coercion could be psychological as well as physical, but it was haunted by the fact, clearly stated in Stein v. New York, 346 U. S. 156 (1953), that "no criminal confession is voluntary" in the "sense that petitioners wanted to make them." A definition of "voluntary" that meant some pressure could be used, but not too much, required constant supervision by the Court. It noted in Spano v. New York, 360 U. S. 315 (1959), that as "the methods used to extract confessions become more sophisticated, our duty . . . only becomes more difficult because of the more delicate judgments to be made." In the Spano case the defendant was persuaded to confess by fatigue and the false sympathy aroused by a boyhood friend on the police force, while in subsequent cases the techniques used included threatening to bring the defendant's wife in for questioning, Rogers v. Richmond, 365 U. S. 534 (1961); threatening to take her infant children from her and give them to strangers, Lynumn v. Illinois, 372 U. S. 528 (1963); injecting "truth serum" into his veins, Townsend v. Sain, 372 U. S. 293 (1963); and refusing to let him call his wife or lawyer until he had confessed, Haynes v. Washington, 373 U. S. 503 (1963). While in some of these cases the police disputed the defendant's version, in all of them the defendants were denied access to counsel who might have given them moral support and perhaps furnished a dispassionate version of the proceedings. Claims that the right to counsel were being denied were noted by the Court but not reached because the confessions were held to be coerced. Clearly the amount of "pressure" a state could use to invoke a confession was becoming less and less.

Then in 1964 the Court moved sharply to merge these two lines of development, extending the right to counsel, but in a way that would serve also as a protection against forced confessions. In Massiah v. United States, 377 U. S. 201, the defendant and another man had been indicted by a federal grand jury for narcotics violation. They had retained a lawyer, pleaded not guilty, and been released on bail. Unbeknown to him, his codefendant had decided to help the federal authorities and persuaded Massiah to make incriminating statements which, with the aid of a hidden radio transmitter, were overheard by a federal agent. The Supreme Court held that the Sixth Amendment forbade the use against Massiah of incriminating statements elicited from him by federal officials "after he had been indicted and in the absence of counsel." Clearly, an indicted person cannot be questioned by the police except in the presence of his lawyer.

The defendant in the present case was arrested for the murder of his brother-in-law on the strength of an accusation made by his alleged accomplice. He was handcuffed and taken to the police station, where the officers tried to persuade him to confess. He was refused permission to consult his lawyer, and when his lawyer came to the station, he was forbidden to see his client, despite persistent efforts to do so, on the ground that they had not finished questioning him.

Mr. Justice Goldberg delivered the opinion of the Court, saying in part:

The critical question in this case is whether, under the circumstances, the refusal by the police to honor petitioner's request to consult with his lawyer during the course of an interrogation constitutes a denial of "the Assistance of Counsel" in violation of the Sixth Amendment to the Constitution as "made obligatory upon the States by the Fourteenth Amendment," Gideon v. Wainwright [p. 477] and thereby renders inadmissible in a state criminal trial any incriminating statement elicited by the police during the interrogation. . . .

There is testimony by the police that during the interrogation, petitioner, a 22-year-old of Mexican extraction with no record of previous experience with the police, "was handcuffed" in a standing position and that he "was nervous, he had circles under his eyes and he was upset" and was "agitated" because "he had not slept well in over a week."

It is undisputed that during the course of the interrogation Officer Montejano, who "grew up" in petitioner's neighborhood, who knew his family, and who uses "Spanish language in [his] police work," conferred alone with petitioner "for about a quarter of an hour. . . ." Petitioner testified that the officer said to him "in Spanish that my sister and I could go home if I pinned it on Benedict DiGerlando," that "he would see to it that we would go home and be held only as witnesses, if anything, if we had made a statement against DiGerlando . . . , that we would be able to go home that night." Petitioner testified that he made the statement in issue because of this assurance. Officer Montejano denied offering any such assurance.

A police officer testified that during the interrogation the following occurred:

"I informed him of what DiGerlando told me and when I did, he told me that DiGerlando was [lying] and I said, 'Would you care to tell DiGerlando that?' and he said, 'yes, I will.' So, I brought . . . Escobedo in and he confronted DiGerlando and he told him that he was lying and said, 'I didn't shoot Manuel, you did it.' "

In this way, petitioner, for the first time, admitted to some knowledge of the crime. After that he made additional statements further implicating himself in the murder plot. At this point an Assistant State's Attorney, Theodore J. Cooper, was summoned "to take" a statement. Mr. Cooper, an experienced lawyer who was assigned to the Homicide Division to take "statements from some defendants and some prisoners that they had in custody," "took" petitioner's statement by asking carefully framed questions apparently designed to assure the admissibility into evidence of the resulting answers. Mr. Cooper testified that he did not advise petitioner of his constitutional rights, and it is undisputed that no one during the course of the interrogation so advised him.

Petitioner moved both before and during trial to suppress the incriminating statement, but the motions were denied. Petitioner was convicted of murder and he appealed the conviction.

. . . We granted a writ of certiorari to consider whether the petitioner's statement was constitutionally admissible at his trial. We conclude, for the reasons stated below, that it was not and, accordingly, we reverse the judgment of conviction.

In Massiah v. United States, 377 U. S. 201, this Court observed that "a Constitution which guarantees a defendant the aid of counsel at . . . trial could surely vouchsafe no less to an indicted defendant under interrogation by the police in a completely extrajudicial proceeding. Anything less . . . might deny a defendant 'effective representation by counsel at the only stage when legal aid and advice would help him.'" . . .

The interrogation here was conducted before petitioner was formally indicted. But in the context of this case, that fact should make no difference. When petitioner requested, and was denied, an opportunity to consult with his lawyer, the investigation had ceased to be a general investigation of "an unsolved crime." . . . Petitioner had become the accused, and the purpose of the interrogation was to "get him" to confess his guilt despite his constitutional right not to do so. At the time of his arrest and throughout the course of the interrogation, the police told petitioner that they had convincing evidence that he had fired the fatal shots. Without informing him of his absolute right to remain silent in the face of this accusation, the police urged him to make a statement. As this Court observed many years ago:

"It cannot be doubted that, placed in the position in which the accused was when the statement was made to him that the other suspected person had charged him with a crime, the result was to produce upon his mind the fear that if he remained silent it would be considered an admission of guilt, and therefore render certain his being committed for trial as the guilty person, and it cannot be conceived that the converse impression would not also have naturally arisen, that by denying there was hope of removing the suspicion from himself." Bram v. United States, 168 U. S. 532.

Petitioner, a layman, was undoubtedly unaware that under Illinois law an admission of "mere" complicity in the murder plot was legally as damaging as an admission of firing of the fatal shots. The "guiding hand of counsel" was essential to advise petitioner of his rights in this delicate situation. . . . This was the "stage when legal aid and advice" were most critical to petitioner. . . . It was a stage surely as critical as was the arraignment in Hamilton v. Alabama, 368 U. S. 52, and the preliminary hearing in White v. Maryland, 373 U. S. 59. What happened at this interrogation could certainly "affect the whole trial," Hamilton v. Alabama, since rights "may be as irretrievably lost, if not then and there asserted, as they are when an accused represented by counsel waives a right for strategic purposes." It would exalt form over substance to make the right to counsel, under these circumstances, depend on whether at the time of the interrogation, the authorities had secured a formal indictment. Petitioner had, for all practical purposes, already been charged with murder. . . .

In Gideon v. Wainwright we held that every person accused of a crime, whether state or federal, is entitled to a lawyer at trial. The rule sought by the State here, however, would make the trial no more than an appeal from the interrogation; and the "right to use counsel at the formal trial [would be] a very hollow thing [if], for all practical purposes, the conviction is already assured by pre-trial examination." . . . "One can imagine a cynical prosecutor saying: 'Let them have the most illustrious counsel, now. They can't escape the noose. There is nothing that counsel can do for them at trial.'" . . .

It is argued that if the right to counsel is afforded prior to indictment, the number of confessions obtained by the police will diminish significantly, because most confessions are obtained during the period between arrest and indictment, and "any lawyer worth his salt will tell the suspect in no uncertain terms to make no statement to police under any circumstances." . . . This argument, of course, cuts two ways. The fact that many confessions are obtained during this period points up its critical nature as a "stage when legal aid and advice" are surely needed. . . . The right to counsel would indeed be hollow if it began at a period when few confessions were obtained. There is necessarily a direct relationship between the importance of a stage to the police in their quest for a confession and the criticalness of that stage to the accused in his need for legal advice. Our Constitution, unlike some others, strikes the balance in favor of the right of the accused to be advised by his lawyer of his privilege against self-incrimination.

We have learned the lesson of history, ancient and modern, that a system of criminal law enforcement which comes to depend on the "confession" will, in the long run, be less reliable and more subject to abuses than a system which depends on extrinsic evidence independently secured through skillful investigation. As Dean Wigmore so wisely said:

"[A]*ny system of administration which permits the prosecution to trust habitually to compulsory self-disclosure as a source of proof must itself suffer morally thereby.* The inclination develops to rely mainly upon such evidence, and to be satisfied with an incomplete investigation of the other sources. The exercise of the power to extract answers begets a forgetfulness of the just limitations of that power. The simple and peaceful process of questioning breeds a readiness to resort to bullying and to physical force and torture. If there is a right to an answer, there soon seems to be a right to the expected answer,—that is, to a confession of guilt. Thus the legitimate use grows into the unjust abuse; ultimately, the innocent are jeopardized by the encroachments of a bad system. Such seems to have been the course of experience in those legal systems where the privilege was not recognized." 8 Wigmore, Evidence (3d ed. 1940), 309. (Emphasis in original.)

This Court also has recognized that "history amply shows that confessions have often been extorted to save law enforcement officials the trouble and effort of obtaining valid and independent evidence. . . ." Haynes v. Washington, 373 U. S. 503.

We have also learned the companion lesson of history that no system of criminal justice can, or should, survive if it comes to depend for its continued effectiveness on the citizens' abdication through unawareness of their constitutional rights. No system worth preserving should have to *fear* that if an accused is permitted to consult with a lawyer, he will become aware of, and exercise, these rights.* If the

---

* Cf. Report of Attorney General's Committee on Poverty and the Administration of Federal Criminal Justice (1963), 10–11: "The survival of our system of

exercise of constitutional rights will thwart the effectiveness of a system of law enforcement, then there is something very wrong with that system.

We hold, therefore, that where, as here, the investigation is no longer a general inquiry into an unsolved crime but has begun to focus on a particular suspect, the suspect has been taken into police custody, the police carry out a process of interrogations that lends itself to eliciting incriminating statements, the suspect has requested and been denied an opportunity to consult with his lawyer, and the police have not effectively warned him of his absolute constitutional right to remain silent, the accused has been denied "the Assistance of Counsel" in violation of the Sixth Amendment to the Constitution as "made obligatory upon the States by the Fourteenth Amendment," Gideon v. Wainwright, and that no statement elicited by the police during the interrogation may be used against him at a criminal trial. . . .

Nothing we have said today affects the powers of the police to investigate "an unsolved crime," . . . by gathering information from witnesses and by other "proper investigative efforts." . . . We hold only that when the process shifts from investigatory to accusatory— when its focus is on the accused and its purpose is to elicit a confession —our adversary system begins to operate, and, under the circumstances here, the accused must be permitted to consult with his lawyer.

The judgment of the Illinois Supreme Court is reversed and the case remanded for proceedings not inconsistent with this opinion.

Reversed and remanded.

Mr. Justice Harlan, dissenting, said in part:

I think the rule announced today is most ill-conceived and that it seriously and unjustifiably fetters perfectly legitimate methods of criminal law enforcement.

criminal justice and the values which it advances depends upon a constant, searching, and creative questioning of official decisions and assertions of authority at all stages of the process. . . . Persons [denied access to counsel] are incapable of providing the challenges that are indispensable to satisfactory operation of the system. The loss to the interests of accused individuals, occasioned by these failures, are great and apparent. It is also clear that a situation in which persons are required to contest a serious accusation but are denied access to the tools of contest is offensive to fairness and equity. Beyond these considerations, however, is the fact that [this situation is] detrimental to the proper functioning of the system of justice and that the loss in vitality of the adversary system, thereby occasioned, significantly endangers the basic interests of a free community."

Mr. Justice Stewart, dissenting, said in part:

Massiah v. United States is not in point here. In that case a federal grand jury had indicted Massiah. He had retained a lawyer and entered a formal plea of not guilty. Under our system of federal justice an indictment and arraignment are followed by a trial, at which the Sixth Amendment guarantees the defendant the assistance of counsel. But Massiah was released on bail, and thereafter agents of the Federal Government deliberately elicited incriminating statements from him in the absence of his lawyer. We held that the use of these statements against him at his trial denied him the basic protections of the Sixth Amendment guarantee. Putting to one side the fact that the case now before us is not a federal case, the vital fact remains that this case does not involve the deliberate interrogation of a defendant after the initiation of judicial proceedings against him. The Court disregards this basic difference between the present case and Massiah's, with the bland assertion that "that fact should make no difference."

It is "that fact," I submit, which makes all the difference. Under our system of criminal justice the institution of formal, meaningful judicial proceedings, by way of indictment, information, or arraignment, marks the point at which a criminal investigation has ended and adversary proceedings have commenced. It is at this point that the constitutional guarantees attach which pertain to a criminal trial. Among those guarantees are the right to a speedy trial, the right of confrontation, and the right to trial by jury. Another is the guarantee of the assistance of counsel. Gideon v. Wainwright. . . .

The confession which the Court today holds inadmissible was a voluntary one. It was given during the course of a perfectly legitimate police investigation of an unsolved murder. The Court says that what happened during this investigation "affected" the trial. I had always supposed that the whole purpose of a police investigation of a murder was to "affect" the trial of the murderer, and that it would be only an incompetent, unsuccessful, or corrupt investigation which would not do so. The Court further says that the Illinois police officers did not advise the petitioner of his "constitutional rights" before he confessed to the murder. This Court has never held that the Constitution requires the police to give any "advice" under circumstances such as these.

Supported by no stronger authority than its own rhetoric, the Court today converts a routine police investigation of an unsolved murder into a distorted analogue of a judicial trial. It imports into this investigation constitutional concepts historically applicable only after the onset of formal prosecutorial proceedings. By doing so, I think the Court perverts those precious constitutional guarantees, and frustrates the vital interests of society in preserving the legitimate and proper function of honest and purposeful police investigation.

Like my Brother Clark, I cannot escape the logic of my Brother White's conclusions as to the extraordinary implications which emanate from the Court's opinion in this case, and I share their views as to the untold and highly unfortunate impact today's decision may have upon the fair administration of criminal justice. I can only hope we have completely misunderstood what the Court has said.

Mr. Justice White, with whom Mr. Justice Clark and Mr. Justice Stewart join, dissenting, said in part:

In Massiah v. United States the Court held that as of the date of the indictment the prosecution is disentitled to secure admissions from the accused. The Court now moves that date back to the time when the prosecution begins to "focus" on the accused. Although the opinion purports to be limited to the facts of this case, it would be naive to think that the new constitutional right announced will depend upon whether the accused has retained his own counsel . . . , or has asked to consult with counsel in the course of interrogation. . . . At the very least the Court holds that once the accused becomes a suspect and, presumably, is arrested, any admission made to the police thereafter is inadmissible in evidence unless the accused has waived his right to counsel. The decision is thus another major step in the direction of the goal which the Court seemingly has in mind—to bar from evidence all admissions obtained from an individual suspected of crime, whether involuntarily made or not. It does of course put us one step "ahead" of the English judges who have had the good sense to leave the matter a discretionary one with the trial court. I reject this step and the invitation to go farther which the Court has now issued.

By abandoning the voluntary-involuntary test for admissibility of confessions, the Court seems driven by the notion that it is uncivilized law enforcement to use an accused's own admissions against him at his trial. It attempts to find a home for this new and nebulous rule of due process by attaching it to the right to counsel guaranteed in the federal system by the Sixth Amendment and binding upon the States

by virtue of the due process guarantee of the Fourteenth Amendment.
. . . The right to counsel now not only entitles the accused to counsel's advice and aid in preparing for trial but stands as an impene-
trable barrier to any interrogation once the accused has become a
suspect. From that very moment apparently his right to counsel attaches, a rule wholly unworkable and impossible to administer unless
police cars are equipped with public defenders and undercover agents
and police informants have defense counsel at their side. I would not
abandon the Court's prior cases defining with some care and analyses
the circumstances requiring the presence or aid of counsel and substitute the amorphous and wholly unworkable principle that counsel
is constitutionally required whenever he would or could be helpful.
. . .

I do not suggest for a moment that law enforcement will be destroyed by the rule announced today. The need for peace and order
is too insistent for that. But it will be crippled and its task made a
great deal more difficult, all in my opinion, for unsound, unstated
reasons, which can find no home in any of the provisions of the Constitution.

HEART OF ATLANTA MOTEL v. UNITED STATES
379 U. S. 241; 13 L. Ed. 2d 258; 85 Sup. Ct. 348. 1964.

KATZENBACH v. MC CLUNG
379 U. S. 294; 13 L. Ed. 2d 290; 85 Sup. Ct. 377. 1964.

Discrimination hurts most perhaps when it denies access to public
accommodations. WHITE ONLY signs on hotels, theaters, barbershops,
lunch counters, and rest rooms constantly remind the Negro that his white
neighbor considers him inferior and objects to close association with him.
The Civil Rights Cases, 109 U. S. 3 (1883), had made clear that such discrimination was a private matter and so not forbidden by the Fourteenth
Amendment, but Shelley v. Kraemer, 334 U. S. 1 (1948), outlawing enforcement of restrictive covenants, had given hope that state enforcement
of these practices might be invalid. Private discrimination is normally implemented by police enforcement of laws against trespass, and this seemed
to make the state a party to the discrimination. During the late 1950's and
early 1960's southern Negroes, led by such people as Martin Luther King,
undertook to bring about desegregation by non-violent means. Among the
techniques employed was the "sit-in" demonstration, one in which Negroes,

sometimes accompanied by sympathetic whites, would enter a public eating place and ask to be served. When service was denied, they would refuse to leave, and the police would ultimately be called to arrest them for trespass.

In five cases decided in 1964 the Supreme Court reversed, on non-constitutional grounds, convictions for sit-in demonstrations. Although it avoided the issue of whether police enforcement of trespass laws to effect private discrimination was constitutional, six justices in separate opinions indicated their stand on this issue. Justices Black, Harlan, and White argued that in the absence of a statute forbidding such discrimination, the impartial enforcement of trespass statutes does not make the state a party to the discrimination and hence does not deny equal protection, while Justices Warren, Goldberg, and Douglas argued that the framers of the Fourteenth Amendment had assumed the continued existence of the right of all citizens to enter places of public accommodation, and the refusal of the state to enforce that right as to Negroes denies them the equal protection of the law. See Bell v. Maryland, 378 U. S. 226; Bouie v. Columbia, 378 U. S. 374; Griffin v. Maryland, 378 U. S. 130; Robinson v. Florida, 378 U. S. 153; and Barr v. Columbia, 378 U. S. 146.

The final chapter in the sit-in cases was written in Hamm v. Rock Hill, 379 U. S. 306 (1964), decided the same day as Heart of Atlanta Motel. Again the Court failed to reach the constitutional issue but concluded that the Civil Rights Act of 1964, by making sit-ins no longer a crime, had abated sit-in prosecutions then in progress, since the state no longer had a policy to be served by such prosecutions. Federal statutes would decree this result as far as federal crimes were concerned, and the Supremacy Clause dictated the same result for state crimes. The effect of the decision was to stop the prosecution of some 3,000 sit-in demonstrators.

Nineteen states have laws forbidding the intermarriage of persons of different races, and while the Supreme Court has never passed on their validity directly, in Pace v. Alabama, 106 U. S. 583 (1883), it suggested what their fate might be should such a challenge arise. Alabama law forbade adultery and fornication in general and adultery and fornication between a white person and a Negro, the latter section carrying a heavier penalty than the former. The Court stated reassuringly that equal protection insures that no person, "whatever his race," shall be "subjected, for the same offense, to any greater or different punishment." Adultery between a white and a Negro, however, was not the *same* offense as adultery between two whites or two Negroes. Equality was maintained by punishing the white and Negro parties the same.

In McLaughlin v. Florida, 379 U. S. 184 (1964), the Court abandoned the approach of Pace v. Alabama and suggested a new test by which anti-miscegenation laws would be judged. Florida, in the section of its criminal code dealing with sexual conduct, forbids a Negro and a white person to "habitually occupy the same room in the night time." No sexual act need be proven, and the same conduct by a white or Negro couple is not made illegal. While conceding that all persons within a class were being treated alike, the Court emphasized that classification, to be valid, must be based on some valid legislative purpose, and racial classifications are constitutionally suspect. Since there was no "overriding statutory purpose requiring the proscription of the specified conduct when engaged in by the white person and a Negro, but not otherwise," the act was an "invidious discrimination forbidden by the Equal Protection clause." On March 7, 1966, the supreme court of Virginia held valid its antimiscegenation laws in a case involving a white man and his part-Negro, part-Indian wife. The court found that nothing in recent Supreme Court decisions warranted abandonment of its long-standing rule.

When the Supreme Court decided the Segregation Cases in 1954 (p. 249), one of the five districts ordered to desegregate its public schools "with all deliberate speed" was Prince Edward County, Virginia. The response of the Virginia legislature was a program of "massive resistance," which included closing integrated schools, cutting off their funds, paying tuition grants to students in private, non-sectarian schools, and providing state and local financial aid (including teacher retirement benefits) for such schools. In 1959 the supreme court of Virginia held the program void under the Virginia constitution, so the legislature repealed it and enacted instead a program under which school attendance was a matter of local option. Faced with the desegregation order, Prince Edward County closed its public schools and provided various kinds of financial support for privately operated segregated schools. In Griffin v. School Board of Prince Edward County, 377 U. S. 218 (1964), the Court held the plan denied equal protection of the law. Noting that "the case has been delayed since 1951 by resistance at the state and county level, by legislation, and by law suits," it emphasized that "there has been entirely too much deliberation and not enough speed." The Court conceded to the state a "wide discretion" in deciding whether state laws should operate statewide or only in some counties, "but the record in the present case could not be clearer that Prince Edward's public schools were closed and private schools operated in their place with state and county assistance, for one reason, and one reason only: to ensure, through measures taken by the county and the State, that white and colored children in Prince Edward County would not, under any circumstances, go to the same school. Whatever nonracial grounds might support a State's allowing a county to abandon public schools, the object must be a constitutional one, and grounds of race and opposition to desegregation do not qualify as constitutional." The district court was told to "enter a decree which will guarantee that these petitioners will get the kind of education that is given in the State's public schools" even if it had to order the Board of Supervisors to levy taxes to do it. After trying in vain to discover what the penalties for refusal would be, the supervisors finally decided to obey, and in the fall of 1964 Prince Edward County reopened its schools on an integrated basis. The county did not, however, abandon its aid to private segregated schools, and a suit to enjoin payment of these supporting funds is already on its way to the Supreme Court.

In 1965 the Supreme Court refused to review a New York City requirement pairing two racially unbalanced schools. One school, 88% white, was paired with a school that was 99% Negro. The pairing resulted in one school being 75% white and the other 46% Negro. Twenty-nine children were bused to the Negro school, but they were not involved in the suit. The parents argued that their children were being moved to a particular school on the basis of race, in violation of the rule of Brown v. Board of Education of Topeka, p. 249. The Court denied certiorari; see Addabbo v. Donovan, 382 U. S. 905 (1965).

The passage of the Civil Rights Act of 1964, Title II of which was sustained in the present cases, brought to an all-time high congressional efforts to abolish race discrimination in the United States. The act itself is remarkable for a number of reasons. First, for the first time since the ill-fated Civil Rights Act of 1875, Congress made a sweeping attack on race discrimination. Second, the act commanded overwhelming bipartisan support. After five months of committee hearings, 2800 pages of testimony, and seven months of debates, the measure passed the House 289 to 126. In an unusual move, the Senate did not even send it to committee, but worked out a bill with informal bipartisan conferences. The House adopted the Senate bill without change. Third, for the first time in history the Senate, with the all-out support of both majority and minority leaders, invoked cloture to stop a southern filibuster on a civil rights measure.

Mr. Justice Clark delivered the opinion of the Court in the Heart of Atlanta Motel case, saying in part:

This is a declaratory judgment action attacking the constitutionality of Title II of the Civil Rights Act of 1964. . . . Appellees counterclaimed for enforcement under § 206 (a) of the Act and asked for a three-judge district court under § 206 (b). A three-judge court . . . sustained the validity of the Act and issued a permanent injunction on appellees' counterclaim restraining appellant from continuing to violate the Act. . . . We affirm the judgment.

1. *The Factual Background and Contentions of the Parties.*

The case comes here on admissions and stipulated facts. Appellant owns and operates the Heart of Atlanta Motel which has 216 rooms available to transient guests. The motel is located on Courtland Street, two blocks from downtown Peachtree Street. It is readily accessible to interstate highways 75 and 85 and state highways 23 and 41. Appellant solicits patronage from outside the State of Georgia through various national advertising media, including magazines of national circulation; it maintains over 50 billboards and highway signs within the State, soliciting patronage for the motel; it accepts convention trade from outside Georgia and approximately 75% of its registered guests are from out of State. Prior to passage of the Act the motel had followed a practice of refusing to rent rooms to Negroes, and it alleged that it intended to continue to do so. In an effort to perpetuate that policy this suit was filed.

The appellant contends that Congress in passing this Act exceeded its power to regulate commerce under Art I, § 8, cl 3, of the Constitution of the United States; that the Act violates the Fifth Amendment because appellant is deprived of the right to choose its customers and operate its business as it wishes, resulting in a taking of its liberty and property without due process of law and a taking of its property without just compensation; and, finally, that by requiring appellant to rent available rooms to Negroes against its will, Congress is subjecting it to involuntary servitude in contravention of the Thirteenth Amendment. . . .

2. *The History of the Act.*

[The Court notes the passage by Congress of earlier civil rights acts, and reviews briefly the struggle to enact the present statute.]

The Act as finally adopted was most comprehensive, undertaking to prevent through peaceful and voluntary settlement discrimination in voting, as well as in places of accommodation and public facilities, federally secured programs and in employment. Since Title II is the only portion under attack here, we confine our consideration to those public accommodation provisions.

3. *Title II of the Act.*

This Title is divided into seven sections beginning with § 201 (a) which provides that:

"All persons shall be entitled to the full and equal enjoyment of the goods, services, facilities, privileges, advantages, and accommodations of any place of public accommodation, as defined in this section, without discrimination or segregation on the ground of race, color, religion, or national origin."

There are listed in § 201 (b) four classes of business establishments, each of which "serves the public" and "is a place of public accommodation" within the meaning of § 201 (a) "if its operations affect commerce, or if discrimination or segregation by it is supported by State action." The covered establishments are:

"(1) any inn, hotel, motel, or other establishment which provides lodging to transient guests, other than an establishment located within a building which contains not more than five rooms for rent or hire and which is actually occupied by the proprietor of such establishment as his residence; (2) any restaurant, cafeteria . . . [not here involved]; (3) any motion picture house . . . [not here involved]; (4) any establishment . . . which is physically located within the premises of any establishment otherwise covered by this subsection, or . . . within the premises of which is physically located any such covered establishment . . . [not here involved]."

Section 201 (c) defines the phrase "affect commerce" as applied to the above establishments. It first declares that "any inn, hotel, motel, or other establishment which provides lodging to transient guests" affects commerce per se. . . .

Finally, § 203 prohibits the withholding or denial, etc., of any right or privilege secured by § 201 . . . or the intimidation, threatening or coercion of any person with the purpose of interfering with any such right or the punishing, etc., of any person for exercising or attempting to exercise any such right.

The remaining sections of the Title are remedial ones for violations of any of the previous sections. Remedies are limited to civil actions for preventive relief. The Attorney General may bring suit where he has "reasonable cause to believe that any person or group of persons is engaged in a pattern or practice of resistance to the full enjoyment of any of the rights secured by this title, and that the pattern or practice is of such a nature and is intended to deny the full exercise of the rights herein described. . . ."

4. *Application of Title II to Heart of Atlanta Motel.*

It is admitted that the operation of the motel brings it within the provisions of § 201(a) of the Act and that appellant refused to provide lodging for transient Negroes because of their race or color and that it intends to continue that policy unless restrained.

The sole question posed is, therefore, the constitutionality of the Civil Rights Act of 1964 as applied to these facts. The legislative history of the Act indicates that Congress based the Act on § 5 and the Equal Protection Clause of the Fourteenth Amendment as well as its power to regulate interstate commerce under Art I, § 8, cl 3 of the Constitution.

The Senate Commerce Committee made it quite clear that the fundamental object of Title II was to vindicate "the deprivation of personal dignity that surely accompanies denials of equal access to public establishments." At the same time, however, it noted that such an objective has been and could be readily achieved "by congressional action based on the commerce power of the Constitution.". . . Our study of the legislative record, made in the light of prior cases, has brought us to the conclusion that Congress possessed ample power in this regard, and we have therefore not considered the other grounds relied upon. This is not to say that the remaining authority upon which it acted was not adequate, a question upon which we do not pass, but merely that since the commerce power is sufficient for our decision here we have considered it alone. . . .

5. *The Civil Rights Cases, 109 U. S. 3 (1883), and their Application.*

In light of our ground for decision, it might be well at the outset to discuss the Civil Rights Cases, supra, which declared provisions of the Civil Rights Act of 1875 unconstitutional. We think that decision inapposite, and without precedential value in determining the constitutionality of the present Act. Unlike Title II of the present legislation, the 1875 Act broadly proscribed discrimination in "inns, public conveyances on land or water, theaters, and other public places of amusement," without limiting the categories of affected businesses to those impinging upon interstate commerce. In contrast, the applicability of Title II is carefully limited to enterprises having a direct and substantial relation to the interstate flow of goods and people, except where state action is involved. Further, the fact that certain kinds of businesses may not in 1875 have been sufficiently involved in interstate commerce to warrant bringing them within the ambit of the commerce power is not necessarily dispositive of the same question today. Our populace had not reached its present mobility, nor were facilities, goods and services circulating as readily in interstate commerce as they are today. Although the principles which we apply today are those first formulated by Chief Justice Marshall in Gibbons v. Ogden [p. 390], the conditions of transportation and commerce have changed dramatically, and we must apply those principles to the present state of commerce. The sheer increase in volume of interstate traffic alone would give discriminatory practices which inhibit travel a far larger impact upon the Nation's commerce than such practices had in the economy of another day. . . .

6. The Basis of Congressional Action.

While the Act as adopted carried no congressional findings the record of its passage through each house is replete with evidence of the burdens that discrimination by race or color places upon interstate commerce. . . . This testimony included the fact that our people have become increasingly mobile with millions of people of all races traveling from State to State; that Negroes in particular have been the subject of discrimination in transient accommodations, having to travel great distances to secure the same; that often they have been unable to obtain accommodations and have had to call upon friends to put them up overnight . . . ; and that these conditions have become so acute as to require the listing of available lodging for Negroes in a special guidebook which was itself "dramatic testimony to the difficulties" Negroes encounter in travel. . . . These exclusionary practices were found to be nationwide, the Under Secretary of Commerce testifying that there is "no question that this discrimination in the North still exists to a large degree" and in the West and Midwest as well. . . . This testimony indicated a qualitative as well as quantitive effect on interstate travel by Negroes. The former was the obvious impairment of the Negro traveler's pleasure and convenience that resulted when he continually was uncertain of finding lodging. As for the latter, there was evidence that this uncertainty stemming from racial discrimination had the effect of discouraging travel on the part of a substantial portion of the Negro community. . . . This was the conclusion not only of the Under Secretary of Commerce but also of the Administrator of the Federal Aviation Agency who wrote the Chairman of the Senate Commerce Committee that it was his "belief that air commerce is adversely affected by the denial to a substantial segment of the traveling public of adequate and desegregated public accommodations." . . . We shall not burden this opinion with further details since the voluminous testimony presents overwhelming evidence that discrimination by hotels and motels impedes interstate travel.

7. *The Power of Congress Over Interstate Travel.*

The power of Congress to deal with these obstructions depends on the meaning of the Commerce Clause. Its meaning was first enunciated 140 years ago by the great Chief Justice John Marshall in Gibbons v. Ogden, in these words:

[The Court here quotes at length from the opinion concerning the nature of interstate commerce and congressional power over it. See p. 394.]

In short, the determinative test of the exercise of power by the Congress under the Commerce Clause is simply whether the activity sought to be regulated is "commerce which concerns more States than one" and has a real and substantial relation to the national interest. Let us now turn to this facet of the problem.

That the "intercourse" of which the Chief Justice spoke included the movement of persons through more States than one was settled as early as 1849, in the Passenger Cases, 7 How. 283, where Mr. Justice McLean stated: "That the transportation of passengers is a part of commerce is not now an open question." Again in 1913 Mr. Justice McKenna, speaking for the Court, said: "Commerce among the States, we have said, consists of intercourse and traffic between their citizens, and includes the transportation of persons and property." Hoke v. United States, 227 U. S. 308. And only four years later in 1917 in Caminetti v. United States, 242 U. S. 470, Mr. Justice Day held for the Court:

"The transportation of passengers in interstate commerce, it has long been settled, is within the regulatory power of Congress, under the commerce clause of the Constitution, and the authority of Congress to keep the channels of interstate commerce free from immoral and injurious uses has been frequently sustained, and is no longer open to question."

Nor does it make any difference whether the transportation is commercial in character. In Morgan v. Virginia, 328 U. S. 373 (1946), Mr. Justice Reed observed as to the modern movement of persons among the States:

"The recent changes in transportation brought about by the coming of automobiles [do] not seem of great significance in the problem. People of all races travel today more extensively than in 1878 when this Court first passed upon state regulation of racial segregation in commerce. [It but] emphasizes the soundness of this Court's early conclusion in Hall v. DeCuir, 95 U. S. 485."

The same interest in protecting interstate commerce which led Congress to deal with segregation in interstate carriers and the white slave traffic has prompted it to extend the exercise of its power to gambling . . . ; to criminal enterprises . . . ; to deceptive practices in the sale of products . . . ; to fraudulent security transactions . . . ; to misbranding of drugs . . . ; to wages and hours . . . ; to members of labor unions . . . ; to crop control . . . ; to discrimination against shippers . . . ; to the protection of small business from injurious price cutting . . . ; to resale price maintenance . . . ; to professional football . . . ; and to racial discrimination by owners and managers of terminal restaurants. . . .

That Congress was legislating against moral wrongs in many of these areas rendered its enactments no less valid. In framing Title II of this Act Congress was also dealing with what it considered a moral problem. But that fact does not detract from the overwhelming evidence of the disruptive effect that racial discrimination has had on commercial intercourse. It was this burden which empowered Congress to enact appropriate legislation, and, given this basis for the exercise of its power, Congress was not restricted by the fact that the particular obstruction to interstate commerce with which it was dealing was also deemed a moral and social wrong.

It is said that the operation of the motel here is of a purely local character. But, assuming this to be true, "[i]f it is interstate commerce that feels the pinch, it does not matter how local the operation which applies the squeeze." . . . As Chief Justice Stone put it in United States v. Darby [312 U. S. 100 (1941)]:

"The power of Congress over interstate commerce is not confined to the regulation of commerce among the states. It extends to those activities intrastate which so affect interstate commerce or the exercise of the power of Congress over it as to make regulation of them appropriate means to the attainment of a legitimate end, the exercise of the granted power of Congress to regulate interstate commerce. . . ."

Thus the power of Congress to promote interstate commerce also includes the power to regulate the local incidents thereof, including

local activities in both the States of origin and destination, which
might have a substantial and harmful effect upon that commerce.
One need only examine the evidence which we have discussed above
to see that Congress may—as it has—prohibit racial discrimination
by motels serving travelers, however "local" their operations may
appear.

Nor does the Act deprive appellant of liberty or property under the
Fifth Amendment. The commerce power invoked here by the Congress is a specific and plenary one authorized by the Constitution
itself. The only questions are: (1) whether Congress had a rational
basis for finding that racial discrimination by motels affected commerce, and (2) if it had such a basis, whether the means it selected
to eliminate that evil are reasonable and appropriate. If they are,
appellant has no "right" to select its guests as it sees fit, free from
governmental regulation.

There is nothing novel about such legislation. Thirty-two States
now have it on their books either by statute or executive order and
many cities provide such regulation. Some of these Acts go back four-
score years. It has been repeatedly held by this Court that such laws
do not violate the Due Process Clause of the Fourteenth Amendment.

. . . As a result the constitutionality of such state statutes stands
unquestioned. "The authority of the Federal Government over interstate commerce does not differ . . . in extent or character from that
retained by the states over intrastate commerce." . . .

It is doubtful if in the long run appellant will suffer economic loss
as a result of the Act. Experience is to the contrary where discrimination is completely obliterated as to all public accommodations. But
whether this be true or not is of no consequence since this Court has
specifically held that the fact that a "member of the class which is
regulated may suffer economic losses not shared by others . . . has
never been a barrier" to such legislation. . . . Likewise in a long line
of cases this Court has rejected the claim that the prohibition
of racial discrimination in public accommodations interferes with
personal liberty. . . .

We find no merit in the remainder of appellant's contentions,
including that of "involuntary servitude." . . .

We, therefore, conclude that the action of the Congress in the
adoption of the Act as applied here to a motel which concededly
serves interstate travelers is within the power granted it by the Commerce Clause of the Constitution, as interpreted by this Court for 140

years. It may be argued that Congress could have pursued other methods to eliminate the obstructions it found in interstate commerce caused by racial discrimination. But this is a matter of policy that rests entirely with the Congress not with the courts. How obstructions in commerce may be removed—what means are to be employed —is within the sound and exclusive discretion of the Congress. It is subject only to one caveat—that the means chosen by it must be reasonably adapted to the end permitted by the Constitution. We cannot say that its choice here was not so adapted. The Constitution requires no more.

Affirmed.

Mr. Justice Black, concurring, said in part:

Long ago this Court, again speaking through Mr. Chief Justice Marshall, said:

"Let the end be legitimate, let it be within the scope of the constitution, and all means which are appropriate, which are plainly adapted to that end, which are not prohibited, but consist with the letter and spirit of the constitution, are constitutional." M'Culloch v. Maryland [p. 20].

By this standard Congress acted within its power here. In view of the Commerce Clause it is not possible to deny that the aim of protecting interstate commerce from undue burdens is a legitimate end. In view of the Thirteenth, Fourteenth and Fifteenth Amendments, it is not possible to deny that the aim of protecting Negroes from discrimination is also a legitimate end. The means adopted to achieve these ends are also appropriate, plainly adopted to achieve them and not prohibited by the Constitution but consistent with both its letter and spirit.

Mr. Justice Douglas, concurring, said in part:

I.

Though I join the Court's opinion, I am somewhat reluctant here, as I was in Edwards v. California, 314 U. S. 160, to rest solely on the Commerce Clause. My reluctance is not due to any conviction that Congress lacks power to regulate commerce in the interests of human rights. It is rather my belief that the right of people to be free of state action that discriminates against them because of race, like the "right of persons to move freely from State to State" . . . "occupies a more protected position in our constitutional system than does the movement of cattle, fruit, steel and coal across state lines." Moreover, when we come to the problem of abatement in Hamm v. City of Rock Hill, 379 U. S. 306, the result reached by the Court is for me much more obvious as a protective measure under the Fourteenth Amendment than under the Commerce Clause. For the former deals with the constitutional status of the individual not with the impact on commerce of local activities or vice versa.

Hence I would prefer to rest on the assertion of legislative power contained in § 5 of the Fourteenth Amendment which states: "The Congress shall have power to enforce, by appropriate legislation, the provisions of this article"—a power which the Court concedes was exercised at least in part in this Act.

A decision based on the Fourteenth Amendment would have a more settling effect, making unnecessary litigation over whether a particular restaurant or inn is within the commerce definitions of the Act or whether a particular customer is an interstate traveler. Under my construction, the Act would apply to all customers in all the enumerated places of public accommodation. And that construction would put an end to all obstructionist strategies and finally close one door on a bitter chapter in American history.

Mr. Justice Goldberg, concurring, said in part:

I join in the opinions and judgements of the Court, since I agree "that the action of the Congress in the adoption of the Act as applied here . . . is within the power granted it by the Commerce Clause of the Constitution, as interpreted by this Court for 140 years. . . ."

In my concurring opinion in Bell v. Maryland, 378 U. S. 226, . . . I expressed my conviction that § 1 of the Fourteenth Amendment guarantees to all Americans the constitutional right "to be treated as equal members of the community with respect to public accommodations," and that "Congress [has] authority under § 5 of the Fourteenth Amendment, or under the Commerce Clause, Art I, § 8, to implement the rights protected by § 1 of the Fourteenth Amendment. In the give-and-take of the legislative process, Congress can fashion a law drawing the guidelines necessary and appropriate to facilitate practical administration and to distinguish between genuinely public and private accommodations." The challenged Act is just such a

4. *The Congressional Hearings.*

As we noted in Heart of Atlanta Motel both houses of Congress conducted prolonged hearings on the Act. And, as we said there, while no formal findings were made, which of course are not necessary, it is well that we make mention of the testimony at these hearings the better to understand the problem before Congress and determine whether the Act is a reasonable and appropriate means toward its solution. The record is replete with testimony of the burdens placed on interstate commerce by racial discrimination in restaurants. A comparison of per capita spending by Negroes in restaurants, theaters, and like establishments indicated less spending, after discounting income differences, in areas where discrimination is widely practiced. This condition, which was especially aggravated in the South, was attributed in the testimony of the Under Secretary of Commerce to racial segregation. . . . This diminutive spending springing from a refusal to serve Negroes and their total loss as customers has, regardless of the absence of direct evidence, a close connection to interstate commerce. The fewer customers a restaurant enjoys the less food it sells and consequently the less it buys. . . . In addition, the Attorney General testified that this type of discrimination imposed "an artificial restriction on the market" and interfered with the flow of merchandise. . . . In addition, there were many references to discriminatory situations causing wide unrest and having a depressant effect on general business conditions in the respective communities. . . .

Moreover there was an impressive array of testimony that discrimination in restaurants had a direct and highly restrictive effect upon interstate travel by Negroes. This resulted, it was said, because discriminatory practices prevent Negroes from buying prepared food served on the premises while on a trip, except in isolated and unkempt restaurants and under most unsatisfactory and often unpleasant conditions. This obviously discourages travel and obstructs interstate commerce for one can hardly travel without eating. Likewise, it was said, that discrimination deterred professional, as well as skilled, people from moving into areas where such practices occurred and thereby caused industry to be reluctant to establish there. . . .

We believe that this testimony afforded ample basis for the conclusion that established restaurants in such areas sold less interstate goods because of the discrimination, that interstate travel was obstructed directly by it, that business in general suffered and that many new businesses refrained from establishing there as a result of it. Hence the District Court was in error in concluding that there was no connection between discrimination and the movement of interstate commerce. The court's conclusion that such a connection is outside "common experience" flies in the face of stubborn fact.

It goes without saying that, viewed in isolation, the volume of food purchased by Ollie's Barbecue from sources supplied from out of state was insignificant when compared with the total foodstuffs moving in commerce. But, as our late Brother Jackson said for the Court in Wickard v. Filburn, 317 U. S. 111 (1942):

"That appellee's own contribution to the demand for wheat may be trivial by itself is not enough to remove him from the scope of federal regulation where, as here, his contribution, taken together with that of many others similarly situated, is far from trivial."

We noted in Heart of Atlanta Motel that a number of witnesses attested the fact that racial discrimination was not merely a state or regional problem but was one of nationwide scope. Against this background, we must conclude that while the focus of the legislation was on the individual restaurant's relation to interstate commerce, Congress appropriately considered the importance of that connection with the knowledge that the discrimination was but "representative of many others throughout the country, the total incidence of which if left unchecked may well become far-reaching in its harm to commerce." . . .

With this situation spreading as the record shows, Congress was not required to await the total dislocation of commerce. . . .

5. *The Power of Congress to Regulate Local Activities.*

Article I, § 8, cl 3, confers upon Congress the power "[t]o regulate Commerce . . . among the several States" and Clause 18 of the same Article grants it the power "[t]o make all Laws which shall be necessary and proper for carrying into Execution the foregoing Powers. . . ." This grant, as we have pointed out in Heart of Atlanta Motel "extends to those activities intrastate which so affect interstate commerce, or the exertion of the power of Congress over it, as to make regulation of them appropriate means to the attainment of a legitimate end, the effective execution of the granted power to regulate interstate commerce." . . . Much is said about a restaurant business being local but "even if appellee's activity be local and though it may not be regarded as commerce, it may still, whatever its nature, be reached by Congress if it exerts a substantial economic effect on interstate commerce. . . ." . . . The activities that are beyond the reach of Congress are "those which are completely within a particular State, which do not affect other States, and with which it is not necessary to interfere, for the purpose of executing some of the general powers of the government." . . . This rule is as good today as it was when Chief Justice Marshall laid it down almost a century and a half ago. . . .

Nor are the cases holding that interstate commerce ends when goods come to rest in the State of destination apposite here. That line of cases has been applied with reference to state taxation or regulation but not in the field of federal regulation.

The appellees contend that Congress has arbitrarily created a conclusive presumption that all restaurants meeting the criteria set out in the Act "affect commerce." Stated another way, they object to the omission of a provision for a case-by-case determination—judicial or administrative—that racial discrimination in a particular restaurant affects commerce.

But Congress' action in framing this Act was not unprecedented. In United States v. Darby, this Court held constitutional the Fair Labor Standards Act of 1938. There Congress determined that the payment of substandard wages to employees engaged in the production of goods for commerce, while not itself commerce, so inhibited it as to be subject to federal regulation. The appellees in that case argued, as do the appellees here, that the Act was invalid because it included no provision for an independent inquiry regarding the effect on commerce of substandard wages in a particular business. . . . But the Court rejected the argument, observing that:

[S]ometimes Congress itself has said that a particular activity affects the commerce, as it did in the present Act, the Safety Appliance Act and the Railway Labor Act. In passing on the validity of legislation of the class last mentioned the only function of courts is to determine whether the particular activity regulated or prohibited is within the reach of the federal power.

Here, as there, Congress has determined for itself that refusals of service to Negroes have imposed burdens both upon the interstate flow of food and upon the movement of products generally. Of course, the mere fact that Congress has said when particular activity shall be deemed to affect commerce does not preclude further examination by this Court. But where we find that the legislators, in light of the facts and testimony before them, have a rational basis for finding a chosen regulatory scheme necessary to the protection of commerce, our investigation is at an end. The only remaining question—one answered in the affirmative by the court below—is whether the particular restaurant either serves or offers to serve interstate travelers or serves food a substantial portion of which has moved in interstate commerce. . . .

Confronted as we are with the facts laid before Congress, we must conclude that it had a rational basis for finding that racial discrimination in restaurants had a direct and adverse effect on the free flow of interstate commerce. Insofar as the sections of the Act here relevant is concerned, §§ 201(b) (2) and (c), Congress prohibited discrimination only in those establishments having a close tie to interstate commerce, i.e., those, like the McClungs', serving food that has come from out of the State. We think in so doing that Congress acted well within its power to protect and foster commerce in extending the coverage of Title II only to those restaurants offering to serve interstate travelers or serving food, a substantial portion of which has moved in interstate commerce.

The absence of direct evidence connecting discriminatory restaurant service with the flow of interstate food, a factor on which the appellees place much reliance, is not, given the evidence as to the effect of such practices on other aspects of commerce, a crucial matter.

The power of Congress in this field is broad and sweeping; where it keeps within its sphere and violates no express constitutional limitation it has been the rule of this Court, going back almost to the founding days of the Republic, not to interfere. The Civil Rights Act of 1964, as here applied, we find to be plainly appropriate in the resolution of what the Congress found to be a national commercial problem of the first magnitude. We find it in no violation of any express limitations of the Constitution and we therefore declare it valid.

Justices Black, Douglas, and Goldberg concur.

GRISWOLD v. CONNECTICUT

381 U. S. 479; 14 L. Ed. 2d 510; 85 Sup. Ct. 1678. 1965.

While the Constitution prescribes certain limits on governmental power, these limits are in a continual state of change. As the Court engages in the endless process of interpreting the constitutional guarantees, certain pro-tections are withdrawn and others are added. Ordinarily this process occurs so slowly and subtly that only a careful observer can detect that a real change is actually taking place. While apparently applying the same princi-ples to a new set of facts, the Court is in reality altering the principle by an almost indistinguishable increment. Now and again the Court will find this process incapable of producing the results that it wants; a former interpre-tation or principle no longer fills what the Court sees as the needs of society, so that principle must be rejected and another put in its place. On such occasions the Court will overrule its previous interpretation of the Consti-tution and substitute another interpretation—usually one which has been long clamoring for acceptance. See, for example, Gideon v. Wainwright (p. 477), and the cases discussed on p. 152.

On very rare occasions, when what seems to the Court to be an important right cannot be brought comfortably under any existing constitutional guar-antee, the Court is forced to draw upon what it conceives to be the general or fundamental principles of the Constitution to supply the necessary pro-tection. In the early days little effort was made to tie such protection to specific parts of the document: in Loan Association v. Topeka, 20 Wallace 655 (1875), for example, the Court forbade spending tax money for private purposes on the ground that it violated limits on governmental power that "grow out of the essential nature of all free governments." With the evolution of the due process clause, this right and the celebrated "liberty of contract" became elements of due process of law. See pp. 260, 269.

In raising the "right of privacy" to the status of an independent right, the Court in the present case draws on a "penumbra" cast by a number of spe-cific constitutional rights, without resting the right squarely on any one of them. Three justices, in addition to endorsing the "penumbra" theory, also invoked the Ninth Amendment and Fourteenth Amendment due process. It is interesting to note that Mr. Justice Black, a staunch proponent of incor-porating the entire Bill of Rights into due process, here dissents on the ground that due process should be *limited* to what is in the Bill of Rights, as well as *extended* to it.

A test of the validity of Connecticut's birth-control statute first came to the Supreme Court in Tileston v. Ullman, 318 U. S. 44 (1943). Tileston, a physician, asked a declaratory judgment that the statute was void because it forbade him recommending contraceptives to three patients whose lives would be endangered by childbearing. The Court dismissed the case on the ground that no threatened injury to Tileston was shown. In 1961 a second challenge to the statute was dismissed for lack of a justiciable con-troversy, the Court finding that despite the notorious and common sale of contraceptives in Connecticut, no one had ever been tried for violating the statute; see Poe v. Ullman, 367 U. S. 497. The present case was brought after Connecticut abandoned, following the opening of birth-control clinics, its long-standing policy of non-enforcement.

Mr. Justice Douglas delivered the opinion of the Court, saying in part:

Appellant Griswold is Executive Director of the Planned Parenthood League of Connecticut. Appellant Buxton is a licensed physician and a professor at the Yale Medical School who served as Medical Director for the League at its Center in New Haven—a center open and operating from November 1 to November 10, 1961, when appellants were arrested.

They gave information, instruction, and medical advice to *married persons* as to the means of preventing conception. They examined the wife and prescribed the best contraceptive device or material for her use. Fees were usually charged, although some couples were serviced free.

The statutes whose constitutionality is involved in this appeal are §§ 53–32 and 54–196 of the General Statutes of Connecticut (1958 rev.). The former provides:

"Any person who uses any drug, medicinal article or instrument for the purpose of preventing conception shall be fined not less than fifty dollars or imprisoned not less than sixty days nor more than one year or be both fined and imprisoned."

Section 54–196 provides:

"Any person who assists, abets, counsels, causes, hires, or commands another to commit any offense may be prosecuted and punished as if he were the principal offender."

The appellants were found guilty as accessories and fined $100 each, against the claim that the accessory statute as so applied violated the Fourteenth Amendment. . . .

We think that appellants have standing to raise the constitutional rights of the married people with whom they had a professional relationship. Tileston v. Ullman, 318 U. S. 44, is different, for there the plaintiff seeking to represent others asked for a declaratory judgment. In that situation we thought that the requirements of standing should be strict, lest the standards of "case or controversy" in Article III of the Constitution become blurred. Here those doubts are removed by reason of a criminal conviction for serving married couples in violation of an aiding-and-abetting statute. Certainly the accessory should have standing to assert that the offense which he is charged with assisting is not, or cannot constitutionally be, a crime. . . .

Coming to the merits, we are met with a wide range of questions that implicate the Due Process Clause of the Fourteenth Amendment. Overtones of some arguments suggest that Lochner v. New York [p. 267] should be our guide. But we decline that invitation as we did in West Coast Hotel Co. v. Parrish, 300 U. S. 379. . . . We do not sit as a super-legislature to determine the wisdom, need, and propriety of laws that touch economic problems, business affairs, or social conditions. This law, however, operates directly on an intimate relation of husband and wife and their physician's role in one aspect of that relation.

The association of people is not mentioned in the Constitution nor in the Bill of Rights. The right to educate a child in a school of the parents' choice—whether public or private or parochial—is also not mentioned. Nor is the right to study any particular subject or any foreign language. Yet the First Amendment has been construed to include certain of those rights.

By Pierce v. Society of Sisters [p. 193] the right to educate one's children as one chooses is made applicable to the States by the force of the First and Fourteenth Amendments. By Meyer v. Nebraska [262 U. S. 390] the same dignity is given the right to study the German language in a private school. In other words, the State may not, consistently with the spirit of the First Amendment, contract the spectrum of available knowledge. The right of freedom of speech and press includes not only the right to utter or to print, but the right to distribute, the right to receive, the right to read . . . and freedom of inquiry, freedom of thought, and freedom to teach . . . —indeed the freedom of the entire university community. . . . Without those peripheral rights the specific rights would be less secure. And so we reaffirm the principle of the Pierce and the Meyer cases.

In NAACP v. Alabama, 357 U. S. 449, we protected the "freedom to associate and privacy in one's association," noting that freedom of association was a peripheral First Amendment right. Disclosure of membership lists of a constitutionally valid association, we held, was invalid "as entailing the likelihood of a substantial restraint upon the exercise by petitioner's members of their right to freedom of association." In other words, the First Amendment has a penumbra where privacy is protected from governmental intrusion. In like context, we have protected forms of "association" that are not political in the customary sense but pertain to the social, legal, and economic benefit of the members. NAACP v. Button, 371 U. S. 415. In Schware v. Board of Bar Examiners, 353 U. S. 232, we held it not permissible to bar a lawyer from practice, because he had once been a member of the Communist Party. The man's "association with that Party" was not shown to be "anything more than a political faith in a political party" and was not action of a kind proving bad moral character.

Those cases involved more than the "right of assembly"—a right that extends to all irrespective of their race or ideology. . . . The right of "association," like the right of belief. . . . is more than the right to attend a meeting; it includes the right to express one's attitudes or philosophies by membership in a group or by affiliation with it or by other lawful means. Association in that context is a form of expression of opinion; and while it is not expressly included in the First Amendment its existence is necessary in making the express guarantees fully meaningful.

The foregoing cases suggest that specific guarantees in the Bill of Rights have penumbras, formed by emanations from those guarantees that help give them life and substance. . . . Various guarantees create zones of privacy. The right of association contained in the penumbra of the First Amendment is one, as we have seen. The Third Amendment in its prohibition against the quartering of soldiers "in any house" in time of peace without the consent of the owner is another facet of that privacy. The Fourth Amendment explicitly affirms the "right of the people to be secure in their persons, houses, papers, and effects, against unreasonable searches and seizures." The Fifth Amendment in its Self-Incrimination Clause enables the citizen to create a zone of privacy which government may not force him to surrender to his detriment. The Ninth Amendment provides: "The enumeration in the Constitution, of certain rights, shall not be construed to deny or disparage others retained by the people." . . .

The present case, then, concerns a relationship lying within the zone of privacy created by several fundamental constitutional guarantees. And it concerns a law which, in forbidding the *use* of contraceptives rather than regulating their manufacture or sale, seeks to achieve its goals by means having a maximum destructive impact upon that relationship. Such a law cannot stand in light of the familiar principle, so often applied by this Court, that a "governmental purpose to control or prevent activities constitutionally subject to state regulation may not be achieved by means which sweep unnecessarily broadly and thereby invade the area of protected freedoms." NAACP v. Alabama, 377 U. S. 288. Would we allow the police to search the sacred precincts of marital bedrooms for telltale signs of the use of contraceptives? The very idea is repulsive to the notions of privacy surrounding the marriage relationship.

We deal with a right of privacy older than the Bill of Rights—older than our political parties, older than our school system. Marriage is a coming together for better or for worse, hopefully enduring, and intimate to the degree of being sacred. It is an association that promotes a way of life, not causes; a harmony in living, not political faiths; a bilateral loyalty, not commercial or social projects. Yet it is an association for as noble a purpose as any involved in our prior decisions.

Reversed.

Mr. Justice Goldberg, whom the Chief Justice and Mr. Justice Brennan join, concurring, said in part:

I agree with the Court that Connecticut's birth-control law unconstitutionally intrudes upon the right of marital privacy, and I join in its opinion and judgment. Although I have not accepted the view that "due process" as used in the Fourteenth Amendment incorporates all of the first eight Amendments, . . . I do agree that the concept of liberty protects those personal rights that are fundamental, and is not confined to the specific terms of the Bill of Rights. My conclusion that the concept of liberty is not so restricted and that it embraces the right of marital privacy though that right is not mentioned explicitly in the Constitution is supported both by numerous decisions of this Court, referred to in the Court's opinion, and by the language and history of the Ninth Amendment. . . .

While this Court has had little occasion to interpret the Ninth Amendment, "[i]t cannot be presumed that any clause in the constitution is intended to be without effect." Marbury v. Madison [p. 323]. . . . To hold that a right so basic and fundamental and so deep-rooted in our society as the right of privacy in marriage may be infringed because that right is not guaranteed in so many words by the first eight amendments to the Constitution is to ignore the Ninth Amendment and to give it no effect whatsoever. Moreover, a judicial construction that this fundamental right is not protected by the Constitution because it is not mentioned in explicit terms by one of the first eight amendments or elsewhere in the Constitution would violate the Ninth Amendment, which specifically states that "[t]he enumeration in the Constitution, of certain rights, shall not be *construed* to deny or disparage others retained by the people." (Emphasis added.)

. . . I do not take the position of my Brother Black . . . that the entire Bill of Rights is incorporated in the Fourteenth Amendment, and I do not mean to imply that the Ninth Amendment is applied against the States by the Fourteenth. Nor do I mean to state that the Ninth Amendment constitutes an independent source of rights protected from infringement by either the States or Federal Government. Rather, the Ninth Amendment shows a belief of the Constitution's authors that fundamental rights exist that are not expressly enumerated in the first eight amendments and an intent that the list of rights included there not be deemed exhaustive. . . .

. . . In sum, the Ninth Amendment simply lends strong support to the view that the "liberty" protected by the Fifth and Fourteenth Amendments from infringement by the Federal Government or the States is not restricted to rights specifically mentioned in the first eight amendments.

Mr. Justice Harlan, concurring in the judgment, said in part:

I fully agree with the judgment of reversal, but find myself unable to join the Court's opinion. The reason is that it seems to me to evince an approach to this case very much like that taken by my Brothers Black and Stewart in dissent, namely: the Due Process Clause of the Fourteenth Amendment does not touch this Connecticut statute unless the enactment is found to violate some right assured by the letter or penumbra of the Bill of Rights.

In other words, what I find implicit in the Court's opinion is that the "incorporation" doctrine may be used to *restrict* the reach of Fourteenth Amendment Due Process. For me this is just as unacceptable constitutional doctrine as is the use of the "incorporation" approach to *impose* upon the States all the requirements of the Bill of Rights as found in the provisions of the first eight amendments and in the decisions of this Court interpreting them. . . .

In my view, the proper constitutional inquiry in this case is whether this Connecticut statute infringes the Due Process Clause of the Fourteenth Amendment because the enactment violates basic values "implicit in the concept of ordered liberty," Palko v. Connecticut [p. 151].

. . . While the relevant inquiry may be aided by resort to one or more of the provisions of the Bill of Rights, it is not dependent on them or any of their radiations. The Due Process Clause of the Fourteenth Amendment stands, in my opinion, on its own bottom.

Mr. Justice White, concurring in the judgment, said in part:

As I read the opinions of the Connecticut courts and the argument of Connecticut in this Court, the State claims but one justification for its anti-use statute. . . . There is no serious contention that Connecticut thinks the use of artificial or external methods of contraception immoral or unwise in itself, or that the anti-use statute is founded upon any policy of promoting population expansion. Rather, the statute is said to serve the State's policy against all forms of promiscuous or illicit sexual relationships, be they premarital or extramarital, concededly a permissible and legitimate legislative goal.

Without taking issue with the premise that the fear of conception operates as a deterrent to such relationships in addition to the criminal proscriptions Connecticut has against such conduct, I wholly fail to see how the ban on the use of contraceptives by married couples in any way reinforces the State's ban on illicit sexual relationships. . . . Connecticut does not bar the importation or possession of contraceptive devices; they are not considered contraband material under state law . . . and their availability in that State is not seriously disputed. . . . Moreover, it would appear that the sale of contraceptives to prevent disease is plainly legal under Connecticut law.

In these circumstances one is rather hard pressed to explain how the ban on use by married persons in any way prevents use of such devices by persons engaging in illicit sexual relations and thereby contributes to the State's policy against such relationships. Neither the state courts nor the State before the bar of this Court has tendered such an explanation. . . . Perhaps the theory is that the flat ban on use prevents married people from possessing contraceptives and without the ready availability of such devices for use in the marital relationship, there will be no or less temptation to use them in extramarital ones. This reasoning rests on the premise that married people will comply with the ban in regard to their marital relationship, notwithstanding total nonenforcement in this context and apparent nonenforcibility, but will not comply with criminal statutes prohibiting extramarital affairs and the anti-use statute in respect to illicit sexual relationships, a premise whose validity has not been demonstrated and whose intrinsic validity is not very evident. . . . I find nothing in this record justifying the sweeping scope of this statute, with its telling effect on the freedoms of married persons, and therefore conclude that it deprives such persons of liberty without due process of law.

Mr. Justice Black, with whom Mr. Justice Stewart joins, dissented, saying in part:

The Court talks about a constitutional "right of privacy" as though there is some constitutional provision or provisions forbidding any law ever to be passed which might abridge the "privacy" of individuals. But there is not. There are, of course, guarantees in certain specific constitutional provisions which are designed in part to protect privacy at certain times and places with respect to certain activities. Such, for example, is the Fourth Amendment's guarantee against "unreasonable searches and seizures." But I think it belittles that Amendment to talk about it as though it protects nothing but "privacy." To treat it that way is to give it a niggardly interpretation, not the kind of liberal reading I think any Bill of Rights provision should be given. The average man would very likely not have his feelings soothed any more by having his property seized openly than by having it seized privately and by stealth. He simply wants his property left alone. And a person can be just as much, if not more, irritated, annoyed and injured by an unceremonious public arrest by a policeman as he is by a seizure in the privacy of his office or home.

One of the most effective ways of diluting or expanding a constitutionally guaranteed right is to substitute for the crucial word or words of a constitutional guarantee another word or words more or less flexible and more or less restricted in meaning. This fact is well illustrated by the use of the term "right of privacy" as a comprehensive substitute for the Fourth Amendment's guarantee against "unreasonable searches and seizures." "Privacy" is a broad, abstract and ambiguous concept which can easily be shrunken in meaning but which can also, on the other hand, easily be interpreted as a constitutional ban against many things other than searches and seizures. I have expressed the view many times that First Amendment freedoms, for example, have suffered from a failure of the courts to stick to the simple language of the First Amendment in construing it, instead of invoking multitudes of words substituted for those the Framers used. . . .

I realize that many good and able men have eloquently spoken and written, sometimes in rhapsodical strains, about the duty of this Court to keep the Constitution in tune with the times. The idea is that the Constitution must be changed from time to time and that this Court is charged with a duty to make those changes. For myself, I must with all deference reject that philosophy. The Constitution makers knew the need for change and provided for it. Amendments suggested by the people's elected representatives can be submitted to the people or their selected agents for ratification. That method of change was good for our Fathers, and being somewhat old-fashioned I must add it is good enough for me. And so, I cannot rely on the Due Process Clause or the Ninth Amendment or any mysterious and uncertain natural law concept as a reason for striking down this state law. The Due Process Clause with an "arbitrary and capricious" or "shocking to the conscience" formula was liberally used by this Court to strike down economic legislation in the early decades of this century, threatening, many people thought, the tranquility and stability of the Nation. See, e.g., Lochner v. New York [p. 267]. That formula, based on subjective considerations of "natural justice," is no less dangerous when used to enforce this Court's views about personal rights than those about economic rights. I had thought that we had laid that formula, as a means for striking down state legislation, to rest once and for all in cases like West Coast Hotel Co. v. Parrish [p. 271].

Mr. Justice Stewart wrote a dissenting opinion in which Mr. Justice Black joined.

SOUTH CAROLINA v. KATZENBACH
383 U. S. 301; 15 L. Ed. 2d 769; 86 Sup. Ct. 803. 1966.

In a show of judicial activism unparalleled in its history the Supreme Court has, in the second half of the twentieth century, sparked a constitutional revolution in the field of civil rights. With bold strokes it has struck at injustices so long intrenched and accepted by the public that they seemed to defy remedy: race discrimination in the use of public facilities (see the School Segregation Cases, p. 249); unfair treatment of suspected criminals (see Gideon v. Wainwright, p. 477); and systematic underrepresentation in the legislative process of urban dwellers (see Reynolds v. Sims, p. 487). While the aim of the Court has been to increase the protection of individuals, the result has been a sharp limitation upon the power of the states; for it is state segregation, state treatment of accused persons, and state districting and apportionment policies that have come under fire. The demand that the states meet new and higher standards of fairness has denied them prerogatives which they had exercised with impunity for over 150 years.

Impressive as this judicial revolution is, however, it is unprecedented only in its scope. We have long accepted the role of the judiciary as the protector of individual rights against government, and we praise or villify the Supreme Court as it upholds, or fails to uphold, those rights we consider fundamental. But congressional and judicial cooperation in such a revolutionary movement is unheard of in the nation's history. During the vindictive, passion-torn days of Reconstruction it was Congress which sought to protect minorities from mistreatment by their state governments, but the laws it enacted, together with three constitutional amendments, met with judicial hostility; see the Slaughterhouse Cases, p. 52, and Norris v. Alabama, p. 243.

Congress has not, of course, sided with the Court in all of its recent battles. To date its activity has been limited to two aspects of Negro discrimination: the problem of racial segregation, discussed in the Civil Rights Act Cases, p. 524, and the problem of voting discrimination. The Civil Rights Act of 1965, held valid in the present case, is the result of nearly a decade of struggle. Timid and experimental, the early laws were limited to federal elections alone and relied almost entirely on the courts for their operation. The Civil Rights Act of 1957 forbade anyone to interfere with a person's right to vote and authorized the Attorney General to seek an injunction to prevent such interference where it was occurring or seemed likely to occur. In United States v. Raines, 362 U. S. 17 (1960), the act was held valid as applied to voting registrars in Georgia who were discriminating on racial grounds.

Failure of these measures to increase Negro voting substantially led Congress to strengthen them in the Civil Rights Act of 1960, which made it a crime to obstruct the exercise of (voting) rights granted by court order and gave the Attorney General access to voting records for the purpose of determining if a pattern of discrimination existed. In addition, the district courts were authorized both to appoint voting referees to hear complaints and to qualify or to have the voting referees qualify persons to vote in areas where a pattern of discrimination resulted in disfranchising them. Failure to permit a person so qualified to vote was contempt of court.

Continued state resistance, abetted by a lack of aggressiveness on the part of local United States attorneys and district courts, still prevented any marked increase in Negro voter registration and led to still stronger voting legislation in the Civil Rights Act of 1964. In Title I of this omnibus measure Congress forbade applying different literacy tests to different applicants, prohibited disqualifying applicants for immaterial errors, and made a sixth-grade education in an English-language school prima facie evidence of literacy for purposes of voting in federal elections. Provision was made for getting quick decisions from federal courts in voter registration cases, some of which had dragged on for over a year. But again, state ingenuity in devising delaying tactics kept Negro registration to a trickle, and again Congress acted.

While the Voting Rights Act of 1965 falls short of providing complete federal election machinery, it harnesses federal power to prevent voting discrimination to a degree never before attempted. Singling out by the use of a "triggering" formula those areas in which voting discrimination is most flagrant, it abolishes literacy tests, waives accumulated poll taxes, and forbids the state to institute new voting requirements until the courts or the Attorney General has found them non-discriminatory. Furthermore, federal examiners can be appointed to list qualified applicants and declare them eligible to vote in all elections, state as well as federal, and federal poll watchers can be assigned to see that their votes are actually counted. If a qualified person is denied access to the polls, United States officials may permit him to cast his ballot and include the vote in the official totals.

Even in areas not singled out by the triggering formula, the Attorney General may institute proceedings to guarantee voting rights, in which case federal examiners and poll watchers may be appointed, all voting tests and devices may be suspended, and the courts may retain jurisdiction of the proceedings to ensure that no new and discriminatory voting rules are adopted.

The only part of the act to be directed primarily at non-southern voting practices is a section which outlaws forbidding a person to vote because he cannot read and write English. Directed primarily at New York's vast Spanish-speaking Puerto Rican population, the section was introduced by Senators Javits and Kennedy of New York and declares to be literate any person who, in any American flag school and regardless of the language of instruction, has completed the sixth grade, or such higher grade as is used by the state to qualify its voters. In the elections of 1965 Herman Badillo, a Puerto Rican, defeated incumbent Joseph F. Periconi for re-election as Bronx Borough President by a margin of 2,000 votes. Voting in this election were over 4,000 Spanish-speaking voters who had been enfranchised by this provision of the act. Following the election, a three-judge court in the District of Columbia held the section invalid on the ground that the power to set voting qualifications was reserved to the states. The Supreme Court tentatively agreed to review the decision; Katzenbach v. Morgan, 382 U. S. 1007 (1966).

Mr. Chief Justice Warren delivered the opinion of the Court, saying in part:

By leave of the Court, South Carolina has filed a bill of complaint, seeking a declaration that selected provisions of the Voting Rights Act of 1965 violate the Federal Constitution, and asking for an injunction against enforcement of these provisions by the Attorney General. Original jurisdiction is founded on the presence of a controversy between a State and a citizen of another State under Art. III, § 2, of the Constitution. . . .

The Voting Rights Act was designed by Congress to banish the blight of racial discrimination in voting, which has infected the electoral process in parts of our country for nearly a century. The Act creates stringent new remedies for voting discrimination where it persists on a pervasive scale, and in addition the statute strengthens existing remedies for pockets of voting discrimination elsewhere in the country. Congress assumed the power to prescribe these remedies from § 2 of the Fifteenth Amendment, which authorizes the national legislature to effectuate by "appropriate" measures the constitutional prohibition against racial discrimination in voting. We hold that the sections of the Act which are properly before us are an appropriate means for carrying out Congress' constitutional responsibilities and are consonant with all other provisions of the Constitution. We therefore deny South Carolina's request that enforcement of these sections of the Act be enjoined.

I.

The constitutional propriety of the Voting Rights Act of 1965 must be judged with reference to the historical experience which it reflects. Before enacting the measure, Congress explored with great care the problem of racial discrimination in voting. The House and Senate Committees on the Judiciary each held hearings for nine days and received testimony from a total of 67 witnesses. More than three full days were consumed discussing the bill on the floor of the House, while the debate in the Senate covered 26 days in all. At the close of these deliberations, the verdict of both chambers was overwhelming. The House approved the Act by a vote of 328–74, and the measure passed the Senate by a margin of 79–18.

Two points emerge vividly from the voluminous legislative history of the Act contained in the committee hearings and floor debates. First: Congress felt itself confronted by an insidious and pervasive evil which had been perpetuated in certain parts of our country through unremitting and ingenious defiance of the Constitution. Second: Congress concluded that the unsuccessful remedies which it had prescribed in the past would have to be replaced by sterner and more elaborate measures in order to satisfy the clear commands of the Fifteenth Amendment. We pause here to summarize the majority reports of the House and Senate Committees, which document in considerable detail the factual basis for these reactions by Congress. . . . [The Court here summarizes the systematic efforts of southern states to disfranchise the Negro.]

According to the results of recent Justice Department voting suits, . . . [discriminatory application of voting tests is now the principal] method used to bar Negroes from the polls. Discriminatory administration of voting qualifications has been found in all eight Alabama cases, in all nine Louisiana cases, and in all nine Mississippi cases which have gone to final judgment. Moreover, in almost all of these cases, the courts have held that the discrimination was pursuant to a widespread "pattern or practice." White applicants for registration have often been excused altogether from the literacy and understanding tests or have been given easy versions, have received extensive help from voting officials, and have been registered despite serious errors in their answers. Negroes, on the other hand, have typically been required to pass difficult versions of all the tests, without any outside assistance and without the slightest error. The good morals requirement is so vague and subjective that it has constituted an open invitation to abuse at the hands of voting officials. Negroes obliged to obtain vouchers from registered voters have found it virtually impossible to comply in areas where almost no Negroes are on the rolls.

In recent years, Congress has repeatedly tried to cope with the problem by facilitating case-by-case litigation against voting discrimination. The Civil Rights Act of 1957 authorized the Attorney General to seek injunctions against public and private interference with the right to vote on racial grounds. Perfecting amendments in the Civil Rights Act of 1960 permitted the joinder of States as party defendants, gave the Attorney General access to local voting records, and authorized courts to register voters in areas of systematic discrimination. Title I of the Civil Rights Act of 1964 expedited the hearing of voting cases before three-judge courts and outlawed some of the tactics used to disqualify Negroes from voting in federal elections.

Despite the earnest efforts of the Justice Department and of many federal judges, these new laws have done little to cure the problem of voting discrimination. According to estimates by the Attorney General during hearings on the Act, registration of voting age Negroes in Alabama rose only from 10.2% to 19.4% between 1958 and 1964; in Louisiana it barely inched ahead from 31.7% to 31.8% between 1956 and 1965; and in Mississippi it increased only from 4.4% to 6.4% between 1954 and 1964. In each instance, registration of voting age whites ran roughly 50 percentage points or more ahead of Negro registration.

The previous legislation has proved ineffective for a number of reasons. Voting suits are unusually onerous to prepare, sometimes requiring as many as 6,000 man-hours spent combing through registration records in preparation for trial. Litigation has been exceedingly slow, in part because of the ample opportunities for delay afforded voting officials and others involved in the proceedings. Even when favorable decisions have finally been obtained, some of the States affected have merely switched to discriminatory devices not covered by the federal decrees or have enacted difficult new tests designed to prolong the existing disparity between white and Negro registration. Alternatively, certain local officials have defied and evaded court orders or have simply closed their registration offices to freeze the voting rolls. The provision of the 1960 law authorizing registration by federal officers has had little impact on local maladministration because of its procedural complexities.

During the hearings and debates on the Act, Selma, Alabama, was repeatedly referred to as the pre-eminent example of the ineffectiveness of existing legislation. In Dallas County, of which Selma is the seat, there were four years of litigation by the Justice Department and two findings by the federal courts of widespread voting discrimination. Yet in those four years, Negro registration rose only from 156 to 383, although there are approximately 15,000 Negroes of voting age in the county. Any possibility that these figures were attributable to political apathy was dispelled by the protest demonstrations in Selma in the early months of 1965. . . .

II.

The Voting Rights Act of 1965 reflects Congress' firm intention to rid the country of racial discrimination in voting. The heart of the

Act is a complex scheme of stringent remedies aimed at areas where voting discrimination has been most flagrant. . . .

At the outset, we emphasize that only some of the many portions of the Act are properly before us. . . .

Coverage Formula.

The remedial sections of the Act assailed by South Carolina automatically apply to any State, or to any separate political subdivision such as a county or parish, for which two findings have been made: (1) the Attorney General has determined that on November 1, 1964, it maintained a "test or device," and (2) the Director of the Census has determined that less than 50% of its voting age residents were registered on November 1, 1964, or voted in the presidential election of November 1964. . . . As used throughout the Act, the phrase "test or device" means any requirement that a registrant or voter must "(1) demonstrate the ability to read, write, understand, or interpret any matter, (2) demonstrate any educational achievement or his knowledge of any particular subject, (3) possess good moral character, or (4) prove his qualifications by the voucher of registered voters or members of any class." § 4 (c).

Statutory coverage of a State or political subdivision under § 4 (b) is terminated if the area obtains a declaratory judgment from the District Court for the District of Columbia, determining that tests and devices have not been used during the preceding five years to abridge the franchise on racial grounds. The Attorney General shall consent to entry of the judgment if he has no reason to believe that the facts are otherwise. . . .

South Carolina was brought within the coverage formula of the Act on August 7, 1965, pursuant to appropriate administrative determinations which have not been challenged in this proceeding. On the same day, coverage was also extended to Alabama, Alaska, Georgia, Louisiana, Mississippi, Virginia, 26 counties in North Carolina, and one county in Arizona. Two more counties in Arizona, one county in Hawaii, and one county in Idaho were added to the list on November 19, 1965. Thus far Alaska, the three Arizona counties, and the single county in Idaho have asked the District Court for the District of Columbia to grant a declaratory judgment terminating statutory coverage.

Suspension of Tests.

In a State or political subdivision covered by § 4 (b) of the Act, no person may be denied the right to vote in any election because of his failure to comply with a "test or device." § 4 (a).

On account of this provision, South Carolina is temporarily barred from enforcing the portion of its voting laws which requires every applicant for registration to show that he:

"Can both read and write any section of [the State] Constitution submitted to [him] by the registration officer or can show that he owns, and has paid all taxes collectable during the previous year on, property in this State assessed at three hundred dollars or more." . . .

Similar tests and devices have been temporarily suspended in the other sections of the country listed above.

Review of New Rules.

In a State or political subdivision covered by § 4 (b) of the Act, no person may be denied the right to vote in any election because of his failure to comply with a voting qualification or procedure different from those in force on November 1, 1964. This suspension of new rules is terminated, however, under either of the following circumstances: (1) if the area has submitted the rules to the Attorney General, and he has not interposed an objection within 60 days, or (2) if the area has obtained a declaratory judgment from the District Court for the District of Columbia, determining that the rules will not abridge the franchise on racial grounds. These declaratory judgment actions are to be heard by a three-judge panel, with direct appeal to this Court. § 5.

South Carolina altered its voting laws in 1965 to extend the closing hour at polling places from 6 p. m. to 7 p. m. The State has not sought judicial review of this change in the District Court for the District of Columbia, nor has it submitted the new rule to the Attorney General for his scrutiny, although at our hearing the Attorney General announced that he does not challenge the amendment. There are indications in the record that other sections of the country listed above have also altered their voting laws since November 1, 1964.

Federal Examiners.

In any political subdivision covered by § 4 (b) of the Act, the Civil Service Commission shall appoint voting examiners whenever the Attorney General certifies either of the following facts: (1) that he has received meritorious written complaints from at least 20 residents alleging that they have been disenfranchised under color of law because of their race, or (2) that the appointment of examiners is otherwise necessary to effectuate the guarantees of the Fifteenth Amendment. In making the latter determination, the Attorney General must consider, among other factors, whether the registration ratio of non-whites to whites seems reasonably attributable to racial discrimination, or whether there is substantial evidence of good-faith efforts to comply with the Fifteenth Amendment. § 6 (b). . . .

The examiners who have been appointed are to test the voting qualifications of applicants according to regulations of the Civil Service Commission prescribing times, places, procedures, and forms. §§ 7 (a) and 9 (b). Any person who meets the voting requirements of state law, insofar as these have not been suspended by the Act, must promptly be placed on a list of eligible voters. . . . Any person listed by an examiner is entitled to vote in all elections held more than 45 days after his name has been transmitted. § 7 (b). . . .

On October 30, 1965, the Attorney General certified the need for federal examiners in two South Carolina counties, and examiners appointed by the Civil Service Commission have been serving there since November 8, 1965. Examiners have also been assigned to 11 counties in Alabama, five parishes in Louisiana, and 19 counties in Mississippi.

III.

These provisions of the Voting Rights Act of 1965 are challenged on the fundamental ground that they exceed the powers of Congress and encroach on an area reserved to the States by the Constitution. . . .

Has Congress exercised its powers under the Fifteenth Amendment in an appropriate manner with relation to the States?

The ground rules for resolving this question are clear. The language and purpose of the Fifteenth Amendment, the prior decisions construing its several provisions, and the general doctrines of constitutional interpretation, all point to one fundamental principle. As against the reserved powers of the States, Congress may use any rational means to effectuate the constitutional prohibition of racial discrimination in voting. Cf. our rulings last Term, sustaining Title II of the Civil Rights Act of 1964, in Heart of Atlanta Motel v. United States, and Katzenbach v. McClung [p. 524]. We turn now to a more detailed description of the standards which govern our review of the Act.

Section 1 of the Fifteenth Amendment declares that "the right of citizens of the United States to vote shall not be denied or abridged by the United States or by any State on account of race, color, or previous condition of servitude." This declaration has always been treated as self-executing and has repeatedly been construed, without further legislative specification, to invalidate state voting qualifications or procedures which are discriminatory on their face or in practice. . . . Guinn v. United States, . . . Smith v. Allwright [p. 212]. The gist of the matter is that the Fifteenth Amendment supersedes contrary exertions of state power. . . .

South Carolina contends that the cases cited above are precedents only for the authority of the judiciary to strike down state statutes and procedures—that to allow an exercise of this authority by Congress would be to rob the courts of their rightful constitutional role. On the contrary, § 2 of the Fifteenth Amendment expressly declares that "Congress shall have the power to enforce this article by appropriate legislation." By adding this authorization, the Framers indicated that Congress was to be chiefly responsible for implementing the rights created in § 1. . . .

Congress has repeatedly exercised these powers in the past, and its enactments have repeatedly been upheld. For recent examples, see the Civil Rights Act of 1957, which was sustained in United States v. Raines, 362 U. S. 17. . . .

The basic test to be applied in a case involving § 2 of the Fifteenth Amendment is the same as in all cases concerning the express powers of Congress with relation to the reserved powers of the States. Chief Justice Marshall laid down the classic formulation, 50 years before the Fifteenth Amendment was ratified:

"Let the end be legitimate, let it be within the scope of the constitution, and all means which are appropriate, which are plainly adapted to that end, which are not prohibited, but consist with the letter and spirit of the constitution, are constitutional." McCulloch v. Maryland [p. 20].

The Court has subsequently echoed his language in describing each of the Civil War Amendments:

"Whatever legislation is appropriate, that is, adapted to carry out the objects the amendments have in view, whatever tends to enforce submission to the prohibitions they contain, and to secure to all persons the enjoyment of perfect equality of civil rights and the equal protection of the laws against State denial or invasion, if not prohibited, is brought within the domain of congressional power." Ex parte Virginia, 100 U. S., at 345–346. . . .

We therefore reject South Carolina's argument that Congress may appropriately do no more than to forbid violations of the Fifteenth Amendment in general terms—that the task of fashioning specific remedies or of applying them to particular localities must necessarily be left entirely to the courts. Congress is not circumscribed by any such artificial rules under § 2 of the Fifteenth Amendment. In the oft-repeated words of Chief Justice Marshall, referring to another specific legislative authorization in the Constitution, "This power, like all others vested in Congress, is complete in itself, may be exercised to its utmost extent, and acknowledges no limitations, other than are prescribed in the constitution." Gibbons v. Ogden [p. 396].

IV.

Congress exercised its authority under the Fifteenth Amendment in an inventive manner when it enacted the Voting Rights Act of 1965. First: The measure prescribes remedies for voting discrimination which go into effect without any need for prior adjudication. This was clearly a legitimate response to the problem, for which there is ample precedent under other constitutional provisions. . . . Congress had found that case-by-case litigation was inadequate to combat widespread and persistent discrimination in voting, because of the inordinate amount of time and energy required to overcome the obstructionist tactics invariably encountered in these lawsuits. After enduring nearly a century of systematic resistance to the Fifteenth Amendment, Congress might well decide to shift the advantage of time and inertia from the perpetrators of the evil to its victims. The question remains, of course, whether the specific remedies prescribed in the Act were an appropriate means of combatting the evil, and to this question we shall presently address ourselves.

Second: The Act intentionally confines these remedies to a small number of States and political subdivisions which in most instances were familiar to Congress by name. This, too, was a permissible method of dealing with the problem. Congress had learned that substantial voting discrimination presently occurs in certain sections of the country, and it knew no way of accurately forecasting whether the evil might spread elsewhere in the future. In acceptable legislative fashion, Congress chose to limit its attention to the geographic areas where immediate action seemed necessary. . . . The doctrine of the equality of States, invoked by South Carolina, does not bar this approach, for that doctrine applies only to the terms upon which States are admitted to the Union, and not to the remedies for local evils which have subsequently appeared. See Coyle v. Smith [p. 39]. . . .

Coverage Formula.

We now consider the related question of whether the specific States and political subdivisions within § 4 (b) of the Act were an appropriate target for the new remedies. Congress began work with reliable evidence of actual voting discrimination in a great majority of the States and political subdivisions affected by the new remedies of the Act. The formula eventually evolved to describe these areas was relevant to the problem of voting discrimination. . . .

To be specific, the new remedies of the Act are imposed on three States—Alabama, Louisiana, and Mississippi—in which federal courts have repeatedly found substantial voting discrimination. Section 4 (b) of the Act also embraces two other States—Georgia and South Carolina—plus large portions of a third State—North Carolina—for which there was more fragmentary evidence of recent voting discrimination mainly adduced by the Justice Department and the Civil Rights Commission. All of these areas were appropriately subjected to the new remedies. In identifying past evils, Congress obviously may avail itself of information from any probative source. . . .

The areas listed above, for which there was evidence of actual voting discrimination, share two characteristics incorporated by Congress into the coverage formula: the use of tests and devices for voter registration, and a voting rate in the 1964 presidential election at least

12 points below the national average. Tests and devices are relevant to voting discrimination because of their long history as a tool for perpetrating the evil; a low voting rate is pertinent for the obvious reason that widespread disenfranchisement must inevitably affect the number of actual voters. Accordingly, the coverage formula is rational in both practice and theory. It was therefore permissible to impose the new remedies on the few remaining States and political subdivisions covered by the formula, at least in the absence of proof that they have been free of substantial voting discrimination in recent years. . . .

It is irrelevant that the coverage formula excludes certain localities which do not employ voting tests and devices but for which there is evidence of voting discrimination by other means. Congress had learned that widespread and persistent discrimination in voting during recent years has typically entailed the misuse of tests and devices, and this was the evil for which the new remedies were specifically designed. . . . Legislation need not deal with all phases of a problem in the same way, so long as the distinctions drawn have some basis in practical experience. . . . There are no States or political subdivisions exempted from coverage under § 4 (b) in which the record reveals recent racial discrimination involving tests and devices. This fact confirms the rationality of the formula.

Acknowledging the possibility of overbreadth, the Act provides for termination of special statutory coverage at the behest of States and political subdivisions in which the danger of substantial voting discrimination has not materialized during the preceding five years. . . .

South Carolina contends that these termination procedures are a nullity because they impose an impossible burden of proof upon States and political subdivisions entitled to relief. As the Attorney General pointed out during hearings on the Act, however, an area need do no more than to submit affidavits from voting officials, asserting that they have not been guilty of racial discrimination through the use of tests and devices during the past five years, and then to refute whatever evidence to the contrary may be adduced by the Federal Government. Section 4 (d) further assures that an area need not disprove each isolated instance of voting discrimination in order to obtain relief in the termination proceedings. The burden of proof is therefore quite bearable, particularly since the relevant facts relating to the conduct of voting officials are peculiarly within the knowledge of the States and political subdivisions themselves. . . .

Suspension of Tests.

We now arrive at consideration of the specific remedies prescribed by the Act for areas included within the coverage formula. South Carolina assails the temporary suspension of existing voting qualifications. . . . The record shows that in most of the States covered by the Act, including South Carolina, various tests and devices have been instituted with the purpose of disenfranchising Negroes, have been framed in such a way as to facilitate this aim, and have been administered in a discriminatory fashion for many years. Under these circumstances, the Fifteenth Amendment has clearly been violated. . . .

The Act suspends literacy tests and similar devices for a period of five years from the last occurrence of substantial voting discrimination. This was a legitimate response to the problem, for which there is ample precedent in Fifteenth Amendment cases. *Ibid.* Underlying the response was the feeling that States and political subdivisions which had been allowing white illiterates to vote for years could not sincerely complain about "dilution" of their electorates through the registration of Negro illiterates. Congress knew that continuance of the tests and devices in use at the present time, no matter how fairly administered in the future, would freeze the effect of past discrimination in favor of unqualified white registrants. Congress permissibly rejected the alternative of requiring a complete re-registration of all voters, believing that this would be too harsh on many whites who had enjoyed the franchise for their entire adult lives.

Review of New Rules.

The Act suspends new voting regulations pending scrutiny by federal authorities to determine whether their use would violate the Fifteenth Amendment. This may have been an uncommon exercise of congressional power, as South Carolina contends, but the Court has recognized that exceptional conditions can justify legislative measures not otherwise appropriate. . . . Congress knew that some of the States covered by § 4 (b) of the Act had resorted to the extraordinary strategem of contriving new rules of various kinds for the sole purpose of perpetuating voting discrimination in the face of adverse federal decrees. Congress had reason to suppose that these States might try similar maneuvers in the future, in order to evade the remedies for voting discrimination contained in the Act itself. Under the compulsion of these unique circumstances, Congress responded in a permissibly decisive manner. . . .

Federal Examiners.

The Act authorizes the appointment of federal examiners to list qualified applicants who are thereafter entitled to vote, subject to an expeditious challenge procedure. This was clearly an appropriate response to the problem, closely related to remedies authorized in prior cases. . . . In many of the political subdivisions covered by § 4 (b) of the Act, voting officials have persistently employed a variety of procedural tactics to deny Negroes the franchise, often in direct defiance or evasion of federal decrees. Congress realized that merely to suspend voting rules which have been misused or are subject to misuse might leave this localized evil undisturbed. As for the briskness of the challenge procedure, Congress knew that in some of the areas affected, challenges had been persistently employed to harass registered Negroes. It chose to forestall this abuse, at the same time providing alternative ways for removing persons listed through error or fraud. In addition to the judicial challenge procedure, § 7 (d) allows for the removal of names by the examiner himself, and § 11 (c) makes it a crime to obtain a listing through fraud. . . .

After enduring nearly a century of widespread resistance to the Fifteenth Amendment, Congress has marshalled an array of potent weapons against the evil, with authority in the Attorney General to employ them effectively. Many of the areas directly affected by this development have indicated their willingness to abide by any restraints legitimately imposed upon them. We here hold that the portions of the Voting Rights Act properly before us are a valid means for carrying out the commands of the Fifteenth Amendment. Hopefully, millions of non-white Americans will now be able to participate for the first time on an equal basis in the government under which they live. We may finally look forward to the day when truly "the right of citizens of the United States to vote shall not be denied or abridged by the United States or by any State on account of race, color, or previous condition of servitude."

The bill of complaint is dismissed.

Mr. Justice Black concurred except as to the validity of § 5.

Constitution of the United States

<hr>

We the people of the United States, in order to form a more perfect union, establish justice, insure domestic tranquillity, provide for the common defense, promote the general welfare, and secure the blessings of liberty to ourselves and our posterity, do ordain and establish this Constitution for the United States of America.

Article I

Section 1. All legislative powers herein granted shall be vested in a Congress of the United States, which shall consist of a Senate and House of Representatives.

Section 2. (1). The House of Representatives shall be composed of members chosen every second year by the people of the several States, and the electors in each State shall have the qualifications requisite for electors of the most numerous branch of the State legislature.

(2). No person shall be a Representative who shall not have attained to the age of twenty five years, and been seven years a citizen of the United States, and who shall not, when elected, be an inhabitant of that State in which he shall be chosen.

(3). Representatives and direct taxes[1] shall be apportioned among the several States which may be included within this Union, according to their

[1] Modified as to income taxes by the 16th Amendment.

respective numbers, which shall be determined by adding to the whole number of free persons, including those bound to service for a term of years, and excluding Indians not taxed, three fifths of all other persons.[2] The actual enumeration shall be made within three years after the first meeting of the Congress of the United States, and within every subsequent term of ten years, in such manner as they shall by law direct. The number of Representatives shall not exceed one for every thirty thousand, but each State shall have at least one Representative; and until such enumeration shall be made, the State of New Hampshire shall be entitled to choose three, Massachusetts eight, Rhode Island and Providence Plantations one, Connecticut five, New York six, New Jersey four, Pennsylvania eight, Delaware one, Maryland six, Virginia ten, North Carolina five, South Carolina five, and Georgia three.

(4). When vacancies happen in the representation from any State, the executive authority thereof shall issue writs of election to fill such vacancies.

(5). The House of Representatives shall choose their Speaker and other officers; and shall have the sole power of impeachment.

Section 3. (1) The Senate of the United States shall be composed of two Senators from each State, chosen by the Legislature thereof,[3] for six years; and each Senator shall have one vote.

(2). Immediately after they shall be assembled in consequence of the first election, they shall be divided as equally as may be into three classes. The seats of the Senators of the first class shall be vacated at the expiration of the second year, of the second class at the expiration of the fourth year, and of the third class at the expiration of the sixth year, so that one third may be chosen every second year; and if vacancies happen by resignation, or otherwise, during the recess of the legislature of any State, the executive thereof may make temporary appointments until the next meeting of the legislature, which[3] shall then fill such vacancies.

(3). No person shall be a Senator who shall not have attained to the age of thirty years, and been nine years a citizen of the United States, and who shall not, when elected, be an inhabitant of that State for which he shall be chosen.

(4). The Vice President of the United States shall be president of the Senate, but shall have no vote, unless they be equally divided.

(5). The Senate shall choose their other officers, and also a president pro tempore, in the absence of the Vice President, or when he shall exercise the office of President of the United States.

(6). The Senate shall have the sole power to try all impeachments. When sitting for that purpose, they shall be on oath or affirmation. When the President of the United States is tried, the Chief Justice shall preside: and

---

[2] Replaced by the 14th Amendment.
[3] Modified by the 17th Amendment.

no person shall be convicted without the concurrence of two thirds of the members present.

(7). Judgment in cases of impeachment shall not extend further than to removal from office, and disqualification to hold and enjoy any office of honor, trust or profit under the United States: but the party convicted shall nevertheless be liable and subject to indictment, trial, judgment and punishment, according to law.

Section 4. (1). The times, places and manner of holding elections for Senators and Representatives, shall be prescribed in each State by the legisture thereof; but the Congress may at any time by law make or alter such regulations, except as to the places of choosing Senators.

(2). The Congress shall assemble at least once in every year, and such meeting shall be on the first Monday in December, unless they shall by law appoint a different day.

Section 5. (1) Each House shall be the judge of the elections, returns and qualifications of its own members, and a majority of each shall constitute a quorum to do business; but a smaller number may adjourn from day to day, and may be authorized to compel the attendance of absent members, in such manner, and under such penalties as each House may provide.

(2) Each House may determine the rules of its proceedings, punish its members for disorderly behavior, and, with the concurrence of two thirds, expel a member.

(3). Each House shall keep a journal of its proceedings, and from time to time publish the same, excepting such parts as may in their judgment require secrecy; and the yeas and nays of the members of either House on any question shall, at the desire of one fifth of those present, be entered on the journal.

(4). Neither House, during the session of Congress, shall, without the consent of the other, adjourn for more than three days, nor to any other place than that in which the two Houses shall be sitting.

Section 6. (1). The Senators and Representatives shall receive a compensation for their services, to be ascertained by law, and paid out of the Treasury of the United States. They shall in all cases, except treason, felony and breach of the peace, be privileged from arrest during their attendance at the session of their respective Houses, and in going to and returning from the same; and for any speech or debate in either House, they shall not be questioned in any other place.

(2). No Senator or Representative shall, during the time for which he was elected, be appointed to any civil office under the authority of the United States, which shall have been created, or the emoluments whereof shall have been increased during such time; and no person holding any office under the United States, shall be a member of either House during his continuance in office.

Section 7. (1) All bills for raising revenue shall originate in the House of Representatives; but the Senate may propose or concur with amendments as on other bills.

(2). Every bill which shall have passed the House of Representatives and the Senate, shall, before it become a law, be presented to the President of the United States; if he approve he shall sign it, but if not he shall return it, with his objections to that House in which it shall have originated, who shall enter the objections at large on their journal, and proceed to reconsider it. If after such reconsideration two thirds of that House shall agree to pass the bill, it shall be sent, together with the objections, to the other House, by which it shall likewise be reconsidered, and if approved by two thirds of that House, it shall become a law. But in all such cases the votes of both Houses shall be determined by yeas and nays, and the names of the persons voting for and against the bill shall be entered on the journal of each House respectively. If any bill shall not be returned by the President within ten days (Sundays excepted) after it shall have been presented to him, the same shall be a law, in like manner as if he had signed it, unless the Congress by their adjournment prevent its return, in which case it shall not be a law.

(3). Every order, resolution, or vote to which the concurrence of the Senate and House of Representatives may be necessary (except on a question of adjournment) shall be presented to the President of the United States; and before the same shall take effect, shall be approved by him, or being disapproved by him, shall be repassed by two thirds of the Senate and House of Representatives, according to the rules and limitations prescribed in the case of a bill.

Section 8. The Congress shall have power (1) to lay and collect taxes, duties, imposts and excises, to pay the debts and provide for the common defense and general welfare of the United States; but all duties, imposts and excises shall be uniform throughout the United States;

(2). To borrow money on the credit of the United States;

(3). To regulate commerce with foreign nations, and among the several States, and with the Indian tribes;

(4). To establish an uniform rule of naturalization, and uniform laws on the subject of bankruptcies throughout the United States;

(5). To coin money, regulate the value thereof, and of foreign coin, and fix the standard of weights and measures;

(6). To provide for the punishment of counterfeiting the securities and current coin of the United States;

(7). To establish post offices and post roads;

(8). To promote the progress of science and useful arts, by securing for limited times to authors and inventors the exclusive right to their respective writings and discoveries;

(9). To constitute tribunals inferior to the Supreme Court;

(10). To define and punish piracies and felonies committed on the high seas, and offenses against the law of nations;

(11). To declare war, grant letters of marque and reprisal, and make rules concerning captures on land and water;

(12). To raise and support armies, but no appropriation of money to that use shall be for a longer term than two years;

(13). To provide and maintain a navy;

(14). To make rules for the government and regulation of the land and naval forces;

(15). To provide for calling forth the militia to execute the laws of the Union, suppress insurrections and repel invasions;

(16). To provide for organizing, arming, and disciplining the militia, and for governing such part of them as may be employed in the service of the United States, reserving to the States respectively, the appointment of the officers, and the authority of training the militia according to the discipline prescribed by Congress;

(17). To exercise exclusive legislation in all cases whatsoever, over such district (not exceeding ten miles square) as may, by cession of particular States, and the acceptance of Congress, become the seat of the government of the United States, and to exercise like authority over all places purchased by the consent of the legislature of the State in which the same shall be, for the erection of forts, magazines, arsenals, dock-yards, and other needful buildings;—And

(18). To make all laws which shall be necessary and proper for carrying into execution the foregoing powers, and all other powers vested by this Constitution in the government of the United States, or in any department or officer thereof.

Section 9. (1). The migration or importation of such persons as any of the States now existing shall think proper to admit, shall not be prohibited by the Congress prior to the year one thousand eight hundred and eight, but a tax or duty may be imposed on such importation, not exceeding ten dollars for each person.

(2). The privilege of the writ of habeas corpus shall not be suspended, unless when in cases of rebellion or invasion the public safety may require it.

(3). No bill of attainder or ex post facto law shall be passed.

(4). No capitation, or other direct, tax shall be laid, unless in proportion to the census or enumeration herein before directed to be taken.[4]

(5). No tax or duty shall be laid on articles exported from any State.

(6). No preference shall be given by any regulation of commerce or revenue to the ports of one State over those of another: nor shall vessels bound to, or from, one State, be obliged to enter, clear, or pay duties in another.

[4] Modified by the 16th Amendment.

(7). No money shall be drawn from the Treasury, but in consequence of appropriations made by law; and a regular statement and account of the receipts and expenditures of all public money shall be published from time to time.

(8). No title of nobility shall be granted by the United States: And no person holding any office of profit or trust under them, shall, without the consent of the Congress, accept of any present, emolument, office, or title, of any kind whatever, from any king, prince, or foreign State.

Section 10. (1). No State shall enter into any treaty, alliance, or confederation; grant letters of marque and reprisal; coin money; emit bills of credit; make anything but gold and silver coin a tender in payment of debts; pass any bill of attainder, ex post facto law, or law impairing the obligation of contracts, or grant any title of nobility.

(2). No State shall, without the consent of the Congress, lay any imposts or duties on imports or exports, except what may be absolutely necessary for executing its inspection laws: and the net produce of all duties and imposts, laid by any State on imports or exports, shall be for the use of the Treasury of the United States; and all such laws shall be subject to the revision and control of the Congress.

(3). No State shall, without the consent of Congress, lay any duty of tonnage, keep troops, or ships of war in time of peace, enter into any agreement or compact with another State, or with a foreign power, or engage in war, unless actually invaded, or in such imminent danger as will not admit of delay.

Article II

Section 1. (1). The executive power shall be vested in a President of the United States of America. He shall hold his office during the term of four years, and, together with the Vice President, chosen for the same term, be elected, as follows:

(2). Each State shall appoint, in such manner as the legislature thereof may direct, a number of electors, equal to the whole number of Senators and Representatives to which the State may be entitled in the Congress: but no Senator or Representative, or person holding an office of trust or profit under the United States, shall be appointed an elector.

The electors[5] shall meet in their respective States, and vote by ballot for two persons, of whom one at least shall not be an inhabitant of the same State with themselves. And they shall make a list of all the persons voted for, and of the number of votes for each; which list they shall sign and certify, and transmit sealed to the seat of the government of the United States, directed to the president of the Senate. The president of the Senate shall, in the presence of the Senate and House of Representatives, open all

[5] This paragraph was replaced in 1804 by the 12th Amendment.

the certificates, and the votes shall then be counted. The person having the greatest number of votes shall be the President, if such number be a majority of the whole number of electors appointed; and if there be more than one who have such majority, and have an equal number of votes, then the House of Representatives shall immediately choose by ballot one of them for President; and if no person have a majority, then from the five highest on the list the said House shall in like manner choose the President. But in choosing the President, the votes shall be taken by States, the representation from each State having one vote; a quorum for this purpose shall consist of a member or members from two thirds of the States, and a majority of all the States shall be necessary to a choice. In every case, after the choice of the President, the person having the greatest number of votes of the electors shall be the Vice President. But if there should remain two or more who have equal votes, the Senate shall choose from them by ballot the Vice President.

(3). The Congress may determine the time of choosing the electors, and the day on which they shall give their votes; which day shall be the same throughout the United States.

(4). No person except a natural born citizen, or a citizen of the United States, at the time of the adoption of this Constitution, shall be eligible to the office of President; neither shall any person be eligible to that office who shall not have attained to the age of thirty five years, and been fourteen years a resident within the United States.

(5). In case of the removal of the President from office, or of his death, resignation, or inability to discharge the powers and duties of the said office, the same shall devolve on the Vice President, and the Congress may by law provide for the case of removal, death, resignation or inability, both of the President and Vice President, declaring what officer shall then act as President, and such officer shall act accordingly, until the disability be removed, or a President shall be elected.

(6). The President shall, at stated times, receive for his services, a compensation, which shall neither be increased nor diminished during the period for which he shall have been elected, and he shall not receive within that period any other emolument from the United States, or any of them.

(7). Before he enter on the execution of his office, he shall take the following oath or affirmation:—"I do solemnly swear (or affirm) that I will faithfully execute the office of President of the United States, and will to the best of my ability, preserve, protect and defend the Constitution of the United States."

Section 2. (1). The President shall be commander in chief of the army and navy of the United States, and of the militia of the several States, when called into the actual service of the United States; he may require the opinion, in writing, of the principal officer in each of the executive departments, upon any subject relating to the duties of their respective offices, and he shall have power to grant reprieves and pardons for offenses against the United States, except in cases of impeachment.

(2). He shall have power, by and with the advice and consent of the Senate, to make treaties, provided two thirds of the Senators present concur; and he shall nominate, and by and with the advice and consent of the Senate, shall appoint ambassadors, other public ministers and consuls, judges of the Supreme Court, and all other officers of the United States, whose appointments are not herein otherwise provided for, and which shall be established by law: but the Congress may by law vest the appointment of such inferior officers, as they think proper, in the President alone, in the courts of law, or in the heads of departments.

(3). The President shall have power to fill up all vacancies that may happen during the recess of the Senate, by granting commissions which shall expire at the end of their next session.

Section 3. He shall from time to time give to the Congress information of the state of the Union, and recommend to their consideration such measures as he shall judge necessary and expedient; he may, on extraordinary occasions, convene both Houses, or either of them, and in case of disagreement between them, with respect to the time of adjournment, he may adjourn them to such time as he shall think proper; he shall receive ambassadors and other public ministers; he shall take care that the laws be faithfully executed, and shall commission all the officers of the United States.

Section 4. The President, Vice President and all civil officers of the United States, shall be removed from office on impeachment for, and conviction of, treason, bribery, or other high crimes and misdemeanors.

Article III

Section 1. The judicial power of the United States, shall be vested in one Supreme Court, and in such inferior courts as the Congress may from time to time ordain and establish. The judges, both of the Supreme and inferior courts, shall hold their offices during good behavior, and shall, at stated times, receive for their services, a compensation, which shall not be diminished during their continuance in office.

Section 2. (1). The judicial power shall extend to all cases, in law and equity, arising under this Constitution, the laws of the United States, and treaties made, or which shall be made, under their authority;—to all cases affecting ambassadors, other public ministers and consuls;—to all cases of admiralty and maritime jurisdiction;—to controversies to which the United States shall be a party;—to controversies between two or more States;—between a State and citizens of another State;[6]—between citizens of different States;—between citizens of the same State claiming lands under

[6] Restricted by the 11th Amendment.

grants of different States, and between a State, or the citizens thereof, and foreign States, citizens or subjects.

(2). In all cases affecting ambassadors, other public ministers and consuls, and those in which a State shall be party, the Supreme Court shall have original jurisdiction. In all the other cases before mentioned, the Supreme Court shall have appellate jurisdiction, both as to law and fact, with such exceptions, and under such regulations as the Congress shall make.

(3). The trial of all crimes, except in cases of impeachment, shall be by jury; and such trial shall be held in the State where the said crimes shall have been committed; but when not committed within any State, the trial shall be at such place or places as the Congress may by law have directed.

Section 3. (1). Treason against the United States, shall consist only in levying war against them, or in adhering to their enemies, giving them aid and comfort. No person shall be convicted of treason unless on the testimony of two witnesses to the same overt act, or on confession in open court.

(2). The Congress shall have power to declare the punishment of treason, but no attainder of treason shall work corruption of blood, or forfeiture except during the life of the person attainted.

Article IV

Section 1. Full faith and credit shall be given in each State to the public acts, records, and judicial proceedings of every other State. And the Congress may by general laws prescribe the manner in which such acts, records and proceedings shall be proved, and the effect thereof.

Section 2. (1). The citizens of each State shall be entitled to all privileges and immunities of citizens in the several States.

(2). A person charged in any State with treason, felony, or other crime, who shall flee from justice, and be found in another State, shall on demand of the executive authority of the State from which he fled, be delivered up, to be removed to the State having jurisdiction of the crime.

(3). No person held to service or labor in one State, under the laws thereof, escaping into another, shall, in consequence of any law or regulation therein, be discharged from such service or labor, but shall be delivered up on claim of the party to whom such service or labor may be due.

Section 3. (1). New States may be admitted by the Congress into this Union; but no new State shall be formed or erected within the jurisdiction of any other State; nor any State be formed by the junction of two or more States, or parts of States, without the consent of the legislatures of the States concerned as well as of the Congress.

(2). The Congress shall have power to dispose of and make all needful rules and regulations respecting the territory or other property belonging to the United States; and nothing in this Constitution shall be so construed as to prejudice any claims of the United States, or of any particular State.

Section 4. The United States shall guarantee to every State in this Union a republican form of government, and shall protect each of them against invasion; and on application of the legislature, or of the executive (when the legislature cannot be convened) against domestic violence.

Article V

The Congress, whenever two thirds of both Houses shall deem it necessary, shall propose amendments to this Constitution, or, on the application of the legislatures of two thirds of the several States, shall call a convention for proposing amendments, which, in either case, shall be valid to all intents and purposes, as part of this Constitution, when ratified by the legislatures of three fourths of the several States, or by conventions in three fourths thereof, as the one or the other mode of ratification may be proposed by the Congress; Provided that no amendment which may be made prior to the year one thousand eight hundred and eight shall in any manner affect the first and fourth clauses in the ninth section of the first article; and that no State, without its consent, shall be deprived of its equal suffrage in the Senate.

Article VI

Section 1. All debts contracted and engagements entered into, before the adoption of this Constitution, shall be as valid against the United States under this Constitution, as under the Confederation.

Section 2. This Constitution, and the laws of the United States which shall be made in pursuance thereof; and all treaties made, or which shall be made, under the authority of the United States, shall be the supreme law of the land; and the judges in every State shall be bound thereby, anything in the constitution or laws of any State to the contrary notwithstanding.

Section 3. The Senators and Representatives before mentioned, and the members of the several State legislatures, and all executive and judicial officers, both of the United States and of the several States, shall be bound by oath or affirmation, to support this Constitution; but no religious test shall ever be required as a qualification to any office or public trust under the United States.

Article VII

The ratification of the conventions of nine States, shall be sufficient for the establishment of this Constitution between the States so ratifying the same.

Done in Convention by the unanimous consent of the States present the seventeenth day of September in the year of our Lord one thousand seven hundred and eighty-seven, and of the independence of the United States of America the twelfth. In witness whereof we have hereunto subscribed our names.

Go Washington—

Presidt. and Deputy from Virginia

Articles in addition to and amendment of the Constitution of the United States of America, proposed by Congress, and ratified by the legislatures of the several States, pursuant to the fifth article of the original Constitution.

Article I[7]

Congress shall make no law respecting an establishment of religion, or prohibiting the free exercise thereof; or abridging the freedom of speech, or of the press; or the right of the people peaceably to assemble, and to petition the government for a redress of grievances.

Article II

A well regulated militia, being necessary to the security of a free State, the right of the people to keep and bear arms, shall not be infringed.

Article III

No soldier shall, in time of peace be quartered in any house, without the consent of the owner, nor in time of war, but in a manner to be prescribed by law.

Article IV

The right of the people to be secure in their persons, houses, papers, and effects, against unreasonable searches and seizures, shall not be violated, and no warrants shall issue, but upon probable cause, supported by oath or affirmation, and particularly describing the place to be searched, and the persons or things to be seized.

Article V

No person shall be held to answer for a capital, or otherwise infamous crime, unless on a presentment or indictment of a grand jury, except in cases arising in the land or naval forces, or in the militia, when in actual service in time of war or public danger; nor shall any person be subject for the same offense to be twice put in jeopardy of life or limb; nor shall be

[7] The first ten Amendments were adopted in 1791.

compelled in any criminal case to be a witness against himself, nor be deprived of life, liberty, or property, without due process of law; nor shall private property be taken for public use, without just compensation.

Article VI

In all criminal prosecutions, the accused shall enjoy the right to a speedy and public trial, by an impartial jury of the State and district wherein the crime shall have been committed, which district shall have been previously ascertained by law, and to be informed of the nature and cause of the accusation; to be confronted with the witnesses against him; to have compulsory process for obtaining witnesses in his favor, and to have the assistance of counsel for his defense.

Article VII

In suits at common law, where the value in controversy shall exceed twenty dollars, the right of trial by jury shall be preserved, and no fact tried by a jury, shall be otherwise reexamined in any court of the United States, than according to the rules of the common law.

Article VIII

Excessive bail shall not be required, nor excessive fines imposed, nor cruel and unusual punishments inflicted.

Article IX

The enumeration in the Constitution, of certain rights, shall not be construed to deny or disparage others retained by the people.

Article X

The powers not delegated to the United States by the Constitution, nor prohibited by it to the States, are reserved to the States respectively, or to the people.

Article XI[8]

The judicial power of the United States shall not be construed to extend to any suit in law or equity, commenced or prosecuted against one of the United States by citizens of another State, or by citizens or subjects of any foreign State.

[8] Ratified in 1795; proclaimed in 1798.

Article XII[9]

The electors shall meet in their respective States and vote by ballot for President and Vice-President, one of whom, at least, shall not be an inhabitant of the same State with themselves; they shall name in their ballots the person voted for as President, and in distinct ballots the person voted for as Vice-President, and they shall make distinct lists of all persons voted for as President, and of all persons voted for as Vice-President, and of the number of votes for each, which lists they shall sign and certify, and transmit sealed to the seat of the government of the United States, directed to the president of the Senate;—The president of the Senate shall, in the presence of the Senate and House of Representatives, open all the certificates and the votes shall then be counted;—The person having the greatest number of votes for President, shall be the President, if such number be a majority of the whole number of electors appointed; and if no person have such majority, then from the persons having the highest numbers not exceeding three on the list of those voted for as President, the House of Representatives shall choose immediately, by ballot, the President. But in choosing the President, the votes shall be taken by States, the representation from each State having one vote; a quorum for this purpose shall consist of a member or members from two-thirds of the States, and a majority of all the States shall be necessary to a choice. And if the House of Representatives shall not choose a President whenever the right of choice shall devolve upon them, before the fourth day of March next following, then the Vice-President shall act as President, as in the case of the death or other constitutional disability of the President.—The person having the greatest number of votes as Vice-President, shall be the Vice-President, if such number be a majority of the whole number of electors appointed, and if no person have a majority, then from the two highest numbers on the list, the Senate shall choose the Vice-President; a quorum for the purpose shall consist of two-thirds of the whole number of Senators, and a majority of the whole number shall be necessary to a choice. But no person constitutionally ineligible to the office of President shall be eligible to that of Vice-President of the United States.

Article XIII[10]

Section 1. Neither slavery nor involuntary servitude, except as a punishment for crime whereof the party shall have been duly convicted, shall exist within the United States, or any place subject to their jurisdiction.

[9] Adopted in 1804.
[10] Adopted in 1865.

Section 2. Congress shall have power to enforce this article by appropriate legislation.

Article XIV[11]

Section 1. All persons born or naturalized in the United States, and subject to the jurisdiction thereof, are citizens of the United States and of the State wherein they reside. No State shall make or enforce any law which shall abridge the privileges or immunities of citizens of the United States; nor shall any State deprive any person of life, liberty, or property, without due process of law; nor deny to any person within its jurisdiction the equal protection of the laws.

Section 2. Representatives shall be apportioned among the several States according to their respective numbers, counting the whole number of persons in each State, excluding Indians not taxed. But when the right to vote at any election for the choice of electors for President and Vice President of the United States, Representatives in Congress, the executive and judicial officers of a State, or the members of the legislature thereof, is denied to any of the male inhabitants of such State, being twenty-one years of age, and citizens of the United States, or in any way abridged, except for participation in rebellion, or other crime, the basis of representation therein shall be reduced in the proportion which the number of such male citizens shall bear to the whole number of male citizens twenty-one years of age in such State.

Section 3. No person shall be a Senator or Representative in Congress, or elector of President and Vice President, or hold any office, civil or military, under the United States, or under any State, who, having previously taken an oath, as a member of Congress, or as an officer of the United States, or as a member of any State legislature, or as an executive or judicial officer of any State, to support the Constitution of the United States, shall have engaged in insurrection or rebellion against the same, or given aid or comfort to the enemies thereof. But Congress may by a vote of two-thirds of each House, remove such disability.

Section 4. The validity of the public debt of the United States, authorized by law, including debts incurred for payment of pensions and bounties for services in suppressing insurrection or rebellion, shall not be questioned. But neither the United States nor any State shall assume or pay any debt or obligation incurred in aid of insurrection or rebellion against the United States, or any claim for the loss or emancipation of any slave; but all such debts, obligations and claims shall be held illegal and void.

Section 5. The Congress shall have power to enforce, by appropriate legislation, the provisions of this article.

[11] Adopted in 1868.

Article XV[12]

Section 1. The right of citizens of the United States to vote shall not be denied or abridged by the United States or by any State on account of race, color, or previous condition of servitude.

Section 2. The Congress shall have power to enforce this article by appropriate legislation.

Article XVI[13]

The Congress shall have power to lay and collect taxes on incomes, from whatever source derived, without apportionment among the several States, and without regard to any census or enumeration.

Article XVII[13]

The Senate of the United States shall be composed of two Senators from each State, elected by the people thereof, for six years; and each Senator shall have one vote. The electors in each State shall have the qualifications requisite for electors of the most numerous branch of the State legislatures.

When vacancies happen in the representation of any State in the Senate, the executive authority of such State shall issue writs of election to fill such vacancies: *Provided,* That the legislature of any State may empower the executive thereof to make temporary appointments until the people fill the vacancies by election as the legislature may direct.

This amendment shall not be so construed as to affect the election or term of any Senator chosen before it becomes valid as part of the Constitution.

Article XVIII[14]

Section 1. After one year from the ratification of this article the manufacture, sale, or transportation of intoxicating liquors within, the importation thereof into, or the exportation thereof from the United States and all territory subject to the jurisdiction thereof for beverage purposes is hereby prohibited.

Section 2. The Congress and the several States shall have concurrent power to enforce this article by appropriate legislation.

Section 3. This article shall be inoperative unless it shall have been

[12] Adopted in 1870.
[13] Adopted in 1913.
[14] Adopted in 1919. Repealed by Article XXI.

ratified as an amendment to the Constitution by the legislatures of the several States, as provided in the Constitution, within seven years from the date of the submission hereof to the States by the Congress.

Article XIX[15]

The right of citizens of the United States to vote shall not be denied or abridged by the United States or by any State on account of sex.

The Congress shall have power to enforce this article by appropriate legislation.

Article XX[16]

Section 1. The terms of the President and Vice President shall end at noon on the 20th day of January, and the terms of Senators and Representatives at noon on the 3d day of January, of the years in which such terms would have ended if this article had not been ratified; and the terms of their successors shall then begin.

Section 2. The Congress shall assemble at least once in every year, and such meeting shall begin at noon on the 3d day of January, unless they shall by law appoint a different day.

Section 3. If, at the time fixed for the beginning of the term of the President, the President elect shall have died, the Vice President elect shall become President. If a President shall not have been chosen before the time fixed for the beginning of his term, or if the President elect shall have failed to qualify, then the Vice President elect shall act as President until a President shall have qualified; and the Congress may by law provide for the case wherein neither a President elect nor a Vice President elect shall have qualified, declaring who shall then act as President, or the manner in which one who is to act shall be selected, and such person shall act accordingly until a President or Vice President shall have qualified.

Section 4. The Congress may by law provide for the case of the death of any of the persons from whom the House of Representatives may choose a President whenever the right of choice shall have devolved upon them, and for the case of the death of any of the persons from whom the Senate may choose a Vice President whenever the right of choice shall have devolved upon them.

Section 5. Sections 1 and 2 shall take effect on the 15th day of October following the ratification of this article.

Section 6. This article shall be inoperative unless it shall have been ratified as an amendment to the Constitution by the legislatures of three-

[15] Adopted in 1920.
[16] Adopted in 1933.

fourths of the several States within seven years from the date of its submission.

Article XXI[17]

Section 1. The Eighteenth Article of Amendment to the Constitution of the United States is hereby repealed.

Section 2. The transportation or importation into any State, Territory or possession of the United States for delivery or use therein of intoxicating liquors, in violation of the laws thereof, is hereby prohibited.

Section 3. This article shall be inoperative unless it shall have been ratified as an amendment to the Constitution by conventions in the several States, as provided in the Constitution, within seven years from the date of the submission hereof to the States by the Congress.

Article XXII[18]

Section 1. No person shall be elected to the office of the President more than twice, and no person who has held the office of President, or acted as President, for more than two years of a term to which some other person was elected President shall be elected to the office of the President more than once. But this Article shall not apply to any person holding the office of President when this Article was proposed by the Congress, and shall not prevent any person who may be holding the office of President, or acting as President, during the term within which this Article becomes operative from holding the office of President or acting as President during the remainder of such term.

Section 2. This Article shall be inoperative unless it shall have been ratified as an amendment to the Constitution by the legislatures of three-fourths of the several States within seven years from the date of its submission to the States by the Congress.

Article XXIII[19]

Section 1. The District constituting the seat of Government of the United States shall appoint in such manner as the Congress may direct:

A number of electors of President and Vice President equal to the whole number of Senators and Representatives in Congress to which the District would be entitled if it were a State, but in no event more than the least populous State; they shall be in addition to those appointed by the States, but they shall be considered, for the purposes of the election of President

[17] Adopted in 1933.
[18] Adopted in 1951.
[19] Adopted in 1961.

and Vice President, to be electors appointed by a State; and they shall meet in the District and perform such duties as provided by the twelfth article of amendment.

Section 2. The Congress shall have power to enforce this article by appropriate legislation.

Article XXIV [20]

Section 1. The right of citizens of the United States to vote in any primary or other election for President or Vice President, for electors for President or Vice President, or for Senator or Representative in Congress, shall not be denied or abridged by the United States or any State by reason of failure to pay any poll tax or other tax.

Section 2. The Congress shall have power to enforce this article by appropriate legislation.

Article XXV [21]

Section 1. In case of the removal of the President from office or of his death or resignation, the Vice President shall become President.

Section 2. Whenever there is a vacancy in the office of the Vice President, the President shall nominate a Vice President who shall take office upon confirmation by a majority vote of both Houses of Congress.

Section 3. Whenever the President transmits to the President Pro Tempore of the Senate and the Speaker of the House of Representatives his written declaration that he is unable to discharge the powers and duties of his office, and until he transmits to them a written declaration to the contrary, such powers and duties shall be discharged by the Vice President as Acting President.

Section 4. Whenever the Vice President and a majority of either the principal officers of the executive departments or of such other body as Congress may by law provide, transmit to the President Pro Tempore of the Senate and the Speaker of the House of Representatives their written declaration that the President is unable to discharge the powers and duties of his office, the Vice President shall immediately assume the powers and duties of the office as Acting President.

Thereafter, when the President transmits to the President Pro Tempore of the Senate and the Speaker of the House of Representatives his written declaration that no inability exists, he shall resume the powers and duties of his office unless the Vice President and a majority of either the principal officers of the executive department or of such other body as Congress may

[20] Adopted in 1964.
[21] Proposed in 1965.

by law provide, transmit within four days to the President Pro Tempore of the Senate and the Speaker of the House of Representatives their written declaration that the President is unable to discharge the powers and duties of his office. Thereupon Congress shall decide the issue, assembling within forty-eight hours for that purpose if not in session. If the Congress, within twenty-one days after receipt of the latter written declaration, or, if Congress is not in session, within twenty-one days after Congress is required to assemble, determines by two-thirds vote of both Houses that the President is unable to discharge the powers and duties of his office, the Vice President shall continue to discharge the same as Acting President; otherwise, the President shall resume the powers and duties of his office.